T0286040

THE ANTI-OLIGARCHY CONSTITUTION

THE

ANTI-OLIGARCHY
CONSTITUTION

Reconstructing the Economic Foundations
of American Democracy

JOSEPH FISHKIN

WILLIAM E. FORBATH

Harvard University Press
Cambridge, Massachusetts ▾ London, England

Publication of this book has been supported through the generous
provisions of the Maurice and Lula Bradley Smith Memorial Fund.

First Harvard University Press paperback edition, 2024
First printing

Library of Congress Cataloging-in-Publication Data

Names: Fishkin, Joseph, author. | Forbath, William E., 1952– author.
Title: The anti-oligarchy constitution : reconstructing the economic
foundations of American democracy / Joseph Fishkin
and William E. Forbath.
Description: Cambridge, Massachusetts : Harvard University Press,
2022. | Includes bibliographical references and index.
Identifiers: LCCN 2021020480 | ISBN 9780674980624 (cloth) |
ISBN 9780674295544 (pbk.)
Subjects: LCSH: United States. Constitution. | Oligarchy—United States—
History. | Law—Economic aspects—United States. | Democracy—
Economic aspects—United States. | United States—Economic policy.
Classification: LCC JC419 .F57 2022 | DDC 320.973–dc23
LC record available at https://lccn.loc.gov/2021020480

CONTENTS

THE ANTI-OLIGARCHY CONSTITUTION

INTRODUCTION

Our constitutional system is headed for a historic confrontation. As in the 1930s, the elected branches of the federal government face an immediate crisis—then the Depression, now the economic devastation wrought by a pandemic—that has laid bare and exacerbated a slower-burning crisis of growing economic and political inequality. Most Americans understand, if sometimes in an inchoate way, that this crisis of inequality threatens our democracy. When too much economic and political power is concentrated in too few hands, what you have is not democracy but oligarchy. Prominent voices now speak openly of oligarchy in this country.[1] Yet it remains possible to change course—to reshape the nation's political economy and disperse economic and political power more broadly among all the people.

As we write these words, liberals and progressives in the elected branches of the federal government are beginning to do this work. They hope to enact measures to distribute both wealth and political power more broadly among all the people: more decent jobs, public investment, and social insurance; more clout for ordinary Americans in politics and in the labor market; more taxing and breaking up concentrated wealth. But as in the 1930s, liberal and progressive lawmakers confront a very conservative federal judiciary that is deeply hostile to exactly this sort of legislation. It is a judiciary put in place by a political party with a weakening grip on power, but a growing determination to thwart legislation and sustain minority rule by translating its vision of political economy into constitutional law.[2]

The phrase "political economy" is essential for understanding the present crisis. It is an old way of thinking that is becoming new again. Before the twentieth-century rise of economics as a discipline, thinkers as varied as Adam Smith, John Stuart Mill, and Karl Marx understood economics and politics as inseparable. These "political economists" studied such subjects as wages, prices, labor and capital, the distribution of wealth, and the distribution of political power. They observed how political decisions shape and constitute market and property relations and thereby shape the distribution of wealth and power—and they observed how economic relations and economic power shape politics. As long as political economy flourished, Americans of all political stripes viewed and argued about the Constitution through a political-economy lens and the political economy through a constitutional lens. In the twentieth century, economics supplanted political economy.[3] It aspired to a more scientific, technocratic approach and a narrower focus: It sidelined questions about the distribution of wealth and political power. Twentieth-century liberals gradually embraced the technocratic promise of economics and abandoned their traditions of political economy—although conservatives never did.[4]

Confronting the present crisis will require liberals and progressives to reclaim many of their older arguments about political economy and enact policies and laws that implement them. This is work for the elected branches. Much of the work is federal legislation. And nearly all of it is vulnerable to constitutional attack by an emboldened conservative political and legal movement that aims, as its predecessors did a century ago, to elevate an anti-redistributive vision of political economy into constitutional arguments to be enforced in court.

In the looming constitutional confrontation, the democratically elected branches have some tools and methods of their own, which they can and likely will use to challenge, defy, or threaten the courts, pushing back against judges' constitutional and statutory claims.[5] But in the name of what? General theories of democracy? A broad vision of congressional power? Precedent and stare decisis, to protect old holdings won in prior rounds of this same conflict, such as the battle over the New Deal? There is room for all these arguments, although each has real limitations. But there is also something else. There is an American tradition of constitutional argument that directly addresses the central problems of oligarchy and inequality we now face. That tradition is the subject of this book.

Throughout the nineteenth and early twentieth centuries, generations of reformers argued that America was becoming a society with a "moneyed aristocracy" or a "ruling class"—an "oligarchy," not a republic. These reformers were making constitutional claims. For them, circumstances resembling America's today, in which too much economic and political power is concentrated in the hands of the few, posed not just an economic, social, or political problem, but a *constitutional* problem.

We call this tradition the *democracy-of-opportunity* tradition. It is as old as the republic itself. But we take the name from President Franklin Roosevelt, who argued that it was a constitutional necessity to overthrow the "economic royalists" and build a "democracy of opportunity" for all Americans in the economic *and* the political spheres.[6] Arguments in the democracy-of-opportunity tradition hold, broadly, that we cannot keep our constitutional democracy—our "republican form of government"— without (1) restraints against oligarchy and (2) a political economy that sustains a robust middle class, open and broad enough to accommodate everyone. The most important and compelling arguments in this tradition hold that (3) a constitutional principle of inclusion—across lines such as race and sex—is inseparable from the first two requirements, and equally necessary for sustaining the political economy that republican government demands.[7]

Constitutional Politics

Building that kind of political economy requires legislation. That is exactly what advocates working in the democracy-of-opportunity tradition argued the Constitution demanded. They held that the Constitution imposed affirmative obligations on all branches of government, but especially on the elected branches, to pass and implement the legislation needed to enforce the Constitution. Often, they insisted, the most important role for courts was to get out of the way of such legislation. Many Americans today view the Constitution as essentially a set of limits on government, enforced almost exclusively by courts. This book argues that it is time to reclaim a different way of thinking about the Constitution— one that made the democracy-of-opportunity tradition possible.

Recovering this tradition involves recovering a different understanding of what a constitutional claim is—what it sounds like, to whom it is addressed, and how it relates to politics. It is conventional today, especially among liberals, to assume that the only *real* constitutional claims are the ones enforceable in court. From that perspective, constitutional claims are political conversation-stoppers; they constrain and set the boundaries of politics.

One of the core aims of this book is to help readers see beyond those assumptions. Americans making arguments in the democracy-of-opportunity tradition, through most of American history, did not view their constitutional arguments (or for that matter, those of their opponents) as outside constraints on democratic politics. Instead, they were the substance of democratic constitutional politics. The participants in these debates often argued about the affirmative constitutional duties of legislatures and executives. They saw that the political branches were crucial fora in which constitutional conflicts and deliberations unfolded. Far from being conversation-stoppers, constitutional claims were central to great national *political* debates about the relationship between the Constitution and the nation's economic and political life.[8]

Why have arguments about the Constitution played this special role in our politics? Although any answer to this question is necessarily speculative, we think the best answer goes something like this. Constitutional politics is how generations of Americans championed and challenged major, structural economic reforms. It is also one of the central ways Americans forged and fought about national identity. In Europe and elsewhere, when nation making got underway in the eighteenth and nineteenth centuries, national belonging was built on ideas of common descent and shared origins. But in the United States, the felt attachments and ideology that were coming to be called nationalism remained more grounded in the liberal republican precepts that animated the American Revolution. Those attachments became bound up with the very legal texts on which the state rested.[9] America, the nation—"We, the People"—was felt to be constituted and defined by law. What else bound such a disparate nation together and explained its solidarity? Unusually among constitutions, ours became a deep root of national identity.[10] No matter their ancestry, shared loyalty to this ongoing experiment in self-rule bound citizens together as a nation.[11] Freely given consent to the laws and Constitution of the new republic made them members of "We, the People." With the Constitution playing this role in our national story, it is hardly surprising that many people with rival views on fundamental questions about the direction of the nation's political economy and much else have worked to ground their views in arguments about the Constitution.

In truth, the United States was never all that exceptional. Alongside the liberal, consent-based account of national belonging was always a rival descent-based account that defined the nation in racial and ethnic terms. It held that only white people (or some subset thereof) were real Americans.[12] This account remains active today in the far-right precincts of national politics, declaring that America is a nation constituted by and for white men, and calling for its restoration. For much of American history, this racist vision of a white republic undergirded policies of exclusion, subordination, and oppression of Blacks, Asians, Latinos, and Native Americans—and grounded these policies in a vision of the Constitution.[13] It turns out to have played a larger role in the politics of recent decades than many of us thought.[14]

The Reconstruction Amendments wrote into the text of the Constitution that the national community includes people of color. That change was honored mostly in the breach until the Second Reconstruction in the mid-twentieth century powerfully advanced the promises of these amendments through statutes building out this constitutional principle of inclusion. Today, the principle of inclusion is one that the vast majority of Americans endorse—but they disagree, often bitterly, about what it entails. Those disagreements, we will suggest, are closely bound up with a different but equally fundamental question: What kind of national community—what kind of social, political, and economic order—does the Constitution promise to secure for all its members?

In a series of pitched battles in constitutional politics, from the founding era through the New Deal, advocates working in the democracy-of-opportunity tradition squared off against a series of rival traditions with different answers to this question. In these debates, all sides shared an understanding that the guarantees of the Constitution are inextricable from the structure of our economic and political life. They argued and fought about *constitutional political economy.*

Constitutional Political Economy

The striking thing about most of the constitutional debates we explore in this book, from the founding era through the New Deal, is that *all sides* were making arguments about constitutional political economy. Southern proslavery constitutionalism, for instance, had its own well-developed vision of constitutional political economy. So did the advocates of the anti-redistributive, "laissez-faire" constitutional politics that crystallized into Lochnerism a century ago. That constitutional politics helped give shape to the modern conservative account of an America founded on rugged individualism, limited government, and private property. It is an account that continues to inspire citizens, lawmakers, and judges to act boldly on its behalf; it not only resonates with conservative values but helps define them. And it mobilizes the impulse of constitutional patriotism—of keeping faith with the Constitution as a root signifier of national identity.

Missing from our constitutional politics today is a comparably robust progressive account of what kind of community the Constitution promises to secure for all. This was not always so. Past generations of progressives offered an account of national community grounded in the democracy-of-opportunity tradition. They argued that the Constitution promises to build a national community with a democratic rather than oligarchic political economy: one in which all Americans enjoy a decent education, material security, and a genuine opportunity not only to earn a decent livelihood, but to do something with value in their own eyes—and also to engage in the affairs of their community and the larger society. This account, like the conservative one, mobilizes the impulse of constitutional patriotism; it shows how the Constitution can undergird, rather than impede, core commitments to a broad distribution of power and opportunity that progressives see as essential to a democratic society.

There are many close ideological and historical links between the conservative constitutionalism of rugged individualism and limited government and the modern conservative view of racial equality, which is famously thin, formal, and individualistic. One of the themes of this book is that there is a similar fit between the thicker, more substantive liberal and progressive view of what the principle of inclusion demands on behalf of Black Americans and other historically subordinate groups, and the other, forgotten constitutional principles of the democracy-of-opportunity tradition, which aim to thwart oligarchy and maintain a broad, open middle class. In contrast to the anti-redistributive slant of the conservative constitutional vision, the principles at the heart of the democracy-of-opportunity tradition put affirmative distributional duties on government. More than that, this book argues that it is a grave error for progressives to see a clash between a robust constitutional politics of race and sex equality and a constitutional politics of fighting class domination. As a matter of constitutional experience, practically, morally, and even conceptually, it turns out to be impossible to sustain a national commitment to one of these without the other.

To the contemporary ear, this talk of national commitments, ideals, and promises may not sound much like talk of the Constitution. Broad principles of constitutional political economy may instead seem to be drawing on what the legal scholar Cass Sunstein calls "constitutive commitments": fundamental commitments, constitutive of, or essential to, important aspects of our national identity, yet not to be found in the Constitution.[15] But that distinction is anachronistic, as applied to the constitutional thinking of the nineteenth- and early twentieth-century reformers who most interest us in these pages.

Those reformers were interpreting the Constitution as they understood it, and they said so. They offered arguments based on constitutional text and history. They offered arguments based on commitments embodied in the Declaration of Independence. And they offered arguments in what might best be described as a structural mode. The structural mode of constitutional argument familiar to most of us today builds claims about topics such as the separation of powers and federalism on institutional relationships within the political sphere. Structural arguments about constitutional political economy hold that the nation's constitutional order rests on and presupposes a political-economic order.[16] Most arguments about constitutional political economy have a structural core.

Reformers working in the democracy-of-opportunity tradition often argued about what the Constitution "requires." They meant this in a double sense.[17] They made interpretive arguments about what constitutional text or its principles require, using all the familiar modalities of constitutional interpretation. They also made their structural political-economy arguments: They argued that our republican form of government, with its guarantees of equal citizenship, requires a broad middle class and cannot coexist with oligarchy. There can be no republic composed of wage slaves and their overlords. For these reformers, the two forms of argument—interpretive and structural—were deeply intertwined. Today, the structural arguments tend to strike modern readers as policy arguments, not constitutional ones. Some might categorize them as "small *c*" but not "capital *C*" constitutional claims. But this way of drawing the boundary around the category of "capital *C*" constitutional argument is, once again, anachronistic. Advocates of the democracy-of-opportunity tradition *and their opponents* throughout the long period from the founding through the New Deal disagreed about many things, but they agreed that part of arguing about the Constitution is making claims about what it requires of our political economy.

Reformers working in the democracy-of-opportunity tradition were not engaged only in constitutional interpretation. They also offered constitutional amendments and deep structural reforms to our system of government—many of them successful—at the state and federal levels. All were aimed at protecting what they saw as an underlying constitutional commitment to a democracy of opportunity: a political economy in which power and opportunity are dispersed among the people rather than concentrated in the hands of a few.

Three Strands of a Tradition

The democracy-of-opportunity tradition has three main strands. First, arguments in this tradition are highly attuned to the threat of *oligarchy:* the danger that, because concentrations of economic and political power are mutually reinforcing, if they become sufficiently extreme, they threaten the Constitution's democratic foundations. There are several ways to fight this threat. One is to target the mechanisms by which economic and political power are converted into one another, defining these mechanisms as forms of corruption. Another is to build and maintain robust secondary associations, like unions, which can give the many the means of challenging the political and economic dominance of the few. Some arguments in this tradition aim to open new channels of democratic politics that can circumvent the political power of oligarchs and their allies. Others aim to break up concentrations of economic power by defining them as monopolies and subjecting them to legal sanction. We call all these measures the *anti-oligarchy* strand of the democracy-of-opportunity tradition.

Second, arguments in the democracy-of-opportunity tradition are attuned to how economic opportunities are structured for ordinary Americans. They hold that the roads to a middle-class life—a middle-class standard of living—must be broad enough to accommodate everyone. That way, the economy will reliably produce the mass middle class that is the social and economic base of republican government—and a structural condition for fair access to opportunity.[18]

"Middle class" in this tradition is not defined by reference to who is above or below. Instead, the term denotes a set of social baselines, which reformers throughout this book describe variously as an "American standard" of material comfort and security, along with the wherewithal and opportunities to make a life with value in one's own eyes. The more Americans who can reach such a standard—in objective terms and from their own point of view[19]—the better. There must be ample room and opportunity for all. The danger is in the other direction: If the middle class shrinks too much, republican government becomes impossible.

The policy implications of these first two strands of the tradition change dramatically over time as the structure of the American economy changes. The initial endowments and opportunities a person needs in order to reach a middle-class standard of living are not the same in an agrarian republic as in an industrial or postindustrial one. Combatting oligarchy also has a very different meaning when the target is plantation feudalism than when the target is industrial robber baron plutocracy. Some early advocates of a democracy of opportunity imagined that these first two principles could be achieved through means such as breaking up large landed estates and limiting government so that it could not grant monopolies or other favors that promoted the accumulation of unequal wealth. By the late nineteenth century, advocates of a democracy of opportunity began to advocate redistributive policies such as the modern income tax, labor laws, and systems of social insurance. Their opponents, in turn, developed a vision of constitutional political economy centered on opposition to redistribution. The economic circumstances change, but these first two democratic principles—anti-oligarchy and the need for a broad middle class, open to all—remain clear.

Third, these strands of argument have sometimes been intertwined with a principle of inclusion: that the democracy of opportunity must extend to all the people, across lines of race, and later, sex and other invidious group-based distinctions. This third principle was embraced only fitfully by reformers and advocates in the tradition we are sketching. But at the moment in American history when the principle of inclusion was inscribed into the text of the Constitution—during Reconstruction—it arrived as part of the democracy-of-opportunity tradition. We argue in this book that all three strands together—anti-oligarchy, a broad and open middle class, and inclusion—are necessary to the most coherent version of the democracy-of-opportunity tradition and the only version that is compelling today.

We use the word *inclusion* to describe this strand because the core idea is to include, on equal terms, those who otherwise would have been excluded from the full range of opportunities the nation offers—in education, employment and occupations, housing, public accommodations, voting and politics, and everywhere that opportunities shape our lives. At that level of abstraction, it is a principle embraced by all sides in modern debates about equal opportunity and constitutional law. Conservative advocates of a thin conception of inclusion frame it in terms of formal equality. Thicker forms of the principle of inclusion have underwritten efforts by courts and lawmakers to restructure important features of our economic, educational, and political systems, with the aim of achieving what President Lyndon Johnson called "equality as a fact and equality as a result" with regard to formerly excluded groups.[20] In Johnson's day, and beyond, those thicker versions of the principle of inclusion often have demanded the attention to the distribution of wealth and social goods that is central to the broader democracy-of-opportunity tradition. These thicker versions of the principle have addressed questions about education policy, the availability of job opportunities, social insurance, access to capital and credit, and a variety of other questions whose answers together determine whether or not members of formerly excluded groups, as well as others, have real, viable paths to the middle class.

At various points in the trajectory of the democracy-of-opportunity tradition, some have tried to build a constitutionalism around the first two principles without the third: a democracy of opportunity for white men only. In fact, it is worse than that. Many of these advocates not only refused to include women and racial others in their democratic vision, they made the subordination of these groups part of their outlook and program. Sometimes this was a strategic matter of making common cause with racists. Some of the most prominent advocates were never anything but racists. But these three principles are not so easily separated. More than once, the fear of racial inclusion has helped drive an anti-egalitarian, antidemocratic politics that defeated the advocates of the democracy-of-opportunity tradition—a dynamic that has been familiar to anyone following American politics in the past fifty years.

What is far less familiar is the opposite story, which we aim to tell in this book: the way the principle of inclusion itself has been bound up in crucial ways—in victory as well as defeat—with the long arc of the democracy-of-opportunity tradition. Abolitionists, Reconstruction Republicans, Gilded Age labor radicals, some important early Populists, some left-leaning Progressives, and many left-leaning New Dealers understood the principle of inclusion, on the basis of race, at least, as a critical component of the democracy-of-opportunity project. The Reconstruction Republicans in particular viewed racial inclusion as fundamentally inextricable from anti-oligarchy, morally and in terms of political economy. This insight turns out to be central to understanding the constitutional project of Reconstruction and the Reconstruction Amendments, as we discuss below.

Today, the principle of inclusion has a seemingly independent life in our constitutional order. Inextricable during Reconstruction from the democracy-of-opportunity tradition, today it lives on, unmoored from that tradition. It is what Americans hear today when anyone speaks of "equal opportunity" in a constitutional register: the project of racial and gender justice and antidiscrimination law. Over the past three-quarters of a century or so, the principle of inclusion has proved remarkably generative. Social movements for sex equality and LGBTQ equality, for example, have made powerful use of this strand of the democracy-of-opportunity tradition.[21] But disconnecting this strand from the broader democracy-of-opportunity tradition risks thinning it out in ways that sharply limit its reach.

Tracing the Democracy-of-Opportunity Tradition

The first six chapters of this book trace the trajectory of the democracy-of-opportunity tradition in American constitutional politics. We begin at the beginning. Arguments in this tradition were at the center of the fight over ratifying the Constitution. As we describe in Chapter 1, that fight, at its core, was about the shape of the nation's emerging political economy. After ratification, rival views about the promise and perils of the framers' new design for a national constitution almost immediately became rival arguments about how to interpret the Constitution. These arguments underwrote the formation of our first political parties. James Madison and Thomas Jefferson loathed parties, viewing them as illegitimate factions. But they were persuaded that the Constitution depended on a more decentralized, democratic political economy than the nationalized, central-bank-and-patronage-based machine that Alexander Hamilton claimed the Constitution authorized and that he intended to build. In response, Madison and Jefferson created what became the first modern political party, the Democratic-Republican Party (or, later, "the democracy") to oppose Hamiltonian designs and, in the words of later Democrats, prevent the nation from becoming a "moneyed Oligarchy."[22]

Jacksonian Democrats like Congressman John Bell of Tennessee argued that the Constitution required a particular political economy: "I deny . . . that it is either proper, or consistent with the object of our Gov-

ernment, to promote the growth of the country in wealth, without regard to the manner of its distribution." "The fundamental principle," Bell
argued, "of the American Governments, local and national," is "equality
of rank, rights, and privileges. . . . Whatever measure of public policy
tends . . . to destroy the equality of rank and influence among our citizens, is not only opposed to the theory of our Government, but subversive of the fundamental principle upon which it is erected."[23] As we re-
count in Chapter 2, it was on this constitutional foundation that the
Jacksonians built their arguments for hard money, limited government,
and free trade. When the Whigs and their allies such as John Quincy
Adams argued for opposing policies, such as protectionist tariffs and a
more active federal government to advance the "general welfare," their
arguments too sounded in constitutional political economy. Article I's
enumerated powers, they held, were "not only grants of power but trusts
to be executed" and "duties to be discharged." The Constitution not only
empowered but *required* Congress to enact tariffs, because of the
opportunity-rich political economy such tariffs would help build.[24]

By the middle of the nineteenth century, Jacksonians-turned-
Republicans were arguing that the Declaration of Independence and
the Constitution required a Homestead Act to distribute public lands
instead of selling them off to the highest bidder. By the new Republican
Party's constitutional lights, it was "both the right and the imperative
duty of Congress to prohibit [Slavery] in the Territories" and parcel the
public land into homesteads for "the landless citizen."[25]

For the next quarter century, through the Civil War and Reconstruction, Republicans would press the idea of Congress's affirmative constitutional duties into service for the cause of making "Freedom National,"
by remaking the political economy of the South. The Reconstructed
Constitution, Radical Republicans would argue, impelled them to dismantle the South's old plantation-based "ruling and dominant class"
with its undying "spirit of oligarchy," and to redistribute their greatest
concentrations of wealth and power to what one Black Union soldier
would call the "bottom rails," from the "top" ones.[26] Thus these Republicans brought together for the first time in the mainstream of
American political life all three core principles of the democracy-of-
opportunity tradition: anti-oligarchy, a broad and open middle class,

and inclusion (at least in terms of race). These linked ideas were central to the politics and ideology behind the Thirteenth, Fourteenth, and Fifteenth Amendments.

These amendments took up and repurposed older precepts of the democracy-of-opportunity tradition, including ideas of equal protection, equal rights, and equal opportunities that had operated as safeguards for white workingmen in state constitutions and in the national constitutional discourse of the parties of Andrew Jackson and Abraham Lincoln. As we show in Chapter 3, the Reconstruction Republicans took hold of these ideas and inscribed them for the first time into the text of the national Constitution, in the service of securing a new guarantee of equal rights for those who had been excluded and enslaved. To the Reconstruction Republicans, this new ideal of racial inclusion was deeply enmeshed in the older antebellum discourse of the democracy-of-opportunity tradition. When Senator Charles Sumner of Massachusetts, a leader of the Radical Republicans, first proposed statutory language in Congress envisioning what would eventually become the Fourteenth Amendment, he began this way: "[T]here shall be no Oligarchy, Aristocracy, Caste, or Monopoly invested with peculiar privileges and powers, and there shall be no denial of rights, civil or political, on account of color or race, but all persons shall be equal before the law."[27] When the early women's movement attempted unsuccessfully to interpret the Reconstruction Amendments to require women's suffrage, they too framed arguments in terms of an unconstitutional "aristocracy" or "oligarchy of sex."[28]

Reconstruction is a case study in the central insight of constitutional political economy with which we began: that economics and politics are inextricably linked, and that a republican constitution requires a republican political economy to sustain it—and vice versa. As the leading Radical Republican on Congress's Joint Committee on Reconstruction, Thaddeus Stevens, put it, "The whole fabric of southern society *must* be changed . . . [i]f the South is ever to be made a safe republic. . . . How can republican institutions . . . exist in a mingled community of nabobs and serfs?"[29] All sides in the bitter battles of Reconstruction understood this insight, and Reconstruction's rise and fall bore it out. Violently disenfranchised, ex-slaves could not hold onto their new rights and opportunities in market and property relations; and by the same token, robbed of economic citizenship, denied any real measure of material independence, and rendered dependent serfs of their ex-masters, freedmen found that their political freedom was fatally vulnerable.

From Reconstruction onward through the New Deal, this point would be the constant constitutional refrain of the great movements for economic justice. What FDR would call "equal opportunity in the polling place" was impossible without "equal opportunity in the market place": Political citizenship was inseparable from social and economic citizenship, and both demanded a broad distribution of wealth and social and economic power.[30] There could be no republican form of government, and no democratic Constitution, in a society of economic "servitors" and "despot[s]."[31]

But the Reconstruction era's understanding that all three principles— anti-oligarchy, the mass middle class, and inclusion—rise and fall together was short-lived. They had been brought together at the point of the bayonet in the occupied South. In the North, they had rested on an unstable compound of moral idealism and hard-nosed pragmatism. Under the combined pressures of class strife in the North and white supremacist terror in the South, Reconstruction fell apart.[32]

The Republican Party in the North soon became the party of big business and its brand of economic nationalism. And many erstwhile Radical Republicans were dismayed when Gilded Age labor reformers seized on their old Reconstruction-era vision of a redistributive nation-state with affirmative constitutional duties to argue that the Constitution obliged Congress and state lawmakers to end "wage slavery." As we show in Chapters 4 and 5, Populist and Progressive reformers and lawmakers took up the democracy-of-opportunity tradition, reworked its ideas and precedents, and put it to use against conservative courts that were striking down maximum hours and minimum wage laws. The reformers argued that, rightly understood, the Constitution not only authorized but demanded these laws, along with legislation to safeguard workers' constitutional rights to organize, strike, and bargain collectively.[33] They argued that the Constitution demanded new taxes and antitrust laws, cooperative ownership of industry, and public ownership of the railroads, among other measures, to counter the powerful new concentrations of economic and political power that were emerging in the Gilded Age. As railroads and other trusts squeezed farmers and small enterprises of their livelihoods—and wielded wildly outsized power over state legislatures and the senators those legislatures sent to Washington—Populists and Progressives dove deep into the materials prior generations had bequeathed them and renewed the democracy-of-opportunity tradition with new initiatives aimed at redistribution, state-building, and structural reform.

Opponents of redistribution and reform also made arguments about constitutional political economy. They argued that a minimum wage and the new national income tax violated the Constitution, because of the kind of political economy such measures advanced: one in which the government takes from some to give to others. All sides in these nineteenth- and early twentieth-century debates agreed that the Constitution spoke to the political economy. The question was what it said.

By the late nineteenth century, the central debates in American politics—not only Reconstruction, but also taxes, monetary policy, labor, railroad transportation, corporate law, and antitrust—were all the subject of major constitutional arguments in which the democracy-of-opportunity tradition squared off against anti-redistributive rivals in a dramatic constitutional class struggle. The Supreme Court was so alarmed by new social movements that it began reading the Constitution to command violent repression of organized labor's strikes and boycotts, and to gut organized farmers' legislative victories aimed at regulating the rates railroads charged for shipping goods to market. Judicial condemnation drew Gilded Age reformers into a full-fledged reexamination of the terms on which an industrial economy and a democratic republic could coexist, producing a radical alternative account of the rights of citizens and the powers and duties of national government.

Both sides made arguments from constitutional text, history, and precedent, but the core of both sides' claims were structural arguments about constitutional political economy. For example, the Populists argued that the rise of the railroads and other trusts amounted to an unconstitutional abdication of sovereignty: Corporations were "private governments" performing "public functions" that usurped the real government's constitutional authority.[34] In the epic struggle over the gold standard, both the goldbugs and their opponents who advocated free silver contended that theirs was "the money of the Constitution."[35] When the Supreme Court struck down the income tax as too redistributive and socialistic for its Constitution, Populists and, later, Progressives made reinstating the income tax—ultimately through constitutional amendment—a centerpiece of their constitutional politics. The Populists and Progressives also embarked on a series of projects of constitutional reform of the political process itself. The new institutions they built—the referendum and ballot initiative, the direct popular election of senators—aimed to shift the political economy of who governed, and on whose behalf, to vindicate an underlying constitutional commitment to eradicating oligarchy and restoring democratic self-rule.

In Chapter 6, we describe how, from the depths of the Great Depression, Franklin Roosevelt's New Deal rescued capitalism and the Constitution from their conservative guardians. Business elites were patently unable to repair the broken economy, and the courts' laissez-faire precepts limited government's power to respond. During Roosevelt's first term, the federal judiciary continued repressing strikes and striking down reforms, including major New Deal legislation. The president accused big business and the courts of constructing a "new despotism . . . wrapped . . . in the robes of legal sanction."[36] A second constitutional class struggle unfolded, but this time, two of the three branches of national government stood on the side of a constitutional vision in the democracy-of-opportunity tradition. Roosevelt declared that the laws the Supreme Court was striking down were part of a new "economic constitutional order"[37] composed of government obligations to halt oligarchy and provide citizens with affirmative rights to work, livelihoods, and social insurance. New Dealers argued for this new economic constitutional order on the basis of the Constitution's Preamble, General Welfare Clause, and Guarantee Clause, and the Reconstruction Amendments. Their arguments set up an epic constitutional confrontation between the democratic branches and the Supreme Court. Roosevelt set out to "save the Constitution from the Court, and the Court from itself"[38]—and in the end, he prevailed.

But as we will discuss below, the terms of FDR's victory over the Court, surprisingly, set the stage for progressives and liberals to lose sight of the idea that the first two strands of the democracy-of-opportunity tradition are constitutional principles at all.

Today, there remains broad agreement that it is important to promote opportunity, avoid oligarchy, and build a robust middle class open to all. These ideas are mainstays of American politics. But they no longer sound to liberals and progressives, or indeed to most Americans, like *constitutional* principles.[39] Indeed, from within the current conventions of constitutional discourse it is not obvious what the claim that they are constitutional principles even means. We discuss how and why this happened in Chapters 7 and 8. Much of this book is a work of reconstruction: a work aimed at understanding the shape and texture of the democracy-of-opportunity tradition. Ultimately, the aim of the book is to reckon with the consequences of this tradition's disappearance—and to explore what is at stake in recovering some version of it as part of our modern understanding of the Constitution.

That is the question we take up in Chapter 9. Readers whose chief interest is the implications of our argument for contemporary constitutional politics may wish to skip ahead and begin with that chapter. Readers chiefly interested in one of the critical periods we discuss are welcome to begin with that one. For readers who wish to understand the whole arc and the richness of the democracy-of-opportunity tradition, and its role in the American story, we offer the chapters in the order they appear.

The Stakes of Constitutional Politics

From one vantage point, the project of this book may seem misguided, even dangerous, to our fellow liberals and progressives. Why should we want once again to "constitutionalize" our claims about political economy? Constitutional law, this objection runs, is the courts' domain—and ours is an era of remarkably conservative and powerful federal courts. Instead, these liberals suggest, let us hold fast to the "New Deal settlement," the ostensible détente over claims of constitutional political economy that followed the Supreme Court's retreat in 1937. Who knows what response abandoning that settlement might invite from the other side!

This objection completely misapprehends the present situation. The constitutionalization of political economy has already occurred. As Chapters 6 and 7 show, the conservatives who objected to the New Deal never agreed to the "settlement" that liberals imagine. Their ideological descendants are now busily framing in constitutional terms their many objections to liberal programs of social insurance, redistribution, labor rights, racial and gender inclusion, and the administrative state, using diverse doctrinal tools from the First Amendment to federalism and the separation of powers. They also employ tools that are ostensibly statutory rather than constitutional, but with constitutional claims looming in the background and driving the result. The strongest response to these arguments is to offer better substantive constitutional arguments—in court, and even more importantly, outside the courts. It is the liberals and progressives who hope instead to deemphasize the Constitution who are pursuing a course of great peril. There is no future for the proposition that political economy is "off the table" in American constitutional politics.

The reason for that is straightforward. Economic libertarians have a substantive vision of a political and economic order they believe the Constitution requires. They have long translated that neo-Lochnerian vision into rights claims that can be enforced in court. Even where such claims cannot be enforced directly in court, they can nonetheless *inflect* court decisions, the way libertarian freedom of contract inflects both the majority's and the joint dissent's reasoning in *NFIB v. Sebelius,* the (first) constitutional challenge to Obamacare.[40]

These moves are possible because the border between constitutional politics outside the courts and constitutional litigation inside the courts is a thin, permeable membrane.[41] Arguments cross it all the time in both directions. When the Constitution is understood by a wide public to do neo-Lochnerian work—to take the side of deregulation and private ordering—this turbocharges the arguments neo-Lochnerians make both outside the courts and inside. It invites those advocates to bring their constitutional arguments, unanswered, from politics into court.[42] And it invites advocates outside the court to use the pronouncements of courts to bolster and buttress their claims in constitutional politics, by giving their claims a special sort of authority: Their opponents might have policy preferences, but those preferences must yield to the Constitution.

In American constitutional culture, that move, if unanswered, can have real power.

The neo-Lochnerian school draws on many past rounds of constitutional conflict. It actually shares certain common roots with the democracy-of-opportunity tradition, particularly in the Jacksonian era, although it developed in a very different and reactionary direction.[43] Whatever the doctrinal setting, the underlying force of its arguments comes by dint of its vision of the relationship between the Constitution and our political economy—a vision that would be very familiar to veterans of many nineteenth- and early twentieth-century constitutional struggles over banking, currency, credit, labor, trusts, and federal power over economic matters. In a variety of domains, this vision was once locked in an elaborate struggle with the democracy-of-opportunity tradition. But today those struggles are more one-sided, with the neo-Lochnerian vision structuring both constitutional law and constitutional politics.

Consider the problem of oligarchy: the problem of concentrated political and economic power. Today, particularly on the left, this problem remains a pressing concern. But its relationship to the Constitution has become surprisingly attenuated. The dominant contemporary story of that relationship goes something like this. Economic elites enjoy too much political sway. But when our legislators attempt to do something about it—to blunt the conversion of economic power into political power—they hit a constitutional roadblock. The First Amendment, as interpreted by the Supreme Court, has come to mean that making political influence less unequal is not even a permissible *goal* for campaign finance regulation. In this story, the Constitution appears only at the end. The problem of oligarchy is not itself a constitutional concern; the Constitution only constrains what legislators can do in response.

Or consider a different problem: the inability of tens of millions of Americans who comprise the so-called working poor to afford health insurance, and to pursue their lives and ambitions free from the enormous and avoidable peril of going without it. Absent the Affordable Care Act's expansion of Medicaid, these Americans cannot obtain a form of security that has become one of the hallmarks of what it is to be part of the American middle class. Here again, there is a constitutional dispute. But the Constitution enters the story very late, and only as a potential roadblock, in the form of a Spending Power question to be answered by courts. Does the Spending Power permit Congress to expand Medicaid?[44]

The usual contemporary liberal response to such constitutional roadblocks is familiar: argue that the Constitution, when properly interpreted, presents no barrier. The First Amendment and the Spending Clause, rightly understood, do not condemn the statutes at hand. This is an inadequate response. It reflects a profoundly consequential twentieth-century narrowing of our collective sense of what a constitutional argument is.

Understood in light of the tradition we are reconstructing, in both of these examples the Constitution belongs at the beginning of the story, not the end. The first question is whether the Constitution *requires* lawmakers to enact measures like the ones the Court struck down. In past rounds of debate about constitutional political economy, arguments of this form were common. Proponents of the democracy-of-opportunity tradition in different eras often responded to constitutional claims that Congress lacked the power to enact laws like these with constitutional claims that Congress had not only the constitutional *power* to do so, but also the constitutional *duty*.

Such arguments were directed primarily to the political branches, and only secondarily to the courts. They reflect a constitutional world that was once familiar but is now much less so, in which many of the central debates were clashes over the affirmative constitutional obligations of the political branches, especially the legislature. And yet such arguments have consequences across all the branches, including the courts. In court, these arguments can help make visible the constitutional claims and interests at stake on *both* sides of many important disputes—not only on the side asserting constitutional constraints on lawmaking.

How did we reach this point? How is it that most of the arguments in the democracy-of-opportunity tradition no longer even sound like constitutional arguments?

The Great Forgetting

In the mid-twentieth century, liberals and progressives came to embrace two ideas about constitutionalism that their forebears would have found strange. First, liberals learned to think of the Constitution in a fundamentally court-centered way. They became enamored of the idea that the Constitution is autonomous from politics, separate from politics, setting the boundaries of politics. This meant that they forgot (or abandoned) their Progressive forebears' understanding of constitutional politics. Second, liberals learned to think of economics as a domain for experts, also autonomous from politics. This meant that they forgot (or abandoned) their progressive forebears' understanding of political economy.[45] As a result of these changes, the discourse of constitutional political economy ceased to make sense to mainstream liberals in the mid-twentieth century.

The idea of constitutional law as autonomous from politics became liberal orthodoxy as an unintended upshot of the terms on which New Dealers fought and won their climactic battle with the "old Court" and its conservative constitutional political economy. In Congress and in public discourse, as Chapter 6 shows in rich detail, New Dealers championed their legislative agenda in terms of implementing a new "economic constitutional order" in which the government would take on major new constitutional duties. There would be new statutes, new agencies, new protections for Americans' material security and access to economic opportunity, new safeguards for fundamental constitutional rights such as the right to strike and organize—all of it in the name of vindicating the promises of the Constitution and the Reconstruction Amendments. But the New Dealers saw nothing to gain by trying to win judicial assent to this outlook, which was wildly at odds with the views of the conservative Supreme Court. So, while New Dealers left no doubt as to the essential constitutional work they believed their new laws were doing, they defended them before the Court on Commerce Clause and Spending Clause grounds. Their political arguments focused on constitutional duty, as well as new fundamental rights, but their claims in court focused more narrowly on federal power.

After the "switch in time" in 1937, when the Court backed down from nullifying their reforms, the New Dealers prevailed. But what they sought and won from the Court was not a decision to make the New Deal's constitutional political economy its own, but simply a decision to step aside and allow other constitutional actors—the ones New Dealers believed were equipped to do the work—to carry out their duties. It was not the time to insist in court that the Constitution safeguarded the rights to strike and organize, or that it condemned gross inequalities of power between labor and capital. The Court had long insisted that the Constitution did just the opposite, forbidding democratic change in the harsh judge-made rules on all those matters. New Dealers believed that Congress had affirmative constitutional duties in this field, but they were content to have the Court simply acknowledge that Congress had the power to act. That was enough.

By the 1940s, even the opponents of the New Deal had moved their fight to other venues. The anti-redistributive constitutionalism of the *Lochner* era lived on outside the courts, animating the "right to work" movement. But it would soon find its way back into court. The New Deal's opponents never truly accepted any "New Deal settlement."[46] And then, in the late 1940s, the remaining legislative efforts of progressives to "complete the New Deal" and fully enact FDR's "Second Bill of Rights" ran aground. These sweeping reforms would have unsettled the South's separate, racially segmented, caste-ridden labor market, so they were thwarted by a coalition of Southern Dixiecrats and conservative Northern Republicans. Between the New Dealers' robust articulation of a modern account of the democracy of opportunity and its enactment fell the shadow of Jim Crow.

By the 1940s, the new industrial unions had emerged as the only powerful, organized constituency behind the idea that Congress had more constitutional duties to fulfill in the economic sphere to build a democracy of opportunity for all Americans. Blocked by the Dixiecrat/ conservative Republican coalition at every legislative crossroads, the unions instead fashioned a robust *private* welfare state by bargaining for private entitlements to job security, pensions, and health insurance for their members. Industrial prosperity, liberal tax incentives, and the hope of thwarting unionization prompted large firms outside the unionized sectors of the economy to adopt some of the main features of this generous, publicly subsidized, private welfare system. And with that, the language of constitutional political economy fell into disuse among liberals and progressives. Progressive claims of constitutional duty to re- cast market and property relations fell silent for the first time in more than a century.

The Court Ascendant

After 1937, one would not have predicted that the story of American constitutionalism across the second half of the twentieth century and into
the twenty-first would be a story of the Court ascendant. At first, restraint was the new judicial watchword. Some New Dealers were debating schemes for shutting down judicial review. Those went nowhere.
Instead, as liberal democracies fell across Europe, and the nation went
to war against fascism, attachment to judicial constitutional safeguards
for individual liberties and the rights of politically unpopular and vulnerable minorities came to seem an essential element of the American
experiment. Enlightened members of the liberal legal elite began to insist that the courts should continue and expand their active watch over
individual rights, when it came to civil liberties and the rights of "religious, or national, or racial minorities," in the famous words of a pre-
scient 1939 footnote by Justice Harlan F. Stone. In *Carolene Products*,
footnote 4, Stone intimated that the Court might transfer its oversight
from legislative transgressions in the economic field to violations of political liberties and minority rights.[47]

Nothing in that footnote preordained the rebirth of robust judicial
activism. But in the late 1930s, as the NAACP and its allies found little
welcome in their quest for equal citizenship for Black America in Congress or the White House, they set their sights on a court-centered approach, just as the Court was beginning to etch out a new role for
itself, in harmony with New Deal liberalism. Instead of the economic
liberties that it had policed before 1937, the Court became the great
constitutional arbiter of civil liberties, and ultimately, of civil rights.

"[T]he paradoxical legacy of Warren Court activism," and indeed of
Brown v. Board of Education, the constitutional scholar Bruce Ackerman
has observed, was that it established an idea of the Court as "the unique
spokesman for We the People of the twentieth century"—an idea that it
is the Court, and only the Court, that has the authority to enforce the
Constitution.[48] The view that the courts were the locus of our most
important constitutional conflicts—and that they were, amazingly, the
most reliable allies of liberal and progressive reform—came naturally to
a generation of reform-minded attorneys who came of age in prosperous,
postwar, Cold War America.

The first two principles of the democracy-of-opportunity tradition had faded, along with the idea that structural reform of America's political economy is an affirmative constitutional duty for lawmakers, not judges, to undertake. What was left of the democracy-of-opportunity tradition was its inclusionary strand and the project of racial justice. Because Jim Crow had a hammerlock on both Congress and the Democratic Party, the first moves were made in court. By the time the civil rights movement reopened the doors of legislative reform in the 1960s, the NAACP and *Brown* had set the stage for a remarkable melding of social reform energies with a new court-centered, countermajoritarian liberal constitutionalism.

In this context, liberalism itself changed shape. Chapter 6 recounts how Roosevelt and the New Dealers stole the label "liberalism" from classical liberals and made it stand for their *progressive* brand of redistributive legislation and administrative state-building. But postwar "liberalism" morphed into something new yet again.[49] Liberal social reformers and advocates for racial minorities, women, the consumer, and the environment all embraced individual rights claims addressed to courts; strong judicial oversight of administrative state institutions and private governance; and legalist, procedural conceptions of fairness and equality—all of which earlier generations of progressives had shunned. The rest of the democracy-of-opportunity tradition—the arguments about constitutional political economy that speak to the concentration and distribution of economic and political power—was forgotten.

Reclaiming Political Economy

As we discuss in Chapter 8, the Great Society was, in policy terms, the high-water mark of twentieth-century liberalism, yet it also illustrated how much was lost when American liberals ceased to think in terms of constitutional political economy. The Great Society unfolded at a distinctive, unprecedented, and brief political-economic moment of broadly shared prosperity. Thanks to New Deal reforms and the post–World War II boom, liberal reformers believed that America was becoming the kind of middle-class nation past generations of reformers had dreamed about—at least for white men. (As it turned out, those liberal reformers were wrong about that. But it was what they believed.) Increasing numbers of white men were enjoying a middle-class way of life, and a measure of dignity and voice at work, underwritten by strong unions, high wages, and a generous meld of public and private-employment-based social insurance. Poverty was a stubborn problem. But overall, broad-gauge class inequalities were at historic lows. All of this underscored the urgency of the work of racial and gender inclusion. For liberal reformers of this era, that was what remained: to open up middle-class job opportunities to Black America; to the overlapping category of the marginalized poor; and, later, to women.[50]

In this same period, political economy itself was fast being replaced by economics. Mainstays of debate about constitutional political economy from the turn of the twentieth century—monetary policy, taxation, antitrust law—all came to be viewed as core domains of the rising science of economics. They became technocratic spheres with expert solutions, rather than subjects that were obviously political to their core. The shift began during the course of the New Deal, as New Deal liberals embraced a more bureaucratized, technocratic vision of economic policymaking. By the 1950s, amid brutal anticommunist purges that silenced left-wing voices on economic matters, a mainstream liberal consensus emerged: Rather than "restructure the economy," the best policy was "stabilize it and help it to grow" through the "Olympian manipulation of macroeconomic levers."[51] With the left marginalized, its voices purged from mainstream politics, the divide between the two mainstream national political parties on matters of political economy was as narrow as it has ever been.

Thus, when President Johnson and his allies in Congress launched the War on Poverty, they insisted the nation could pay for it out of the increased revenues that would flow from continued economic growth. No tax hikes were needed, no controversial redistribution, no structural changes in the political economy. The Great Society did not aim, as nineteenth- and early twentieth-century reformers had aimed, to redistribute wealth *and power* between "capital" and "labor," the "few" and the "many," or private business elites and government. Those demands, in various forms, had been at the center of the political *and constitutional* claims of the Jacksonians, the Populists, the Progressives, and the New

Dealers. They are at the heart of the democracy-of-opportunity tradition. But they were absent from the Great Society agenda.[52]

Not everyone agreed with this change in focus. In contrast to mainstream white liberals, many Black civil rights leaders such as Martin Luther King Jr. and Bayard Rustin—along with left-leaning labor leaders, academics and intellectuals, and some New Deal veterans in Congress and the executive branch—rejected the notion that America's broadgauge class problems were a thing of the past, and all that remained was the unfinished work of racial justice and the inclusion of the marginalized poor. These Black leaders worried that by assuming the nation's class problems were solved and forgetting the older elements of the democracy-of-opportunity tradition that addressed them, Great Society liberalism was undermining its own ambitions.[53] They were right.

This forgetting happened at an unfortunate moment. Just as Congress, the executive, and the courts began to get behind the civil rights movement's demands for "Jobs and Freedom," just as Title VII of the Civil Rights Act of 1964 made equal employment opportunity a norm that reached into the nation's factories and offices, union hiring halls, and joint labor-management committees, the seeming abundance of decent jobs began to dwindle. The doors of middle-class opportunity in industrial regions and workplaces began closing. By the 1970s, the political economy was on its way to becoming the one we know today—one where, as President Barack Obama observed, "opportunity comes to be seen as a zero-sum game, in which your dreams come at my expense."[54]

This zero-sum dynamic provided the basis for the most enduring and successful political strategy of the past fifty years: convincing many white people that the most salient threat to their economic security and middle-class status comes from a runaway, often court-enforced liberal drive toward racial and gender inclusion. This strategy has produced an enduring realignment of our political parties. It has helped convince the literal and figurative descendants of Southern white redistributionist New Dealers to adopt a politics, even a constitutional politics, of antiredistribution. It has paved the way, as well, for a clever and consequential redirection of the anti-oligarchic strand of our politics, in which Republicans from Ronald Reagan to Donald Trump have argued that the real oligarchy people ought to be concerned about is not our economic oligarchs, but rather some combination of liberal elites, the courts, and the government.

This strategy and the realignment it provoked had one other effect as well. It ushered into existence a Democratic Party that, for the first time in its entire history, does not have at its core a large base of the most racist white voters. The Democratic Party remains a complex coalition with plenty of internal tensions. But it now has the potential—and here we make no promises about how soon or how likely this potential is to be fulfilled—to knit back together and advance all three strands of what Americans once understood to be a constitutional vision of a democracy of opportunity.[55]

A Twenty-First-Century Democracy of Opportunity?

This brings us to the present—a moment of deep inequality and profoundly unequal opportunity, when oligarchy has reentered mainstream political discourse, when the economic anxiety of the eroded middle class is roiling politics and fueling new forms of populism. Americans understand in a far more systematic way today than we did during the last Gilded Age that these themes are connected. Recent work in economics by Raj Chetty, Miles Corak, Thomas Piketty, Emmanuel Saez, Joseph Stiglitz, and others has illuminated some of the ways that extreme inequality of wealth *makes* opportunities more unequal: It has the effect of hardening class lines and giving elites both the means and the incentive to maintain and magnify their own advantages and keep others out.[56] Americans now understand more clearly than ever how *economic* and *political* inequality (and inequality of opportunity) are intertwined. Social and political science and popular and highbrow public discourse alike are focusing attention on the connections between the economic order and the political order, and how power flows between them.[57] We have the tools to recognize the threat our present political-economic situation poses to fundamental values of equal citizenship.

It is increasingly obvious that many questions that twentieth-century liberals had characterized as technocratic economic matters are instead fundamentally political questions. Questions of antitrust, for instance, or the regulation of banks and money, or the regulation of employment and its rewards—all these and many others turn out to be political choices, with large implications not only for the distribution of wealth but also for the distribution of political power.[58] In other words, they are questions of constitutional political economy. But the current conventions of constitutional discourse largely conceal their constitutional dimensions.

Some of the fights about these questions will take place in the courts. This book does, to an extent, speak to courts. The narrowest version of the argument of this book, viewed entirely from *within* current conventions of constitutional discourse, speaks to courts. It suggests how courts ought to understand and take proper account of the constitutional character of statutes and regulations that aim to shape our political economy in a way that builds and preserves a democracy of opportunity. Litigants ought to make these constitutional stakes apparent to courts. Courts ought to include them in their calculus when weighing whether to uphold these statutes and regulations against constitutional challenges.[59] In court, the democracy-of-opportunity tradition operates primarily as a shield rather than a sword: It aims not to strike down these statutes and regulations but to show why it is constitutionally essential to uphold them. Equally important, the tradition can function as an interpretive guide. Courts ought to make self-conscious decisions about how to *interpret* such statutes and regulations in light of their constitutionally significant purposes.[60]

However, the primary focus of this book is *not* courts. It is to help recover the crucial idea that constitutionalism is not exclusively a judicial domain. This is a necessary precondition for recovering any robust discourse of constitutional political economy.[61] If constitutional claims are judicially enforced conversation-stoppers, setting boundaries on politics, then the only kind of constitutional political economy that is conceptually possible is one of blocking legislative action. This works quite well for economic libertarians and sometimes for other opponents of the democracy-of-opportunity tradition. But it does not leave any space for the democracy-of-opportunity tradition itself—save the principle of inclusion, which on this approach is necessarily left hanging on its own, disconnected from the rest of the tradition and woefully thinned out.

This book is a project of reconstruction. We wrote it because we think those who developed this important tradition in American constitutional thought got a lot of the big things right. Most fundamentally: The constitutional order *does* rest and depend on a political-economic order. That political-economic order does not maintain itself. It requires action (as well as forbearance from action) from each part of the government. The content of what is required changes radically over time in a dynamic way in response to changes in the economy and in politics. But we believe the basic principles of the democracy-of-opportunity tradition remain affirmative constitutional obligations of government today: to prevent an oligarchy from emerging and amassing too much power; to preserve a broad and open middle class as a counterweight against oligarchy and a bulwark of democratic life; and to include everyone, not just those privileged by race or sex, in a democracy of opportunity that is broad enough to unite us all.

Thus, the first crucial move we are making in this book, necessary for getting the project off the ground, is this: We are asking liberals and progressives to step away from the idea that the Constitution is a thing outside of politics. That insistence plays into the hands of the courts; and more often than not in American history, courts have worked to protect the prerogatives of ruling elites, as they do today.

Instead, Americans must acknowledge and embrace constitutional politics.[62] All are engaged in it: progressives and conservatives, judges and legislators, people with law degrees and people without. To make arguments about the Constitution is not to cede all authority to courts, but rather, to claim—and to demonstrate, by claiming—that there is no judicial monopoly on constitutional authority.

One of the few redeeming features of the current era of political polarization is that it may help more Americans on the left half of the political spectrum to understand this point. In the special case of judicial appointments and confirmations, more and more Americans of all political stripes are beginning to see that there is constitutional politics going on. The next step is understanding the continuity between the conflict over judicial appointments and the broader conflict in our politics over the direction of the nation's political economy.

These struggles are as old as the republic. Arguing about constitutional political economy has always been part of American politics. It is part of what Americans do. Today, amid economic fracture and a battered middle class, in the shadow of the threat of oligarchy, we can see on the horizon a major confrontation between Congress and the Court over the direction of the nation's political economy. One side in this confrontation, the Lochnerian side, will have no trouble translating its vision of political economy into constitutional language and doctrine to thwart legislation. The question is what the other side will say and do—whether the advocates of a twenty-first-century democracy of opportunity will be able to see and articulate the constitutional stakes, and act accordingly.

Our project in this book is to recover and explain those constitutional stakes, while capturing something of the richness and resonance of the democracy-of-opportunity tradition itself. This tradition has long supplied an indigenous American language for making constitutional claims that address the structural dynamics of economic life. It also provides a window into a set of long-running premises about the economic foundations of the American constitutional order. This book invites readers to begin imagining how our constitutional order today might look different if it were informed by this crucial piece of the nation's constitutional legacy.

1

CONSTITUTION MAKING AND THE POLITICAL ECONOMY OF SELF-RULE IN THE EARLY REPUBLIC

The democracy-of-opportunity tradition has its deepest roots in the anti-aristocratic, republican ideals of the revolutionary generation. The revolutionaries of 1776 were hardly of one mind about what kind of republic they hoped to create, but they all held it a constitutional essential that the new United States avoid reproducing the hierarchies, titles, and aristocratic forms of privilege of the government they were leaving behind. They considered it equally essential for the new republican societies, which were the new United States, to be filled with "middling sorts," citizens who had enough to be comfortably independent, but not so much as to be aristocratic. Here were the anti-oligarchy and broad middle-class precepts in their youth.

For the revolutionary generation, political liberty—the very heart of the Revolution—depended on economic equality. The revolutionaries were conversant with the laissez-faire ideal of liberty as noninterference on the part of government. As good Lockean liberals, they prized the security of private property and the classical liberal freedoms of conscience and trade. As much as they were liberals, however, the revolutionaries were also ardent republicans. During the long contest for independence, the rights they prized most were not private but public ones: the republican rights of active self-government. And according to their republican heritage, what "liberty" meant was not merely noninterference with one's private rights, but something more. That was where economic equality came in—equality among white men, that is.

The republican conception of liberty was not noninterference but nondomination—freedom from both private and public overlords.[1] This republican brand of freedom required material independence. Either a want of ample resources for ordinary citizens at the base of society or a permanent concentration of wealth at the top would doom it. Unlike the liberal precept of noninterference, a government founded to secure this kind of freedom had distributional work to do.

Every well-informed revolutionary embraced this distributional outlook on the requisites for republican self-rule. Consider Noah Webster, hardly a firebrand or particularly radical, whose lasting fame would spring from his dictionary. "The basis of a democratic and a republican form of government," wrote Webster, "iz, a fundamental law, favoring an equal or rather a general distribution of property."[2] "An equality of property," he insisted, "is the very *soul of a republic*—While this continues, the people will inevitably possess both *power* and *freedom;* when this is lost, power departs, liberty expires, and a commonwealth will inevitably assume some other form."[3] Given this understanding of the political economy of freedom and self-rule, it is no wonder that the revolutionary generation believed republican governments had essential distributional tasks, and that they inscribed such precepts in their founding charters—the state constitutions they crafted in the late 1770s, as soon as independence was declared.

Once the Revolution was won, the founding generation—and every future one until the Great Forgetting—would fight over the inevitable tensions among these foundational commitments. Just when, where, and how should the need for "a fundamental law, favoring . . . a general distribution of property" give way to the security of private property? Just when, where, and how should active, popular self-rule on the part of the people give way to what many revolutionary elites saw as the indispensable role of the wealthy (and supposedly wiser and more broad-minded) elites in governing the new republics? National figures like George Washington, James Madison, and Alexander Hamilton grappled with these questions, and began to proclaim that while republics with too much concentrated wealth risked decaying into oligarchy, republics with too much unchecked democracy also degenerated. So, they called for a new constitutional balance. In the eyes of their popular critics, such calls for balance seemed a step in the direction of oligarchy dressed in republican clothes. Popular self-rule versus oligarchy would become a major motif of America's constitutional politics—first, in the battle over whether to ratify the new national charter these men had begun to imagine, and forever after, in clashes over how to interpret it.

So, the American experiment plunged the founding generation into battles over constitutional political economy and constitutional design. This chapter explores the trajectory of those battles, from the Declaration of Independence and the radical state constitution making of the late 1770s to the framing and ratification of the national Constitution in 1787–1789. In the course of these battles, we shall see, the founding generation produced a common culture of constitutional interpretation. This culture incorporated rival ideas about constitutional political economy, among them the broad distributional precepts we saw Noah Webster expounding.

The Material Conditions of Republican Freedom— Other People's Labor, Other People's Land

These precepts would endure for most of our constitutional history as touchstones of the democracy-of-opportunity tradition. Like other republican thinkers of the era, Webster channeled the seventeenth-century English thinker James Harrington, who had made the same freedom-and-equality point a hundred years earlier. "Equality of estates," Harrington wrote, "causeth equality of power, and equality of power is the liberty not only of the commonwealth, but of every man. . . . Where there is inequality of estates, there must be inequality of power, and where there is inequality of power, there can be no commonwealth."[4] Webster drew from Harrington a clear lesson for his fellow colonists: "Vast inequality of fortunes" was fatal to free constitutions.[5]

Webster's close friend John Adams also soaked up the ideas of these republican thinkers and gave them clear and careful application to the colonists' situation. An attorney and rising star in revolutionary Boston, Adams would defend the revolutionaries' view of the political economy of republican self-rule with Harrington's maxim "that Power always follows Property."[6] "The balance of power in a society," wrote Adams to a friend, "accompanies the balance of property in land. The only possible way, then, of preserving the balance of power on the side of equal liberty and public virtue, is to make the acquisition of land easy to every member of society; to make a division of land into small quantities, so that the multitude may be possessed of landed estates. If the multitude is possessed of the balance of real estate, the multitude will take care of the liberty, virtue, and interest of the multitude, in all acts of government."[7]

The seedbed of this uniquely American brand of republicanism was the presence in the colonies of cheap and fertile land, or what economic historians call a favorable land-to-person ratio. Securing that land for white settlers involved a meld of imperial violence and lawfare—treaties and other legal technologies, like debt and mortgage—inflicted on the indigenous peoples.[8] This won land cessions sufficient for the wants of white settlers, while leaving great swathes of fertile land in the hands of Native Americans. (In the 1830s, President Andrew Jackson would inaugurate a new policy of mass expulsion—egged on by Southern slaveholders and speculators who craved the vast, fertile "Indian territory" of the Southeast.)[9]

During the late eighteenth century, a great many white male settlers came over from Europe as indentured servants. Most of them served out their terms and then worked for wages. The land-to-person ratio assured relatively high wages and affordable land, turning these hirelings into landowners. The relatively broad suffrage rules of most of the colonies, which gave most propertied stakeholders a right to vote, enabled a majority of these white male settlers to become voters in elections for the colonial assemblies.[10]

There remained, however, the seemingly ineluctable need for subordinate toilers. Revolutionary statesmen assumed this labor would be supplied by women, children, young servants, and slaves—even if they had to be forced to supply it. America's revolutionary experiment in popular self-rule, civic equality, and democracy of opportunity for almost all its white males depended on the subordination of women, the violent subjugation of Black Americans, and the conquest and eventual "removal" of Native Americans.

The enslavement, expropriation, and death meted out to people of color was the other face of American freedom, as constitutional scholar Aziz Rana reminds us in his chronicle of America as a white "settler empire."[11] These two faces—the first that of a white settler who was enfranchised and owned land, and the other of a propertyless laborer who was likely not only disfranchised but enslaved for life—enabled patricians like Madison and Jefferson to imagine and embrace an unprecedented experiment in broad-based republicanism.[12] Black slavery muted elite worries about an experiment in popular self-rule in the context of what otherwise would have been a mass of propertyless but *unbound* white toilers. First, conquest, and later, Indian extermination and removal, made the fertile land broadly available to those same white masses.

Yet, as Rana underscores, even as Madison and Jefferson and the revolutionary leadership focused on white, male settlers, they articulated their broad conception of freedom in the universal language of natural rights and human equality. Mobilizing a populace to wage revolutionary war in that language set in motion egalitarian currents of thought and action that put pressure on social hierarchies, not only among white men, but beyond.[13]

Thus, it was no accident that this revolutionary moment saw the blossoming of what hitherto had been a tiny abolitionist movement against Black slavery. James Otis, a Boston attorney and leading critic of the imperial authorities in the decade leading up to the Revolution, wrote in his 1764 pamphlet *The Rights of the British Colonies Asserted and Proved*, "The colonists are by the law of nature free born, as indeed all men are, white or black. . . . Does it follow that 'tis right to enslave a man because he is called black?"[14] In the North, this egalitarian current put slavery on the road to abolition.[15] In the upper South, it led many leading figures to see the institution as an anomaly in the new republics, which they piously hoped was on the road to extinction. And in the Deep South, it forced leading statesmen to steel themselves to defend slavery as the foundation of the planter class's wealth and power—and, they rightly noted, the basis of much Northern mercantile and financial wealth.

So, as we shall soon see, the official constitutional order would supply strong safeguards for Black bondage and strong supports for a gendered, racialized, and class-bound construction of the political community, bequeathing a tragic and contradictory course of constitutional and political-economic development from which we are still trying to extricate ourselves.

Revolutionary Principles and the First Constitutions

The ideals of the revolutionaries did more than inspire the War of Independence. They also led to a significant political innovation: the world's first written and popularly ratified constitutions, drafted by eleven of the thirteen new United States during 1776–1777. They were written mostly by state legislatures, with a few written by delegates elected to special conventions.[16] The constitutions reveal that core ideas of the democracy-of-opportunity tradition were not just widely shared, but also considered fundamental for the new republics: abolishing aristocracy, ensuring a wide distribution of property, and giving the mass of "the people" (that is, the white male people) active participation and decisive power in government. The work of writing these constitutions, Jefferson observed at the time, was "the whole object of the present controversy."[17]

The general design of this first generation (1776 to the early 1780s) of republican constitutions went a long way down the revolutionary road of popular self-rule. The processes and institutions of government were constituted so that the "whole mass" of "the people" could ensure that lawmakers acted with an eye to their "happiness and safety."[18] The constitutions had an allocation of power among the branches of government (powerful legislatures, weak executives, and nothing in the way of judicial review) and other key features (frequent elections, small districts, rotation in office) aimed at making them exquisitely responsive to the outlooks of ordinary citizens, whose active participation in self-rule they encouraged. Constitutional review of the actions of government was still understood as an undertaking for "the People themselves."[19] And the unruly people undertook it, as we shall see, with regard to profound questions of constitutional political economy.

Every state constitution but South Carolina and Connecticut included annual elections for the lower house. South Carolina held its elections every two years; Connecticut, every six months. Several had annual elections for the upper house and the governor, as well. In addition, most had requirements for rotation of office—what today we call "term limits"—to return officials frequently "to a private station . . . into that body from which they were originally taken," in the words of Virginia's constitution, so they continued to feel "the burdens of the people" and "restrain[ed] from Oppression."[20] Only Massachusetts's constitution— the most conservative of the lot—provided the governor with a veto over legislation.

The Revolution's egalitarian push brought an expansion of suffrage rights to include the majority of white males. Before the Revolution, somewhere between 50 and 80 percent of adult white men had the vote.[21] During the Revolution, many states reduced and some eliminated property requirements, giving the ballot to all taxpayers, or to all with either a modicum of property or a "mechanic trade."[22] Nor was voting the only constitutionally enshrined form of participation. The revolutionary generation loved popular involvement too much to see the people extinguished as a constitutional actor. Most states also specified other kinds of participatory rights: "to assemble together," "to consult for their common good," and, in some, to "instruct their representatives" about how to vote on pending legislation, and failing that, to "apply to the legislature for redress of grievances by address, petition or remonstrance."[23]

The state constitutions of the 1770s and early 1780s also brimmed with provisions aimed at dismantling the aristocratic elements of the colonial social order. Thus, all of the new state constitutions rehearsed the later federal Constitution's Title of Nobility Clause, often in passionate language revealing something of the drafters' resentments toward the upper ranks of the old imperial order.[24] New Hampshire's constitution provided that "no office or place whatsoever in government, shall be hereditary—the abilities and integrity requisite in all, not being transmissible to posterity or relations."[25] Virginia's constitution decreed that "no Man or Set of Men are entitled to exclusive or separate Emoluments or Privileges from the Community, but in Consideration of public Services; which not being descendible, or hereditary, the Ideal of Man born a Magistrate, a Legislator, or a Judge is unnatural and absurd."[26]

The new constitutions also sought to broaden the distribution of wealth, power, and opportunity. Many revolutionary leaders were confident that the abolition of aristocratic laws and privileges would, by itself, go a substantial way toward closing the gulf between rich and poor. Over time, Noah Webster argued, an end to primogeniture and entail would produce that "equality of property" that is "the very soul of a republic."[27] Primogeniture and entail were legal devices for holding together the landed wealth and social and political power of "great families," essentially by ensuring that eldest sons, and they alone, inherited the bulk of great landed estates. Every state abolished them, sometimes by statute and sometimes by writing the abolition of these devices explicitly into their constitutions.[28] Webster seems to have been right in believing that the abolition of these reviled aristocratic institutions would, over a generation or two, produce fairly large distributional consequences; where economic historians have carefully examined the question, as with Virginia, it did just that.[29]

The revolutionary elites who designed the new constitutions were encouraging and responding to the expectations of plebian patriots that the new constitutions would ensure, in the words of Willi Paul Adams, a leading historian of the period, "not only that everyone enjoy equality before the law or have an equal voice in government, but also that everyone have an equal share in the fruits of the common enterprise."[30] Another has observed that such "equality" was "to be achieved if necessary through government acting as a distributive mechanism under the guidance of a population whose inalienable right to political participation was the Revolution's signal domestic achievement."[31]

Thomas Jefferson and Initial Endowments as Constitutional Essentials

While the revolutionaries of the 1770s and early 1780s agreed about the need for a broad distribution of property, wealth, and opportunity, they disagreed about what was necessary to achieve that result. Many agreed with Jefferson, who led the campaign against primogeniture and entail in Virginia but insisted that maintaining a republican constitution over time demanded much more. "[L]egislators," he wrote to Madison, "cannot invent too many devices for subdividing property."[32] Steep taxes on large landholdings and exemptions for small-holdings, along with public land policies, and even "agrarian laws" restricting large estates—all were apt tools for sustaining a republican citizenry and upholding the equal right of every poor man to the pursuit of happiness.[33]

In this spirit, Jefferson in June 1776 drafted "A Bill for new-modelling the form of Government" of Virginia, which included a section on "Rights, Private and Public." There, one finds the following declaration: "Every person of full age neither owning nor having owned 50 acres of land shall be entitled to an appropriation of 50 acres or to so much as shall make up what he owns or has owned fifty acres in full and absolute dominion."[34]

Libertarians imagine Jefferson as a foe of "energetic" government. He was that—but only with respect to a distant, central government, which he feared "always" would use its power in "oppressive" ways.[35] He was not skeptical about governmental power itself, particularly at the local or state level. Quite the contrary. As historian Joyce Appleby observes, Jefferson was "never loathe" to use both "constitutional and statutory measures to make the poor independent" and achieve and sustain "the institutional framework for a free society."[36]

An integral part of Jefferson's "system by which every fibre would be eradicated of antient and future aristocracies" from Virginia's constitutional "fabric" was his famous "systematical plan of general education."[37] The discussion of that plan gave him occasion to frame two enduring precepts of the democracy-of-opportunity tradition: first, that some social goods are so important to building and maintaining a democracy of opportunity that government must treat such goods as *initial endowments;* and second, that the *elite* must be wide open and drawn from all classes.

In the Revolution-era annals of the democracy-of-opportunity tradition, education was a social good second only to free or cheap land in undergirding the constitutional order of the new republics. These were the original "essentially necessary" initial endowments. Thus, just as Jefferson's draft constitution called for a right to fifty acres of land, so, as

Virginia's governor, Jefferson demanded and got an "amendment of our constitution . . . in aid of the public education."[38]

As with other states, Virginia's commitment to constructing something like Jefferson's conception of universal public education evolved over the next several decades.[39] The idea was firmly established, however, that basic education was, in Jefferson's words, "essentially necessary" for the "whole mass" of "the people themselves" to participate in government and be the ultimate "judges" and "guardians" of their "liberty" and "happiness." Without this initial endowment—without "mass" education—"government degenerates" into oligarchy, no matter its republican forms. Basic education also is "essentially necessary" to enable the "great mass" of the citizenry "to work out their own greatest happiness," which must "not depend on the condition of life in which chance has placed them," but instead must flow from "occupation and freedom in all just pursuits."[40]

Jefferson translated these precepts about mass education as a democratic republican constitutional essential into a blueprint, which became part of the Virginia constitution. It resembled a pyramid of public / private education. At its base were elementary schools where "every person [in the district was] entitled to send their children three years, gratis" to receive a basic education. Above these were "grammar schools, of which twenty are proposed to be erected in different parts of the country." There, tuition-paying students who could attend because of the "wealth of their parents" would learn alongside "geniuses . . . from among the classes of the poor," chosen each year from every elementary school in the area. After two years of grammar school, a "rake" of students "whose parents are too poor to give them further education" would select "the best genius" to "be instructed, at the public expence, so far as the grammar schools go," for a total of nine years of schooling, and half of these would be selected to be sent "at the public expence" to the College of William and Mary.[41] The idea was that "nature has sown" talents "as liberally among the poor as the rich"; yet the talents "perish without use, if not sought for and cultivated," to the detriment of both the individual and the state.[42] Thus, the "general system" was an educational charter for the idea of natural equality and the ideal of an opportunity structure with open avenues to the top.[43]

Jefferson's educational plan echoed the theme that loomed larger than any other in the orations marking the new republics' first Independence Day celebrations: the ideal of a "natural aristocracy" of "talent and merit." A farmer or mechanic hearing a notable patriot deliver a Fourth of July oration in any medium-sized town from 1777 onward was as likely as not to be told that the struggle for independence was ushering in a brave new world in which "all offices lie open to men of merit, of whatever rank or condition." "[E]ven the reins of state may be held by the son of the poorest men, if possessed of abilities equal to the important station."[44] Because it fit this ethos so well, something like Jefferson's blueprint, or at least a commitment to free common education, was inscribed in almost every state constitution.

Securing the Right to the Pursuit of Happiness

When Jefferson set to work on the Declaration of Independence in mid-1776, he had in his hands the Virginia constitution's Declaration of Rights, drafted earlier that year by his friend and fellow Virginian, George Mason. Mason's Declaration commenced with the "inherent rights" enjoyed equally by all men. Mason already had altered the familiar Lockean trinity of life, liberty, and property to include "pursuing and obtaining happiness," a change Jefferson took a step further in the Declaration by altogether dropping "property" in favor of "the Pursuit of Happiness."[45]

The substitution, which recurred in several of the new state constitutions, was about substance, not just stylistic felicity.[46] Many of these new constitutions made more explicit the right of the people and the duty of the state to promote the public happiness with language securing to "the people of this State . . . the sole exclusive and inherent right of governing and regulating the internal police of the same."[47] We can get a deeper purchase on the distributive and regulatory dimensions of the constitutional discourse of the early republic by pausing over these two words, "police" and "happiness," whose eighteenth-century meanings we have quite forgotten.

"Police," as historian Christopher Tomlins has reminded us, had nothing to do with uniformed officers of the law, which, apart from militia or regular military troops, simply did not exist in North America until the middle of the nineteenth century.[48] "Police" instead was the eighteenth-century ancestor of what today we call the "police power" of the states. As eighteenth-century lawyers understood the term, it harked back to Aristotle, or, more precisely, as Tomlins points out, to English translations of Aristotle explaining that the term derived from "polis" and "polity" and "can signify the constitution in general, or the constitution under which the many rule with a view to the common good," or "'[w]hen the masses govern the state for the common interest or public happiness.'" "Police" named both the source and exercise of governmental power whose key object was securing the common "weal" and "happiness."[49]

For a contemporaneous definition of the "happiness" whose pursuit the new republics aimed to make amply available for all, we can turn to a humbler source. William Manning was a farmer and tavern keeper in Billerica, Massachusetts, and a self-taught commentator on constitutional and political-economic matters. The views expressed in his pamphlets roughly tracked those of figures like Jefferson and the more plain-spoken Thomas Paine. Manning's work provides a good snapshot of the widely shared public meaning of key words like these. Manning defined that "Happiness" enshrined in the Declaration and state constitutions as "a person . . . enjoying the goods of his own labors, and feeling that his life and liberties (both civil and religious) and his property are all safe and secure; and not in the abundance he possesseth, nor in expensive . . . grandeur, which have a tendency to make other men miserable."[50] Government had the duty, Manning held, following Jefferson and Paine and their reading of Locke—a more literal reading than Locke may have intended—to prevent the wealthy from accumulating property to a degree that deprived the poor of their natural inheritance in available land and resources.[51] Enabling "the pursuit of happiness" was not just an aspiration; it implied a rich set of obligations of government.

And so, just as revolutionary lawyer-leaders like Mason and Jefferson were pushing aside the inherited "mixed" constitution of king, nobility, and commons and imagining "purely republican constitutions" in which "the many rule with a view to the common good," so too were they developing a notion of "Police" inflected by the natural rights discourse of the Revolution and the radical notion of "the people" possessing the "sole exclusive and inherent Right of governing and regulating."[52] The word appeared in the state constitutions and encapsulated the idea that the social and economic activities and relations of the new republics should be regulated (and also deregulated) with an eye to the "Safety and Happiness" of the "whole mass" of "the people."

How did this square with thinking about property rights? A rough answer emerges if we consider the replacement of "property" with "the pursuit of happiness" in the Declaration. Jefferson himself distinguished between the two. While property was essential to individual and collective well-being, it was not itself a natural right, "but one which is established by and subject to the civil power."[53] As such, the right of property was decidedly subordinate to the inalienable individual right to the pursuit of happiness.[54] Republican legislation and "police" could therefore impinge on the vested interests of large property-holders in order to maintain this inalienable right for the "poor many" to pursue happiness, and there could be no claims that such measures were violations of higher law.[55]

The striking absence of "just compensation" clauses in the state constitutions of the revolutionary era highlights these considerations.[56] Government could not take private property except for public uses, and not without either the owner's consent or duly enacted legislative authorization.[57] Beyond that, however, there was no right of compensation. As property rights were hedged by the right of individuals to the pursuit of happiness, so too were they hedged by the ability of the government to legislate for the common good.

Jefferson stood by his explanation of the phrasing of the Declaration after the Revolution. A dozen years later, when Jefferson was the United States' envoy in France, his friend the Marquis de Lafayette, the liberal French aristocrat and hero of the American Revolution, sent Jefferson his working draft of what would become France's 1789 Declaration of the Rights of Man and of the Citizen. The American envoy returned the draft with the words "Life, Liberty and Property" edited. Jefferson omitted "Property" and replaced it with the superior right to "the Pursuit of Happiness."[58]

The Push for a New Constitutional Order

Of these revolutionary constitutions, some worked reasonably well, while others—especially the national Articles of Confederation—did not. The Articles were more a treaty among sovereign states to fashion a common foreign and military policy than a real scheme of government. They had been drawn up to enable the colonies to fight Britain and had performed poorly even at this. As historian Jill Lepore notes, "regiments went unfed, soldiers unpaid, veterans unpensioned."[59]

Having gone to war to break free from one central government, the thirteen newly constituted republics were not about to confer too much power on a new one. The states would not even allow Congress to tax citizens to pay for the fighting. Instead, Congress had to rely on "requisitions" to the states. Even during the war, the states were decidedly uneven in meeting their obligations, and the situation worsened after the peace. Unable to tax, the nation was deep in debt, its credit dismal.

Ordinary citizens had no great use for taxes, but other deficits in Congress's power hurt them, and they knew it. One was Congress's lack of authority to regulate commerce. After the war, Britain barred American ships from ports in the West Indies and from the lucrative transatlantic carrying trade. Britain also barred important American goods like fish and whale oil from British markets. Britain allowed other goods into its markets—timber, tobacco, and wheat were the most important—but American producers of these goods still suffered, as the British exploited their monopoly over transatlantic shipping to fleece American growers.[60] The obvious response would have been to enact reciprocal restrictions against Britain, but Congress had no power to do so. Nor was Congress empowered to address the collective action problems raised by the actions of individual states. When any one state enacted trade restrictions, a rival state with a rival port could pick up the trade. Thus, fishermen and maritime workers, shopkeepers, shipbuilders and artisans, hewers of timber and growers of wheat and tobacco—a very broad swath of ordinary Americans—saw their livelihoods suffer as a result of the weaknesses in the design of the Articles of Confederation. Ill fortune also flowed from the lack of power to regulate commerce among the states.[61] During the 1780s, states began discriminating against their neighbors' trade. Spiraling trade wars frayed political bonds, even as they deprived everyone of the advantages of a common market. Every citizen with some link to the burgeoning market economy felt the pinch.

A further push for postwar constitutional reform came from a different direction. By the mid-1780s, many elites were troubled by the *state* constitutions, which had imparted sweeping policy-making ("police") powers to state lawmakers. They were especially vexed by the way state legislatures were confronting the severe economic depression that followed the war: providing economic relief for farmers and for the various tradespeople known as "mechanics."

Many such mechanics, along with small farmers and artisans, had gained local prominence as elected officers in the revolutionary militias and then became natural candidates for office in the small election districts created by the state constitutions. Now, these local leaders were making policy with an eye to their neighbors' burdens, exactly as the state constitutions envisioned. They eased the pace of debt payments, put stays on farm foreclosures, and issued various kinds of paper currency.[62]

National leaders like Washington, Hamilton, Adams, Madison, and even Jefferson began to bemoan the "excess of democracy" and the "spirit of localism" that pervaded state government. Local-minded state lawmakers had no idea of the damage they were causing the nation's credit abroad, to say nothing of the confidence of creditors and bondholders at home. "[T]he general disease," Hamilton told a friend, "which infects all our constitutions [is] an excess of popularity."[63] Madison agreed. An enfranchised "multitude" could abuse the "democratic parts of our constitutions" in a "leveling spirit."[64] Thus, leaders like Madison and Hamilton thought that Congress ought to be empowered not only to raise taxes and regulate commerce but also to block popularly inspired economic policymaking in the states and shift a good deal more policy-making power to the center.[65]

Put simply, much of the revolutionary generation's national leadership had come to think that America needed more elite control over political economy, and that, in turn, required a national government *with substantial powers over the states.* Thus, some of the very men who taught the colonial rebels about the anti-oligarchy principle seemed to be adding a big pinch of oligarchy to their vision for the republic.

That was not how Washington, Madison, or Hamilton saw things, of course. From their point of view, as we already noted, they were simply restoring the balance. Did not history teach us that while republics with too much concentrated wealth risked decaying into oligarchy, so too did republics with an excess of democracy risk toppling into tyranny? To more democratic-minded contemporaries, such calls for a new constitutional balance seemed a step away from popular liberty—a move contrary to the principles of a revolution fought against imperial rule. And, as we noted, popular self-rule versus oligarchy would become a lasting motif of the nation's constitutional politics.

The attitude of national elites, coupled with the glaring infirmities of the Articles of Confederation, made a major national effort at constitutional reform seem inevitable. But it took a more violent expression of popular liberty—one that highlighted the interactions between state constitutions and a still-revolutionary constitutional culture—to finally provoke these national figures to gather in Philadelphia.

Daniel Shays and the Massachusetts Constitution

During the summer and fall of 1786, a few thousand backcountry farmers in western Massachusetts rose up in armed resistance against the state's eastern, commercial elite, which dominated the state government, for its handling of the postwar economic depression.[66] The depression was as severe as any the United States would see until the 1930s, producing extraordinary economic pain that was exacerbated by heightened taxation to cover the states' war debts.[67] Foreclosures on farm mortgages reached staggering proportions. Taxes were so painful and foreclosures so pervasive partly because the new nation's supply of hard currency was drained off to pay foreign debts, mostly to English creditors.

Almost all the states responded, as they frequently had done during the colonial era, by issuing paper currency.[68] Not so Massachusetts, which had the most conservative of all the state constitutions. It was, as we noted, the only state constitution with a gubernatorial veto, and it retained stiff property qualifications for suffrage and officeholding. It also tilted representation heavily against the rural West, where the pain of the depression was most acute.[69] As a result, Massachusetts's lawmakers were alone in refusing to issue any kind of paper money or enact any other kind of debt relief.

The state's rural counties petitioned for redress, calling for relief measures that other states had enacted, like a paper-money land bank to lend money to farmers based on the value of their land, a measure for boosting economic activity the New England colonies had used with success in the past. Instead, the Massachusetts legislature in the winter of 1786 *hiked* taxes, demanding prompt payment in specie in order to pay down the state debt without delay.[70]

The farmers then did what their generation's constitutional culture taught them. They called conventions, county by county. No less than the national convention in Philadelphia that would unfold the next summer, these backcountry conventions were brimming with discussion of constitutional political economy and the links between constitutional design and the distribution of wealth and power. The main current of opinion in these county conventions held that the Massachusetts constitution was so "aristocratical" that it had become an instrument of rule by the moneyed elite. Only an aristocratically framed constitution could have yielded a government so hell-bent on enriching a small number of well-heeled citizens, like the shrewd Abigail Adams, who had bought the state's consolidated war bonds at steep discounts from the original holders.[71]

With their solemn pleas for constitutional reform ignored, some of the farmers who had gathered in the western county conventions turned, as had the rebellious colonies, to the next stage of constitutional opposition—forcible resistance.[72] Led by the farmer and Revolutionary War veteran, Captain Daniel Shays, some three thousand farmers, calling themselves "Regulators" rather than rebels, turned forcibly against private debt enforcement and set about closing down county courthouses. When the legislature passed a harsh riot act, delegating broad power to the governor to suspend habeas corpus, Shays rallied a group of the insurgent farmers to march on a federal arsenal. A better-equipped army blocked them. When it came to actually arresting the insurgents, local militia units refused, and several thousand privately financed troops put down Shays's Rebellion.[73]

Thomas Jefferson had a "famously measured reaction" to the uprising in Massachusetts.[74] Writing Abigail Adams from Paris, Jefferson told his friend, "I like a little rebellion now and then," as the "spirit of resistance to government is so valuable on certain occasions that I wish it to be always kept alive."[75] Lacking Jefferson's distance—and his greater enthusiasm for the constitutional function of popular resistance—the great majority of national figures were horrified. Other states were beginning to see county courts shut down and foreclosures resisted. Washington feared that the rebellion would spread all the way to Virginia, and he began to wonder whether the nation needed a king after all. "We are," he wrote Madison, "fast verging to anarchy and confusion!"[76]

The Constitutional Convention

In New York, Congress responded to this anxious climate by approving Hamilton's proposal for a convention in Philadelphia "for the sole and express purpose of revising the Articles of Confederation."[77]

The elites' hope of containing the excesses of democracy found its clearest expression in the plan proposed at the convention by the Virginia delegation. The antidemocratic sentiments expressed in support of the so-called Virginia Plan help undergird the case so often made by historians that the Philadelphia Convention was a constitutional "coup" or "counterrevolution" against the democratic impulses set loose by the Revolution.[78] But viewing the framing through the lens of "counterrevolution" risks obscuring the broad accommodations made for popular anti-oligarchic sentiments during the drafting and ratification processes. The Constitution-as-coup idea slights the compromises and continuities between the new constitutional order and the revolutionary republican outlook reflected in the egalitarian ethos and "democratic parts of our [earlier] constitutions."[79] As we shall see, that radical outlook constrained and shaped the convention's work, most obviously by contributing to the swift rejection of the Virginia Plan itself. This same radical outlook was also behind many of the arguments made by Anti-Federalists during the ratification debates, and it shaped an important interpretive frame for the Constitution that remained active in our law and politics and continued to shape constitutional developments over the coming century.

Of all the states, Virginia had the most wealth, the biggest population, and—with none other than George Washington at its head—the most distinguished of all the delegations present in Philadelphia. As such, the Virginia Plan, prepared by Madison and presented by the state's young governor, Edmund Randolph, set the terms of discussion and debate over the next four months.

The Virginia Plan envisioned a national government with a full-blown executive, legislature, and judiciary. That was a fundamental change; but it stuck. More controversial were the new powers the Virginia Plan aimed to confer on Congress. Under the Articles, Congress enjoyed very few powers, and those powers were carefully enumerated and pertained to mutual defense. Any "power, jurisdiction [or] right" not "expressly delegated" by the Articles was reserved to the states, which retained their "sovereignty, freedom and independence."[80] The Virginia Plan upended this, conferring a new, sweeping grant of power "to legislate in all cases to which the separate States are incompetent; or in which the harmony of the United States may be interrupted by the exercise of individual Legislation."[81] Lest there be any doubt about who would determine the scope of state versus national competence, the Virginia Plan also empowered Congress "to negative all laws passed by the several States contravening, in the opinion of the national legislature, the articles of union"—in other words, to strike down any state laws Congress deemed unconstitutional.[82]

Edmund Randolph was blunt about the reason that he and others wanted a stronger federal government. "Our chief danger arises from the democratic parts of our [state] constitutions," he explained. "None of the constitutions have provided sufficient checks against the democracy."[83] Madison argued that the "evils which had perhaps more than anything else, produced this convention" were the "Interferences" of the state legislatures with the "security of property rights, and the steady dispensation of Justice."[84] As far as framers like Madison, Randolph, Washington, and Hamilton were concerned, not only interstate trade barriers, but a much broader swath of state laws governing economic life, including debtor relief laws, land banks, and what Madison called "the havoc of paper money," were all "aggressions [on] the rights of other states" and "destructive of the general harmony."[85] The Virginia Plan promised to halt these aggressions and the "excess of democracy" that produced them by giving financial and monetary policy-making power to the small body of elite lawmakers that Madison and the others expected to occupy the halls of Congress. Giving Congress the power to "negative" such state measures and to regulate currency and credit systems was exactly the strong medicine the republic needed.

The great majority of delegates at Philadelphia swiftly rejected the Virginia Plan's central aim of sweeping aside the old regime of "enumerated powers." Plenary congressional authority to legislate wherever Congress sees fit was certain to be seen as an unacceptable threat to popular self-rule and the people's "inherent right" of governing and regulating "the internal Police" of their states. The congressional "negative" on state legislation was cast aside the same day for the same reason.[86] Madison was vexed. Congress's "negative" went to the heart of subduing the states. During the debate on the proposal, he had called it "the great pervading principle that must control the centrifugal tendency of the states," without which they "would continually fly out of their proper orbits."[87] It was his brainchild, and he had a hard time letting it go.[88] The "Father of the Constitution" warned that there would be no end to constitutional contests over political economy, and no strong and durable national vehicle for putting them to rest.[89] He was right about that. Much would remain open-ended and contested under the new order.

In place of a general supervisory power over the states, the delegates inserted provisions in Article I, Section 10, directly forbidding the states from enacting the measures that states were most often enacting—and the most distasteful to the Virginians and other elites. Thus, Section 10 banned state emissions of paper money, forbade the states from making anything but gold or silver legal tender in payment of debts, and barred them from passing debtor relief laws that "impair[ed] the Obligation of

Contracts."[90] These constitutional prohibitions aimed to block states from enacting the types of political-economy interventions—debtor relief—that the farmers and "Regulators" of western Massachusetts had so urgently demanded from their government.

However, rather than being imposed by a congressional veto, these substantive restraints would be enforced only by the Supremacy Clause, which bound "the judges in every state" to enforce constitutional limits against contrary state laws.[91] Even assuming that the Supreme Court would exercise some measure of supervisory authority over the state judges, *state* adjudications were a pale substitute for the Virginia Plan's omnibus *national* veto. Much as Madison gloomily expected, state legislatures went on enacting debtor-relief laws—almost two hundred over the course of the nineteenth and early twentieth centuries; and state lawmakers regularly took up matters of political economy the new Constitution seemed to assign to national government.[92]

Ultimately, what the framers ended up forging in the way of new national powers looked less like the wholesale transfer envisioned by the Virginia Plan and more like the particular grants widely anticipated at the beginning of the process. The national government got the power to raise and pay for an army; it got foreign affairs powers, to make treaties and declare war, without unanimity but with a supermajority in the Senate; and in the realm of political economy, it got a national taxing power, national control over tariffs, and national power to regulate interstate and foreign commerce. During ratification, this last trio of powers would prove widely popular; they promised to address British trade barriers, quell internal trade wars, and raise new federal revenue via custom duties, which seemed likely to ease the tax burden on farmers.[93]

Determining the class of men who would exercise these new powers became as important to the new constitutional order as the powers themselves. Debates about the all-important architecture of representation brought together debates over constitutional design and political economy. What weight would state population be given? What weight would go to the states' respective contributions to national wealth? How much clout would economic elites—the Southern planters and Northern merchants—enjoy over the emerging national political economy and the future course of economic development? How much would be enjoyed by ordinary citizen farmers, artisans, and mechanics? Apportioning representation engaged all those questions; no wonder it provoked the convention's fiercest clashes.

The framers aimed to make sure that the new national lawmakers would be men like themselves, men who got the big picture. For the most part, they thought constitutional design and the sheer scale of the nation—Madison's "extended Republic"—would bring about their aims. Compared to state election districts, the ratio of voters to representatives in the House districts was daunting. Winning elections in such big districts would require higher profiles, broader reputations, and, in all likelihood, greater wealth. The political economy would be in safer hands. Senators would be chosen by the state legislatures to represent the states as wholes. Thus, they too would need to be men of broad reputations, as would the president and vice president.

The conflicting interests of the different state delegations prevented any easy solution to the problem of representation. Delegates from the smaller states recoiled from the Virginia Plan's reliance on state population for apportioning representation in *both* houses. But disparities of size were not the chief problem. "The States," Madison observed, "were divided into different interests not by their difference of size . . . but principally from the effects of their having or not having slaves."[94]

The Political Economy of Slavery

Slavery implicated deep rifts. Between 1776 and 1787, the United States had "imported" and enslaved some two hundred thousand people, bringing the total enslaved population to seven hundred thousand. By 1787, slavery had been practically abolished in New England and was eroding in Pennsylvania and New York. At the same time, it was fast becoming the basis of social and economic organization in five of the thirteen states, where enslaved people accounted for fully 40 percent of the population. These five Southern states' slave plantation economies had produced the new nation's richest regional elite and most of the whole country's wealth.

These Southern economies also diverged from the rest in being based predominantly on the export crops of tobacco, rice, and indigo (cotton would come later, in the nineteenth century). The South imported most of its manufactured goods and relied on others to carry its imports and exports. Accordingly, the South leaned in favor of free trade. In contrast, the North's diversified economy, with a growing manufacturing sector and a great many shippers and merchants, inclined its statesmen to favor tariffs and other mercantilist restraints on trade.[95]

As the historian Michael Klarman underscores in his invaluable account, this clash of economic interests, more than rival views about the morality of slavery, drove the debates over the shape of representation. True, the Northern delegations included men prominent in the antislavery movement, like Benjamin Franklin and Alexander Hamilton. But they were there to create a strong union, and they knew that the Southern delegations would not abide any scheme that outlawed slavery or expressly empowered the contemplated new union to do so. The Southern delegations were not much concerned with writing explicit protections against emancipation into the proposed constitution's text. Their concern lay with apportioning political clout to enable Southern representatives to safeguard the region's distinct political economy and to thwart any future national policies aimed at undermining slavery.[96]

The delegates from slave plantation states managed that task exceedingly well. Slavery figured in two essential constitutional calculations, which captured something of the contradictory character of human property in a supposedly liberal order. How would slaves-as-persons figure in calculating state populations for purposes of apportioning representatives? And how would slaves-as-property figure in calculating the states' respective fiscal burdens for purposes of apportioning taxes?

Southern delegates wanted enslaved people to be counted for purposes of representation but not taxation. Otherwise, there being only five slave states, and slaves being fully 40 percent of those states' population, the South's political weight would come up short of its fiscal burden. Only by counting enslaved persons on a par with free whites would the five states' voting power be commensurate with their contributions to the union's wealth.

Northern delegates wanted slaves counted for taxation but not representation. How could it be, asked a New York delegate, that a Southern planter could go "to the Coast of Africa, and . . . tear[] away his fellow creatures . . . damning them to the most cruel bondages, [and thereby] have more votes in a Govt. instituted for protection of the rights of mankind, than the Citizen of Pa. or N. Jersey" who condemns the practice?[97] Similarly, a New Englander argued that demanding that slaves be included in Virginia's population count was no different from insisting that Massachusetts's "fishery" be included in its tally. Both were productive property under state law; both were "interests" the states' representatives would seek to advance in national policymaking. It was absurd as well as unfair and immoral for the Southern planters to expect a special boost in representation for their particular interest. Tempers flared, debate went nowhere, and the convention repeatedly deferred the divisive issue.

By bringing together the two controversial constitutional calculations—representation and taxation—the notorious Three-Fifths Clause broke through the impasse. The three-fifths formula was familiar from its use in determining the state "requisitions" that financed the national government under the Articles, apportioned according "to the whole number of white and other free citizens and inhabitants, of every age, sex and condition, including those bound to servitude for a term of years, and *three-fifths of all other persons* not comprehended in the foregoing description."[98] Gouverneur Morris of Pennsylvania suggested using it as a basis for apportioning *both* representation *and* taxation. At once, a great many delegates from both sections applauded the "justice" of Morris's compromise, as most delegates already agreed that taxation and representation should be linked.[99]

The three-fifths "compromise" was in fact a masterful piece of pro-slavery constitutional political economy, in particular for its power in electing presidents. Many found James Wilson's proposal that the people themselves choose the president attractive, but the idea had a fatal defect from the slaveholders' perspective: If the president were chosen by popular vote, then Virginia and the other major slaveholding states would have "no influence in the election on the score of the Negroes."[100] So, Wilson next suggested that the people elect delegates to a separate body, an Electoral College, to be composed of worthy men. That measure passed, and Madison swiftly maneuvered to ensure that the number of each state's delegates to the Electoral College would be determined by the number of its representatives in the House, which the Three-Fifths Clause now governed.[101]

Instead of "no influence . . . on the score of Negroes," the slaveholding South gained disproportionate influence. Virginia and Pennsylvania had roughly equal free populations. Thanks to its slave population, Virginia would commence with three more seats in the House and, therefore, three more electors in the Electoral College. Thomas Jefferson's victory over John Adams in 1800 was widely—and plausibly—seen as a consequence of the three-fifths compromise, and the electoral disparity does much to explain why, for thirty-two of the first thirty-six years of government under the new Constitution, the president was a slave-owning Virginian.[102]

Historians and interpreters of the Constitution have long disagreed over what meaning to attach to the euphemistic language in which the Three-Fifths Clause, along with slavery's other constitutional safeguards, was couched. Many say that prominent Southerners at Philadelphia shared Northern counterparts' qualms about the moral contradictions of slavery in a free republic and piously hoped the institution would wither away. In that case, they did not want to be remembered as bequeathing a national charter that bluntly declared its commitments to maintaining and protecting Black bondage. As Madison later explained, many delegates, including himself, "had scruples against admitting the term 'slaves' into the instrument."[103] In its place, they used euphemisms like "such Persons" (in the Slave Trade Clause), "other persons" (in the Three-Fifths Clause), and "person[s] held to service or labour" (in the Fugitive Slave Clause).[104] Some interpreters go further. They underscore that the framers might have provided slaveholding with even more sweeping and explicit safeguards; they chose not to do so. From this, it is argued, the framers deliberately left room for an antislavery reading of the Constitution to emerge.[105] One thing is sure: the framers' "covert language" enabled President Abraham Lincoln and his party to invent an antislavery reading of the text, making the most of the framers' textual scruples and pious hopes.

But whatever their aims, and whatever their efforts to make slavery's presence in the Constitution *seem* modest, the framers supplied the interests of slave owners with more formidable protections than any other ruling class interest. The framers' contradictory commitments to slavery and freedom, contained in the Three-Fifths and other clauses, were so deeply embedded into the architecture of the Constitution that it would require a violent revolutionary struggle to repair it. But in the summer of 1787, the compromises brought to a conclusion the drafters' work in the Philadelphia State House.

Ratification and the Joint Construction of American Constitutional Culture

The Constitution then went to the people. It was printed in newspapers and on broadsheets, "often with 'We, the People' set off in extra-large type."[106] The Constitution would be of no consequence, wrote Madison, "unless it be stamped with the approbation of those to whom it is addressed . . . THE PEOPLE THEMSELVES."[107] And so, between September 1787, when the old Continental Congress sent the Philadelphia Convention's handiwork to the states, and June 1788, when New Hampshire's vote in favor of ratification gave the Constitution legal effect, "the People themselves" engaged in profound debates about whether the Constitution deserved their stamp of approval.

The battle over ratification would turn out to be a generative moment of culture-making, as work by historians Woody Holton, Saul Cornell, and Gerald Leonard has underscored.[108] As Americans fought over the proposed constitution's meaning, they jointly created what would become competing interpretations of it, once enacted. Anti-Federalists made dire prophecies about the likely reach and application of key provisions, which they assailed in light of cherished republican precepts, anti-oligarchy chief among them. The Federalists responded both by pointing to compensating virtues of the new national organs and by providing assurances about how gently they would operate in a new federal framework. Almost immediately after ratification, the arguments and counterarguments of the ratification contest would morph and recombine into contending accounts of how the enacted text ought to be understood and how the federal framework ought to work. Anti-oligarchy would go from being a touchstone for misgivings and skepticism about the proposed new charter to being a principle for interpreting the powers it conferred. The Federalists' words of assurance about the nature of the new federalism they championed—and the continued authority of state legislatures over economic life—would be invoked against their own readings of the new Constitution. In retrospect, the ratification debates were laying much groundwork for arguments a generation later for a constitutional political economy in which the federal government's powers would be limited by "strict construction," leaving room for continued popular control over the shape of economic development and the levers of distributive justice.

The Federalists, the proponents of ratification, had important advantages. First was that the Constitution promised clear benefits. Compared to the parlous, postwar status quo, the new national government (with its powers to tax, regulate commerce, raise and pay an army, and make sure treaties were honored) was bound to bring more prosperity, safety, and security. Even many western farmers in the demographic heartlands of Anti-Federalism believed (correctly) that the new Constitution would fortify the white nation in its murderous battles with Native Americans. Thus, for example, the settlers in the western regions of Virginia and Maryland supported the Constitution in their states' ratifying conventions on account of Indian raids and worries that there were only "four or five hundred [U.S.] troops scattered along the Ohio to protect the frontier inhabitants" and that "[t]hose troops are ill paid, and in a fair way for being disbanded."[109]

Addressing farmers, Federalists constantly recurred to the promise that the new national government would also relieve one of farmers' most pressing grievances—their outsized tax burden. The grant of power to levy taxes, Federalists predicted (rightly again), would enable the new national government to rely chiefly on the most lucrative (and least painful) of taxes: tariffs on foreign goods entering U.S. ports. Under the Articles, such tariffs were levied by *states* with important ports. Thus, the greatest boon from a switch to federally collected custom duties would go to so-called nonimporting states. Unable to levy custom duties on goods arriving from overseas, Delaware, New Jersey, and Connecticut got whatever money they sent Congress from painful direct taxes. It was no coincidence that they were three of the first four states to approve the Constitution.[110]

Federalists had strategic advantages as well. The majority of nationally prominent public figures supported the proposed new Constitution, as did the majority of newspapers. Delegates to the state ratification conventions were drawn from voting districts that had been crafted to favor the states' wealthier eastern and coastal districts, where public sentiment more often supported the controversial new charter—and to disfavor the poorer western districts, where it was more often opposed.[111]

Yet, in spite of all the benefits it promised, and in spite of the acknowledged defects of the Articles of Confederation, the contest over ratification was incredibly close; ordinary citizens and the delegates they chose were profoundly divided about the proposed constitution.[112] It promised weighty advantages, but to a great many voters, it also seemed a bridge in the wrong direction, leading backward to the aristocratic past and government by the high and mighty.

Alexander Hamilton rightly cautioned that the "democratical jealousy of the people" was sure to be "alarmed at the appearance of institutions that may seem calculated to place the power of the community in few hands."[113] Anti-oligarchy would prove to be the opposition's rallying cry.[114] While Federalists cited the excesses of democracy and the ills of disunity, Anti-Federalists feared the loss of the democratic ethos and egalitarian spirit of the Revolution, which had led to the hard-won, decentralized, state-based constitutional order. What would become of the people's "sole exclusive and inherent Right of governing" their states' political economies with an eye to the "happiness of the people"?[115]

At the Virginia Ratifying Convention, Patrick Henry, revolutionary hero and eloquent foe of the new Constitution, channeled these popular worries: "I dread the operation of it on the middling and lower class of people: It is for them I fear the adoption of this system."[116] In New York, Melancton Smith, the state's leading Anti-Federalist, agreed. The large, new federal legislative districts, even for the supposedly democratic lower house of Congress, would favor men "unacquainted with the common concerns and occupations of the people." Such "aristocrats" "do not feel for the poor and middling class," said Smith. "[T]he reasons are obvious. They are not obliged to use their pains and labor to procure property. . . . They consider themselves above the common people [and] do not associate with them."[117] The same worry animated the *Dissent of the Minority to the Pennsylvania Ratifying Convention,* which circulated widely in other states. Even though it was among the most populous states, Pennsylvania would send only ten representatives to Congress. The system of representation, warned the dissenters, would privilege the "lordly and high-minded" who "will have no congenial feelings with the people."[118] The astute young John Quincy Adams, watching the ratification contest unfold while at Harvard College, made the same observation about the size of the districts. If only *"eight* men should represent the people of this Commonwealth," he warned, "they will infallibly be chosen from the aristocratic part of the community."[119]

Patrick Henry's fellow Virginian, the framer-turned-foe George Mason, tapped into the same worries when he warned that the form of government set out in the proposed constitution was a "moderate aristocracy" that was bound to turn into a "corrupt, tyrannical aristocracy," over time.[120] Indeed, that was just the point, Tom Paine declared. The proposed constitution was "a copy, though not quite as base as the original, of the form of the British government."[121] Aping the British form of government, it could end up, like the original, as oligarchy.

Federalists responded to these Anti-Federalist concerns most eloquently in the eighty-five essays that came to be known as the *Federalist Papers,* authored by Hamilton, Madison, and John Jay under the name "Publius." The gist of Publius's case was this: the American experiment in republican self-rule was in peril, and the proposed new constitution would rescue it. All true "friends of . . . public and personal liberty" should rally to it, wrote Publius.[122]

Constitutional scholars love to underscore Madison's genius in anticipating the insights of modern political science about the logic of collective action. And Madison's constitutional political economy tool kit indeed anticipated some of our own analytic tools for understanding how constitutional design shapes strategic advantages, molding the distribution of wealth and power over time. But a closer look at the ratification debates shows that Madison was hardly alone in his shrewdness about the logic of collective action. The practical experience of a decade's worth of state politics had led some prominent Anti-Federalists to the same insights. But the Anti-Federalists pressed them in a different direction, highlighting a crucial weakness in Madison's account: He addressed the problem of oppression by majority factions, but ignored the problem of oppression by elites.

Factions, Madison famously wrote, are the bane of the republican form of government—majority factions above all, and most especially, majority economic factions composed of the poor many.[123] Experience confirmed that the poor many could and would use their votes to despoil the wealthy few. A great virtue of the proposed "extended republic," with its large electoral arenas, was that it would stymie such factions in their efforts to make laws and policies for their own selfish and partial purposes. The smaller the arena, the easier it is for a selfish majority to gather its forces and trample the rights and interests of others, like the wealthy few. The larger the arena, the greater the coordination problems confronting would-be factions, the greater the number of cross-cutting group interests, and the harder it becomes for a selfish majority to oppress others. Accordingly, Madison is praised for showing that if you want a pure republic, the logic of collective action favors an "extended" one.[124] A larger republic's larger districts, Madison explained, would necessarily produce lawmakers and officials with fatter wallets and bigger reputations than state officeholders. More than that, however, they would be men with broader horizons and greater characters—the "purest and noblest," in his words.[125] Under the new constitution, ruling elites would be disinterested and pure, and they would be pure and disinterested *because* they were elite.[126]

But what about the distinct capacity of elites to harness republican institutions for selfish ends? Anti-Federalists rightly pointed out that the same logic of collective action had something significant to say about this unacknowledged problem of elite domination. Melancton Smith put it well at New York's ratifying convention in June 1788. "The great easily form associations," said Smith, apropos of the large districts into which New York would be carved for choosing national representatives, but "the poor and middling class form them with difficulty." In such large districts, "the common people will divide, and their divisions will be promoted by the others." By contrast, "the *natural aristocracy*"—Smith used the common phrase with irony—would "easily unite their interests."[127] A Massachusetts Anti-Federalist similarly explained the ease of collective action on the part of the state's "compact" elite. Among the elite, "there is a constant connection and intercourse," to say nothing of patronage and family networks. Thus, they are easily able to "centre their votes" and align their "interests" in legislation and policy; farmers, by contrast, were "scattered far and wide" and despite being in the majority, would find it much harder in large districts to "act in concert."[128]

The peril of elite domination was compounded by the expansive powers the Philadelphia Convention conferred on these lordly new lawmakers and officials. True, the federal government's powers were carefully enumerated. But what difference would that make, given such provisions as the Necessary and Proper Clause? How easy it would be for an ambitious set of moneyed aristocrats in the proposed new Congress, equipped with that elastic clause, to read their power to regulate commerce to reach deep into the contract and property relations of every humble citizen! Or to read their powers to tax and borrow to authorize a national bank for outsized speculators and stockjobbers to exploit![129] How easy for these new national lawmakers to read their power to create inferior federal courts as authority to legislate the all-important rules of everyday social and economic life that would obtain in those courts— rules that hitherto had been the sacred province of each state's "police" and common law.[130] All that would remain for the lowly state governments to do would be "*yoaking hogs* [and] determining the width of *cart wheels.*"[131]

Federalists devoted much eloquence and ingenuity to addressing the fears raised by their foes. The powers of the proposed new federal legislature, they insisted, would not upset the republican order of things. The new federal machinery's main focus would be on the nation's foreign affairs.[132] The Anti-Federalists were torturing the draft constitution's natural meaning in order to find such sweeping authorization for federal power over domestic affairs.[133] Not federal but state government and state law, insisted Publius, would reign over domestic matters and the affairs of everyday life.[134] "The powers reserved to the several States will extend to all the objects which, in the ordinary course of affairs, concern the lives, liberties, and properties of the people, and the internal order, improvement and prosperity of the State."[135] State government, declared Hamilton rather disingenuously, would continue to hold the levers of distributive justice.[136] The people's "inherent right to govern and regulate" the political economies of their respective states would remain untrammeled.

And what, finally, was one to make of the glaring lack of a bill of rights? "A bill of rights," Jefferson reproached Madison, "is what the people are entitled to against every government on earth."[137] The lack of a bill of rights cost the Federalists many allies and would-be supporters. It encapsulated the perils Anti-Federalists underscored—about individual rights, about popular self-rule and the collective liberties it demanded, about threatened encroachments on the states.[138] All could agree that the states were essential guardians of "popular liberty," "Public Happiness," and "distributive Justice," but the Anti-Federalists were not buying the assurances by Madison and Hamilton and their colleagues that states would continue to have the authority to perform the work. The Federalists scoffed at the notion that their proposed text needed amendments or a bill of rights, only to reverse themselves in the nick of time.[139] Facing potential defeat at the all-important New York and Virginia ratifying conventions, they grabbed hold of a compromise and fallback position that the Anti-Federalists had provided: the state conventions should ratify, but on the condition that the first order of business for the new Congress should be to propose amendments embodying a bill of rights. And so they did, and so it was.

The promise and swift delivery of amendments helped ensure wide acceptance of the new republic by erstwhile foes. The amendments—the Tenth Amendment in particular, as it reaffirmed the powers of the states to safeguard popular liberty—baked some more of the old egalitarian and democratic republican constitutional ethos into the new order.[140] They entitled the Anti-Federalists to feel that the final product was also their work, to be interpreted according to their lights.

The entire process of ratification crystallized what we have dubbed the unintentional process of joint construction of a constitutional culture, equipped with nascent rival interpretations and rival constitutional political economies, each with plausible claims on the new charter. What had been arguments against the Constitution would become arguments about its meaning and application. The Federalists won the crucial battle of ratification, but the Anti-Federalists' outlook went on to win a great many of the battles of interpretation that followed.

In these interpretive encounters, the old revolutionary political economy of broad, egalitarian distribution and democracy of opportunity remained central. And so too, of course, did the Federalist case for strong centralized powers to construct and maintain a national political economy that worked for the collective good in ways beyond the competence of individual states. Quite unwittingly, the ratification contest had sown the seeds of the two-party system, which would take shape around exactly this divide over the direction of the nation's constitutional political economy.

The Political Economy of the Birth of Partisanship

After ratification, as the federal government began to take shape, many in the front ranks of national leadership, like Jefferson and George Mason, worried that the new national framework might provide the machinery by which the privileged classes would climb to new oligarchic powers. As Madison watched the first treasury secretary, Alexander Hamilton, pursue policies that seemed to justify those fears—policies aimed at creating a strong central, fiscal-military state, with a national bank, a national debt, and a national patronage-based moneyed elite, openly modeled on Britain's—Madison reversed (or at least, dramatically shifted) ground.[141] During the 1790s, he joined Jefferson in creating a national opposition, based on the very values and institutions he had gone to Philadelphia to subdue.

The pair coordinated newspaper campaigns against the bank and Hamilton's other policies. As leaders of the burgeoning Democratic-Republican opposition movement, they forged an enduring outlook on federalism and republican self-rule and political economy under the new Constitution: an outlook rooted in states' rights and the democracy-of-opportunity tradition bred by the revolutionary contest. By tightly linking text, structure, and political economy in one discourse, the Democratic-Republicans made the distributional purposes and effects of national policies into matters of great constitutional moment. According to this outlook, the bank and other Federalist policies not only breached constitutional limits and usurped powers that the Constitution assigned to the states, but also imperiled the constitutional order by promising to concentrate wealth and power in a moneyed aristocracy with control over the levers of public policy and private finance. Hamilton's *Reports on the Public Credit* and *Report on Manufactures* openly laid out the scheme, with his arguments for the bank's legality revealing some of the ways that the would-be Federalist oligarchy meant to exploit the Constitution's open-ended clauses, like the Necessary and Proper Clause, to justify it.[142]

In truth, there was much to be said for Hamilton's vision of America as a manufacturing powerhouse, destined to overtake Great Britain. His *Report on Manufactures* mounted a formidable critique of Adam Smith's and David Ricardo's free trade orthodoxy. Free trade was well and good for Britain, with its dominant economic position. But if one examined what Britain did to get on top—instead of what Britain now prescribed for the rest of the world—one found that the formula was tariffs and other protections for the nation's infant industries, which was just the policy Hamilton's Whig heirs, like Lincoln and Clay, would adopt for the United States. Burgeoning domestic manufacturing could supply a richer market for domestic agriculture, to the advantage of all.[143]

Likewise, there was something to be said for Hamilton's plan for a national bank and a funded national debt, which the Federalist-led Congress adopted. It did put the new national government on a solid financial footing. Yet, Hamilton's aping of British prime minister Robert Walpole's patronage-based, fiscal state-building was too much to swallow. Madison and Jefferson shared the view of their fellow Virginian and Democratic-Republican John Taylor, who explained the scheme's dire logic: "The funding system was intended to effect, what the bank was contrived to accelerate. 1. Accumulation of great wealth in a few hands. 2. A political moneyed machine. 3. A suppression of the republican state assemblies, by depriving them of political importance, resulting from the imposition and dispensation of taxes."[144] The goal, on Taylor's account, was to reduce the state assemblies to cogs in a consolidated system of government. The only truly representative bodies in the new federal system would be undone by the machinations of the paper banking interest.[145]

Only by restoring the constitutional balance between national and state power would lawmakers accountable to the humbler classes of citizens retain essential powers over economic life and development; only then would the safeguards for sustaining a broad middle class and fair equality of opportunity be assured. And only then, with its social basis intact, would the Constitution—conceived as a grand experiment in republican self-rule—survive.[146]

It is no wonder that the Democratic-Republicans insisted on the constitutional stakes of their opposition to Hamilton's policies. Although their work in the 1790s seems plainly partisan, neither Madison nor Jefferson saw party-building as constitutionally legitimate. Party-building was still, by definition, faction-building; and factions were what the new Constitution or any good republican constitution was designed to overcome, and what virtuous citizens scorned. But traditional antipartyism did make room for an exception. "Just as the people might organize to effect their right of revolution (as they did in 1776)," historian of this party-building moment, Gerald Leonard, explains, "they might organize a temporary party of the Constitution to attempt salvation by peaceful, political means when the Constitution was in danger of usurpation."[147]

So, the Democratic Party came into being as a "party of Principle," its very warrant for existence the *constitutional* stakes of defeating the "moneyed Oligarchy" in power.[148] Americans would later grow accustomed to the idea of permanent political parties. But for decades, the Democrats—or "the democracy," as the party called itself—would continue to proclaim the constitutional necessity for a mass party of "the people" or "the producing classes" to counter the inevitable tendency of "wealth" to convert economic into political domination.[149] "To be allied to power, permanent, if possible . . . is one of the strongest passions which wealth inspires," Martin Van Buren, the great architect and theorist of Jacksonian democracy, later observed in his remarkable *Inquiry into the Origin and Course of Political Parties*. "Here [in the U.S.], where [wealth] is deprived of [aristocratic privileges], it maintains a constant struggle

for the establishment of a moneyed oligarchy, the most selfish and mo-
nopolizing of all depositories of political power, and is only prevented
from realizing its complete designs by the democratic spirit of the
country"—a spirit, Van Buren argued, which could only find effective
political expression via a permanent party organization.[150]

Looking back from mid-century on "the democracy's" origins in the
decades we have just canvassed, Van Buren set out a canonical rendering
of the Jeffersonian narrative of constitutional redemption. Hamilton's
policies in the 1790s, Van Buren declared, were well intentioned and bril-
liantly crafted, but blatantly unconstitutional. Why, Hamilton himself
argued that his political-economic policies reflected what the national-
ists at Philadelphia had really wanted—not what they managed to get
into the text! Convinced that the best interests of the nation demanded
flouting the Constitution that "the people recently had ratified," Hamilton aimed to "sap and mine" and ultimately supplant the Constitution
with what he believed was "a superior Monarchical form of Government." If the Democratic Party's founding father had not thwarted
him, "this glorious old Constitution of ours . . . would long since have
sunk beneath the waters of time. . . . Our system might then have dis-
solved in anarchy, or crouched under despotism or some milder type of
aristocratic government—a monarchy, an aristocracy, or, most ignoble
of all, a moneyed oligarchy—but as a Republic it would have endured
no longer."[151]

Together, during the 1790s, Jefferson and Madison honed an account
of the constitutional order and the roles it assigned to national, state, and
local government in support of a more democratic and decentralized political economy: one dedicated to a democracy of opportunity, one
where, as Hamilton ruefully observed, people would expect "distributive justice" from the "hands" of state government, where great fortunes at
the top would diminish, the share of those at the bottom would rise, and
the middling classes would predominate in both state and civil society.
Jefferson proclaimed that his victory in the 1800 presidential race—the
"Revolution of 1800"—was an enduring national decision in favor of this
view of the principles enshrined in the national Constitution.

The new Democratic-Republican Party—popularly known by its early
leaders and rank and file as the Republican Party—toppled Hamilton

and the Federalist grandees, gathered into its ranks the nation's enfranchised majority of small farmers and artisans, and incorporated them into a new, broader-based elite alliance with rising enterprisers and slaveholding planters. Over the next two decades, a new generation of state-based entrepreneurial leaders of Jefferson's party took on board much of Hamilton's program and built up *at the state level* much the same kind of monetary, corporate, and transportation infrastructure Hamilton had hoped to create on a national scale. Meanwhile, on the national plane, Republicans aimed to stabilize money and credit, and subsidize manufactures.[152]

This new generation of Republican leaders embodied a stunning shift in direction, as the party's founding father saw it. Yet, the younger politicos who engineered the shift defended their reversal of Jeffersonian tradition in the name of that tradition. The new entrepreneurial wing of the Republican elite acknowledged, as one of them put it, that yes, they had grown "reconciled to . . . measures and arrangements which may be as proper now as they were premature or suspicious when urged by champions of Federalism." [153] On the other hand, as the historian Charles Sellers mordantly chronicles, they proclaimed undying fealty to the Jeffersonian vision of government acting to protect every man's equal rights and opportunities. Every new bank, canal, and railroad, every shiny, new investment opportunity they chartered and underwrote with unsecured loans or bonds backed by local taxpayers' dollars was said to promote the ordinary mechanics' and farmers' opportunities.[154]

These new entrepreneurs and their banks were experimenting with the possibilities of a system that no one understood very well, a shift to financial transactions based solely on values represented by paper instruments—banknotes, bills of exchange, and corporate stocks. "Real money" or specie was giving way to "paper promises to pay," multiplied far beyond the amount of specie or present capital to satisfy them. Established banks earned large dividends by extending loans and notes beyond their specie reserves. The resulting inflation threatened sound growth, and to stem this, the Republican Congress chartered the second national bank in 1816, hoping it would reform the currency by forcing the state banks to resume specie payments.[155]

The new national bank and its new-school Republican directors instead succumbed to the get-rich mood, maximizing the bank's profits by extravagant lending. Thus, the second national bank began its career, according to its later president Nicholas Biddle, as a "monied institution governed by those who had no money . . . a mere colony of the Baltimore adventurers." Among them was the propertyless adventurer and cashier of the bank's Baltimore branch, James W. McCulloch. McCulloch was one of several Baltimore directors and insiders who got loans without collateral—half a million in McCulloch's case, none of it repaid.[156] And it was on James McCulloch's behalf that Chief Justice John Marshall, fully aware of the irony, vindicated the national bank and the tarnished but polishable Hamiltonian vision of a great continent-spanning, commercial-republic-cum-capitalist-state, in *McCulloch v. Maryland,* handed down a few weeks after the Panic of 1819 had arrived.

The delusion that "legerdemain tricks upon paper can produce as solid wealth as hard labor in the earth," complained Jefferson from Monticello, made it impossible to "reason Bedlam to rights."[157] Early in 1819, with the bust almost at hand, Jefferson wrote that the speculative frenzy had produced "a filching from industry its honest earnings, wherewith to build up palaces, and raise gambling stock for swindlers and shavers."[158]

When the bust came, it brought the nation's first "traumatic awakening to the capitalist reality of boom and bust."[159] As the Republicans' second national bank set about saving its own skin by calling in loans and demanding settlement of its heavy balances against state banks, the brutal deflation brought down most of the nation's new market economy. "Export prices collapsed; businesses failed; settlers lost their allotments of public lands for inability to complete payments; the remorseless process of debt liquidation brought down modest enterprisers and large ones; distress was greatest in the cities where roughly a million, perhaps three out of four, of the growing new class of wage earners, were out of work . . . the destitute fled back to kin in the countryside for subsistence."[160]

The "Workey," or urban working-class press, saw the emergence of a new, more radical and class-conscious brand of popular constitutionalism. Jefferson saluted it and was gladdened by the growing sway of old-school Republican leaders whose influence would mount during the Bank War of the 1830s. This new generation of old-school Republicans and the older purists alike mocked the grandiloquent vision of national authority and national development, set out by Marshall in *McCulloch v. Maryland* in the course of upholding the constitutionality of the national bank, while it leeched the life out of the new market economy to save its own skin.[161] In the old-school view that Jackson would make his own, the bank was a "great monopoly ... concentrat[ing] the whole moneyed power of the Union." With its vast power to corrupt and its "numerous dependents," it was engendering a new oligarchy with a sway sufficient "to defeat any measure" in Congress. But even at the state level, the "paper system" enabled "one class in society" to corrupt the polity and exploit and rule over the rest.[162]

Thus was a pattern—we might say, a dialectic—of constitutional political-economic discourse and debate formed, which would endure for well over a century to come. After the Federalists' demise, no mainstream party ever again openly proclaimed itself the party of elite rule. All sides appropriated the language of democracy of opportunity—and made their rival constitutional political-economic claims and defenses at least partly in its terms. They might accuse their foes of "despoiling the rights of property" or of being the "ruination of enterprise," they might defend the wealthy, but not the wealthy's right to rule; always they proclaimed fealty to "equal rights" and broad distribution of prosperity for the "producing classes." When such claims grew strained and thin, when the enfranchised "mass" of the citizenry of this white man's republic, or some significant portion of it, was pressed too far, thicker distributional claims emerged, and new policies and restraints were defended in the name of constitutional restoration. So it was when Jackson and Van Buren set out to save the democracy of opportunity once more.

2

CLASHING CONSTITUTIONAL POLITICAL
ECONOMIES IN ANTEBELLUM AMERICA

Most of the major constitutional conflicts of the antebellum period were clashes over constitutional political economy. Today, when constitutional scholars read and write about the fights from this period over such subjects as tariffs and internal improvements, they see a battle about states' rights and the limits of national power. They understand the contest largely in terms of a Southern elite whose constitutional politics were aimed at keeping Congress's hands off slavery. All that is true; but it is only half the story. Entwined with that battle was a constitutional debate about the nation's distribution of opportunity, wealth, and power and what kind of political economy would best serve the equal rights and standing of the white workingman.

Chapter 1 began the work of retrieving a world in which figures like Thomas Jefferson, James Madison, and Alexander Hamilton, among many others, viewed the Constitution through the lens of political economy, and political economy through the lens of the Constitution. Andrew Jackson added an important new layer to the story: he brought constitutional political economy to the center of partisan politics. He also tightened the knot of race and class, entangling the antebellum Democratic Party's embodiment of the democracy-of-opportunity tradition more than ever with racial subordination—with the promotion of Black slavery and Indian expulsion and extermination.

This chapter begins by charting the rise of "Jacksonian democracy." We examine the Jacksonians' passionate views on political economy and their conflicts with the Whig Party and its rival "American System" of political economy. With the Whigs, we uncover a forgotten world of ideas about legislative constitutional duties, intimately bound up with the legislative tasks of national policymaking and institution-building. Jacksonians and Whigs alike shared the belief that when it came to constitutional political economy, they—the legislators, including the president in the exercise of his "legislative" role—were the primary interpretive actors or "expositors" of the Constitution *as well as* the primary policymakers.

They understood their politics not as working within a constitutional order so much as working out a constitutional order, and renovating it, over time.[1] Thus, Congress's affirmative, legislative constitutional duties were a central focus, in ways we have forgotten—but which generations of American reformers (Reconstruction Republicans, Populists, Progressives, New Dealers) inherited and understood well. Renovating our political economy in the ways liberals and progressives envision today will involve much controversial legislative action animated by constitutional purposes and principles. So, one goal of the first part of this chapter is to begin recovering this way of thinking and arguing about the Constitution.

We start, though, with the Jacksonians' war on the national bank. That war was part of a broader questioning of how American capitalism was taking shape. The Jacksonians drew together a dominant political coalition—small farmers and urban workers and shopkeepers on one hand, and Southern planters and slaveholders on the other—united around the common constitutional ground of strict construction, states' rights, "equality of rights" for the white laboring many, and righteous opposition to unconstitutional "class legislation" on behalf of corporations and financial and manufacturing elites. The democracy-of-opportunity tradition was at the militant core of their constitutional politics.

The second part of this chapter examines the emergence of two new visions of constitutional political economy, built around rival systems of labor and production: "Free Labor" and slavery. Calling itself the party of "Free Labor," the new antislavery Republican Party rested on a coalition of erstwhile Northern Democrats and Whigs. It rewrote the democracy-of-opportunity tradition, basing its constitutional political

economy on the expansive opportunities and material independence afforded working people by an active national government committed to
"Free Labor." Securing those promises also demanded vanquishing a
new "oligarchy": not the financial elite, this time, but the slaveholding
planter elite, the Southern "Slave Power," hell-bent on making slavery
national by subverting the Constitution. Not surprisingly, the planters
fashioned a new, militantly proslavery constitutional political economy
of their own.

Jacksonian Constitutionalism and Whig
Principles of Legislative Duty

One cannot understand the central elements of Jacksonian constitutionalism—its conceptions of equal protection and class legislation, strict
construction, and states' rights—without understanding the contest over
constitutional political economy that Andrew Jackson and his new
Democratic Party believed they were waging.

With the Panic of 1819 and the economic pain that followed, a breach
had opened between ordinary voters—mostly farmers and workers—and
the party elites, who were then blazing new paths of national and regional development. Into the breach stepped a popular nonpolitician.
In 1828, a white farmer-worker populace, voting directly, in mass numbers, in a presidential election for the first time, found in General Jackson
more than military charisma. Ordinary Americans were mustering democracy against "the paper system" and its "new aristocracy" of enterprise. To the astonishment of old party leaders like John C. Calhoun and
Henry Clay, the voters rallied to Old Hickory's cry: The Constitution was
imperiled "and the people alone by their Virtue, and independent exercise of their free suffrage" could rescue and redeem it.[2] Not until Franklin
Roosevelt would a presidential candidate again speak so plainly about
the realities of class divisions and the incompatibility of political democracy and economic oligarchy. Voters who readily accepted that they were
the poor "many" fighting off the wealthy "few" exercised their suffrage
for what the new Democratic Party press heralded as a "democratic
Millennium."[3]

JACKSONIAN EQUAL PROTECTION

Today, the idea of equal protection of the laws is central to our modern understanding of the Constitution. We now think of equal protection as the wellspring of the inclusionary principle: a constitutional provision aimed against laws that injure groups defined by race and sex and other "discrete and insular minorities."[4] But there was also another equal protection, *before* the Equal Protection Clause. For Andrew Jackson and his followers, equal protection was not about race or sex, but was nonetheless a touchstone of the democracy-of-opportunity tradition. Equal protection was a constitutional principle about protecting the "many" against class legislation that privileged the "few."[5]

The mass of ordinary white farmers and those Jackson called "the laboring classes of society" were fearful of the new "paper-money system"; the new boom-and-bust business cycle; and the growing inequalities of wealth, opportunity, and political power between the poor many and the rich few.[6] The new "paper-money system," Jackson told the nation in his farewell address, threatened "to undermine . . . your free institutions" and place "all power in the hands of the few . . . to govern by corruption or force."[7]

The bank controversy perfectly distilled the Jacksonians' fears. Congress chartered the Second Bank of the United States in 1816 to facilitate paying off debt from the War of 1812 and to stabilize the national currency. But the bank was a for-profit enterprise funded, and governed, primarily by its private shareholders, the largest and most powerful of whom were wealthy merchants like Jacob Astor and Stephen Girard. It competed with smaller state banks; its critics charged that it heavily favored the speculators of the Northeast over the farmers of the South and West.[8] Jacksonians argued forcefully against renewing its charter for reasons they framed in a constitutional discourse they inherited from their party's founders. As one leading Jacksonian put it, although the bank is "maintained out of the hard earnings of the poor," "[i]t is essentially an aristocratic institution" that "bands the wealthy together" and tends "to give exclusive political, as well as exclusive money privileges to the rich." The bank, he argued, "falsifies our grand boast of political equality; it is building up a privileged order, who, at no distant day, unless the whole system be changed, will rise in triumph on the ruins of democracy."[9]

Jacksonians responded to these fears with a welter of sustained constitutional arguments—in the courts, in Congress and state legislatures, and in critical presidential vetoes.[10] These arguments were about constitutional political economy. They condemned not only the bank but a wide array of corporate and bank charters, tax exemptions, subsidies, and protectionist tariffs as unequal laws, as "invasion[s] of the grand republican principle of Equal Rights—a principle which lies at the bottom of our constitution."[11] Such laws created "inequalities of wealth and influence" that would lead "inevitably" to the invasion of the rights of the "weak" by the "strong."

Specifically, such laws would enable an emerging oligarchy—the "moneyed aristocracy"—to amass economic and political power over the "middling and lower classes."[12] In vetoing the bank, President Jackson urged the government to "confine itself to *equal protection,* and, as Heaven does its rains, shower its favors alike on the high and the low, the rich and the poor" rather than "grant[ing] titles, gratuities, and exclusive privileges, to make the rich richer and the potent more powerful."[13]

The Jacksonians viewed the direction of economic development that this emerging oligarchy was charting with a distinct sense of *constitutional* crisis: they argued that it subverted the nation's republican Constitution (or, more precisely, republican constitutions). In great part, this was a story of the corrosive effects of inequalities of wealth. An American political economy built on true constitutional principles, argued Jacksonian Congressman John Bell of Tennessee, would not aim for the "European" goal of maximizing national wealth "without regard to the manner of its distribution": "[T]he accumulation of great wealth in the hands of individual citizens" subverts the natural "equality of rank and influence" that is "the very end and aim of all our political institutions."[14]

Mainstream Jacksonians strove to lay down strong distributional constraints on government policy—ones that ran to formal equal opportunity and also to "equality in the actual condition" of the citizenry.[15] As Bell's speeches illustrate, these constraints were precepts of their political economy and—equally, inseparably—of their constitutional outlook.

"The fundamental principle," Bell argued, "of the American Governments, local and national," is "equality of rank, rights, and privileges. . . . Whatever measure of public policy tends . . . to destroy the equality of rank and influence among our citizens, is not only opposed to the theory of our Government, but subversive of the fundamental principle upon which it is erected." For this reason, Bell argued, "I deny . . . that it is either proper, or consistent with the object of our Government, to promote the growth of the country in wealth, without regard to the manner of its distribution." He viewed "the accumulation of overgrown individual fortunes" as "a positive national evil," and argued that governments are "free, just, and equal in proportion to the degree of equality in the actual condition of their members or citizens."[16]

The central problem was that economic inequality inevitably has corrosive effects on political equality. In Jackson's words, an economic system divorced from "the great principle of equality" threatened to create "a dangerous connection between a moneyed and political power." The "moneyed interest" would become a political aristocracy, he warned, as "a control would be exercised by the few over the political conduct of the many by first acquiring that control over the labor and earnings of the great body of the people."[17] This is, in short, the problem of oligarchy.

These concerns became the mainspring of a distinctive Jacksonian constitutionalism. They inflected many modalities of Jacksonian constitutional argument, such as textual arguments about federal power—for instance, President Jackson's argument that Congress's textual authority to mint currency should *not* be read to permit Congress to delegate this power to a private bank (by chartering the national bank and authorizing it to issue notes that, foreseeably, had become the nation's paper currency). Jacksonian equal protection and equal rights meant that stern constitutional scrutiny was required any time the government granted exclusive privileges, exemptions, immunities, or monopoly powers to determine whether these were truly "necessary" or whether they instead embodied an unjustifiable "bend[ing of] the acts of government" by "the rich and powerful . . . to their selfish purposes." But Jacksonian equal protection was not laissez-faire for its own sake. It had two overriding purposes: to prevent the capture of the government by the rich and to safeguard broad opportunities for all.[18]

Of course, "all" did not mean all. Jacksonians wedded white farmers' and workers' democratic and egalitarian aspirations to the racist causes of Southern slavery and Indian removal. This was a tragedy of American political and constitutional development from which we are still disentangling ourselves. Slaves' productive work—as well as women's productive work—was not merely excluded from the Jacksonians' generous conception of equality for the nation's white male producers; racial and gender subordination were among the bases on which they rested their vision of the white man's republican liberty and citizenly independence.[19] It was not the Jacksonians but instead their Whig foes and abolitionist critics who first probed the contradictions between championing an egalitarian political economy for the white "laboring classes" and perpetuating Black bondage; it was nineteenth-century women's rights advocates who made the case that the Constitution's promise of equal rights meant equal rights for women.[20]

And when Jackson launched his murderous new policy of mass expulsion of Native peoples—egged on chiefly by Southern slaveholders and land speculators, who craved the vast and fertile "Indian territory" of the Southeast for the expansion of their slave plantations—it was the Whigs who opposed him. (The House vote on Jackson's hallmark Indian Removal Act of 1830 was so close—102 yeas and 97 nays—that the nays would have triumphed if the Three-Fifths Clause had not inflated slaveholders' power.)[21] Southern politicians, intent on asserting state authority over Indigenous nations' lands, often lumped the issues of Native sovereignty and slavery together as "local concerns" that Northerners and the federal government had no constitutional authority to meddle with—a states' rights position Jackson largely endorsed.[22] In all these ways, "Jacksonian democracy" was a Herrenvolk democracy— "democratic for the master race but tyrannical for the subordinate groups."[23]

What the Jacksonians also understood, vividly, and articulated in constitutional terms, was that in their time, a nexus of elite wealth and political power threatened the political and economic equality of white male farmers and "mechanics." In Jacksonian constitutional political economy, this was the fundamental threat to the constitutional order.[24] To respond to this threat, as the constitutional historian Gerald Leonard has chronicled, the Jacksonians created the first modern mass political party. Such a creature seemed to its conservative foes a constitutional nightmare: a permanently organized faction. But the Jacksonians defended the new creature as just the opposite: not a nightmare, but actually a constitutional necessity, to mobilize the nation's dispersed "producing classes" as a new "[d]emocracy of numbers" to defeat oligarchy and save the republic from the "[a]ristocracy of wealth."[25]

THE "AMERICAN SYSTEM" AND THE WHIG CONSTITUTION OF OPPORTUNITY

What about the Jacksonians' foes: turncoat Democrats like John Quincy Adams, the great Whig statesman Henry Clay, and the rising star in the Whig galaxy, the young Illinois lawmaker Abraham Lincoln? They too believed that constitutional principles must determine public policy and guide economic development. They had views, in other words, about constitutional political economy. And it was not only up to judges to preserve the constitutional order: judicial review played a relatively minor role in their view, as it did in the Jacksonians'. It was chiefly up to the people and their representatives to safeguard constitutional liberty and ensure that the Constitution's other precepts and purposes were fulfilled, as the nation pursued its combined experiments in constitutional government and capitalist development.

The Whigs clashed with the Jacksonian Democrats over the developmental and distributional possibilities and perils of banks and currency, corporate charters, protective tariffs, and internal improvements; the Whigs' arguments were similarly suffused with constitutional claims. The core disagreement was over the kind of political economy the developing nation should embrace. Henry Clay's "American System" called for a robust, active role for national government—what development economists today would call a developmentalist state. This meant building up infant domestic industries by imposing protective tariffs; linking farmers and local enterprises to far-flung markets with national

subsidies for internal improvements like canals and railroads; and promoting growth and prosperity by fostering concentrations of capital for
investment and encouraging a credit-based national economy and a flexible medium of exchange via national and state banks.[26] Senator Daniel
Webster of Massachusetts earned the sobriquet of the great Whig "Expounder of the Constitution" thanks to his many famous oral arguments
on behalf of corporations.[27] As these arguments dramatized, alongside
the other elements of the American System, Whigs promoted judicial
protection of what they deemed investors' vested rights. Unless capital
investments were secure against popular "interference," they argued,
everyone would suffer.[28]

An ex-Federalist like Webster might scorn egalitarian appeals to
the enfranchised masses. But the party leadership soon appropriated
the Jacksonians' mass-party organizational structure, and along with it the
Jacksonian rhetoric of equal opportunity for the poor farmer and workingman. The rising young Illinois Whig Abraham Lincoln adapted that
rhetoric to defend the very development policies Jackson and the "Old
School" Democrats assailed. Jacksonians watched and were alarmed by
the young lawmaker's unhesitating sponsorship of dozens of charters for
large, new corporations. "What is the passing [of] an act of incorporation, but the *making of a law*?" Lincoln demanded, as he painted a
glowing portrait of future railroad corporations of "a great national
character."[29] Here, for Lincoln, was the promise of new markets and new
opportunities for the poor farmer to improve his condition by producing
for profitable home markets of manufacturing workers in the East.[30]
Jacksonian lawmakers pointed out Lincoln's blindness to the threats
posed by large concentrations of capital to the "poor man's" prospects
for material independence and the republic's need for a rough "equality
of condition."[31] Lincoln responded by pointing out their blindness to the
state's need for outside capital to underwrite development, and the impossibility of a hard-money or specie currency sustaining the pressures
of a growing farm population and its hunger for prosperity.[32]

Plainly, the Whigs' political economy was of the rising-tide-lifts-all-
boats variety.[33] Clay and Lincoln were not unduly troubled by growing
inequalities of wealth, as long as the rising fortunes at the top resulted
from new industry and growing commerce. Concentrations of capital

in well-run banks or in "[t]he joint stock companies of the North" did not distress them. In part this was because they thought such concentrations of capital essential to expanding jobs and opportunities for ordinary people. Here, it is important to recall the typically small scale of manufacturing production that Lincoln knew in central Illinois, or Clay in Kentucky—where, Clay observed, "almost every manufactory known to me is in the hands of enterprising self-made men, who have acquired whatever wealth they possess by patient and diligent labor."[34] Even in manufacturing centers like New York at this time, the typical shop was fairly small.[35] Given this, it was not yet so far-fetched for these Whig spokesmen to believe that the expansion of American manufacturing promised wide-open avenues for a broad swath of hireling journeymen to acquire the know-how and raise the capital to own "manufactories" of their own. An entrenched "monied aristocracy" seemed a distant worry to a young Whig like Abraham Lincoln in the hazardous, hurly-burly world of new fortunes made and lost in the market economy. As Lincoln's own path from hardscrabble farming to counsel for new banks and corporations seemed to demonstrate, those who rose to the top in this brave new competitive world were more likely to be a "natural" elite than an "artificial aristocracy."[36]

A great many proponents of Jacksonian constitutional political economy hewed to the old republican precept that a rough "equality in the actual condition" of the citizenry was essential to republican constitutions. By their lights, as we have seen, policies that promised to magnify inequalities of wealth were constitutionally suspect. Whigs spurned this "leveling" outlook. But their own views were far from indifferent to distributional concerns. They shared with their foes the other old republican maxim: the citizen's political equality and independence must rest on a measure of economic independence, and that demanded property-holding. Their vision was a burgeoning commercial republic, not a backward-looking agrarian one, but it was no less a republic with a broad, wide-open, propertied middle class.[37] Thus, they loudly affirmed that a true "American" system of political economy must provide as ample as possible a supply of decent livelihoods for the laboring classes, along with wide opportunities for laborers to become proprietors, and broad avenues to wealth and distinction for the gifted and ambitious but penniless beginners.[38] Not surprisingly, Whigs contended that their own economic policies were best suited to these core commitments. And more than that, they argued that Jacksonian nostrums like free trade, hard money, and "limited government" only hurt the very classes the Jacksonians claimed to champion.

Here we begin to see the implications for Whig constitutional political economy. Consider Clay's response to the Southern Democrats' argument that protective tariffs were beyond Congress's power (because their purpose was not revenue, but a practical bar on foreign imports of some lines of manufactured goods). Clay invoked constitutional text, history, structure, and congressional and judicial precedent. And then he turned to consequences, contending that these, too, were of constitutional import. "It is for the great body of the people, and especially for the poor," he argued, "that I have ever supported the American system. It affords them profitable employment, and supplies the means of comfortable subsistence." He went on to argue that "the great body of the people" benefit from tariffs in terms of economic security. The American System "*secures* to them, certainly, necessaries of life, manufactured at home, and places within their reach, and enables them to acquire, a reasonable share of foreign luxuries," while the free-trade alternative "*promises* them necessaries made in foreign countries, and which are beyond their power; and *denies* to them luxuries which they would possess no means to purchase."[39]

Similarly, Clay attacked Jackson's war on the national bank, arguing that chartering the bank was well within congressional power. He made arguments from precedent and from constitutional structure. He also argued that Jackson's constitutional political economy argument against the bank must be rejected, because the "hard-money policy" the president proposed would actually injure the very farmers, laborers, and small entrepreneurs for whose "equal protection" in opportunities and livelihoods he claimed to act:

> [I]f the effect of this hard-money policy upon the debtor class be injurious, it is still more disastrous, if possible, on the laboring classes. Enterprise will be checked or stopped, employment will become difficult, and the poorer classes will be subject to the

greatest privations and distresses. Heretofore it has been one of
the pretentions and boasts of the dominant party [Democrats],
that they sought to elevate the poor by depriving the rich of
undue advantages. Now their policy is . . . to reduce the wages
of American labor to the low standard of European labor, in
order to enable the American manufacturer to enter into a successful competition with the European manufacturer in the sale
of their respective fabrics.[40]

Here it is helpful to step outside contemporary assumptions about
how constitutional arguments work. A lawyer today would guess that
the only *constitutional* claims made on behalf of Clay's American System
of political economy were arguments of the familiar permissive kind:
you say the Constitution prohibits Congress from enacting this policy;
we say the Constitution allows it. That was not the case. Whigs like Clay,
and erstwhile Democrats won over to Clay's American System like John
Quincy Adams, made stronger claims. The Constitution not only allowed Congress to enact policies like the protective tariff, they argued,
it compelled them. Article I's enumerated powers were "not only grants
of power but trusts to be executed" and "duties to be discharged for the
common defense and general welfare." The "non-use[] of the power" was
"a violation of the trust." "[T]he words common defence and general welfare" were the "expositors of the purpose for which Congress are expressly enjoined TO PROVIDE." And where the "general welfare" was
clearly better served by the exercise of an enumerated power than by its
"non-use," Congress had not only the power but the *constitutional duty*
to act.[41]

The language of the "solemn Preamble," on this account, was not intended to confer boundless or unrestrained powers, or "indeed . . . any
power at all" beyond those granted in Article I, but neither was the Preamble devoid of legal meaning. It announced principles like "liberty"
and purposes like "the common defence" and "the general Welfare,"
which the Constitution directed the political branches to use their enumerated powers to secure, promote, and provide, under the watchful
eyes of the people. This was especially the case, both Clay and Adams
argued during the tariff debates of 1832, with regard to the "great and

solemn *duty* [of Congress] to *provide* for the common defence and general welfare," since the Article I enumeration of the power to levy taxes and duties "repeats" the "same identical language" of the Preamble.[42]

Alongside the textual argument, Clay offered a federalism-based account of why the national government had a constitutional "duty of protecting our domestic industry"—with an originalist twist:

> The States, respectively, surrendered to the General Government the whole power of laying imposts on foreign goods. They stripped themselves of all power to protect their own manufactures, by the most efficacious means of encouragement—the imposition of duties on rival foreign fabrics. Did they create that great trust? Did they voluntarily subject themselves to this self-restriction, that the power should remain in the Federal Government, inactive, unexecuted, and lifeless? Mr. Madison, at the commencement of the Government, told you otherwise. In discussing, at that early period, this very subject, he declared that a failure to exercise this power would be a "*fraud*" upon the Northern States, to which may now be added the Middle and Western States.[43]

AFFIRMATIVE LEGISLATIVE CONSTITUTIONAL DUTIES

The idea that Congress has affirmative constitutional duties to legislate in the political-economic sphere—and the practice of responding to claims of *no power* with *not merely power, but duty*—proved vital for nationalist-minded lawmakers and administrations for a century to come. This constitutional move proved essential for Reconstruction Republicans, who rested their pervasive talk of constitutional duty not only in the General Welfare Clause, but also in the Guarantee Clause and the Thirteenth and Fourteenth Amendments. How and why these constitutional duties have been forgotten is a question reserved for later chapters. But one part of the answer is already in view. Legislators on all sides of these various political-economic debates believed that they were not only the primary policymakers; they—and not the courts—were also the most important constitutional interpreters or "expositors."

("Legislator" here included the president in the exercise of his "legislative" role.) Indeed, virtually all agreed that at least some political-economic issues such as the tariff could not be assessed, in some of their most important constitutional dimensions, except by the political branches.[44] Exercises of enumerated powers, making and enacting national policy, were occasions to interpret or "exposit" the Constitution and implement its purposes. These were occasions for first-order arguments about the Constitution's meaning.

Today, the default assumptions are different. The Supreme Court is the primary expositor of the Constitution. Two tasks, once deeply connected, have been separated. The political branches make national economic policy; the Court decides whether they have transgressed the limitations of what the Constitution allows them to do. These new default assumptions mean that it makes little sense for lawyers, lawmakers, or constitutional scholars today to think hard about the affirmative constitutional duties of Congress or the president with respect to economic and social policy and its distributional goals and perils. Whatever our rival views about these matters, we cannot imagine the courts doing the primary work of making and enforcing these kinds of distributional policy choices regarding trade, industry, and economic development.

And neither could the lawmakers, statesmen, politicians, and reformers whose arguments we explore here. However, they imagined and inhabited the constitutional order in a rather different fashion from us. For them, "the Constitution" was at once a text and tradition one interpreted and, at the same time, a system of government, whose powers, purposes, and precepts one implemented and pursued over time, through political and legislative action.

In our current highly judicialized constitutional culture, it makes sense to think hard and argue seriously about constitutional limits on Congress's power, which courts can and do elaborate and enforce, but not about Congress's affirmative constitutional duties—which are also relevant to the work of courts, but are not an area where courts can do the first-order work or the heavy lifting. Partly for this reason, we have forgotten the very idea of affirmative legislative constitutional duties and with it, much of the conceptual landscape of constitutional political economy as it was practiced for most of American history.

Congressional Constructions of Spending
for the General Welfare

Arguments about the general welfare focused not only on the power to tax but also on the Spending Power. Much like banks or tariffs, the Spending Power occasioned a great volume of constitutional debate and line-drawing in the political branches, which carried on well into the twentieth century. As Chapter 6 details, New Deal lawmakers would later inherit and build on these constitutional constructions in the context of designing and defending key parts of New Deal constitutional political economy. New Deal social provision would find its constitutional basis in legislative precedents about what it means to provide for the general welfare.

Like the national bank question, the Spending Power debate first arose out of Hamilton's blueprints for political-economic development. Hamilton's famous *Report on Manufactures* called for federal loans and investments in manufacturing and federal spending on canals and roads to promote interstate markets for manufacturers' goods and farmers' crops. The constitutional authorization for such spending was clear, said Hamilton. The very first power conferred by Article I was the power to tax and spend for the general welfare. The phrase, he explained, was meant to ensure that the spending is "within the sphere of the national Councils"; this "generallity" required that such appropriations were "made . . . *General* and not *local;* its operation extending in fact, or by possibility, throughout the Union, and not being confined to a particular spot."[45]

Not surprisingly, Jefferson and Madison balked at this construction, which augured yet more centralization of power over economic development, and yet more prospects for corruption. The two of them had no difficulty responding to Hamilton's constitutional argument. Article I's careful enumeration of powers would be meaningless if Hamilton's reading were correct. The better reading was that the Spending Power was limited to spending in fulfillment of the objects laid out in the rest of Article I's enumerated powers. "*General*" Welfare was an additional restraint on the Spending Power, not the exclusive one. Spending must serve the general, national good; and it must also be tethered to the exercise of an enumerated power. Congress was not free to fund any undertaking it liked, simply because it thought the project conduced to the public good. Otherwise, what was the point of enumeration?[46]

This restrictive view of the Spending Power found its most famous expressions in a handful of high-profile, antebellum presidential vetoes of internal improvements, like Monroe's veto of the Cumberland Road and Jackson's veto of the Maysville Turnpike, on the old Jeffersonian ground that internal improvements were not among Congress's enumerated powers.[47] But more often, Jefferson's Democratic successors departed from what the party father ruefully described as the "'ancient doctrine' of strict constructionism."[48] What Jefferson rued was that over time, congressional Democrats began to join hands with Whigs in enthusiastically building roads, canals, and other internal improvements, which led even Madison's successor, President James Monroe, to adopt an essentially Hamiltonian stance. "My idea," Monroe explained, has come to be that "Congress has an unlimited power to raise money and that in its appropriation they have a discretionary power, restricted only by the duty to appropriate it to purposes of common defense and of general, not local, national not state benefit."[49]

Democrats could not consistently hew to Jefferson's and Madison's line on the Spending Power for a simple reason, which the legal historian Michele Landis Dauber has persuasively reconstructed. From the start, Congress was making "charitable" appropriations for the relief of Latin American earthquake victims, white refugees from the great Haitian slave revolt, and U.S. citizens whose properties were laid waste by the War of 1812, as well as a growing array of disaster relief bills for domestic victims of major fires, floods, and droughts. No one pretended that any of these expenditures had any constitutional warrant, besides the Spending Power itself.[50] With these appropriations in view, the nationalist-minded Justice Joseph Story would write in his canonical *Commentaries on the Constitution* that the Hamiltonian position on the Spending Power had prevailed.[51] The sole constitutional limitation on Congress's power to appropriate revenue lay in the General Welfare Clause itself, Story concluded. This might remain an important limitation, depending on one's view of the general welfare. That constitutional fight, Story argued, following Hamilton, was one for Congress, not the courts. Democrats and Whigs agreed on the institutional point.[52] It was exclusively within the power of the political branches, not the courts, to decide the constitutional question of what federal spending promotes the general welfare. Despite many opportunities, the Supreme Court showed no interest in interfering.

In this arena of constitutional politics, Democrats maintained a more restrictive view than their Whig and, later, Republican rivals of what amounted to constitutional spending for the general welfare. Charitable appropriations for disaster relief were one thing. But major innovations in federal spending drew constitutional objections, prompted by leeriness over any new expansion of federal authority that might someday legitimate national interference with the South's "domestic institutions." Thus, for example, in 1859, when Republicans first pushed through Congress a land-grant bill in support of public colleges and universities, Democratic president James Buchanan vetoed the measure. Invoking the old Jeffersonian view, Buchanan declared that federal appropriations of national assets—whether taxes or public lands—were "confined to the execution of the enumerated powers delegated to Congress"; they could not be "diverted" to carry into effect "any other measure of . . . domestic policy" that Congress happens to "see fit to support." That "would be to confer upon Congress a vast and irresponsible authority, utterly at war with the well-known jealousy of Federal power which prevailed at the formation of the Constitution."[53] Such states' rights objections remained strong among Southern Democrats whenever ominous new forms of federal social spending arose, as they would in the 1930s and 1940s, and beyond.[54]

Meanwhile, in the traditional domain of disaster relief, the antebellum Congress developed a sophisticated system of nonjudicial constitutional precedents, which governed what counted as a relief appropriation for the general welfare. Congressional staff kept tables of past appropriations, and lawmakers drew on them to argue for and against present bills. Touchstones for analogizing and distinguishing past cases of federal aid included whether a given calamity was sudden and unforeseeable, whether the losses somehow implicated a general, federal interest, and, above all, whether the calamity's victims were blameless victims of fate or were, in some fashion, responsible for their own plight. Here was another paradigmatic example of lawmakers acting as sole "expositors" of the Constitution and understanding their interpretive and policy-making activities in respect of the general welfare as a constitutional "duty" and "trust to be executed." The tradition continued, uninterrupted, well into the New Deal, when, as Dauber shows, the disaster-relief precedents played a crucial role, and when the clash of interests and constitutional outlooks on powers *and duties* that unfolded in the executive branch and in Congress, and not in court, would decisively shape the system of social insurance America would build.[55]

Slavery and Free Labor

The contest over slavery would forever alter the democracy-of-opportunity tradition. This fight would ultimately transform the entire American constitutional order through what constitutional historians call a Second Founding, or second republic, that not only abolished slavery, but made the former slaves into rights-bearing citizens and authorized the national government to safeguard their rights. Astonishingly, from the point of view of the first founding moment, this Second Founding would make the national government responsible, in constitutional principle, for the economic and political enfranchisement of the ex-slaves. Indeed, the Reconstructed Constitution would make everyone's fair measure of liberty and equality in economic and social life a matter of constitutional import in dramatic new ways.[56]

The Reconstructed Constitution would become an increasingly active site of battles over the political economy of work and livelihoods, along with opportunity and the allowable limits of class domination. In those later battles, the legacy of the contest over slavery provided crucial normative resources, enabling and restraining constitutional arguments and imaginations on all sides. Thus, to understand the modern history of the democracy-of-opportunity tradition, we must understand the constitutional fate of slavery. Since its abolition, when Americans have fought over what we mean by equality of rights and opportunities, the battle has turned, in some important measure, over what we abolished when we abolished slavery.[57]

Here, we examine how the antebellum antislavery movement came to see an inescapable clash between the Free Labor system of the North and the slave system of the South. That clash led antislavery politicians and constitutional thinkers (and the founders of the Republican Party were both) to invent a new constitutional-interpretive narrative and a new constitutional political economy commanding Congress to cabin slavery and promote Free Labor, under the banner of a new political party. This new party would press the idea of Congress's affirmative constitutional duties far more forcefully than any of its Whig forebears, just as it would forge stronger and stronger links between its political-economic and constitutional precepts and arguments.

This antebellum antislavery movement posed a fundamental question: What kind of nation and political economy was the Constitution ultimately for: slave or free? Edgy Southern statesmen (also often both politicians and constitutional thinkers) soon concluded that Lincoln and his party were pressing toward a stark, violent conflict over slavery itself—and that Republicans would ultimately claim the power and duty to dispossess slaveholders of their wealth and to uproot the legal order of the states they ruled.

Northerners and Southerners alike in antebellum America would speak of slavery as the South's "peculiar institution." From a long historical perspective, slavery was anything but peculiar. It has endured from the dawn of history right down to the present and was found in every region of the earth. Slavery existed in most societies at one time or another. However, the antebellum South was one of only a handful of "slave societies," societies whose overall social structure and political economy squarely rested on slave labor and the institution of slavery. And yet if slavery had become the very basis of the Southern elite's wealth and power, its legitimacy could never be taken for granted. Roman masters felt no need to defend Roman slavery; American masters felt the need at every turn.[58]

On its face, slavery clashed with the Declaration's "self-evident" truths. How exactly could American slavery comport with the nation's founding commitments? How could one square slavery with a form of government that promised to secure for all the governed the "inalienable rights" to life, liberty, and the pursuit of happiness? From 1776 onward, there always were voices raising these questions. The only answer that the slave-holder could give them, the only defense that seemed to allow American slavery to coexist with American democracy, was a racial one: Black racial inferiority justified slavery, and justified applying the principles of the Declaration only to whites.[59]

Tying the capacity for reason to the capacities for self-rule and self-control, the Declaration's author, Jefferson, famously compared the races in his *Notes on the State of Virginia* (1785) and found Blacks lacking in these very capacities that make freedom possible. In the *Notes* and elsewhere, Jefferson dwelled obsessively on the question of whether Blacks' "incapacities" were innate or environmental, a function of race or oppression and deprivation. His democratic values and, no doubt, something of his personal experience inclined him to the hope that no group was fixed in a permanent place of inferiority; his racism led him to the "suspicion" that nature had rendered Blacks permanently defective and incapable of freedom.[60] By the nineteenth century, this possibility of innate Black inferiority would grow into a full-fledged ideology central to prevailing accounts of America as a white man's nation.[61]

So, American slavery was "peculiar" for three reasons. It became the social and economic base of Southern society, yet it clashed with the nation's founding ideals, and it was defined and justified by race. All three features contributed to the formation of a distinct political and cultural identity on the part of Southern elites; a distinct Southern "civilization" and a distinct Northern one emerged in opposition to one another, as the differences between their social orders widened. "Free Labor" and proslavery ideologies shaped one another, and they crystallized into rival visions of constitutional political economy.[62]

The Southern ruling class saw slavery as the heart of their social order and themselves as a beneficent American aristocracy atop a well-ordered, hierarchical society. All this, they told themselves, not only made the planter elite the nation's wealthiest, it also lent them a certain distance from the harsher, more competitive—and egalitarian—way of life of their Northern counterparts. They could rely largely on racial solidarity, along with a dose of deference, to cement their bonds with the lesser ranks of white fellow citizens. After all, the bottom third of the region's population were degraded Black slaves. Thus, every white man was privileged by definition. The Southern elite did not need to pretend that they and their offspring shared a common social destiny with the region's ordinary white farmers and mechanics.[63]

But a common social destiny was just what Northern elites proclaimed. The heart of Northern society, they said, was "Free Labor" and a shared destiny of work and opportunity. And they wove this into a new social, political, and constitutional outlook, binding together labor and capital, just as these discordant classes were emerging on the Northern scene. From the 1830s onward, "Free Labor" encapsulated the egalitarian ethos of democratic capitalism as the Northern elites preached it. If Southern "civilization" despised manual labor and linked it with Black slavery, Northern elites would draw out the contrast by celebrating the dignity of manual labor in the free North, along with the ease of mobility, what the young Whig Abraham Lincoln saw as "the right to rise" in the world, according to one's talents and industry, and the unity or "harmony of interests" between "labor" and "capital."[64]

Free Labor Political Economy versus the Mudsill Theory

The idea of a "harmony of interests" between labor and capital was a mainstay of most leading Northern antebellum political economists.[65] Lincoln was bolder, emphasizing the actual identity of labor and capital in the paradigmatic figure of Free Labor, which stood at the center of the new Republican Party's emerging vision of constitutional political economy. That composite figure was the yeoman farmer, small producer, artisan, and petty entrepreneur who toiled but also owned productive property. What distinguished the North's "Free Labor System," Lincoln insisted, was precisely this: The "large majority [of the male working population] . . . in these free states" was neither "labor" nor "capital," but both. And a place in this broad propertied middle class was the likeliest destiny of every poor "beginner,"[66] in the democratic, antihierarchical North:

> The prudent, penniless beginner in the world, labors for wages awhile, saves a surplus with which to buy tools or land, for himself; then labors on his own account another while, and at

length hires another new beginner to help him. This, say its advocates, is free labor—the just and generous, and prosperous system, which opens the way for all—gives hope to all, and energy, and progress, and improvement of condition to all. If any continue through life in the condition of the hired laborer, it is not the fault of the system, but because of either a dependent nature which prefers it, or improvidence, folly, or singular misfortune.[67]

This conception of antebellum Northern capitalism as an exceptionally "just and generous . . . system" had no more confident or shrewder spokesman than Lincoln; it had some shrewd critics among the proslavery social theorists and political economists of the South.[68]

Thus, Lincoln inveighed against the Southerners' "Mudsill theory" of political economy for its unsettling critique of the "system" he prized. (A mudsill was the sill at the base of a house or barn; it sat directly on the dirt.) South Carolina senator James Hammond first coined what became known as Mudsill theory—that Northern wage slaves and Southern bondspeople, like "mudsills" in any society, had much the same lot in life—in a famous speech on the Senate floor that expounded the virtues of Southern slavery as a system of labor relations compared to the supposedly free and morally elevated system of the North. Channeling the more systematic arguments of proslavery thinkers like George Fitzhugh, Senator Hammond declared to his Northern colleagues, "The difference between us is, that our slaves are hired for life and well compensated. . . . Yours are hired by the day, not cared for, and scantily compensated, which may be proved in the most painful manner, at any hour in any street in any of your large towns."[69] The actualities of the Northern "Free Labor" system, in other words, belied its ideology. "[Y]our whole hireling class of manual laborers and 'operatives,' as you call them, are essentially slaves."[70] For his part, Fitzhugh added that the spread of the factory system combined with the economic logic and individualist ethos of Northern capitalism made wage slavery the inevitable fate of Northern workers—a fate already afoot in the industrial centers for which Fitzhugh supplied facts and figures.[71]

Hammond's speech and Fitzhugh's stream of books and articles galled Lincoln, who pored over Fitzhugh's work. What vexed Lincoln was not the Mudsill theory's brash apologetics about the benevolent "socialism" of the South's peculiar institution so much as the theory's critique of "wage slavery," which, Lincoln knew, echoed the political-economic outlooks and analyses of genuine socialists and labor radicals in the United States and Europe at the time. It was this critique to which Lincoln responded in speeches like the one at the annual fair of the Wisconsin Agricultural Society, containing the classic account of the Free Labor System we just glimpsed.[72]

Lincoln did not attack the Mudsill theory on the ground that the North's "hireling class" was not really as downtrodden as Hammond claimed. As the historian Eric Foner has taught us, like their forebears, Lincoln's generation still understood "liberty" in terms of economic independence.[73] To be free, one had to own productive property. The hireling was, in many respects, almost as unfree and dependent as the slave.[74] Thus, for Lincoln and the other architects of Free Labor ideology, the weak spot in the "wage slavery" argument lay elsewhere—in its assumptions that only "[a] few men own capital," that labor and capital were necessarily separate classes, and that "the whole labor of the world exists within that relation," either owned or hired by capital.[75] The Mudsill theory, Lincoln explained to his Wisconsin audience, holds that "all laborers are naturally either *hired* laborers or *slaves*," and either way, they must toil under capital's direction. Accepting this, the only "disputation" is "whether it is best that capital shall *hire* laborers . . . or *buy* them."[76]

But these assumptions, he insisted, missed the core facts and a central norm of the North's "Free Labor System": under it, "there is no such thing as a freeman being fatally fixed for life, in the condition of a hired laborer."[77] "There is demonstration for saying this," Lincoln told his listeners. "Many independent men in this assembly doubtless a few years ago were hired laborers. And their case is almost, if not quite, the general rule."[78]

Lincoln was defending what he saw as the vibrant, progressive actualities of the Free Labor System against the distortions of proslavery apologists and radical critics; at the same time, he was flattering his farmer audience by extolling a world of producers who both worked with their hands and owned and ran their farms and small artisanal shops. Yet, Wisconsin farmers, shopkeepers, and artisans knew something about booms and busts. They knew that the bank loan and mortgage, the higher taxes for "internal improvements," and the torrent of new railroad and other corporate charters sponsored by lawmakers like Lincoln were all threats as well as promises. They knew that prosperity, independence, and "improvement of condition" were never as secure as the politicians claimed. They may have shared Lincoln's low regard for those who fell short of middle-class independence, and still have been shaken by his unflappable conviction that it was no "fault of the system" if they did. Many had offspring and relatives in the industrializing cities and manufacturing centers, where the notion was beginning to ring hollow that anyone who remained a "hired laborer" all his life had only himself to blame. As the wrenching shift to an industrial economic order proceeded, the "wage slavery" critique had increasing bite.[79]

So, Lincoln took pains to assure audiences that his party had a cogent vision of American constitutional political economy that put working people like them first. When push came to shove, he declared, "labor is the superior—greatly the superior—of capital," even as he made no bones about the middle-class virtues that the Free Labor System sternly demanded of them.[80]

In sum, the genius of the North's "Free Labor System" was that it entwined together a legal order of equal rights and a political economy committed to preserving wide-open opportunities for all to dwell in propertied independence. Opportunity was its normative hinge and its vulnerability; in this sense, Lincoln's old-fashioned republican account of freedom as propertied independence conceded a good deal of ground to the system's critics. Equal rights alone were not sufficient to constitute a free political economy; there had to be genuine opportunities and "no such thing" as fixed classes of laborers and capitalists.

The worry that the North's "System" might be failing to sustain such fluidity and wide-open opportunities would push its champions toward stronger and stronger assertions of a constitutional imperative that Congress remedy the situation. Accompanying these assertions would be novel arguments that Congress had the constitutional power and duty to take unprecedented actions in service of this Free Labor imperative—no matter the cost to the rival interests of Southern slavery.

But these arguments and assertions had a hard row to hoe. True, it was not difficult to belittle the interests of slaveholders. Like Lincoln, many Northerners deplored slavery: "If slavery is not wrong, nothing is wrong."[81] Northern slavery had largely been abolished a generation ago, and this bred stronger Northern convictions that slavery clashed with the Declaration of Independence as well as their own state constitutions.[82] Not only did slavery conflict with first principles, but most Northerners believed it had bred an arrogant Southern elite that denigrated manual labor and enjoyed an overweening power in the national government, which it wielded to enforce its benighted version of states' rights and thwart policies—tariffs, internal improvements, and so on—many thought essential to Northern prosperity, and, indeed, part of Congress's constitutional trust to carry out.[83]

Even so, most Northerners loved the Union more than they hated slavery. And they rightly believed that the framers had baked a compromise over slavery into the Constitution. The gist of that compromise was that slavery was a matter for each state to decide. If the citizens of North Carolina wanted to uphold the iniquitous system, that was their business.[84] If the two sections had evolved clashing civilizations, they were joined by a national Constitution and polity, which they prized, and the two major parties had worked assiduously to knit together the interests and aspirations of ordinary voters and elites in both North and South.[85]

What finally tore the sections and the Union apart was not the rightness or wrongness of slavery, as such, in the states where it existed. It was the future of slavery in the Western territories and the Western states-to-be. It was the growing conviction among both sections that their systems of labor and ways of life had to expand and enjoy ever more robust national protection and support (and hence, votes in Congress) in order to survive. Periodically, and with increasingly disruptive force, the question of slavery in new territories (and new states) would arise in national politics. When the question took center stage in the 1840s, Northern Whigs joined with erstwhile foes to pioneer a new precept of constitutional political economy: that democracy of opportunity demanded a frontier free of slavery, a frontier full of free homesteads for "Free Labor."[86]

Free Soil: The Constitutional Political Economy of Blocking Slavery's Expansion

Horace Greeley was editor of the *New York Tribune*, the nation's leading Whig paper in the 1840s (and its leading Republican paper in the 1850s and 1860s). In urban centers like New York, reform-minded Whigs like Greeley were anguished by the ways that industrialization and the emerging factory system were a boon for economic growth but were narrowing the Northern workingman's path to economic independence. Eruptions of labor-capital strife and denunciations of "wage slavery" and "property rights rulership" among workers in New York and elsewhere were the predictable result.

In this milieu, the prominent writer, preacher, and public intellectual Orestes Brownson published and also occasionally channeled the views of labor activists in the *Boston Quarterly Review,* of which he was founder and editor. His writings, and others he published in the *Review,* marked the coming into consciousness of a distinctly workers' perspective on constitutional political economy. In the *Review,* Brownson published the October 1840 "Address" of the Workingmen of Charlestown; they called for government, as the "agent of society" and "the organ through which society effects its will," to repeal "all laws which bear against the laboring classes." Brownson called the Workingmen "social democrats" because, as the legal historian Christopher Tomlins writes, he saw in the Workingmen "an identical commitment to democracy as substantive 'equality before society' rather than mere political equality."[87] In 1841, Brownson wrote in the *Review:*

> Democracy as a form of government, *political* Democracy, as we
> call it, could not be the term of popular aspiration. Regarded in
> itself, without reference to anything ulterior, it is no better than
> the aristocratic form of government, or even the monarchical.
> Universal suffrage and eligibility, the expression of perfect
> equality before the State, and which with us are very nearly re-

alized, unless viewed as means to an end, are not worth contending for. What avails it, that all men are equal before the
State, if they must stop there? If under a Democracy, aside from
mere politics, men may be as unequal in their social condition,
as under other forms of government, wherein consist the boasted
advantages of your Democracy? . . . [The public] seeks and ac-
cepts *political* Democracy only as a means to *social* Democracy,
and it cannot fail to attempt to realize equality in men's social
conditions, when it has once realized equality in their political
condition.[88]

Significantly, Brownson articulated the first intimations of the government's affirmative redistributional role. He did so by approaching government as a tool, not the inevitable enemy, of "the laboring classes."[89]
In his writings, Brownson emphasized the importance of not merely repealing legislation and regulation "of the wrong kind," but also seizing
control of government in order to enact policies that benefited the laboring classes.[90] In other words, his program was redistributive rather
than laissez-faire. "The goal," Tomlins explains, "was hence not inactivity
but activity differently directed, the enactment of such new laws as would
be necessary to enable working people to achieve and maintain social
equality."[91]

Brownson's new outlook suggests that the urban working class was
emerging and fashioning its own subaltern variation on a democratic
constitutional political economy. Only after abolition was inscribed in
the Constitution—and the question became what was it we abolished
when we abolished slavery—would this variation find mainstream expression in a new constitutional political economy challenging Greeley's
and the Republicans' premise of class harmony. Soon enough, we will
encounter mainstream agrarian and labor movements making just such
class-based claims for "social equality" on the Constitution—claims
against "wage slavery" and capitalist "property rights rulership."[92] But
in the constitutional political economy of Greeley and Republican antislavery, what we have is a distinctly bourgeois kind of radicalism—what
the historical sociologist Barrington Moore described as "the last revolutionary offensive on the part of . . . bourgeois capitalist democracy."[93]

When that antislavery offensive prevailed and made Free Labor a new constitutional baseline, it became possible to raise new claims about just what kind of freedom and equality—what kind of democracy of opportunity—working people got.

Orestes Brownson's heterodox emphasis on the government's creation and regulation of rights as tools for the laboring classes would become common currency among Gilded Age and Progressive reformers, and the constitutional coin of the realm in New Deal America, when Brownson's "social democrats" briefly reigned. In the antebellum North, however, Greeley's reforming bourgeois outlook aimed to defuse emergent class tensions without interfering with property and contract relations between wage laborers and the owners of capital. Class harmony, as a social and political fact, together with the Whigs' cherished belief in a "harmony of interests" between labor and capital—the very integrity of the North's vaunted equality of rights and opportunity, its "Free Labor System"—both seemed to hinge on finding some dramatic way to keep the path of economic ascent wide open. The main solution, Greeley and others concluded, lay in the "public lands" of the West.[94] "The public lands," Greeley declared, "are the great regulator of the relations of Labor and Capital, the safety valve of our industrial and social engine." A sound homestead policy might reinstate harmony between capital and labor, by offering every citizen the genuine alternative of "working for others or for himself."[95]

The view that the Western territories henceforth had to be "free soil" reserved for "free labor" gradually drew Whigs like Greeley and Lincoln into alliance with Northern Jacksonians, whose classic Jeffersonian ideals about easy access to land led them to the same conclusion.[96] In this fashion, the outlines emerged of the first major national party with a purely sectional base. What began as the Liberty Party and the Free Soil Party of the 1840s ripened into the new Republican Party of the 1850s.[97]

With a platform whose main plank promised a bar on "the extension of Slavery," the party dubbed itself the Party of Free Labor.[98] If the party's founders differed about many aspects of development policy, they all agreed that reinvigorating and maintaining the "Free Labor System" urgently demanded that public lands go henceforth to free labor. And just as Whigs had done with the American System, the new Republican Party put its core policy forward in the language of constitutional duty. It was "both the right and the imperative duty of Congress to prohibit [slavery] in the Territories," the party platform proclaimed.[99]

For the next quarter century, through the Civil War and Reconstruction, Republicans would press the idea of Congress's affirmative constitutional duties onward, from a contest over the national territories to a violent conflict over slavery itself, and a prolonged moment of constitutive politics and statecraft in which Republicans would ultimately claim the constitutional power and duty to remake many of the basic structures and institutions of Southern politics and society—and to redistribute some of the region's great concentration of wealth and power from what one Black Union soldier would call the "top rails" to the "bottom" ones—all in the name of rescuing and purifying the Constitution. No wonder, given these vaulting claims, we will find that the Republicans reprise the Jeffersonian-Jacksonian idea that theirs was no ordinary political party, but instead a party of principle, an indispensable constitutional counterweight to a new "ruling and dominant class," a new "oligarchy" determined, even after military defeat, to subvert the constitutional order.[100]

A CONSTITUTIONAL DUTY TO MAKE "FREEDOM NATIONAL"

But let us return to the territorial conflict of the mid-1850s, and the party's founding. It was the Ohio abolitionist—and future Chief Justice—Salmon Chase who first hammered out the theory that cast the Republicans' land policy as a constitutional imperative. Chase offered a bold new constitutional narrative, assuring Northern voters that they could support antislavery candidates for national office without breaking faith with the founders—that, indeed, the founders' vision demanded nothing less. Lincoln recast that abolitionist narrative and made it his own, as he became the Republicans' most popular expositor of the national government's duty to make the new territories in the West a constitutional sanctuary for the rights and opportunities of free labor.[101]

On Chase's and Lincoln's new account, the framers had always envisioned that the Constitution would lean toward freedom. Hoping to put slavery on the road to "ultimate extinction," they made "slavery restriction" the "original policy of the Government."[102] Slavery was to be safeguarded in the states where it existed, and where state citizens chose to preserve it. However, slavery was to be restricted wherever the national government had authority to do so. Thus, they pointed out, the framers outlawed slavery in the Northwest Territory—in language the Republicans would later inscribe in the Thirteenth Amendment. In keeping with the principle that slavery could only exist by dint of state law, the framers intended that the liberty guarantee of the Due Process Clause would bar slavery from ever existing under direct national authority. And direct national rule was precisely how the Constitution provided that the territories were to be governed. This meant, as Chase wrote to fellow abolitionist attorney and future Republican senator Charles Sumner, in 1850, that "under the Constitution Congress cannot establish or maintain slavery in the territories."[103]

How was it, then, that Congress had allowed slavery into some of the national territories? The answer was that this original understanding "has been subverted and the Constitution violated for the extension of slavery" by "the political supremacy of the Slave Power."[104] In the new Republican lexicon, the "Slave Power" was the political expression and political arm of the planter elite, and it had seized on the structural advantages that the Three-Fifths Clause lent the Slave Power in the House and the Electoral College (and, indirectly, on the federal bench), not merely to safeguard their legitimate interests but to dominate national politics and wield national power in ways that inverted the framers' design. They were hell-bent, in the Republicans' telling, on making "Slavery National" and on trampling the rights and opportunities of Free Labor. Every new portion of the West claimed by the Slave Power, in defiance of the framers' Constitution, deprived Free Labor of the space it needed to flourish. At the same time, when the slave territory became a slave state, it lent the Slave Power yet more clout in national affairs—all in the face of a Constitution that promised just the opposite. All this had the purpose and cumulative effect of making the "Mudsill theory" of labor and capital an American reality.[105]

Chase was a young widower and a Dartmouth-educated banking and corporate attorney in 1830s Cincinnati when he began representing ex-slaves, fugitives from nearby Southern river ports who had found work along the Ohio River as artisans and river pilots and had the usual disputes with steamship companies and building contractors. Chase had lost a few major banking clients, business was slow, and putting the law of contract to work for Black workingmen in the borderland between slavery and freedom had moral and religious appeal, although it won him few friends in the border city's business elite. One thing led to another, and soon he had struck up friendships among Ohio's talented band of Black and white abolitionists and was litigating fugitive slave cases. By the time the future Chief Justice had earned himself the title of "America's 'Attorney General for Runaway Slaves,'" Chase had been working for some years in state and federal constitutional materials trying to expand legal safeguards for alleged fugitives.[106]

It was no accident that the Republicans' constitutional narrative came from the party's small wing of abolitionists. They were the only seasoned advocates for the Black slaves of the South—as opposed to the white free labor of the North—and had been poring over the Constitution's bearings on slavery and freedom for two decades.[107] Abolitionist attorneys first fashioned the "Freedom National" narrative in trying to narrow the ambit of the Fugitive Slave Clause. When some of them, like Salmon Chase, began to run for federal office, they took the narrative to the hustings. As they joined forces with more moderate politicians like Lincoln in founding the Republican Party, the "Freedom National" narrative went mainstream. The story of the framers leaning in favor of Black liberty merged (but did not vanish) into a more politically salient and popular account of the framers' determination to safeguard the national territories for free white labor.[108]

The Declaration of Independence took the same journey. The abolitionists seized on the Declaration in their efforts to reinvigorate the revolutionary idea of freedom as a truly universal entitlement. Even as slavery spawned a racialized definition of American nationhood, the struggle for abolition produced its opposite, a purely civic understanding, an American people unbounded by race. Thus, abolitionists pointed out Jefferson's, Madison's, and other founders' condemnations of slavery and their efforts (via manumission laws, limitations on the slave trade, and exclusion of slavery from the then existing federal territories) to put it "on the road to extinction." With these, the abolitionists fashioned a theory that the Declaration was "declaratory" of rights the framers hoped to secure for "all men"; they inscribed these universal rights into many of their state constitutions—and would have done so with the national Constitution as well, but to secure the Union they had to compromise over slavery, leaving it to future generations to complete their work.[109]

Lincoln embraced this antislavery account of the Declaration, although unlike some radical abolitionists, he never spoke of the Declaration as binding law. Rather, in pungent, accessible terms, he popularized the hermeneutics of an evolving antislavery constitutional political economy, which, ultimately, would make good on the Declaration's proposition of human equality. The Declaration's promise of "Liberty to all" was the heart of the national enterprise; slavery was antithetical to it, and the Constitution must be read in the light of this point.[110]

"We" Americans, Lincoln told scores of thousands who gathered to hear him debate the decade's leading political figure, Stephen Douglas (and the hundreds of thousands who read the debates), had created a nation dedicated to universal liberty through "our" Declaration, and "we" were forced to compromise with slavery to "get our Constitution." The founders lacked the "power to confer [the] boon" of freedom on the slave. "They meant simply to declare the right, so that the enforcement of it might follow, as fast as circumstances should permit." And lest any future generation of leaders try to twist the nation and its constitutional order "back into the hateful paths of despotism," the founders meant that the language of the Declaration would be "at least one hard nut to crack."[111]

Lincoln was not a racial egalitarian. He accepted the racial proscriptions of the antebellum North. Almost to the end, he opposed Black suffrage; and he occasionally spoke of colonizing Blacks outside the country. But like the abolitionists, he insisted that the Declaration's creed encompassed all humanity. Taunted by Douglas for touting racial equality, Lincoln maintained that the basic rights set out in the Declaration applied to all people, "black as well as white." Insisting that the right to the fruits of one's labor was a natural right, not confined to any particular set of persons, Lincoln drove the point home by using as his example a Black woman: "In some respects she is certainly not my equal, but in her natural right to eat the bread she earns with her own hand . . . she is my equal and the equal of all others."[112]

For the abolitionists, that was the heart of the matter. But for Lincoln and his party, the abolitionist meaning was one element of a broader fusion centered on the morality and political economy of "Free Labor." The Declaration's "principle of 'Liberty to all'" spoke to the appropriate fate of slavery; at the same time, it belonged at the center of our constitutional politics and interpretations because, in Lincoln's words, brimming with middle-class uplift and the spirit of democratic capitalism, the Declaration's "Liberty to all" was "the principle that clears the *path* for all—gives *hope* to all—and, by consequence, *enterprize* and *industry* to all."[113] And so, when the new Republican Party's platform proclaimed it was the constitutional "right and imperative duty" of Congress to prohibit slavery in the territories, the platform's drafters enveloped each step of their reasoning in the language of the Declaration.[114]

Proslavery Constitutional Political Economy as "Minority Rights"

With the new antislavery forces framing the territories question in the language of constitutional duties and constitutional political economy, it is no wonder that the proslavery forces did likewise. Senator John Calhoun of South Carolina was the chief architect of the proslavery theory. In the familiar dialectics of constitutional discourse, Calhoun's ideas and those of his Republican interlocutors took shape in opposition to each other. Where Chase and Lincoln found a congressional duty to outlaw slavery in the territories, Calhoun found a duty to protect the slaveholder's property. Congress was without power, said Calhoun, to outlaw slavery anywhere in the federal territories. Instead, the national government was duty bound to administer the territories for the whole people, with an equal regard to the rights of the Southern slaveholder as to those of the Northern farmer and mechanic.[115] If it would be unconstitutional to bar a farmer from bringing his cow or a mechanic his tools into federal territory, so it was with the planter and his slave.

During the tariff debates of the 1830s, Calhoun already had fashioned a constitutional theory of "minority rights" pertaining to the rival interests of the different sections and their different economies. While it was not a justiciable question, it was no less a matter of constitutional principle, Calhoun had argued, that Congress could not impose all the costs and burdens of an economic policy on one section, and confer all the benefits on others. The fact that the burdens-bearing section, in this case the agrarian, crop-exporting South, might constitute a more or less permanent minority in the House and Senate could not justify such unequal legislation. At a certain point, where the burdens on the disadvantaged minority were sufficiently great, the Constitution was offended.[116] The same precept applied to the territories question, now that the party of antislavery had "avow[ed] that their determination is to exclude slavery from all the territories of the United States . . . and, of course, to prevent the citizens of the Southern States from emigrating with their property in slaves into any of them."[117]

As antislavery and proslavery forces in the political branches pressed their rival claims on the Constitution, and guerilla warfare broke out between pro- and antislavery settlers in "Bloody Kansas," pressure mounted on the Supreme Court to take up the matter, and the Court famously did so in *Dred Scott.* Much of what the Justices had to say channeled the debates in the polity. Like the politicians and lawmakers, the Court's various opinions entwined constitutional and political-economic arguments in a single discourse.[118]

For his part, Justice John McLean, in dissent, defended the constitutionality of Congress's power to exclude slavery in the service of Free Labor. Responding to an argument from counsel echoing Calhoun's theory of unfair political-economic burdens on the "minority" section, McLean did some number crunching: "[A]s regards any unfairness of such a policy [of barring slavery] to our Southern brethren . . . it is only necessary to say that, with one-fourth of the . . . population . . . they have in the slave States a larger extent of fertile territory than is included in the free States. . . . The repugnancy to slavery would probably prevent fifty or a hundred freemen from settling in a slave Territory, where one slaveholder would be prevented from settling in a free Territory."[119]

In the majority, the opinions of Chief Justice Roger Taney and Justice John Catron both took up Calhoun's case that the property rights of slaveholders were entitled to "entire EQUALITY" of treatment from

Congress as the property rights of "those of the North" and their "cattle or horses . . . tools of trade, or machines."[120] Congress could no more bar "the culture of sugar and cotton" from the territories than it could exclude "the Northern farmer and mechanic."[121]

Perhaps the last word belonged to "Old Bullion," the famous Jacksonian senator from Missouri, Thomas Hart Benton. Benton described the rival constitutional political-economic programs afoot in the polity and on the Court as two blades of a pair of shears that soon would sever the Union.[122] Benton was right. Disunion came; war followed; the party of Free Labor prevailed.

AFTER SLAVERY, WHAT DID FREEDOM MEAN?

Only after the war ended and slavery was abolished, a Northern labor leader observed, did it become possible for the nation to address the "labor question" in its modern form. As long as chattel slavery existed, and those with capital were allowed to own and dispose of the bodies and families of working people, that species of total dominion was always present, as a moral and legal baseline. Before the war, many forms of domination and deprivation, many inequalities, and many constraints on opportunity that American labor endured could be defended—indeed, could even appear—as *not slavery; therefore, freedom.*[123]

Abolitionism's heroic attack on slavery illustrated this, for it brought into play among the nation's most advanced reformers a narrower, more constricted conception of Northern labor's freedom than the one that animated Free Labor ideology. We have glimpsed abolitionism's racial liberalism, which clashed with the North's and the Republican Party's prevailing racism and laid the groundwork for building the inclusionary principle into the democracy-of-opportunity tradition. But here we are concerned with a second marked difference between the Republican mainstream and the abolitionist outlook. As Eric Foner's classic work puts it, Lincoln talked about Northern labor's freedom in terms of economic independence—being able to own one's own shop or farm—whereas the abolitionist typically talked about the freedom of the Northern worker in terms of self-ownership—that is, simply not being a slave, being free to sell his own labor.[124] The difference was one of emphasis, but it had vast implications for what kind of liberty and equality the triumph of Free Labor would hold in store for Southern slaves and Northern working people alike. Self-ownership and equality of rights in market and property relations were a necessary condition of freedom. But were they sufficient? Or did freedom also demand, as Lincoln's accounts always seemed to insist, a political economy and legal-constitutional order that guaranteed robust opportunities for material independence and economic autonomy? The latter answer might require initial endowments, distribution-focused policies, and some modifications to those rules of market and property relations, depending on the political economy of a given time and place.

As Foner uncovered, the mutual suspicion and incomprehension with which the leading abolitionists and Northern labor leaders often regarded one another was revealing and prophetic. Chiding the Northern labor movement for its protests against "wage slavery," the great abolitionist leader Wendell Phillips declared that the "elevation and improvement" of laborers in the free states was impeded only by their failure to acquire "economy, self-denial, education and moral and religious character."[125] The middle-class abolitionists' characteristic attitude toward labor, Foner writes, was exemplified in a pamphlet published by New York abolitionist William Jay.[126] In the course of a discussion of the benefits of immediate emancipation, Jay set out to answer the recurrent question, what would happen to the slave when free?

> He is free, and his own master, and can ask for no more. Yet he is, in fact, for a time, absolutely dependent on his late owner. He can look to no other person for food to eat, clothes to put on, or house to shelter him. . . . [He is required to work], but labor is no longer the badge of his servitude and the consummation of his misery, for it is *voluntary*. For the first time in his life he is a party to a contract. . . . In the course of time, the value of negro labor, like all other vendible commodities, will be regulated by the supply and demand.[127]

What is noteworthy in this, as Foner points out, is, first, the abolitionist's ready acceptance of the condition that prompted (and would increasingly generate) so much complaint among the labor movement: the treatment of human labor as a "vendible commodity"; and second, the rather dubious use of the word "voluntary" to describe the labor of an individual who owns nothing and is "absolutely dependent" on his employer. Foner writes: "To the labor movement, Jay's description of emancipation would qualify as a classic instance of 'wage slavery'; to Jay, it was an economic definition of freedom."[128] It was a definition of freedom that would enable Northern elites to confront the emerging factory and wage labor system with a new mode of social thought, one that affirmed what Lincoln's more traditional republican outlook denied, that a free society was compatible with large, permanent classes of dependent workers.

In the decades ahead, it would be the abolitionists' definition of freedom as the right to sell one's labor that judges enshrined as workers' constitutional liberty of contract. Indeed, some of the leading jurists wielding the new doctrine to strike down labor laws were, as we shall see, youthful colleagues of Jay's in the abolitionist movement. But if the abolitionist legacy helped valorize liberty of contract and lent a remarkable sense of righteousness to the jurists who invented Lochnerism, nothing about the antislavery battle preordained these developments.

To the contrary, Northern victory and the end of slavery would leave unsettled what kind of new constitutional political economy Reconstruction lawmakers would forge and what kind of destiny of work and opportunity awaited the Black and white laboring classes of the war-ravaged South and industrializing North. The labor reformer who anticipated that the end of slavery would make possible addressing the labor question in a more ambitious, modern fashion was not mistaken. Reconstruction would see a division in Republican ranks about the meaning of the Free Labor precepts the party was enshrining in the new Reconstruction Amendments.[129]

Wendell Phillips, for example, abandoned his hostility toward the Northern labor movement and became a champion of the very labor reforms he had earlier scorned. The labor movement had been right, he concluded: the work of antislavery did not end with emancipation, and something of slavery remained in the "wage labor system." A constitutional political economy for the emerging industrial working class required measures like the eight-hours law the labor movement was demanding from Congress. Phillips was no outlier. During Reconstruction, many Republican lawmakers would continue to hew to the broader antebellum account of labor's freedom and the affirmative constitutional duties it laid on them. But many other Republican lawmakers, journalists, and jurists began to repurpose antislavery as a constitutional bulwark against redistribution, and to discount the distributional commitments that had been an important strand of Free Labor constitutionalism. It is to these battles that we now turn.

3

THE SECOND FOUNDING:
A BRIEF UNION OF THREE PRECEPTS

It is no exaggeration when historians say that the Civil War and Reconstruction Amendments marked a Second Founding and a fundamentally changed constitutional order. From a slaveholding, racially exclusive republic, America reconstituted itself into a racially inclusive republic of free labor and equal citizens. The authority of the national government over the states was transformed, and with it, the meaning of American democracy. The lion's share of rights and opportunities in the antebellum Jacksonian "democracy" had belonged to white men, as a matter of principle as well as practice. But the struggle to end slavery and uproot the Slave Power resulted in more than abolition. It produced a new constitutional order, proclaiming that equality of rights and opportunities, henceforth, was universal.[1]

The Second Founding moment was a high-water mark for the democracy-of-opportunity tradition. This time, the inclusionary principle—in terms of race—was at its center. The thrust of the Civil War and Reconstruction Amendments, according to the framers of those amendments, was not simply to abolish slavery but to make "Freedom"— free labor, the democracy of opportunity, and all the basic rights they were thought to entail—"National."[2] Equality was inscribed in the national Constitution and put under national protection for the first time, and its promise extended to all "the People," which the Second Founding redefined as "all persons born in the United States . . . of every race and color, without regard to any previous condition of slavery or involuntary servitude."[3]

Equal rights for the ex-slaves was the most breathtaking element. But the Reconstruction Republicans understood that equal rights alone would amount to a hollow victory unless the political economy of the postbellum South was also remade, in line with the other two core principles of the democracy-of-opportunity tradition. An oligarchy—centered on the overwhelming economic and political power of the slave-owning class—had to be uprooted and its grip on economic and political power broken. A broad, open, biracial middle class had to be constructed where none existed. The planter elite, with their vast wealth in land and labor, had held down not only the slave population, but the great mass of "poor whites" as well.[4]

All three principles were thus intertwined. All sides to the bitter battles of Reconstruction understood that the freed people's actual enjoyment of equal citizenship—the inclusion principle—needed a material underpinning to be real, and that Black citizens needed real political clout to hold on to whatever material independence they could achieve. Reconstruction's rise and fall confirmed this. Without suffrage and political rights, the ex-slaves could not hold on to their new rights and opportunities in market and property relations. By the same token, stripped of economic citizenship, denied any real measure of material freedom, and rendered dependent serfs of their ex-masters, the freedmen would find that their political freedom was fatally vulnerable. Absent a biracial, redistributive "poor man's party" (as foes would call the new Southern Republicans), poor whites would be prey to the old lure of white supremacy, and the economic and political power of Southern oligarchy would be restored.

Thus, not only were the democracy of opportunity's three cardinal principles brought together in the work of the Republican Party, but that party also revived the old idea of the political party as bearer of constitutional redemption. Antebellum Democrats had justified and defended the creation of the mass political party as essential to rescuing the republican Constitution from the grip of moneyed elites and guarding the constitutional order against oligarchy. The postbellum Republicans justified their revolutionary efforts to enfranchise the ex-slaves as essential to building the Southern political base for the Republican Party—which they argued was necessary to block the unrepentant Southern

Democrats' attempts to restore the old Slave Power and undermine the Reconstructed Constitution. Continued Republican control of Congress was thus both a partisan goal and a high-minded constitutional necessity. Party constitutionalism opened on to legislative constitutionalism. Securing the freed people's rights and outfitting Black ex-slaves and poor whites as equal citizens and real free laborers, with a measure of education and material independence, was *legislative* constitutional work. Indeed, as we shall see, this work was not just within congressional power—it was a matter of Congress's affirmative constitutional duty.

By 1866, these connections were already beginning to become clear to Congress's Joint Committee on Reconstruction. "Slavery, by building up a ruling and dominant class, had produced a spirit of oligarchy averse to republican institutions," the committee reported in April of that year. "[L]eaving [that ruling class] in the exclusive possession of political power, would be to encourage the same spirit, and lead" to restoring the old oligarchy.[5] The same was true regarding the distribution of social and economic power. As the leading Radical Republican on the Joint Committee, the craggy-faced Congressman Thaddeus Stevens, tartly put it, "The whole fabric of southern society *must* be changed. . . . How can republican institutions . . . exist in a mingled community of nabobs and serfs?"[6]

Presidential Reconstruction—or "Restoration"?

Even before the war's end, emancipation had come to mean more than a formal end to slavery. It meant, in the martyred president's words, "a new birth of freedom," drawing both ex-slave and ex-master into the Free Labor system and somehow remaking the South into a free society.[7] But what that transformation would entail—economically and socially, politically and constitutionally—remained deeply contested.

Lincoln had hoped for a gentle and conciliatory Reconstruction and expected that "loyal" Southern whites would take the lead. His successor, the impolitic border-state politician and vicious racist Andrew Johnson, embraced these notions with zeal. For "Reconstruction," Johnson substituted "Restoration."[8] In April 1865, his first month as president,

Johnson appointed a provisional governor for each rebel state, directed the states to hold constitutional conventions, and demanded that the conventions nullify the ordinances of secession, repudiate the Confederate war debt, and adopt the Thirteenth Amendment. He offered a broad amnesty, pardoning anyone who took an oath of loyalty to the Union, as well as anyone elected to office, and imposed neither Black suffrage nor any wide disenfranchisement of former Confederate leaders or soldiers. By late 1865, all the Southern states had fulfilled the president's instructions, and Johnson declared the process complete. He recommended that the senators and representatives chosen by the restored state governments be seated in Congress.[9]

In Congress, however, the Republicans were appalled at what these reorganized state governments had wrought. Far from protecting the ex-slaves' basic civil rights, the reorganized states enacted Black Codes designed to enserf the freed people and make them slaves of the white community. The Black Codes reinstated a race-based caste system, keeping African Americans an inferior and dependent class by hindering or disabling them from owning, renting, or transferring property, pursuing skilled callings, or seeking access to courts. New vagrancy, indenture, and apprenticeship laws would re-bind them and their offspring to white planters; new employment laws authorized whipping them and docking their pay; and new enclosure laws prevented them from hunting or grazing animals and livestock.[10]

Furthermore, in the 1865 elections, the reorganized states chose mostly "unrepentant rebels" to lead and represent them.[11] Mississippi elected a Confederate brigadier general to be governor, and the Georgia legislature chose Alexander Stephens, the ex–vice president of the Confederacy, to represent it in the Senate. Doubly disturbing, most of the newly elected senators and congressmen were Democrats, and the arithmetic of emancipation boosted the threat this posed to Republican hegemony. The Thirteenth Amendment eliminated the Three-Fifths Clause and promised to increase the Southern delegation in the House and Electoral College by roughly fifteen. Having lost the war, the unrepentant South seemed to be winning the peace.[12]

So, when the Thirty-Ninth Congress convened in December 1865, Republicans rallied to block the seating of the Southern delegation and to take the lead in Reconstruction policy away from the White House. Approving a resolution introduced by Thaddeus Stevens, Republicans formed the Joint [House and Senate] Committee on Reconstruction.[13]

Congress's Constitutional Powers and Duties— Dismantling Slavery, Constructing Freedom

Given our current forgetfulness about constitutional political economy, we would do well to pay attention to how the Reconstruction Amendments' racially inclusive, rights-conferring project and their political-economic, redistributive project were inseparable sides of the same constitutional coin, from the perspective of the amendments' framers. The two were inseparable because slavery had been both an economic class system and a racial caste system—a brutal system of labor exploitation and one of racial domination.[14] As a matter of political economy, abolishing slavery meant, first of all, dismantling two groups of legal subjects: slaves and slaveholders. In the process, property on the order of a trillion dollars, as the slave market measured things, was expropriated, without compensation.[15] The Thirteenth Amendment extinguished slaveholders' property rights in, and conferred rights of self-ownership on, roughly four million ex-slaves—among the largest redistributions of ruling-class property the modern world has ever seen. Uprooting a social order based on slavery had required what Lincoln called a "violent and remorseless, revolutionary struggle."[16] After the war, the consummation of this revolutionary project—dismantling an old social order based on slavery and building a new one resting on free labor and a baseline of equal rights for the freed people—required some unprecedented legislation and institution building.

But what kind of legislation, and what kind of institutions, were needed? The Republican visions of Black freedom were various and often uncertain in early 1866. Some New Englanders—like Harriet Beecher Stowe and her abolitionist family (proud owners of a new-model Southern plantation designed to lift the freed people into the world of free labor)—thought that the key was simply self-ownership and equality with whites in the basic rights to bodily security and to make contracts to labor; eventually, perhaps, to own or lease property; and to make one's own way.[17] That was the classical liberal definition of free labor, and they thought it a sufficient touchstone of freedom for the ex-slaves, even if it consigned the great majority of them to work on factory-like plantations. However, for most Republicans, this liberal strand was entwined with a thicker republican one, as it had been for Lincoln. Labor's freedom was incomplete without an actual measure of material independence, and such freedom required broad access to land or a trade. Just what measures would be required to ensure that kind of freedom for the Black South remained an open and contested question as the Thirty-Ninth Congress got underway.

Enacting Freedom

It was the Radical Republicans, the party's formidable left wing, who had the most coherent sense of the larger tasks at hand.[18] As the historian Eric Foner writes, they were "a self-conscious political generation with shared experiences and commitments, a grass-roots constituency, a moral sensibility and a program for Reconstruction."[19] With the exception of Thaddeus Stevens of Pennsylvania, they represented voters in New England, like the renowned abolitionist Massachusetts senator Charles Sumner, along with voters living "in the belt of New England migration that stretched across the rural North through upstate New York, Ohio's Western Reserve, northern Illinois, and the upper Northwest." Here lay "growing communities of family farms and small towns, where the superiority of the free labor system appeared self-evident, antebellum reform had flourished, and the Republican party commanded overwhelming majorities."[20] Sumner's fellow Boston abolitionist, Wendell Phillips, summed up the Radical program in three words: "land, education and the ballot."[21]

Rooted in their regions' social experience and reform traditions, the Radicals envisioned the South reshaped in the idealized image of small-scale, democratic capitalism; its people, Black and white, endowed with identical rights, and no longer slaves or propertyless dependents but "landholders . . . no longer . . . subject to the despotism with which a privileged class has heretofore ruled that whole country."[22] "My dream," one Radical explained in early 1866, "is of a model republic, extending equal protection and rights to all men. . . . The wilderness shall vanish, the church and school-house will appear; . . . the whole land will revive under the magic touch of free labor."[23] Said another, "We must guard the equal rights of the people. . . . Instead of the spirit of Caste and the law of Hate . . . we must build up homogeneous communities in which the interest of each will be recognized as the interest of all. . . . [W]e must have no order of the nobility but that of the laboring masses. . . . Instead of large estates . . . small farms, closely associated communities, thrifty tillage, free schools, social independence . . . and equality of political rights."[24]

These Republicans were speaking in the language of the democracy-of-opportunity tradition that stretches all the way back to Jeffersonian and Jacksonian Democracy. They shared the old Democratic vision of a broad middle class composed of independent small landholders and proprietors, and its opposition to any privileged class. But the Radical Republicans took these ideas to their logical conclusion, recognizing in a way that Jefferson and Jackson and their followers never did, that racial hierarchy thwarts the possibility of a democracy of opportunity.

Initially, Republican lawmakers outside the Radical wing had little inclination to go much further than conferring basic civil rights on the ex-slaves and hoping for the best. Suffrage seemed a bridge too far. Northern racism—views of the ex-slaves as childish, helpless, potential tools of old masters, not fully equal and certainly not ready for the ballot—stood in the way. Within two years, however, events in the South would enable the Radicals to bring the rest of the Republican lawmakers on board for much more of their revolutionary vision, which bound together the core strands of the democracy-of-opportunity tradition we are examining in this book.

While the three strands of the tradition—racial inclusion in the full rights of citizenship, a broad middle class, and anti-oligarchy—may seem distinct today, for the Radicals, they were inseparable. There may be no better example of the interweaving of these three ideas than Senator Sumner's proposed draft of what became the 1866 Civil Rights Act. The draft declared: "That in all States lately declared to be in rebellion there shall be no Oligarchy, Aristocracy, Caste, or Monopoly invested with peculiar privileges and powers, and there shall be no denial of rights, civil or political, on account of race or color; but all persons shall be equal before the law."[25] With his bill ready in hand as Congress convened, Sumner laid out the Radical case with a speech stretching over two days, February 5 and 6, 1866, and consuming forty-one columns of small print in the *Congressional Globe*.[26] His themes, to which he returned over and over, were *oligarchy, aristocracy, caste,* and *monopoly*. His Senate colleague, William Fessenden from Maine, observed, "[I]f the brain of the honorable Senator from Massachusetts should ever chance to be dissected, I think those words would be found very strongly impressed on it."[27]

Sumner's bill promised equality "in the court-room" and "at the ballot-box."[28] The "ballot-box" went further than most Republicans (outside the Radical caucus) thought their constituents or the Constitution, even with the new Thirteenth Amendment, would support. Sumner had no such doubts. He explained that his bill's constitutionality rested on "quadruple powers."[29] These were the War Power, because the South remained under military occupation; the power of Congress to judge the qualifications of its members; the new Thirteenth Amendment's Enforcement Clause (to which we will return); and Article IV's Guarantee Clause, providing that the "United States shall guarantee to every state in this union a republican form of government."[30]

"Power and Duty Here Concur": Protecting Basic Rights, Providing Basic Goods

The last of these "quadruple powers" Sumner dubbed a "sleeping giant," and he devoted the bulk of his two-day speech to interpreting and expounding it.[31] The Court had long ago acknowledged that the Guarantee Clause was a provision for Congress, and not the Court, to interpret and apply;[32] and the clause's language—"*shall* guarantee"—made plain that Congress was "not only empowered but commanded, to perform the great guaranty. Power and duty here concur."[33] Thus, Sumner stepped into the familiar Whig tradition of congressional exposition of Congress's constitutional duties, and other framer-lawmakers—moderates and Radicals alike—soon followed, expounding Congress's duties under the new Reconstruction Amendments as well as the Guarantee Clause. As Sumner explained:

> Believe me, Sir, this is no question of theory or abstraction. It is a practical question, which you are summoned to decide. Here is the positive text of the Constitution, and you must affix its meaning. You cannot evade it, you cannot forget it, without abandonment of duty. Others . . . have dwelt on the idea of a Republic, and they have been lifted in soul. You must consider it . . . practically, as legislators, in order to settle its precise definition, to the end that the constitutional "guarantee" may be performed. *Your powers and duties are involved in this definition. The character of the Government founded by our fathers is also involved in it.* There is another consideration, which must not be forgotten. In affixing the proper meaning to the text, and determining what is a "Republican government," you act as a court in the last resort from which there is no appeal.[34]

What was the clause's proper meaning? What would "our fathers" have had Congress do to reform the rebel states' governments and make them truly republican?[35] The gist of Sumner's argument was that the "essential condition" of a "republican form of government" called for by the Guarantee Clause was the "Equal Rights of All"; above all, "every man" must have suffrage, and with it, a secure livelihood to make his ballot independent.[36] No voting rules that monopolized the ballot for a privileged minority and no "permanent or insurmountable" qualification for voting, such as race, could stand in a republic.[37] "Call it Oligarchy, call it Aristocracy, call it Caste, call it Monopoly; but do not call it a republic."[38]

Sumner's reading of the Guarantee Clause fit into the general antislavery account of the founders' purposes, which Salmon Chase and Abraham Lincoln had fashioned in the 1850s. On this view, the Constitution was a developmental blueprint, designed to help put slavery on the road to extinction. Thus, like Lincoln and Chase, Sumner summoned the founding fathers for support. Slavery was an "anomalous condition," and the provisions safeguarding it were "compromising expedients,"[39] he explained, quoting Hamilton. The Constitution's language, on this account, had been crafted to avoid any express recognition of "property in man," to leave space for an antislavery politics to take hold.[40] Once the laws "restore the rights which have been taken away" from Black bondsmen, Sumner again quoted Hamilton, "the negroes could no longer be refused" the ballot on ground of color.[41]

The purpose of the Guarantee Clause was similarly developmental: a constitutional guardrail to ensure a more "truly 'republican'" nation "in the development of the future" by empowering Congress to prevent state-based oligarchies of caste or class from taking root, and thus keep the nation on track, one day "to make the whole numerous people . . . homogeneous and one."[42] Now, with the Southern oligarchs on the ropes and the Thirteenth Amendment in place, "the 'guaranty' must be performed," the "'rights which have been taken away'" restored, and the ballot secured for "everyman." Finally, a biracial republican citizenry, "homogeneous and one."

For the most part, Republican senators praised Sumner's learning and rejected his bill, because it conferred the ballot. But the great majority of them shared Sumner's view that Congress had both constitutional power and constitutional duties to protect basic *civil* rights and to provide basic social goods to secure the freed people in their freedom.[43] Radicals and moderates alike, these framer-lawmakers leaned on the inherited Whig discourse of legislative constitutional duties to justify their revolutionary steps toward establishing a newly inclusive democracy of opportunity. Again and again, they declared that the Thirteenth Amendment's enforcement provision imposed on Congress a "constitutional duty" or a "constitutional obligation" to enact and enforce measures Congress deemed necessary to "protect these people" and "every man in the land" in their freedom.[44]

From the 1850s onward, Lincoln had taught Republicans to regard this equality of basic rights as one "declared" by the founding fathers in 1776 to belong to "all men," Black and white, "so that the enforcement of it," in Lincoln's words, "might follow, as fast as circumstances should permit."[45] Now, circumstances permitted, and a large—veto-proof, as it turned out—majority of Republicans found in the Thirteenth Amendment the power and duty to make the freed people citizens, and to guarantee them equal enjoyment of the core rights of contract, property, and personal liberty.[46] The Civil Rights Act of 1866 would safeguard enjoyment of the rights, and the Second Freedmen's Bureau Bill of the same year would provide food and sustenance, schools, and access to public lands and abandoned plantations.[47]

The equality-conferring language of the final version of the 1866 Civil Rights Act—"the same right to make and enforce contracts, to sue, be parties, and give evidence, to inherit, purchase, lease, sell, hold, and convey real and personal property, and to full and equal benefit of all laws and proceedings for the security of person and property, as is enjoyed by white citizens"[48]—encapsulates the outlook of the Republican mainstream at this moment. Their vision was one of Black free laborers making contracts, owning or leasing land, and meeting white employers, merchants, and landlords on a plane of legal equality.

Most striking here are the new convictions about the appropriate uses of national power to constitute a new economic order populated with new legal subjects, via federal enforcement of these hitherto local and state-based rights—all in the face of planters' and state and local authorities' determination to use the Black Codes to enserf the ex-slaves instead. The year 1866 also saw reauthorization of the Freedmen's Bureau (formally, the Bureau of Refugees, Freedmen, and Abandoned Lands). The 1866 Civil Rights statute gave both the federal agency and the federal district courts unprecedented power to adjudicate and enforce rights claims under the statute. This expansion of national authority, Republicans explained, was not only within Congress's power under the Thirteenth Amendment; it was an affirmative duty to safeguard the freedmen's precarious economic enfranchisement and new constitutional standing as citizens and "freemen."[49] Lyman Trumbull, chair of the Senate Judiciary Committee and coauthor of the Thirteenth Amendment, explained that "the constitutional obligation . . . is upon us to pass the appropriate legislation to . . . protect these people in their freedom."[50]

But freedom demanded more than legal rights and fair tribunals. It required food and sustenance for the desperately poor—and for all, it required a free common school education and access to free land. Today we are taught that the Reconstruction Amendments confer no

"affirmative right to government aid" and impose no "affirmative obligation" to protect basic liberties; the Supreme Court has said so, categorically.[51] The Reconstruction lawmakers, who framed the amendments,
thought differently. They thought the Constitution obliges government
to protect basic rights from state and private invasion and imposes
what we might call a pre-distribution of basic social goods.

Thus, said one Republican lawmaker, invoking the Thirteenth Amendment, "The second section of that amendment . . . creates the duty
for just such legislation as this bill contains, to give [the freed people]
shelter, and food, to lift them from slavery . . . and to educate."[52] The
"bill" was the Second Freedmen's Bureau Act of 1866. It provided for
relief in the form of food and clothing for destitute ex-slaves; it funded
and mandated the Bureau's Education Division to erect and staff free
common schools for them; and it funded and authorized the Bureau's
Land Division to purchase land and set aside "unoccupied public lands
[in the Deep South]" for "loyal refugees and freedmen," and, like Sumner's bill, it conferred possessory rights on freedmen who had occupied
abandoned plantation land under General Sherman's authority.[53] Constitutional authority for all this rested on the Thirteenth Amendment—
as well as the General Welfare Clause, the Federal Territories or Property
Clause, and the Guarantee Clause. The affirmative duties to provide
education and land ran through them as well.[54]

Education and Land as Constitutional Essentials

Since the party's founding in 1854, Republicans had constantly highlighted the lack of free common schools in the "despotic" South. Slaves
were forbidden to learn to read and write, and the great mass of poor
whites were deprived of any opportunity to do so. Such deprivation was
fatal to the republican form of government.[55] Work by historian Forrest
Nabors retrieves this Republican narrative.[56] The majority of Southern
whites, so the narrative went, being poor and illiterate, had been "de-
ceived and misled" into following the Slave Power on the path to secession, the object of which was "to overthrow republican institutions, and
to erect on the ruins of the Republic oligarchy."[57] Now, with congres-

sional Reconstruction underway, Congress's mission was finally to topple oligarchy and lay new foundations for a "permanent" and "pure Republic."[58] Republicans in Congress argued: "Shall we commit the fatal mistake of building up free States, without first expelling the darkness in which slavery had shrouded their people? Shall we enlarge the boundaries of citizenship, and make no provision to increase the intelligence of the citizen?"[59] One added: "We cannot leave the population of the South, white or black, in the condition they are now in. We must educate them."[60] Or as another put it, "[W]e must restore the great body of that people by the establishment in those States of free schools."[61]

BLACK SCHOOLS

With Freedmen's Bureau support, thousands of Northern Blacks and whites joined Southern Blacks and a handful of Southern whites in founding and staffing what hitherto had been outlawed: Black schools.[62] Throughout Reconstruction, the majority of teachers would be Black.[63] Some had been public school teachers in the North, some teachers in "secret schools" in the South; most had never been teachers.[64] Booker T. Washington, who was a young boy in Virginia in the late 1860s, recalled, "It was a whole race going to school." His first teacher was William Davis, "a young colored man from Ohio, who had been a soldier."[65]

The dawn of Black suffrage in 1867 would usher Republican Party majorities into the Southern statehouses. These lawmakers "embedded black schools in state systems of public education"[66]—systems that also provided the first public schools for poor Southern whites. Teaching was not a full-time occupation. Black teachers moved in and out of the classroom; "they were also lawyers, planters, farmers, sharecroppers, newspaper editors and ministers."[67] They were community leaders and had a great stake in the fortunes of the Southern Republican Party, believing that both the education and the fragile new citizenly standing of the Black South depended on it. They "served as voter registrars and election supervisors. They headed Union Leagues and Republican clubs, drilled the freedmen on the mechanics of voting, and distributed ballot papers. . . . Of the approximately fifteen hundred blacks who held public office during Reconstruction [roughly 10 percent of them] had taught in schools. Every state had its complement of teacher-politicians."[68]

By the same token, the close association of Black schools with the project of Black citizenship and the Republican dream of an inclusive democracy of opportunity made them targets of white violence and arson and "fueled white distrust of the public school systems inaugurated by Republican [state] governments."[69] Still, the schools endured. Even after Republican rule had been toppled and Reconstruction ended, Southern lawmakers slashed Black schools' budgets but left the schools in place—for fear of renewed federal intervention and also, in some cases, to court the Black vote. (Disenfranchisement was far from immediate.) In such parlous circumstances, the schools helped produce a measure of Southern Black literacy and generations of vital community leaders.[70]

Land

Land seemed no less vital than education. Congress's constitutional duty regarding homesteads was not a hard question for the Reconstruction Republicans. From the start, it was party doctrine that Congress was duty bound not only to bar slavery from the western territories, but also to parcel the public lands into free homesteads. From their first days in Congress, in the mid-1850s, party founders George Julian and Galusha Grow set out to remake federal lands policy. No longer should Congress sell off the lands for revenue. The right policy was to grant land in limited parcels—160 acres—to "actual settlers, on condition of occupancy and improvement."[71]

Free homesteads were not just better policy—they were a constitutional essential. Allowing speculators to buy up the most fertile swaths of public lands forced city workers who wanted to go west and "buy a farm" to "pay the speculator three or four hundred per cent on his investment."[72] Free homesteads, by contrast, were a promising way to combat the scourge of shrinking opportunity, "starvation wages," and mounting inequality in the industrializing regions of the North. Because of this, Republicans contended that selling public lands to the highest bidders was a species of class legislation—"aid[ing] the strong against the weak" in the unequal "struggle between capital and labor."[73]

Grow, Julian, and other Jacksonian-turned-Republican lawmakers thus turned the old Jacksonian constitutional bar against "unequal" and "partial" class legislation into an affirmative duty to dispose of the public lands in a fashion that helped the landless poor reach the middle class. Invoking "our great charters of Human Rights," they argued that the Declaration and Constitution obliged Congress to set aside earlier policies, centered on federal revenue, and to recognize "in its legislative enactments . . . the natural right of the landless citizen of the country to a home upon its soil."[74]

Harking back to Jefferson's radical reading of Locke, and like them, discounting the prior claims of Native Americans, these Republicans tapped into the old Lockean trope likening America's vast "vacant land" to a "state of nature." Echoing Jefferson's famous maxim that the earth is "for the support of man," they declared, "[E]very man has, by nature, a perfect right to a reasonable portion of it, upon which to subsist." When so many "more than one billion acres" of public land lay "untouched," it was a "wanton abuse of [Congress's] trust" *not* to recognize every American's "right to land enough to rear a habitation and live on"; for the right to land was a "necessary and indispensable means for the enjoyment of inalienable rights of life, liberty and pursuit of happiness."[75]

Following the election of 1860, Galusha Grow was en route to becoming the first Republican Speaker of the House and George Julian the chair of the House Committee on Public Lands. Congress had already passed their homestead bill earlier that year, and Buchanan had vetoed it. The 1860 party platform called on the new Congress to reenact the measure and the hoped-for Republican president to sign it. Against Democrats' protests that the bill would make the public lands a refuge for Northern paupers, the platform denounced "any view of the free-homestead policy which regards the settlers as paupers or suppliants for public bounty."[76] To the contrary, a free homestead was every citizen's right. And in 1862, Lincoln signed the Republicans' Homestead Act into law.[77]

So, by 1866, the constitutional political-economic idea of homesteads as initial endowments for the freed people was ready at hand. Sumner's civil rights bill had expressly defined the freedman's right of property to include "a homestead."[78] His colleague Lyman Trumbull, the moderate chair of the Senate Judiciary Committee and coauthor of the Thirteenth Amendment, agreed. Underscoring the land provisions of the Second Freedmen's Bureau bill, and later that year, championing the Southern Homestead Act, Trumbull said, "[A] homestead is worth more to these people than almost anything else . . . so long as the relation of employer and employed exists between the blacks and the whites, you will necessarily have a dependent population."[79] When President Johnson vetoed the Second Freedmen's Bureau bill, on the ground that Congress had no power to enact it, Trumbull responded that the Thirteenth Amendment not only empowered but *required* Congress "to discharge the constitutional obligation that is upon us to pass the appropriate legislation to protect every man in the land in his freedom."[80] As with the Civil Rights Act, the 1866 Congress overrode the president's veto.

Free homesteads were vital for the Northern worker facing the dependency of wage slavery. But they seemed indispensable for the Southern freedmen emerging from chattel slavery and facing continued dependency on the old masters. The Civil Rights Act made the freedmen citizens, and access to free homesteads was every "landless citizen['s]" right. Without land, as Lyman Trumbull observed, the "negroes" risked remaining forever hirelings, subordinated, a "dependent population."[81] The freedom promised by the Thirteenth Amendment meant not merely self-ownership but a real prospect of economic independence, which meant owning productive property. Congressman William Allison, another architect of Reconstruction, put it in classic Lincolnian terms: "Labor must not only be free but the cultivator of the soil must have a proprietary right in the soil itself."[82] Securing a permanent foundation for republican government pointed in the same direction as the requisites of Black freedom. Thus, as Allison explained, distribution of Southern lands for homesteads was an extension of the "settled policy of the Government" in distributing public lands, giving "the oppressed poor" access to "happy and independent homes," and allowing them to "contribute to the growth, wealth, and greatness of the nation."[83]

The hard question was not whether to make homesteads out of public lands; the hard question was whether to break up the big plantations of the Slave Power oligarchs and redistribute them to their ex-slaves. The idea had important advocates and powerful reasons in its favor. First of all, since 1863, several Union generals had been doing just that, with abandoned plantations in the Georgia Sea Islands, in Mississippi, and elsewhere. Granting the plantation land to the freed people enabled them to support themselves, it proved their capacity for economic independence, and it produced cotton and other export crops to help fund the war effort. Second, most Radicals in Congress were persuaded that the only way to prevent the resurrection of the Slave Power was, as James Wilson of Iowa put it in 1864, to "destroy that aristocratic and semifeudal system which has heretofore existed in the South" by "breaking up the land monopoly of the rebel slaveholders" and making "the mass [of poor Blacks and whites into] landholders . . . placing land within reach of the poor."[84] Only thus would an "aristocratic few" cease to "rule the betrayed mass of the southern people."[85] The wealthiest 10 percent of Southerners owned some four hundred million acres, and Thaddeus Stevens called for parceling those acres out to the freedmen. "If the South is ever to be made a safe republic," he declared, "let her lands be cultivated by the toil of the owners."[86]

George Julian, the great homesteads champion, agreed. Homesteads out of the public lands were not enough. The public lands of the Deep South were mostly inhospitable swamps. Abandoned plantations, given over to ex-slaves by the army or the Freedmen's Bureau, were being reclaimed by their antebellum owners, with President Johnson's support. Nothing short of systematic confiscation and redistribution of the great plantations would suffice to create a broad-based Black yeomanry and to break the power of the old ruling class, the planter oligarchy. "We must not only cut up slavery," said Julian, ". . . we must see to it that these teeming regions shall be studded over with small farms and tilled by free men."[87] Otherwise, the "evil" old "land monopoly . . . will be continued and vitalized by falling into fresh hands," and "a grinding aristocracy, resting upon large landed estates," will continue to rule the South and undermine the Reconstructed state and national republics, all over again.[88]

Ordinary freed people shared the Radicals' view about land redistribution. "Only land," said former Mississippi slave Merrimon Howard, would enable "the poor class to enjoy the sweet boon of freedom."[89] In an 1865 "colloquy" with General William Tecumseh Sherman and Secretary of War Edwin Stanton, twenty "Colored Ministers" concurred. Asked as to "what you understand by slavery, and the freedom that was to be given by the President's Proclamation," ex-slave Garrison Frazier, a Baptist preacher and the group's spokesman, replied: "The freedom, as I understand it, promised by the proclamation, is taking us from under the yoke of bondage and placing us where we could reap the fruit of our own labor, and take care of ourselves." "Freedom," he went on, meant that ex-slaves were entitled "to have land, and turn and till it by our labor . . . and we can soon maintain ourselves."[90]

It was not to be. A majority of Republican lawmakers pushed back against the Radicals' efforts to confiscate and redistribute the biggest plantations. The idea smacked too much of taking property from A and giving it to B, even if A was a member of the old Slave Power oligarchy and B an ex-slave. A "common school" education along with equal legal rights to contract freely and to lease, rent, and acquire land were all the freedmen really needed, according to the (stubbornly bourgeois) liberal republican constitutional political-economic outlook of the majority of the Republican elite.

Black Suffrage and Electoral Arithmetic: A Biracial Republic or a White Oligarchy

This mainstream Republican rendering of an inclusive democracy of opportunity may have been bourgeois, but it was also revolutionary. The Republican struggle to destroy slavery and reconstruct the Southern political economy ended up being exactly what we heard historical sociologist Barrington Moore call it in Chapter 2: "the last revolutionary offensive on the part of . . . bourgeois capitalist democracy."[91] A violent counterrevolution took shape. Amid Congress's 1866 efforts to confer core civil rights on the freed people and use federal power and resources to secure them, amid the federally sponsored founding of Black schools and the interventions of Freedmen's Bureau agents to adjudicate ex-slaves' claims as legal equals of ex-masters, the Ku Klux

Klan was born. An orgy of racist violence and terror erupted against freedmen and -women who had the temerity to set up households and farms of their own.

The Republican dream of Black homes and families on small farms owned or leased by free Black men was the "nightmare scenario" of Southern white men of all classes who still "aspired to the status of masters."[92] The Klan and kindred organizations rose up to demonstrate the impossibility of Black independence and the inevitability of Black dependency and subordination, through terror campaigns and rituals of rape, castration, murder, and arson on a mass scale.[93]

As the Joint Committee on Reconstruction heard testimony and Northern journalists sent back reports about these terror campaigns by Southern "Redeemers," more and more Republican lawmakers came to the view that the only alternative to permanent military occupation as a safeguard for Black civil rights might be a federal constitutional guarantee of Black political rights. Only by wielding political clout and taking part in local and state government might Blacks have a shot at securing their new civil rights for themselves. As one moderate Republican acknowledged in the debates on the Fifteenth Amendment, "Suffrage is the only sure guarantee which the negro can have, in many sections of the country, in the enjoyment of his civil rights" and the social and economic freedom the rights were meant to secure.[94]

That is what clinched the case for Black suffrage in the Reconstruction Congress—that *plus* the arithmetic of emancipation. As Thaddeus Stevens argued to his wavering colleagues, Blacks had to be enfranchised or "the basis of representation" somehow changed. Otherwise, the expanded Southern delegation resulting from the demise of the Three-Fifths Clause "will always give [the Democrats] a majority," and "at the very first election" in which Southern voters were allowed to participate, they would "take possession of the White House and the halls of Congress." The result would be constitutional "ruin": "oppression of the freedmen; re-amendment of their State constitutions; and reestablishment of slavery.... [But] grant the right of suffrage to persons of color [and there will] always be Union men enough in the South [to] secure perpetual ascendancy to the party of the Union [and] render our republican Government firm and stable forever."[95]

Securing "perpetual ascendancy" for "the party of the Union" was a partisan rationale for Black suffrage; it was also a paradigmatic expression of party-based constitutionalism. From the start, we saw, the Republicans had reprised the Jeffersonian-Jacksonian idea that theirs was no ordinary party but a party of constitutional principle, with a mission to save the republican Constitution from subversion. The constitutional menace here was not Jefferson's nemesis, an emergent financial elite with its stockjobbers and money-jobbers, but the planter elite with its undying "spirit of oligarchy averse to republican institutions" (and to the Republican Party). Even after military defeat, the old Southern ruling class was hell-bent on reinstating itself—by rebuilding the Southern Democratic Party and bringing poor whites into line, not by redistribution, but by re-raising the banner of white supremacy and Black subjugation. Only by entrenching Black suffrage could Congress "render . . . republican Government . . . stable" in the postbellum South. A Republican Party, with a biracial Southern base, was thus a partisan project *and* a constitutional necessity. Without it, the new national guarantee of Black freedom was dust, and the South would sink back into a particularly vicious kind of race-and-class-ridden oligarchy. These considerations enabled Stevens and the Radicals to bring the rest of their party on board the project of Black suffrage. First came the crucial Sections 2 and 3 of the Fourteenth Amendment, which Congress sent to the states for ratification on June 16, 1866; then, in 1867, the Military Reconstruction Act; and finally, in 1870, the Fifteenth Amendment.

The Fourteenth Amendment's Sections 2 and 3 addressed the shape of the Southern electorate and political class. Today, in our court-obsessed constitutional culture, we devote all our attention to Section 1, with its open-ended promises of national citizenship, civil rights, and equal protection. But, as recent work by constitutional scholar Mark Graber reminds us, the framers' attention was riveted on the language and design of Sections 2 and 3, which set the terms of suffrage and eligibility for state political officeholding—which makes perfect sense in light of their realistic party-based and legislation-based vision of constitutional development.[96] Section 1's general promises of equal citizenship were for Congress and the Executive to implement and enforce. Securing the freed people's rights was legislative and administrative work for the political branches. No one expected the courts to do the first-order work of expositing and applying the new amendments. That was the significance of Section 5's all-important enforcement clause: "The Congress shall have power to enforce, by appropriate legislation, the provisions of this article."[97]

The Thirteenth Amendment (and later, the Fifteenth Amendment) had virtually identical enforcement clauses. These were something new under the constitutional sun. The antebellum Constitution already had provisions conferring rights on individuals against the states—the Ex Post Facto Clause, for instance, or the Contracts Clause—but none contained such language granting Congress enforcement power. As one framer of the Thirteenth Amendment put it, "what makes this constitutional amendment a practical, living thing is the power given to Congress to enforce it"; it "must . . . be the effective power of Congress, cooperating with the Executive, that will protect the freedmen from oppression."[98]

If Republicans were not in charge of those branches, then all was lost. To the Radicals' chagrin, the final version of Section 2 stopped short of requiring Black suffrage. But it eliminated the possibility of the Southern states *enlarging* their representation in Congress and the Electoral College *without* also instituting Black suffrage—by subtracting from the basis of each state's representation the number of "male inhabitants . . . being twenty-one . . . and citizens of the United States" whose "right to vote" was "denied . . . or in any way abridged, except for participation in rebellion, or other crime."[99]

Section 3 disqualified from federal officeholding any rebels who, prior to the war, had held any state or national office that required an oath of support for the federal Constitution.[100] Radicals rued both sections as weak compromise measures: Section 2 for failing to require Black male suffrage and Section 3 for not disenfranchising a much broader class of rebels.[101]

The Military Reconstruction Act of 1867, however, conditioned readmission of Southern delegations into Congress on ratification of the Fourteenth Amendment, along with holding state constitutional conventions with Black male suffrage and providing for Black male suffrage in the new state constitutions. As its name implied, the 1867 Act also provided for continued military (as well as Freedmen's Bureau) jurisdiction. Then, in 1870, the Fifteenth Amendment entrenched Black male suffrage in the federal Constitution.

RADICAL RECONSTRUCTION AND "BLACK REPUBLICAN" RULE

So, starting in 1867, Southern whites watched in stupefaction as Union Army troops guarded polling places and supervised voter registration, enrolling Blacks and excluding prominent whites. The ensuing period became known as "Radical" or "Black Reconstruction." More than seven hundred thousand ex-slaves cast ballots, and while they never dominated state office holding, Blacks were a majority of eligible voters in South Carolina, Florida, Alabama, Mississippi, and Louisiana.[102]

Starting in 1867, roughly eight hundred Black men served in state legislatures before mass disenfranchisement spread its tentacles throughout the region. Black men filled more than a thousand public offices in town and county governments. More than a dozen ex-slaves served in Congress, one sat on the South Carolina Supreme Court; another was, briefly, governor of Louisiana.[103] "Now is the black man's day—the whites have had their way long enough," said one politician. A Northern journalist visiting the South Carolina legislature reported: "The body is almost literally a Black Parliament. . . . The Speaker is black, the Clerk is black, the door-keepers are black . . . the chairman of Ways and Means is black, and the chaplain is coal black."[104]

Whites called it "Negro rule";[105] and they called the state and local Republican coalitions that Black leaders formed with representatives of white yeomen and tenant farmers the "Black Republicans." This was the short-lived Southern base Thaddeus Stevens had imagined for the Party of Free Labor, a "poor man's Party," as planters scornfully called it. The planters had to deal with sheriffs, prosecutors, justices of the peace, and judges who were responsive to Black constituents. They had to contend with Blacks on juries. No longer could Blacks be indicted and convicted just because whites accused them of crimes.

"Black Republican" state judges and justices of the peace adjudicated contract disputes between freedmen and former masters, as well as white sharecroppers and landlords, in a fashion that reflected the well-known mutability and distributional consequences of common-law doctrine. They began reshaping state common law along the redistributive lines the Reconstruction framers envisioned. "Equal rights under law" was anything but self-defining; as always with contract and property relations, the devil was in the details. Called on to apply the principles of free contract and property to the emergent relations between landlord and sharecropper, "Black Republican" judges did so in ways that gave the latter a real measure of bargaining power and control over work and crop.[106]

As Republican state judges plumbed the meaning of the individual's "right to the fruits of his labor," Republican state lawmakers enacted lien laws and land-lease regulations that favored poor borrowers; they created land commissions and used the tax power to encourage the breakup of very large estates. In South Carolina, they created a new land commission and state loans for freedmen.[107] Everywhere, as we have noted, they created the region's first public school systems.

THE LIMITS—AND END—OF RECONSTRUCTION

The Reconstruction Congress's rejection of the Radicals' proposals to use federal power to undertake large-scale land redistribution had major consequences. It meant the great majority of freed people had to go back to work for the planters. In principle, as free Black citizens, they could challenge the conditions and terms of their work; they could go to court, or haggle and move on when and where they wished; they could establish their own households and marry whom they wished; and they enjoyed the same political and civil rights as any other citizen. In principle, the ballot and political equality gave them the wherewithal to use their votes to ally with poor whites in common cause against common exploiters, now that their economic circumstances had become strikingly similar.

When you consider all the forces stacked against them, it is extraordinary how much the freed people and their white allies accomplished, making the most of the lofty principles, sparse institutions, and increasingly shaky commitments embodied in the new national constitutional political-economic order. And especially so, when you consider that while the Reconstruction Congress gave the ex-slaves more and more rights, it left fewer and fewer troops on the ground to back them up. The Klan and related white terror organizations kept up the same kind of attacks they had been deploying since 1866 against Black economic independence to quell Black voting and Black and biracial political associations. In response, the Reconstruction Congress enacted more robust civil and voting rights statutes (which are still in use today). But without a strong troop presence, even vigorous federal prosecutions and sympathetic lower federal courts became an increasingly fragile bulwark.[108]

In the mid-term elections of 1874, the Democrats took back the House, for the first time since the early 1850s. The Northern public was weary of Reconstruction. Meanwhile, Northern elites were thoroughly alarmed by the emergence of mass strikes on the railroads and in the cities, and by burgeoning labor and agrarian demands for redistributive measures in the halls of Congress and their own Northern state legislatures. With labor problems of their own, Northern Republican elites began to look more sympathetically on the Southern planters' yearning for control over restive Black labor and an end to federal interference on Blacks' behalf.

Then, with Republican leaders' devotion to the party's old precepts and alliances badly frayed, a cynical compromise between Republican and Democratic leadership brought an end to Reconstruction. The outcome of the 1876 presidential election was in dispute, the Democratic candidate having won the popular vote, and the decision thrown to an ad hoc electoral commission. Key Republicans agreed to a swap with the Democrats. The Democrats on the commission would throw their support behind the Republican candidate, "ever after known as Rutherfraud B. Hayes," so that he became president, and, in exchange, the Republicans promised to bring an end to military occupation.[109]

For another decade, after the troops had left, freed people would manage to remain key actors on the political stage, unevenly across the South. They voted, marching to the polls en masse, often flanked by Black militias, to face down white violence. The 1880s would witness a remarkable effort to rebuild an inclusive democracy of opportunity in the South, on the part of an audacious new biracial movement of poor farmers and workers: the Populists and their People's Party, which swept across the South and beyond. In Chapter 4, we will explore the Populists' vision of a radical alternative constitutional political economy, which built on, and remade, the democracy-of-opportunity tradition that the Radical Republicans had made the center of their constitutional politics. That Populist vision of constitutional political economy, along with the Populists' formidable success at movement- and party-building, would prove threatening enough to unite Southern elites around unvarnished white supremacy and mass disenfranchisement. But that lay in the future, and for now, even after the curtain fell on Reconstruction, the future remained in flux.

The Women's Rights Movement in the Age of Emancipation and Reconstruction

Far from "universal," the "new birth of freedom," as Reconstruction's framer-lawmakers conceived it, was deeply gendered. But advocates for women's rights were heavily involved in the antebellum abolitionist movement and central to the campaign for the Thirteenth Amendment. At an extraordinary moment of constitutional remaking, the movement for women's rights grabbed hold of Reconstruction's revolutionary promise to contest women's social, sexual, and political subordination. Like the abolitionists who were their longtime allies, advocates of women's rights laid claim to the republican legacy of the American Revolution, making substantial use of the Declaration of Independence, the concept of taxation without representation, and ideas of republican citizenship. They also built new analogies, often uncomfortably close analogies, between the situation and rights of women and those of slaves.

Women's rights advocates had good reason to believe that during Reconstruction such arguments would win them, as a start, the right to vote. They had long-standing commitments on that specific point from abolitionist friends and allies in the Republican Party like Charles Sumner. But their allies did not deliver. Sumner would later protest that he "wrote over nineteen pages of foolscap to get rid of the word 'male' and yet keep 'negro suffrage' as a party measure intact; but it could not be done."[110] The word "male" entered the Constitution in the Fourteenth

Amendment's suffrage provisions; the Fifteenth Amendment, too, would confer Black male suffrage but not universal suffrage. For suffragists, this was a bitter result. The inclusion of Black men in the circle of full citizenship sharply underscored women's continued exclusion.[111] But the presumptions of male governance over women, household, family, and body politic were ones the great majority of Republican lawmaker-framers were unwilling to contest.

And so it fell to this era's movement for women's rights to contest these assumptions without the help of those powerful allies. Building on a long abolitionist tradition of direct action in the name of rights denied, Susan B. Anthony and scores of other women's rights activists marched to the polls in the early 1870s in a set of actions known as the "New Departure," demanding to cast their ballots as equal citizens under the new Reconstruction Amendments—and also under Sumner's old "sleeping giant," the Guarantee Clause. Awaiting trial for breaking the voting laws, Anthony delivered an address to an audience of supporters. Like Sumner's address to Congress with which we began, her address showed the centrality and the reach of the anti-oligarchy principle during the Second Founding. For women, Anthony declared, this government "is not a republic." Instead, she argued,

> It is an odious aristocracy; a hateful oligarchy; the most hateful ever established on the face of the globe. An oligarchy of wealth, where the rich govern the poor; an oligarchy of learning, where the educated govern the ignorant; or even an oligarchy of race, where the Saxon rules the African, might be endured; but surely this oligarchy of sex, which makes the men of every household sovereigns, masters; the women subjects, slaves; . . . cannot be endured. And yet this odious aristocracy exists in the face of Section 4, of Article 4, which says: The United States shall guarantee to every State in the Union a Republican form of government.[112]

Anthony's extensive use of the race-sex analogy here traces a path of reasoning that the women's movement a century later would pursue with great effect.[113] While her effort to construct a hierarchy of oligarchies ("the most hateful," worse than slavery) was bitterly wrongheaded, her core analogical approach had tremendous power. It is instructive to pause to consider exactly how the analogy worked in the 1870s. When Anthony reaches for a more general concept that can encompass both the enslavement of "the African" and the oppression of women by men, what she grasps hold of is oligarchy. She moves seamlessly between condemning slavery and condemning aristocracy and oligarchy, in that way mirroring the moves her erstwhile Reconstruction Republican allies were making in their own thinking, and situating her claims in the longer arc of the anti-oligarchy Constitution. The Southern slave-owning oligarchy that Reconstruction toppled is, in Anthony's telling, not entirely unique; while every form of oligarchy is different, there are common elements. One of these—and part of what patriarchy had in common with slavery and white supremacy—is that these forms of domination were hardly limited to the ballot box. They opened onto the master's household and into the economic sphere. As with the slave, a wife's body and her toil were not her own; they belonged to her husband and master. To oppose these forms of oligarchy was to challenge "systems of dependency . . . centered [in part] on control over work and its rewards."[114] In other words, constitutional claims about both race and sex in this era were never just about politics: They were about political economy.

The struggles to end subjection of women's bodies and dispossession of women's labor in marriage and household were bound up with women's campaign for the franchise. The organizations that led women's struggles for equal citizenship argued that ending women's status as a dependent and subordinate class demanded not only suffrage, but also that women enjoy the fruits of their own labor.[115] Equal rights meant legal autonomy in market and property relations, and economic independence within the marriage relation. The common law denied all these rights. Married women lacked not only the right to vote, but also the right to contract; their labor and its fruits belonged to their husbands.[116] Law and social usage "oppressed [women] with such limitation and degradation of labor and avocation as clearly and cruelly mark the condition of a disabled caste." So, women's rights organizations campaigned for statutes that would overturn the husband's common-law rights to his wife's labor, both within the household and outside it.[117] The "economy of the household," a Woman's Rights Convention resolved, "is generally as much the source of family wealth as the labor and enterprise of man"; yet the law effaced women's contribution, embedding it in property to which men held title.[118] No less economically productive than men, the convention went on, women were entitled to participate equally in managing assets that were the product of the work of both women and men. In this manner, as Reva Siegel has shown, women's rights advocates cannily employed the mainstream constitutional language of self-ownership and labor rights to dismantle and reconstruct the legal and cultural discourse that cast women as unproductive dependents.[119]

By 1876, at the nation's centennial, the National Woman Suffrage Association sharpened its constitutional critique into a set of "articles of impeachment against our rulers."[120] Reaching back to the Revolution as well as the Second Founding, the declaration decried "taxation without representation" and assailed the denial of "the writ of habeas corpus" for wives legally imprisoned by their husbands. The suffragists declared that universal male-only suffrage had ushered in "an aristocracy of sex" that amounted to "a more absolute and cruel despotism than monarchy" because it left every man a "master." Insisting that "[w]oman's wealth, thought, and labor have cemented the stones of every monument man has reared to liberty," the suffragists demanded "all the civil and political rights that belong to citizens of the United States."[121] The declaration ended with a striking denunciation of the judiciary. It "has proved itself but the echo of the party in power," first denying Black citizenship "when the slave power was dominant" and now, in keeping with the views of those now in power, deciding that "a woman, though a citizen, had not the right to vote."[122]

The suffragists did not pin their hopes on judicial avenues of constitutional change. They knew the courts were unlikely to accept their understandings of women's constitutional rights and equal citizenship. As Anthony predicted, it would instead take decades of political struggle, culminating in another moment of higher lawmaking, so that the Constitution could be amended to undo "the disfranchisement of one entire half of the people."[123] (We discuss the Nineteenth Amendment in Chapter 5.)

For now, the last word is Anthony's. She anticipated in 1873 that such a moment of higher lawmaking would bring American law into alignment with the Declaration of Independence, as well as the state constitutions and the federal Constitution itself, each of which she contended was built on a logic of republican citizenship that entails dethroning oligarchs of all kinds. By the "declarations" in those documents, she argued, "kings, priests, popes, aristocrats, were all alike dethroned," and so were men "deprived of their divine right to rule." But her story did not end there. Switching to the future tense, Anthony situated women's claims in the arc of a tradition of anti-oligarchy constitutionalism that extended into the future: "By the practice of those declarations *all class and caste distinction will be abolished*; and slave, serf, plebian, wife, women, all alike, will bound from their subject position to the proud platform of equality."[124]

The link between dethroning oligarchy and establishing a "proud platform of equality" is an idea with remarkable reach. It can reach into the political economy of the nation and into the political economy of the household; into the workplace and the relations of labor and capital; into federal macroeconomic policy and into what had been core domains of state law. As both the Reconstruction Republicans and the suffrage movement understood, it is not primarily the courts who will decide how far ideas like this extend. It is all of us, through the practice of constitutional politics.

4

CONSTITUTIONAL CLASS STRUGGLE
IN THE GILDED AGE

At the beginning of the nineteenth century, the birth of the capitalist market economy had brought forth a crisis of mounting inequality and hardening class lines. Jacksonian democracy was the polity's dramatic response. The advent of corporate capitalism at the end of the nineteenth century produced another such crisis. It prompted another constitutional reckoning—and ultimately, a reinvention of the democracy of opportunity's ideal of the mass middle class and a transformation in its views about the appropriate scale, scope, and duties of national government.

During the 1880s and 1890s, Americans haltingly confronted the fact that the United States, like Europe, possessed a vast, seemingly permanent class of propertyless wage earners. It was no longer possible to contend that the industrial hireling was on a path to owning his own workshop, or the agricultural tenant or laborer his own farm. At the same time, nation-spanning corporations were coming to dominate the economy, arrogating to themselves the essential tools of industry, transportation, communications, and finance. Both developments contributed to a profound sense of social, political, *and constitutional* crisis.

The country witnessed violent class struggle on the railroads, and in the streets, factories, mines, and mills, as well as an explosion of radical third-party politics—and in response to all that, a startling set of class-conscious, pro-corporate constitutional decisions from the Supreme Court. At the heart of these clashes were two rival visions of constitutional political economy: one requiring a major redistribution of wealth and power; the other forbidding even modest redistribution.

Fundamental questions were at stake. The legitimacy of the basic institutions of an emerging corporate capitalism was bitterly contested, and the key issues cast in terms of constitutional political economy. Was "the wage-system of labor" compatible with "the republican system of government"?[1] Were the new giant corporations consistent with the Constitution's pledge of equal rights? Or did these unprecedented concentrations of wealth and power mean a slide into oligarchy, upending republican self-rule? If the promise of equal opportunity meant universal access to middle-class status—and if only a mass middle class could protect the republican Constitution—then either the vanishing world of small producers and proprietary capitalism would somehow have to be restored, or the mass middle class would somehow have to be reinvented.

The two rival visions that emerged in this period both grew out of the Free Labor legacy bequeathed by Reconstruction. Both had deeper roots, as well, in Jacksonian constitutional political economy. As these two visions diverged, one crystallized into "Lochnerism," the laissez-faire and anti-redistributive outlook whose themes reverberate today in decisions like *Citizens United, Janus v. AFSCME,* and the Commerce Clause discussion in *Sebelius*.[2] Dubbing themselves "new liberals," the late nineteenth-century architects of this vision cast aside the distributive commitments of the old democracy-of-opportunity tradition, in both its Jacksonian and Free Labor forms. Holding on to the old egalitarian distributional principles in an industrialized society would come at too high a constitutional price: too much "class politics" and "class legislation," too much taking-from-A-and-giving-to-B, too much statism. Reformers' "socialistic" efforts to achieve the old distributional ideal in industrial America threatened to destroy private rights and principled limits on government—and probably prosperity and economic order, as well. The "socialists" had to be defeated.

Institutionally, this new anti-redistributive outlook came to stand for expanding the role of the federal courts and the new corporate legal elite in making the rules, policies, and institutions that would govern market and property relations in the new corporate economy. Lochnerism also came to stand for judicial supremacy in constitutional interpretation. This helped ensure that governance of matters like corporate consolidation and labor organization remained, as far as possible, under the conservative auspices of federal courts and judge-made law, constitutionally walled off from the redistributive energies and innovations of democracy. Politically, this outlook came to define the main line of a transfigured Republican Party—the dominant party in American presidential politics and judicial appointments for most of the half century following the Civil War.

Against Lochnerism, the second, rival vision that emerged in these decades attempted to modernize the democracy-of-opportunity tradition while sticking to its distributive commitments. This vision, which would become the foundation of the modern democracy-of-opportunity tradition, rejects Lochnerism's classical liberal conception of free labor as the unfettered liberty to sell one's labor power in the market. Instead, it continues to hold to the more ambitious republican understanding of free labor as independence, or what political theorists today call nondomination.[3] This second vision likewise rejects Lochnerism's efforts to naturalize the courts' common-law definitions of property and free contract as constitutional baselines, and its slightly later efforts to naturalize the corporation as a rights-bearing individual. Corporations were state-chartered forms of private government. As they expanded and consolidated their grip over economic life, they threatened to "usurp" powers the Constitution assigned to public, democratic authorities.

Thus, in institutional terms, this vision of the democracy of opportunity came to stand for the primacy of legislation and administrative state-building in meeting the challenges of modern government. It opposed judicial supremacy in constitutional interpretation in favor of the many-sided legacy of popular constitutionalism and claims of affirmative duties on the part of the political branches.

This clash of visions animated the era's central battles over the relations between labor and capital, the trusts, the currency and the banks, the federal income tax, and the emergence of new regulatory bodies that were the vanguard of the new administrative state. Now that class inequalities have returned to Gilded Age levels, our political system is beginning to refight a number of these battles. Revisiting these contests may help liberals and progressives understand constitutionalism anew as a field where some of the important work of reimagining the relationship of democracy and economic life can resume.

These contests also remind us how the earliest incarnations of the modern democracy of opportunity drew together all three strands of the tradition—anti-oligarchy, a broad and open middle class, and a tentative but crucial vision of racial inclusion—as part of a political movement that aimed to rival and supplant the dominant political parties of the era. When that effort failed and the People's Party collapsed, white Populists' commitment to racial inclusion collapsed as well—a tragic turn that set the stage for a Progressive outlook that openly embraced white supremacy. Racial inclusion became a dissenting tradition among white radicals and reformers in the early twentieth century, while they carried on with updating the two other main precepts of the democracy-of-opportunity tradition. This hobbled the democracy of opportunity for the next century.

We begin by tracing the rise of classical legal liberalism and the development of what became Lochnerism, in courts and outside them. We show how the democracy-of-opportunity tradition took a new form in reaction to these developments—a form that particularly emphasized legislation and the administrative state, rather than the federal courts, as engines of constitutional political economy. We then explore the clash of these rival visions in several of the constitutional battles at the center of Populist politics: labor; federal power over railroads and commerce; the gold standard; and the income tax—along with the fraught trajectory of the principle of racial inclusion in the Populist constitutional imagination.

The Origins of Classical Legal Liberalism and Constitutional Laissez-Faire

By 1874, Northern weariness with Reconstruction and readiness to "leave the South alone" enabled the Democrats to regain control of the House of Representatives. Southern Blacks continued to vote and form political associations for virtually two decades after Reconstruction, but all three branches of the national government began dismantling federal protections for the freed people's recently enacted rights.[4] From the mid-1870s onward, racial backlash in the South and intensifying class strife and agrarian unrest in the North and Midwest drove Republican leaders to remake their party into a bastion of pro-business laissez-faire. Agrarian Populism, burgeoning labor organizations, and industrial warfare brought disillusionment with the party's old views about the distributional duties of a republican nation-state active on behalf of working people and the ideals of "Free Labor." The GOP would gradually make defense of property and political-economic respectability for large-scale enterprise the heart of its ideology, and economic nationalism the core of its political agenda.[5]

We can see this transition—and the shape of the political and constitutional vision that emerged from it—in the trajectories of many Radical Republicans. Consider Edwin Godkin, the editor of *The Nation* and a leading Radical opinion maker. During the Civil War and Reconstruction, Godkin told labor audiences that a government "of and from the people . . . cannot destroy its (or their) liberties."[6] When he first turned his attention to the discontents of industrial labor, Godkin's analysis of the wage laborer's predicament had rested on a traditional Free Labor outlook and resembled the labor movement's own assessment. The industrial laborer, Godkin wrote in 1867, "is legally free while socially bound."[7] "Since the rise of political economy," he "has been treated [in books] as the equal of the capitalist . . . but in real life his position has been that of a servant with a fixed status."[8] Godkin agreed with labor spokesmen that this system of social bondage undermined workers' capacities as citizens: "When a man agrees to sell his labor, he agrees by implication to surrender his social and political independence." Widespread "diffusion" of ownership of productive property was essential to a "virtuous"—"independent," "self-reliant," and "intelligent"—citizenry, and to a nation's liberty.[9] The remedy to labor's "servile dependence" on capital, he agreed, lay in cooperative ownership of industry. He enjoined workers to "never cease agitating and combining until the regime of wages . . . has passed away," and all "the great accumulations of capital are held by [labor] associations."[10]

But by the 1870s, Godkin had had enough of labor's combining and agitating. He and other Radical Republican writers were growing alarmed to hear their own language of popular sovereignty and active democratic government appropriated by labor agitators denouncing "property rights rulership" and "wage slavery"[11]—and by the massive eight-hour day strikes that were sweeping New York and other industrial cities. In 1872, he undertook to enlighten "the working-class mind."[12] Where he had once argued for the abolition of the wage system, now he assailed workingmen for seeking to "prevent[] capital from flowing into the hands of the only class in the community which is competent to use it."[13] Above all, Godkin was outraged by the New York labor movement's victorious campaign for an eight-hour day ordinance covering municipal contracts and employment, and by their demand for a general eight-hour law. Instead, Godkin declared, the "reward of labor" ought to depend "on demand and supply."[14]

To Godkin and to many of the "best men" of the North, labor's new politics were disturbing—and so were other signs of "runaway democracy," such as the agitation by farmers in the Midwest and soon throughout the country, through the Granger movement, against the monopolistic practices of the railroads that transported the goods they produced.[15] In the pages of Godkin's *Nation,* the *Atlantic Monthly,* and the *North American Review,* a growing disenchantment with federal intervention and "Black Republicanism" in the South was closely bound up with a desire to dial back the "excesses" of republicanism more generally—that is, of the set of ideas that these leading journals of Northern opinion had themselves championed. Those ideas now seemed to be taking a more radical turn, both among Midwestern farmers and, closer to home, among the labor organizers of the industrializing North.[16] In the 1860s, these journals' editors and contributors had helped to develop a theory of an active, democratic state that lent legitimacy and coherence to the expanded powers of the federal government and the project of Radical Reconstruction. Now many of the same thinkers and spokesmen coalesced into a new movement that gained adherents among prominent Northern lawyers, businessmen, and academics, many of them former Radicals and abolitionists.[17]

Liberalism and the Aggrandizement of Capital

This new movement styled itself "liberalism." It was an appropriate label: its thinking represented an unraveling of Lincolnian "Free Labor" ideology, discarding some of its democratic strands and fortifying its liberal ones.[18] The abolitionists' austere, classical liberal definition of freedom as self-ownership and liberty of contract was beginning to seem freedom enough for the industrial working class. And even as they set aside central Free Labor commitments, the new liberals could feel, rightly, that their new constitutional outlook retained a connection to an older democratic tradition of constitutional political economy. As we saw in Chapter 2, the first expressions of laissez-faire doctrine, the first systematic protests against government activism in America arose from the Jacksonian campaigns against national bank and state corporate charters, against government-created "monopolies" that privileged the few over the many. The first judicial opinions striking down "class legislation" in the name of a laissez-faire reading of state constitutions were antebellum decisions by Jacksonian jurists overturning legislative favors for a privileged class of entrepreneurs or corporate entities. The new liberals spoke in this Jacksonian constitutional vocabulary. But ironically, they began to transform it into a defense of the few against the claims of the many.[19]

This transformation was neither immediate nor complete. The new liberals remained uneasy about the growing power of large corporations, especially in the political sphere. If they assailed labor's and farmers' experiments with state power, the new liberals were no less alarmed by capitalists seeking "state favors," "abus[ing] the taxing power," clamoring for "tariff schemes, subsidy schemes, internal improvement schemes." The "aggrandizement of capital by law," they warned, was the "parent" and inspiration of labor's "socialism." The state and the law had to be reclaimed from capture by private interests, whether of labor or capital. Indeed, the new liberals were troubled not only by state subsidies for capital but also by the unprecedented power of the emerging large corporation itself. The common law was replete with doctrines and ideology hostile to corporate expansion. Late nineteenth-century liberal jurists often wielded them vigorously.[20]

To be ambivalent about corporations' effects on individual freedom and opportunity, free markets, and republican government was to remain alive to the classical liberal view of corporations as artificial, carefully hedged creatures of the state, endowed with special, often monopolistic rights and privileges—at odds with the ideal of a free and competitive economic order. Perhaps none felt this ambivalence more than the liberal reformers who were also corporate attorneys—such as David Dudley Field, the brother of Supreme Court Justice Stephen Field. As spokesmen of the new liberalism, men like Field extolled a legal order that protected a free and competitive marketplace. Equal rights and equal opportunities for the free-standing individual were at the heart of their social vision. But in their work as attorneys for the new industrial corporations, as legal historian Robert Gordon powerfully demonstrates, they strove to undercut and supplant the very legal concepts and doctrines that sought to keep corporations within the competitive framework that reformers prized.[21] These elite lawyers were at once the self-proclaimed opponents and the actual agents of the "aggrandizement of capital by law."

Field may have had his own law practice in mind when he fretted in the pages of the *North American Review,* "We have created a new class of beings . . . [and] individuals find themselves powerless before these aggregations of wealth"—because "we have neglected to fence them about with . . . restraints."[22] How to restore the equality that "we" negligently have destroyed? How to bridge the ever more distant and antagonistic relations between capital and labor? Field's answer was to call on fellow members of the new corporate elite to appropriate the cooperative impulse afoot among labor and agrarian reformers: to turn corporations from associations "of capital only" into associations "of capital and labor united." Field beheld the labor upheavals of the mid-1880s and responded with anxious concern to wage earners' protest that capital had reduced them to a "relation of dependence . . . incompatible with that sense of self-respect . . . which should be the patrimony of every American citizen."[23] He did not share Edwin Godkin's short-lived sympathy with strictly worker-owned businesses; rather, he hoped that profit sharing and granting workers certain voting rights in the corporation would restore equality and respect between labor and capital. Of course, like Godkin, Field held that accomplishing these desirable reforms could not be the business of government. That was the "dream of madmen" and would violate "the supreme law."[24]

Henry George was among the Gilded Age's leading radicals, just as Field was among its leading liberal reformers. Author of the era's best-selling work in political economy, *Progress and Poverty,* and Labor Party candidate for mayor of New York City in the election of 1886, George questioned Field's reliance on the corporate elite's goodwill to reform industry and restore the attributes of ownership and citizenly independence to industrial workers. In a revealing public debate between the two men, George emphasized that he too had once adhered to such laissez-faire principles. But the concentration of capital in industry after industry had forced him, reluctantly, to the conclusion that achieving the ends of the old Jacksonian democracy of opportunity required abandoning its conception of appropriate means. Securing "the full and equal liberty of individuals" and mutual cooperation in an age of "great corporations and combinations" would require a government with similarly great scope—a government that would "regulate" and, perhaps, "carry on" certain businesses and "in larger and larger degree assume co-operative functions."[25] Sternly, Field replied that although he did not believe George was "one of the Communists," he thought his ideas might entail "spoliation . . . tak[ing] from one man his property and giv[ing] it to another."[26]

The prominence of elite attorneys like Field in new liberal circles and the emerging ideology's countermajoritarian bent help explain why the new liberalism won its strongest support in the judiciary. But the explanation runs deeper. The legal profession faced new rivals in the form of new professionals—economists, social scientists, and others—forming academic departments and professional associations, and claiming scientific expertise in the government of social and economic affairs. The old challenge of maintaining the authority of common-law governance against hasty, amateurish democratic legislation was joined by the new challenge posed by rival would-be governing elites with new state-building ambitions.[27]

Thus, the leading judges and legal scholars who fashioned this new mode of legal and constitutional thought—which legal historians have dubbed "classical legal liberalism"—no longer claimed to supply wise rules of conduct for life's myriad circumstances. Instead (and here the key work is Duncan Kennedy's *Rise and Fall of Classical Legal Thought*),[28] these legal thinkers used highly general and abstract legal-constitutional principles—above all, freedom of contract and security of private property—along with precedents and reason to specify the conditions under which people, or lawmakers, were free to behave as they pleased. The object of legal science was to draw clear boundary lines around these zones of private and public action. Liberal jurists claimed to do this in a neutral, noncoercive fashion by treating all (adult male) persons as legal equals and deriving all legal obligations from the voluntary exercises of someone's will—either the will of a private individual or the will of the state.[29]

By the turn of the century, as classical legal liberalism became fully elaborated, private and public law principles were integrated in an elegant formal system.[30] The systematic quality of classical legal liberalism—integrating judge-made common-law and constitutional doctrine in what seemed a coherent whole—is worth bearing in mind because it helps one understand the confidence and militancy with which courts expanded and defended their common-law and equity powers over the nation's political economy, along with their powers as constitutional arbiters of the state's role therein. All were part of the same whole.

This is how it became a *constitutional* imperative to safeguard and enforce what were really judge-made common-law precepts of contract and property against unwarranted efforts at statutory revision. Statutes were coercive state-made restrictions of the "natural" and "social" sphere of market exchange; common law, by contrast, was a gradually unfolding outgrowth of organic custom, which, even though judges enforced it and kept revising it, was somehow not "the state" but part of the spontaneous, "natural" order of a self-regulating, competitive market society. Thus, as we'll soon see, *Lochner*'s author, the classical liberal Justice Peckham, would speak of the "general law of competition" as though market competition under the constitutionally enshrined common law was itself "the transubstantiation of . . . natural law."[31]

These views came to dominate the Court. A succession of mostly Republican presidents appointed Justices who hailed chiefly from the nation's nascent bar of corporate and Wall Street lawyers. Justice Peckham himself has been described as the "confidant of tycoons": "Morgan, Rockefeller, and Vanderbilt."[32] Through these Justices' decisions, classical liberal political economy's "law of competition"—adapted to the exigencies of corporate capital, as the corporate bar understood them—became a feature of our constitutional order for decades. But the Court's treatment of corporate giants as equal rights-bearing persons alongside workers and small producers made its systematic "scientific" qualities seem like "plutocracy tempered by humbuggery" to a growing host of critics.[33]

LABOR, CONSTITUTIONAL LAISSEZ-FAIRE, AND *LOCHNER V. NEW YORK*

The first systematic exposition of the new laissez-faire liberalism was a constitutional treatise. In 1868, Thomas M. Cooley, then chief justice of the Supreme Court of Michigan, published *A Treatise on the Constitutional Limitations Which Rest upon the Legislative Power of the States of the American Union*.[34] Cooley's political odyssey was richly typical of the new laissez-faire liberals: a radical Jacksonian in his youth; an abolitionist; a Free Soil Party organizer and Republican Party founder who broke with the Republicans during the Grant administration; and finally an independent mugwump, or new liberal reformer and jurist.[35] His judicial opinions exemplified the highly abstract yet deeply felt fusion of abolitionist and laissez-faire meanings of "discrimination by the state." Cooley's *Treatise* would enjoy greater sales and circulation and more frequent citation than any other treatise of the latter half of the nineteenth century. In it he wrote that the "sacred right" to private property stood as "the old fundamental law"—and through it, popular sovereignty was limited.[36] Like his judicial opinions, Cooley's *Treatise* assailed "class legislation" in all its forms, from the use of the taxing power to subsidize private enterprise to the segregation of schools by race, to the enactment of maximum hours laws on behalf of workers.[37]

In the 1870s and 1880s, it was not federal but state high courts that proved most willing to take up this task of patrolling the constitutional boundaries of state power. The statutes that provoked the most judicial ire were labor reforms aiming to redress the weak bargaining power of workers.[38] Thus, for instance, in its 1886 *Godcharles v. Wigeman* ruling, the Pennsylvania Supreme Court struck down a measure requiring manufacturing and mining corporations to pay their workers in cash rather than scrip from the company store.[39] The court condemned the law as "degrading" and "insulting" to the workers, for it attempted "to do what ... cannot be done; that is, [to] prevent persons who are *sui juris* from making their own contracts."[40] Then, echoing the language of Justice Field's famous *Slaughter-House* dissent, in which Field had quoted Adam Smith on the just liberty of workingman and employer, the state high court declared that the worker "may sell his labor for what he thinks best, whether money or goods, just as his employer may sell his iron or coal."[41]

Over the next several decades, courts gradually etched out a sphere of labor reforms they were willing to uphold as valid police power measures. Factory or mine safety laws always passed muster. Courts generally (but not always) upheld hours laws for women and children, on the theory that they were distinctly vulnerable, legal dependents, not sui juris—and also in the case of women, the "mothers of the race"—giving the state a public-interest rationale for such laws. Likewise, beginning in the 1890s, courts began to uphold maximum hours laws for men drawn to encompass trades thought especially dangerous, like mining.[42]

But as *Lochner v. New York* illustrates, the new legal liberalism led state and federal courts to strike down labor laws whose purpose they saw as redistributing bargaining power—and with it, wealth or workplace authority.[43] *Lochner* involved a ten-hour law for bakery workers. The state defended it on the ground that long hours by hot ovens ruined workers' health—a traditional category of police powers regulation. The *Lochner* majority found this specious. The work of bakers seemed to them no more or less unhealthy than countless other trades. Indeed, the Court suspected that the statute was nothing more than "a labor law, pure and simple," meaning redistribution "pure and simple."[44] As such, it could not stand. And neither could state or federal measures aimed at enhancing workers' bargaining power by protecting workers from being fired for joining a union, or by modifying the harsh common-law restraints on strikes and boycotts.[45]

Jurists were disturbed by the radical rhetoric and ideals attached to this brand of "class legislation"—and by the laws themselves. For legislatures to redraw the most basic terms of (what had become) the most pervasive and important of contractual relations, the employment contract, or to authorize unions to demand a share of power and control over industrial property against the will of the property owners, meant there was no core of categorically *private* economic rights protected from the changing whims of political majorities. Such legislative power seemed to erase the baselines that defined the limits of state power. As we shall see, leading conservative judges, including a majority of the Supreme Court, identified the unraveling of this brand of legal liberalism with the end of bourgeois civilization. They did not give up without a fight.

Labor, Populism, and the Updating of the Democracy of Opportunity

The first opponents of the emerging anti-redistributive, laissez-faire constitutional political economy came from two main groups: urban, working-class labor activists and rural Populists. Both found themselves drawn into a set of constitutional debates and confrontations in this period that updated and extended the democracy-of-opportunity tradition. They wrote the first drafts of what later developed into Progressive and New Deal principles of constitutional political economy. These Gilded Age radicals saw that legal equality of rights—to make contracts, to own property—was no guarantee of equal citizenship in industrial America. They argued that one had to interpret the Constitution's guarantees of civil and political liberty and equality in light of their "social" meaning. The Constitution's original promise, they proclaimed, had been property to all, secured by "equal rights"—this was the "democratic social fabric" that the guarantees of liberty and equality wrought into our constitutions were meant to underwrite.[46] By the end of the century, the reach of these ideas had grown; middle-class and professional critics joined the radicals and built what became early twentieth-century Progressive constitutionalism, grabbing hold of or taking inspiration from many of the radicals' ideas. They left others behind—some of the most old-fashioned ideas, and some of the most deeply democratic ones. To understand how the modern world of Progressive constitutionalism emerged, we should look to its roots.

The decades following the Civil War witnessed a dramatic growth in organized labor, alongside the galloping pace of industrialization. The largest and most prominent of the era's labor organizations was the

Knights of Labor.[47] Born in 1869, it reached its peak in the 1880s when its active membership numbered almost one million. What set the Knights and kindred organizations apart from the labor organizations that succeeded them was, above all, the fashion in which they joined economic with broad-gauged political endeavor, aiming to reconstruct not only the industrial labor market, but the broader political economy to "abolish the wages system" and usher in a "Co-operative Commonwealth"—a democratic, industrial republic. Thus, the Knights waged far-flung strikes and boycotts, but they also created labor parties, ran candidates in thirty-four of the country's thirty-five states, and elected members to city and state governments. They also founded factory cooperatives and established a panoply of cultural associations. It was in this context that the Knights and other labor organizations began to campaign for distinctly working-class legislation—factory, mine, and maximum hours laws.[48]

The Wage System of Labor and the Republican System of Government: An "Irresistible Conflict"

Most controversial of labor's legislative initiatives was the massive campaign to legislate a shortened workday, which so exercised E. L. Godkin in New York. In several industrial states, labor succeeded in passing hours legislation.[49] But in Chicago, Philadelphia, and other cities, as in New York, employers resisted, and workers mounted massive, almost general, strikes seeking to enforce the new laws. The bitterness of these 1870–1872 strikes, together with the subversive character of the claims being made on behalf of the new laws, called forth an ideological levée en masse against labor and its demands from most quarters of elite and middle-class opinion.[50] In *The Nation*, Godkin fulminated against the laws. Eight-hour legislation was futile; one could not "nullify one of the natural economical laws by a law of the State."[51] Most of the genteel press, and politicians of many stripes, rose to join the attack. Unions were patently coercive organizations, destroying "all individuality" and blotting "out all those great efforts by which a man works his way up."[52] Enlisting the state to dictate the hours of the working day, Horace White argued in the *Chicago Tribune*, was "a restriction upon the inalienable rights of man." The unions and their new laws would destroy the freedom of contract and leave the workingman "as completely enslaved as the negro was five years ago."[53]

In response, labor's tribunes began forging a constitutional political economy of their own, picking apart the new liberals' notions of the "free market" and "liberty of contract." The new liberals, they pointed out, were tearing the right of free labor away from its republican moorings— and leaving in its place only the bare liberty to sell one's labor, which was no basis for workers' equal citizenship. In these new liberals' accounts of labor's constitutional freedom, they argued, "something of slavery still remains."[54]

Thus, these labor-movement thinkers contended that the eight-hour laws and other labor protections were in fact what the Constitution's promise of equality *demanded*. Within the wage-labor system, wrote one eight-hour advocate, the laborer was an "itinerant chattel." "[W]hen a man is without means to subsist upon, his wants compel him to work, and he must ask for employment as a favor from someone who has the property required to carry on productive work. In plain language, *property is a tyrant, and the people are its slaves*."[55] As George McNeill, another Eight Hour League spokesman, argued to the Massachusetts legislature's Labor Committee in 1874: "The laborer's commodity perishes everyday beyond possibility of recovery. He must sell today's labor today, or never." The terms of such a sale were thus dictated by the employer.[56]

Labor leaders like McNeill were as devoted as the liberals to "the theory of freedom of contract," an ideal of freely associating parties to industrial enterprise. But they insisted that no actual "freedom of contract" could exist between labor and capital, except possibly in those industries where "a powerful labor organization has practically obtained a monopoly of their craft," rendering bargaining power more equal.[57] Workers in those industries had gained the eight-hour day by striking. In the rest of the economy, it would take legislation. And it was a monstrous absurdity for the courts and "the so-called political economists, whose theories agree with their pecuniary interests," to hold that it is a natural law enshrined in the Constitution that eight-hour laws "would destroy the great right of freedom of contract."[58]

McNeill and other leaders of the movement saw a relationship between the trajectory of industrial capitalism and the fate of republican citizenship. Industrialization itself was not the problem. The problem was twofold: the capitalists' "monopolization of the producers' wealth," and the way they used technology to grind down wages and dissolve skilled occupations into unskilled machine-tending. This "cheapen[ing]" of labor mattered for republican citizenship because it meant ever-longer hours of "mindless toil" for meager wages, and it tore workers' children from school because wages were too low for families to make ends meet without sending children to work. In addition to leaving workingmen in a state of economic dependence, this deprived them of the time to educate themselves and participate in public affairs. Capitalist "progress" thus seemed ironically to yield more "dependence," more "ignorance," and more "grinding poverty." The capitalist's wealth was being purchased at the price of making the working class unfit for citizenship.[59]

This is why McNeill declared, in 1873, that "there is an inevitable and irresistible conflict between the wage-system of labor and the republican system of government."[60] A similar declaration appeared in the preamble to the constitution of the Knights of Labor.[61] While the courts were enshrining as a constitutional right the worker's liberty to sell his labor, the labor movement was forging an opposing constitutional political economy that held that being forced to sell his labor under the liberal legal rules of the game contradicted the worker's status as a citizen. Preserving a "republican form of government," McNeill proclaimed, demanded that we "engraft republican principles into our industrial system."[62] Only with the "republicanization of industry"—meaning cooperative ownership—could there be a genuine "republicanization of government."[63] This is what it would take, the Knights argued, to restore to workingmen the kind of economic independence and equality necessary for authentic participation in the polity.

The 1880s labor movement fully understood that creating a world of worker-owned industry would require a transformation of the nation's banking and credit systems, along with many other dramatic changes in the emerging corporate political economy. Mainstream labor leaders like Knights of Labor president Terence Powderly did not shy away from calling for just such a peaceful revolution. The vision drove many labor reformers toward alliances with like-minded agrarian organizations, in hopes of creating a third-party movement with the heft to bring to earth what organized workers and farmers alike dubbed a "Co-operative Commonwealth." Like the Jeffersonian and Jacksonian Democrats and Lincolnian Republicans before them, the founders of the People's Party—the Populist Party's formal name—styled their party-building movement a campaign of constitutional restoration. As we shall see, these Gilded Age practitioners of party constitutionalism set about renovating the old Jacksonian claim that a new mass party movement was constitutionally essential—lest popular sovereignty and republican self-rule be forever lost to the usurpations of a corporate elite, which had corrupted the two old parties.

The Populist movement and People's Party took shape in the late 1880s and early 1890s, as trade unionists and labor activists began to see the severe obstacles to "reform by legislation" in the American system. By then, state high courts were striking down hard-won labor law reforms—and those they did not void, they read with hostile eyes. Meanwhile, even the most industrialized states had scant administrative capacity to enforce labor legislation. Middle-class reformers might carry on the slow work of building state labor bureaus and factory inspectorates. But hard-pressed workers increasingly agreed with Samuel Gompers, the chief of the newly founded (1886) American Federation of Labor (AFL). The Knights of Labor dream of marrying trade unionism to third-party politics and a broad legislative agenda was a hopeless diversion, said Gompers. Plausible in England or Europe, perhaps, but not in the United States, with its engrained antistatism, its uniquely powerful anti-redistributive courts, and its two old parties, built on ethnocultural loyalties and cross-class coalitions.[64]

The way to topple wage slavery here in America, declared trade unionists like Gompers, was collective self-help: wielding strikes and boycotts to enforce labor's own labor standards. Class-based *legislative* initiatives like the eight-hour day for all workers—beyond the "dependent" or "vulnerable" groups like women and children—simply would not pass judicial muster.[65]

The 1894 AFL convention in Denver saw a crucial debate between the proponents of broad "independent labor politics" on the model of

England's recently formed Independent Labour Party and the champions of a minimalist politics and what Gompers called "pure and simple unionism."[66] Adolph Strasser of the cigarmakers' union, Gompers's mentor and colleague, declared: "There is one fact that cannot be overlooked. You cannot pass a general eight hour day without changing the constitution of the United States and the constitution of every State in the Union. . . . I am opposed to wasting our time declaring for legislation being enacted for a time possibly, after we are dead."[67]

Henry Demarest Lloyd, a widely known journalist and key figure in forging the farmer-labor alliance that founded the People's Party, rose to respond. The courts' constitutional rulings were counterfeit, he declared—products of class bias. Preserving a republican form of government and equality of rights *demanded* a broad reform program. "I sometimes wish I had been born in any other country than in the United States. I am sick and tired of listening to lawyers . . . declaring everything we ask unconstitutional." The solution was to elect lawmakers and choose judges with truer constitutional understandings, and if need be, "to change the constitution" to rein in the courts. Unimpressed, Strasser pointed proudly to the craft unions (like the cigarmakers') that had gained the eight-hour day "by themselves . . . pass[ing] and enforc[ing] [their own] law without the government."[68]

Gompers's and Strasser's base lay in craft unions and skilled workers; their unusual bargaining power made workplace victories easier. But their single-minded focus on improving workers' lot via strikes and boycotts was becoming the dominant one, because it was paying off.[69]

Strikes were nothing new. But until the late 1880s and early 1890s, most were spontaneous, local affairs. Now, more and more strike calls, demands, and strategies issued from national and regional unions, knit together by the AFL. In a great many industries, unions were banding together on a much larger scale than businesses. A struck hat manufacturer in Boston might confront a national AFL-sponsored boycott of his goods; a struck printer in Milwaukee, a refusal of press workers throughout the city and state to take up his back orders. A Chicago construction firm that spurned its union carpenters' work rules and wage demands might find the teamsters refusing to haul materials to the building site.[70]

The AFL leaned to the view that workers' "final emancipation" lay in the self-organization of the "House of Labor." The route to the material independence, dignity, and authority associated with republican citizenship was not using legislation to "engraft republican principles into our industrial system," but instead through workers' collective clout in the marketplace.[71]

This boycott of politics was temporary. It would end in response to the self-organization of capitalists—and courts' growing readiness to suppress labor's most effective forms of collective action. As we shall see in Chapter 5, by the turn of the century, hundreds—and by the 1920s, thousands—of antistrike and antiboycott decrees provoked a decades-long campaign of civil disobedience, jail time, and lobbying by the AFL to repeal "government by injunction."[72]

Already, in the 1870s and 1880s, "government by injunction" had emerged on the nation's railroads. Several factors made the federal judicial interventions in railway strikes unique. Until the late 1880s, judicial repression was aimed only against strikers and boycotters of railway lines in federal equitable receivership. Thus, the federal judges were already involved with the railroads' management and inclined to view them as "public property for the time being."[73] Even as the railway labor injunction spread beyond lines in receivership, the far-flung and quasi-public character of the industry, as well as its centrality to interstate commerce and the federal mails, continued to differentiate railroad strikes and their regulation.[74]

When employers sued to enjoin nonrailroad strikes, weighty doctrines stood in the way. Among them, Gilded Age courts would refuse to grant injunctions because the suits alleged nothing more than "ordinary crimes" like trespass or assault, which properly belonged in criminal court.[75] As one state court explained, the mere fact "[t]hat the [criminal] law against this offense is not enforced and observed is no ground for the interposition of a court of equity."[76] Similarly, a federal judge in Colorado stoically declined to expand his equity powers into the domain of state criminal law: "[T]he Constitution of the United States has committed the maintenance of peace and good order to the . . . state governments. If the state government has fallen into the hands of socialists . . . or . . . imbeciles . . . we do not thereby acquire the right to assume control."[77] Thus, he refused to enjoin a miners' strike.

In re Debs: "A Lesson Which Cannot Be Learned Too Soon"

Even during railway strikes, the air and the courts were filled with objections that the Constitution committed the maintenance of peace and order to state authorities, and the prosecution of crimes to trial by jury. The great Pullman Strike of 1894 is a good example worth pausing over because it occasioned the Supreme Court's unanimous 1895 decision *In re Debs*.[78] In the very same term, *Pollock v. Farmers' Loan & Trust Co.*,[79] which we discuss below, struck down the federal income tax. These two decisions launched the *Lochner* era with an explosion of class-conscious constitutional political economy.[80]

Even though the AFL and the old railroad workers' brotherhoods held back from the Populist movement, the Populists loudly condemned *In re Debs* and promised to end federal judicial interventions against railroad strikes and boycotts.

The farmers' and the workers' threatening new movements had much in common, declared Justice David Brewer, the author of *Debs*, to the elite of the New York bar in 1893.[81] In Brewer's mind, workers' far-flung sympathy strikes and farmers' legislative campaigns for railroad rate regulation and other restraints on corporate power were part and parcel of one menacing new "movement of 'coercion' . . . which by the mere force of numbers seeks to diminish protection to private property."[82] It was a movement, said Brewer, marching under "[t]he black flag of anarchism" and "the red flag of socialism," and flouting "the unvarying law, that the wealth of a community will be in the hands of a few."[83] A dark moment like this, in the Justice's view, demanded "[m]agnifying, like the apostle of old, my office," for the "salvation of the nation" rested on the "vigor of the judiciary."[84] And magnify his office is what Brewer did.

The Pullman Strike was called by the American Railway Union (ARU), a fledgling industrial union created by Eugene Debs and other former railroad brotherhood leaders to overcome the old unions' divisive craft boundaries and their exclusion of masses of unskilled railway workers. Swayed by George Pullman's ruthless wage cuts and refusal to confer with his factory employees, the ARU's membership voted to take on the cause of Pullman's desperate workers with a nationwide boycott of Pullman's "palace cars."[85]

An eloquent voice of working-class republicanism, Debs defended the boycott as the "practical exhibition of sympathy," Christian brotherhood, and republican mutualism.[86] But in the eyes of a ruling class on edge—exemplified by Justice Brewer—Debs's industrial unionism and the extensive web of railway workers' sympathy boycotts of Pullman cars and of railway lines that refused to uncouple the cars, embodied the labor movement at its most threatening.

The railroads were prepared—and so was President Cleveland's attorney general, Richard Olney, a leading corporate attorney who had retained his seat on several railroad companies' boards of directors. The railroads agreed in advance to refuse to uncouple any Pullman cars, and to link them, wherever possible, to cars carrying the mail. Working closely with the attorney general, dozens of lines sought and won federal equity decrees against the strikers "in nearly every large city west of the Allegheny Mountains."[87] At the same time, Olney appointed "a long-time attorney for a railroad company" as a special assistant to sue on the government's behalf for a decree against the ARU in Chicago, the nation's railroad hub and ARU headquarters.[88]

Within days, railroad cars everywhere were plastered with injunctions prohibiting the ARU and any of its sympathizers from threatening, combining, or conspiring to quit in any fashion that would embarrass the railways' operations, and from refusing to handle the cars of other struck lines. Several injunctions also forbade attempts to induce fellow workers to support the strikes and boycotts. With the decrees in place, President Cleveland dispatched some sixteen thousand federal troops to enforce them.[89] The judges agreed with the president. "The situation in Chicago," in the private words of then circuit judge William Howard Taft, was so "alarming and distressing" as to demand "much bloodletting" on the troops' part to "make an impression" on "the mob."[90]

But the troops arrived over the vehement opposition of Illinois's labor-populist governor John Altgeld. To him, the "situation in Chicago" was one of mass demonstrations by strikers and their supporters, but there was neither large-scale destruction of railroad property nor significant violence. Altgeld telegrammed the president demanding an end to the invasion, which did "violence to the constitution." The "exercise of the police power and the preservation of law and order" belonged to "local government."[91] Altgeld denied that the president could dispatch troops to Illinois without his request. Article IV of the Constitution seemed to say as much, expressly predicating federal protection "against domestic Violence" on "Application of the [state] Legislature [or] Executive."[92]

Ignoring Altgeld's arguments, the president shot back that "the post office department" had requested federal intervention, and his decision to send the troops also rested on "abundant proof that conspiracies existed against commerce between the states."[93] The federal troops and what the labor and Populist press—and even the *New York Times*—called the "gatling gun injunctions" brought down the Pullman Strike, and the ARU never recovered.[94]

Before the contempt convictions of Debs and other ARU leaders reached the high court, Governor Altgeld explained the high constitutional stakes for the anti-oligarchy principle. "If the acts of the President," said Altgeld to the Illinois legislature, "are to stand unchallenged and thus form a precedent, then . . . our [nation's] career as a republic is over. We will have a rapidly increasing central power controlled and dominated by class and by corporate interests." He argued: "Never before were the United States government and the corporations of the country so completely blended . . . and never before was the goddess of justice made a mere handmaid for one of the combatants. . . . It is evident that if the Attorney General . . . did not outline and advise the policy [the corporations] pursued, it received his approval and was carried out through his assistance."[95]

Some of the lower court decrees rested on the Interstate Commerce Act of 1887; the others relied on the Sherman Act of 1890.[96] Attorney General Olney wanted a broader ruling from the Supreme Court, one based directly on the Constitution.[97] And he got it.[98] Counsel for Debs and the other imprisoned strike leaders were former senator Lyman Trumbull (whom we met in the Reconstruction Congress) and Clarence Darrow, famous friend of labor and the oppressed. They pointed out that neither statute spoke to strikes or labor organizations, and neither authorized injunction proceedings against obstruction of the railroads. Congress had addressed interference with the U.S. mails with criminal statutes, which supplied no basis for the equity proceedings and jail sentences below. Besides, the injunction proceedings insulted due process, having unfolded without notice to Debs and the others, and the Sixth Amendment, having deprived them of trial by jury.[99]

For a unanimous Court, Justice Brewer adopted the attorney general's theory.[100] "[E]nter[ing] into no examination" of the Sherman Act "upon which the Circuit Court relied,"[101] Brewer reasoned that the Constitution itself was sufficient authority for the injunction and the jail terms. The Constitution did more than authorize Congress to enact laws to protect commerce and the mails on the railroads; it imparted inherent power to the executive to act against obstructions.[102]

When it came to railway strikes, it turned out, the Court's Constitution had antistrike and antiboycott rules baked in, which the president was authorized to enforce, unilaterally, by sending in the army.[103] It was "more to the praise than to the blame" of the president that he repaired to court for an injunction, but he was entirely within his rights simply to wield "[t]he strong arm of the national government . . . to brush away all obstructions to the freedom of interstate commerce or the transportation of the mails. If the emergency arises, the army of the Nation, and all its militia, are at the service of the Nation to compel obedience to its laws."[104]

Obedience to what laws? Justice Brewer does not say; none of the statutes he flags cover the case. Only the Constitution. Fueled by fear and loathing of labor insurgency, *In re Debs* offers up an emergency powers doctrine ("If the emergency arises . . .") that today's commentators rarely discuss—and a scary one.[105]

What about Governor Altgeld's quaint view that the Constitution requires a request on a state's part before troops get sent? What about the notion that the executive branch *executes* laws, rather than "determining for itself questions of right and wrong on the part of [the striking workers and their unions] and enforcing that determination by . . . the bayonet of the soldier," which, Brewer tells us, rather astonishingly, was entirely in the executive's power to do?[106] Plainly, the Court agreed with the attorney general and the White House that order on the railroads demanded a bluntly authoritarian construction of executive power—a hard-as-nails pronouncement on the utter illegitimacy of both the sympathy strike and the state's refusal to welcome federal troops to put it down.

Brewer framed his forgotten emergency powers doctrine with a revealing hypothetical. "If all the inhabitants of a State, or even a great body of them, should combine to obstruct interstate commerce or the transportation of the mails, prosecutions for such offences had in such a community would be doomed in advance," he speculated.[107] Can it be, then, that government's only recourse is via enforcement of the criminal law? No, a "single State" cannot overawe the nation's interests! In such an "emergency," conjuring memories of nullification, the Army is at hand to preserve "the peace of the nation."[108]

Of course, President Jackson's Nullification Proclamation threatened armed intervention in the face of actual, far-reaching nullification of federal law by a state government (not imagined nullification by protesters or jurors).[109] No matter. Nor is "the army the only instrument" for safeguarding the nation. There are also the sturdy equity powers of the courts, which avert the prospect of (again, imagined) jury nullification. To hold that defendants facing prison for defying judicial orders are entitled to trial by jury would "deprive the proceeding of half its efficiency."[110] All this fancied nullification of federal law betrayed more than ordinary distrust of democratic institutions and state governments in the hands of labor-populist governors and working-class voters and juries. *In re Debs* brims with language associating them with rebellion against the United States.[111]

Sympathy strikes and boycotts, as we saw, were becoming a tried-and-true form of labor solidarity and class-based collective action. Even the stodgy brotherhood of railroad engineers had a provision in their constitution obliging members to honor boycotts in support of other unions.[112] How else were employees of nation-spanning corporations supposed to gain a commensurable measure of bargaining power, if not by combining on a similar scale? *In re Debs* professed to put aside all questions about the statutory or common-law bounds of strikes and boycotts.[113] Yet, Brewer's opinion closes with "a lesson which cannot be learned too soon or too thoroughly" by would-be sympathy strikers like those before the Court, "who threw up their employment . . . to assist others whom they believed to be wronged."[114] The sympathy strike was no legitimate "means of redress." "[N]o wrong, real or fancied, carries with it legal warrant to invite . . . the cooperation of a mob."[115] Redress must be found "through the courts and at the ballot-box."[116]

With that equation of sympathy strikes and boycotts with the "mob," the Court's fear of the era's burgeoning movements of farmers and workers boiled over into contempt. It was rich for the Justices to relegate those movements to the courts and the ballot box, when the courts were striking down labor legislation and railroad rate regulation won by the votes of farmers and workers, and the Supreme Court itself was furiously gutting the Interstate Commerce Act.[117] Just days before handing down *Debs,* the Court had struck down Congress's new federal income tax (about which, more soon), and earlier the same term, it had found that the Sherman Antitrust Act, on which the lower courts relied to condemn the Pullman Strike, could not constitutionally touch the notorious Sugar Trust, which controlled 95 percent of the nation's sugar production.[118] All that was rich; and now, the Court was openly baking the "gatling gun injunction" and condemnation of broad-gauged collective action into constitutional law.

So, in movement circles, among Populists and their People's Party, the "lesson which cannot be learned too soon" from *Debs* and the other blaring decisions of the Court was not what Brewer had in mind, but instead this: it was time to push aside the constitutional political economy the Court was constructing in favor of their own. It was time for a full-fledged reexamination of the terms on which an industrial economy and a democratic republic could coexist, and for a radical alternative account of the rights of citizens and the powers and duties of national government. Both the Court and the Populists wanted to build up national power beyond inherited constraints, but for diametrically—and dialectically—opposed reasons: the one to hem in the initiatives of organized labor; the other to subdue capital.

Updating the Democracy of Opportunity—Populist Constitutional Political Economy

National legislation to halt "government by injunction" on the railways became a central Populist demand.[119] The AFL declined to support the People's Party. It agreed about abolishing the labor injunction but stuck with nonpartisanship and "pure and simple unionism." The Knights of Labor, by the mid-1890s, was a shadow of its glory days, its many railroad locals and experiments in industrial unionism beaten down, like the ARU, by state violence, and the whole outfit torn by divisions over trade unionism versus third-party politics. Thus, it fell to the agrarian Populists to create a formidable new party organized (like its predecessors) around a new brand of constitutional politics: the first full-blown constitutional political economy aimed at modernizing the democracy of opportunity for an age of "combination" and large-scale industry.[120] Populism marked an effort to rebuild a biracial "poor man's party" akin to the Reconstruction era's "Black Republicans." Across the South, Midwest, and West, the Populists made a formidable entry into state and national politics and brought labor's program (and, they hoped, labor's votes) with them.[121]

Running and electing candidates to national office meant confronting fierce constitutional attacks on the Populist program—which pushed the Populists to develop and refine their constitutional arguments. Indeed, the Populists had a double burden of persuasion: they also had to persuade *themselves* and their core constituents of erstwhile Democrats to lay to rest the old Jefferson-and-Jackson gospel of states' rights and strict construction. They had to return to the sacred texts and show why a vast expansion of national governmental power was constitutional. Like the Knights, these agrarian reformers envisaged a new "Co-operative Commonwealth," which restored a broad diffusion of productive property and a wide-open middle class via legal frameworks and government support not only for strong unions but also for new, cooperative forms of ownership in both agriculture and industry, along with new forms of government regulation and control over the nation's banking and transportation systems.[122] Such dramatic reforms were constitutional abominations according to inherited Jeffersonian and Jacksonian standards—and they went far beyond what was allowable under the tenets of late nineteenth-century liberal legal and constitutional orthodoxy.

By the Populists' reckoning, however, the reforms were not simply allowable, but essential. Throughout the 1890s, Populists produced scores of books and entire weekly and monthly journals whose densely argued pages melded constitutional, political-economic, and sociological arguments, calling for the democratization of a range of national institutions: the banking and currency systems, corporations law, railroad regulation, industrial relations, and the constitutional framework itself.[123]

Like the Knights of Labor, Populists held that the Constitution's "doctrine of equality" was "not limited to a dogma that all men should be made equal before the law." The "real theory," according to one of Populism's leading political economists, was this: "[I]n our Constitution the principle is imbedded" of securing "the widest distribution among the people, not only of political power, but of the advantages of wealth, education, and social influence."[124] This idea of "equal rights," he insisted, was "the great basic idea of our laws, the very corner-stone of the republican structure." And that structure was at risk. Corporations had arrogated to themselves the tools of industry, transportation, communication, and finance. Concentrating "egregious wealth in the hands of the few at the cost of creating a proportionate poverty among the many," corporations wielded their power to destroy the "democratic social fabric." This "departure from the fundamental intent and purpose of our republican system," however, was no sign of the "failure of the constitution," but of the "failure of this Nation to enforce" it.[125]

In their quest for a constitutional check on corporate power, the Populists held fast to the classic theory of the corporation as an "artificial creature," created to perform a "public function," and subject to common law and legislative direction and constraints far sterner than could be visited on an individual citizen.[126] In the 1880s and 1890s, the weight of doctrine still leaned the same way. As we'll see, state constitutional provisions and state and federal high court decisions fairly brimmed with declarations that equality of rights and opportunity, as well as popular sovereignty and the "rights of the community" to govern, were all at stake in upholding and bolstering the inherited restraints on corporate expansion. So, Populist tribunes and lawmakers were on conventional legal ground, accusing the corporate bar and bench of corrupting the old common law as well as express state-constitutional commands when they began eroding the old constraints and endowing corporations with personhood and property rights that stymied regulation.

Combination, Populists acknowledged, was an "irresistible" fact of the age.[127] But, while corporate lawyers argued for the unique efficiency of corporate consolidations, Populists argued that there was no natural path for combination to follow, no natural laws dictating the trajectory of commercial and economic development. As corporate attorneys sought and judges granted myriad modifications of doctrine to accommodate consolidation, Populist journalists like Henry Demarest Lloyd (whom we met at the 1894 AFL convention) disputed claims that these shifts were dictated by technical imperatives and economic laws.[128] Lloyd became a keen observer and sharp critic of these organizational changes championed by corporate consolidators, and he saw particular group interests as the real driver. Some of the consolidations would provide economies of scale and consumer savings; others only profited the consolidators who fashioned them. But never were they the only efficient avenues of industrial change. There were other workable alternatives that promised more—materially and morally—for the broader citizenry.[129]

Another leading Populist lecturer explained that "the development of corporations under our changing laws has created especial advantages for the accumulation of property in the hands of a favored class . . . and increased the[ir] political and social power." Yet, the very purpose of "inscribing in the Constitution the principle of equality" was "to secure a general diffusion of wealth and to maintain the practical equality of all the people." Thus, it was "vital[ly] necess[ary to] discover[] exactly where and how the constitutional principle was violated, and restor[e] the supremacy of republican doctrine."[130]

As federal courts, gripped by the new liberalism, began striking down popular state railroad regulatory commissions and statutory controls on corporations, Populists like Oregon governor Sylvester Pennoyer complained of one such court-minted constitutional violation: the "monstrous doctrine" that "sovereignty of the state can be peddled out to corporations and frittered away."[131] This was Jacksonian constitutional fare: the idea that lawmakers could not constitutionally hand over or barter away to corporations governmental powers, which the people had lodged in their representatives, and which belonged to the community.[132] The Populist innovation was to invoke the idea in connection with Congress's Commerce Power, and do so in a way that anticipated Progressives' and legal realists' critical take on corporations as "private governments" performing "public functions."[133] Thus, for example, Populist senator John Kenna declared that railroad regulation "was a resumption by Congress of a power to regulate interstate commerce which the Constitution confers upon Congress, and which the railroads have usurped and absorbed."[134]

Populist presidential candidate James Weaver generalized the constitutional point. With the rise of the "trusts," key functions of government—regulating interstate commerce and transportation, issuing and controlling currency—had been given over to private corporations and "leased to associated speculators." These were constitutional usurpations. Not only did the Constitution authorize Congress to perform these functions, but when otherwise Congress's governmental powers were being exercised by private corporate actors in violation of the common good, it was the "great duty" of Congress to act.[135]

Weaver's campaign book during his 1892 run for the White House put this constitutional duty at the center of his campaign: "The great object . . . is to restore to Congress its Constitutional and exclusive control over the great limbs of commerce, money, transportation and telegraphy. . . . These great facilities, so essential to life, prosperity and happiness have been wrenched from the people and passed to the control of the monopolists. To reclaim them is the great duty of the hour."[136] The Populist Party wove these ideas explicitly into its platform, which asserted that "the political rights and personal liberties of the citizen" depended on the government ending the "tyranny and political power now exercised by the great railroad corporations" by taking control of the railroads away from the monopolists.[137]

James "Cyclone" Davis, a charismatic Texan who was one of Populism's favorite constitutional experts and orators, authored a book-length constitutional indictment of corporate "usurpation," a "'communism of capital' . . . unknown to our Constitution."[138] Often carrying a dozen volumes of Jefferson's and Madison's papers to the podium, Davis, like many Southern Populists, struggled to reconcile an inherited strict constructionism with Populism's more expansive constitutional vision of national power and its uses. Davis returned to the founding era to recover for leery Southern audiences the nationalizing thrust of the framers' political-economic outlook. In Madison's papers he found the report of the 1786 Annapolis Convention highlighting the need for a new national "'power of regulating trade is . . . of such comprehensive extent . . . that to give it efficacy . . . may require a correspondent adjustment of other parts of the Federal system.'"[139] He argued from history: "As James Madison and Thomas Jefferson tell us, the old Federal government [under the Articles] was insufficient," and the constitutional convention found their task "impossible" without expanding national power.[140]

Turning to constitutional text, Davis argued that Congress must exercise its enumerated powers, especially the Commerce Power—"the mainspring to build up our government"—to fulfill the purposes laid out in the text of the Preamble. Instead, he charged, Congress had betrayed its constitutional trust by franchising out its enumerated powers to private monopolies. "Congress allows, yea even charters, licenses a lot of cold, faithless, soulless, heartless, merciless corporations, to stand between the government and the people, and usurp the blessings conferred by [the Commerce] power, forcing the people to look to these conscienceless beings for money and transportation to carry on their commerce."[141] A fresh reading of the founders' papers—informed by the Populists' new vision of national regulation—had brought Davis around to the idea we encountered first in Whig and then Reconstruction-era Republican constitutional discourse: Congress had affirmative constitutional duties to implement the purposes of national government. But, of course, Populist constitutional thinkers like Davis pressed the notion in quite different directions. "[I]n every one of [Article I's enumerated] powers," Davis contended, "it is the duty of Congress *to act directly on the people and for the people . . .* not through the States . . . *much less through corporations or syndicates.*" "To 'farm out' or delegate its powers" by authorizing corporate control of the veins of commerce and finance was to betray the Constitution.[142] Congress had abandoned the "general welfare" and destroyed equality before the law by allowing "monopoly in the . . . distribution of money" and "monopoly in transportation"—which fostered "monopoly in the distribution of wealth."[143]

Populists like Weaver and Davis had no illusions about how their program of constitutional restoration might fare in the federal courts. The party platform lamented that corporate corruption "touches even the ermine of the bench."[144] Implementing the "great duty" of restoring governmental authority over the nation's political economy, while averting any more decisions like *Debs,* thus demanded freeing the Constitution from the courts. The power and duty of the citizenry and political branches to arrive at their own constitutional interpretations was a major theme in Populist speeches and writings, and one they passed on to Progressives as mainstream and various as Teddy Roosevelt and his rival Woodrow Wilson. It became a major part of early twentieth-century constitutional politics.[145] To understand how it emerged, it helps to understand just who occupied the federal bench.

The "ermine of the [federal] bench" during the decades bracketing the turn of the century belonged overwhelmingly to the new and still tiny elite ranks of prominent railroad, banking, and other large-scale corporate attorneys: men with "sound" views on the great political-economic questions of the day and deep familiarity with corporate and large-scale commercial affairs. Most of the Supreme Court appointments between Reconstruction and the 1892 election were drawn from this elite province of the profession.[146] With the lower federal bench, the story was the same. By the 1880s, 91 percent of them were Republicans.[147] Their pre-judicial law practices, wealth, and ties of family and friendship put 98 percent of them at the very top of the nation's class and status hierarchies.[148] The lower federal bench, in their collective biographer's words, "increasingly . . . resembled a dominant ruling class."[149]

Today it may seem unexceptional for most federal judges and justices to hail from the corporate elite. Not so then. This spectacle of the federal judiciary as the arena where the ruling class went to rule—of corporate attorneys on the federal bench designing and governing the new corporate political economy, unleashing troops against striking workers, and overturning or gutting legislative efforts to curb and revise the courts' work—was something new, and ominous.[150]

It is against this backdrop that the antimonopolists, both agrarian and labor—so named because of their opposition to economic monopoly and corporate power—also decried the judiciary's "asserted Monopoly on interpreting the Constitution," for which "no warrant can be found in the Constitution itself."[151] By legislative initiative and interbranch confrontation, and by amending the state and federal constitutions, Populists and their allies sought to reclaim the "Power of the Co-Ordinate Branches and of the Sovereign People to render their own Interpretations."[152] They envisioned constitutional amendments to tame the judiciary and to restore popular sovereignty, all of which remained part of the Progressive agenda into the early 1930s. These included the election of federal and state judges; abolition or curtailment of judicial review; direct election of senators; new amendment rules to make the Constitution itself more easily amendable; and the new innovations of direct democracy—the initiative, referendum, and recall—in state constitutions.[153]

Then, they could set about lawmaking to restore and renew farmers' and workers' democratic citizenship. Substantively, this meant freeing the "colored laborer with the white" from the "iron rule of the Money power" through public credit and support for cooperative enterprise.[154] It meant nationalizing the railways.[155] It meant constructing "a political economy organized to provide work for all who are willing" and in economic downswings create jobs through public works.[156] It meant an end to the repressive common-law restraints on workers' collective action and the savagery of "government by injunction," encouraging robust unions and industrial cooperation. Ultimately it meant reshaping the legal and governmental order to enable ordinary working people to exercise the rights and responsibilities of control over productive property, and the political power to shape the nation's trajectory of economic development in the direction of democracy rather than oligarchy.

"The Money of the Constitution"

In the context of this distinctive Populist constitutional vision, one can understand why the question of the nation's currency, and the banking system that regulated and disbursed it, became one of the hottest flash points of Gilded Age politics. The central question of the day was whether to hold fast to the hard money of the gold standard or switch to a looser monetary policy of greenbacks or bills backed by silver.

Here, as in so many areas of constitutional political economy, the Populists' battles reprised Jacksonian ones—with important continuities, but with some important polarities reversed. The core continuity was this: Currency is the lifeblood of any economy. Andrew Jackson and his party had argued—to enormous political effect—that the only way to protect the "equal rights" of ordinary, white farmers was to restrain the power of the financial elite, the distant Northeastern banks on whom so many farmers depended for credit. In regional terms, this meant defending the Midwest and South from the financiers of New York City and New England. In terms of actual monetary policy, it meant the gold standard. The party of Jackson had argued that the Constitution required American money to be backed by gold. The reasons were rooted in a particular set of arguments about the constitutional political economy of money. Jacksonians saw gold as the way to maintain some stability for poor farmers in a world of numerous panics, financial reversals, and rampant speculation. They viewed gold as "real" currency, natural rather than "speculative"; they feared that departing from it would empower bankers and speculators, destroying the ordinary farmers' economic opportunities and ultimately their "equal rights."

By the Gilded Age, the political and constitutional valence of gold had flipped. To the mostly Midwestern and Southern agrarian radicals and reformers who shaped the People's Party, the gold standard itself seemed a powerful tool for centralizing economic power in the banking elite of the Northeast, especially New York City. Farmers depend on credit to get through each season; by the 1870s it was clear that credit was not being distributed around the country in anything like an even way. Money—and therefore, the capacity for loans and development—was heavily concentrated in the Northeast, where it fueled enormous industrial growth.[157] Outside the Northeast, credit was harder to come by and interest rates were higher. The banks simply did not have as much to lend.[158] The Civil War had led the nation to suspend the gold standard and issue greenbacks—bills backed by nothing but the full faith and credit of the United States, like dollars today—to fund the war. After the war, the government gradually moved back toward the gold standard, preparing for "resumption" in 1879 by keeping more or less constant the amount of money in circulation as the economy expanded.[159] This meant deliberate deflation, as money became scarcer and more valuable—meaning that every debt became more onerous in real terms by the time it was paid. This monetary policy also made credit even harder to come by outside the Northeast.

Against this backdrop, the Populists put a call for the rejection of the gold standard at the center of their political program. This call came in a variety of flavors. Early People's Party campaigns for abundant green-backs and interconvertible bonds as a countercyclical instrument, with no private banks enmeshed in monetary policy, gave way to a campaign for an end to private banks of issue, plus bimetallism: money backed by silver and gold together. This would mean far more currency in circulation than gold alone.[160] James Weaver grandly proclaimed in his campaign book, "This whole book could be devoted to the silver question."[161] But in fact, the book was about oligarchy. Threading together the strands of the democracy-of-opportunity tradition, Weaver argued that "[t]he slave holding aristocracy . . . was destroyed by the war only to be succeeded by an infinitely more dangerous and powerful aristocracy of wealth."[162] Only by distributing "abundant circulating medium" out among the people—"money that works and not money that shirks" (in the hands of speculators and financiers)—would it be possible to avoid aristocracy and protect the liberties of the people.[163] Particularly after the Panic of 1893 and the economic depression that followed, these ideas became a centerpiece of Populist constitutionalism.[164]

By 1896, William Jennings Bryan, the avatar of Populist outrage against the economic aristocracy of the Northeast and the poverty of farmers in the hinterland, captured the Democratic nomination for president (in a fusion ticket that proved disastrous for the political fortunes of both the Democrats and the People's Party) with what became by far the most famous political speech of its era.[165] From the Democratic convention floor, with the nomination highly in doubt, the young congressman from rural Nebraska thundered, "[W]e stand here representing people who are the equals before the law of the greatest citizens in the State of Massachusetts." But that equality was under threat. "What we need," he said, "is an Andrew Jackson to stand, as Jackson stood, against the encroachments of organized wealth."[166] Bryan advocated Jacksonian distributional ends through the means of a decidedly un-Jacksonian monetary policy. He found a mandate for it in the Constitution itself. "When we have restored the money of the Constitution," he argued, "all other necessary reforms will be possible; but until this is done there is no other reform that can be accomplished." From this assertion he built to his peroration, reaching out to link together "the struggling masses" of "toilers everywhere"—the cities as well as the farms—against the "holders of idle capital," "saying to them, you shall not press down upon the brow of labor this crown of thorns, you shall not crucify mankind upon a cross of gold."[167]

What exactly was "the money of the Constitution"? Why was there a constitutional mandate for bimetallism? For a contemporary reader, listening for constitutional arguments in the modalities we recognize today, there are plenty to be found, beginning with claims on constitutional text. The text of the Constitution gives Congress the power "To coin Money"[168] without specifying what metals, if any, should back it. But a later section prohibits *states* from "mak[ing] any Thing but gold and silver Coin a Tender in Payment of Debts."[169] Populists and other advocates of bimetallism found in this explicit textual privileging of "gold and silver Coin" a strong argument, by their lights, that the Constitution imposed a *duty* on the government to issue money backed by both gold and silver, not gold alone. "Congress has no authority under the Constitution to deny equal coinage of silver with gold," one representative argued in 1898: "They are the money of the Constitution. They are the money therein authorized."[170] The phrase "deny equal coinage" artfully transposes the argument for bimetallism into a constitutional prohibition, but the claim here was unmistakably one of an affirmative duty to expand the money supply by issuing money backed with silver.

The real reasons for this duty—the real drivers of this argument— were a series of intertwined claims about constitutional political economy. The first was a version of Jacksonian equal protection, updated for the Gilded Age. In a major campaign speech at Madison Square Garden about the currency question, Bryan quoted Jackson—not the Fourteenth Amendment, whose verbatim text would have worked as well—for the proposition that "every man is equally entitled to protection by law."[171] Bryan saw in the gold standard a policy that violated this idea and instead enriched the few—a policy that tended, again quoting Jackson, "to make the rich richer and the potent more powerful" as against "the humbler members of society—the farmers, mechanics, and the laborers." These humbler citizens suffered enormously from deflation under "[a] monetary system which is pecuniarily advantageous to a few syndicates," but not "to those who create the nation's wealth."[172]

Even though their actual monetary policy was very distant from Jackson's, the Populists understood their constitutional vision of the political economy of currency, like Jackson's, as a firm stand against "an aristocratic or monarchial system of finance."[173] In both visions, a monetary system that enriches an elite at the expense of ordinary Americans is ultimately a threat to liberty. In line with republican tradition, the Populists reached for analogies to slavery to describe this threat.[174] James Weaver argued that the declining supply of money (in dollars per capita), as the nation inched back toward the gold standard, meant that "the whole country has been reduced to the servitude of debt."[175] As in Jacksonian and Reconstruction-era Republican constitutional political economy, there is no separation here between the economic and the political; a wide-open opportunity structure is essential to liberty. Bryan summed up the connection in a later speech: in America we have "no aristocracy resting upon birth or kingly favor" and we ought to have no "plutocracy ruling in the name of the dollar. Here the road to advancement is a public highway, and it is within our power to keep it open to all alike."[176]

These arguments did not go unanswered. We have seen the class-conscious constitutionalism on both sides of the labor question. No surprise that, like their Populist foes, conservative supporters of the gold standard—Republicans and Cleveland Democrats—argued that their preferred monetary policy had a constitutional pedigree and mandate. They argued that expanding the money supply and thereby causing inflation (which the Populists and other free silver advocates favored) would erode the value of dollars and dollar-denominated assets held as property, thereby violating constitutionally protected property rights by redistributing value from the holders of those assets to others—most often, from creditors (and the wealthy) to debtors (and the poor).[177] An 1896 pro-gold treatise actually took the title "The Money of the Constitution."[178] It threaded together quasi-originalist arguments about the currency laws of the 1790s with arguments that echoed Jacksonian monetary policy—*minus* its distributional goals—to conclude that the Constitution demands a currency with "soundness" and "integrity": one backed by a single and unvarying metal, gold.[179] To the elite members of the Sound Money League, the calls for free silver by the Populists and

Bryan-aligned Democrats amounted to a form of "socialism" that would mean "the overthrow of the Republic."[180]

In the end, the Republic was not overthrown. Bryan won twenty-two of forty-five states in 1896, but William McKinley captured the populous Northeast and thus the presidency. The National Banking System creaked on until 1913 when a less Populist, more business-friendly Democratic Party would finally create the Federal Reserve. Without abandoning gold, it accomplished part of what the Populists had long sought: it provided an increase in liquidity and a more flexible monetary policy.[181] A classic Progressive Era reform, the Federal Reserve was also an important step in the process of moving monetary policy out of the sphere of politics and toward a domain of expert management. But the gold standard itself remained. The real triumph of the Populists' core idea—a monetary policy that aimed to get currency flowing throughout the country, and that abandoned gold—would not come until 1933. By then, the gold standard had contributed mightily to the initial deflationary spiral that brought on the Great Depression. While the Federal Reserve Act seemed to mark the beginning of the largely expert-led technocratic conception of monetary policy we know today, FDR's decision to abandon the gold standard in 1933 brought monetary policy roaring back to the center of constitutional politics. We will turn to that historic confrontation, surprisingly forgotten today, in Chapter 6. For now, let us turn briefly to another central plank of Populist constitutional politics, the income tax. The fight over this tax became fully and unambiguously a constitutional fight after a stunning intervention by the Supreme Court—in the same explosive term as *In re Debs*—as the Court launched the nation into the *Lochner* era and the pitched battles over constitutional political economy that stretched into the 1940s.

The Court and the Income Tax

Throughout the nineteenth century, the federal government relied on two main sources of tax money: tariffs, which benefited the manufacturing Northeast and harmed the agricultural South and Midwest, and various consumption taxes, which fell most heavily, then as now, on the less well-off everywhere. During the Civil War, a federal government in dire need of funds imposed a personal income tax on high earners. After it expired, the question was presented squarely: How should the federal government raise revenue? The Republican Party, dominant in national politics for most of the half century following the war, favored a continued reliance on tariffs, which benefited the North and various specific industries that counted themselves part of the Republican coalition. Southerners, Democrats, and Populists opposed tariffs, for different combinations of reasons.

The courts, for their part, had for a century taken a hands-off, deferential approach to Congress's power to tax. Article I of the Constitution twice states that "direct" taxes must be apportioned to the states by population; it also states that all "Duties, Imposts, and Excises" must be "uniform."[182] But the Court held, in a century of decisions from 1796 to 1880, that a wide variety of taxes the federal government had imposed did not count as "direct" taxes and so were not subject to the state-population-apportionment rule.[183] Nor did the uniformity requirement seem to have any particular bite in court. Thomas Cooley wrote an influential treatise on taxation that suggests why. As long as taxes have a "public purpose," he argued, there is "no reason for judicial interference" with a decision that is fundamentally legislative in nature, even though taxes "often are oppressive to the persons and corporations taxed."[184] Cooley was no friend of either protectionist tariffs or regressive consumption taxes, but he did not see a role for courts in policing legislatures' choices about these questions on constitutional grounds.[185]

In the late nineteenth century, the tide was turning against the tariffs. Classical liberals like William Graham Sumner, the influential Yale social scientist, favored a flat tax on all income with an exemption set at the minimal cost of living, as an alternative to the protectionism and sectoral special pleading involved in the tariff.[186] The People's Party wanted no part of a flat tax. It demanded a "graduated income tax" so "that aggregated wealth shall bear its just proportion of taxation."[187] Major early Progressive political economists like Henry Carter Adams and Richard Ely agreed, and built arguments for the income tax.[188] In 1894, a divided federal government passed a muddled compromise bill that modestly lowered tariffs and enacted a limited income tax that applied only to very high earners, with an exemption level set at $4,000. Wealthy taxpayers, concentrated in the industrial Northeast, would pay it.

Some who owed this new tax sued. Represented by some of the most distinguished members of the corporate bar, such as Joseph Choate,[189] they attacked the peacetime income tax as unconstitutional on two grounds: a lack of uniformity and the claim that it was a "direct" tax that therefore had to be apportioned according to population. In *Pollock v. Farmers' Loan & Trust Co.*, the Supreme Court accepted the second argument and killed the tax, sharply raising the constitutional stakes of the fight. Today, the constitutional fight over the income tax seems archaic, the issue settled by the Sixteenth Amendment. But some of the constitutional principles that animated it remain with us, just below the surface of contemporary debates about progressive taxation. It is worth remembering why Congress's tax power loomed so large in the constitutional politics of the Gilded Age, and why the Court itself, which was sharply divided, saw compelling constitutional arguments of a kind we have quite forgotten, on both sides of the issue, demanding as well as forbidding a progressive tax system.

Chief Justice Melville Fuller wrote for the majority in *Pollock* in a fashion that seemed to avoid the most important questions of political economy surrounding the income tax—questions about progressivity, protectionism, and the federal government's capacity to raise funds.[190] But the Court's approach did have an explicit grounding in political economy. The majority viewed the apportionment requirement as a powerful protection for state fiscal sovereignty, a rule that reserved to the states "the opportunity to pay the amount apportioned, and to recoup [it] from their own citizens in the most feasible way, and in harmony with their systems of local self-government."[191] Requiring apportionment made it impossible for the federal government to collect a tax on any form of income because, then as now, it would be both unjust and politically impossible to apportion income taxes by state population.[192] The Court's constitutional holding therefore tended to hobble the federal government's power to tax—as Justice John Marshall Harlan put it in dissent, "to re-establish that condition of helplessness in which congress found itself during the period of the Articles of Confederation."[193] To the majority, disabling the federal government from enacting an income tax was a feature, not a bug. But why?

The most powerful underlying reasons have to do with constitutional equality norms and their relationship to taxation—equality norms that were at the center of the main arguments *both* sides made in *Pollock*. For one side, the constitutional problem was a tax statute singling out the rich for a special burden (an income tax with a high exemption that only they would have to pay). For the other, the constitutional problem was a judicial construction singling out the rich for a special *benefit*: *Pollock's* constitutional holding (that income taxes are "direct") effectively blocked Congress from making the rich shoulder any real share of the tax burden of modern government at the national level—where, as we have seen, Gilded Age reform movements envisioned major projects of state-building.

Justice Stephen Field's argument was forthright in its constitutional political economy, making use of both Jacksonian equal protection and the constitutional commitments of Reconstruction. In that way, his opinion echoed his *Slaughter-House* dissent, which had linked what he saw as a violation of the "right of free labor" with Jacksonian constitutional precepts against class legislation—both of which he thought were rights protected by the Fourteenth Amendment.[194] In *Slaughter-House,* Field wrote in an antimonopoly vein; the rights at stake belonged to small producers, and he made much of that. A quarter century later, in *Pollock,* the right belonged to big capitalists, and Field wrote in an anti-redistribution vein that cast the federal judiciary as the nation's safeguard against the class-based, majoritarian "movement of 'coercion'" afoot in the land.

The income tax, wrote Field, "is class legislation." It is "arbitrary discrimination" between "those who receive an income of $4,000 and those who do not." The income tax is as unconstitutional as any other law that places a benefit or burden on "citizens by reason of their birth, or wealth, or religion."[195] "It was hoped and believed that the great amendments to the Constitution which followed the late Civil War had rendered such legislation impossible for all future time."[196]

Justice Field concluded with a passage that resonates with his nephew Justice Brewer's jeremiads to the New York Bar and in *Debs:*

"The present assault upon capital is but the beginning," he wrote. "It will be but the stepping-stone to others, larger and more sweeping, till our political contests will become a war of the poor against the rich—a war constantly growing in intensity and bitterness."[197] To a modern reader, this antisocialist language reads as political argument, not constitutional principle.

But part of why these lines read today as political rather than constitutional is because we no longer think about constitutional political economy in the way that these Justices did. To Justice Field, as to his nephew, the potential for a war of the poor against the rich was a *constitutional* problem, requiring a constitutional counterweight. The Court must step in to protect the Constitution from the "usurpation" of a Congress that, numerically speaking, is sure to be dangerously stacked in favor of a nonrich majority. "Unless the rule of the constitution governs," Field writes, the majority is free to design tax laws that "will not include any of their own number."[198] This is a problem at the intersection of political power and economic distribution; it is quintessential constitutional political economy. And in this claim we can see unmistakably the emergence of Lochnerism: the reorientation of both Jacksonian equal protection *and* the Reconstruction Amendments into a new bulwark of constitutional protection for accumulated capital against redistributive politics. In this new scheme, the courts must play a unique role as the protectors of the Constitution against what counsel Joseph Choate characterized at oral argument as "communistic, socialistic, . . . populistic" laws that undermine "fundamental rights of private property and equality before the law."[199]

Justice Harlan, in dissent, also viewed *Pollock* through lenses that combined Jacksonian and Free Labor ideas of equal treatment and applied them to taxation—but with a very different constitutional political economy, one that looked on many aspects of the Populist enterprise with equanimity and sympathy. For Justice Harlan, the core problem with the majority's interpretation of the Constitution in *Pollock* is that it "discriminates against the greater part of the people of our country" by giving "privileges and immunities never contemplated by the founders of the government" to the holders of great wealth. The *Pollock* majority made it effectively impossible for the federal government to tax large fortunes, whether held in the form of land or in the form of stocks and bonds. The "practical effect" of this, Harlan writes, "is to give to certain kinds of property a position of favoritism and advantage."[200] Ordinary working Americans, people who earn their money by the "skill and industry displayed by them in particular callings, trades, or professions, or from the labor of their hands, or the use of their brains," can be compelled by Congress to shoulder their part of the burden of government. But because of *Pollock,* none of that burden can be placed on the "persons, trusts, combinations, and corporations, possessing vast quantities of personal property, including bonds and stocks of railroad, telegraph, mining, telephone, banking, coal, oil, gas, and sugar-refining corporations, from which millions upon millions of income are regularly derived."[201]

The constitutional problem with this was at once economic and political. A special constitutional protection against taxes gave wealthy "persons, trusts, combinations, and corporations" unfair economic privilege, and also unfair "power and influence." Ordinary Americans, Justice Harlan writes, "ought not to be subjected to the dominion of aggregated wealth any more than the property of the country should be at the mercy of the lawless."[202] Justice Harlan was no Populist—he was an old-school liberal Republican. He voted with the rest of the Justices in *Debs,* and his reference to lawlessness suggests that there is a balance to be struck between protecting the wealthy from "the mob" and protecting ordinary people from "the dominion of aggregated wealth." The liberal-republican Constitution demands such a balance, and in Justice Harlan's view, the Court upset it. Harlan predicted bluntly that the Court's decision would "provoke a contest in this country,"[203] and it did.

Pollock electrified Populist politics. The fight for the income tax, alongside the fight for free silver, became the centerpiece of the Populist constitutional and political vision that enabled William Jennings Bryan and his faction to take over the Democratic Party. The confrontation between the Populists and the Court over *Pollock* would also test and probe the evolving boundaries between constitutional politics and constitutional law, the ground rules under which an American political party can call for a change in constitutional law while respecting the authority of the Court. These tensions are readily apparent in the Populists' coy responses to particular questions about how they proposed to revive the income tax the Court had just declared unconstitutional, as they promised repeatedly and explicitly to do. Reluctant to call for an Article V amendment—at this point in American history, such amendments had been ratified only in the nation's first years or in the wake of the Civil War—Bryan argued that Congress should pass a new income tax in defiance of *Pollock*'s interpretation of the Constitution, and then hope for a different outcome in court. Emphasizing the close divide on the Court, he argued, "The income tax was not unconstitutional when it was passed; It was not unconstitutional when it went before the Supreme Court for the first time [when the Court divided 4–4]; It did not become unconstitutional until one judge changed his mind, and we cannot be expected to know when a judge will change his mind."[204] *Why* Bryan and other Populists thought a new tax statute might result in a different outcome in court was not fully articulated; in this space one can imagine a variety of modern theories of the interaction between the courts and the election returns.[205]

Meanwhile, *Pollock* catapulted questions of progressive taxation more broadly into constitutional politics. Advocates of progressive taxation, perhaps spurred in part by the immensely popular writings of Edward Bellamy, had begun to call for inheritance taxes in addition to the income tax. In 1898, Congress enacted an inheritance tax to fund the Spanish–American War by taxing, as one senator put it, "a class of wealth, a class of property, and a class of citizens that do not otherwise pay their fair share of the burden of government."[206] The Court upheld it, but it soon expired.[207] It fell to President Theodore Roosevelt to make the more forthright case, in terms of modern political economy, for a progressive tax on all fortunes, "beyond a certain amount" that would "increase very heavily . . . after a certain point."[208] He argued that its purposes were three. First, it raised revenue. Second, it aimed to reduce "very large fortune[s]"—to defang, if only slightly, the forces he elsewhere called the "malefactors of great wealth." And third, it aimed to "preserve a measurable equality of opportunity . . . an approximate equality in the conditions under which each man obtains the chance to show the stuff that is in him when compared to his fellows."[209]

The tools of progressive taxation—both income taxes and inheritance or estate taxes—thus play an indispensable role in more than one strand of the democracy-of-opportunity tradition. It is no coincidence that they emerged in American politics in earnest with Populism: they were perhaps the most straightforward line of attack on the new concentrations of economic and political power of the great fortunes of the Gilded Age.[210] Progressive taxation could reduce these new fortunes over time or over generations, preventing the emergence of an aristocracy and thereby advancing the anti-oligarchy principle. At the same time, the same taxes promote an open opportunity structure and a broad middle class.

Tax policy was, at first, an extremely controversial means to these ends. Against a baseline of tariffs and consumption taxes, progressive income and inheritance taxes look like the introduction of redistribution into a system formerly focused on revenue. And from the perspective of the holders of accumulated capital, that is what they are. So class interests and fundamental ideological commitments fused in the furious political counterattack against the income tax as "socialist" meddling with private property, one that is best understood as of a piece with the attack on the American Railway Union as well as the constitutionalized-common-law backlash across a number of domains where nascent reform ideas ran into fierce opposition from liberal courts. We have discussed several of these domains in this chapter—the regulation of interstate commerce, corporations, labor, the currency, and the income tax—and we will shortly add antitrust law to our story. These early battles framed decades of constitutional debate about two strands of the democracy-of-opportunity tradition—anti-oligarchy and the open opportunity structure. But what of the third strand, inclusion?

Populism and Inclusion: An Ideal and Its Collapse

The Populist moment was a significant moment of possibility for a genuinely multiracial politics—a politics that had the potential to draw together all three strands of the democracy-of-opportunity tradition. As it turned out, it was the last such moment for perhaps eighty years. What

made this moment possible was the substantial level of political participation by Black as well as white voters. We often think of Jim Crow as
the consequence of Reconstruction's end. It was, but it was slow in
coming. For almost two decades after the end of Reconstruction,
Southern Blacks continued to vote and form political associations in
large numbers. It was not until the 1890s, after the defeat in Congress of
the Lodge Force Bill, which would have defended Black voting rights,
that Southern Redeemers fully succeeded in their campaign to disenfranchise Black voters—and along with them, large numbers of poor
whites.[211]

The rights talk of Black labor and agrarian reformers in the Gilded
Age "wove together the rhetoric of 'equal rights' and 'race pride.'"[212] They
continued to assail Klan violence and forcible exclusion from skilled callings. But they also drew out the links between the labor-populist reform program and their own Reconstruction-bred understanding of
equal citizenship—a decent living, and with it, dignity, autonomy, and
equal standing in civil society, secured by something beyond formal
equality: rights and resources, accessible land and credit, and new forms
of civic association.[213]

Many white Southern Populists saw the possibility of a cross-racial
coalition politics, one that would pit poor farmers of both races against
the wealthy interests who aimed to monopolize the fruits of the labor of
both. Congressman Tom Watson, a young Georgia Populist and William Jennings Bryan's running mate in 1896, saw the fight between
"Democracy and Plutocracy" as one that required this cross-racial coalition.[214] Speaking for the People's Party, he told Black and white
farmers: "You are kept apart that you may be separately fleeced of your
earnings. You are made to hate each other because upon that hatred is
rested the keystone of the arch of financial despotism which enslaves you
both."[215] As C. Vann Woodward describes in his classic account of the
People's Party through the lens of Watson's career, the young Watson
pressed the cause of antilynching legislation and Black voting rights,
often shared the podium with Black speakers and spoke to racially mixed
audiences, and nominated a Black man to the state executive committee
of his party.[216] It goes without saying that these racial views made the
People's Party extremely controversial in most of the white South. But

well into the 1880s and 1890s (depending on the state), there was enough of a Black presence at the ballot box to keep alive the possibility of a genuine alliance, threading together all three strands of the democracy of opportunity.[217]

By the end of the century, this possibility was gone. A wave of mass disenfranchisement—laws passed by Democratic legislators, backed up with election fraud and a concerted wave of violence and terror—took Black voters entirely out of the political equation in the Deep South. By the turn of the century, the words "equality" and "equal rights" appeared less and less in the Black press, and the most insistent claim for equal protection of the laws was no longer against discrimination in credit, schooling, streetcars, or public accommodations. Now, it was against the denial of bare physical protection from the lynch mob, white violence, and a rule of terror condoned by local and state officialdom.[218]

Waving the banner of white solidarity, the "Redeemers" yoked their campaign of fraud and terror against Black voting to an ideological campaign against the fragile interracial alliance at the heart of Southern Populism. By century's end, Southern Populism's white leaders and constituents had largely succumbed. The People's Party lived on into the 1900s, lapsing into vile racism and supporting an end to African American suffrage. Tom Watson himself, who had stood firm against armed lynch mobs in the name of interracial solidarity and Black suffrage, bitterly concluded that agrarian reform demanded Black disenfranchisement: Southern whites couldn't band together against their economic overlords until they first united with them to disenfranchise Blacks.[219]

The campaign to "redeem" the South in which a jaundiced Watson enlisted was an elite-led affair, prompted by the threat of a poor people's party that joined tenants, sharecroppers, and mine and mill workers on both sides of the color line. The Redeemers did not disenfranchise poor Blacks alone; to defeat Populism, they also aimed to strip the vote from lower-class whites, and they succeeded. The poll tax proved a defining feature of the Jim Crow order forged around the turn of the century, and in some states more whites than Blacks in absolute numbers—sometimes a majority of all white voters—were barred from the ballot box by the tax. Combined with the all-white primary and racial violence, the poll tax and the literacy test would operate for decades, well into the

New Deal era and beyond, to deprive liberal Democrats of their natural constituency among hard-hit Southerners of both races. Meanwhile, the codification of white supremacy and widespread disenfranchisement secured a closed, one-party system dominated by the landholding elites of the Black Belt and by New South entrepreneurs and industrialists, two groups joined in their determination to preserve a labor force that was poorly educated, racially divided, and "schooled in dependency."[220]

The U.S. Supreme Court played an important part in this process, almost strangling the Equal Protection Clause in its infancy, striking down or narrowly reading various civil rights acts, refusing to intervene against massive and unconcealed disenfranchisement in violation of the Fifteenth Amendment, and confirming that the constitutional guarantees of Black citizenship would not impede Jim Crow.[221] The Court thus lent its sanction to the reconstituted caste system of the South; and the New South thereby secured its special status as a distinct society within the Union's new constitutional order.

5

PROGRESSIVE CONSTITUTIONAL FERMENT
IN THE NEW CENTURY

As the Populist moment passed, the movement's commitment to multi-racial democracy—always fragile and ambivalent on the part of white Populists—became a dissenting current within the democracy-of-opportunity tradition, shunted out of the mainstream of reform ideals by the increasingly virulent, taken-for-granted racism of mainstream white America in the first decades of the twentieth century. But other important planks of the Populist program endured, along with the basic conviction that unreconstructed corporate capitalism spelled an unavoidable slide into oligarchy, and that vindicating the Constitution's guarantees of republican self-rule and equal rights demanded wholesale reform.

What the Populists and labor radicals did for agrarian and working-class movements, Progressive thinkers like Herbert Croly, Jane Addams, Louis Brandeis, and John Dewey did for their era's middle-class and elite reformers: they interpreted the emergence of big business and corporate capitalism in terms of an inherited democratic constitutionalism, and responded by developing an alternative constitutional political economy.

The social and economic problems of the Gilded Age remained: growing concentrations of wealth and power, mass working-class and rural poverty and shrinking opportunities for old-fashioned middle-class livelihoods and opportunities, and the sense that corporations and the corporate elite were governing the economy and corrupting the government. But compared to their Gilded Age forebears, most early twentieth-century Progressives (and socialists too) had a greater confidence that the raw, new industrial society America had become was the outgrowth of—you guessed it—"progressive" historical forces. Large-scale industrial enterprise and social organization could be made to serve the old democracy of opportunity's commitments to a broad distribution of wealth and social and political power.

Some Progressive reformers—Louis Brandeis, Robert La Follette— carried into the early twentieth century an older reform vision of a decentralized America, with vibrant regional economies of small producers, medium-sized firms, and cooperatives. Like the Populists, they saw classical liberalism as a disaster; their reinvigorated antimonopoly vision required an active national government to create the framework for democratic decentralization. But most Progressives made their peace with what Brandeis called the "curse of bigness." Their solutions to the problems of oligarchy and economic domination, poverty, and exploitation were not so much to dismantle the giant corporations as to empower unions and institute "industrial democracy" between labor and capital, giving workers a real share of authority in industry, while building up new governmental organizations—bureaus, commissions, an administrative state—to enable the public to regulate the new large corporations, and own and run some of them, while adapting the corporations' organizational achievements to the task of governance. The idea was to bring order and expertise to the management of the public's business, but at the same time, to create participatory administrative processes, empowering unions, industrial associations, and consumers to help shape government policy.

Most Progressives did not call themselves "socialists" but they were all "social"-ists, concerned, like their forebears, with reknitting the "democratic social fabric" that the democracy of opportunity and republican self-rule demanded. They contrasted the dogmatically individualistic liberal "legal" understanding of justice with a truer and deeper "social" understanding. When Progressives spoke of *social* justice, as opposed to *legal* justice, they meant a conception of fairness and right that looked beyond legal forms and legal equality to address the actualities of wealth and poverty, power and powerlessness in industrial America. This meant, among other things, a legislative overhaul of common-law rules of labor and employment and many other economic relations. Indeed, to a great extent it meant discarding common-law adjudication itself. The abstract categories of common-law contract and property rules were veils for the courts' class biases; they also failed to capture the particularities of social and economic life and the specific problems faced by concrete social groups. These required specialized agencies, rules, and regulations. Legal Progressives like Roscoe Pound and Charles Evan Hughes played the role of consummate elite reformers, tacking between the old classical legal liberalism and the new Progressive or "social" liberalism. They would end up making administration and bureaucracy, social science and social reform safe for the courts and the Constitution—and vice versa.[1]

As with the tools of government, Progressives were innovators with the tools of constitutional interpretation. Many brought a new style and sensibility to the interpretive enterprise: modernist, pragmatic, and antifoundational, newly alive to the constructed character of both legal and economic orders, determined to disenthrall Americans from worshipping the framers' Constitution. Progressives also aimed to get Americans to enact major formal changes in that document—and in several key cases they succeeded. Far from worship, they hoped to wean Americans from the original design.[2] The original design thwarted the kind of state-building and lawmaking the nation needed to hold on to the "Republican Form of Government" guaranteed by the Constitution. Built into the framers' design, argued Progressives of many stripes, were some glaringly archaic institutions. No matter their original justifications, some of which were bluntly antidemocratic, their present effect was to enable plutocrats and conservatives to head off essential new state-building and social and economic reform—and thereby defeat the Constitution's enduring principles of popular self-rule and democracy of opportunity. In sum, Progressives embraced critical, historicist approaches to the text, and there was a deep continuity between their approaches to constitutional interpretation and to structural constitutional reform.

This chapter begins by showing what was distinctive about the Progressive refashioning of the democracy-of-opportunity tradition: its confident view of the potential for democratic government to intervene in political economy, its more radical skepticism of the role of courts in constitutional interpretation, and its turn against racial liberalism. The middle sections of the chapter explore two of the central questions of constitutional political economy of this period: the Labor Question and the Trust Question. For ease of exposition, our discussion of the Trust Question in this chapter traces the whole arc of this domain of Populist and Progressive constitutional politics from the late nineteenth through the early twentieth century. Finally, the last section of the chapter turns to the constitutional promise of structural democratic reform. The Progressives unleashed an unusual burst of higher lawmaking through Article V, and a fusillade of constitutional reforms at the state level that aimed to overthrow the power of oligarchy and restore the constitutional promise, as they saw it, of rule by the people.

From Gilded Age Radicalism to "Progressive Democracy"

From our perspective, what most separated Progressives from Gilded Age radicals was the near death of racial liberalism among white reformers. Throughout the nation, white Progressives concurred, or at least acquiesced without protest, in the soured Tom Watson's conclusion: social reform for white Southerners depended on Black disenfranchisement and segregation. From the perspective of Southern Progressive history, "the great race settlement of 1890–1910 . . . was itself the seminal 'progressive' reform of the era."[3] The plausibility of this outlook on the national scene hinged on a revaluation of Reconstruction—a new constitutional narrative, which the new social science and historical professions helped to frame.

In this revaluation, Reconstruction became a wildly misguided and self-regarding experiment on the part of Northern reformers. A backward people, Blacks had "suffered much [but] . . . received more" under the civilizing "tutelage" of slavery. Reconstruction interrupted the civilizing process, duping the "race" with delusions of political grandeur beyond its reach. Former slaveholders had been obliged to "redeem" the South from governmental corruption and the madness of interracial equality. Disenfranchisement of a "backward race" was a grim but "necessary reform." Now the responsibility of Progressives was to "persuade the white masses" that benign segregation was "better than brutality."[4] The gradual uplift of the "Negro" in "separate and special" institutions would lead him toward "industrial efficiency" without injuring the betterment of white farmers and workers.[5] To this tidy tale, the Progressive historians added their "economic interpretation" of the Radical Republican project—not a grand redefinition of "We, the People" but a shrewd capitalist scheme to clinch national policymaking for Northern capital and open the South to Northern industrial development and exploitation.[6]

Thus debunked, Reconstruction could be set aside. As a professor of political science at turn-of-the-century Princeton University, Woodrow Wilson wrote in his widely used American history textbook that the Compromise of 1877, which led to the withdrawal of federal troops from active duty in the South, meant that the "supremacy of the white people was henceforth assured in the administration of the southern States," and the "Union was now restored . . . to normal conditions of government." With the "abandonment of federal interference with elections, the 'southern question' fortunately lost its prominence" in national politics, to be replaced by the great Progressive issues of the day: "[T]he reform of the civil service, the reduction of tariff duties, the control of corporations . . . and the purification of the ballot." Wilson would address these Progressive concerns in the White House, where, as the first Southern president since the Civil War, his administration brought Jim Crow to the capital and federal bureaucracy.[7]

A saving remnant of white Progressives were racial egalitarians. The Black founders of the NAACP—W. E. B. Du Bois, Alexander Walters, Ida Wells-Barnett—were joined by white socialists and Progressives like Florence Kelly, Jane Addams, and William Walling in the creation of the new organization in 1909, with the hope of forging a "new abolition movement" to fight the tide of mass disenfranchisement, lynching, segregation, and anti-Black race riots across the country. Writing about one such riot in Springfield, Illinois, Walling declared, "[T]he spirit of the abolitionists, of Lincoln and Lovejoy, must be revived and we must come to treat the negro on a plane of absolute political and social equality." It was a radical and lonely stand to resist the Progressive Era's prevailing schemes of social-evolutionary racism and instead call for enforcement of "the right of the Negro to the ballot on the same terms as other citizens."[8]

Many accounts identify a different gulf between Progressive Era reformers and their more inclusionary Gilded Age predecessors. They emphasize the Progressives' fondness for managerial and administrative solutions to social problems, and their role in recasting American "freedom" to mean abundance and security in the sphere of consumption, not dignity and independence in the sphere of production. The Progressives' vision of reform, the story goes, substituted a new consumerist welfare state for the old producerist commonwealth. And they traded the ideal of democracy for that of administration.[9]

There is truth to this picture, but it paints over important continuities. Many of the most modernizing, "advanced" Progressive thinkers remained deeply engaged with the old producerist constitutional political economy of property, work, and citizenship. Many also plunged into the creation of novel forms of democratic participation in the new administrative state—forging, for example, regulatory bureaus and commissions that lent governmental and bargaining power to workers' and small producers' organizations. As John Dewey put it, in a terse philosophical statement that found its way into Progressive handbooks of administrative practice, "The means have to be implemented by a social economic system . . . for the production of free human beings associating with one another on terms of equality."[10]

Or consider Herbert Croly, founding editor of the leading journal of Progressive opinion, the *New Republic,* and intellectual architect, along with Roosevelt himself, of Teddy Roosevelt's New Nationalism. "How," Croly repeatedly asked, "can the wage-earners obtain an amount or a degree of economic independence analogous to that upon which the pioneer democrat could count?" Social insurance and social legislation were necessary, but no substitute for transforming "the wage system itself . . . in the interest of an industrial self-governing democracy." This was essential, in Croly's account, to "convert[ing] civil and political liberty" under the old Constitution into their "socially desirable consummation" under a new economic order.[11]

Like the Gilded Age Populists and labor reformers, then, Croly was no simple welfare state liberal. He hewed to the democracy of opportunity's traditional republican emphasis on propertied "economic independence" as the material foundation and touchstone of full membership in the American polity. And like the Gilded Age radicals, he envisioned using "organization," "combination," and collective action to reinvent for industrial workers the kind of social and political authority and responsibility that individual ownership of productive property once conferred.

Croly, Roosevelt, and the other architects and spokespeople of "Progressive Democracy" also continued to press the Populists' lines of attack on judicial supremacy. Croly set out Progressive Democracy's case against judicial supremacy in the form of a constitutional narrative that synthesized the case for a popular democratic allocation of interpretive authority with the case for a democratic constitutional political economy. "[I]n the beginning," Croly's constitutional narrative began, "[t]he American democracy" could accept "an inaccessible body of [judge-made] Law" and the judiciary's "uncontrollable" sway over the political economy because "the Law promised property to all."[12] This was the Constitution's "original promise": economic opportunity and a republic of freeholders secured by limited government and equal rights to own and hold property made the Constitution a "working compromise" between the "pioneer democrat" and "the monarchy of the Law and an aristocracy of the robe."[13] In industrial America, however, the ideals of liberty and equality that were "wrought into our constitutions" could no longer "consist in the specific formulation of legal and economic individualism" defended by the courts.[14] In industrial America, these Lochnerian judicial renderings of liberty and equality left American workers "exposed to exploitation" and "economically disfranchised."[15]

Thus, interpreting and safeguarding these constitutional ideals could no longer be left to the "benevolent monarchy" of the courts. Instead, it belonged to the branches of government that made and administered the law, watched over by—and also directly involving groups and organizations of—an active citizenry. This was important for reasons of popular sovereignty, but also for practical reasons: In industrial America, securing the old liberties required data gathering, complex and necessarily fallible choices, and expert policymaking.[16]

For both Croly and Dewey, the ultimate argument for this more participatory and democratic form of constitutional politics and self-government was "educational." The American people were ready, argued Croly, for an "increase in popular political responsibility."[17] We did not need "an aristocracy of lawyers" or an "aristocracy of the robe" to apply basic constitutional principles to our "fundamental political problems."[18] Echoing such Progressive debunkers as Charles Beard, Croly made no bones about the framers' elitism: They "were not seeking to establish a system of popular political education." But the "monarchy of the Constitution" had proved "educational in spite of itself."[19] By now, broader literacy, participation in party politics and local government, and habits of "orderly procedure . . . wrought into the American national consciousness" over generations had produced an "increasing political maturity."[20] Now it was time for the citizenry to assume more of the "duty of thinking over their political system," up to and including questions of constitutional principle.[21] "[A] Progressive Democracy had to reject the finality of [the] specific formulations" of "states rights" and "individual rights" offered up by the courts.[22] The public had to stop investing those "formulations" with an undeserved "sacredness."[23]

To implement this more "active," "experimental," participatory form of constitutional interpretation, Croly argued for converting our "semi-democratic constitutionalism" into genuine "constitutional democracy."[24] Like the Populists, he and most other Progressive leaders believed that conversion required structural changes, some of which would need federal Article V amendments. Croly commended amendments to make the amendment process easier, and amendments either abolishing judicial review or subjecting individual judicial rulings to popular review and recall.[25]

For his part, Teddy Roosevelt put radical constitutional change and "the Right of the People to Rule" at the center of his 1912 run for the White House. The Progressive Party was born of Roosevelt's ambitions to return to power, along with the aspirations of a great range of Progressive reformers—insurgent Republicans; disaffected Democrats; crusading journalists, academics, social workers, and others—who saw in the new party a way to advance an ambitious Progressive vision of the democracy of opportunity. Like the Populists before them, the new party also aimed to transform the party system, reorienting it into one pitting progressives against conservatives.[26] The Progressive Party platform was a radical one. It called for national social insurance, national regulation of industry and labor relations, a national corporation law, "pure democracy"—meaning what we would call "direct democracy," specifically the initiative, referendum, and recall—and other dramatic constitutional changes.[27] Its aim was to make "the people . . . the masters of their Constitution"; to build a national government adequate to secure "equal opportunity," "industrial justice," and economic democracy; and to end "the tyranny of plutocracy."[28]

More than his friend Croly, Roosevelt was steeped in American political and constitutional thought; he understood the traditions from which he was departing. From the moment he threw his hat in the ring in the 1912 race, first as a candidate for the Republican nomination, it was clear that Roosevelt's vision of social and constitutional reform would require a new brand of constitutionalism outside the courts—and outside the political branches as well. Invoking the Lincoln of the Douglas debates and the first inaugural address, Roosevelt defended the view that the judiciary should not enjoy the final word on "vital questions" of policy and constitutional principle.[29] But Lincoln's brand of departmentalism assumed that although the people were the ultimate authority, their role was mediated: conflicts over constitutional meaning would take place among the branches of the federal government, among elected officials and party leaders. For Roosevelt and his Progressive followers, this inherited constitutional order was sliding into an oligarchy of entrenched "corporations" and "bosses."[30] The solution would involve an array of institutional, constitutional, and political changes to "make popular feeling effective" in interpreting constitutional commitments and deciding constitutional conflicts. Direct primaries were essential: they would enable the people to bypass "the vulgar thieving partnerships of the corporations and the bosses" and elect candidates who were not chosen by this "corrupt partnership."[31] But what about the courts?

Here Roosevelt made a radical and arresting case. High courts like those in his own state of New York were staffed by "honest but wrong-headed judges" irremediably in thrall to the outlook of their own "separate class."[32] The "American people," he declared, "have shown themselves wiser than the courts in the way they have approached and dealt with such vital questions" as "the proper control of big corporations and of securing their rights to industrial workers."[33] "[T]he American people are fit for complete self-government," argued Roosevelt, and so, they must be able not only to amend but also "to apply and interpret the Constitution."[34] They must be "the masters and not the servants of even the highest court in the land"; they must be the "final interpreters of the Constitution."[35]

"I do not say the people are infallible," Roosevelt declared to an Ohio convention considering constitutional reforms, but they are "more often sound in their decisions than is the case with any of the governmental bodies to whom, for their convenience, they have delegated portions of their power."[36] So, the people ought to have "the real, and not merely the nominal, ultimate decision on questions of constitutional law."[37]

Thus, Roosevelt counseled the Ohio convention, high court decisions ought to be subject to review by the people through referendum. A progressive constitution must "permit the people themselves by popular vote, after due deliberation and discussion, but finally and without appeal, to settle what the proper construction of any Constitutional point is."[38] The idea of popular "recall" of judicial decisions was a moderate alternative to judicial recall, which Roosevelt largely abjured,[39] and to abolishing judicial review, which he also opposed. But of all the innovations in "the machinery of government" that Roosevelt championed, the "recall of judicial decisions" proved most controversial. His bold statement of the people's interpretive authority hobbled Roosevelt's chance of securing the Republican nomination. By attacking the courts, Roosevelt alienated the conservative wing of his party, and they abandoned the former president.

Progressives' democratic faith in the people as constitutional arbiters may have been easier to come by because the imagined field of action was political economy—not civil liberties, about which most leading Progressives were largely indifferent until World War I, and not race relations, about which most white Progressives nursed a callous and bigoted notion of evolutionary "progress."[40] Perhaps, as pragmatists, many of them would not have been surprised to learn that later generations would see them as having articulated a partial and time-bound view of the people's authority over constitutional interpretation. But in any case, for us to understand their views, the essential starting point is to understand that when they imagined the people taking control of constitutional decision-making, they imagined that the subject of this decision-making was constitutional political economy.

Louis Brandeis, like most leading legal Progressives, had no use for Croly's and Roosevelt's attacks on the institution of judicial review. Brandeis was a stern critic of the laissez-faire Constitution and classical legal liberalism, first as a crusading public-interest lawyer and later as a Supreme Court Justice. But his critique demanded an enlightened rather than a marginalized constitutional judiciary, one that would enforce tempered norms of federalism and separation of powers; civil liberties; and the rights of racial and religious minorities, rather than the rights of employers and capitalists. He imagined a judiciary capable of infusing constitutional law, and common law, with Progressive respect for the policy-making capacities of legislatures and administrators—and Progressive insights about the social meaning of constitutional liberty and equality and the social nature of contract and property.

All this is familiar ground, evident in Brandeis's judicial opinions. What we have forgotten is Brandeis's legislative constitutionalism—the arguments he made about the affirmative constitutional duties of lawmakers and government generally. For Brandeis, no less than Croly or the labor and agrarian radicals, the nation's industrial and economic orders were fraught with constitutional infirmities that only legislation could remedy.

The key object of law and government, Brandeis held in good republican fashion, was sustaining a politically and economically independent citizenry. The Constitution must safeguard not only a framework of government, but also the project of fitting citizens for "their task" of self-rule.[41] Thus, Brandeis insisted, there must be an end to the use of common-law rules and entitlements to define the substantive content of constitutional guarantees. Instead, in a widely published 1915 address, the year before he was appointed to the Court, Brandeis insisted we must interpret "those rights which our Constitution guarantees—the rights to life, liberty and the pursuit of happiness" in terms of the social and economic conditions for their meaningful exercise in modern America. All Americans "must have a reasonable income" and regular employment; "they must have health and leisure," decent "working conditions," and "some system of social insurance." However, the "essentials of American citizenship are not satisfied by supplying merely the material needs . . . of the worker."[42] There could be no more "political democracy" in contemporary America, Brandeis told the U.S. Industrial Commission that same year, without "industrial democracy," without workers' "participating in the decision[s]" of their firms as to "how the business shall be run."[43] Only by bringing democracy into industry could the United States produce not only goods but citizens.

For Brandeis and other Progressives, "industrial democracy" was a modern route to recovering for industrial workers the citizenly, character-forming qualities that ownership of productive property was thought to impart in the old Jeffersonian and Free Labor traditions: not only a measure of material security and independence, but some share of authority and responsibility in one's workaday life. Gilded Age radicals and later, Eugene Debs's Socialist Party, aimed to restore all this through their vision of a Co-operative Commonwealth. But like the Socialists and every seasoned Progressive reformer in the sphere of labor and industrial relations, Brandeis knew the empowerment of workers would not arrive as a gift from employers. It had to be won by strong unions.

Long a business attorney, Brandeis often had clashed with unions, but he also participated in constructing, in the New York garment trades, one of the era's few successful experiments in industrial democracy— large-scale collective bargaining and standard-setting across firms, and broad participation of ordinary workers in union and industry affairs. The experiments were rare, because the legal order did not recognize— indeed, it flatly denied and suppressed—the collective freedoms on which such industry-wide organizing and bargaining clout depended. It worked in the garment trade chiefly because garment-making was so rife with tiny shops that capital *needed* labor to rationalize the industry and put a floor under cost-cutting competition.[44] But everywhere that unions strove to set decent standards and institute union participation in running the shop, they collided with judge-made law. This set even the

AFL, which disclaimed "reform by legislation," on course for a constitutional confrontation with the courts over the right to strike and
organize.

The Labor Question

So, the Progressive Era saw the pursuit of labor reform along two different routes, and both flouted the rules of the classical liberal legal order.
A growing movement of middle-class reformers along with the sizable
socialist contingent of trade unions, outside the AFL mainstream, pressed
for legislation requiring employers to provide workers—particularly, the
great mass of "unskilled," "new immigrant" factory workers abandoned by the AFL—not only safe workplaces but "reasonable incomes,"
"leisure" (via shorter hours), and "some system of social insurance," as
Brandeis put it. At the same time, an even more threatening movement by
all manner of trade unions pushed to enact—via direct action, on the
ground—the collective freedoms they insisted the Constitution afforded
them, to organize, strike, boycott, and bargain collectively on a far
broader basis than the law allowed.

The two movements embodied the same "'coercion' . . . by the mere
force of numbers" that so aroused Justice David Brewer in the 1890s. In
the 1900s, the Supreme Court would "magnify [its] office" once more in
an effort to undo workers' growing clout in the market and the polity.[45]
The Court authorized a massive expansion of "government by injunction" beyond the railroads, across the whole industrial landscape. It also
took a leaf from state high courts and fashioned a federal liberty-of-
contract jurisprudence to police legislative interventions in the wage
contract.

Thus, by 1910, Lochnerism was in full bloom. It is no coincidence that
the case that gave its name to this era of Supreme Court activism was
a case about labor legislation, nor that so many of the key cases of the
New Deal's later "constitutional revolution"—*Schechter Poultry Corp. v.
United States, Morehead v. New York, West Coast Hotel Co. v. Parrish,
NLRB v. Jones & Laughlin Steel*—would also involve labor regulation.[46]
The common-law ordering of labor-capital relations, invested with the

permanence of fundamental law, was the central battleground for the Progressive Era's struggle over constitutional political economy.

"Those Who Would Unlaw the Land"

Lochnerism is remembered for condemning labor legislation—and fair enough. But in fact, the *Lochner*-era courts were far more ferocious in attacking class-based collective action on the ground. They issued thousands of antistrike and antiboycott decrees, meted out thousands of arrests and hundreds of jail terms, called forth and sanctioned untold state violence, and generally did their utmost to repress, demean, and demoralize workers' capacities for broad-based mutual aid.[47] Moreover, they encased the judge-made common-law and equity rules that comprised this repressive labor policy in a hard constitutional shell. By 1930, federal and state courts had struck down or gutted some forty-odd legislative efforts at revising this repressive policy, by reading the court-minted rules into the Constitution along lines rehearsed in *Debs*.[48]

This great expansion of judicial regulation of labor began in the 1890s with the proliferation of the citywide boycotts we glimpsed in Chapter 4. Just as judges were beginning to condemn railway boycotts in the late 1880s, boycotts of "unfair" goods and shops began to grow and flourish in the industrial cities. These citywide boycotts were a rich illustration of what twentieth-century treatise writers would soon be calling "secondary" labor actions. If a city labor federation called a boycott against a brewer who persistently hired "unfair" men or spurned union work rules, the federation would do more than proclaim his beer "unfair"—representatives would visit saloons and call on them to cease serving his beer or face boycotts themselves.[49]

Such labor activity provoked courts' anxiety and rage partly because it mobilized whole working-class populations. "Their action," as one court remarked, "in the language of the times, was purely sympathetic," resting on the notion of a moral circulation of goods and money ("Keep the money of fair men moving only among fair men," read a typical circular), a world of exchange relations under the rules and norms of working-class organizations like New York's Central Labor Assembly.[50] Courts found "class legislation" constitutionally intolerable when it emanated from state legislatures. No wonder they assailed efforts to enforce what workers called union "laws" and "legislation," when the "laws" and their enforcement sprang from rival, nongovernmental centers of authority like unions, labor assemblies, and trade councils.[51] A corporate employer could promulgate work rules, but a union of workers could not!

Boycotts were thus seen and felt as proto-political challenges to official authority; they were waged with a rhetoric not merely of "fair wages" but of "redeeming the republic" from the grasp of "money power judges."[52] One typical trial judge dubbed boycotting a "socialistic crime."[53] Another declared, "[I]f [boycotts] can be perpetuated with impunity, . . . there will be the end of government."[54] In this mood, courts resolved doctrinal dilemmas, loosened inherited restraints, and extended the labor injunction beyond the railways.[55] Judges began meting out hundreds of harsh terms in state penitentiaries to enforce their new antiboycott decrees. As with the sympathy strike, the demise of the city-wide boycott was brought on by legal repression.[56]

By the mid-1890s, another, less street-centered and less "disorderly" form of boycotting had emerged. This more far-flung boycott relied on publicizing "unfair" products through labor newspapers and organizers dispatched to speak at other cities' and states' labor assemblies. The new weapon proved well suited to pressuring the growing number of employers producing for regional or national, not local, markets. Knights of Labor and AFL journals carried "We Don't Patronize" lists announcing boycotted products.[57] They also created centralized "Boycott Committees" to ensure that unions across the country received notice of boycotts in different locales.[58] The 1890s and early 1900s were punctuated by a series of highly successful national boycott campaigns waged by national craft unions, winning strategic concessions from large, obdurate manufacturers and generating broad-based coalitions among once-parochial workers and unions.[59]

These startling successes on labor's part spawned the self-organization of capitalists. The early 1900s saw the creation of dozens of industrial employers' associations, including the aptly named American Anti-Boycott Association (AABA) and the still-thriving National Association of Manufacturers (NAM). These well-heeled outfits set out to vanquish such boycotts and other sympathetic actions, chiefly through new law firms and law departments specializing in antistrike and antiboycott litigation. Students of "cause lawyering" have taught us that new rights do not get brought down to earth, elaborated, and enforced unless social movements develop a "litigation infrastructure" to set the courts in motion.[60] The antiboycott and "open shop" movement of the Progressive Era was a social movement of capital, which crafted, sought, and won from a sympathetic judiciary the rich elaboration of employers' rights against organized labor. Scores of hitherto allowable or tolerated forms and goals of collective action fell under judicial ban.

Since the newly mobilized employers were producing goods for interstate markets, attorneys for boycotted companies naturally turned to the Sherman Act—which prohibits "every contract, combination . . . , or conspiracy, in restraint of trade or commerce among the several States"— as the government and railroads had done with such success against railroad workers in the 1890s.[61] Antiboycott injunctions under the antitrust law proliferated. The AFL press reported on them in painstaking detail, accompanied by editorials, speeches, pamphlets, poems, and songs proclaiming the labor movement's determination to carry on with boycotts of "unfair" employers and to flout the decrees—which typically enjoined precisely all such publications and speechifying. For the first half dozen years or so of NAM's "open shop" campaign, the AFL policy was open defiance, in the name of labor solidarity and the First Amendment. Antitrust was aimed at capital, but it was hitting labor. The "We Don't Patronize" lists kept on appearing.[62]

One firm on the list belonged to NAM's first president, James Van Cleave: the Buck's Stove and Range Company, a large manufacturer, locked in battle with the metal polishers' union. In 1907, Van Cleave and his NAM attorneys won a sweeping Sherman Act injunction against Samuel Gompers and other national and local union officials in the Supreme Court of the District of Columbia, prohibiting defendants from continuing to publish the company's name on the AFL "Unfair List" or otherwise continuing to promote the boycott of Buck's Stove. Gompers and other AFL leaders embarked on a whirlwind tour, decrying NAM generally and the treatment of workers in Van Cleave's plant, in particular; reminding workers around the country no one could force them to buy a Buck's stove; and proclaiming that labor's freedom and the freedom of speech and press would long outlive Van Cleave, the District of Columbia trial judge, and the reign of labor injunctions.[63]

The trial judge in D.C. conducted contempt hearings in December 1908. He was in a lather over Gompers's and his comrades' widely reported and reprinted speeches, editorials, and publications, and he erupted with all the gathering fury of a judiciary faced with open, or as he put it, "utter, rampant, insolent defiance" of judicial orders. With the AFL's three most well-known national leaders before him—eminently stolid and respectable men, as many Americans saw things—Judge Daniel Wright declared that the case at hand confronted society with a choice between "the supremacy of law over the rabble or its prostration under the feet of the disordered throng." The case confirmed that what was afoot was "a studied, determined ... conflict ... in the light of open day, between the decrees of a tribunal ordained by the Government of the Federal Union and of the tribunals of another federation grown up in the land." Between the two, "one or the other must succumb." Sentencing Gompers to twelve months and the others to six months in prison, Judge Wright concluded, chillingly: "Those who would unlaw the land are public enemies."[64]

At the height of the Progressive Era, this unbridled wrath was too much for a broad reformist branch of the nation's political elites, especially in view of the still-unrequited public longing to see the Sherman Act finally enforced against "a Rockefeller, . . . a Harriman, or an Armour," as opposed to "a labor leader."[65] President Teddy Roosevelt was "besieged with telegrams of protest and . . . requests that he exercise at once his prerogative of pardon." William Jennings Bryan "telegraphed the sentenced men that they 'did right in testing the law.'"[66] Gompers and the others were released on bail, while the case was appealed to the Supreme Court. Dryly noting that Van Cleave was president of Buck's Stove and also president of NAM, the Court overturned the criminal contempt convictions on technical grounds but unanimously rejected defendants' First Amendment arguments and upheld the propositions that such boycotts ran afoul of the Sherman Act, and that unions and their leaders were liable to the panoply of injunctions and treble damages under the act.[67]

INDUSTRIAL DEMOCRACY IN THE SHADOW OF HOSTILE COURTS

Gompers and other labor leaders continued for a time their principled disobedience of judicial bans on publicizing boycotts in speech and print. But Unfair Lists gradually disappeared from union journals.[68] Alongside sympathy strikes, boycotts lost their prominent place in the labor movement's arsenal and common culture, and judicial suppression of these weapons loomed large in labor's broader strategic deliberations.

"Gatling-gun injunctions" jumped the rails and spread out to cover more and more big strikes and organizing campaigns in the mine fields and factory towns, generalizing Justice Brewer's lesson in *Debs*: broad, inclusive strikes would run up against violent state opposition, and state force would arrive with high legal sanction. Both federal and state courts were making plain that the law was implacably opposed to inclusive industrial unionism and the kinds of aggressive, industry-, community-, and class-based tactics it entailed. Applying both antitrust and old common-law limits on collective action to emergent forms of industrial organization and protest, the courts helped instill the view among skilled workers that inclusive, class-based unionism and the organizing tactics it entailed were too costly. Such tactics invited brutal repression, sponsored and validated by the nation's high courts.[69]

Gompers and the AFL's dominant bloc of strong craft unions drew up their conclusions. Broad unionism and broad reform politics alike assumed a minimally tolerant and tractable state. But the American state of courts and parties was enemy territory.[70] Even when labor won, it lost. Not only were labor- and populist-inspired reforms struck down or nullified by interpretation, they were turned violently against labor. Experiences with injunctions grounded on the Interstate Commerce and Sherman Acts, as most federal decrees were, gave rise to a voluntarist parable. In their youths, trade unionists would say, they had agitated for legislation against the trusts and monopolies, and they had prevailed— only to have the Sherman Act invoked most successfully against unions.. Like the Interstate Commerce Act, the Sherman Act "simply resulted in the arrest and indictment of union workmen"; it supplied a modern warrant for calling workers' "effort[s] to protect their common interests action[s] . . . in restraint of trade." Laws intended to protect the nation's "toilers" proved "instead the incubators of our modern injunction and trial without jury."[71]

The proponents of protective legislation like hours laws frequently encountered this injunction-inspired parable about the treacherous court-dominated state. One close observer of AFL politics remarked: "Year after year the Federation . . . has gone on record as vehemently opposed to the eight-hour day by legislative enactment and in favor of direct action as the exclusive means of securing the shorter work day."[72] Each year, the progressive "minority led by the Socialist delegates" strove to reverse the "traditional policy of the Federation."[73] And each year, they encountered Gompers's objection. "Legislative enactments, he has always contended, means the subjection of organized labor to the courts. And subjection to the courts, he has always held, means subjection to tyranny. Upon this contention he has repeatedly staked his leadership in the American Federation of Labor."[74] In the shadow of so many broken big strikes and bootless broad initiatives, many thought it wise to conserve and build on what "worked"—minimalist politics, craft unionism, high dues, and restrained but well-calculated strike policies.[75]

Of course, not everyone in the labor movement drew the same lessons. A substantial minority of AFL trade unionists remained attached to the old Knights of Labor vision of a broad, inclusive movement. The Pullman injunction and 1890s courts converted Eugene Debs to socialism, and many followed him into the American Socialist Party, which Debs led for decades to come, carrying the banner of the Co-operative Commonwealth into the twentieth century.[76] Along with the large Socialist contingent, there were many state-level leaders in the Progressive camp in the early twentieth-century House of Labor; they continued down the political road Gompers spurned, pursuing broad labor legislation and social insurance in state legislatures. But the dominant national craft union leaders followed Gompers's more austere line of "pure and simple" craft-based unionism.[77]

In the aftermath of the bitter defeats suffered by working-class and agrarian radicalism in the 1890s, a great many native-born white working people retreated into more insular cultures and narrower and more defensive group identities and interests. The mainstream of the early twentieth-century labor movement was shot through with the same currents of racism that ran through middle-class Progressive politics. When Southern Redeemers destroyed the citizenship rights of Black toilers, white trade unionists did not protest. Indeed, many unions enacted formal color bars, and during the 1900s most native-born white trade unionists supported immigration restrictions, against the "cheap," "servile," "unassimilable" southern Europeans as well as the Chinese. Along gender lines as well, native-born skilled white workingmen abandoned the broader, more inclusive understanding of who belonged to the community of citizen-workers, which had characterized organized labor two decades earlier.[78] In rough tandem, the national AFL's political goals under Gompers grew narrow and sharply drawn: not positive regulation, but repeal of the judge-made restraints on collective action and an end to immigration.

But let us be clear. "Pure and simple unionism" was no rejection of constitutional politics or constitutional political economy. Adopting a more disciplined and restrained strike policy in the 1900s did not free AFL unions from the courts. The unions continued to depend on tactics the courts condemned, including refusals to haul or work on unfair goods, strikes over workers' control and workplace authority, closed shop strikes, organizing strikes, and all manner of picketing. So, even though the AFL drew back from broader class-based collective action, the courts grew ever more deeply involved in policing everyday industrial strife. In turn, Gompers and other union leaders and activists at every level of the labor movement immersed themselves in common-law doctrine, equity jurisprudence, and constitutional law.[79] For over three decades, they built a constitutional case against "government by injunction" and for "industrial democracy" in countless articles and pamphlets, speeches, and congressional and state legislative hearings and commissions.

No politician could ignore organized labor's constitutional outlook because labor not only made repeal of "government by injunction" its chief political demand but also carried on with a decades-long campaign of civil disobedience, organized around an articulate defiance of judicial authority and judge-made law. Defiance of antistrike and antiboycott injunctions became official AFL policy. Cast by the courts into a state of semi-outlawry, respectable trade unionists endured thousands of arrests and hundreds of prison terms, casualties, and deaths in the name of organized workers' rival understanding of the constitutional order. With each decade, more and more reform-minded lawmakers came to embrace some variation of labor's constitutional political economy of "industrial democracy" and shared workplace authority— early twentieth-century labor's distinctive contribution to the democracy-of-opportunity tradition.[80]

Eventually, in the 1930s, as we shall see, mass strikes and mass defiance of judicial decrees in auto, steel, rubber, and other core industries deprived "government by injunction" of its last shreds of legitimacy, enabling New Dealers in Congress to enact a fairly robust version of "industrial democracy" into law. The New Deal statutes would safeguard union organizing and workers' "concerted action" as "fundamental rights" against both state suppression and employer reprisal. Even the Supreme Court, which frequently had struck down just such legislative measures, would fleetingly adopt the opposite notion: that these safeguards were not merely allowable, but actually constitutional essentials, grounded in the democratic constitutional political economy labor had forged over the previous decades.[81] Today, the fundamental rights to organize and strike have become toothless paper tigers, and organized labor is near its nadir. Rebuilding a democracy of opportunity will involve reinvigorating both. This makes it especially worth recalling the arguments that framed this constitutional drama.

"We Are Not without Our Sacred Precedents"

What these workers and reformers were up against cannot be fairly described as constitutional laissez-faire. The courts were not merely protecting the freedom of contract and the rights of property from interference by legislative majorities, they also were refurbishing and building up a distinctive common law of employment marked by hierarchy and subordination, by illiberal fixed status as much as liberal free contract. While the United States developed into a burgeoning industrial nation, employment law remained lodged in the master's household. It could be found in legal treatises on "domestic relations." Courts mingled free-contract principles with the older doctrines of master and servant. The common law of employment, treatise writers freely conceded, bore the "marks of social caste." The common law "presupposes two parties who stand on an unequal footing in their mutual dealings." "This relation" admittedly is "hostile to the genius of free institutions."[82]

The master's relation to his servant was one of governance, discipline, and control. To judges, the necessity of governing the industrial workplace, of disciplining an unruly workforce—often recently arrived from rural settings overseas—and of subduing a trade-union movement intent on challenging employers' authority all made the old common law of master and servant resonate with modern times. So courts continued to recognize an employer's property interests in his employees' or servants' labor, his right to their loyalty and obedience, and his right to enjoin and unleash state violence against their organizing efforts.[83]

"The relation of employer and employee," the Supreme Court could still proclaim as late as 1936,[84] is "one of the domestic relations." Master-servant law proved alive and well in the coal fields, garment trades, and elsewhere, as the Court upheld the use of centuries-old anti-enticement doctrines to underpin injunctions against organizing efforts as infringements on the employers' right to the nonunion status of their workers. In *Hitchman Coal* (1917), the Court saw in the union organizers' efforts to enlist the miners a new incarnation of an ancient wrong: enticing away a rival's servants. Justice Mahlon Pitney, the redoubtable old equity lawyer, wrote for the Court that "any court of equity would grant an injunction to restrain this as unfair competition."[85] By upholding the equity device in this context, *Hitchman* helped legitimate the savagery with which the mine operators policed their company towns.[86]

The peculiarities of equity jurisprudence also prompted the late nineteenth-century and early twentieth-century courts to wed the ancient idea of the master's property in his servant's labor to a new conception of property as anything with "pecuniary value." Since equity could not issue decrees except to protect property interests, and property here was still defined in old-fashioned terms as real and tangible things, the courts issuing antistrike decrees often had to expand the definition of a "property right" to include the value to the business of the uninterrupted flow of employees through the factory gates.[87] In response, trade unionists were drawn to the Thirteenth Amendment and the "fundamental principle of American law . . . that there shall be no property rights in man."[88]

Forbidding "whomsoever" from doing "whatsoever" in support of a proscribed strike, including quitting or threatening to quit in concert, or encouraging others to do so, the labor injunction seemed to trench on the Thirteenth Amendment. In a case applying the Sherman Act to forbid a quarry workers' strike, Justice Brandeis wrote in a memorable dissent: "If, on the undisputed facts of this case, refusal to work can be enjoined, Congress created by the Sherman Law . . . an instrument for imposing restraints upon labor which reminds of involuntary servitude."[89] Labor spokesmen attacked the "feudal" or "slavish" tenor of the doctrine that employers had a property right in their contracts with workers or in the expectation that their workers would return each day to toil in the employers' plants. They attacked the antistrike decree itself as an indirect way of enslaving strikers, a judicial effort "virtually to re-enact slavery."[90]

When two organizers of streetcar workers were jailed for speaking in defiance of a federal injunction, and strikers' morale ebbed in the face of the judge's warning that they were all knocking on the penitentiary's door, John Frey of the Machinists reminded them:

> We are not without our sacred precedents. When judicial decisions held that the colored man was a chattel to be bought and sold . . . when he was looked upon as an article of commerce and a commodity, it was the clergymen of this state who organized the underground railway. It was the clergymen and their congregations . . . who defied the decision of the United States Supreme Court and held that every human being was free and that they would do all in their power to avoid and evade the decisions of the highest judicial tribunal.[91]

So, in addition to the workers' constitutional right to "come and go at will," antislavery constitutionalism supplied the AFL with precedent for other claims: that official legality could be counterfeit, that it could be opposed by a truer understanding of the law, and that such an understanding could sanction disobedience. Thus, workers claimed constitutional rights to speak and publish, to assemble and "consult freely" with one another, to unite peaceably, and to determine jointly to "withhold their labor"—rights under the First, Thirteenth, and Fourteenth Amendments and the Guarantee Clause that the courts spurned and their definition of "property" swallowed up. And labor and its allies attacked the courts' master-servant conception of employers' authority over workers—the view that industrial property conferred the kind of sovereignty over workers that entitled capital to command, and to prohibit organizing—as an illiberal, antirepublican doctrine, a species of "modern feudalism." To the contrary, they argued that the constitutional order demanded a wide berth for activity such as organizing, and the collective bargaining and joint workplace governance it fostered. Echoing Brandeis's maxim that there can be no more "political democracy" in contemporary America without "industrial democracy," organized labor argued that "[p]olitical equality is not sufficient": Without "industrial equality that places [the worker] upon a par with his employer there can never exist that freedom and liberty of action which is necessary to the maintenance of a republican form of government."[92]

During the early twentieth century, this idea—that there can be no republican form of government, no constitutional democracy without "industrial democracy," no "political equality" without "industrial equality"—emerged as the widely shared constitutional outlook of Progressive reformers and trade unionists. Here was where core features of the modern democracy of opportunity—what FDR would come to call the modern "economic constitutional" meaning of citizenship, along with modern ideas about opportunity and the middle class—were forged.

The old idea, which had animated Free Labor republicanism and much of the antebellum democracy-of-opportunity tradition, was this: Ownership of productive property—whether in the form of land or the tools of a trade and a place to ply it—was the material basis of middle-classness and of full membership in the political community. Only someone who owned such property, and enjoyed the economic independence that was thought to accompany it, had the minimum social measure of dignity and freedom from domination, as well as the material circumstances to develop his capacities for judgment and deliberation sufficiently to participate in civic life. Within this framework, to be a "hireling" or a "servant" was, as Lincoln saw it, and nineteenth-century treatise writers confirmed, to be in a dependent, subordinate, caste-like position incompatible with republican citizenship. If that was to be the permanent lot of the nation's industrial wage earners, it spelled constitutional trouble for the individual citizen-worker and for the republic writ large, which required a broad middle class as an essential bulwark against oligarchy.[93]

That was the *old* idea. The new insight generated by the trade unionists and social reformers who marched under the "industrial democracy" banner in this period was this. It is true that middle-classness and full membership in the political community depend on material independence—freedom from domination—and a measure of dignity, authority, control, and security in one's economic circumstances. But you do not have to be a member of the old propertied middle class to obtain these citizenly goods. They need not come from individual ownership of productive property. Instead, the question of who can obtain these citizenly goods turns on how we order social and economic life—how we structure our political economy.

The rise of large-scale industry and employment relations had upended the old propertied, self-employed household farm or workshop. And good riddance, from the point of view of the women and poor laborers, disproportionately poor laborers of color, who had never enjoyed civic membership in that world of the small producer's household and the old middle class. A decent, stable livelihood, some leisure for self-improvement, civic life, some control and authority over one's work life—all these were social resources. None was naturally restricted to any single class. Indeed, just what it meant to belong to the laboring or the owning class in an age of "combination"—in terms of authority and clout at work, or in terms of the division of the fruits of industry—depended on the legal architecture of "property" and "contract" and "employment," and on what constitutional political economy the nation embraced.

Trade unionists and champions of labor law reform boasted that by overcoming grave inequalities of bargaining power—by providing the individual worker with real opportunities for "actual liberty of contract" and "full freedom of association"[94]—unions and collective bargaining would overcome the contradiction between "political democracy" and "industrial tyranny." They aimed to bring all the expectations of living under the Constitution—the freedom to associate and voice grievances, deliberate over common concerns, share authority, choose representatives, and be heard before suffering loss—into industrial life. By combining labor law reform—repealing the old judge-made law of industrial and employment relations—with minimum wages and maximum hours laws, safety standards, and social insurance, the unionists and social reformers aimed to transform industrial wage slaves into middle-class citizens.

There is some historical truth, in other words, to the bumper sticker slogan that unions brought you the modern middle class. This is not simply a story about economic distribution; it is that, but it is also a story about a revision of the American idea of middle-classness itself. The seeds of these changes were planted by labor's advocates and allies a century ago, but it was not until the New Deal and World War II that they dramatically reshaped our political economy.

The Trust Question

The change that most set in motion the whole story of this chapter and Chapter 4 was one of corporate growth and consolidation. Everyone, from the political parties to organized labor to the Justices of the Supreme Court, had to react to this change and recalibrate their views of political economy in response. It is difficult to overstate just how hotly contested the legitimacy of the big corporation was from the 1870s until World War I.

In this period, giant corporations were arrogating to themselves the tools of industry, transportation, communication, and finance. They seemed to threaten basic rights and the constitutional order—and it was not only the Populists who thought this, but most bands of the political spectrum. Remedies varied enormously. But radical, reform-minded, mainstream, and conservative analysts agreed that "the modern corporation and association of incorporations called trusts" put both republican self-rule and equal opportunity in peril.[95] In one conservative jurist's words, the new "giant combinations" of capital were driving "the small tradesman, manufacturer and artisan . . . to the wall," undermining the proprietary, competitive capitalist order on which, in his eyes, the constitutional pledge of "equal rights" hinged.[96]

But what was to be done about it? At stake was government's relationship with the new leviathans. Would the emerging holding companies, trusts, and giant new corporations be curbed and dismantled to preserve a more decentralized economic order? Would old doctrines be renewed, or new ones invented, to cast large corporations as creatures of the state—either as state-owned enterprises or as public utilities subject to extensive government regulation and control? Or would the corporations be "naturalized" and treated as though they were rights-bearing private entities or "persons," constitutionally protected against undue state interference?

Social movements took shape and politicians took stands on all sides of these questions. The Populists, as we have seen, hoped to reinvigorate a decentralized, regionally based economy of smaller-scale agriculture and cooperatively owned marketing and manufacturing units—all buttressed by vigorous new uses of national power to make public much of the private banking and railroad systems and other elements of the infrastructure of modern commerce currently in private corporate hands. Only that radical solution to the Trust Question was consistent with a faithful reading of the Constitution, by Populist lights, and only that radical remedy could restore the old democracy of opportunity's promise of equal rights and opportunities for the nation's farmers. The Gilded Age's largest labor organization, the Knights of Labor, shared the agrarian Populists' vision of a Co-operative Commonwealth. They too held that private ownership of large units of capital employing wage labor was an unconstitutional state of affairs.

A generation later, nationalizing Progressives like Teddy Roosevelt and Herbert Croly accepted the "inevitability" of big corporations across the industrial landscape—but emphatically not the inevitability of the big corporations' threat to democratic rule, or the seizure of the nation's economic policy by Wall Street and the trusts. They were central-state builders and aimed to create a broad-gauged national administrative agency, a powerful bureau of corporations that would put corporate organization and capitalization under ongoing national regulation and supervision.[97] The "trusts," said Roosevelt, "are the creatures of the State, and the State not only has the right to control them, but is in duty bound to control them."[98] Finally, the new corporate elite itself formed a social movement from above, which sought to legitimate the new giant corporations and keep their governance in *private* hands, guided by corporate lawyers and overseen by courts and friendly, court-like commissions.[99]

When the dust settled, neither the Populists' nor the state-building Progressives' solution to the Trust Question had prevailed. Instead, federal antitrust law stood as the nation's chief legislative response to the dawn of the giant corporation. Antitrust was more conservative, by far, than rival reforms, both in its reach (policing the predatory and monopolistic abuses of big capital, but not dismantling, nationalizing, or heavily regulating it) and in its institutional shape (based in the federal judiciary, with its deeply—and deliberately—ambiguous meaning and application in the hands of Article III judges). Still, it was a thorn in the industrial titans' sides—and Progressives were able to strengthen it a bit, with later statutes that cut against the conservative renderings of the law that the federal courts predictably favored. Over the decades it brought a measure of fairness and opportunity to the new corporate economy. For our purposes, what matters most about this history is recovering the forgotten constitutional stakes in these battles.

Antitrust, Anti-Oligarchy

In the Gilded Age, as now, corporations law governed the size and powers of firms, and corporations law was a state, not federal domain. But this came to seem problematic—and not only to the Populists. National action was needed if nation-spanning corporations and trusts—oil, steel, whiskey, sugar, and especially railroads—had the power to set the terms of commerce across the country, to drive out rivals, and to buy out state legislatures, while ruling their tens of thousands of employees like feudal lords. In Congress, the idea that the trusts spelled constitutional trouble was hardly restricted to the Populists. Senator John Sherman, finance committee chair and lead sponsor of the Antitrust Act of 1890 that bears his name, was a moderate Republican. But no less than the agrarian radicals, he cast the trust problem in stark constitutional terms. The concentration of wealth and power in the new trusts and corporations, he claimed, had become like "a kingly prerogative inconsistent with our form of government";[100] corporate power was "fast producing [a] condition in our people in which the great mass of them are the servitors of those who have this aggregated wealth at their command." Justice Stephen Field's "right of free labor" echoed here, just as it did in Populist discourse: "It is the right of every man," said Senator Sherman, "to work, labor, and produce in any lawful vocation and to transport his production on equal terms. . . . This is industrial liberty and lies at the foundation of the equality of all rights and privileges." Because corporate combinations were destroying the "equal rights" and "industrial liberty of the citizens," Congress was duty bound to act against them.[101]

And act it did. Through rigorous application of the old common-law bars against monopolies, and against combinations in restraint of trade, Senator Sherman's bill aimed to quell the unnatural combinations and trusts and restore the capitalist market to its natural competitive conditions, which would reinvigorate equal economic liberty and opportunity.[102] The Populists and Gilded Age radicals disagreed: they thought capitalist competition was part of the problem; cooperation and new forms of government involvement in economic life were the solution. Moderate Republicans like Senator Sherman found a solution to the trust problem more consistent with classical liberalism. Indeed, it was one of the few solutions allowable under the central tenets of late nineteenth-century liberal-legal and constitutional orthodoxy, with its commitment to a neutral, nonredistributive state and a neutral, self-regulating competitive capitalist market order.

Antitrust aimed to protect constitutional freedoms of trade and enterprise; it did this by blocking the coercive business practices of monopolists. Soon enough, the paradoxical character of this approach became clear. The more vigorously one applied the law, the more one interfered with some of the freedoms the law aimed to protect, by preventing market actors from acquiring property and making contracts. The act could be applied wherever a federal attorney (or, later, a business rival) might persuade a judge that a given business initiative thwarted competition by restraining trade, as countless acquisitions and agreements do. The same constitutional political-economic principles that animated the act also supplied constitutional objections to it, since every prosecution was a statutory intrusion on the sacred sphere of freedom of contract and the rights of property.

The Populists and Gilded Age radicals did not expect great things from antitrust. How far would the corporate-attorneys-turned-jurists on the federal bench go in dismantling the trusts and giant corporations before invoking the "sacred rights" and "Supreme Law" of contract and property to blunt the act? The great danger, as Populist lawmakers saw it, was that whatever the senator's good intentions, Sherman's new law would be wielded by "money power judges" in the service of capital, against the farmers' fledgling market cooperatives and the workers' growing unions.[103]

The Populists were partly right, but only partly. The act would not upend corporate capital. The federal courts would indeed wield it with growing ferocity against hundreds of peaceful strikes and boycotts. However, the skeptical Populists sorely underestimated how far the Supreme Court would go in pursuing Senator Sherman's quaint classical vision of market fairness, weighing in against the (supposedly) unnatural new combinations of capital. For roughly the first two decades of federal antitrust, a majority of the Court, invoking the precepts of classical liberal constitutional political economy, seemed hell-bent on dismantling the trusts.

From the 1890s to the early 1910s, the Supreme Court's antitrust decisions would generate as much public attention and controversy as did the Warren Court's civil rights decisions half a century later. True, the Sherman Act decisions were statutory ones; true, they ran against private actors. Even so, they were understood as "constitutional" by both the public and the Court, and were "viewed in much the same way as the modern Court views cases arising under the various civil rights acts," as Owen Fiss underscored in his Holmes Devise volume on the Fuller Court, which decided the formative Sherman Act cases.[104] The Sherman Act was seen as enforcing constitutional norms, because so many of the lawmakers who crafted the act and jurists who interpreted and applied it understood the competitive market itself "from a constitutional perspective." This is what is most essential to understand if one hopes to understand early antitrust and constitutional political economy. "[T]he market," Fiss explains, "was more a political than an economic construct. It was not a device for achieving the optimum allocation of resources but rather a projection of political and social ideals."[105] The courts would safeguard competition against "all-powerful combination[s] of capital," in service of those ideals, as Justice Rufus Peckham put it in the Supreme Court's first case applying the new antitrust law: to prevent the "ruin" of the "class" of "small dealers and worthy men" and protect the old middle class against socially and politically destructive combinations of corporate capital.[106]

Antitrust scholar Tim Wu has recently joined Fiss and others, including us, in underscoring the constitutional role antitrust would play in the early twentieth century.[107] But while Fiss emphasizes the broad middle class thread of the constitutional argument, Wu's focus is anti-oligarchy. The constitutional meaning of the Sherman Act, Wu argues, was "as a new kind of limit: a check . . . on the growth of monopoly corporations into something that might transcend the power of elected government to control."[108] This aspect of antitrust's constitutional meaning took up the old antimonopoly movement's anti-oligarchy outlook and carried it into the twentieth century and on to the Court. There, Wu reminds us, it found voice through most of the twentieth century, until antitrust jurisprudence underwent its own Great Forgetting in the 1970s. Thus, Wu quotes Justice William O. Douglas for a terse retrospective account of antitrust law's anti-oligarchy meaning: "[P]ower that controls the economy should be in the hands of elected representatives of the people, not in the hands of an industrial oligarchy."[109]

Antitrust became a central arena in which Americans fought their battles over constitutional political economy. Did preserving a broad middle class and thwarting oligarchy require dismantling big business, harnessing it for public purposes through forceful regulation, or leaving it largely alone? Until very recently, it was hard to imagine antitrust law carrying this kind of weight. For decades, we have been taught by courts and scholars to think of antitrust as a technocratic domain in which dueling economists argue over whether a given business arrangement will or won't diminish competition in a fashion injurious to consumer welfare. This idea—that antitrust law's core animating principle is consumer welfare or the costs of goods and services—dates from the 1970s and 1980s, when neoclassical law and economics came to dominate the field and reshape its doctrines. Consumer welfare was always present in antitrust law, but for most of a century it ranked behind the original, constitutionally anchored interpretive principles: anti-oligarchy and the goal of preserving a wide-open opportunity structure and a broad diffusion of productive property, so that a broad middle class could flourish. Now, in the 2020s, as the country awakens to new oligarchs astride government and new "monopoly powers" like Amazon, Facebook, and Google in control of so much of our commerce in goods, information, and ideas, antitrust mavericks like Wu and his colleagues have begun to revisit and reboot these earlier principles.[110]

We join them here. As always, our point is not an originalist one. We revisit this history not because we think it is somehow "binding," but because we think these principles have independent merit and stand in need of reinvention today. Glimpsing their formation and seeing them at work reminds us that antitrust was conceived as a project in constitutional political economy, concerned with the economic, social, *and political* power of giant firms—power over smaller businesses, would-be entrepreneurs, and employees; power over the nation's opportunity structure; and power over political life. It is worth recovering this history if antitrust law and, more broadly, economic regulation are to do the kind of work we need today.

Bigness: From Unnatural to Inevitable

Popular attention was first riveted on the question of industrial concentration in the 1880s by the publication of Populist journalist Henry Demarest Lloyd's muckraking articles on monopoly. The first, "The Story of a Great Monopoly" (1881), assailed the Standard Oil Company, detailing the firm's ruthless predatory practices as it swallowed up competitors, commandeered transportation routes, and forced independent dealers and producers to the wall.[111] Standard Oil also became the first actual "trust" in 1882 when that firm's legal counsel conceived of the trust form as a vehicle for putting hitherto competing companies under unified control in a way that avoided state corporation laws' bans on one corporation holding stock in another. Five other nationwide trusts were organized during the 1880s, including the Whiskey and Sugar Trusts. While the "trusts" often brought down or left unaffected the costs of goods to consumers, their power was ominous.

The search for profits and control motivated this movement of expansion and consolidation. In many industries, new technologies and new ways of organizing production yielded economies of scale, which advantaged large firms. Bigness, however, magnified the costs of sharp increases in the cost of materials, market downturns, or "ruinous competition" brought on by new market entrants and the "overproduction" of goods. Some firms sought to manage these hazards through vertical integration; others through horizontal arrangements, which involved agreements among producers of a given good to limit production and / or maintain prices. These could take the simple form of a contract or the more complex and tighter form of a cartel, or, finally, a merger among competing firms.

Old-fashioned, antimonopoly-minded, conservative (classical liberal) jurists were hostile to all those forms of combination and consolidation. The common law, after all, distinguished sharply between the property rights of "natural" persons and the rights enjoyed by the "artificial person" embodied in the corporation. The latter were carefully circumscribed. The taint of "special privilege" lingered long after the Jacksonian era ushered in "free incorporation" and general incorporation statutes. Common-law doctrines as well as state incorporation statutes preserved many limitations on corporate conduct that applied solely to the corporation, still viewed as an "artificial" entity, a creature of the state.[112]

State statutes set limits on capitalization; common-law ultra vires doctrine forbade leasing corporate property to other corporations or transferring stock to a holding company; common-law doctrine demanded unanimity among shareholders to authorize sales of corporate assets. What's more, many states had laws forbidding "foreign corporations" from doing business within their borders, a prohibition that seems to us to run afoul of the Constitution's protection of interstate commerce and its guarantee of equal treatment of out-of-state citizens. But until 1910, the Supreme Court hewed to the doctrine that the corporation was a "mere artificial being" of the state that created it, entitled to no legal recognition outside that state's borders. The legal and constitutional legitimation of the large-scale corporation thus involved uprooting much old law.[113]

At first, the old law seemed to hold fast. To ensure it would, many states inscribed antitrust provisions into their constitutions, which constitution drafters and state attorneys general linked to the state constitutions' more general entitlements to "the gains of [one's] own industry" and "equal rights and opportunity under law." Thus, for example, in a quo warranto suit against the Chicago Gas Trust Company, Illinois's attorney general argued that the state's corporation law did not authorize defendant's holding stock in and thereby thwarting competition among the city's several gas companies. He defended his interpretation of the general incorporation statute by invoking the state's constitution. "To create one corporation for the express purpose of enabling it to control all the corporations engaged in a certain kind of business . . . is in contravention of the spirit, if not the letter of the [Illinois] constitution"—the spirit of its equal rights provisions and the letter of its antitrust norms.[114]

Similarly, during Missouri's historic antitrust suit against Standard Oil, the state attorney general framed his argument before the state high court not around the price of oil, which had not risen despite Standard Oil's furtive ownership and control of nominally independent firms, but around the constitutional peril of oligarchy and the constitutional pledge of equal opportunity: "History shows that the greatest danger to the existence of free institutions and the rights of the individual are the influences that come from the power wielded by combined and concentrated wealth." Quoting the Missouri constitution's guarantee of "equal rights and equal opportunity," he argued that an antitrust judgment against Standard Oil would "accomplish[] more for the industrial freedom of this country—more for the protection of the individual against wrong and oppression–more for the securing of 'equal rights and equal opportunity'—than has been accomplished by the decision of any court in the history of this commonwealth."[115]

In all, during the late 1880s, six different states brought suits to revoke the charters of corporations that had become constituents of the great trusts, contending, successfully, that state corporation law and ultra vires doctrine forbade them. True, said the New York Court of Appeals in the celebrated Sugar Trust case, "an individual having the necessary wealth" could legally have bought up and consolidated all the sugar refineries joined in the trust. But it was "one thing for the State to respect the rights of ownership . . . and the business freedom of the citizen." It was "quite another thing" for the state to "creat[e] artificial persons" and allow these corporations "with little added risk" to "mass their fortunes . . . vastly exceeding . . . in their power over industry any possibilities of individual ownership."[116]

During the last decade of the nineteenth century, however, important economists and public intellectuals began to ponder whether the large-scale enterprise was not "unnatural" but instead "inevitable." Prevailing economic wisdom still held that competition was the natural order of economic life, except for the rare case of the "natural monopoly" like the railroads. But new "institutionalist" economists like Henry C. Adams, chief statistician for the newly formed Interstate Commerce Commission (ICC), began to see the railroads as just one of many industries "which conform to the principle of increasing returns [to scale], and for that reason come under the rule of centralized control." In Adams's view, since competition was destined to vanish, and no "laws compelling competition" could bring it back, "the only question" was "whether society shall support an irresponsible, extra-legal monopoly, or a monopoly established by law and managed in the interest of the public."[117]

Adams hoped to supply an economic rationale for lawmakers, government attorneys, and judges to put the old public utility doctrine back to work forging and defending an expansive agenda of economic regulation and reform. Lending the authority of economic "science" to the trend toward "centralized control" in a gamut of industries beyond the railroads, Adams aimed to unsettle the deep-seated legal-liberal idea of competition as the natural order of things. Wherever economies of scale pressed hard in favor of large-scale enterprise, law could not bring back the small proprietor. Instead, law should focus on the public functions of these giant private enterprises and regulate them accordingly, whether that entailed price or rate controls, as with the ICC, or moving past that to ongoing supervision, municipal ownership, or public works. This became a key notion in many veins of Progressive and New Deal constitutional political economy: neutralize the oligarchic and oppressive power of big private firms by treating them as public utilities or "businesses affected with a public interest," and regulate them to work for the public good.[118]

Not surprisingly, the new titans of industry found something to like in the new institutional economists' ideas about the "inevitable" centralizing, consolidating thrust of modern industrial development. While they spurned Adams's prescription of extensive public regulation of their giant businesses, the new corporate elite echoed his diagnosis: Concentration was inevitable, and the trust a natural product of economic "evolution."

As we have seen, however, the state high courts unanimously disagreed. The new corporate law firms on Wall Street looked for a workaround. State legislatures came to their aid. Several corporate attorneys drafted an amendment to New Jersey's corporation law to permit incorporation "for any lawful business or purpose whatever." Among other things, this handily could be read to allow one corporation to own the stock of another. Some of the Wall Street attorneys distributed liberal amounts of corporate boodle, and the state legislature obliged them, leading to the reorganization of almost all the nation's trusts as New Jersey corporations—gaining the state a windfall in tax revenue, while earning it the title of "Traitor State" from the famous muckraker Lincoln Steffens.[119] Soon, the state legislatures of Delaware and New York followed suit, eliminating or weakening key restraints on corporate growth and consolidation. Corporations hobbled by other states' more traditional legal regimes easily reincorporated in the liberalized jurisdictions.

"Competition, Free and Unrestricted"

Even as states dramatically loosened their regulatory constraints, most members of Congress and the federal bench continued to view state government as the primary locus of authority over the trusts. Thus, when Congress took up the Trust Question in 1888–1890, the division of federal versus state authority loomed large. Senator Sherman saw clearly the inadequacies of state regulation. His first antitrust bill envisioned direct federal control over corporate structure, authorizing federal courts to dissolve all agreements or combinations "extending to two or more states" that "tend to prevent full and free competition" in "growth, production, or manufacture." After constitutional federalism objections from Judiciary Committee colleagues, the redrafted statute took out this language and more ambiguously condemned "[e]very contract, combination in the form of trust or otherwise, or conspiracy in restraint of trade or commerce," and also outlawed monopolization of any part of interstate commerce.[120] The 1890 Congress left it to the courts to determine what specific forms of business conduct and combination violated the common-law-based language of the act.

For two decades, neither the courts nor commentators could agree whether the new federal statute simply codified common-law norms or enacted stricter prohibitions. The common law distinguished between "reasonable" and "unreasonable" restraints on trade, condemning only the latter. The statute contained no such distinction. Congress had preferred ambiguous statutory language so that it could please competing constituencies, including the broad middle-class public that was demanding restoration of some form of proprietary capitalism and the metropolitan business interests favoring continued development of the new giant corporations under enhanced oversight. The result was that the nation's battles over what was to be done about corporate capital and constitutional political economy became focused on an ongoing interpretive conflict, which generated an impassioned debate both inside the Court and between the Court and the public. This debate echoed the battles over labor's rights and presaged later moments of high-stakes constitutional conflict including the civil rights revolution of the mid-twentieth century.

The Supreme Court pursued a jarring course. From 1897, when it decided the *Trans-Missouri* case, through the end of Chief Justice Melville Fuller's tenure in 1910, a majority of the Court, led by Justices Peckham and Harlan, insisted that the act went further than the common law, condemning all restraints of trade. "Competition, free and unrestricted" was the rule, and the rule, as the Peckham-Harlan majority saw it, had a constitutional mandate. Unless the Court stood firmly behind what

Peckham described as "the law of competition,"[121] and firmly against the efforts of looming monopolies to dominate the nation's commerce and industries, the social and political conditions that underwrote equality of rights and opportunities would soon perish.

Peckham spoke for the Court in *Trans-Missouri* and other key early Sherman Act cases and emerged as the architect of the new antitrust doctrine. In *Trans-Missouri,* Peckham set out what he took to be the Sherman Act's overriding social and political purposes. "[D]istress and, perhaps, ruin," the Justice observed, were inevitable accompaniments of "any great and extended change in the manner or method of doing business," and such was the case with the rise of large-scale corporate enterprise. "It is wholly different, however, when such changes are effected by combinations of capital, whose purpose in combining is to control the production or manufacture of any particular article in the market, and by such control dictate the price at which the article shall be sold." The effect of those kinds of combinations, said Peckham, was to put both the public and polity in peril of subjection, because of the combination's power to drive out all the "small but independent dealers," depriving the public of their services, their families of their livelihoods, and the polity of a proprietary middle class of such "worthy" men. "Whether they be able to find other avenues to earn their livelihood is not so material," Peckham continued. It was not for the "real prosperity" or social and political well-being "of any country that such changes should occur which result in transferring an independent businessman, the head of his establishment, small though it might be, into a mere servant or agent of a corporation for selling the commodities which he once manufactured or dealt in, having no voice in shaping the business policy of the company and bound to obey orders issued by others."[122]

Trans-Missouri, it bears noting, involved not a manufacturing combination but a joint tariff agreement, or price-fixing contract, among competing interstate rail lines. Thus, it fell squarely into Henry C. Adams's wheelhouse, over at the ICC. Indeed, this was just the kind of agreement Adams had tried to persuade Congress to expressly authorize, as it drafted the Interstate Commerce Act. His idea was that the new ICC could monitor such agreements, ensuring fair rates for shippers, while allowing the rail lines to avert the "ruinous" rate wars that forced them either to bankruptcy or to gouging the shippers on noncompetitive portions of their lines. Even without express authorization, the ICC had found a way to do just that. But Justice Peckham was having none of it. He brushed aside the argument that the Sherman Act was preempted here by the Interstate Commerce Act, as well as the argument that the joint tariff agreements were—at least implicitly—allowed. Peckham also took on the institutional economists' broader argument for the inevitability of bigness and "centralized control" and the futility of "laws compelling competition" where there were increasing returns to scale. The railroads, after all, were the classic example of such "natural monopolies." Peckham understood full well the railroads' (and economists') argument that high fixed costs and economies of scale pointed toward the need for a public / private system of negotiated rate-fixing to avoid "deadly competition so liable to result in the ruin of the roads." But rather than trying to determine whether there was merit to this argument, he read the Sherman Act as flatly prohibiting all price-fixing contracts.[123]

This striking judgment was not based on the precise words of the statute, any more than Peckham's liberty of contract decisions like *Lochner* rested on any parsing of the Due Process Clause. Rather, as Fiss notes, Peckham's conclusion expressed a social and constitutional vision that he found "embodied in the Sherman Act"—a vision of a market order that Peckham thought "was willing to sacrifice efficiency so as to avoid the social and political costs of monopoly."[124] "Combinations," he argued, may "reduce the price" of a good "temporarily, or perhaps permanently" because of the efficiencies they can bring. But "[t]rade or commerce under those circumstances may nevertheless be badly and unfortunately restrained by driving out of business the small dealers and worthy men whose lives have been spent therein. . . . Mere reduction in the price of the commodity dealt in might be dearly paid for by the ruin of such a class and the absorption of control over one commodity by an all-powerful combination of capital."[125] Instead, Peckham concluded, "Competition, free and unrestricted" was "the general rule." It was inscribed, somehow—perhaps, as Fiss suggests, as a "transubstantiation of natural law"—from the classical liberal Constitution into the statute. To safeguard middle-class opportunity and freedom of enterprise, the "law of competition" had to remain the "controlling element in the business world."[126] The majority applied this reasoning in a string of subsequent decisions striking down agreements, combinations, and mergers—any effort, not just an "unreasonable" one, in restraint of trade and competition.

THE FIRST TRUSTBUSTER

The majority's old-fashioned antitrust disposition would not have mattered so much for turn-of-the-century battles over constitutional political economy, had it not been for an assassin's bullet, which felled President William McKinley in 1901. McKinley was no friend of antitrust. True to the emergent Republican outlook as the party of big business, McKinley "tacitly acknowledged that Wall Street, rather than the White House, had executive control of the economy."[127] He saw the Sherman Act as a measure to appease the Populists. He confirmed his do-nothing posture by greeting news of J. P. Morgan's plan to buy out Andrew Carnegie and create the U.S. Steel trust with a White House dinner in Morgan's honor.[128]

No wonder J. P. Morgan groaned at the news that McKinley was expiring and his vice president, Teddy Roosevelt, had taken over. A seasoned publicity hound from his stint as a reforming police commissioner of New York and his service to the American empire in the Spanish–American War, Roosevelt was the kind of patrician politician we have seen before and will see again—one with an abiding faith in majoritarian government and in the majority's good sense to prize him as its tribune. Roosevelt admired bigness but also fervently embraced the proposition that the public must rule Wall Street, not vice versa. He had no interest in dismantling big corporations, but he was determined to take the corporate elite down from its oligarchic tower and put the nation's political economy under the nation's constitutional authority.[129]

What better way to bring alive antitrust's overriding constitutional purpose in checking oligarchy than to make headline-grabbing news prosecuting the most powerful economic overlords of the day? In 1902, Roosevelt became the nation's first "trustbuster." He started big, ordering his attorney general to investigate whether the Sherman Act was offended by J. P. Morgan's effort to join forces with John Rockefeller to monopolize the Western railways, via a New Jersey trust corporation, the Northern Securities Company. The attorney general concluded it did. Thus began the federal government's first campaign against a major trust and against the nation's leading investment banker. Over the ensuing months, "trustbuster" and "octopus hunter" came into wide use in print and cartoons, giving color to Roosevelt's declarations that the "trusts are the creatures of the State, and the State . . . has the right . . . [and] the duty . . . to control them."[130]

By the standards of later blockbuster antitrust suits, the Northern Securities litigation proceeded swiftly. The case reached the Supreme Court, and the Court decided for the government in 1904. The merger of Western railroads was blocked. Writing for the majority was Justice John Marshall Harlan. The Court's most eloquent proponent of the old antitrust absolutism, Justice Harlan channeled and spoke for the Populist and old liberal republican constitutional currents that flowed into the Sherman Act. He found Morgan and Rockefeller's trust company in blatant violation of the act's bar on attempts to monopolize interstate commerce. It "placed the control of the two roads in the hands of a single person, to wit, the Securities Company . . . [and] destroy[ed] every motive for competition between two roads."[131]

Soon we will delve more deeply into the constitutional outlook animating Harlan's antitrust opinions. For now, what is noteworthy is that despite Harlan's certainties, the decision was a close one, 5–4. It met ridicule and alarm in powerful dissents by Justices Oliver Wendell Holmes and Edward Douglass White. Holmes accused the majority of enacting a literal ban on combination, and with it a mad effort to "disintegrate society so far as it could into individual atoms." Far more passionately than in his *Lochner* dissent, Holmes derided the majority's "law of competition" views as an "interpretation of the law which . . . would make eternal the bellum omnium contra omnes" (war of all against all).[132] Future Chief Justice White was no less passionate, declaring that the majority's reading of the Sherman Act was flatly unconstitutional. Justice White was of the same mind as the trust's attorneys: In the name of free competition and freedom of enterprise, the majority had opened the door to limitless government power to restrict contractual freedom and to nullify the essential constitutional rights to own and sell property—all in disregard of modern technology and business conditions, which entailed a substantial measure of consolidation.

Meanwhile, statutory and common-law developments in the states and lower federal courts continued to push the opposite way from Justice Harlan's and the Supreme Court's majority view. In the wake of New Jersey's and other states' new statutes, the merger movement took off. State law now sanctioned the creation of corporations without limits on powers or capital, and it seemed to follow that within their chartered rights, the corporations had the same power to acquire property as individuals. Confronted by the mass migration of corporations to New Jersey, state high courts grew resigned: corporations, in fact, could do anything they wanted. The elegant new institutional economists' "inevitability" theory corresponded to gritty reality. In this climate, corporate attorneys tore through the remaining statutory and doctrinal impediments to mergers, and an increasingly pro-bigness bench took up the corporate bar's urgings and welded onto the corporation a rights-bearing identity akin to the old liberal individual's freedom from state interference in the realms of contract-making and property acquisition.

Returning to office for a full term beginning in 1905, Roosevelt had no truck with the corporate elite's and new pro-bigness conservative judges' notions about corporations' "natural" or constitutional rights, and he burnished his reputation as a trustbuster by initiating new proceedings against two of the most notorious trusts, James M. Duke's American Tobacco Company and John D. Rockefeller's Standard Oil Company. In the lower courts, the government prevailed against both. By 1910, with Roosevelt out of office and Supreme Court review pending, antitrust doctrine stood at a crossroads, both in the courts and in public discourse. Did the law condemn all combinations, or only "bad" ones?

The Standard Oil suit reached the Court in 1911, just after President Taft promoted Justice White to fill the Chief Justice seat. Other recent appointments of pro-bigness–minded Justices enabled the new Chief to marshal a majority of eight behind his opinion, which obliged the government by undoing Standard Oil, but enraged the antitrust old guard by declaring that the old common-law "rule of reason" was the "guide" to interpreting the Sherman Act.[133]

"ANOTHER KIND OF SLAVERY"
—THE ABSOLUTISTS' LAST STAND

In a lone concurrence that riveted public attention, the old absolutist Justice Harlan assailed the Court for betraying precedent, legislative intent, and the Constitution itself. Recent precedent included more than one sustained discussion by the now-vanished Peckham-Harlan majority about why it refused to read the word "unreasonable" into the statutory language: The Sherman Act Congress, according to that majority, knew full well what it was doing in going beyond the common law with the sweeping and unqualified antimonopoly / pro-competition language it chose to employ. Congress's objective, Harlan's Standard Oil concurrence reminded his brethren and the public at large, was nothing less than to respond to a new antislavery campaign, using the full extent of its constitutional powers. Harlan argued that in 1890, when the act was passed, there was "among the people generally, a deep feeling of unrest." Slavery was gone, but "the conviction was universal that the country was in real danger from another kind of slavery sought to be fastened on the American people." This was "the slavery that would result from aggregations of capital in the hands of a few individuals and corporations controlling, for their own profit and advantage exclusively, the entire business of the country, including the production and sale of the necessaries of life."[134]

Harlan's use of "slavery" underscores the old-fashioned republican work "slavery" continued to do in constitutional discourse, denoting forms of social and political subordination, often resting on economic domination, incompatible with full membership and equal rights in a republican system of government. "Wage slavery," as we have seen, was one such form of economic domination and social and political subordination, alive in Gilded Age and Progressive Era constitutional discourse. Harlan's conception of subjection to "aggregations of capital" was another. And lest there be any doubt that the Sherman Act Congress was enforcing the republican antislavery Constitution and its rights-bearing provisions, Harlan's legislative history had the 1890 Congress rely for its authority to enact the sweeping statute (as the old Harlan-Peckham majority had construed it) not solely on the Article I Commerce Power, but also with "due force being given to other provisions of the fundamental law . . . for the safety of the Government and for the protection and security of the essential rights inhering in life, liberty and property." By abandoning its initial reading of the act, Harlan concluded, the Chief Justice's majority was shamelessly violating the separation of powers, indulging in "judicial legislation," "'emasculat[ing]'" the statute, and doing so on behalf of the oligarchs of corporate capital.[135]

President Taft stood by his Chief Justice and declined to call for any amendment to the Sherman Act. Indeed, doctrinally, Taft read the Chief's "rule of reason" decision as foreclosing little, and he pursued an active policy of antitrust prosecutions against major corporations. Progressives in Congress, however, heeded Harlan's call and denounced the Court for reading into the Sherman Act just the phrase that the trusts wanted to find there. Public confidence in the nation's antitrust law evaporated. New legislation seemed inevitable. Should Harlan's doctrine be revived? Should the trust problem be taken from the courts and put under the ongoing regulation and supervision of some new national administrative agency?

The three-way race for the White House in 1912 put these questions on the public docket. In 1912, Roosevelt challenged Taft for the Republican nomination, accusing Taft of drifting toward a stand-pat conservatism. Exhibit A was Taft's defense of the judiciary, contrasted with Roosevelt's advocacy of a powerful new regulatory state and a sharp diminution of judicial authority. Losing the Republican nomination, Roosevelt helped create and then ran on the Progressive Party platform, which promised national corporation law and national regulation of industry and big business, including a powerful national bureau to monitor and separate the "good trusts" (with their greater efficiency and economies of scale) from the "bad" (with their predatory business practices and their purely opportunistic and anticompetitive welding together of firms). Woodrow Wilson, the Democratic candidate, echoed his adviser Louis Brandeis in decrying the "curse of bigness." Bigness on this view was generally a bad thing in itself. The Brandeisian reform vision evoked the hope of restoring a more decentralized political economy in which smaller firms continued to flourish. Wilson won—and Roosevelt and Wilson together garnered three votes to every one for Taft. Greater legislative and administrative intervention in the new corporate economy seemed inevitable.

AMBIGUOUS PROGRESSIVE LEGACIES

In 1914, President Wilson signed into law two new antitrust measures, the Federal Trade Commission (FTC) Act and the Clayton Act. The first created a regulatory commission with power to identify and proscribe "unfair methods of competition" and "deceptive business practices." The second outlawed particular unfair business methods: price discrimination, tying contracts, and some kinds of interlocking directorates. The expressly constitutional dimensions of the old antimonopoly / antitrust discourse of the 1880s and 1890s had receded in the debates surrounding the two new measures. But principles at the heart of the democracy-of-opportunity tradition—anti-oligarchy, anti–economic domination, broad opportunities for middle-class "independence"—remained. Responding to arguments based on consumer welfare, the Senate sponsor of the FTC Act declared that "we must do something to preserve the independence of the man as distinguished from the power of the corporation." He added:

> We often go wrong, I believe, in assuming that because a great corporation, a vast aggregation of wealth, can produce a given commodity more cheaply than can a smaller concern, therefore it is for the welfare and the interest of the people of the country that the commodity shall be produced at the lower cost. I do not accept that article of economic faith. I think we can purchase cheapness at altogether too high a price, if it involves the surrender of the individual, the subjugation of a great mass of people to a single master mind.[136]

And yet the Clayton and FTC Acts' language was, in the end, sufficiently qualified and ambiguous to leave room for the more conservative Court of the 1920s to construe most of the acts' provisions as no more than codifications of inherited judge-made rules. Combined with common-law developments favoring corporate consolidation, the "rule of reason" decisions had gone far toward settling the "trust question," pushing it from the center of national politics. Congress had chosen modest reform in the 1914 statutes, spurning the bolder Progressives' vision of a national commission with power to issue and revoke national corporate charters and to supervise corporate pricing, accounting, and capitalization and investment policy.

By 1920, the giant, nation-spanning corporation had become what the late nineteenth-century courts—and liberal and radical reformers alike—declared it could never be: a natural, rights-bearing actor on the legal-constitutional stage, endowed with all "the rights of ownership" and "business freedom of the citizen" as an individual proprietor.[137] But this legitimation of bigness came at a price: antitrust statutes pushing back against this new corporate rights-bearer with background norms that were shot through with democracy-of-opportunity ideas, especially anti-oligarchy and the idea of an open opportunity structure with a broad middle class. These precepts remained, despite the work of hostile courts; they would be reinvigorated in modern fashion during the New Deal.

The Structure of Politics Itself

From the start, we have encountered this basic axiom of constitutional political economy: Capitalist wealth has an inevitable tendency to convert economic into political domination. As Martin Van Buren put it, when deprived of aristocratic privilege and the chance to be permanently "allied to power," wealth "maintains a constant struggle for the establishment of a moneyed oligarchy."[138] A corollary is that there is no constitutional construction designed in the spirit of democratic and egalitarian reform that economic elites will not try to convert over time into a new instrument of political rule. That was the fate of Van Buren's own deeply innovative construction, the mass political party. Created and justified as a constitutionally essential counterweight to the "money power," the Democratic Party became, in Grover Cleveland's day, a fairly reliable instrument of the "money power" itself. And the same happened, of course, to the party of Lincoln, Sumner, and Stevens. This inspired fierce critiques of "the two old parties" as objects and vehicles of plutocratic domination, and third-party movements emerged—the People's Party of the 1880s and 1890s, the Progressive Party of the 1910s, and the Socialist Party, launched around the turn of the century, which ran

Eugene Debs as its perennial candidate from 1900 through 1912 and again in 1920—all to save the republic from a new corporate elite, which had "usurped" the constitutional order once more.

But this story of parties hardly does justice to the constitutional inventiveness of the Populist and Progressive movements and the formal-textual and structural innovations they championed to repair and rebuild our republican form of government. So far, we have devoted most of our attention to the work these movements did to reinvent our political economy in the face of new, nationwide agglomerations of corporate power. But they also recognized that the structural reforms they envisioned for the political economy would not get far without structural reforms to the system of government. (Reared in the labor republican tradition, Eugene Debs and his generation of Socialists reached the same conclusion: You could not make transformative democratic changes in the modern economy without commensurate changes in the structure of government. A smaller battalion than the others, Debs's party formed the left flank of the constitutional reform army and welcomed many Populists and Progressives into its ranks.)

Radical or mainstream, Populists and Progressives had no illusions that all they needed to prevail were third parties and a platform of substantive economic reforms. The new giant corporations were agglomerations of both economic *and political* power. Those corporations found it a surprisingly straightforward business to capture and control state governments, especially state legislatures—and especially (but not only) in the newer states of the American West. (The New Jersey legislature's sale of its state corporations law to Wall Street was a good case in point from the East.) Being able to buy and sell state legislatures was a particularly big structural-constitutional advantage in a system that put the selection of U.S. senators in the hands of state legislatures—and that vested crucial power over the appointment of the federal bench and high executive officials in the hands of the U.S. Senate. A Senate stacked with the allies of giant corporations could also easily thwart or cabin efforts in Congress to legislate reform of the new corporate economy.

Populists and Progressives thus turned serious attention to structural flaws in the constitutional scheme. Some of these, like the mode of selecting senators, seemed baked into the original design. Others, like the uncanny ability of corporate wealth to corrupt party politics and elections, were modern results of past structural reforms. These flaws drove both generations of reformers past mere third-party politics to a politics of constitutional amendment and revision at both state and national levels. The reformers embraced the "excess of democracy" that most appalled the framers, upending the foundational notion that a republican form of government required legislation by elected representatives. In another reversal of the constitutional politics of the early nineteenth century, the structural obstacles to economic reform now pushed for constitutional reform in an *antiparty* spirit, advocating forms of democracy that were less mediated and more direct.

Start with the Senate. As we have seen, a central reform struggle during the decades bracketing the turn of the century was the push to move regulatory power *upward*—away from the state legislatures that were often no match for the trusts, and instead toward new agencies and institutions within the federal government that could be built to give them a fairer fight. The ICC and antitrust law were early fruits of this approach. These efforts were an uphill climb, especially in Congress, and most especially in the Senate, for a structural constitutional reason: senators were chosen by state legislatures. And as we have noted, in the wild political economy of the Gilded Age, the Senate was the branch of the federal government most easily captured by the trusts.

As the canonical argument for the direct election of senators framed the problem, "[T]he Senate has become a rich man's club, a paradise of millionaires," which made it "the stronghold of the trusts and of corporate interests."[139] And of course that stronghold also shaped the composition of each presidential administration and the makeup of the federal courts. This is why the idea that ultimately became the Seventeenth Amendment—the Article V change providing for the direct election of senators by the people—was at the center of the Populist constitutional project, even though it would not succeed until the conflict over Populism had passed and the Progressives had inherited and revised that project.[140]

The Progressives similarly succeeded, where their Populist forebears had failed, in ratifying the Sixteenth Amendment, which finally reversed the odious *Pollock* case and gave the federal government unambiguous power to enact any income tax, creating the powerful engine of progressive fiscal policy that would function as the financial base for the New Deal and the "American century." By the middle of the twentieth century, the federal government set progressive rates that effectuated enormous redistribution—rates more progressive, in fact, than the social democracies of Western Europe at mid-century.[141] Both these consequential constitutional amendments were ratified in 1913 (because the income tax amendment's ratification took several years). Both were, at their heart, anti-oligarchy amendments. They reflected a self-conscious effort to alter the political economy through constitutional redesign, as a means of addressing the nation's new and unprecedented agglomerations of wealth and corporate power.

The four amendments of the Progressive period of higher law-making—the Sixteenth, Seventeenth, Eighteenth, and Nineteenth—amounted to one of the most significant and sustained exercises of Article V in our history. Each of these amendments, in different ways, shifted some measure of power toward the federal government and away from the states. Each was the outgrowth of long-standing, overlapping reform movements. The temperance movement, active for much of the nineteenth century, had its core constituency in rural, religious, common people, skeptical of the new urban industrial system and the new waves of immigrants that populated it.[142] This movement and its allies won the Eighteenth Amendment prohibiting the sale of alcohol.

Of the four amendments, Prohibition is the most distant from our story, but there are at least two points of connection. First, and most bleakly, when the Eighteenth Amendment was ratified in 1919, it became a tool for "old stock," moralistic Progressive reformers to discipline and scourge new immigrants and a tool in the hands of Southern whites and the Klan, who enforced it punitively against Southern Blacks; it thus was part of the successful effort to undo what little remained of the racial inclusion strand of Reconstruction constitutional politics.[143] Second, as Lisa McGirr has shown, although World War I played a larger role in expanding the scale of the federal government, the Eighteenth Amendment was a powerful spur to the development of a more muscular federal *domestic* policy, specifically federal law enforcement, and in that way helped suggest the possibility of the much greater expansion of federal power that occurred in the New Deal. If the federal government could reach deep into the states to police every tavern and distillery in the nation, perhaps it could regulate other forms of production, labor, and commerce as well.[144]

The Nineteenth Amendment, which secured women's right to vote, is far more central to our story. It was, from the perspective of the suffrage movement, a completion of the unfinished business of Reconstruction, which had introduced racial inclusion into our constitutional text but had conspicuously failed to do the same with sex. The suffragists who succeeded in getting this amendment ratified in 1920 hoped to do more than alter who casts ballots. By 1920, suffragists had already persuaded most states to open up at least some local elections to women; many states had opened up all elections.[145] But a federal constitutional amendment had broader implications. Just as the ardent champions of the Reconstruction Amendments had aimed to do with race, the suffragists who provided the activist leadership and the rank-and-file foot soldiers of the campaign for the Nineteenth Amendment aimed to bring women into the circle of full legal and economic citizenship. Including women in this way meant using the federal Constitution to alter the political economy of the family and household. "As proponents and opponents of the Nineteenth Amendment well appreciated," legal scholar Reva Siegel explains, "the decision to enfranchise women under the federal Constitution involved breaking with common-law traditions that subordinated women to men in the family and intervening in domestic matters traditionally reserved to state control."[146]

Just as in Reconstruction, advocates of the amendment imagined that enfranchisement would also bring about a different politics. To some extent, that prediction was borne out. Although the immediate political effect proved less dramatic than many advocates expected, the Nineteenth Amendment did lay the groundwork for a politics more open to a different kind of social contract, one with a greater role for government in the provision of social insurance, health and safety legislation, and perhaps especially education.[147] There were significant divisions among women activists over whether to favor sex-specific protective labor legislation, but these activists were largely united around a generally Progressive agenda that would include child labor laws, consumer protections, industrial health and safety laws, and laws protecting women's rights. Despite the conservative and red-baiting political turn of the 1920s, they got some of this enacted into federal and state law.[148]

But just as it had been ambiguous exactly what it meant to emancipate Black people from slavery, it was ambiguous exactly what it meant to emancipate women from the second-class citizenship of coverture and disenfranchisement in the household, as the states had been doing gradually over the past several decades, with reforms like married women's property acts. Despite the generally Progressive constitutional politics of the suffragists themselves, the Supreme Court of the 1920s chose the most Lochnerian possible answer to this question. The leading early case interpreting the Nineteenth Amendment was *Adkins v. Children's Hospital.* The Court read the profound changes in the political economy of the family that had culminated in the amendment through the lens of Lochnerian political economy.[149] The case was a challenge to a law setting a minimum wage for women. The Court noted that common-law ideas of coverture, women's role as mothers, and women's dependence on their husbands may once have justified such legislation—indeed, so the Court had suggested just fifteen years earlier when it upheld a maximum-hours law for women.[150] But now, the Court held that such interference with a woman's liberty of contract was no longer permissible "[i]n view of the great—not to say revolutionary— changes which have taken place since that utterance, in the contractual, political, and civil status of women, culminating in the Nineteenth Amendment."[151]

Adkins was a victory for the proposition that the Nineteenth Amendment was not exclusively about voting or political rights, but also had implications for reorienting the political economy of the family.[152] However, in the hands of Lochnerian courts, such a reorientation basically made women, like men, into legal subjects whose property and contract rights could trump Progressive efforts to redistribute economic and political power. The 1920s were a bad decade for the democracy-of-opportunity tradition. The constitutional project of race-based inclusion was likewise at its lowest ebb. It would take almost half a century, and a new set of social movements, to bring race- and sex-based inclusion back to the center of our constitutional politics.

Restoring Government by the People

The Progressive period of sustained Article V lawmaking contrasted sharply with Reconstruction in its orientation toward partisanship. None of the four amendments of the Progressive Era was enacted by a dominant political party. To be sure, the People's Party, the Progressive Party, the Socialist Party, and the National Women's Party of the late suffrage movement all played important supporting roles. But none of them ever won a presidential election. Rather, as we observed, these movements shared an *anti*-party orientation, amounting to a distinctive form of constitutional politics, fueled by widespread disgust with the corruption of the two old parties and ordinary partisan politics. They shared a Progressive faith that political economy might be repaired—a democracy of opportunity restored, the "money power" tamed, the Co-operative Commonwealth brought to earth—through constitutional reform. This faith extended far beyond the politics of Article V amendments. It was at the center of constitutional agitation at the state level in much of the nation in the early twentieth century.

Indeed, although we have laid out these four Article V amendments because they are unique in American history, viewing Progressive Era constitutional politics through the lens of these amendments distorts it. It took many years for the movements that produced these amendments to reach the point of altering the text of the federal Constitution. Advocates of the Nineteenth Amendment spent half a century articulating and refining claims on behalf of women's suffrage that imagined a different political economy of the household and the state, and began to build that political economy through changes in state law, such as the law of coverture, long before women won the vote.[153] And the reform agenda that ultimately led to the Sixteenth and Seventeenth Amendments first transformed state governments—building new political institutions, changing old ones, and restructuring the rules of the political game.

Progressives understood this last set of mostly state-level constitutional reforms as simultaneously a radical innovation and a return to constitutional principles in a world of Gilded Age economic inequality, where vast structural changes would be needed for ordinary Americans to take back the instrumentalities of politics. To understand the constitutional vision that animated these reforms, it helps to understand the problem as Populists and Progressives understood it.

In the remainder of this chapter we tell that story in two parts. First, we describe the origins of American direct democracy in the middle-class politics of the state of Oregon, which gave birth to a series of pivotal constitutional changes that swept the American West: the initiative, referendum, and recall; regulations of campaign finance and other "corrupt practices"; and finally, perhaps most revolutionary of all, the direct primary. These innovations were intertwined, politically and constitutionally, with programmatic arguments for an array of economic reforms, including a massive shift in the burdens of taxation from the middle class to the handful of wealthy dynasties that owned the state's timberlands and transportation companies and controlled Oregon politics. But the novel institutional reform proposals that came to be known as the "Oregon System" also aimed for something more fundamental and constitutional: to restore government by the people.

From Oregon, we pan outward to the national struggle over the Sixteenth and Seventeenth Amendments, and then turn briefly to the far more proletarian constitutional politics of early twentieth-century Montana, where there was barely any middle class. The constitutional stakes of oligarchy there were that much more urgent; the corrupt intertwining of economic and political power that much starker. The people of Montana grabbed hold of the Oregon System and remade the state's politics, dismantling an oligarchy and constructing safeguards against the domination of big capital that now stand as fading landmarks—because today, a century later in our own Gilded Age, the U.S. Supreme Court is undoing them.

Tool Makers for Democracy

The movement for constitutional reform that would reshape the system of government of much of the United States—and eventually, through the Seventeenth Amendment, the entire country—began in earnest in Oregon, just before the turn of the twentieth century. At the home of a fruit grower in Clackamas County, the Farmers' Alliance, progenitor of the People's Party, held what would turn out to be an important series of meetings in which "the topics were those under discussion by farmers everywhere: exorbitant railroad rates, the tight money supply, and control of the legislature by the plutocracy."[154] There the assembled farmers, skilled workers, craftspeople, and shopkeepers learned from a People's Party lecturer about the practice of direct democracy in Switzerland, which a number of books by Americans had begun to popularize.[155] The Swiss model of direct democracy took its place among a number of European social reforms and European innovations in what we now call the "law of democracy," which played a crucial role in Progressive thought. What the Swiss model suggested was the possibility of a democratic structure that circumvented the corrupt parties.[156]

And that was compelling because Oregon's Farmers' Alliance and its new People's Party were brimming with substantive ideas for tax reform, antitrust, railroad and utility rate regulation, and barring corporations from spending money on elections (or so-called corrupt practices legislation, which was the precursor of campaign finance regulation). Yet, there was not a snowball's chance in hell that the legislature would enact any of them, because the Oregon legislature was wildly, flagrantly corrupt. Like other young Western states, observers from the Northeast often observed, with a note of condescension, Oregon had no long tradition of stable governance that could withstand the emergence of Gilded Age concentrations of wealth. As one such observer described it, "The principal, and quite frequently, only business of the [Oregon] legislature was auctioning off the [U.S.] senatorship to the highest bidder without regard for the wishes of the electorate."[157] Muckraking journalists would later publish the text of written contracts in which legislators had literally agreed to sell their votes for U.S. senator in exchange for thousands of dollars payable in gold.[158] When laws were passed at all, they were "dictated to a large degree by timber and railroad interests."[159]

And of course, the legislature's selection of U.S. senators also shaped the federal bench, which, as we know, the People's Party saw as a pivotal actor in an unelected "regime of privilege" that would block anything "obnoxious to plutocracy" for a simple reason: "Plutocracy appoints the Federal judges."[160] The entire state and federal constitutional machinery seemed broken and inaccessible, if you were an ordinary farmer or tradesman.

One extraordinary Oregon tradesman was William Simon U'Ren, a blacksmith's son and a blacksmith himself, who became a farmer, then a newspaper editor, and an attorney with his own firm, but remained a stalwart champion of the laboring and producing classes. U'Ren was there at the Farmers' Alliance meetings in Clackamas County when the assembly learned about direct democracy. He grabbed hold of the idea—that the people themselves could enact laws—and ran with it. Here was a way to work around the timber and railroad barons' hammerlock on the legislative process—by taking the process away from them.

U'Ren's legal talent helped him master the new-model constitutional blueprints from abroad and emerge as architect of what became the "Oregon System." But he expounded and publicized the project with a tradesman's tropes. Government, said U'Ren, is "the common trade of all men."[161] But "men worked still with old tools, with old laws, with constitutions and charters which hindered more than they helped." Why didn't our able lawyers "invent legislative implements to help the people govern themselves? Why had we no tool makers for democracy?"[162] In this, U'Ren echoed the same pragmatic, irreverent approach to the Constitution one heard from public intellectuals like Croly and Beard (although less often from Progressivism's legal luminaries). It came naturally to the tradesman-inventor of the Oregon System to picture the Constitution as a machine that had broken down but could yet be repaired and rebuilt to accomplish its basic purposes: to secure a government by the people, along with the political economy that made such a government possible.

Certain forms of direct democracy were already common. Not only in the West, but throughout the United States, an increasing number of state constitutional amendments and changes to local government charters were increasingly put to a vote of the people.[163] But it was *legislators* who put these questions to the people. The initiative and referendum were different: they gave the people the opportunity to answer questions their legislators had not asked. Thus, the "Oregon System" consisted of the initiative, in which voters petition to put on the ballot a question whose answer has the force of law; the referendum, in which voters do the same, except it is to repeal an act of the legislature; the recall, where voters petition to remove a local or state official from office before the end of the official's term (remember here, as well, the hybrid version we heard Teddy Roosevelt commend to Ohioan constitution makers, where voters "recall" not a judge but a high court opinion); and perhaps most important of all, the direct primary, in which voters choose which candidate shall represent the party, rather than simply making the general-election choice between candidates chosen by party bosses. Today, half of the states have adopted some version of the popular initiative or referendum, and every state has adopted some form of the direct primary.[164] The Oregon System thus became the wedge of a nationwide constitutional change. It introduced into the text of many states' constitutions the idea that, as in Oregon, legislatures share the lawmaking power: Some of it, "the people reserve to themselves."[165]

U'Ren and his allies elected only a small minority of the state legislators, but they somehow succeeded in enacting the Oregon System through a series of politically audacious bargains with the very politicians whose corruption they aimed to rout. After holding up a U.S. Senate election, and cutting cross-party deals to install some of those same corrupt politicians as statehouse speaker and U.S. senator, they got the initiative and referendum through both houses of the legislature in the form of a constitutional amendment.[166] That amendment then went to a vote of the people in 1902, where it won over 90 percent of the vote.[167] The initiative swiftly became the vehicle for enacting the other elements of the system, including the direct primary. U'Ren and his reform crowd even used the initiative to force the popular election of U.S. senators, prior to (and helping advance the cause of) the Seventeenth Amendment. They created a statewide popular vote for U.S. senator, which was legally nonbinding, but whose results the candidates for state legislature could pledge to support. If legislative candidates did make this pledge, that would be *noted on the ballot* in their own elections; a slim majority soon took the pledge and the first more or less popularly elected candidates joined the U.S. Senate.[168] The pace of all these changes was jaw-droppingly swift. By 1910, U'Ren would declare triumphantly, "[I]t is now up to the mudsills to legislate."[169]

Opponents of these constitutional changes argued vociferously—first in politics, then in court, and then back in politics again—that direct democracy violated the basic design of the U.S. Constitution. It was not hard to make the case that the framers had a vastly more elitist republican form of government in mind, and the Oregon System's foes often framed their arguments in terms of the Guarantee Clause's "Republican Form of Government." Some invoked Madison, arguing that *Federalist* No. 10 specifically rejected "pure democracy" in favor of a more indirect design: our republic was one of "constitutional representative government," not "an unconstitutional irresponsible democracy."[170] After losing their political battle against the Oregon System, opponents took their case to court, arguing that the new system violated the Guarantee Clause and several others, the core argument being that direct democracy was "subversive of the principles upon which the republic is founded."[171] The Supreme Court demurred, declaring the question nonjusticiable,[172] which had the effect of returning the question to constitutional politics. As the Oregon System swept the West (and as portions of it were adopted, as well, in the Midwest and Northeast), a debate took place on two levels: practical democratic toolmaking, and fidelity to constitutional principles.

Direct-democracy advocates responded to their opponents with a different reading of American constitutional history. Some candidly acknowledged, with Beard and Croly, that the Constitution was marred from the start by "the fear of too much democracy" on the part of the propertied elite.[173] However, most of the advocates of direct democracy took the opposite approach.[174] They argued for the centrality of popular sovereignty both to the original Constitution and to the views of founders like Jefferson. Jonathan Bourne Jr., who was the first U.S. senator elected for a full term under Oregon's new system of popular voting, made the case for direct democracy in simple terms: its purpose "is to restore the absolute sovereignty of the people."[175]

Above all, the reformers relied on the argument that it was not their proposed structural reforms but rather the Gilded Age concentration of political and economic power that was thwarting the American constitutional design. "Scarcely a vestige of the system that was intended for the common good remains," argued one Populist representative; "a privileged money power," completely unanticipated by the "framers of the Constitution," is now "dominating and controlling legislation for its own selfish interest."[176]

The high stakes of constitutional reform for the state's political economy seemed plain. The conservative editor of *The Oregonian* warned darkly that if the champions of direct democracy like U'Ren and Bourne "can get a direct vote on money, wages, interest, rents, profits, and the general scheme of business . . . they will be able to set aside the whole of that science known as political economy."[177] This seems a revealing misstatement of the point. The democratic reformers who would become the core of the Progressive coalition had in mind a *different*, competing vision of political economy than the "science" the *Oregonian* editor imagined—a vision that encompassed all the fields of economic reform he cited and more.

THE PEOPLE AND ARTICLE V

William U'Ren and his Populist and Progressive allies were not, in the end, able to implement the most far-reaching elements of their new political economy. More radically democratic and redistributionist in outlook than many of the nationally prominent reform figures like Herbert Croly, who would praise his handiwork,[178] U'Ren ran for governor in 1912 and asked voters to imagine a different, more equal society. "Suppose there should be no estates above $50,000," he would say on the stump. "Possibly there would not then be any unemployed."[179] But he lost.[180] Reformers' dreams of proportional representation systems—in part as a bulwark against gerrymandering—likewise went largely unrealized.[181] And yet the changes wrought by this wave of constitutional reformers, extending from the end of the Populist era through the Progressive moment, were vast enough to reshape much of the practice of American government.

It was on the foundation of these changes in the first years of the twentieth century that overlapping coalitions of Progressive reformers were able to push through the Sixteenth, Seventeenth, Eighteenth, and Nineteenth Amendments. All had been the subjects of decades of social movement agitation. And while these were the only four amendments ratified, they did not exhaust the changes of the national Constitution on the Progressive agenda. Congress approved, but the states did not ratify, a child labor amendment to grant Congress the power to "limit, regulate, and prohibit the labor of persons under eighteen years of age."[182] In terms of breadth of support, perhaps the most significant unrealized structural change to the Constitution was an amendment to amend the amendment process, altering Article V to "provide a more easy and expeditious method of amending the Federal Constitution," as the Progressive Party platform put it.[183] The goal was to make the people more fully "the masters of their Constitution"[184]—and the Constitution a more wieldy, effective instrument for building a modern democracy of opportunity. That was a goal establishment Progressives had in common with Populists and Debsian Socialists alike.[185]

Absent such an amendment, the Article V process was such a steep uphill climb that activists and reformers had good reason to distrust it. After Reconstruction, this process was dammed up until the Progressive Era. But then, with a Senate whose composition was beginning to shift, even in advance of the Seventeenth Amendment because of primaries and other changes at the state level, an unprecedented series of nonpartisan coalitions were able to build the requisite supermajorities to break through.

The Sixteenth Amendment is a case in point. Ever since the infamous *Pollock* case, Populists and populist-inclined Democrats in Congress had pressed for the decision to be overturned. Their arguments sounded unambiguously in constitutional political economy. Representative Cordell Hull of Tennessee, one of the leading advocates of the income tax, argued in 1909 that "all authors of political economy of reputation" favor an income tax. He quoted Adam Smith, Francis Wayland, and Thomas Cooley, before reprising a set of constitutional arguments from what he called Justice Harlan's "memorable" *Pollock* dissent. Hull argued that to prohibit the government from taxing "accumulated wealth," which has "enjoyed the protection and other blessings of the Government and thus far escaped most of its accompanying burdens," amounted to special favoritism of the rich, while the consumption-focused tax system *Pollock* effectively required the government to employ amounted to "an infamous system of class legislation."[186] "The world," he added, "has never seen such colossal fortunes as we behold in the present age. Their owners are richly able to pay taxes."[187] The other side of the fight about constitutional political economy in *Pollock* was also well represented in Congress; opponents of the income tax contended that the tax itself amounted to "class legislation" because it targeted the wealthy. But by 1909 it was clear that most of Congress favored reversing *Pollock*. The question was how.

One faction, led by Hull, argued that it was the "duty of Congress"—whose members are "under oath to support the Constitution"—to "exhaust[] every reasonable and legitimate means" to persuade the Court to reverse its error, by enacting a new income tax statute.[188] "I say it is a gross dereliction of duty," he argued, "for Congress to tamely and meekly acquiesce in the patent errors" of *Pollock*.[189] Others argued that a constitutional amendment was needed. At a crucial moment, President Taft, a Republican and a perhaps reluctant supporter of the income tax, who had favored the statutory route, sent a message to Congress saying that after further reflection, he had concluded that "an amendment is the only proper course."[190] His reasons were institutional, harking back to his years as an appellate judge and presaging his time as Chief Justice. "For Congress to assume that the Court will reverse itself, and to enact legislation on such an assumption, will not strengthen popular confidence in the stability of judicial construction of the Constitution,"[191] he wrote. Taft's proposal won the day in part because of the calculated support of some income tax *opponents*, who hoped the amendment would never be ratified. They imagined that the Article V process was broken, in 1909, the way it actually *is* broken today; channeling reformers' energies into an amendment would divert and thwart them.[192] This turned out to be a colossal miscalculation. After a five-year ratification campaign, the Sixteenth Amendment became part of the Constitution, radically increasing the revenue-generating power of the federal government in a way that would forever transform the federal system.

The Seventeenth Amendment followed a similar trajectory: powerful Populist roots, white-hot with arguments that sounded in constitutional political economy, tempered somewhat by the drawn-out process of the amendment's adoption. Advocates of the direct election of senators spent two decades arguing that the indirect system had become a constitutional crisis. Populist representative Omer Kem, from the western plains of Nebraska, and reportedly the first person elected to Congress who had lived in a sod house, made the Populist case in characteristic terms. "False and evil systems," argued Kem, "have crept in through defects in the Constitution, by which the natural rights of the people have been taken from them, resulting in an unequal distribution of the wealth of the country."[193] Linking the present crisis of concentration of economic power to past Jacksonian strands of constitutional political economy, he reasoned that if not for the "unjust, discriminating legislation of the past that gave special privileges in the way of subsidies and grants of different kinds to a favored few"—specifically, giveaways to railroads, banks, and "wealthy corporations" of many kinds—then today "there would not be so many wealthy corporations to influence legislation."[194] But as it is, the current course will "inevitably result in wiping out the great middle class entirely and the establishment of two extremes: the extremely poor and extremely wealthy, landlord and tenant, aristocrat and plebian." This was a substantive constitutional problem, involving class domination and political inequality, that called for a structural constitutional solution, involving constitutional design:

> [T]he time has come, Mr. Chairman, in my opinion, when the Constitution should be so amended as to conform more nearly to the principles set forth in the Declaration of Liberty and its own preamble. . . . It was to be a popular government by, of, and for the people, returning to them all rights and privileges they had lost under the monarchy from which they had suffered by the discrimination of that government in favor of the few . . . resulting, as it always must result, in the absolute slavery of the masses. It was this evil of concentrating the power to govern in the hands of the few that the fathers sought to guard against in framing the Constitution.[195]

This particular way of threading the needle—advocating constitutional redesign, but arguing for it in terms of constitutional fidelity—became the centerpiece of Populist arguments for the Seventeenth Amendment, as it was in their interpretive arguments for enlarging the scope of congressional authority over political economy. Here, the current power of large, distant corporations could stand in for the old dangers of rule by distant British royals across the sea. Notice, too, the familiar republican role of "slavery" in Kem's reasoning. This is a Constitution weighted toward the Preamble, the Declaration of Independence, and the Gettysburg Address, a Constitution whose foundation is popular sovereignty. And in the decades to come, countless Progressives, along with leaders, lawyers, and activists attached to Eugene Debs's Socialist Party, made use of the same tropes of constitutional fidelity—calling for radical revision of inherited constitutional structures and institutions, while proclaiming constancy to the principles of the Declaration.

Crucial to this needle-threading, this stance of fidelity amid radical revision, was the claim that something had gone awry to thwart the idea of popular sovereignty at the foundation of the original constitutional design. "With the development during recent times of the great corporate interests of the country," Senator Joseph Bristow of Kansas argued, these interests "have spent enormous amounts of money in corrupting legislatures to elect to the Senate men of their choosing."[196]

> Through the influence of the Senators so elected, who have become known as corporation Senators, legislation to control the trusts and monopolies has been smothered in committees and defeated. . . . [A]nd by controlling the election of Senators these great interested have to a large extent been able to secure the appointment of judges who are more devoted to their interests than to the public welfare.[197]

The solution was a constitutional change that was also a kind of restoration. As another representative put it: "The economic, social, and industrial changes which have taken place since the present method of electing Senators was established seem to require a reconsideration of the method; not for the purpose of changing the fundamental principles of our Government, but for the purpose of maintaining the very principles which the fathers sought to establish."[198] By removing one of the avenues "through which corporate influence now holds its sway," direct election will "once more restore the United States Senate to the dignified position intended by the fathers of our country."[199]

Even opponents of the amendment understood that it was basically about constitutional political economy. As the debate wore on over many Congresses, they argued (with ample prescience, it must be said) that direct election would not succeed in its goal of reducing the influence of wealth on politics. "[I]f there are millionaires in the country who would obtain a seat in this body by the use of money," argued Senator Stewart of Nevada, "the opportunity to accomplish such a result afforded by primary elections would be vastly superior to the opportunities now existing to corrupt State legislatures."[200] In light of this, "The clamor to destroy the Senate of the United States as ordained by the fathers of the Constitution ought not to prevail."[201]

The House passed what became the Seventeenth Amendment by the requisite two-thirds vote in several successive Congresses. Unsurprisingly, the Senate itself was the bigger challenge. In the end, part of what finally helped nudge the Senate vote over the supermajority threshold in 1912 was the sheer volume of embarrassing, highly public Senate corruption scandals, combined with the surprisingly frequent occasions when deadlocked state legislatures were failing to send anyone to the Senate at all.[202] In one Congress, more than one in ten senators had faced either a court trial or a Senate investigation for some serious form of corruption.[203] A series of muckraking articles in William Randolph Hearst's *Cosmopolitan* made the public case in the most sensationalistic terms that the Senate had become a pack of wildly disreputable characters, "elected by the interests," whose "stealthy and underhanded" work on behalf of those interests amounted to "an intentional betrayal of the people."[204] The series, titled "The Treason of the Senate," dwelled at length on the details of particular baroque episodes of senatorial corruption. Such tales undoubtedly strengthened public resolve. But it would be a mistake to understand the amendment in terms of the narrow prevention of bribery-like corruption, or for that matter, the simple aim of reducing the extent to which the Senate was a "club of millionaires." Although the amendment *did* for a long spell modestly alter the type of person who typically served in the Senate,[205] this is too narrow a lens through which to view its purpose and effect.

The Seventeenth Amendment was, in the end, an anti-oligarchy amendment. Its purpose was to decouple half the national legislature from a system of election that allowed it to become a central vehicle for the political power of the emerging oligarchy. "Corruption" was at the center of the politics of the amendment and its ratification, but corruption means more than one thing. In light of the arc of Populist and Progressive agitation for direct democracy that led to it, the Seventeenth Amendment is best understood not simply as a brake on bribery and vote-buying, but rather as an attempt to recast the political *and economic* order of early twentieth-century America, making both more accessible and responsive to the American people, rather than corrupted by oligarchy.[206]

The coalition that won this amendment was animated by a vision of constitutional political economy that was far broader than any changes made through Article V. We can see the contours of this vision most clearly in the state-level constitutional politics that drove the adoption of the Oregon System throughout the West and parts of the Midwest and Plains. Its focus was not just politics, but political economy. To see it in the starkest possible relief, we will end this chapter with a brief visit to Montana, a rougher place than Oregon, with a much scanter middle class. Here the constitutional stakes of oligarchy—not only in politics, but also in economic life—were that much rawer, which is why the Oregon System caught like a wildfire.

The Copper Kings

On October 23, 1903, the Amalgamated Copper Company abruptly shut down all of its mining, logging, and other operations in the state of Montana. The state's economy ground immediately to a halt. An appreciable portion of the population of the state was thrown out of work as winter approached.[207] It was a classic political power play by a monopolist. Amalgamated, owned primarily by the Rockefellers and other Eastern investors, had consolidated ownership of most of the state's lucrative copper industry. The company, which sometimes was called simply "the Company," controlled most of the politicians in the state's legislature through a combination of overwhelming economic clout, ownership of nearly all of the state's newspapers, and a great deal of outright bribery.[208] The situation was similar to the Oregon story, but more extreme. In

Montana in 1903, Amalgamated had a single remaining significant rival. Apparently that rival had in his pocket two state judges in the town of Butte, who consistently rendered verdicts in his favor and against Amalgamated in many high-dollar disputes.[209] In response, Amalgamated shut down its operations that October in a kind of unregulated capital-side strike, to pressure the legislature to immediately pass a new venue statute that would enable it to remove cases from the courts in Butte to friendlier judges elsewhere.

Amalgamated got exactly what it wanted out of the Montana legislature, which went into special session within weeks to enact the desired law.[210] The company eventually crushed its smaller rival as well.[211] But it also set in motion a process whose implications the company did not anticipate. Led by activist miners and mill workers and a handful of friendly shop owners and attorneys, working-class Montanans prodded the same legislators who cowered before the economic and political power of Amalgamated to begin a process of structural constitutional reform, adopting in Montana the state initiative, referendum, and direct constitutional amendment—devices the people would eventually use to circumvent the awesome combined political and economic power of "the Company" and restore popular sovereignty.[212] By 1912, at the height of Progressive constitutional agitation to counterbalance oligarchic power structures across the West, the people of Montana, through the direct initiative, enacted among other things a sweeping campaign finance law called the Corrupt Practices Act, one provision of which prohibited corporations from using their corporate funds to support or oppose candidates for state office.[213]

This is a story of constitutional reform in the name of the anti-oligarchy principle. The Populists and Progressives of Montana who both pushed for the initiative system itself and used it to enact the Corrupt Practices Act viewed these projects as a "fight to preserve to the people of Montana the right of self-government."[214] The goal was to wrest some form of popular sovereignty from a political system that had lost its republican character, a system in which a single company so "clearly dominated the Montana economy and political order" that it had "convert[ed] the state government into a political instrument" serving the interests of absentee stockholders rather than the people of Montana.[215]

How should we view these changes, and their constitutional significance, more than a century later? The answer turns on how we understand the project of the anti-oligarchy Constitution. Exactly a century after the passage of the act, in a 2012 case called *American Tradition Partnership v. Bullock,* the U.S. Supreme Court struck down the corporate political spending provision of Montana's Corrupt Practices Act as a violation of the First Amendment.[216] For the Supreme Court, this was an exceedingly straightforward case, disposed of in a one-paragraph per curiam reversal of the Montana Supreme Court. The Court had recently decided *Citizens United,* striking down a similar ban on corporate political expenditures.[217] There was "no serious doubt" that *Citizens United* applied and required striking down the Montana law.[218]

The Montana Supreme Court was aware of *Citizens United.* It had viewed *American Tradition Partnership* as distinguishable because the statute had a distinct factual predicate: in Montana, the Corrupt Practices Act had been enacted against a backdrop of severe and prolonged oligarchic capture of the machinery of the state government. The question is what significance that history—and the movement for constitutional restoration that arose out of that history—has for how either courts or any of us ought to interpret the First Amendment today. We will return to this question in Chapter 9.

6

THE NEW DEAL "DEMOCRACY OF OPPORTUNITY"

When the great New Deal historian Arthur Schlesinger Jr. defined the subject of his classic trilogy, *The Age of Roosevelt,* as "the crisis of the old order," the "old order" he had in mind was the constitutional political economy of Lochnerism.[1] The stock market crash, the financial break-down, and the Great Depression brought mass economic suffering and dread for the future. By election eve 1932, it was plain to a majority of Americans that the country's business and financial elites were quite un-able to repair the nation's broken economy. Yet, Lochnerism's classical liberal precepts limited the scope of government's authority to regulate and reform the private corporate and financial order.

The New Deal set out to save capitalism and the Constitution from their own conservative guardians. The overbearing power of financial and business elites was making capitalism's crises unmanageable, while America's experiment in constitutional democracy was imperiled by prevailing legal orthodoxy. Neither might survive without a more powerful central government capable of robust economic reform and policymaking.

No wonder the New Deal brought to a boil many of the constitutional and political-economic conflicts left simmering from the Progressive Era. Roosevelt's long tenure in the White House defined an era of con-stitutional politics par excellence. Rival visions of our most basic con-stitutional commitments in the sphere of economic life were the stuff of headlines and everyday debate—in the electoral and legislative arenas, in the new mass media, on street corners and picket lines, and, of course, in the courts. Already during the 1932 race for the White House, Her-bert Hoover, the Republican president, and Roosevelt, his Democratic challenger, both agreed that the battle over New Dealers' nascent efforts to revive and reshape the nation's political economy was, in Hoover's words, "more than a contest between two parties. It is a contest between two philosophies of government"—a contest over whether to change "our form of government and our social and economic system."[2]

The Supreme Court's sweeping condemnation of key New Deal measures in 1935 lent practical and symbolic power to the New Deal's foes and led Roosevelt and the New Dealers to make their showdown with conservatism on the field of constitutional political economy. Roosevelt accused the "economic royalists"—whom he likened to "the eighteenth century royalists who held special privileges from the crown"—of building a "dynastic scheme" that threatened to subvert our constitutional democracy and replace it with a "new despotism," "a new industrial dictatorship."[3]

Here was the democracy-of-opportunity tradition—the anti-oligarchy Constitution—in its purest modern form. In his speech at the 1936 Democratic National Convention, Roosevelt declared, "For too many of us the political equality we once had won was meaningless in the face of economic inequality. A small group had concentrated into their own hands an almost complete control over other people's property, other people's money, other people's labor—other people's lives." He framed the result in terms of the Declaration of Independence: "[L]ife was no longer free; liberty no longer real; men could no longer follow the pursuit of happiness."[4] Roosevelt credited the Populist and Progressive antimonopoly movements for understanding the constitutional stakes. These movements understood that "the inevitable consequence" of placing "economic and financial control in the hands of the few" was "the destruction of the base of our form of government" and its replacement with "an autocratic form of government."[5]

A *democratic* government, on FDR's and the New Dealers' account, had not only the constitutional power but the duty to enact a host of new social and economic rights: to decent work and livelihoods, to organize unions and bargain collectively, to education and training and retraining, to housing, health care, and social insurance. These rights, Roosevelt argued, were imperative to restore the "forgotten[] ideals and values" once secured by the "old and sacred possessive [common-law contract and property] rights."[6] Such modern social and economic rights,

FDR explained, amounted to an "economic constitutional order," essential "to protect majorities against the enthronement of minorities" and secure what he called a "democracy of opportunity."[7]

Thus, Roosevelt tied his ringing new phrase "democracy of opportunity" to the old promise of a political economy that ensures every American a "right to make a comfortable living."[8] FDR was echoing the revolutionary generation's view that the right to the pursuit of happiness entailed conditions of ownership, production, and exchange that enabled all to achieve what that generation called a "competency" and "a degree of comfortable independence."[9] Like the founders, Roosevelt underscored that this kind of broad and wide-open middle class was not only essential to basic distributive fairness and economic freedom, it was also a necessary basis of *political* liberty and republican self-rule, and a necessary bulwark against oligarchy. In the founders' day, much of this freedom-ensuring work set out under the banner of strict construction and laissez-faire. That was the outlook of the Jeffersonian founders of FDR's own party, as he often observed. But as modern industrial civilization replaced Jefferson's agrarian ideal, laissez-faire and strict construction morphed into protections of concentrated wealth and corporate privilege. New Dealers argued that the old freedom-ensuring constitutional order now required broad national powers and new affirmative readings of the old basic rights.[10]

Edward Corwin, a Princeton political scientist, was the era's preeminent constitutional commentator. By the "ideological revolution" we have just witnessed, he wrote, "it becomes the duty of government to guarantee economic security to all as the indispensable foundation of constitutional liberty."[11] Equally important, noted Corwin, was the nation's—and, suddenly, the Court's—"dramatic" reimagining of "liberty" in its constitutional dimensions as "something that may be infringed by other forces" besides government. Safeguarding labor's collective constitutional freedoms against the *private* forces of capital was "something that may require the positive intervention of government against those other forces."[12]

These were the New Deal's additions to the layered meanings of the liberty promised by the Constitution. The product was an American variation of social democracy packaged in the language of freedom. It proved so popular as an up-to-date expression of the American creed that its creators managed to brand the product as "liberalism" in the public mind.

The only way to topple oligarchy, rebuild democracy, and reinvent a broad and secure middle class, argued New Deal liberals, was through a national government empowered to regulate and redistribute economic power and wealth on a national scale. Constitutional lawyers, scholars, and historians today remember the claims about the scope of national power, but we have forgotten the claims about affirmative rights and constitutional legislative duties to effectuate those rights and to use federal power to reorder the nation's political economy along democratic lines.

The New Dealers themselves inadvertently encouraged this forgetting. Arguing in Congress and in public discourse, FDR and New Deal lawmakers championed their legislative agenda in terms of implementing their new social-democratic "economic constitutional order,"[13] brimming with positive social and economic rights and affirmative governmental duties to make good on the Constitution's core promises and commitments. But when it came to framing the constitutional defenses of these statutes before the Court, New Deal lawyers concluded that they had nothing to gain by trying to win judicial assent to this outlook. So, while their public-political arguments focused on legislative constitutional duties and fundamental rights, after one colossal, failed effort to put such arguments before the Court, their claims in court came to focus solely on the scope of federal power.

And, of course, after the Court's famous "switch in time" in 1937,[14] these claims prevailed. But what New Dealers gained from the Court was not a decision to make the New Deal constitutional political economy its own. The main thing they asked of the Court was for the Court to step aside and let legislative and administrative actors carry on with the constitutional work they were better equipped—and disposed—to do. And yet, the Court did take note of the constitutional arguments addressing economic inequality, class domination, and the distribution of the risks and rewards of industrial life, which thrived in Congress and public discourse.

Roosevelt's new "constitutional economic order" hinged on a governmental duty to assure decent work and livelihoods, collective bargaining, social insurance, and other social goods to all Americans. The New Deal's actual legacy would be a far more partial and segmented, racialized, and gendered patchwork of social provision and labor standards. The New Dealers and the vast social movement of industrial workers that became their key social and political engine strove for over a decade to "complete the New Deal," and failed. And then, as Chapters 7 and 8 will show, the language of progressive constitutional political economy vanished from mainstream public discourse and debate in the face of a conservative counterrevolution. This coounterrevolution would uproot much of the constitutional vocabulary and institutional foundations New Deal liberals had forged to defend a modern and inclusive democracy of opportunity, leaving that for us to reimagine.

Prelude: The Gold Clause Confrontation

On March 4, 1933, when President Roosevelt took office, the United States was in the throes of two overlapping crises of banking and currency that gave rise to the first constitutional confrontation between New Deal constitutionalism and the old Lochnerian regime. First, a sudden cascade of bank failures was sweeping the nation, as fearful depositors rushed to withdraw funds. Second, and no less important, a slower-burning crisis of deflation—plummeting prices—was deepening the Depression. Deflation was ruinous for debtors, who owed more and more over time as each dollar of their debt grew larger in real terms. It was devastating for farmers. To stop deflation, the United States would have to adopt a monetary policy that put more money into people's hands. Roosevelt was no William Jennings Bryan, but he could see from the moment he took office that it was time for the United States to stop crucifying itself on the cross of gold.

He moved within thirty-six hours. In the wee hours of March 6, 1933, Roosevelt issued a proclamation declaring a temporary bank holiday to give Congress time to pass emergency legislation shoring up the banks, creating what is now federal deposit insurance.[15] The same proclamation began to seize control of the money supply by barring all banks from paying out or exporting any gold. Within weeks, Roosevelt suspended the gold standard and confiscated all the privately held gold in the United States. Individuals holding gold or gold certificates had to surrender them in return for dollars, at a price set by the government.[16] Congress went on to order all the gold coins melted down into bars, as if to make the point as clear as possible: Gold was no longer money, and would never be again.[17] Officially, a gold standard lived on in some form until 1971, but in substance it was gone by April 1933. Roosevelt soon used the government's new power over the monetary system to devalue the dollar and cause inflation, by declaring that an ounce of gold would now be worth not $20.67, but $35.[18] Congress did its part by swiftly passing a law repudiating "gold clauses."[19] Since the Civil War, these clauses had been written into the vast majority of long-term financial contracts in the United States. They aimed to fortify a creditor against possible devaluations of the dollar or changes to the gold standard by entitling the creditor to the value of a specific amount *of gold* rather than a specific number of dollars. Gold clauses threatened the federal government's ability to successfully devalue the dollar. Congress declared all such clauses—in business contracts, mortgages, even federal bonds—"against public policy" and unenforceable. This unleashed a constitutional firestorm.

The late nineteenth-century Populist confrontation over "the money of the Constitution" had been a fight about which monetary policy the Constitution *required*. The fight took place in political campaigns and in legislatures. Its institutional focus was legislative constitutional duty.[20] In contrast, the 1933 confrontation took place on different constitutional terrain more familiar to a modern reader. The plaintiffs in the so-called Gold Clause Cases correctly saw the federal courts as the only branch likely to protect their Lochnerian rights of property and contract against usurpation by legislation and executive action. Such claims had deep roots in the anti-redistributive constitutional arguments against state actions such as debtor relief laws going back all the way to the founding.[21] They also had strong and recent Supreme Court precedents in the landmark cases of the *Lochner* era. Roosevelt's devaluation of the dollar combined with Congress's repudiation of the gold clauses meant that the holders of bonds and contracts with gold clauses would receive far fewer dollars—69 percent fewer—than if their gold clauses could be enforced. So the holders of these promises moved swiftly to enforce their gold clauses in federal court. Four cases—the "Gold Clause Cases"—soon reached the Supreme Court.[22]

The plaintiffs' claims were vintage Lochnerism. They primarily argued that Congress could not constitutionally repudiate gold clauses because this would impair their contracts or destroy their property. Undergirding those core property and contract rights claims was the deep Lochnerian commitment to the unconstitutionality of redistribution itself. The plaintiffs argued, in so many words, that the statute invalidating gold clauses would "take the property of one class of persons and give it to another class without compensation and without due process of law."[23] (The claim was that repudiating gold clauses would take property from creditors and give it to debtors.)

The stakes for American constitutional political economy could hardly have been higher. As one commentator sympathetic to the Lochnerian side of the contest put it at the time, the Gold Clause Cases weighed the question of whether "the rights of the individual citizen" would have to give way, "if not to a totalitarian State, at least to the social welfare of the community as a whole." Victory for the government would mean that courts were now apparently to interpret "the Constitution . . . in the light of present-day economic facts and concepts of social justice." Perhaps, he added ruefully, those storied "[o]ld concepts of liberty," the liberties of property and contract, "applicable to freeholders and craftsmen owning their own tools, are an empty shell to the landless and the wage-slave" of the present day, who had ushered Roosevelt into office.[24]

Justice McReynolds, the most obdurate of the Four Horsemen fighting the New Deal, wrote a passionate opinion adopting the Lochnerian theory of the case. He was frustrated by the proposition that the Gold Clause Cases were about monetary policy at all: "[A]ny abstract discussion of congressional power over money would only tend to befog the real issue." The real issue was that "under the guise of pursuing a monetary policy, Congress really has inaugurated a plan primarily designed to destroy private obligations, repudiate national debts, and drive into the Treasury all gold within the country."[25]

Yet McReynolds could not entirely leave behind the old constitutional political economy arguments of gold's nineteenth-century advocates. He called Roosevelt's policy "a debased standard," unconstitutional because it fails the first prong of *McCulloch v. Maryland* ("Let the end be legitimate . . .").[26] "The end or objective of the Joint Resolution was not 'legitimate.' The real purpose was not 'to assure uniform value to the coins and currencies of the United States,' but to destroy certain valuable contract rights."[27] In other words, McReynolds argued, certain monetary policy objectives are legitimate exercises of congressional power, while others are not. *That* argument perfectly tracked the constitutional claims of the nineteenth-century goldbugs who had successfully blocked the Populist incarnation of the anti-oligarchy Constitution when it came to monetary policy. The argument was also linked to a story of practical perils, which Justice McReynolds dolefully recounted: As soon as "the United States were off the gold standard," he wrote, "their paper money began a rapid decline in the markets of the world."[28] That was true. But in the depths of the deflation of the Depression, it was not an especially trenchant criticism. The "decline" or devaluation of the dollar was precisely the goal, and it worked.

But McReynolds got only four votes. Announcing his dissent from the bench to a rapt gallery, he intoned: "The Constitution as many of us have understood it, the Constitution that has meant so much to us, has gone."[29] There is some dispute about exactly what else he said (which definitely included a reference to the emperor Nero—who apparently, like Roosevelt, had devalued the currency). In a version of the oral dissent found in his papers, he concludes, "Shame and humiliation are upon us now. Moral and financial chaos may confidently be expected."[30] That peroration restates axioms of pro-gold constitutional political economy. But in fact, it was the claims of the plaintiffs, not those of the government, that were poised to cause financial chaos. As future Supreme Court Justice Robert Jackson succinctly explained, despite the legal uncertainty that lingered as the Gold Clause Cases proceeded through the courts, "the business world, which could not wait for lawyers' arguments to end, had accepted the whole monetary program and gone ahead making settlements and commitments."[31] Contrary to Justice McReynolds's expectations, the markets reacted to the government's victory with "unmixed relief."[32]

Still, the main line of Justice McReynolds's dissent was not the constitutional political economy of the goldbugs. It was the constitutional political economy of *Lochner*. It was the view that property and contract are paramount constitutional values that trump any newfangled constitutional commitments to egalitarianism. "To destroy a validly acquired right is the taking of property," McReynolds wrote. And for this proposition he pointedly cited a case from 1871 in which the Court had held that a man who had sold a slave, before emancipation, was still entitled to collect payments owed: Despite the ratification of the Thirteenth and Fourteenth Amendments, the contract was still valid.[33] One can well see why McReynolds might have chosen that particular case. In it, the Court had held that to invalidate the slave contract would impermissibly "take away one man's property and give it to another."[34] Such a thing, the Court held, was not required by the Thirteenth or Fourteenth Amendment. And if it *had* been required, the Court suggested, perhaps the amendments themselves might not be enforceable, because such interference with contract is "forbidden by the fundamental principles of the social compact, and is beyond the sphere of the legislative authority both of the States and the Nation."[35] A purer distillation of the Lochnerian view of the priority of anti-redistribution over other constitutional principles—most especially, over the core principles of the anti-oligarchy Constitution—would be difficult to invent.

Attorney General Homer Cummings, arguing the Gold Clause Cases personally on behalf of the government, framed the central questions of constitutional political economy in starkly different terms.[36] His argument recalled Gilded Age Greenbackers' and Populists' claims about private banks' usurpation of Congress's constitutional authority over the nation's currency.[37] Monetary policy, the attorney general declared, is either under the control of Congress—to whom the Constitution had expressly granted sovereign power over this field—or it is under the control of powerful bondholders and contract holders who can decide the nation's monetary policy by winning their cases in court. More fundamentally, he suggested, the nation's money itself is either a core area of sovereignty and democratic policymaking under the Constitution, or else it is some sort of pre-constitutional form of privileged private property, out of the reach of the law. It cannot be both. Cummings argued that the answer was clear. "These gold contracts," he argued, "deal with the very essence of sovereignty, for they require that the Government must surrender a portion of that sovereignty. To put it another way, these gold contracts have invaded the Federal field. It is not a case of Federal activity reaching out into a private area. . . . These claimants are upon Federal territory. They are squatters in the public domain, and when the government needs the territory they must move on."[38] These may be private contracts, but, as the government's brief put it, such contracts "interfere[] no less directly and substantially with the regulation of the value of money than do monopolistic agreements or unreasonable rate contracts with the regulation of interstate commerce."[39]

Cummings argued that an array of textual grants of constitutional power were best read together as a broad grant of power to Congress over this monetary field. It was not only the Article I power "to coin money and regulate the value thereof," but also the powers to borrow, to tax, to provide for the general welfare, even to maintain armies and declare war. Together these "imply all the essentials of a comprehensive federal power over the whole subject of the medium of exchange, standards of measure and value, coinage of money, and the control of credit."[40] Congress and the executive had acted "against the background of utter national need," in the thick of "an industrial and monetary and financial crisis of the most terrifying character." These branches had exercised their powers to build a new financial structure for the nation, "essential to the happiness and prosperity and welfare of our country." Vindicating the plaintiffs' Lochnerian claims of property and contract "would mean the break-down and the wreckage of the structure thus carefully created. Moreover, it would create a preferred class who, because of a contract of a special character, are able to take themselves outside, as it were, of the financial structure of their own country."[41]

And there, deep in the heart of the argument, in that claim about the "preferred class," we begin to hear the strong echo of the older constitutional political economy arguments in the democracy-of-opportunity tradition, from Jacksonian equal protection tradition through, especially, the arguments of Justice Harlan in dissent in *Pollock*. Would the Court enable wealthy speculators wielding constitutional rights claims to build themselves up as a special privileged class? Would the Justices thwart the democratic branches' efforts to build a financial system with enough resilience and broad enough access to credit to save the great mass of ordinary, middle-class Americans from financial ruin? Cummings urged the Justices to consider what a decision for the plaintiffs would mean for the broad swath of Americans who now depended on the federal government to dig the nation out of the Depression—and at the same time, how undemocratic, even oligarchic, a decision for the plaintiffs would be: "Should the claims of the owners of these gold obligations be approved, it would create a privileged class which, in character, in immunity, and in power, has hitherto been unparalleled in the history of the human race. I feel the walls of this courtroom expand; I see, waiting upon this decision, the hopes, the fears, and the welfare of millions of our fellow citizens."[42]

In that contrast—the welfare of millions, versus the building up of a privileged class with unparalleled immunity and power—Cummings grasped two of the three central threads of the democracy-of-opportunity tradition and fashioned them into a constitutional defense of federal power. It was a powerful argument—and in the Gold Clause Cases, it won over the majority of the Court. A year earlier, in *Blaisdell*, Chief Justice Hughes had written a 5–4 majority opinion upholding a Minnesota debtor relief law that had given borrowers more time to pay their debts.[43] The Court upheld the Minnesota law against a Contracts Clause challenge in part because it was a reasonable and proportionate response to the temporary emergency of the Depression. In the Gold Clause Cases, Chief Justice Hughes wrote for the same 5–4 majority over Justice McReynolds's dissent. But this time he did not rely on any claim of temporary emergency. Instead, his opinion held in sweeping terms that, exactly as Cummings had argued, the federal government has "broad and comprehensive national authority over the subjects of revenue, finance and currency . . . derived from the aggregate of the powers granted to the Congress."[44] The private contracts interfered with that authority, so Congress could void them.[45]

Chief Justice Hughes found more troublesome the government's argument in *Perry*, the case concerning gold clauses in U.S. bonds. In that case, Hughes thought, the federal government was essentially repudiating *its own* promise—violating the express terms of its own contract. That was one step too far. "When the United States, with constitutional authority, makes contracts, it has rights and incurs responsibilities similar to those of individuals," he wrote, and concluded that one Congress was "without power" to abrogate the contracts a prior Congress had made.[46] This had wild implications: A win for the *Perry* plaintiffs would have exploded the national debt by granting a massive special windfall to the holders of the federal bonds that had gold clauses. But then, in rather *Marbury*-esque fashion—asserting the Court's power while holding it back—Hughes held that although the bondholders won the constitutional argument, they were not entitled to a cent of damages.[47] Because Congress and the president had (constitutionally) confiscated all the gold and ended the market in it, the bondholders could not expect to be paid in actual gold. If it was dollars they were getting instead of gold, they were not entitled to any extra dollars beyond the number set by the new, postdevaluation dollar standard that Congress and the president had (constitutionally) made the monetary policy of the United States.

In essence, the bondholders were not entitled to damages because damages would require their stepping outside their nation's monetary policy. And that, no one could do. But the modern logic of that conclusion was in deep tension with the old-order logic of holding that Congress was "without power" to repudiate the gold clauses in its bonds. *Perry* was in this way a liminal case, with one foot in the old order and one in the new. (One could say the same of *Blaisdell*.) *Perry*'s outcome seemed "baffling"[48] at the time. But the upshot was clear. In *Perry*, the Court stood firmly on the sanctity of contracts—in theory. In practice, the Court allowed the New Deal's first critical political-economic project—asserting a muscular new federal power over monetary policy and exercising that power to get much more money into the hands of ordinary Americans—to proceed.

Although the Chief Justice probably did not know this, Roosevelt was prepared to respond to an adverse ruling in the Gold Clause Cases by openly defying the Court. In a fireside chat he had prepared to broadcast to the nation had the Court gone the other way, Roosevelt described in some detail the practical consequences of enforcing the gold clauses, from the "wholly unearned profit" this would grant certain investors and speculators to the mass industrial and municipal bankruptcies and the devastation of ordinary "[h]ome owners, whether city workers or farmers," whose mortgages would instantly have become far too expensive to pay.[49] Invoking "the duty of the Congress and the President to protect the people of the United States to the best of their ability," he argued in the draft address that "[t]o stand idly by and to permit the decision of the Supreme Court to be carried through to its logical, inescapable conclusion would . . . imperil the economic and political security of this nation."[50] This talk of the "duty" of Congress and the president was a major theme in New Deal constitutional thought: the idea that the legislative and executive branches have affirmative constitutional duties, rather than simply operating within the Constitution's constraints. Roosevelt framed his most direct challenge to the Court's constitutional supremacy by reaching back in political history, quoting President Lincoln's first inaugural address: "[I]f the policy of the government, upon vital questions affecting the whole people, is to be irrevocably fixed by decisions of the Supreme Court, the instant they are made . . . the people will have ceased to be their own rulers, having to that extent practically resigned their government into the hands of that eminent tribunal."[51]

Because Chief Justice Hughes sided with the government in the Gold Clause Cases, Roosevelt never delivered that speech. The government could proceed with its first radical change to the nation's constitutional political economy—a change that had, decades earlier, been at the very center of the Democratic Party's political platform and its constitutional aspirations for building a democracy of opportunity. By 1933, gold no longer played so central a role. Monetary policy was only one of several dimensions of the wrenching crisis. Still, for a court still largely thinking about constitutional political economy in Lochnerian terms, the Gold Clause Cases represented a highly significant early retreat. The Court effectively accepted that one of the most important sets of macroeconomic rules could constitutionally be set through politics, not through the court-enforced claims of property and contract so central to the old constitutional political economy. The implications of this change were enormous. As Roosevelt and his party began to fashion novel national solutions to the broader crisis, they would test how far the Court was willing to go.

The National Industrial Recovery Act:
A Corporatist Solution to the Crisis

Roosevelt's first efforts to confront the broader crisis led the federal government to assume unprecedented responsibilities across the economic sphere: public employment and public works, relief payments, labor policy and the regulation of markets, prices, and wages. Never had the federal government asserted such sweeping authority in peacetime. Along with great hope, the assertion of centralized power aroused grave constitutional worries. FDR and the New Dealers met the worries with the justification that the economic crisis was akin to war. They also made another, more paradoxical claim. The greatest constitutional worry was not New Deal innovation but the status quo. Without some nationally orchestrated scheme of economic cooperation and industrial democracy, they contended, our constitutional order would not survive the present crisis. Saving our Constitution, in other words, demanded resetting the old Lochnerian rules of the game. A great many defenders of the old order begged to differ, including the U.S. Supreme Court. It was one thing to accept, perhaps grudgingly, that Lochnerian political economy would have to give way to the federal government's muscular new assertion of constitutional power over currency. It was quite another to accept that the federal government had the constitutional power to rewrite the rules of everyday economic life wholesale, across the industrial landscape, in the name of building a democracy of opportunity.

The centerpiece of the early New Deal's scheme of economic cooperation and industrial democracy was the National Industrial Recovery Act (NIRA).[52] The Recovery Act was cobbled together early in the "first hundred days" to make plain that the New Deal was equal to the challenge of fundamental reform. It was an ambitious reform and, at first, a popular one. It was also, according to conservatives, unconstitutional; it ultimately met its demise at the hands of the Supreme Court in *Schechter* (the "Sick Chicken Case") on "Black Monday" in May 1935.[53]

The NIRA included a massive public works program to help put Americans back to work. But its main scheme was America's first large-scale experiment with a form of economic regulation known as corporatism, conferring formal governmental authority on private actors to regulate key terms of economic life.[54] Thus, the Recovery Act authorized private trade associations composed of employers and trade unions composed of workers to hammer out industrial "codes of fair competition"—maximum hours, minimum wages, prices, production standards—for public officials in a new National Recovery Administration to vet, adopt, and enforce.

The Recovery Act's architects drew on the associational spirit of the Hoover administration. Allowable, voluntary cooperation among firms under Hoover became *mandatory* under the NIRA. Hoover had pushed back the outer limits of antitrust law; the Recovery Act went well beyond them, and it suspended antitrust enforcement. Equally startling: whereas Herbert Hoover left labor out in the cold, the NIRA's soon-to-be-famous Section 7(a) not only obliged employers to "comply with the maximum hours . . . minimum rates of pay, and other conditions" contained in the industry-wide codes, but also provided that "employees shall have the right to organize and bargain collectively through representatives of their own choosing, and shall be free from the interference, restraint or coercion of employers" in doing so.[55]

Long a champion of organized labor and a seasoned social reformer, Senator Robert Wagner of New York was the Recovery Act's sponsor and one of its main designers.[56] In the NIRA, Wagner hoped to boost unions and give them an important role in making economic policy. The idea, as Wagner saw it, was to redistribute power in the nation's political economy by giving workers' organizations and associations of small and medium-sized firms something closer to an equal voice with big business in hammering out "codes of fair competition" for all the nation's industries.

As soon as the Recovery Act passed through Congress, the White House launched a massive campaign to mobilize public support around the National Recovery Administration (NRA)[57] and its famous "Blue Eagle" emblem, which would operate as a brand for every business abiding by the new codes. With broadcasts, advertisements, and parades, the administration summoned all manner of businesses in every corner of the economy to join the president's grand experiment in industrial cooperation.[58] The Recovery Act's sweep underscored New Dealers' determination to bring national government deep into manufacturing, mining, and agriculture, where much Commerce Power precedent held that the national government could not go, and deep into labor and other market and property relations, where due process precedent held no government could go.[59] But the act's drafters had had little time for the niceties of what they saw as reactionary doctrine. Rather than trying to frame their far-reaching assertions of congressional authority in the language of Commerce Power precedent, they set out as the "policy of Congress" a declaration of "a national emergency . . . of widespread unemployment and disorganization of industry." And they made that emergency a warrant for a brash, doctrinally unhinged invocation of Congress's duty "to provide for the general welfare by promoting the organization of industry for the purpose of cooperative action among trade groups" and "united action of labor and management" under "adequate governmental sanctions and supervision."[60]

All this would come back to haunt the government's lawyers when it came to defending the act in court. It embodied the new president's forceful rejection of what, in his inaugural address, he called "an outworn tradition" of constitutional political economy that saw markets as largely self-regulating and self-correcting and hewed to the classical liberal vision of a limited national government.[61]

The Court would not respond to the Recovery Act until 1935. But other leading defenders of the old order wasted no time. In the *Saturday Evening Post,* Herbert Hoover proclaimed the NIRA an epochal "Challenge to Liberty." Under FDR, the United States was lining up behind other "peoples and governments" that were succumbing to "economic regimentation" and "blindly wounding, even destroying . . . fundamental human liberties."[62]

Hoover was right. The thinking behind the NIRA borrowed features of corporatism and economic planning from regimes that rejected liberal democracy.[63] But the New Dealers saw the constitutional stakes in a different light: Could constitutional democracy measure up to the challenges of rebuilding the collapsed capitalist order and putting the nation back to work? Or were the dictatorships correct that the old "bourgeois" republican constitutions, with their quaint reliance on democratically elected legislatures, were just not up to the toughest problems of the day? If that was so, then Americans, like others, would eventually turn to authoritarians of left or right.[64]

As Ira Katznelson has underscored, the most basic constitutional challenge, in the New Dealers' eyes, was to come up with the outlines of a political economy that harnessed new forms of economic governance to unshakeable liberal democratic commitments.[65] That was what the NRA's general counsel, Donald Richberg, had in mind when he told Congress: "The great adventure of the Recovery Act lies in this effort to find a democratic . . . solution of the problem that has produced dictatorships in at least three great nations since the World War."[66]

Like Richberg and Senator Wagner, most New Deal–minded economists, policymakers, and politicians shared the view that at bottom, the Great Depression was a result of underconsumption—and underconsumption a consequence of the maldistribution of wealth and bargaining power, in favor of the corporate elite and against worker-consumers. The mass-production corporate economy required a mass market to consume its goods, but neither big, oligopolistic corporate employers nor smaller, competitive ones had the incentives to pay the wages to sustain mass consumption. That required measures compelling employers to pay higher wages without fear of falling behind their rivals. The result would boost mass purchasing power, to everyone's collective advantage. This, in turn, required some combination of legal floors on wages and a massive redistribution of bargaining power to enable workers to secure high wages for themselves, across the whole industrial economy.

So went the economic logic behind Section 7(a). Its political logic was that the only way to restore democracy was to bring the constitutional norms of fair representation and equal rights into industrial life. But the act was "fraught with . . . danger to workers and consumers," Senator Wagner warned, if its suspension of antitrust to allow for "organization and cooperation" on the part of businesses and employers "is not counterbalanced by the equal organization and equal bargaining power of employees."[67]

Much as Wagner feared, the NRA lacked the administrative capacity to do its job, and the White House lacked the political will to make the business elites deal equitably with either labor or small business. Representatives of big corporations dominated the new federal agency and its constituent associations. Chief executives Alfred Sloan of General Motors, Gerard Swope of General Electric, and Walter Teagle of

Standard Oil held top positions.[68] Big firm influence permeated not only the NRA but also the great majority of trade associations doing the codification. Government supervision lay with a handful of staff attorneys, who ended up approving hundreds of codes drafted by the corporate bar.[69]

Roosevelt refused to weigh in on labor's behalf. He instructed Richberg to give up demanding labor representation in the code-making process. The NRA declined to require collective bargaining as a condition for ratifying the industry codes, and Roosevelt, reluctant to rile the fiercely anti-union captains of industry, refused to intervene. He confirmed labor's separation from the code-drafting machinery by establishing a separate National Labor Board (NLB) within the NRA.[70] Chaired by Senator Wagner, the Labor Board was charged with implementing Section 7(a) by hearing complaints under that provision and, with little but its moral authority and symbolic power to withhold the NRA's Blue Eagle brand, to "compose all conflicts threatening the industrial peace of the country."[71]

The result of this conciliatory approach was that Wagner's fledgling Labor Board worked hard but produced little peace.[72] Big industry was convulsed with labor strife; firm after firm, from auto to steel to mining to textiles, saw waves of bitter, often violent strikes, the great majority of them brought on by the firms' refusals to recognize and bargain with the unions their workers were joining. Union activists were fired and workers threatened if they talked up unionism. Employers in these core industries flatly rejected the Labor Board's interpretation of Section 7(a), which required companies to bargain with unions that signed up a majority of workers or won their votes in Labor Board–run elections. Employers refused, standing adamantly on their constitutional rights under the ancien regime, which the courts routinely upheld.[73]

So, Section 7(a) didn't underwrite effective enforcement of labor rights. But it did do important work. Its inclusion in the Recovery Act marked a dramatic recognition that unions were central actors in the new political-economic order struggling to be born. Unions campaigned with the slogan "The President Wants You to Join the Union."[74] Section 7(a) encouraged an enormous boost in union membership and a remarkable new sense of entitlement among industrial workers.[75] It provided unprecedented legitimacy to the labor movement's long-standing rights claims, and it made the increasingly militant strike waves into more than economic battles; now, they were also openly political and constitutional contests between competing visions of the fundamental rights and duties of labor and capital.

Dismayed by the weakness of his ad hoc Labor Board, Senator Wagner introduced a new bill in early 1934 to "put[] teeth" into workers' rights to organize by making the Labor Board a permanent agency with ample powers of enforcement.[76] Only a year and a half later, when the Supreme Court struck down the Recovery Act, and Section 7(a) with it, did the president throw his support behind Wagner's bill. That happened in mid-1935, after the Court handed down *A. L. A. Schechter Poultry Corp. v. United States.*[77]

SCHECHTER POULTRY: THE COURT CONFRONTS NEW DEAL CONSTITUTIONALISM

The Schechter brothers ran a wholesale poultry yard and kosher slaughterhouse in Brooklyn. They were convicted of violating various provisions of their industry's Live Poultry Code, including the ones that set maximum hours and minimum wages. Maximum hours and minimum wages were a requirement of Section 7(a), so the Schechters' constitutional challenge was aimed at that section. But when the Supreme Court agreed to hear the case in April 1935, the entire act was on the block, and briefs and oral arguments brimmed with the same high-stakes constitutional claims that were increasingly a subject of public debate.

The counsel for petitioners, Frederick H. Wood, a prominent member of the elite New York Bar who rarely represented kosher butchers, framed the issues in a way that echoed the conservatives' constitutional arguments in Congress and the public square.[78] He asked: "May the Federal Government usurp the power of regulating purely intrastate production?" And "may it annihilate the principles of a free government, by wiping out in a single stroke the freedom of contract and enterprise of a free people and regimenting those participating in every private business by regulation more onerous . . . than that previously imposed even upon public utilities?"[79] At oral argument, his closing peroration again echoed the act's foes outside the Court: "If, as many believe, the Federal Government should be converted into some form of national socialism—whether Soviet, Fascist, or Nazi—it may be accomplished only by the submission of a constitutional amendment. . . . It may not be made by an act of Congress."[80]

When the NRA's general counsel, Donald Richberg, took up the government's oral argument before the Court, he encouraged the Justices to consider the touchstones of New Deal constitutionalism that New Deal lawyers soon would learn not to mention in court: affirmative economic rights and affirmative governmental duties to secure them, and a national Constitution that not only empowered but obliged Congress to address the problem of gross class inequality and domination.[81] These arguments forced the Court to confront a more sweeping question than the one posed in the Gold Clause fight. Would the Court allow the New Deal to revise the fundamentals of American constitutional political economy?

Richberg suggested it would have to, because only a muscular assertion of national power over economic policy could lift us out of the Depression. The NIRA, he argued, was Congress's response to an economic breakdown that "private industry" had proved unable to repair. In 1933, Congress had confronted a "nationwide system of production, exchange, and employment" in a "downward spiral." The "National Government alone" had "the power and the obligation" to "protect against the evils of this unparalleled depression." Invoking Madison's Notes and his Virginia Plan, Richberg reminded the Court of the understanding of the "Fathers" that the Constitution would secure to Congress the power to address problems, above all economic problems, which the states separately were incompetent to solve.[82] Congress had not only the power but the duty to bring about an "expansion of industry."[83]

Opposing counsel cast the NIRA as an end to "freedom of contract"; Richberg responded with the New Dealers' consistent counterpoint. The old economic liberties had never safeguarded "actual economic freedom" for workers, and now, their court-crafted freedom of contract stood exposed as a "liberty to starve." "No men can claim that they are free when they have no opportunity to make a living," Richberg told the Justices. Preserving the "realities of liberty" and the "freedom of the employee to make a contract for decent wages" required "action, not inaction," on the part of government.[84]

The Court was having none of Richberg's New Deal constitutionalism. *Schechter* was decided on May 27, 1935, dubbed by journalists the New Deal's "Black Monday." The Court unanimously struck down the NIRA. Its unanimity signaled that the Recovery Act had breached boundaries that even the liberals—Brandeis, Cardozo, and Stone—meant to enforce.[85]

Putting the Schechters' freedom-of-contract arguments on the shelf, the Justices settled on two other principles: federalism and separation of powers. *Schechter*'s classic separation of powers ruling goes under the name of the "nondelegation doctrine." It says that Congress may not "delegate" its lawmaking authority to the executive branch. Administrative agencies lodged in the executive, as well as independent agencies like the Federal Trade Commission (FTC), may develop and enforce specific rules and policies, but they must do so under reasonably clear, general standards set out by Congress. The NIRA, said Chief Justice Hughes for the Court, crossed that line, impermissibly blurring the boundary between Article I and Article II powers. As Justice Cardozo put it in his concurring opinion, the NIRA was "delegation running riot."[86]

"Delegation running riot" has become a mantra of contemporary libertarians and *Lochner* revivalists, who repeat it frequently these days in their legal and political battles to dismantle or "deconstruct" the modern administrative state. They point to *Schechter* as the last great expression of a once-robust judicial check on unbridled state-building. Liberals don't lament the doctrine's demise, but they tend to agree on its historical significance.[87]

That history has it wrong.[88] There never was a robust nondelegation doctrine.[89] *Schechter* was a one-off. Until *Schechter,* not a single federal statute was ever struck down on nondelegation grounds. Starting in the 1880s, the federal government began construction of modern administrative agencies. The Court would hear nondelegation-based objections to newly enacted regulatory statutes conferring broad policy-making discretion on new agencies. The Court would confirm that there was a core of legislative power that could not be delegated, and then proceed to uphold the statutory delegation at issue.[90]

This was not Justice Gorsuch's or Kavanaugh's imagined nondelegation doctrine. All that the actual doctrine ever demanded was a modicum of legislative direction and specificity.[91] That was true in *Schechter* and remained true after *Schechter,* when Congress got the message and supplied a modicum more direction. In contrast to *Lochner*-era Commerce Power or substantive due process doctrine, nondelegation did not undergo some dramatic abandonment.[92]

Even before its judicial burial, the NIRA was going badly—for reasons close to the heart of the Court's objections. The act's main architects, like Wagner, hoped to reset the economy and "restore democracy" by dramatically redistributing economic power. What they got instead was a Recovery Administration dominated by the corporate elite. That was what the politics of the moment produced. Achieving the kind of transformation the New Dealers envisioned would have involved forcing business elites, who had always enjoyed unilateral authority over industrial relations, to recognize and bargain with unions. But the White House had no strong incentive to force this to happen. Charged by Congress in general terms to engineer a business recovery, the Executive took the path of least resistance and put the executives in charge of what amounted to a big-corporation-friendly form of corporatism. To overcome the nondelegation problem, Wagner's vision of a new "equality of organization and bargaining power" would have to be clearly stated policy; it would need sharp legal teeth. Wagner was drafting exactly that bill: an act with teeth to enforce the collective freedoms and right to union recognition it conferred on labor. A stark choice lay ahead for politicians and for the Court. *Schechter*'s nondelegation doctrine was no problem for Wagner's new bill. But a hardline version of the old Lochnerian limitations on the Commerce Power would be an insurmountable problem.

And that was just what the Commerce Power portion of *Schechter* delivered. Determined to write for the Court, Chief Justice Hughes produced an opinion built around the doctrinal style and substance of the conservative Four Horsemen. Hughes, Roberts, and Brandeis were sufficiently outraged by the New Dealers' heedless centralization of power that they joined the old guard in deploying all the old learning against FDR's recovery program. Thus, the Court didn't just parry Congress's stab at making the General Welfare Clause an alternative to the Commerce Clause as a fount of regulatory power. Hughes's opinion was laced with all the old categorical distinctions of the Court's nineteenth-century commerce doctrine. Mining, manufacturing, growing crops, preparing food like the Schechters' kosher chickens: all of these were *not* "commerce" but "essentially local" activities; and it fell to the "authority of the States to deal with domestic problems arising from labor conditions" in these domains.[93]

Richberg and the other New Deal lawyers charged with defending the Recovery Act had hoped to defend Section 7(a) before the high court in a case involving employment at a big firm deeply embedded in interstate commerce. Instead, they got stuck with the "Sick Chicken Case." So, the government had to argue that the Schechters' breach of the code's minimum wage provision put pressure on the whole trade's wage structure. And that defeated Section 7(a)'s core purpose— boosting the purchasing power of the nation's working-class consumers to generate the kind of demand that would revive interstate commerce and stabilize the overall economy. This *was* the main purpose; and that was the problem. The same argument could be made about *anybody's wages, anywhere.* The scheme was designed around the idea that the economy was a "nationwide system." Butchers' wages in New York affected miners' wages in West Virginia and farmers' incomes in Nebraska![94]

In response, Chief Justice Hughes rehearsed the old learning, whose gist was that "essentially local" economic activity like "mining, manufacturing or growing crops" could not be brought under Congress's control on the theory that want of salutary federal regulation had brought about a "diminution" of interstate commerce. That kind of reasoning led to complete centralization.[95] Justice Cardozo's concurring opinion, joined by Justice Stone, showed some sympathy for the New Dealers' thinking. The New Dealers were right that in modern industrial society, economic activity in any one place affects commerce as a whole. But the Schechters were right, too; ours was a federal system, and upholding it required boundaries between inter- and intrastate activities. The majority's categorical reasoning would not do. Happily, said Cardozo, the "law is not indifferent to considerations of degree."[96]

Of the nine Justices, only two conceded that at least some intrastate economic activity involving wages in manufacturing or other sectors might have sizable enough effects on commerce for Congress to regulate. And even Cardozo and Stone intimated agreement with the court below: their fellow Progressive, the famous Learned Hand, who not only struck down Section 7(a) but forthrightly said that generally speaking, manufacturing, mining, food processing, and the like belonged to the "separate states" to regulate, until we changed the Constitution itself.[97] Thus, on Black Monday, a unanimous Court had done more than simply strike down the NIRA. Seven, and quite possibly all nine, Justices seemed to have rejected the New Deal's most basic political-economic premise: that economic reform was a national problem requiring national solutions.

ROOSEVELT'S RESPONSE TO *SCHECHTER*

Five days after the *Schechter* decision was handed down, President Roosevelt held an hours-long press conference, carefully unpacking passages from Hughes's opinion and its greater implications. The decision, said the president, was "much more important than . . . any decision of my lifetime or yours . . . more important than any decision probably since the Dred Scott case."[98] Roosevelt was preparing the public for a showdown on the plane of constitutional political economy, and doing so with great care, in a spirit of "high constitutional seriousness."[99] As Bruce Ackerman has argued, the president was educating the press corps in order to educate the public, laying the ground for a well-considered popular mandate to confront the Court.[100] Based on the thousands of letters and telegrams he had received lamenting the demise of the codes and calling for action to replace them, FDR concluded that the public "have not yet information from either the press or the radio or from me, which would put this situation in plain, lay language." He went on to explain his worry "that so many of these letters and telegrams"—and the actions they suggested to address anew the problems of big business domination and downward spiraling wages—"are futile."[101]

Taking up the majority's interpretation of the Commerce Clause, Roosevelt observed that if the Justices held fast to this view of the Commerce Power, vast areas of national economic life—"construction," "mining," "manufacturing," "the growing of crops," all the "major . . . activities" besides transportation—would remain beyond the reach of the New Deal, leaving action on all these matters to the states.[102]

Here, FDR gave a sophisticated account of the jagged path of Commerce Power thinking, since "the old Knight case," where the commerce versus manufacturing and the direct versus indirect effects ideas originated. True, the Court sometimes reverted to these ideas. But the "whole tendency over the years since Knight has been to view the interstate commerce clause in the light of present-day civilization." FDR was alluding to Cardozo's perspective, which, he noted, arose from "an entirely different philosophy."[103] "The prosperity of the farmer," Roosevelt explained, "does have an effect today on the manufacturer in Pittsburgh. The prosperity of the clothing worker in the city of New York has an effect on the prosperity of the farmer in Wisconsin, and so it goes. We are interdependent—we are tied in together. And the hope has been that we could, through a period of years, interpret the interstate commerce clause of the Constitution in the light of these new things that have come to the country."[104] "That was why," the president went on, "the Congress for a good many years" has thought "that in drafting legislation we could depend on an interpretation" that enlarged "the Constitutional meaning of interstate commerce to include . . . those matters which indirectly affect interstate commerce." Now, however, with *Schechter,* "all that seems to be 'out the window.' . . . We have been relegated to the horse-and-buggy definition of interstate commerce."[105]

However, he argued, this question was not one for the Court finally to decide. The issue of national authority over national problems was for the nation to determine. "In some ways it may be the best thing that has happened to this country for a long time that such a decision has come from the Supreme Court, because it clarifies the issue."[106]

> Yes, and the issue is this: . . . Is the United States going to decide, are the people of this country going to decide that their Federal Government shall in the future have no right under any implied power or any court-approved power to enter into a solution of a national economic problem, but that that national

economic problem must be decided only by the States? . . . Shall
the Federal Government [have] no right under this or following
opinions to take any part in trying to better national social conditions? Now that is flat and that is simple![107]

But what else would the administration do to try to reverse the Court's
obduracy? An amendment enlarging the scope of Congress's regulatory
power? An amendment ending or restricting judicial review of federal
statutes? A statute changing the number of Justices? Or perhaps a national referendum to reverse *Schechter,* while avoiding the protracted
amendment process prescribed by Article V? All these possibilities were
being discussed in the administration and Congress. Having laid before
the nation his critique of what the Court had done, FDR was keeping
his options open.

The Wagner Act and New Deal Constitutional Political Economy

By striking down the Recovery Act, the Court deprived FDR of an industrial relations policy and inadvertently nudged him to support Senator Wagner's radical labor bill, which would prove a formidable work
of constitutional construction. The Wagner Act of 1935 brought together
two strains of labor constitutionalism. It reflected progressive and socialist labor's views about the affirmative role of government in industrial life. It also partook of the old AFL case for collective constitutional
liberties, with its many textual bases and sources in constitutional tradition: the Guarantee Clause; the First, Thirteenth, and Fourteenth
Amendments; and inherited antislavery and republican accounts of economic liberty.

The class struggle that swirled around the transformative new law
would flow into the election campaign of 1936 and reshape the New Deal
into an explicitly pro-labor, social-democratic movement. Likewise, the
Wagner Act battle would see New Dealers articulate for the first time
their own full-bore constitutional political economy of affirmative so-

cial and economic rights and governmental duties. These would reshape both public discourse and the Court's own doctrines more deeply than we remember.

A "Veritable Charter of Freedom of Contract"

In the wake of *Schechter*, hearings continued on Senator Wagner's bill to "put teeth"[108] into labor's rights, and to reorganize the NRA Labor Board into an independent agency, fully empowered to enforce those rights. Amid hundreds of mass strikes demanding the collective freedoms and right of union recognition that the now defunct Section 7(a) had promised, it was untenable for the New Deal to lack a labor policy. Meanwhile, business's mounting opposition to New Deal reform combined with the solid support FDR enjoyed from the expanding ranks of organized labor to put the president behind Wagner's radical new bill. For the first time in our history, the national government—or rather, two branches of it—lined up squarely on labor's side of the struggle over the nation's constitutional political economy.

Business big and small poured unprecedented resources into defeating the bill. In newspaper, magazine, and radio ads, in pamphlets and brochures sent to employees and customers, and in testimony before Congress, business leaders and their attorneys and publicists conjured the old trope of the union as a "labor trust" or "monopoly"; they railed against Wagner, FDR, and the New Deal for seeking to impose a "collectivist" future on American industry. Chiefly, however, they leaned on the Constitution, the Court's Constitution, and insisted that the bill flouted it.

Schechter only reconfirmed for them that the Wagner bill breached the Constitution's federalism safeguards: It regulated employment in manufacturing and other domains that belonged solely to the states. Business likewise pointed to an unbroken line of precedents enshrining employers' right to contract with individual employees and striking down legislative efforts to make them deal with unions.[109] James Emery, chief counsel of the National Association of Manufacturers (NAM) and veteran anti-union advocate, protested that the Wagner bill flatly violated one of "the most fundamental rights that man possesses, whether labor or employer," the right to contract and refuse to contract, and the right "to decline to associate with others."[110]

Senator Wagner's response channeled both organized labor's long-standing, antislavery-inspired constitutional outlook and the views of Progressive reformers like Brandeis on safeguarding labor's freedom of collective action as a building block for industrial democracy. The collective freedoms codified in the new bill, said Wagner, were no violation of freedom of contract but a "veritable charter of freedom of contract."[111] "The law," he noted, "has long refused to recognize contracts secured through physical compulsion or duress. The actualities of present-day life impel us to recognize economic duress as well. We are forced to recognize the futility of pretending that there is equality of freedom when a single workman, with only his job between his family and ruin, sits down to draw a contract of employment with a representative of a tremendous organization having thousands of workers at its call."[112]

Without the right of workers to choose to bargain collectively and the corollary duty of employers to bargain with their representatives, "there would be slavery by contract."[113] Notice Wagner did not dispute the premise that the Constitution, rightly understood, enshrined economic liberty; instead, working within the democracy-of-opportunity tradition, he challenged the understanding of that precept advanced by business interests and the courts.

"Nothing could be more fallacious," said Wagner, than the notion that the new legislative restraints that his bill imposed on employers violated economic liberty. True, the bill altered the distribution of bargaining power enforced by the entrenched common-law rules of the game. But those rules were anachronistic. "The fathers of our Nation did not regard freedom of contract as an abstract end. They valued it as a means of insuring equal opportunities, which cannot be attained where contracts are dictated by the stronger party."[114]

Wagner was right. Jefferson, informed by Adam Smith, prized the emancipatory power of free markets and yet was "never loathe" to use "constitutional and statutory measures to make the poor independent" and build "the institutional framework for a free society."[115] Making "the poor independent" was a constitutional essential; only an economically independent citizenry could sustain a republican form of government. For antebellum republicanism, that meant propertied independence. Wagner rang out the changes on the democracy-of-opportunity tradition wrought by postbellum labor republicanism and the Progressives' industrial democracy ideal. Political self-rule could not survive alongside industrial "despotism."[116] Too many working people were "industrial slaves." They would regain their economic independence—and the citizenly-character-forming qualities it imparted—not via individual property-holding, but collectively, via the material security and voice, authority, and responsibility that came with unions. "Let men know the dignity of freedom and self-expression in their daily lives," the senator told the *New York Times,* "and they will never bow to tyranny in any quarter of their national life."[117]

Of the antistatist AFL old guard, only Andrew Furuseth came around to supporting Wagner's bill. Recalling the Jacksonians' core anti-oligarchy insight that the laboring "many" needed mass organizations—a mass political party and now, mass unions—with the clout to counter the wealthy "few," Furuseth declared that Wagner's bill would come to the republic's rescue by finally "incorporat[ing] the industrial workers in the polity of the United States" as a "check upon the power of 'Big Business.'"[118]

Wagner welcomed the labor constitutionalist's support but rebuffed Furuseth's renewed efforts to get Congress to rely on "labor's glorious Amendment" as the constitutional basis for its labor bill.[119] Nor would Wagner repeat the blunder of the "first hundred days" and the NIRA, making light of the Court's jurisprudence by framing a regulatory measure around the General Welfare Clause. The Commerce Power was no safe shelter from the inevitable judicial storm, but it was the only one in sight. As soon as *Schechter* came down, Wagner summoned his team of attorneys, including Donald Richberg and two Frankfurter protégés in their late twenties—Wagner's chief legislative aide, Leon Keyserling, and the solicitor of the Department of Labor, Charles Wyzanski. Wagner directed them to save the bill's substance, but redraw it to hew as closely as possible to the Court's language and strictures.[120]

The NIRA had asserted national authority over every workplace in the land. It did not even pay lip service to the federalism safeguards the

Court had been etching into Commerce Power doctrine for decades. The path forward ran through Cardozo's concurrence. Above all, the bill must not appear to "obliterate the distinction between what is national and what is local in the activities of commerce."[121] A bill that embraced the requirement that the regulated activity affect interstate commerce just might prompt a few more Justices to join in the view that magnitude matters, and at least some employment in manufacturing and other sectors could have large enough effects on commerce for Congress to regulate. The way around *Schechter* was to follow Learned Hand's signal: Make the affecting-commerce requirement a "question . . . in each case."[122] This case-by-case approach to "affecting commerce" would enable the new Labor Board to build test cases that easily fit existing Commerce Power precedents—and others that stretched beyond them. It might also convince a majority of the Court that Congress was finally taking its doctrines seriously.

Wagner also directed Keyserling and the others to redraft the bill's first section without mention of the general welfare. Instead, Section 1 begins with the finding that "[t]he denial by employers of the right of employees to organize and the refusal by employers to accept the procedure of collective bargaining leads to strikes and other forms of industrial strife . . . , which have the intent or the necessary effect of burdening or obstructing commerce."[123]

Section 1 was an impressive piece of constitutional political economy unto itself. With Frankfurter's encouragement, Wyzanski had urged Wagner "to stick as closely as possible to the [commerce power] precedent already established" and avoid any "broad language" in Section 1 about the "worker's freedom."[124] Wagner rejected the advice. As Keyserling later recalled, the senator's idea was not only to track but also "to make constitutional law."[125] So, Section 1 became a braid of Commerce Power doctrine with labor's Constitution of collective liberty, Progressive constitutional ideas about industrial democracy, managerial reformers' concerns about industrial peace, and Realist insights about the public construction of private employers' unequal bargaining power.[126] At Wagner's insistence, Section 1 wove these threads together with the New Dealers' distinctive macroeconomic take on the Depression: that its root causes lay in the maldistribution of wealth and bargaining power;

and that overcoming it demanded a legal order that positively encouraged broad-based unionization and collective bargaining to boost "wages
and the purchase power of wage earners" and to stabilize "competitive
wage rates and working conditions within and between industries."[127]

Thus, making it "the policy of the United States" to "encourag[e] the
practice and procedure of collective bargaining" and "protect" workers'
"full freedom of association, self-organization, and designation of representatives of their own choosing" was a way to "restore" to "wage
earners" the Constitution's promises of equal rights in economic as well
as political life.[128] But it also was a public policy addressing the *general*
interest in averting two great evils: "recurrent business depressions" and
commerce-killing "industrial strife and unrest."[129]

The body of the bill created a New Deal agency that turned the law of
industrial relations upside down, in both substance and procedure,
transferring authority as far as possible from the courts to the new National Labor Relations Board (NLRB).[130] The act guaranteed workers the
right to organize, strike, boycott, and picket, and to select their own
union by majority vote. Like the late, lamented Section 7(a), it safeguarded these rights from employer interference, constraint, or coercion.
It outlawed what had been employers' constitutionalized common-law
right to discriminate against employees on the basis of union membership or union activism. In contrast to the NIRA, it made violations of
these various norms into statutory infractions ("unfair labor practices") and authorized the new NLRB to prosecute and to hear employee
complaints, to determine union jurisdictions, and to conduct on-site
elections. It also required employers to bargain exclusively with the
chosen union over wages, hours, and working conditions. It was not lost
on employers (nor on the wary AFL craft unions) that the bill's architects aimed to authorize broad-based industrial unions in order to organize workers—and raise and stabilize wages and labor standards—as
far as possible across the whole industrial landscape.

Framing the Constitutional Conflict

In spring and early summer of 1935, as the hearings unfolded, there was
little doubt about the constitutional meaning of Wagner's bill, from the

perspective of its champions. Witness after witness on the act's behalf—lawmakers, labor leaders, and middle-class experts and professionals—cast the problem it addressed as not simply economic or social, but, inextricably, constitutional as well.[131] The constitutional infirmities of the existing legal order were basically twofold. First, they ran to the kind of livelihood promised by the Constitution's guarantees of equal rights and liberty in the democracy-of-opportunity tradition. The grossly "unequal freedom" and bargaining power of the "single workman" mocked this promise.[132] Without the rights to strike and bargain collectively, he was consigned to poverty wages and had no real hope of an American "standard of living."[133]

And second, the constitutional infirmities of the existing legal order went to its denial of any realistic measure of democratic agency and equal citizenship for working-class Americans. Corporate power in the halls of government made a mockery of republican self-rule. By promoting and protecting unions, Wagner's bill would finally "incorporate the industrial workers in the polity of the United States" as a "check upon the power of 'Big Business.'"[134] Likewise, participation in collective decision-making and possession of collective clout via unions were indispensable to making the real world of production more like what it ought to be in republican theory: a character-forming sphere of freedom and agency, not slavery and domination. The right of labor representation, said Wagner, was fundamental to "democratic self-government" in an industrial society; it marked the "difference between despotism and democracy."[135] The great Legal Realist, Columbia law professor Robert Hale, told the Senate Committee on Education and Labor that the situation of an employee at a nonunion steel plant was akin to that of a "nonvoting member of society."[136]

The Senate report on the Wagner bill dwelled long on the constitutional commitment to collective self-rule that it would bring to earth. "A worker in the field of industry, like a citizen in the field of government," had an "inherent right" to "self-government." In both fields, it declared, he was entitled "to be free to form or join organizations, to designate representatives, and to engage in concerted activities."[137] But instead, as one local union leader testified, "[i]ndustrially," the citizen-worker is "dis[en]franchised."[138] From this perspective, the statute's cornerstones, set forth in its central section, were those rights organized labor had long claimed under the Guarantee Clause and the First, Thirteenth, and Fourteenth Amendments: to associate, organize, and act in concert, and to "representatives of their own choosing." Together, the act's provisions promised to bring the responsibilities and expectations of American citizenship—elections and self-rule, due process, free speech, the rights of assembly and petition—into the factory, mine, and mill.

No sooner had FDR signed the Wagner Act in July 1935 "than employers announced that they would defy it."[139] U.S. Steel's vice president of industrial relations proclaimed that he would "go to jail or be convicted as a felon" rather than obey the Wagner Act.[140] Employers openly flouted the new law and the efforts of the new Labor Board to enforce it. Organizers and activists continued to be fired, beaten, and blacklisted. Where new union locals sprang up, employers continued to refuse recognition. Employers defended their defiance in the name of contract, property, and states' rights—and their claims were uniformly upheld by the lower courts.

In May 1936, the Supreme Court handed down *Carter Coal Co.*[141] It struck down the Guffey Coal Stabilization Act,[142] a NIRA / Section 7(a) replacement specific to the coal industry. The decision seemed to spell doom for the Wagner Act. Justice Sutherland, writing for the Court in *Carter Coal,* did not doubt that the constant strikes in the coal fields wreaked havoc on industry and commerce. Coal, after all, powered the nation's factories and its rail and shipping lines. But as Sutherland saw it, miners' strikes have only "secondary and indirect effects" on interstate commerce. No matter how vast these "effects" may be, coal mining was local activity, labor relations were local relations, and so, "the evils [addressed by the act] are all local evils over which the federal government has no legislative control."[143]

After *Carter Coal,* six out of six circuit courts to address the issue all held *unanimously* that the Wagner Act was unconstitutional as it applied to manufacturing. The heart of the nation's economy was exempt from the act.[144] Labor's councils, along with New Dealers in Congress, began taking up in earnest the questions of court-packing, jurisdiction-stripping, and formal constitutional amendment that the president had deferred. In the union halls and factories, strikers continued to demand the rights of labor that two branches of government had now upheld. Employers backed by the federal courts condemned these rights and flouted them. Two rival legal and constitutional regimes vied with one another in the nation's industrial centers; the clash flooded into the national political debate.

In the summer and fall of 1936, FDR campaigned for reelection against his Republican challenger, Kansas governor Alf Landon. Having come down on one side in the industrial struggle, Roosevelt abandoned cross-class appeals and launched a crusade against the "economic royalists" and their new "industrial dictatorship."[145] An overt attack on the Supreme Court, he reckoned, would distract attention from the substance of the New Deal program. So FDR left that to surrogates while he took the high road, casting the campaign as a time for fundamental constitutional choices by "the people themselves"—about the meaning of American freedom, the rights of citizens, and the powers and duties of government.

Landon and his supporters made certain that the Court and its decisions would also be central issues in the campaign. As the campaign got underway, conservative Republicans and business organizations like the Liberty League repeatedly accused FDR and the New Deal of "running against" and "tearing down the Constitution." The Republican Party platform declared, "America is in peril" because FDR was "insist[ing] on the passage of laws that are contrary to the Constitution," "violat[ing] the rights and liberties of citizens," and "constantly seeking to usurp" the rights "reserved to the people and the States."[146]

ROOSEVELT'S "DEMOCRACY OF OPPORTUNITY" VERSUS "ECONOMIC TYRANNY"

Roosevelt responded in kind. His speech accepting the Democratic nomination in June 1936 was one Wagner helped draft.[147] It was built around the same basic constitutional narrative about the rise of oligarchy and demise of liberty in the age of corporate capital that was at the heart of the claims of Gilded Age social movements, Progressive reformers, and "advanced" New Dealers. FDR made it his own, summoning the story to support the democracy-of-opportunity vision of constitutional political economy he now brought to the center of the national stage. "In 1776," the president began, "we sought freedom from the tyranny of a political autocracy—from the eighteenth-century royalists who held special privileges from the crown." Since then, however, "the rush of modern civilization . . . has raised for us new difficulties, new problems which must be solved if we are to preserve to the United States the political and economic freedom for which Washington and Jefferson planned and fought."[148]

Over the course of the nineteenth century, Roosevelt explained, industrialization brought forth "a new civilization," and with it, a new peril for political and economic freedom. "For out of this modern civilization economic royalists carved new dynasties. New kingdoms were built upon concentration of control over material things"—plainspoken words for an oligarchy resting on finance and industrial capital. In ways "undreamed of by the fathers," the "economic royalists" used "corporations, banks and securities, new machinery of industry and agriculture, of labor and capital" to construct a "new despotism wrapped in the robes of legal sanction."[149] Undoing this new despotism was the basic challenge of the day. Answering it was not within the grasp of laissez-faire constitutionalism and its one-sided notion that liberty is secure as long as government is restrained. "Against economic tyranny such as this, the American citizen could appeal only to the organized power of Government."[150]

Taking his constitutional grammar from reformers like Wagner, whose social-democratic rendering of republican freedom emphasized economic independence and nondomination, Roosevelt explained,

> An old English judge once said: "Necessitous men are not free men." Liberty requires an opportunity to make a living—a living decent according to the standard of the time, a living which gives man not only enough to live by, but something to live for. For too many of us the political equality we once had won was meaningless in the face of economic inequality. A small group had concentrated into their own hands an almost complete control over other people's property, other people's money, other

people's labor—other people's lives. . . . The royalists of the economic order have conceded that political freedom was the business of the Government, but they have maintained that economic slavery was nobody's business. They granted that the Government could protect the citizen in his right to vote, but they denied that the Government could do anything to protect the citizen in his right to work and his right to live.

Today we stand committed to the proposition that freedom is no half-and-half affair. If the average citizen is guaranteed equal opportunity in the polling place, he must have equal opportunity in the market place.[151]

FDR was articulating and describing an American constitutional order centered on affirmative governmental obligations—government's "inescapable obligations to its citizens," he called them—to ensure economic security for all and "the establishment of a democracy of opportunity."[152] This constitutional order, he argued, must secure Americans' freedom from private economic domination. A few weeks later, Roosevelt would return to the idea of a battle over the meaning of freedom, in a way that spotlighted the theme of industrial servitude. The election, he said, called on Americans to decide between returning "to that definition of liberty under which for many years a free people were gradually regimented into the service [of capital]," or else embracing a "changed concept of the duty and responsibility of government toward economic life."[153]

Given what this portended, the president said, it was no wonder that the "economic royalists" were claiming that the New Deal's "democracy of opportunity" marked an attempt "to overthrow" the Constitution. "What they really complain of is that we seek to take away their power." The people themselves were equipped to decide what "the Constitution stand[s] for" and whether the New Deal was a threat to its principles or their vindication.[154]

On November 3, 1936, FDR won by the largest popular landslide in U.S. history. Roosevelt won over 60 percent of the popular vote and forty-six of forty-eight states in the Electoral College. Democrats secured three-fourths of the seats in both House and Senate.[155] The president and the New Dealers in Congress hailed their crushing victory and wasted little time in depicting it as a mandate for their constitutional outlook and a repudiation of the Court's. The Wagner Act and the Social Security Act (SSA), the other great landmark of 1935, were both on the Supreme Court docket, set to be argued in February. Given its stone-cold reception in every lower court, the Wagner Act (NLRA) seemed doomed to a near certainty. The SSA was also in peril. (We will return to its fortunes soon.) A showdown with the Court seemed inevitable.

In Congress, jurisdiction-stripping and other court-curbing bills and calls for Article V amendments of all sorts abounded. Given the high constitutional stakes both sides had raised in the election and the Democrats' unprecedented sweep, New Deal lawmakers proclaimed their victory a mandate for a "great economic and social revolution."[156] The "dominant five-judge" "economic-social-constitutional philosophy" "was repudiated by the people of America," proclaimed New Deal senator and soon-to-be-Justice Hugo Black.[157] It was "not only the right of Congress under the Constitution, but the imperative duty of Congress, to protect the people" from the "miserable and degrading effects" of joblessness, exploitation, and poverty.[158] The people have adopted this constitutional philosophy, but, New Dealers complained, the courts "have not understood . . . this revolution."[159]

The Constitution: A "Layman's Document"

In early February, days before oral argument began on the Wagner Act, Roosevelt broke his silence on the Court and announced the first big legislative initiative of his second term: a bill authorizing the president to appoint an additional Supreme Court Justice for each sitting Justice aged seventy or more who had served at least ten years.[160] There was something to be said for addressing the entrenchment of Justices appointed decades ago by long-departed presidents and senators. Still, Roosevelt's court-packing proposal was a blunt instrument that distressed a great many Democrats as well as Republicans. The fact was that six of the sitting Justices at the time met its age and years-on-the-bench threshold, so the bill immediately would have given the president more than enough appointments to swing the Court promptly into the New Deal's corner.

Unlike the fireside chat Roosevelt had prepared in advance of the decision in the Gold Clause Cases, which was forthright and highly concrete in its critique of the Court, here Roosevelt indulged his fondness for sly indirection and, at first, championed the radical measure as mere housekeeping to help the aging Court keep up with judicial business.[161]

The slyness garnered bad press, so FDR put forward the constitutional case for his "Plan for Reorganization of the Judiciary." In his second term's "first radio report to the people," the president told his millions of listeners: "I hope that you have re-read the Constitution of the United States in these past few weeks. Like the Bible, it ought to be read again and again."[162] As he had in the days after Black Monday, Roosevelt expounded text and history to make his case before the public.

Like the Protestant Bible, the Constitution was a "lay-man's document." No priesthood or legal elite enjoyed a monopoly of interpretive authority. To the contrary: at critical moments in the past, the "lay rank and file," "the American people," and their reform-minded "leaders" had "interpreted the Constitution for themselves" and set their own constitutional vision against the doctrines of the judiciary and legal elite, and had "ultimately prevailed." They "overruled" the Court.[163] So it was today: "We have reached the point as a Nation where we must take action to save the Constitution from the Court and the Court from itself."[164]

But wasn't the amendment process the proper route? No, the president answered. The plutocrats, who had tried to thwart the "mandate of the people" in the last election, now aimed to make the amendment process their "last stand." And the Article V rules would enable them to make that process an endlessly protracted one. Even then, "five per-cent of the voting population" could block ratification.[165]

Besides, the Constitution's text was not the problem. The problem was the conservative Justices' gloss on it. Roosevelt pointed out that the text was ample to support the New Deal program in all its parts. The Commerce Power was aimed to reach problems the several states could not address one by one, and the power to provide for the general welfare was the framers' way of giving Congress power to deal with "problems then undreamed of [that] would become national problems."[166] Pundits predicted that the Court would not heed these substantive views. They were wrong. An unreorganized Court soon would uphold the Wagner Act under the Commerce Power and Social Security under the General Welfare Clause.

As the president bore down on the Court with his dramatic and controversial measure, labor was taking dramatic and controversial steps of its own. The industrial unions were embracing a new form of industrial action, the "sit-down strike," or factory occupation.[167] It marked an escalation of the constitutional class war and became indelibly associated in the public mind with the clash between the Court's old constitutional order and the one promised by the Wagner Act and the New Deal.[168] Beginning in late December 1936, all the nation's big auto manufacturers were hit with full-blown factory occupations.[169] Soon, thousands of sit-down strikes spread to almost every industry and city in the nation.[170] The strikers, with their defenders in Congress and public debate, cast the sit-down strikes as claims for a new statutorily enacted regime recognizing workers' constitutional freedoms of organization and self-representation.[171]

A COURT TRANSFORMED

In the second week of February 1937, the Justices heard argument on the constitutionality of the Wagner Act. Outside the Court, in public discourse, the case was about clashing rights and freedoms. Would the Court stick to the old order of employers' rights or succumb to the combined pressure of sit-downs and court-packing and recognize labor's new rights? Inside the Court, however, the New Deal attorneys defending the act—Solicitor General Stanley Reed, Wyzanski from the Labor Department, and Warren Madden, recently appointed chair of the new NLRB—would stick to the Commerce Power script. They would breathe not a constitutional word about the heterodox "fundamental rights"—collective not individual, against private not state invasion, and safeguarded chiefly by an administrative state actor—at stake in the NLRA.[172] Even so, Reed, Madden, and Wyzanski were not sanguine about the prospects for *NLRB v. Jones & Laughlin Steel Co.*[173] as they took it up to the Court. The famous case involved an NLRB sanction and reinstatement orders against a big steel-making company for firing union activists in an organizing drive. Reed and the others hoped the case might squeak through. The steel corporation was a vertically integrated outfit that not only made steel but also mined and transported its own ore and distributed its own product via its own rail system. The lawyers argued that the whole concatenation of interstate activities that a steel-workers' strike at Jones and Laughlin's plant would disrupt was suffi-cient to bring the Commerce Power into play, especially since the plant accounted for a substantial portion of the nation's steel output.

And thanks to the famous "switch in time"—revealed just a month earlier, when the Chief Justice and Justice Oren Roberts switched from the conservative to the liberal camp in upholding a minimum wage law[174]—the Court agreed. Now, writing for the Court as he had in *Schechter,* Chief Justice Hughes began the Court's analysis by under-scoring that it did not have to uphold or overturn the act "in its en-tirety."[175] That had been the case in *Schechter* with the NIRA; if it had been so here, the act "would necessarily fall" under the Tenth Amend-ment and the inherent limits of the Commerce Clause.[176] But the NLRA was different: it authorized the NLRB to sanction only unfair labor prac-tices "affecting commerce."[177]

Congress intended the statute to reach as far as the Constitution al-lowed. The Chief's opinion devoted pages to describing the corporation's "far flung [interstate] activities" and the evidence linking them to labor conditions in the steel-making operations of the huge plant. Then, Hughes adopted for the Court what had been the approach of Cardozo and Stone in their *Schechter* concurrence: It should not matter whether interstate-commerce-destroying activities occur in a "productive in-dustry" like steel-making, or whether the activities' causal connections to commerce are "indirect." "The question is necessarily one of degree." Here, the impact of a strike at the giant steel firm "would be immediate and might be catastrophic."[178]

Having made the most of the facts in *Jones & Laughlin,* Hughes's five-Justice majority quietly signaled it was going further down the path of constitutional transformation. In two forgotten companion cases,[179] involving much smaller firms, including a tiny clothing man-ufacturer, the Court did just what *Jones & Laughlin* claimed to abjure—practically upholding the Wagner Act "in its entirety." In terse, unsigned, one-page opinions, handed down the same day, the five-Justice majority upheld the act's application to these very different facts, without explaining how or why, save for referencing the "reasons stated" in *Jones & Laughlin*.[180] A strike at these small outfits could not have a remotely comparable impact on interstate commerce. The dissenters were nearer the mark in objecting that if these kinds of facts passed the majority's Commerce Power test, then so would almost any manufacturing outfit in the country. That was Wagner's vision and purpose.

The Court went further still: It reached out to embrace the collective constitutional rights claims the New Deal lawyers now avoided articulating in court. Workers' right to self-organization, to choose representatives and bargain collectively, to engage in collective action for these purposes, and other forms of mutual aid—all "without restraint or coercion by their employer . . . is a fundamental right," said the Court.[181] It continued: "Employees have as clear a right to organize and select their representatives for lawful purposes as the respondent has to organize its business and select its own officers and agents. . . . Hence, the prohibition by Congress of interference with the selection of representatives for the purpose of negotiation and conference between employers and employees, 'instead of being an invasion of the constitutional right of either, was based on the recognition of the rights of both.'"[182]

It was a stunning acknowledgment of the constitutional stature of the statutory rights the Court was upholding, and the era's leading constitutional scholar and court-watcher did not miss it. Weeks later, Edward Corwin first used the phrase New Deal "constitutional revolution," writing in the *New Republic*. American constitutional law, he observed, had "undergone a number of revolutions, but none so radical, so swift, so altogether dramatic as that witnessed by the term of Court just ended." What made the new dispensation radical was not the expansion of the Commerce Power. Rather, as Laura Weinrib shows in her account of the era's transformations in civil liberties law, what was radical was the Court's bold reimagining of "liberty" along the New Dealers' heterodox lines.[183] Liberty in its constitutional dimensions, wrote Corwin, was now "something that may be infringed by other forces as well as by those of government; indeed, something that may require the positive intervention of government against those other forces."[184]

The change "mark[ed] a development of profound significance in our constitutional history."[185]

Days after *Jones & Laughlin* was announced, the *New Republic* reported that "the event which Americans had been anticipating" had happened. "[T]he paths of 'judicial reform' and 'collective bargaining' crossed," and the Court upheld the Wagner Act. Workers "no longer had to drop their tools and fold their arms to squeeze this concession from adamant bosses." The Nine Old Men "had about-faced, donned habiliments of liberalism," and in one stroke, they "removed the need for 'infusion of new blood.'"[186]

Newsweek's headline read: "Judgment Day: Supreme Court Gives Its Blessing to Labor Relations Act and Hands Roosevelt a Victorious Defeat [on court-packing]."[187] Underneath was a picture that took up more than half of the page, of sit-downers perched in the windows of a factory. "Sit-downers," its caption read, "looked out at a future of court-given rights."[188]

FDR and the New Dealers did not need to depend on the amendment process or the court-packing plan to "save the Constitution from the Court," and Wagner and the New Deal lawyers seemed vindicated in their choices to rest the NLRA on the Commerce Power. Leaving definition and elaboration of labor's new "fundamental" rights in legislative and administrative hands, they had built a new constitutional construction on political ground, and still gained something like judicial recognition of labor's collective freedoms. The rights were hardly "court-given," but the Court had chosen to characterize them exactly as Senator Wagner and his industrial union allies saw them: "fundamental" and "constitutional." And this, despite all that was heterodox about the rights: they were collective, redistributive, running against private actors, and safeguarded by the administrative state.[189]

After *Jones & Laughlin*, NLRB chairman Madden began to cast the Wagner Act as inaugurating a new generation of "civil liberties" as "fundamental" as those that "men mobilized to secure in 1776 and 1787." Senator La Follette launched a new congressional Commission on Civil Liberties, to investigate private corporate spying, intimidation, and violence against labor organizing. Little more than a month after *Jones & Laughlin,* Justice Brandeis wrote an opinion for the Court in *Senn v. Tile*

Layers Protective Union rejecting an employer's challenge to Wisconsin's "little Norris–La Guardia" anti-injunction law, which forbade injunctions against peaceful picketing, even when the picketing was so-called stranger picketing against an "unfair" employer, not the boss of any of the picketers.[190] The Court went much further: Not only did the employer have no constitutional claim against the "little Norris–La Guardia's" safeguards for stranger picketing, but the union seemingly had a First Amendment right to engage in that picketing! Peaceful picketing—"making disclosure of the facts of the labor dispute"—was an exercise of the "freedom of speech guaranteed by the federal Constitution."[191]

Only recently, federal courts had been outlawing secondary actions like peaceful stranger picketing against nonunion employers and striking down state anti-injunction statutes like this one. Now, Brandeis appeared to be nudging the Court toward a regime of new constitutional safeguards that would confer on unions a vast, new measure of "coercive economic power."[192] If dicta became doctrine, a leading labor law scholar predicted, the constitutional political economy of industry might open onto the hitherto outlawed labor utopia of a "federated universal closed shop" and gain for workers "the sort of unquestioned collective bargaining power" that "universal unionism" would bring.[193] And soon dicta did become doctrine, and the prophecy seemed on its way to realization. By 1941, the Court had extended First Amendment protection to peaceful labor picketing in primary strikes, and began extending it to secondary actions.[194] Labor's collective constitutional liberties—combining freedom of communicative action with redistribution of economic clout—were in motion in Congress, on the streets, and on the Court.

Social Insurance, Social Rights, and Social Movements

At the same time that FDR was advancing Wagner's labor bill in Congress and in the courts, he and his administration were also working to build a permanent system of social insurance. This would provoke a constitutional battle of an intensity that rivaled the fight over the Wagner

Act. When Edward Corwin declared in 1937 that the nation had just witnessed a "constitutional revolution," what he was describing was also a new "duty of government to guarantee economic security to all as the indispensable foundation of constitutional liberty."[195] Not only had labor gained new, collective constitutional liberties; the revolution also transubstantiated "economic security" into a fundamental right.[196]

Corwin used this phrase—"economic security"—because the White House did. From the start, FDR's closest advisers on social policy, such as Frances Perkins, saw an opportunity in the crisis to create a national system of social insurance. Perkins would chair the president's cabinet-level Committee on Economic Security.

When the Depression hit, millions of immiserated Americans immediately needed emergency relief. Led by Perkins, the administration poured federal money into works programs and the empty coffers of states, localities, and private charities. But the lack of any national system to address the crisis was testament to the need for long-term institution-building. Progressives like Perkins had long followed pioneering figures like Brandeis in the view that social insurance was an essential foundation for a modern democratic order—a constitutional essential, as Brandeis proclaimed from the Progressive Era onward.[197]

When the Great Depression hit, there were no state or federal unemployment insurance programs. During the first years of the Depression, two million older, middle-class Americans joined the Townsend movement for a national government-funded old-age pension. Dr. Francis Townsend was an amateur policy entrepreneur whose own penniless retirement inspired him to write up a proposal in a letter to the editor of the local paper. He proposed a $200 per month pension for every American over sixty; the only proviso was one had to "use it or lose it" in order to generate consumer demand and help restart the economy. Townsend's proposal seemed madcap to "responsible" reformers but inspired seven thousand Townsend clubs, regional and national conventions, and mass protest.[198]

Pressure for national social provision also sprang from the flamboyant, populist senator from Louisiana, Huey Long, and his controversial "Share Our Wealth Society." Invoking the Declaration and the inherited language of the democracy-of-opportunity tradition, his platform, pamphlets, and speeches called for expanded public works, drastic limits on the workweek, and an old-age pension like the Townsend-ites'. Most famous and hair-raising were his demands for a wealth tax, capping the fortunes of the richest Americans, and a "decentralization of wealth" guaranteeing every family "around $5,000; enough for a home, an automobile, a radio . . . and the opportunity to educate their children; a fair share of the income of this land . . . so there will be no such thing as a family living in poverty and distress."[199] New Dealers used Huey Long as a foil for promoting their "conservative" vision of social insurance.

By far the biggest and most powerful mobilization, though, was the industrial union movement and the new Congress of Industrial Organizations (CIO). By 1936, the CIO, with its call for jobs, industrial democracy, and economic security as every American's rights, would become the organizational and financial mainstay of the Democratic Party in much of the country, as well as the principal funder of FDR's reelection bid.[200] Through the 1920s, the nation's millions of unorganized, largely "new immigrant" factory workers had been scorned by the AFL and ignored by Washington. The New Deal turned them into ardent—and overwhelmingly Democratic—voters, who looked to Washington for such basic goods as welfare, security, and employment.[201] Mobilized by CIO locals and local activists, this American-born generation of ethnic workers and their immigrant parents became the new mass base of the New Deal Democratic Party and transformed the substance of electoral politics.[202]

Experience with early New Deal programs and rhetoric engendered among these millions of working-class families a remarkable new sense of entitlement. They made no apologies for taking relief and jobs, and social security, insurance, and mortgages, from the state. As contributing members of society, they had rights to such things, and they rallied behind those politicians, labor leaders, and other reformers who championed expanding the programs that backed up these rights.[203]

THE COMMITTEE ON ECONOMIC SECURITY AND THE GENERAL WELFARE CLAUSE

In June 1934, Roosevelt appointed Perkins as chair of a new, cabinet-level Committee on Economic Security, announcing its formation in an address to Congress. It seized on reformers' long-standing reliance on the Preamble to undergird a positive vision of national responsibilities: "If, as our Constitution tells us, our Federal Government was established among other things, 'to promote the general welfare,' it is our plain duty to provide for that security upon which welfare depends. . . . [T]he security of the home, the security of livelihood, and the security of social insurance are, it seems to me, a minimum . . . of the promise that we can offer to the American people. They constitute a right which belongs to every individual and every family willing to work."[204]

Casting social insurance, work, and livelihoods as basic rights and their provision as government's duty, FDR continued to assimilate the new social rights to the "old and sacred possessive [traditional, constitutionally enshrined common-law] rights" of property and labor. In preindustrial America, these common-law rights had gone a long way to secure the "welfare and happiness" of ordinary Americans; now, only the recognition of new governmental responsibilities would enable "a return to values lost in the course of . . . economic development" and "a recovery" of the old rights' original social meaning.[205] Here again, Roosevelt made pointed use of the reformers' hermeneutics—the argument of changing conditions imperiling old constitutional principles, and new interpretations and institutions restoring them.

In the summer of 1934, the NIRA was having a rough time in the lower courts. So, as the president began using his bully pulpit to lay out the popular constitutional case for the "Economic Security Bill" he had promised Congress, the young New Deal lawyers on Perkins's staff set to work on a constitutional defense of the bill that the courts might accept. They discovered that the president had a point. Roosevelt's idea that the political branches had expansive authority to define and provide for the general welfare was received doctrine. The doctrinal landscape was full of judicial obstacles to national *regulation* of economic relations. But the same was not true when it came to federal *spending*. Despite many opportunities, the Supreme Court had never struck down a single piece of federal spending legislation.

Perkins's lawyers discovered what we saw in Chapter 2. They read the great debates between Hamiltonians and Jeffersonians over whether the Spending Power had to be tethered to the exercise of another enumerated power (Jefferson and Madison and their Democratic heirs), or instead was much broader, and constrained only by the general welfare requirement (Hamilton and the Federalists, Whigs, and Republicans). But they found, as we did, that both sides agreed on one thing: that this constitutional question was one solely for the political branches to debate and adjudicate. It was not for the courts.[206]

The Democratic (Jefferson–Madison) side of that long debate over the Spending Power also had a significant weakness. At no point did Democrats consistently hew to Jefferson's and Madison's views of enumerated power, for a simple reason: From the start, as Michele Landis Dauber has shown, Congress was making "charitable" appropriations for relief projects of all sorts. No one pretended that these expenditures had any constitutional basis in the enumerated powers besides the Spending Power itself.[207]

Still, Democrats maintained a more restrictive view than their Whig and, later, Republican rivals. Charitable appropriations for disaster relief were one thing. Major innovations in federal spending drew constitutional objections, prompted by a combination of fiscal conservatism and leeriness over any new expansion of federal authority that might someday legitimate national interference with the South's "domestic institutions." Such states' rights objections remained strong among Southern Democrats whenever ominous new forms of federal social spending arose.[208]

Meanwhile, in the traditional domain of disaster relief, the Congress developed a sophisticated system of nonjudicial constitutional precedents, which governed what counted as a relief appropriation for the general welfare. Touchstones for analogizing and distinguishing past cases of federal aid included whether a given calamity was sudden and unforeseeable, whether the losses somehow implicated a general, federal interest, and whether the calamity's victims were blameless victims of fate or were, in some fashion, responsible for their own plight.[209]

Unemployment: A "Natural" Calamity

Perkins's team reached back to these precedents in arguing for the economic security bill. This strategy was not entirely novel. It had been tried during the first "Great Depression" of the industrial era in 1873–1877. A few adventurous lawmakers had then responded to the new calamity of mass unemployment with pleas for federal aid for the "'suffering and starving poor'" of the crisis-stricken industrial regions. But this was the heyday of classical liberal political economy. Congress barely attended to these pleas.[210] It is worth briefly exploring why, in order to see why the 1930s shift in our understanding of the constitutional political economy of federal spending on social insurance was so significant.

In the 1870s, it was a given among the postbellum legal and political elites that the idle but able-bodied poor were generally responsible for their own lack of employment. In fact, the Great Depression of 1877 was the moment in our political-economic history when two dozen states enacted uniform "tramp acts"—bringing state coercion, not state aid, to bear on the "wandering" unemployed.[211]

"Unemployment" had not yet entered public discourse or even the technical vocabulary of postbellum political economy. As Alexander Keyssar explains, "no one doubted" in the 1870s and 1880s "that business panics occasionally threw some men and women out of work, but . . . these were [seen as] transient episodes. . . . If a worker was idled repeatedly or for a prolonged period of time, it was almost certainly his own choice or his own fault."[212]

By the 1890s, Keyssar observes, this began to change. The realities of the modern business cycle began to register. "Unemployment" came into common usage; it became more plausible to depict mass idleness as a national disaster, not a host of personal failings.[213] As the severe depression of the early 1890s set in, the Senate's Populists, whose constitutional arguments for greater federal power over political economy we examined in Chapter 4, contended for countercyclical spending on federal public works and federal unemployment relief. Kansas Populist William Pfeffer assembled a sheaf of newspaper articles from around the country to buttress the claim that unemployment was a problem of national dimensions, not "limited to one locality, to one town, to one city, to even one State." Rather, the problem "spreads out over the entire country, that one-third of the industrial population of the whole people are unemployed."[214]

Pfeffer then turned to precedents. "It is too late now," said the Populist senator, "to say that we dare not do anything of this kind. Upon an examination of the record it will be found that there are many instances where the Congress . . . has gone to the relief of suffering people in different parts of the country."[215] Pfeffer read out from a table of disaster precedents, which he had printed in the *Congressional Record,* beginning with "the Portsmouth fire in 1803" and carrying through a host of other fires, earthquakes, and "Indian depredations."[216]

Pfeffer's arguments were unavailing. By 1890 the Republicans had become the party of business and laissez-faire. Most of them regarded Populists' ideas about new uses of national power—to nationalize the railroads, put credit and currency under public control, support farmers' and producers' co-ops, repeal the judge-made law of labor relations, build federal public works, and now institute unemployment relief—as all of a piece and all a mortal threat to the liberal Constitution and the liberal political economy it enshrined. The conservative Democrats agreed and added their own constitutional objections, which ran to states' rights. Unemployment relief went nowhere in that Congress.

And yet, even during that moment of raw class conflict, when socialism was in the air and Lochnerism and "government by injunction" were ascendant, the Supreme Court held back from asserting the authority to strike down spending measures. In a key case about a scheme of subsidies and tariffs that benefited the Sugar Trust, the attorney general argued that such subsidies were unconstitutional and had always been.[217] He urged the Court to adopt a construction of the Spending Power to match its "class legislation" versus "public purpose" doctrine under the Fourteenth Amendment. Such a construction, the attorney general pointed out, could become a judicial bulwark not only against corrupt subsidies like this, but also against other kinds of redistributive class legislation as well. Judicial scrutiny of federal spending could help stop the "socialistic wave."[218]

But the Court stuck by its old deferential stance. The author of *Lochner* itself, Justice Rufus Peckham, wrote for a unanimous bench. Since "the adoption of the Constitution," Peckham observed, citing a comprehensive table of congressional disaster precedents, Congress has exercised its Spending Power in response to claims for aid and relief. The table, said Peckham, was evidence of Congress's unbroken practice of adjudicating whether particular cases fell within the "class of claims which Congress can and ought to recognize as founded" on principles of generality and justice. Such questions, he concluded, were ones in their "nature . . . for Congress to decide for itself."[219]

The "Economic Security Bill": Necessity or Nightmare?

There things stood in the summer of 1934. When it came to judicial obstacles, Perkins and the lawyers on the Committee on Economic Security (CES) knew that things looked much better for the New Deal's forthcoming experiment in social insurance, under the Spending Power, than for its embattled regulatory regime under the Commerce Clause. As far as spending for the general welfare was concerned, even the *Lochner* Court's old stalwarts had flagged long ago that the main action was going to be in Congress; and in Congress, the airwaves, and the press, New Dealers began laying the ideological groundwork for the "Economic Security Bill" that the CES would deliver to Congress at year's end. Everywhere, New Dealers were declaring that no future downswing should find the nation without programs to meet the needs of Americans thrown out of work. Unemployment was not a failing of the individual, but a structural feature of the capitalist business cycle. Government's plain duty was to provide jobless Americans with either decently paid work or dignified insurance.

What FDR and Perkins had in store, Herbert Hoover warned, was "a system of regimentation and bureaucratic domination in which men and women" would become "pawns and dependents of a centralized and potentially self-perpetuating government." National social insurance, said a leading conservative civic group, was at war with "the fundamental principles of our form of Government embodied in our Constitution." The National Association of Manufacturers (NAM) agreed. "Congress had no authority to create either welfare or social insurance programs." It "may only levy taxes for the common defense and the general welfare in execution of express grants of authority made to it." The Tenth Amendment made that perfectly clear.[220]

In the public sphere, New Dealers were making their popular-constitutional arguments. But what about the courts' Constitution? *Schechter* had not yet reached the high court. The lower courts were divided, but most had concluded that the NIRA went beyond what the Commerce Clause allowed.[221]

Edwin Witte, the CES's executive director and a seasoned Wisconsin labor economist, wrote to the constitutional law professoriate and Justice Brandeis, asking for counsel.[222] Brandeis confirmed what every constitutional expert told Witte and his staff: The Taxing and Spending Power was the way to go. But Brandeis's famous aversion to centralization and his devotion to the states as "laboratories of democracy" led him to push back against the CES's notion of a system run directly by the federal government. He suggested a scheme that would encourage the states to create their own unemployment and old-age insurance plans via "a federal payroll tax on employers, from which they could deduct whatever amount they were paying into state plans." "Have you considered the case of Florida v. Mellon?" Brandeis asked, alluding to a unanimous 1927 decision of the Court, upholding a federal statute allowing use of state inheritance taxes as credit against federal ones.[223] The "Brandeis idea," as Witte called it, could include some minimum federal standards for state insurance plans to qualify, while still leaving much room for the kind of state-level experimentation and local governance Brandeis and his followers loved.

President Roosevelt liked Brandeis's idea. FDR understood that Congress's powerful Southern Democrats would not abide any national social insurance—particularly unemployment insurance—that deprived local white planters and employers and white elites of control over Black labor. They would scuttle any scheme that put federal administrators in charge of the terms on which Black workers got unemployment checks. The "Brandeis idea" offered an ideal accommodation: Encourage the Dixiecrats to support nationwide social insurance by leaving the states in charge of administration, so Jim Crow could go undisturbed.

The constitutional law professoriate Witte had consulted were against the Brandeis idea. On one hand, like Brandeis, the professors confirmed that the Spending Power was almost "bomb-proof."[224] Edward Corwin had just published his Storrs Lectures at Yale, prophesying how the

Spending Power would enable the New Deal to "elud[e] all constitutional snares."[225] On the other hand, Corwin and the rest all favored a "straight national" plan.[226] The "Brandeis idea" smacked too much of the Child Labor Tax Case, where the Court had found Congress to be using its Taxing Power to invade the states' police powers, instituting federal labor standards by indirection.[227]

The CES's staff economists also weighed in unanimously in favor of the straight national plan.[228] Uniform national insurance would maximize the number of Americans covered as well as the program's redistributive potential. For similar reasons, the economists favored paying for the program via general revenue, not contributory payroll taxes. General revenue matched the ideal that social insurance was a basic duty of national government.

FDR favored the contributory option less because of fiscal prudence than because he could see that with workers making contributions, the benefits would seem a matter of right. "We put those payroll contributions there so as to give the contributors a legal, moral and political right to collect their pensions. . . . With those taxes in there, no damn politician can ever scrap my social security program," FDR said.[229] It was a characteristically conservative and pragmatic strategy for constructing a new right.

What the CES and the White House finally hammered out and sent to Congress was a hodgepodge of rival ideas, which persists today. Only the old-age insurance—what today we call Social Security—was purely federal. To accommodate the Dixiecrats, the unemployment insurance scheme rested on the "Brandeis idea" of federal payroll taxes, which employers could offset with payments into a state-run unemployment insurance plan, as long as that state plan met minimal federal standards. The other provisions of the White House's bill consisted of federal grants-in-aid for states to administer, for the needy elderly, dependent children, and the blind, again with minimal federal standards.

SOCIAL SECURITY IN CONGRESS AND IN COURT

The accommodations for Jim Crow were not enough. Some Dixiecrats candidly declaimed against federal administrators interfering with the

South's "domestic institutions" by providing any welfare or setting any terms of social provision for "blacks."[230] Others simply invoked state sovereignty. One declared that the White House bill was "the most brazen attempt to submerge the sovereignty of State governments to the will of the General Government. . . . Why have any State legislature at all, if they must pass such laws as Congress and the executive branch . . . shall direct?"[231]

So, the Dixiecrats in Congress exacted more concessions. They demanded and won the categorical exclusion of agricultural labor and domestic servants from both the old-age and unemployment insurance schemes. These two occupations accounted for the great majority of African American workers in the South. They stripped the national minimum standards from the unemployment and grants-in-aid schemes.[232]

Wagner and many Northern New Dealers vowed to undo the racialized exclusions and mend the loose crazy quilt of state programs when they could. Meanwhile, they championed the bill in terms of universal social rights and the old language of affirmative legislative duties. "What is the whole purpose of our Government? Is it not in order to guarantee equal rights and making possible 'the pursuit of happiness'?" asked one advocate for Social Security. Congress had a "duty . . . to see that poverty, at least[,] is abolished in this country."[233] Far from being beyond government's purview, "the matter of effecting happiness for our people is one of the basic objectives of government."[234]

Like FDR, many New Deal lawmakers framed the argument in terms of updating the old political economy of citizenship. Social insurance was a modern substitute for freely available land; in "promoting the economic independence" of citizens, it enabled each one to be "an agent for his Government."[235] Like Roosevelt, they also pointed out how economic distress had brought down constitutional democracies abroad. "American democracy can be preserved only" by ensuring this kind of economic independence.[236] Congress, they said, was "fashioning the foundation stones upon which will rest the happiness and welfare of future generations" by enacting "social reforms that are necessary to preserve our economic and political institutions."[237] Wagner, one of the bill's sponsors in the Senate, insisted Social Security was a matter of right.[238]

But would the Justices hold fast to their traditional deference? *Schechter* came down in May 1935, while Congress was in the thick of work on Social Security. We saw the president's public unease about what *Schechter* augured for a national effort to address industrial unemployment. The same month, the Court also decided *Railroad Retirement Board v. Alton Railroad Co.,*[239] which struck down Congress's effort to require the interstate railroads to provide old-age pensions for railroad workers. Writing for a 5–4 majority, Justice Roberts penned a sweeping opinion that found the compulsory employer-funded pension system a "naked appropriation of private property" under the Fifth Amendment, and also an illegitimate exercise of the Commerce Power.[240]

It would not do, said the Court, for Congress to pretend that the statute conduced to the safety and efficiency of the nation's interstate transportation system. What Congress really was addressing was "merely the social welfare of the [railroad] worker."[241] The Court openly mocked the newfangled policy of "old-age security."[242] The purpose of a pension system was to engender a servant's "loyalty."[243] That meant providing a pension had to remain in the private employer's discretion; it could not flow from "legislative largesse."[244] This haughty Lochnerian scorn for the idea of providing workers with "old-age security" via publicly orchestrated pensions also did not augur well. How different, really, from *Alton*'s "legislative largesse" was the Social Security bill's payroll tax scheme?

And yet, just two years after *Schechter* and *Alton,* the Social Security Act won seven Justices' approval. The same old Hughes Court, which had split so sharply and wrote so gingerly about the Commerce Power, gave the New Deal's General Welfare Constitution a shining seal of approval. Speaking through Justice Cardozo, the Court emphatically affirmed that it was the province of Congress, and not the Court, to "shape . . . the concept of welfare" to meet the nation's exigencies, and affirmed, as well, that the "concept of the general welfare . . . is not static" but "changes with the times."[245] In the early republic, wrote Cardozo, the "hinterland . . . gave an avenue of escape" for those thrown out of work, and providing for them was a local matter. But the "nation-wide calamity that began in 1929" amply justified Congress's judgment that unemployment and old-age insurance had become national obligations.[246]

Only two of the Four Horsemen took a constitutional last stand against national social insurance and the idea of a modern American welfare state.[247] Justice McReynolds's dissenting opinion offers a truly antique view of social provision, as well as a backhanded acknowledgment that determining the boundaries of the Spending Power and the General Welfare Clause had always belonged to the political branches. Nine-tenths of his ten-page-long opinion consists of "pertinent portions of" President Franklin Pierce's veto message of May 3, 1854, rejecting a land-grant measure appropriating "public lands to the several States for the benefit of indigent insane persons."[248] So McReynolds made his constitutional point via Pierce's lengthy constitutional argument, the gist of which was this: "I cannot find any authority in the Constitution for making the Federal Government the great almoner of public charity throughout the United States."[249]

Justice Butler also dissented, but unlike McReynolds, he had a modern point to make about why any large national program of social provision like the SSA violated the Tenth Amendment.[250] Even if Congress may spend for the general welfare, reasoned Butler, it may not deprive the states of the practical capacity to exercise their reserved powers. Here, the heft of the old-age pension tax was so great a practical burden on the states' taxing powers that it was tantamount to coercion. What was more, the SSA's unemployment insurance scheme breached the Tenth Amendment by making the states an offer too big to refuse—a 90 percent share of federally collected taxes, if they instituted state programs. As proof, Butler pointed to the large number of states that had swiftly acquiesced to Congress's wishes by instituting such programs.[251]

This offer-too-big-to-refuse-is-tantamount-to-coercion theory is precisely the argument opponents advanced against Obamacare's Medicaid expansion in *NFIB v. Sebelius*, winning at least four votes.[252] This argument has the potential to do considerable future mischief any time a large federal intervention in our political economy runs through the states in the way Brandeis suggested. In anticipation of that possibility, it may be helpful to recall Justice Cardozo's rejoinder for the Court: "[T]o hold that motive or temptation is equivalent to coercion is to plunge the law in endless difficulties. . . . We cannot say that [Alabama] was acting . . . under the strain of a persuasion equivalent to undue influence, when she chose to have relief administered under laws of her own making, by agents of her own selection, instead of under federal laws, administered by federal officers with all the ensuing evils, at least to many minds, of federal patronage and power."[253]

At bottom, the Court's reasoning rests on a baseline conception of the General Welfare: Provision must be made for Americans facing poverty by dint of disability, old age, joblessness, or obligations of care. If any states "are unwilling, whether through timidity or for other motives, to do what can be done," Congress would have to provide.[254] The Court upheld the idea of a national government fully authorized to build national systems of social insurance. The future reach of such insurance, including its reach into the racial caste system of the South, was now a constitutional battle for Congress to fight.

The Fair Labor Standards Act

In 1937, after the Wagner and Social Security Acts were upheld, the administration brought forward the bill that became the Fair Labor Standards Act (FLSA). During the 1936 campaign, FDR had promised to enact new national labor standards in the wake of *Schechter,* and the FLSA created a national minimum wage and maximum hours regime.[255] Discourse and debate around the bill confirmed how much a constitutionalism of "affirmative rights" and "economic security" had taken root. New Dealers cast the Labor Standards bill as part of an expanding "system" of "fundamental rights" that ensured American workers the "minimal equality" and "security which the Constitution of the United States provides for."[256]

When Frances Perkins proposed a national wage and hours law in 1933, the president told her to put it aside—he was focused on recovery. Besides, federal courts were still striking down state wage and hour laws on liberty of contract grounds. Senator Wagner helped Perkins ensure that national maximum hours and minimum wage provisions went into the Recovery Act, until *Schechter* struck them down on Commerce Power and federalism grounds. One year later, in *Morehead ex rel. Tipaldo,*[257] the Court voided New York's minimum wage statute on the basis of liberty of contract.

Morehead "was too much even for Herbert Hoover." In 1936, both parties' platforms assailed the decision.[258] After all, the New York wage law that *Morehead* nullified covered only women workers, and only when employers were paying below a subsistence wage. *Morehead* built on *Adkins v. Children's Hospital,* which in 1923 had similarly struck down a piece of protective wage legislation, reading the new Nineteenth Amendment to help justify the idea that women, like men, had Lochnerian contract rights with which the government could not interfere.[259] *Adkins* and *Morehead* dramatized the Court's determination to shield the wage bargain from the redistributive energy of democratic politics. If the natural operation of the market was such that women's labor could not command a living wage, said the *Adkins* Court, this was not a problem the Constitution would allow society to foist on employers. "Certainly the employer, by paying a fair equivalent for the service rendered, . . . has neither caused nor contributed to her poverty."[260]

But then, in 1937, came the "switch in time." *West Coast Hotel v. Parrish*[261] upheld a Washington State minimum wage law identical to the New York law *Morehead* voided, and very much like the one the Court had struck down in *Adkins.* As he did in *Jones & Laughlin,* Chief Justice Hughes wrote for the Court in *West Coast Hotel* and gingerly took on board the New Dealers' notion of economic liberty and government's role in securing it. Washington's minimum wage law allegedly violated "freedom of contract." Hughes asked, "What is this freedom? The Constitution does not speak of freedom of contract. It speaks of liberty. . . . But the liberty safeguarded is liberty in a social organization which requires the protection of law against the evils which menace the health, safety, morals and welfare of the people."[262]

West Coast Hotel turned *Adkins*'s reasoning inside out. Along with the distinctly Progressive notion of the "social organization" of economic liberty, the Court adopted the Realist refusal to privilege the common-law organization of the labor market. Any rule regulating the employment contract—whether statutory or judge-made—was a public policy decision that shaped the bargaining power between the parties. The common-law ordering of market relations was no guarantor of a "fair" or "just" exchange of "equivalents" at all. The common law's background rules of contract and property instead gave rise to pervasive inequality "with respect to bargaining power" and the "exploitation of a class of workers" in "an unequal position" in relation to employers.[263] The *West Coast Hotel* Court could have upheld the Washington minimum wage statute on narrow gender grounds, since the minimum wage applied only to women. Justice Sutherland in *Adkins* had imagined that the trajectory of women's emancipation, culminating in the Nineteenth Amendment, required the Court to strike down sex-based protective labor legislation. But this was not the only possible interpretation of that trajectory and amendment.[264] The Court in *West Coast Hotel* could have reached back to any number of precedents for the proposition that protective labor legislation is justified by women's inherent vulnerability and role as "maternal" guardians of "the strength and vigor of the race."[265] And indeed, *West Coast Hotel* cited some precedents in that vein. But instead of resting its holding on those old grounds, it reasoned in revolutionary, gender-free terms about the problem of unequal bargaining power and class exploitation.

Chief Justice Hughes sounded like Frances Perkins or Senator Wagner. The wage contract—the most important contract in most Americans' lives and the one at the heart of the Lochnerian notion of economic liberty—would no longer be insulated by the Supreme Court from democratic change. In other words, yes, there *were* constitutional stakes in the legal construction of relations between labor and capital. But the entire framework was composed of governmental choices. And those choices belonged to the polity.

Back in 1935, when the Court was hearing arguments in *Schechter*, Perkins directed the Labor Department's chief attorneys to draft two labor standards bills. One relied on the Spending Power and set maximum hours and minimum wages for government contracts. It was enacted in 1936.[266] The other was a general wage and hour bill resting on the Commerce Power, which she kept safe in her desk drawer until *West Coast Hotel* and *Jones & Laughlin* came down and the president asked, "What happened to that nice unconstitutional bill you had tucked away?"[267]

The desk-drawer bill became the FLSA. It was enacted in 1938. Designed like the New York measure the Court had struck down in *Morehead*, it set a national minimum wage and an eight-hour day, with time-

and-a-half for overtime, and these standards applied to men and women. The bill provided for appointment of tripartite "industry committees" composed of union, employer, and public representatives to hammer out rules and standards for their respective industries.[268] With its tripartite "industry committees," to be lodged in a new Wage and Hour Division of the Labor Department, the FLSA—as labor law scholar and historian Kate Andrias has shown—was an improved version of what Wagner and other pro-labor architects sought in the NRA, their first and ill-fated attempt to enact their brand of corporatism.[269] Like the old Recovery Act, the FLSA built into the public administration of the law a system of industry-wide negotiation and bargaining between representatives of labor and capital. The problem with the NRA had not been its corporatist meld of public and private governance, but its vague and open-ended mandate, its domination by big business, and its abject failure to include labor representatives in the code-making machinery. By contrast, the FLSA's mandate was pointed and the administrative guidelines clear; workers and employers were equally and fairly represented. These boards redistributed power between capital and labor over questions of wages and hours, upending the old constitutionalized common-law ordering of labor-capital relations.[270] The Wagner Act did this through bargaining, the FLSA through administration.

According to New Deal constitutional political economy, "private" bargaining and "public" administration were not separate things. New Dealers were committed to breaking down the old formalist boundaries between public and private, to bring the old principles of equal citizenship and democratic self-rule into the government of economic life in new ways. They were determined to use law to constitute new institutions for negotiation, bargaining, and cooperation between capital and labor—while conferring a great deal more bargaining power on labor than it ever had before.

Between 1933 and 1938, union membership grew from 2,689,000 to 8,034,000, and the new industrial unions became key players in the New Deal administration and Congress.[271] Thanks to them, New Deal labor policy was now in the hands of social democrats like Wagner, Perkins, Hillman, and others, whose thinking all along had been to foster industry-wide organizing and collective bargaining, across the whole economy. The FLSA's backers boasted that the 1938 law, like the Wagner Act, would expand unions' role in government and economic life.[272] As David Walsh, chair of the Senate Labor Committee, put it, "the Government is attempting to set up machinery which . . . ought to be helpful in providing collective bargaining through a Government agency for the men and women who are not organized."[273]

The FLSA embodied the New Deal's promise to unorganized workers: "We will see to it that you, too, are given some of the benefits and some of the privileges of collective bargaining."[274] While the FLSA entitled workers one by one, union and nonunion alike, to minimum standards, it rested, like the NLRA, on a democratic, participatory, and collective notion of workers' political-economic agency. Together, so New Dealers hoped, the statutes would empower unions in politics and public administration, as well as in workplace, firm-based, and industry-wide bargaining.

In 1940, when the inevitable constitutional challenges to the FLSA reached the Supreme Court, its membership was reconstituted.[275] FDR had just finished appointing a string of six New Deal Justices—Black, Reed, Frankfurter, Douglas, Murphy, and Stone. Writing for a unanimous Court, Justice Stone upheld the FLSA in a sweeping opinion that announced the consolidation of a national police power over economic life—"the plenary power conferred on Congress by the Commerce Clause," Stone called it.[276] It no longer mattered, Stone flatly declared, that the Commerce Power thus construed was indistinguishable from "the police power of the states."[277]

"[T]he plenary power conferred on Congress" meant the Court was extending to the fraught sphere of *regulation* the same full measure of judicial deference to legislative constitutional constructions it had long afforded, and long restricted to, the sphere of *spending*. It was up to Congress and the White House now to interpret and implement the Constitution's basic purposes and requirements, remaking the political economy and revising the distribution of wealth and power, by their own lights. By those lights, the FLSA was like the NLRA, an effort to secure the "economic rights of citizenship."[278] Both contributed to making good on the "principle that all men being born equal must share a minimum of equality, at least, extending to all spheres of life—political, economic, and social."[279]

Did that work? Well, the FLSA's administrative apparatus created seventy industry committees and issued wage orders covering some twenty-one million workers, roughly the same as the old NRA, but with far greater results—thanks to the unions' involvement and their watchfulness over enforcement.[280] As Kate Andrias has shown, the forgotten tripartite committees and the sectoral bargaining and policymaking they housed proved a good fit in the emerging institutional order of economic governance in New Deal America. "Combined with the Wagner Act," writes Andrias, "FLSA's administrative scheme made clear that employers would have to negotiate as equals with unions both in the marketplace and in government. In this way, the FLSA and the NLRA together 'provided the most hospitable climate ever fashioned in American history for trade unions and for decent enforceable conditions of employment.'"[281]

The New Dealers Take Up the Mantle of Antitrust

After the demise of the NIRA in 1935, the New Dealers abandoned their idea of suspending antitrust in favor of reinventing it. Antitrust was a constitutional matter from the start in the democracy-of-opportunity tradition. But during the New Deal, antitrust discourse began its shift from constitutional political economy into "economic policy," in tandem with the gradual decline of political economy and the rise of economics. We discuss this transformation in Chapter 8.[282] In 1935, it was in its early stages. What we find is not a forgetting but a sublimation—or as critics complained, a smuggling—of the value-laden precepts of anti-oligarchy into the neutral-sounding discourse of economics. With this also came new levers against corporate power.

FDR's cousin, Theodore Roosevelt, had been the first great trustbuster. His headline-grabbing prosecutions dramatized antitrust's constitutional purpose in checking oligarchy. TR prosecuted the most powerful economic overlords of his day and broke up J. P. Morgan's railroad monopoly and John D. Rockefeller's Standard Oil.[283] As president, Franklin Roosevelt followed his cousin's course, with greater results. In 1937, FDR chose Robert Jackson, a star New Deal attorney, to lead the DOJ's Antitrust Division, and encouraged him to bring an antitrust prosecution against Andrew Mellon and his vast aluminum monopoly, ALCOA. Like Morgan, Mellon was the era's most powerful investment banker, and his machinations with ALCOA resembled Rockefeller's in the creation of Standard Oil.[284]

As secretary of the treasury to the three prior Republican presidents, Mellon's political connections had insulated ALCOA for decades.[285] Now, New Dealers were holding congressional hearings on Mellon's corruption as treasury chief. The widely reported hearings, combined with public outrage over ALCOA's price hikes on aluminum when the U.S. Air Force was rebuilding its fleet, made Jackson's antitrust suit front-page news.[286] Beyond ALCOA, Mellon had long run the "unofficial . . . economic Government" of interlocking corporate directorates and investment bankers, which Roosevelt denounced so fervently.[287]

Soon after Jackson filed his suit against Mellon, Roosevelt sent a message to Congress on monopolies. "[T]he liberty of a democracy," said the president, "is not safe if the people tolerate the growth of private power to a point where it becomes stronger than their democratic state itself."[288] ALCOA had long been such a power. The trial took some four years. In the thick of it, Roosevelt promoted Jackson to be solicitor general, and hired Thurman Arnold to replace him as head of the Antitrust Division of DOJ. A prominent Yale Legal Realist and brilliant publicist, Arnold prevailed over ALCOA and presided over the division for the rest of the New Deal.

ANTITRUST STATE-BUILDING AND LITIGATION AS REGULATION

The great New Deal historian Alan Brinkley called this the New Deal's "Anti-Monopoly Moment."[289] But neither FDR nor Arnold were antimonopolists of the old school. Like Teddy Roosevelt, they accepted the inevitability of giant firms, but not their threat to democratic rule, nor their abuse of social and economic power to the detriment of workers, consumers, and smaller firms. The classical antimonopoly solution to these evils was to dismantle the giants. The Rooseveltian alternative was to constitute the federal government as a countervailing power to regulate and constrain the giant firms to work for the public good.

At DOJ, Thurman Arnold remade the government's antitrust practice and helped create a new blend of antitrust "economics" and old-school constitutional political economy. Gardiner Means was one in a gifted group of New Deal institutional economists working on corporations and antitrust.[290] His technical paper "Industrial Prices and Their Relative Inflexibility" became the urtext of New Deal antitrust policy.[291] According to Means, concentrated industries and their anticompetitive practices were much to blame for the Depression. In markets where a few giant companies dominated, they could and did engage in an array of anticompetitive practices, like administering fixed prices above what supply and demand would generate.

The lesson, which Means left implicit but Arnold drew out, was that the federal government had to act as a countervailing power, by monitoring whole industries for price-fixing and predatory practices and dismantling concentrated market structures where they were "inherently anti-competitive."[292] To make this new vision of federal antitrust enforcement seem modest and tradition-bound, Arnold would describe the division's role as simply the "traffic policeman" and depict what was largely an administrative practice as one that ran through the courts, and not some bureaucratic machinery.[293]

Meanwhile, Arnold was a master administrative state-builder, cajoling Roosevelt and Congress to enlarge the Antitrust Division's technical and legal staff from 18 to 583 during his tenure.[294] Between 1938 and 1945, the division did massive monitoring and research and brought hundreds of suits and criminal indictments against key players in scores of industries, but rarely had to go to trial, relying instead on consent decrees to restructure entire industries. Arnold accompanied all this with public accounts of what his division was doing and why.

THE NEW ECONOMICS AND THE OLD CONSTITUTIONAL POLITICAL ECONOMY

What is striking about these accounts of the New Deal's antitrust philosophy is how the old constitutional political economy continued to shape the new "economics." The old distributional, social, and political touchstones remained active—sometimes in the old vocabulary, but usually translated into the language of the new economics. Thus, when Arnold encapsulated his division's overarching purpose in his public speeches and writings, he would say that antitrust is a weapon against the "evils of concentrated economic power in a democracy."[295] In a democracy, mind you—not in a free market economy.

When it came to reciting the more particular "evils of concentrated economic power," however, Arnold would turn to economic vocabulary: the ability of giant firms in concentrated industries to fix prices, with the result that "resources are not efficiently allocated"; and "the tendency of such empires to swallow up local businesses, and drain away local capital."[296] As Eskridge and Ferejohn explain in their account of the Sherman Act's trajectory as a constitutional "super-statute," Arnold was mixing arguments based on economic science with other, potentially contradictory arguments that were not. Inefficient allocation of resources, Eskridge and Ferejohn note, "was [an] economic [argument] and drew from administered-price and other economic theories." On the other hand, worrying about "draining away local capital" or "'swallow[ing] up local businesses' . . . sounded economic but did not reflect sound economic analysis"[297]—according to whose wisdom the efficient thing often is for local businesses to get swallowed up, or for investment capital to move somewhere more efficient. What Arnold was doing here was importing the old concerns that animated antitrust law at its inception: building a constitutional political economy that prizes the broader distribution of power and opportunity afforded by constellations of local small and medium-sized firms and widely distributed sources of capital.

In sum, as Eskridge and Ferejohn suggest, Arnold's antitrust thinking "reflected the pervasive New Deal philosophy that big business was too politically powerful and arrogant, rigging both the economic and political systems."[298] Or, as Arnold's successor Wendell Berge said in 1946, in classic anti-oligarchy terms, "monopolies" were "threats to American democracy" itself, because great concentrations of economic power "translate into political power."[299]

Anti-oligarchy reasoning imbued high-profile judicial opinions as well as public discourse. So, for example, the administration's suit against Mellon's aluminum monopoly ended in a striking reaffirmation of the old constitutional political economy.[300] Arnold and his team lost in the trial court. The giant corporation had forged a near-total monopoly—well over 90 percent of the national market—in both raw and sheet aluminum. However, reasoned the conservative trial judge, there was nothing per se illegal about a monopoly, and this one was not the result of bad conduct, but of praiseworthy ingenuity and foresight, along with great economies of scale.[301] The Second Circuit reversed, and its decision was the final word. (At least four Supreme Court Justices recused themselves, leaving the Court without a quorum, so Congress provided for a special panel to decide the case.)[302]

"A KINGLY PREROGATIVE, INCONSISTENT WITH
OUR FORM OF GOVERNMENT"

Authored by Learned Hand, the ALCOA opinion was a major victory for the New Deal's antimonopoly campaign. Even if ALCOA's monopoly was solely the result of economies of scale, said Judge Hand, and its total control over the market had "fall[en] undesigned into [its] lap," which Hand found implausible, the simple "possession of unchallenged economic power," the "concentration of producing power" in one company, and the "mere existence" of such "power to fix prices" condemned ALCOA. A monopoly was illegal per se.[303]

The Sherman Act Congress, said Judge Hand, forbade all trusts, "good" and "bad." It was of the view that competition, rather than concentration, aids "industrial progress." But such "economic reasons" alone were not what animated the act's bar on monopoly—and not the sole guide to its interpretation. The act was "actuated" by a desire to stem "'the inequality of condition, of wealth, and opportunity'" that had grown "'out of the concentration of capital.'" Its framers and its leading judicial interpreters had "social or moral" purposes for "prefer[ring] a system of small producers . . . to one in which the great mass . . . must accept the direction of a few."[304]

Judge Hand summoned Senator Sherman himself to expound antitrust law's general view of Mellon's monopoly: "If the concerted powers of this combination are intrusted to a single man, it is a kingly prerogative, inconsistent with our form of government, and should be subject to the strong resistance of the State and national authorities."[305] Thus, did Learned Hand, more openly than Thurman Arnold, press the economists' concentrated markets analysis into the service of anti-oligarchy and envelop the new economics in the old constitutional political economy.

Other famous New Deal jurists simply refused to wrap antitrust's distributional principles in new-model economic arguments. Take Thurman Arnold's fellow Realist-turned–New Dealer William O. Douglas, who chaired the brand-new Securities and Exchange Commission before FDR appointed him to Louis Brandeis's seat on the Supreme Court. As Justice Douglas, he would reproach the Court for forgetting "the problem of bigness" whose "lesson should . . . have been burned into our memory by Brandeis."[306]

In 1948, the case involved the giant U.S. Steel. By Justice Douglas's lights, it was "the most important antitrust case which has been before the Court in years," and it revealed "the way of growth of monopoly power—the precise phenomenon at which the Sherman Act was aimed."[307] Yet, the majority was allowing U.S. Steel to "gobble[] up" smaller "independent units" because the vertically integrated giant was going about the business of building its monopoly power in "gentlemanly ways."[308] The government lost the case in the Supreme Court because it had not shown at trial that U.S. Steel engaged in predatory practices or bought up the independent competitor with an intent to monopolize the market. But "the impact . . . [wa]s the same."[309]

> Size in steel should . . . be jealously watched. In final analysis, size in steel is the measure of the power of a handful of men over our economy. That power . . . can be benign or it can be dangerous. The philosophy of the Sherman Act is that it should not exist. For all power tends to develop into a government in itself. Power that controls the economy should be in the hands of elected representatives of the people, not in the hands of an industrial oligarchy. . . . The fact that they are not vicious men but respectable and social-minded is irrelevant.[310]

Like Sherman, Hand, and Harlan, Justice Douglas carried on the anti-oligarchy tradition. Much as it did in the case of Harlan's 1911 dissent, Congress responded to Douglas's *U.S. Steel* dissent by amending the antitrust law to restore something more of its framers' constitutional political economy, albeit cast in a more modern economic idiom.[311]

New Deal banking reform was similar to New Deal antitrust in this way. On the one hand, champions of the landmark Glass-Steagall Act promoted the separation of commercial and investment banking in terms of core ideas of the old anti-oligarchy constitutional tradition. On the other hand, defenders of the reform also made claims of a more technocratic economic sort. "Economic experts" gained an edge they lacked in past rounds of bank reform, when constitutional political economy predominated—and the irreducibly political and distributional choices, the constitutional stakes involved in how we design and run our banking system, were kept in plain view.[312]

Meanwhile, the constitutional stakes and distributional choices remained vividly clear in the precincts of labor rights and social provision. Even after the Court had backed down, social and economic rights were yet to be fully realized, safeguarded, and, in some cases, to be enacted at all. The New Deal Court was hospitable to such new rights. As we have seen, it even began to recast its own First Amendment jurisprudence to reflect New Deal understandings of labor's collective freedoms. And when economic reform was challenged on old Lochnerian grounds, the New Deal Court was content to say that regulation and redistribution in the world of social and economic relations were legislative business about which the Court's Constitution was silent.

But how did it happen that by mid-century this no-constitutional-stakes perspective came to prevail *outside the courts,* as well? What happened to the New Deal language of affirmative distributional duties and social and economic rights in politics, executive action, and public debate? Why did public memory lose hold of the social-democratic constitutional political economy at the heart of the New Deal "revolution," replete with duties to prevent oligarchy from recurring and to secure industrial democracy, decent livelihoods, and a middle-class standard of economic security for all Americans?

New Dealers like Wagner were sorely aware of the partial, patchwork, and deeply racialized character of what they had accomplished circa 1938, and they carried on for another eight years with efforts to "complete the New Deal," to enact missing social and economic rights and to make the ones they had enacted inclusive. That never happened. The unfinished New Deal reforms remained, but the language of progressive constitutional political economy vanished from mainstream public discourse and debate.

The explanation lies in a dramatic set of confrontations that unfolded almost entirely outside the courts. That drama and the beginnings of the Great Forgetting are the subjects of Chapter 7.

7

CONSTITUTIONAL COUNTERREVOLUTION AND THE LEGACIES OF A TRUNCATED NEW DEAL

According to constitutional scholars, when the Court upheld the Fair Labor Standards Act in 1941 and the Agricultural Adjustment Act in 1942 with unanimous and sweeping validations of Congress's "plenary power" to regulate the national economy, it marked an epochal constitutional "settlement."[1] That was true as far as the interbranch clash between the New Dealers and the Court was concerned. But when you consider the constitutional battles still blazing in the polity and the Congress, the notion of a constitutional settlement, circa 1942, makes little sense.

Three of the principal actors in the New Deal drama—the nation's business elites, their Republican allies in Congress, and the leaders of the Southern wing of the Democratic Party—would have laughed out loud at the notion of a constitutional settlement in the early 1940s. None had made peace with the idea of plenary national authority over the economy. All agreed that labor's new statutory and constitutional freedoms were counterfeit. They saw the Court as simply a judicial wing of the Roosevelt White House, and they embarked on a militant crusade to restore the old order. The crusade only gathered momentum as New Dealers tried to complete their project of building a democratic political economy—even beginning, hesitantly, to embrace the principle of racial inclusion, which was enough to arouse the Dixiecrats.

Between 1938 and 1947, this new conservative coalition waged a constitutional counterrevolution. With considerable success, they fought to repeal key New Deal measures, and to prevent the expansion of existing programs or the creation of new ones; and they managed to shove the champions of a racially inclusive social-democratic America from the mainstream to the margins of national politics, leaving a modern democracy of opportunity unfinished, for us to reclaim and reinvent.

Social-Democratic State-Building and the Second Bill of Rights

The advent of a "New Deal Court" and its embrace of Congress's plenary power over the national economy encouraged a flowering legislative and administrative constitutionalism composed of governmental duties and affirmative rights. A good example was the "right to work" or "right to a job"—a right New Dealers thought essential to the constitutional political economy that was still a work in progress in the late 1930s and early 1940s.

In addition to labor standards and social security, the New Dealers wanted legislative commitments for full employment.[2] In 1935 when Senator Wagner introduced the Social Security Act, he had underscored that social insurance was insufficient: "At the very hub of social security is the right to have a job." Unemployment insurance was "designed not to supplant, but rather to supplement" government's duty to assure work for the "bulk of persons . . . disinherited for long periods of time by private industry."[3]

The forgotten right to a job got a boost in the late 1930s, when balancing the budget to cut the deficit—the counsel of orthodox economic thinkers—brought about the "Roosevelt recession" of 1937. After that, FDR turned increasingly to advisers who argued that solving unemployment required public investment tied to macroeconomic objectives and permanent public employment programs. In the White House, the Department of Commerce, the Budget Bureau, and the National Resources Planning Board, a group of policymakers led by "social Keynesians" like Harvard's Alvin Hansen[4] drafted structural reforms and policy innovations, imbuing their proposals with the constitutional discourse FDR and New Dealers in Congress were broadcasting to the nation. They supplied not only legislative proposals like the Full Employment Bill of 1945, but also much of the rhetoric and outlook animating key speeches, including the social and economic policy portions of Roosevelt's 1943 and 1944 State of the Union addresses. By 1945, when Congress took up the administration's Full Employment Bill, the right to a job seemed secure, not only in reform rhetoric, but in the discourse of the liberal legal establishment.

Even the staid American Law Institute (ALI) characterized the right to a job as a constitutional essential.[5] In 1945, the ALI appointed a committee of legal luminaries to draft a "Statement of Essential Human Rights" to set out a standard for postwar constitutions around the globe to emulate. The staff of the Senate committee holding hearings on FDR's Full Employment Bill asked the ALI group to prepare "an analysis of the legal and philosophical considerations that led to the inclusion" of the right to work in the ALI statement.[6] The liberal legal notables pointed to "the [forty] nations whose current or recent constitutions contain provisions granting various social and economic rights," and put these alongside the legislative measures passed in the United States in the last dozen years "to secure such rights to its citizens." The Full Employment Bill would help complete the legislative constitutional work at hand.[7]

The ALI draftsmen conceded that some lawmakers and legal thinkers continued to recoil at the idea of a right, "which requires positive action by government, involving complex organization and the expenditures of public funds." Such a right seemed "paternalis[tic]," potentially "tyrann[ical]," and, at the same time, "useless because it is impossible to go into court and force the government . . . to insure that a man has a job."[8]

Criticizing "the traditional legal habit of looking upon rights as negative," the ALI draftsmen offered arguments that continue to run through contemporary debates over so-called positive versus negative rights.[9] Several of the rights in the Bill of Rights, they pointed out, "actually require government to take very positive action indeed . . . [entailing] all the involved and expensive machinery for the administration of civil and criminal justice." From the perspective of "the legislators who must implement" the Constitution, a system of full employment was "child's play in comparison with the system that gives effect to due process of law." The Constitution "was equally binding" on the Congress, which "had the right to determine for itself the meaning of its provisions." By the ALI's learned lights, Congress was obliged to enact "a positive program to secure the right to work to all."[10]

If the ALI seems a surprisingly stodgy outlet to boldly support New Deal constitutional political economy, such contributions ran the gamut, including much advocacy from prominent academics and public intellectuals on the left. Political scientist and historian Charles Beard, remembered for his debunking masterpiece *An Economic Interpretation of the Constitution*,[11] promoted his ideas for New Deal America in a constant stream of books, articles, and speeches, draft legislation, and wide conversation with friends on both sides of Pennsylvania Avenue. Beard's vision was a radical American social democracy in a distinctly republican frame.

A generous welfare state without full employment and a socially independent and empowered working class, said Beard, was almost as great a peril to the republic as unchecked corporate oligarchs.[12] It was true that "doles, pensions, allotments . . . may for the time being, create an enlarged purchasing power" and boost recovery; but by itself, redistribution via taxation bred dependency.[13] If America was to remain a republic, it would have to be a "workers' republic."[14] For that, it needed a full employment economy, as well as new forms of worker, cooperative, and government ownership, along with robust unions, to produce "ways of industry conducive to the promotion of individual and social virtues."[15]

A public law polymath, Beard laid out many of the constitutional avenues for instituting this kind of "workers' republic." Fluent in institutional economics, Beard also helped supply the technical underpinnings for a "constitutional readjustment" of property rights in labor, capital, and land.[16] The social-democratic constitutional republic would not abolish private property; instead, it would rearrange property rights.

What was most needed, however, and what Beard saw Roosevelt reaching for, was not so much legal-economic expertise as a new grand vision that synthesized "the strength of Hamilton's government with the democratic control so vaunted by Jefferson."[17] Wedding Jeffersonian ends and Hamiltonian means was an old Progressive trope. But Beard added a new one—the "Living Constitution"—which he put into general circulation.[18] "Since most of the [Constitution's] words and phrases dealing with the powers and the limits of government are vague and must in practice be interpreted by human beings," wrote Beard in 1936, "it follows that the Constitution as practice is a living thing."[19] Earlier in the century, Beard's *Economic Interpretation of the Constitution* helped take the framers down from their pedestals. Spotlighting the class-bound, elitist motivations afoot at the Philadelphia Convention helped make the case for democratic constitutional reform in the Progressive Era. But now, with fellow socialists and radical reformers in the corridors of national power, Beard put forward a different take on the founding fathers.

Beard's 1936 *Living Constitution* praised the "fathers" for the "flexible character" of the rights of citizens and the powers and duties of government they laid down. "The fathers intended to leave room for interpretation, growth and modification within the letter of the Constitution."[20] The Constitution was meant to empower "citizens, judges, administrators, [and] lawmakers" who aimed to "bring[] about changes in the relations of persons and property in the United States" no less than those committed to "preserving existing relations."[21] The idea that legal and constitutional precepts were mutable and open-ended was familiar, but Progressives had been using it chiefly to deconstruct the constitutional certainties of the conservative judiciary; Beard helped make it an authorization from "[t]he fathers" for social-democratic state-building.[22]

During the depths of the Depression, full employment and the right to work were everywhere in policy blueprints. But before these guarantees got out the door, war preparations and the wartime mobilization of American industry brought abundant jobs and revived the nation's economy. "Dr. Win-the-War," Roosevelt told Americans, was taking the place of "Dr. New Deal."[23] Nevertheless, the architects and leaders of wartime agencies like the War Labor Board (WLB) and the Office of Price Administration (OPA) included many New Deal experts in progressive constitutional political economy.

The New Dealers built social-democratic distributional commitments into the design and policies of these wartime agencies. They formed tripartite agencies and commissions composed of business, labor, and "public" representatives, in which the latter two often enjoyed power roughly commensurate with that of capital. (This was not surprising, since these governmental structures rose alongside the massive new industrial unions, which enjoyed considerable clout on the ground and in the White House.) The tripartite WLB and OPA regulated wage and price relations within and between industries; they fashioned a broad policy of redistributing income into workers' and consumers' hands, along with a policy of redistributive wage compression, which meant raising wages most in low-income sectors. So, for example, Black wages rose twice as rapidly as white wages under this WLB / OPA regime, and weekly earnings in relatively low-wage industries like cotton, textiles, and retail trade rose about 50 percent faster than in high-wage industries like auto and steel.[24]

As the New Dealers looked ahead to peacetime, they aspired to make their innovations permanent.[25] They hoped to carry on with this public / private style of economic governance: a peacetime "mixed economy," committed to full employment and replete with democratic controls over economic decision-making to assure that the erstwhile oligarchs never again enjoyed such lopsided authority over the political economy and ordinary Americans' share of wealth, power, and opportunity.[26]

A good illustration of this robust constitutional discourse emanating from the wartime executive branch came in the National Resources Planning Board's 1942 Annual Report.[27] It began with a declaration of rights, a classic Rooseveltian Living Constitution proclamation: We must reinterpret "our provisions for human freedom. . . . [T]o the old freedoms we must add new freedoms and restate our objectives in modern terms."[28] Roosevelt's speechwriter (and editor of his *Public Papers*), Samuel Rosenman, described how Roosevelt himself grabbed hold of the 1942 report and set about simplifying and "dramatiz[ing]" its meld of social and economic rights, structural reforms, and policy innovations for his widely published 1944 State of the Union address.[29]

The 1944 State of the Union made plain the principles of a postwar constitutional political economy worth fighting for. In the speech, Roosevelt unfurled "a second Bill of Rights under which a new basis of security and prosperity can be established."[30] The postwar period must not bring a return to outworn, pre–New Deal notions of the rights of persons and property and the duties of government, here or abroad, FDR said. "In the first World War," the president reminded Americans, "we came closer [than ever before] to national unity" via a strong government role in making the industrial economy work for all. But armistice and peace brought a "rightist reaction" and a rollback to the old laissez-faire. If "such reaction should develop" again, Roosevelt warned, "if history were to repeat itself and we were to return to the so-called 'normalcy' of the 1920's—then it is certain that even though we shall have conquered our enemies on the battlefields abroad, we shall have yielded to the spirit of Fascism here at home."[31]

Unregulated financial markets, misguided notions of the rights of capitalist property, and other outworn political-economic institutions during the 1920s ended in disaster on a global scale, Roosevelt said. By the 1930s, much of the industrial capitalist world had seen frightened business elites strike their own new deals with "Fascism" and "gangster rule."[32] Repression, fear, and want bred acquiescence among ordinary citizens. And liberalism and the rule of law gave way. During the 1930s, America managed instead to rest liberalism and the rule of law on a new and sturdier basis—not the economic royalists' right to rule, but the social and economic rights and liberties of all Americans. Embracing government's inescapable responsibility for the way our political economy distributed risks and rewards, power and opportunity, security and insecurity, the New Deal had restored people's faith in constitutional democracy. FDR quoted himself: "We have come to a clear realization of the fact that true individual freedom cannot exist without economic security and independence. 'Necessitous men are not free men.' People who are hungry and out of a job are the stuff of which dictatorships are made."[33]

"In our day," he continued, "these economic truths have become accepted as self-evident." And then in Living Constitution style, he set out a "second Bill of Rights," calling on Congress to continue "implementing this economic bill of rights" in order to lend modern substance to the democracy of opportunity that the original Bill of Rights was designed to ensure. In addition to "adequate food and clothing and recreation," "adequate medical care," and "a decent home," Roosevelt's "second Bill" included "[t]he right to a useful and remunerative job," "[t]he right to earn enough," "[t]he right of every farmer to raise and sell his products," and "[t]he right of every businessman . . . to trade . . . [free from] domination by monopolies at home or abroad," and all of these rights "regardless of station, race, or creed."[34]

The "second Bill" captures what the president and his constitutional political economists meant when they spoke of completing the New Deal. The commitment to racial inclusion seems most remarkable, in view of the New Dealers' strenuous efforts to accommodate Jim Crow. To propitiate the Dixiecrats, we saw, the NLRA, the SSA, and FLSA were tailored to exclude Southern Black labor, and to vest administrative control in the hands of local officials. What changed?

The Conservative Counterrevolution Begins

The short answer is that the Southern Dixiecrats turned openly against New Deal reform, and FDR and Northern New Deal Democrats responded by turning against them. As the Dixiecrats began forging a conservative alliance with anti–New Deal Republicans, it began to seem wise for the party of reform to revisit the old Reconstruction-era idea of allying with the Black South. That radical development fueled the conservative counterrevolution, but it also helped produce a largely forgotten civil rights movement rooted in New Deal constitutional political economy, and a glimpse of what a fully realized democracy of opportunity might have looked like.

It did not take long for clear-eyed students of congressional politics to begin spotlighting Jim Crow's lead role in shaping the fortunes of New Deal reform. The first scholarly account of the links between Dixiecrat power and the half-finished shape of the New Deal came from the Texas-born political scientist V. O. Key. Key homed in on the informal veto power that the Southern Democrats enjoyed in the New Deal Congress by dint of their numbers, seniority, and control over crucial committees. He described how the Dixiecrats exercised this power to veto civil rights legislation; hence, the New Deal's notorious failure to enact a federal antilynching law.[35] But, as the historian and political scientist Ira Katznelson and others have richly documented, the Dixiecrats used their veto power far more broadly.[36]

Hailing from an impoverished region with a Populist tradition, most Southern Democrats were staunch supporters of the New Deal until the late 1930s. But the Southern delegation was under the sway of a ruling elite—an "oligarchy" of "Southern Bourbons"—who were determined to insulate the region's separate, racially segmented, caste-ridden labor market.[37] We saw this process unfold in Chapter 6. In exchange for the Southern delegation's support for New Deal programs, the Bourbons exacted decentralized administration and standard-setting for key labor protections and social provision, and demanded that other measures exclude the main categories of Southern labor.

Otherwise, asked Senator Carter Glass of Virginia, how "were they going to get blacks to pick and chop cotton when Negroes were receiving [on federal work programs] more than twice as much as they had ever been paid[?]"[38] The Bourbons were blunt. Congressman "Cotton Ed" Smith railed against the administration's original Fair Labor Standards bill: "Any man on this floor who has sense enough to read the English language knows that the main objective of [the original bill] is, by human legislation, to overcome the splendid gifts of God to the South."[39] By allying with Northern Republicans or threatening to do so, the Dixiecrats got what they wanted.

The "gentlemen's agreement" between the White House and the Dixie elites had seemed "unshakeable"[40] in the early 1930s. But as the 1936 election approached, and business opposition to the New Deal intensified, Roosevelt grew more attentive to two crucial constituencies: the insurgent industrial unions of the CIO and the Black voters of the large cities of the North. As these groups gained importance in his 1936 reelection bid, Roosevelt's social and economic rights talk grew more robust and universal—and the Southerners attacked. Governor Eugene Talmadge of Georgia convened a "Grass Roots Convention" to "uphold the Constitution" against "Negroes, the New Deal and . . . Karl Marx."[41] Senator Carter Glass of Virginia challenged the white South to show "spirit and courage enough to face the new Reconstruction era that Northern so-called Democrats are menacing us with."[42]

The next few years brought more "interference." Minimum wage legislation, CIO organizing drives, rural poverty programs, and recurrent political initiatives and mobilizations among the disenfranchised, both white and Black, began to undermine the political and economic sway of Key's oligarchy of Southern industrialists and Black Belt landowners. Although early New Deal programs like the Agricultural Adjustment Act had been tailored by these Southern elites and their powerful representatives in Congress to pour aid into Southern agriculture without upsetting the plantation system, the very inequities of these programs from tenants' and sharecroppers' perspective sparked protests and national debate. CIO organizers, NAACP leaders, and progressive New Deal administrators lent support to grassroots movements like the biracial Southern Tenant Farmers Union. They wheedled new programs from sympathetic New Dealers in Washington like Secretary of Agriculture Henry Wallace.[43]

Just as FDR had cemented his alliance with industrial labor and redoubled his attacks on corporate "tyrants," and just as executive branch support for upstart Blacks and poor whites was mounting in what hitherto had been secure provinces of "States' rights" and "local self-government," judicial safeguards against all these dangers seemed to crumble. In the fall of 1937, after the Court handed down *West Coast Hotel Co. v. Parrish* and *Jones & Laughlin,* who could say that the Court's steadfastness in upholding the old Constitution was still to be counted on?[44] For all these reasons, the New Deal's foes in Congress were galvanized. A group of conservative Southern Democrats in the Senate met with like-minded Republican senators to consider a more formal alliance against the New Deal.[45]

The counterrevolution contemplated party realignment in the name of the old Constitution, and its leaders drafted a "statement of principles and objectives,"[46] which became known as the "Conservative Manifesto." If the Court was giving up the constitutional battle against economic radicalism and centralized government, these conservatives would carry it on. The manifesto proclaimed the conservative Democrats' and Republicans' shared devotion to the Constitution of states' rights, liberty of contract, and the property rights of the owners of capital.[47] The attempt at forming a new conservative party foundered, but the coalition and its role as bulwark for the old Constitution held firm.

The leaders of the new coalition declaimed against "Roosevelt constitutional tyranny."[48] Together, they defeated the administration's efforts in the late 1930s and early 1940s to build new administrative capacities in the executive branch to oversee fiscal policies, work programs, and public investment in the name of full employment.[49] The administration and Northern New Dealers tried to remedy the many gaps, exclusions, and anomalies in the SSA and FLSA.[50] They tried to enact national health insurance.[51] And they drafted measures like the Full Employment Bill of 1945, setting forth an unequivocal federal commitment to full employment.[52] But the conservative coalition managed to block, hollow out, or undo all these measures; they succeeded in dismantling the National Resources Planning Board, whose social-democratic-minded planners had written the first draft of FDR's "second Bill of Rights."[53] Had these defeated measures and agencies prevailed in their efforts to "complete the New Deal," they would have produced a post–World War II American state much more akin to those fashioned in the social democracies of postwar Europe. Between that vision of a social-democratic America and its enactment fell the shadow of Jim Crow.[54]

"A New Reconstruction Era": The New Deal's Forgotten Civil Rights Movement

The vanguard of the New Deal era's forgotten movement to topple Jim Crow were the half-million Black workers who joined CIO unions. Where the 1960s civil rights movement led with integration and bringing down "whites only" laws, the New Deal civil rights movement emphasized labor and constitutional political economy. Thus, along with voting rights and voter registration drives, the civil rights movement of the 1930s and 1940s was built around decent work, livelihoods, and economic citizenship.

Another difference: the Fourteenth Amendment, with its promise of equal protection, anchored the civil rights lawsuits of the 1960s. The Thirteenth Amendment, with its bar on slavery and its promise to make free labor universal, was at the heart of New Deal civil rights lawyering, as legal historian Risa Goluboff has chronicled.[55] Organized labor called the Thirteenth Amendment "the glorious Labor Amendment" and made its promise—"No Property Rights in Man"—the basis of anti-injunction campaigns. Likewise, when Roosevelt's attorney general, Frank Murphy, established a new civil rights unit in the Department of Justice, its attorneys seized on the Thirteenth Amendment to go after the brutal coercion and exploitation of Black workers in the turpentine camps and cotton and rice fields of the Deep South. The NAACP also used the Thirteenth Amendment to push the cause of Black tenant farmers and tobacco workers, challenging debt peonage.[56]

Workplaces and working-class neighborhoods were where Black Americans fought their most decisive battles in the New Deal era. The CIO was where the action was, with its intensive organizing campaigns, militant rights-consciousness, and ringing demand for "Equal rights for Negro workers."[57] By the 1930s, Black workers were a significant part of the nation's industrial workforce and central to union organizing throughout the nation—in Southern metal and coal mining, longshore work, and tobacco manufacturing, as well as in Northern auto and steel manufacturing and meatpacking.[58] Friend and foe alike agreed that the new industrial unions would not have prevailed without the militant support they won from Black workers.[59] A reporter for *Crisis*, the NAACP's national journal, observed that the CIO had become a "lamp of democracy" throughout the old Confederate states. "The South has not known such a force since . . . the great days of the Reconstruction era."[60]

"Hidden away in Southern black communities," writes historian Robin D. G. Kelley, "was a folk belief that the Yankees would return to wage another civil war in the South and complete Reconstruction."[61] No such invasion came. However, Black and white labor organizers did arrive from the North, particularly organizers from the communist left, whose uncompromising focus on working-class unity undergirded their forceful demands for full equality for Black workers.[62] The new CIO unions welcomed them; in states like Alabama, the 1930s Communist Party itself took shape as a "'race' organization," with a predominantly Black membership.[63] Its arrival reawakened the barely remembered tradition of "the Union Leagues and black militias during Reconstruction [and] the Knights of Labor [and] Populists" of the late nineteenth century.[64]

Part of what gave Reconstruction so much significance in collective memory was the fact that the power of the nation-state was mobilized behind Black enfranchisement. The Wagner Act began to rekindle that dream. The 1935 National Labor Relations Act excluded agricultural workers to accommodate Jim Crow.[65] But even so, the "one man, one vote" policy implemented in thousands of National Labor Relations Board elections enfranchised Southern Black industrial workers, who became first-time voters and rights-bearing participants in labor's public sphere.[66] The new unions offered these Black workers industrial citizenship through participation in union governance—deliberating and deciding on workplace grievances and broader goals, and winning election to positions of biracial union leadership. As historians Robert Korstad and Nelson Lichtenstein have shown, these experiences combined with the patriotic egalitarianism of the New Dealers' wartime propaganda to generate a militant rights-consciousness among Black workers as powerful as that evoked by the Baptist spirituality of Martin Luther King Jr. a generation later.[67]

FAIR EMPLOYMENT AND FULL EMPLOYMENT— RACIAL INCLUSION IN THE DEMOCRACY OF OPPORTUNITY

In 1941, the leading Black trade unionist and socialist A. Philip Randolph led a union-sponsored "March on Washington for Jobs and Equal Participation in National Defense," which the CIO underwrote.[68] Randolph called on "Negro America" to march on the capital: "[I]f American democracy will not give jobs to its toilers because of race or color . . . it is a hollow mockery."[69]

The march was called off, but FDR responded by creating the Fair Employment Practices Committee (FEPC) to end job discrimination in defense industries.[70] The first civil rights beachhead in the federal government since the Freedmen's Bureau, the FEPC was a weak agency, but its interracial staff conducted well-publicized hearings and investigations, exposing racist conditions and spurring on Black protest.[71] By 1943, Randolph demanded a permanent, peacetime FEPC to be organized "roughly like the NLRB," with similar authority to identify and adjudicate rights violations. Like the Wagner Act, this law would secure "the right to work without demeaning discrimination." The one protected the "dignity of union membership"; the other would protect the dignity of fair employment.[72]

Bills to transform the wartime FEPC into a permanent federal agency came before Congress in 1945, the same year that it took up the administration's Full Employment Bill.[73] Both were cast as measures redeeming fundamental rights, as more and more Northern New Dealers brought racial equality squarely into their constitutional political economy. The social right to a job for all who can work, they declared, and the civil right to work, irrespective of race, color, and creed, were two sides of the same equation. Both were economic rights of American citizenship.[74]

When Congress finally acted against employment discrimination, almost two decades later, in 1964, the right to a job had fallen out of the equation. But in the mid-1940s, these two forms of citizenship were inseparable, and New Deal liberals were clear on the constitutional stakes in both the Full Employment Bill and the bill for a permanent federal fair employment agency.

So were key Black legal thinkers. Pauli Murray is revered today as the intellectual progenitor of what we now think of as intersectionality and of the law of sex-based equal protection that Ruth Bader Ginsburg would later develop through litigation.[75] In 1945, as Congress took up the FEPC and Full Employment bills, Murray was a recent Howard University Law School graduate pursuing a graduate degree in jurisprudence at Berkeley.[76] Today, we do not think of the work she was doing as having anything to do with full employment. But that shows we have lost an important connection, because in 1945, Murray thought it "obvious" that the "right to equal opportunity in employment" was intimately linked to "full employment" and the right to work and livelihood.[77] The inclusion thread and the wide-open-middle-class thread of the democracy-of-opportunity tradition could not easily be pulled apart. Murray wrote in the 1945 volume of the *California Law Review,*

> When the opportunity for employment is further conditioned by an arbitrary qualification based upon race, color, creed, national origin or ancestry . . . the minority worker faces an additional handicap. It is obvious, however, that job discrimination based upon racial or religious prejudice is subsidiary to the more pressing issue of full employment. When jobs are plentiful, all kinds of economic discrimination are minimized. When jobs

> are scarce . . . it is relatively easy to divide employees into con-
> venient groupings . . . and to aggravate the prejudice which leads
> to an exclusion of minority groups from job opportunities. The
> basic problem to be solved, therefore, is the problem of full
> employment.[78]

She concluded her "anti-discrimination discussion" by underscoring that the "current Full Employment bill" recognized "the right to employment" and "livelihood" as "the essence of American tradition."[79]

If Black and white New Deal liberals, social democrats, and socialists were clear on the stakes for democracy of opportunity, so were conservatives. The Dixiecrats hurled constitutional objections at the bills proposing a permanent FEPC. The idea of national legislation against private employment discrimination was "in palpable violation of the Constitution." But "[w]hat is the Constitution between friends," one Dixiecrat inquired acidly, "especially if the question has to do in some way, directly or indirectly, with the suffrage of a Negro?"[80] The Bourbon congressman explained that insofar as the proponents of a permanent, peacetime Fair Employment Practices Commission sought to rest the measure on the Fourteenth Amendment, on the grounds that the "right to work" free from discrimination was a privilege or immunity of national citizenship, their argument flouted the *Slaughter-House Cases*'[81] clear account of the narrow scope of that clause. Southern congressmen also accused the FEPC bills' drafters of ignoring the state action requirement of the *Civil Rights Cases,*[82] and to the extent the drafters purported to rest the bills on the Commerce Clause, they could not prevail unless Congress could now do anything at all under that clause. But surely, even in 1945, enough of the old Constitution's liberty and property protections survived, at least in the halls of Congress. Surely, Congress knew that it could not reach deeply into the realm of private life (compelling unwanted racial association) and invade the rights of private property beyond where even the states "operating in the vast realm of their reserved sovereignty" could properly venture.[83] Even "the States," as one Republican argued, could not enact the FEPC antidiscrimination norm without destroying "the right of free choice in hiring, discharging, or promoting employees."[84]

The House sponsor of a permanent FEPC, Progressive Republican congressman Charles La Follette, rose to defend the bill's constitutionality.[85] What he and other proponents of the bill said in its defense confirms that New Deal constitutionalism in the hands of Congress's ablest lawyers (La Follette would soon be sent by FDR to join Robert Jackson as deputy chief counsel at Nuremberg) was not what we have been taught in law school. It was not a constitutional outlook that thrust economic rights and liberties beyond the purview of constitutional concern. Instead, this outlook recast such rights in a new "affirmative" mold, adequate to building a democratic political economy in the era of corporate capitalism.

When conservatives objected to the FEPC bill's unconstitutional interference with "free choice" in hiring and firing, La Follette argued that the Court had already upheld a federal statutory intrusion on that freedom in the form of the Wagner Act, which outlawed the discharge of a worker for union affiliation. The Court had agreed "it was unlawful to refuse to employ a man because of his . . . union activities," La Follette said.[86] Thus, it seemed to follow "as a matter of constitutional authority that Congress has the power to declare a thing to be discrimination" and "irrelevant and invidious" as far as employment opportunity was concerned.[87]

But La Follette and other defenders of the FEPC bill went further, addressing the nature of Americans' new fundamental economic rights and Congress's new governmental duties in the wake of the constitutional revolution. Here, again—as was the case during the debates over passage of the Wagner Act itself—La Follette, along with Senator Wagner and others, reasoned as though the NLRA was a fundamental rights-bearing measure. The Wagner Act, on this reading, affirmed that the "the right of employment in industry or the right to work" had "the dignity of at least a quasi property right" that the Constitution authorized and required Congress to safeguard.[88]

Thus, La Follette did not rely on the Commerce Power to defend the FEPC bill's constitutional bona fides. Rather, he claimed a fundamental rights-based constitutional warrant for Congress to protect the "right to work at a gainful employment"[89] against invidious discrimination. Granting that Congress had a duty to protect this "right to work" from discrimination, however, did not eliminate the state action requirement. But this La Follette swept away as a relic of laissez-faire. If the nineteenth-century Constitution already forbade laws or customs requiring or upholding private race discrimination, and empowered Congress to sanction them, it followed that in New Deal America, "Congress also has the affirmative power to treat affirmatively with those [private] discriminations and to prohibit them."[90] As Professor Corwin said, the New Deal "revolution" marked a "profound" recognition of "'liberty' . . . as something that may be infringed by other forces" than government and "may require the positive intervention of government against these other forces."[91] That was the deepest meaning of *Jones & Laughlin.*

Other FEPC proponents reached the same result via Justice Harlan's dissent in the *Civil Rights Cases*.[92] There, Justice Harlan suggested that state action may be found where the private actor is a creature of state law, like a corporation.[93] In the Wagner Act, Congress also underscored the publicly constructed character of the corporation and its power over employees.[94] Perhaps the New Deal Court, having absorbed the Realists' insights about the public policy–making nature of private law and constitutional rights adjudication, would put Harlan's theory to work in service of racial equality and a democracy of opportunity.[95] Wagner and others put forward that theory when they drafted the Senate FEPC bill, which provided that the "right to work and to seek work without discrimination . . . is declared to be an immunity, of all citizens of the United States, which shall not be abridged by any State or by an instrumentality or creature of the United States or of any State."[96]

Introduced repeatedly from 1945 onward, the administration's bills to create a permanent FEPC either died at the hands of Dixiecrat committee chairmen or were vanquished by Dixiecrat filibusters.[97] Dixiecrats also killed FDR's right to a job by gutting the administration's Full Employment Bill in committee.[98] These defeats hardly shocked New Dealers. Eight years had passed since the Solid South and the conservative coalition had stopped the New Deal's legislative engine in its tracks. And since the late 1930s, figures like Eleanor Roosevelt, Secretary of Agriculture Henry Wallace, Wagner, and La Follette insisted the future of New Deal reform hinged on attacking Jim Crow and Southern disenfranchisement and promoting civil rights.[99]

"When You Come Down to It There Is Little Difference between the Feudal System and the Fascist System"

By 1938, they had succeeded in prodding Roosevelt to speak out about Southern primary elections in hopes of defeating the Southern reactionaries.[100] Roosevelt began to assail the South's congressional bloc for stymieing New Deal reforms.[101] In the summer primary season, FDR "marched through Georgia," boldly attacking the South's "feudal economic system" and the myth of white economic paternalism: "When you come down to it there is little difference between the feudal system and the Fascist system," he declared. "If you believe in the one, you lean to the other."[102]

The president may have met with success in "trying to woo southern labor and tenant farmers into the camp of his new liberalism," as one of his Southern foes complained.[103] However, the effort to unseat the Southern reactionaries in Congress was doomed by the poll tax, literacy tests, and other roadblocks that kept Blacks and a majority of low-income whites from voting.[104] While he failed to defeat any Dixiecrats, FDR's campaign to elect Southern liberals helped galvanize the labor-based voting rights movement. It sought to carry out from below what Eleanor Roosevelt, Henry Wallace, Wagner, and even the cautious and pragmatic president himself pursued from above: a real assault on Jim Crow and Black disenfranchisement, and the liberal realignment of the Democratic party.[105]

"There is another South," a leader of the movement assured its CIO backers, "composed of the great mass of small farmers, the sharecroppers, the industrial workers white and colored, for the most part disenfranchised by the poll tax and without spokesmen either in Congress, in their state legislatures or in the press."[106] This South, he claimed, was the great majority of the region's population.[107] Were it mobilized and enabled to vote, the South would become "the most liberal region in the Nation."[108] A Black labor and civil rights activist told a biracial audience in Birmingham that the movement's gains in registering Black and poor white voters in Alabama were reminiscent of those "first bright days of Reconstruction ... [which] gave to our region its first democratic governments." It was time, he said, for "history to repeat itself."[109]

But that time had not arrived. The fraud, intimidation, and violence that greeted the Southern campaign to revive the democratic promise of Reconstruction confirmed once more, half a century on, how dependent such a regional movement ultimately was on a national commitment to decisive action based on a broad interpretation of constitutionally protected civil and political rights. Presented with such a federal commitment, even in the late 1930s or early 1940s, perhaps a majority of hard-hit white Southerners might have proved willing to forsake old political identities rooted in states' rights and white supremacy and wager instead on the promise of a national program embracing all three strands of the democracy-of-opportunity tradition, including racial justice. But white supremacy remained too deeply etched in the national government and party system from which such a program would have had to emerge.

Taft–Hartley and the Battle Over the Postwar Political Economy

"War is the health of the State," wrote the radical journalist Randolph Bourne as the world went to war in 1914.[110] As far as the American state is concerned, Bourne was right. Wartime advanced state-building during both World Wars. One difference was that World War II state-building unfolded in the context of a powerful labor movement in close alliance with the New Deal administration. To regulate the wartime economy, we have seen, the New Deal state-builders built tripartite agencies and commissions composed of business, labor, and "public" representatives, in which the latter two often enjoyed power roughly commensurate with that of capital. As they looked ahead to peacetime, many New Dealers and their labor allies hoped to preserve that institutional framework, which seemed critical to the unfinished work of creating a modern democracy of opportunity.

By war's end, however, business leaders were desperate to end the encroachments of the social-democratic-minded phalanx of state agencies in league with a social-democratic-minded labor movement.[111] Business elites yearned for a reprivatization of labor-management relations and an end to wartime government controls on capital.[112] At every opportunity in the mid-1940s, captains of industry would speak feelingly about the demise of "individual autonomy" and the rise of a profoundly unconstitutional, bureaucratic, near-totalitarian state of political-economic affairs.[113] Publicly and privately, they expressed a deep and genuine sense of constitutional peril. If the union chieftains and their New Deal allies had their way, and if something like the "collectivist" regime they had fashioned during the Great Depression and the war became part of normal peacetime government, then "economic liberty" would perish forever, and the nation would be given over to "compulsion," "slavery," and an end to "equality of opportunity."[114]

As these business elites saw it, the heart of the problem was the enormous political and economic clout that organized labor had acquired over the previous decade. That power originated in the despised Wagner Act, the collective action it safeguarded, and the affirmative boost the Labor Board lent the industrial unions. All this had to be repealed, or at least sharply redrawn, with labor's new rights curtailed and employers' old rights recouped. Employers' "right to manage" became a watchword of the movement to repeal the Wagner Act, which included virtually every major corporation in every major industry.[115] "America is at the crossroads!" declared a General Motors (GM) advertisement, during a bitter hundred-day strike by the United Auto Workers (UAW) in 1945–1946. At stake was "the freedom of each unit of American business to determine its own destiny." When workers organized and struck, free of the old legal restraints and empowered by the new state protections, it was no wonder that the "union bosses" were seeking "to tell us what we can make, when we can make it, where we can make it, and how much we can charge."[116] But this could not continue; it flouted the right of "every business unit in America" to "manage its own affairs."[117]

GM's president Alfred Sloan and others laid these complaints at the feet of the Wagner Act and the Labor Board. The Court had upheld the act with its "switch in time" in 1937, and by the mid-1940s, the Court was overwhelmingly dominated by Roosevelt-appointed New Deal Justices. Constitutional scholars write about this mid-1940s period as the moment when the "New Deal settlement" was consolidated, but no one mistook the facts on the ground for a constitutional settlement.

As far as contemporary business leaders and the conservatives in Congress were concerned, there was nothing remotely like a New Deal constitutional settlement. Not as long as the constitutionally outrageous new rights and powers of labor and the National Labor Relations Board and other features of New Deal and wartime state regulatory authority were left intact. Sloan compared the moment to the repeal of the Eighteenth Amendment: "It took fourteen years to rid this country of prohibition. It is going to take a good while to rid the country of the New Deal, but sooner or later the ax falls and we get a change."[118]

The Dixiecrats also loathed both the CIO and the New Deal's centralized statecraft. They, too, were determined to curtail the industrial unions' newly minted, federally guaranteed but constitutionally counterfeit, collective freedoms. That seemed the only sure way to weaken labor's clout and ward off the CIO / New Deal coalition's vision of a racially egalitarian, social-democratic postwar political economy and a realigned, postwar Democratic Party. This was the political and constitutional backdrop for the Taft–Hartley Act.

The catalyst was the election of 1946. In industry after industry, management was trying to retake authority lost during the war and keep a lid on wages as government involvement receded. Giant industry-wide strikes resulted, as labor sought to support President Harry Truman's efforts to sustain price controls and working-class living standards during demobilization. When voters went to the polls in 1946, roughly a million workers were on picket lines, cities were shut down, and inflation neared 20 percent. The upshot: Republicans won majorities in both houses for the first time since the 1920s, and their victory emboldened the champions of repealing the Wagner Act.

The Taft–Hartley Act proved to be a constitutional battle royale, and the confrontation on which the fate of the New Deal order turned. The old Lochnerian definitions of the rights and liberties of labor and capital were not dead. They were present and active in this and other crucial legislative constitutional battles of the mid-1940s. A few years after the Court rang down the curtain on the old Lochnerian doctrines, the newly dominant congressional Republicans and their Dixiecrat allies invoked the old rights and liberties, largely indifferent to what the New Dealers on the Court had to say. Because the Court had announced its retreat from policing such questions, it was Congress's constitutional battle anyway.

As the bill that became the Taft–Hartley Act[119] took shape, its Republican sponsors put aside talk of outright repeal of the Wagner Act, instead attacking a host of key provisions. The 1947 legislation outlawed industry-wide bargaining; reinstated many old common-law restrictions on strikes and boycotts, including a ban on all so-called secondary boycotts; condemned "supervisory" workers' unions; and imposed anticommunist oaths. The act also abolished the closed or union shop (wherein employers agreed to make union membership a condition of employment). It spared agreements that made dues payment, as opposed to union membership, a requirement of employment, but it provided for states to enact even harsher "right to work" laws, forbidding unions from negotiating for such mandatory dues payments or so-called agency fees in the first place. Those state laws would no longer violate or be pre-empted by national labor law.

Taft–Hartley's champions characterized all these provisions as constitutional essentials and defended the bill in ringing constitutional terms. Thus, Kansas Republican Wint Smith, taking a swipe at the 1944 G. I. Bill of Rights, declared, "I am not asking you to give money for the ex-serviceman from a paternalistic government. I am only asking for something that is not just guaranteed by the Constitution but given to him by his Creator—the right to work where and when he pleases—just plain freedom."[120]

The Republicans' "right to work," which got enshrined in the Taft–Hartley Act, was cut from the old cloth. It was the quintessential freedom from state "interference" in the old common-law-governed wage contract between worker and employer. This Lochnerian right to work was a world apart from the right to work that FDR put at the heart of the Second Bill of Rights. That right signified government's affirmative duty to ensure work for everyone who needed a job. In 1946–1947, the grisly old meaning returned from the grave and devoured the new. Already, in early 1946, the conservative coalition had gutted the administration's Full Employment Bill; instead, Congress had enacted a hollow substitute, the renamed Employment Act of 1946.[121]

It was one thing, however, to prevent a new right from being enacted and brought down to earth; it was quite another to bring back the much-despised liberty of contract. That required a movement. None other than the famous Cecil B. DeMille, director of countless Hollywood blockbusters and founder of Paramount Pictures, joined forces with veteran anti-union attorneys and employers' associations to launch and fund the "right to work" movement to restore as much as possible of the old libertarian-conservative outlook on unions.[122]

DeMille's "right to work" movement has remained a vigorous player in our constitutional politics ever since. Beyond Taft–Hartley itself, the "right to work" movement scored other important gains over the next decades, including passage of "right to work" statutes in about two dozen states. More recently, the Roberts Court has begun nationalizing the "right to work" regime. We will return to this development in Chapter 9.[123]

But Taft–Hartley was a stunning victory for the new movement. In the congressional hearings and reports surrounding Taft–Hartley, the law's champions rekindled for the mid-twentieth-century "right to work" campaign the antimonopoly rhetoric that had imbued Populist and Progressive constitutional political economy; it was actually an old conservative trope, the labor monopoly. As one Republican congressman put it: "The American workman ... has been subject to the complete domination and control of unregulated monopolists. To get a job he has had to pay them. He has been forced to join these groups against his will. . . . He has been denied the right to arrange the terms of his own employment. . . . In short his mind, his soul, and his very life have been subject to a tyranny more despotic than one could think possible in a free country."[124]

The right to join with fellow workers in a union might be fundamental, but no less so was "the unrestricted right of Americans to work."[125] In another typical turn on the antimonopoly trope, one prominent Republican lawmaker painted a picture of "a national labor leader who wants to control in a monopolistic way all employees, to have them under his ... dominion, to be to them a dictator." It was up to the 1947–1948 Congress, "the first Republican Congress in 14 years," to set the American worker free.[126]

Remember: from the 1880s onward, judge-made common-law and constitutional doctrine had condemned the closed or union shop. Workers could not strike or negotiate for an employer to hire only union members, nor could lawmakers alter these prohibitions. The Wagner Act, once the Court upheld it, ushered in a brief era in which unions legally could strive for this goal.

Conservatives were not wrong to be leery about the potential for tyranny that resided in the closed shop. But the devil was in the details. It was true that many old-fashioned craft unions had used the closed shop to monopolize a given craft and bar others from entry (ethnoracial others, or simply other would-be craftspeople, who would enlarge the skilled labor supply). By contrast, the new industrial unions wanted closed shops, but they were *open* unions. Given the essentially unlimited supply of poor, unskilled workers in the hitherto unorganized mass production industries, the open-union / closed-shop route seemed the only durable way to maintain solidarity, put a floor on wages, preserve labor standards, and halt the inevitable race to the bottom.

The closed shop was also bound up with industrial democracy and economic citizenship. In NLRB-supervised elections, workers chose whether they wanted this new form of government on the job, like mini-constitutional conventions in the heart of everyday economic life. If a majority chose union representation and collective bargaining, everyone was bound. You could be an active, dissenting, or passive member of the union, just like citizens in the polity, but you couldn't opt out and make your own separate deal, as a matter of democratic principle as well as the practical logic of collective action.[127]

This full-blown industrial democracy did not survive. With Taft–Hartley, the new Republican Congress handed the "right to work" forces a major victory by outlawing the closed or union shop once more. A more radical restoration of the old anti-union doctrine would have prohibited even mandatory dues or agency fees, as a matter of federal law. Labor's political clout was sufficient to prevent that outcome, but it could not forestall the Taft–Hartley provision for state enactments of just such a "right to work" regime. And this, in turn, enabled conservative state lawmakers to make the South and Southwest into "right to work" regions.

Those state laws kept unions fragile, and they animated a rival, regional constitutional political economy in which the rights of anti-union workers and employers enjoyed preponderant weight.[128] This closed the door on New Dealers' hopes of organizing the South, building up the nascent union-based civil rights movement, and realigning the party system by ousting reactionary, racist Democrats.

However, the conservative coalition's Constitution required more than simply restoring the old Lochnerian "right to work." For them, the New Dealers' efforts to democratize the power structures of industry were a "termite process on America's Constitution, on her Bill of Rights, on the basic liberties of our people in the field of labor . . . sabotaging the very foundations of the Republic and the inherent rights of the individual man."[129] Taft–Hartley also restored the "fundamental rights of management."[130]

Organized labor made loud and clear its views about the constitutional stakes of Taft–Hartley. Hundreds of thousands of workers staged mass rallies and demonstrations against the "Slave Labor Law."[131] Taft–Hartley, the unions agreed, was a restoration, but what it restored were key elements of an old, discredited constitutional political economy built on a legal order that violated basic rights.

Like his predecessors, American Federation of Labor leader George Meany was steeped in constitutional political economy. The AFL, he observed, "has been unfairly accused of going to unnecessary extremes in describing the Taft–Hartley Law as a 'slave labor law.'"[132] Not so, Meany insisted, unpacking case law and statutes for mass audiences and congressional hearings alike. Labor's antislavery-inspired constitutional protests, he pointed out, had always found support from the nation's most revered jurists, as well as a majority of the current 1940s Court. In principle, Meany noted, the "right of workers to organize and choose representatives of their own" had been recognized "long before [the Wagner Act's passage in] 1935" as "fundamental rights that inhere in our very system of government . . . beyond the power of Congress to grant or withdraw."[133] But for decades, courts hedged these rights with such overbearing restrictions and restraints in the name of property that "in too many instances these rights proved to be abstract, meaningless phrases."[134] Several times, Congress sought to repeal repressive swaths of judge-made law; several times, the courts undid Congress's work.

The Wagner Act was Congress's boldest effort to get the law of industrial relations right, giving workers' freedoms the kind of concrete meaning the Constitution really required. And finally, the Supreme Court had upheld Congress's work and even begun to apply the Constitution in ways that repudiated the Court's own repressive past. So it was a brutal turnabout when Congress dug up the reactionary doctrines from the judicial graveyard and reinstated them as federal law.

Consider the boycott, "the right to refuse to work on materials produced under substandard, non-union conditions." "Supporters of the Taft–Hartley Law make much of the fact that all so-called secondary boycotts are now outlawed," said Meany. "[O]ne look behind the convenient phrase into the concrete reality discloses" the great constitutional wrong and practical damage done. Since "the earliest beginnings of trade unionism in this country," workers and enlightened lawmakers alike understood that unions could make no headway unless they could ensure that fair employers were not undercut by unfair competitors with substandard conditions and ill-paid labor. The boycott was indispensable to enable union workers to come to the aid of their own employers against unfair rivals as well as fellow workers striving to organize at rivals' firms. For courts to condemn such efforts insulted liberty and economic logic.[135]

Congress understood this decades ago, Meany pointed out, when it enacted the Clayton Act, which seemed to repeal the judge-made restraints and legalize such boycotts. Then, in the *Bedford Cut Stone Co.* case, the century's two greatest Justices, Brandeis and Holmes, took up labor's constitutional outlook and dissented when the Court gutted the act.[136] In that case, a majority of the Court had held that members of a small stonecutters' union could not refuse to work on stone produced at a quarry where workers were on strike. The Court, in what Holmes and Brandeis called "plain defiance" of the statute, called this an unlawful secondary boycott. Meany quoted their "stirring and provocative dissent": "If, on the undisputed facts of this case, refusal to work can be enjoined, Congress created by the Sherman Law and the Clayton Act an instrument for imposing restraints upon labor which reminds one of involuntary servitude."[137]

Meany led his audiences at rallies and the Capitol through other antilabor decisions and Brandeis and Holmes dissents, leading up to Congress's response with the 1932 Norris–La Guardia (Anti-Injunction) Act, "which completely adopted the language, the reasoning, and the philosophy of the Holmes-Brandeis dissents. . . . No longer did the Court have difficulty . . . recognizing . . . the fundamental right of workers. . . . [Its] reversal of the old doctrine of unlawful boycotts was complete."[138]

Not only had the Court upheld both Norris–La Guardia and the Wagner Act, it was building the New Deal concept of labor's constitutional freedom into First Amendment doctrine. Meany cited *AFL v. Swing*, which upheld picketing even when there was "no immediate employer-employee dispute," and other cases striking down state statutes that outlawed secondary boycotts and echoed the Brandeis and Holmes dissents. If organized labor was "extreme" in its picture of Taft–Hartley's constitutional outrages, so were Holmes, Brandeis, and the Court.[139]

President Truman vetoed the act, and his veto message echoed labor's objections, condemning Taft–Hartley as a blow to labor's hard-won freedom of collective action and a reinstatement of the discredited old regime.[140] But Dixiecrats joined with Republicans to override Truman's veto and drive home the linchpin of the conservative counterreformation.

The result was a sharply restrained labor movement and a rollback of the New Deal's legislative, administrative, and judicial constitutionalism. By the end of World War II, organized labor was growing by leaps and bounds, and was poised to expand. Taft–Hartley halted that expansion, but left alone existing union strongholds. Until the 1970s, unions would continue to prosper in core industries like auto and steel, and labor would remain a great force in national politics. But with the revival of sharp restraints on organizing and collective action and the purging of labor's left wing, labor lost the clout and even the ambition it would have needed to finally organize the whole national economy, particularly the South, and finish the work of "completing the New Deal." Not organizing the unorganized, but "mature collective bargaining," grievance arbitration, and other services for existing members, became the main work of the industrial unions.

Taft–Hartley hardly repealed the Wagner Act, but it dramatically altered the design of the act as a piece of legislative constitutionalism—narrowing its breadth as a constitutional construction, a statute that helps fill out the meaning of the Constitution.[141] The Wagner Act had come down squarely on the side of unions and provided a redistribution of bargaining power that just might have been sufficient to underwrite "industrial democracy" across the economic landscape. Taft–Hartley was framed by its champions as restoring "balance" between the rights of pro-union and anti-union workers, and between the rights of workers to organize and managers to manage.

The Taming of Labor and the Eclipse of Progressive Constitutional Political Economy

On the constitutional front, the first casualty was the bold idea of constitutional-economic liberty that the Wagner Act had briefly enshrined, the early Labor Board had begun to elaborate, and even the courts had begun to explore: that labor had "fundamental rights" and constitutionally grounded "civil liberties" that prevailed over private employers' efforts to suppress union activism and trumped state laws limiting secondary strikes and boycotts. After Taft–Hartley, there would be no more talk by the board or the courts about constitutional liberties aimed at rectifying asymmetries of power and providing wide freedom for peaceful collective action. Indeed, after Taft–Hartley, the board simply stopped talking about concerted action in a constitutional register, and the Court shut down its short-lived recognition of labor's constitutional rights.

Much as Truman's veto message had predicted, the labor movement once more found itself enmeshed in coils of legal restraints. By bringing back the old common-law bars on every kind of secondary boycott, Taft–Hartley dealt a severe blow to inter-union solidarity. Once again, union workers in one firm were banned from boycotting the products of another in support of fellow workers' strikes or organizing drives. The strong could not come to the aid of the weak, and just when, where, and how unions could picket or strike became increasingly baroque legal questions.

It was the Warren Court that filled out Taft–Hartley's initial meaning. The Warren Court was fond of quoting Justice Brandeis's famous dissents, but Brandeis's views of workers' rights and industrial democracy found no purchase in its labor jurisprudence. The Warren Court wanted no part of Brandeis's notions that peaceful labor protest and collective action warranted constitutional protection, and that there were constitutional worries about judicial suppression of strikes.

In the early 1940s, we noted, the Hughes and Stone Courts had gingerly embraced something of the constitutional political economy that animated the Wagner Act, and began to outline a right to peaceful labor protest with both a public-political-communicative and a redistribution-of-economic-clout dimension.[142] Under Chief Justice Earl Warren, the Court would take up a dramatically different set of precepts about the constitutional dimensions of labor disputes. This new outlook was no revival of Lochnerism and was not the handiwork of conservatives. Under the banner of "industrial pluralism," it was the work of a high-profile cadre of *liberal* legal academics—Harvard's Archibald Cox, John Dunlop, and Derek Bok; Yale's Harry Shulman and Harry Wellington; and others—who fashioned the basic conceptual and ideological framework of U.S. labor law during the mid-twentieth-century decades of postwar prosperity.[143]

For the industrial pluralists and the Warren Court that took up their ideas, labor disputes had no constitutional dimensions. Heedlessly, in hindsight, this liberal legal outlook assumed that American corporations had made their peace with unions and collective bargaining, and it interred the vocabulary of fundamental rights and constitutional political economy. Instead, Cox, Dunlop, Bok, and the liberal justices who tracked their thinking cast industrial relations as a technocratic domain of expert administration, partly under the board's supervision, but chiefly under the aegis of seasoned labor arbitrators like themselves and the private labor bar. Theirs was a process-based or proceduralist interpretation of the NLRA—what Shulman called a "bare legal framework" to facilitate "private ordering." It was not government's role to monitor the balance of bargaining power in the service of broad distributional ends, as Wagner envisioned, and there was no space for constitutional doctrine in this sphere of "'continuous, pragmatic and flexible regulation'" by labor experts.[144] When courts resumed issuing antistrike and antipicketing decrees in the context of this new technocratic regime, unions' constitutional objections found no traction. Labor relations were no longer a sphere of "popular government" and public political engagement that demanded constitutional protection. Looking back, scholars would observe that labor rights had vanished into a constitutional "black hole."[145]

As far as most national labor leaders were concerned, the disappearance was hardly a burning issue. Today, the lack of any judicially acknowledged constitutional safeguards for labor action seems a major scandal, to which we will return in Chapter 9. But in the 1950s and 1960s, the big industrial unions established unprecedented collective bargaining relations with the largest corporations in key industries. Their working-class members were enjoying middle-class living standards and material security. "Contract administration" became the business of business unionism. Labor rights gradually lost their public, political, and constitutional dimensions in high-brow and popular discourse; their domain began to seem largely one of administration, expertise, and "private ordering."

The trajectory of social provision outside of labor law followed a related path. For a time, in the mid-1940s, New Deal liberals persevered in efforts to "complete" the New Deal's unfinished legislative program in this field: to expand and "universalize" old-age and unemployment insurance, to enact national health insurance, and to create a national budget and planning agency to preside over a national commitment to full employment, along the lines of the postwar welfare states under construction in Western Europe. They aimed to bring Roosevelt's Second Bill of Rights down to earth. But the same conservative coalition that curbed the labor movement grew in strength and handily defeated the New Deal liberals' and CIO leadership's dream of a social-democratic style of postwar governance in America.

By the mid-1950s, most of the rights in FDR's Second Bill of Rights went private. Only socialists still sounded like Roosevelt. Instead, the industrial unions and big corporate employers began fashioning a *private* system of social provision through collective bargaining in core sectors of the economy. The industrial unions bargained for private entitlements to job security, pensions, and health insurance for their members.[146] Beyond the unionized sectors of the economy, industrial prosperity, liberal tax incentives, and the hope of thwarting unionization prompted large firms to adopt the main features of this generous, publicly subsidized, private welfare system. This private welfare state was a good deal for millions of industrial workers; in tandem with Social Security and federally guaranteed housing loans, it brought about the new mass middle class.[147]

In the process, though, the domain of social provision and "social rights" largely lost its public-political and constitutional dimensions and became, like labor relations, an arena of administration and private ordering.

"New Deal liberalism" and its social-democratic constitutional political economy unraveled. The second half of the twentieth century's court-centered Constitution would be a charter of "neutral principles," "negative liberties," and minority rights; and so too, the nation's labor law was "neutral" in regard to the bargaining power of labor and management. Gone and forgotten were the efforts to link constitutional liberty with working people's economic security and workers' freedom of collective action; gone too, the notion that the First Amendment had anything to do with safeguarding labor protest and boosting workers' collective clout.

Thus did the language of progressive constitutional political economy recede from mainstream public discourse and debate. Claims of constitutional governmental duty to provide and maintain an "American standard" of life for all, to safeguard against the return of a business oligarchy, and to watch over a rough equality in the "actual conditions" of Americans went unspoken for the first time in more than a century, as the rigid, anticommunist, pro-business "consensus politics" of the Cold War eclipsed the confident liberalism of New Deal America.

8

THE GREAT SOCIETY
AND THE GREAT FORGETTING

The great constitutional confrontation of the New Deal—FDR and his allies' clash with the courts and their conservative patrons over the direction of the nation's political economy—proved to be the last of its kind, so far, in American history. The struggle over constitutional political economy continued outside the courts, in Congress and in public debate, during the conservative counterrevolution of the 1940s. After that, the democracy-of-opportunity tradition seemed to go into eclipse.

This chapter thus marks a major turn in our narrative. It is an effort to untangle the story of how and why this eclipse occurred. (Chapter 9 will explore what it would mean to bring the tradition back.) The eclipse was not total. Elements of the tradition lived on in the postwar years and beyond. But the democracy-of-opportunity tradition we traced in Chapters 1 through 6—with its rich body of precedents on questions of political economy, its distinctive language of legislative constitutional obligations, and its demands for judicial assent—largely disappeared from progressive politics.

By the 1960s, it became unimaginable to mount a progressive constitutional challenge to the courts. Instead, after the Supreme Court became the nation's first mover on civil rights, the politics of racial inclusion became bound up with a politics of judicial supremacy. Support for civil rights entailed support for a Court-centered Constitution. The former progressives who became postwar liberals[1] mounted a new constitutional *defense* of the Supreme Court, which they came to see as the indispensable constitutional guardian of civil liberties and civil rights.

As the constitutional politics of the 1930s and 1940s receded into history and the Warren Court laid down landmark decisions in the shadow of the Cold War, civil liberties and civil rights replaced economic matters as the paradigm of what a constitutional rights claim *is*. Collective labor rights were expelled from the category of constitutional "civil liberties." Substantive arguments in favor of redistribution and social provision lost their constitutional character. At the same time, just as these changes were transforming constitutional politics, progressive political economy was itself in retreat, supplanted by the technocratic expertise offered by the rising science of economics. These shifts had a powerful effect on President Lyndon Johnson's Great Society and on progressive constitutional politics for the rest of the twentieth century.

Racial inclusion was central to the constitutional politics of Reconstruction and the political program of the Radical Republicans, as well as that of the early Populists and of early twentieth-century Progressive Black activists and their handful of white supporters. But for the entire first half of the twentieth century, with most of the Black population disenfranchised under Jim Crow, racial inclusion was shut out of mainstream politics and mainstream visions of reform. By the mid-1960s, however, pivotal Court decisions,[2] along with the climactic decades of the Great Migration of African Americans northward, set the stage for the reinvigoration of this strand of constitutional politics. The civil rights movement brought the principle of inclusion to the center of mainstream constitutional politics with its riveting sit-ins, protest marches, and voting rights campaigns; the movement became a vital force in American life and forged a complex relationship with racial liberals in Congress.

The Civil Rights Act, the Voting Rights Act, the Fair Housing Act, and related statutes powerfully advanced the inclusion strand of the democracy-of-opportunity tradition. But in keeping with the new politics of judicial supremacy, Congress framed these statutes in ways that carefully respected the Court as the expositor of the Constitution's meaning.[3] The statutes themselves fell tragically short because, like the New Deal statutes before them, they advanced only part of the democracy-of-opportunity tradition—this time, only its inclusionary strand, disconnected from the rest.

Conservatives did not share liberals' opposition to challenging the Court. Instead, running against the Court (really the Warren Court) became a staple of conservative politics—a remarkable feat, given the Warren Court's end in 1969 and the Court's increasingly conservative cast ever since. Over the next half century, the conservative coalition evolved, consolidated its hold on the Republican Party, and made the idea of constitutional change *through* the courts one of its central bogeymen. But the bogeyman here was *liberal* constitutional change through the courts, in the Warren Court mode. *Conservative* constitutional change through the courts—and in particular, through changing the personnel of the courts—became one of the central elements of the new coalition's political program.

This conservative coalition included former Democrats of the South who opposed Court-sponsored desegregation; it evolved to encompass a full spectrum of opposition to different elements of the Warren Court's constitutional agenda. In time, the conservatives' theory of constitutional change became more explicit: Constitutional change occurs by changing personnel on the courts. Much later and more slowly, liberals adopted the same view, so that by the twenty-first century it once again seemed possible to speak of partisan constitutional politics.

But the subject matter of constitutional politics had been transformed. Instead of the questions of constitutional political economy that drove participants in nineteenth-century constitutional politics, the main battlegrounds of constitutional politics became such topics as abortion, affirmative action, sexual orientation, and religion in the public square. On questions ranging from antitrust to labor law to arbitration to campaign finance, by the early twenty-first century, a more conservative Court had moved far toward building an economically libertarian and anti-egalitarian constitutional political economy. But, until recently, these efforts remained off the radar of mainstream constitutional politics.[4]

This chapter tells two stories. The first is about the changing politics of judicial supremacy and judicial activism. The second is the story of the collapse of Progressive political economy. In the end, the two stories collide.

In the postwar era, we will see, economics supplanted political economy, especially among liberals, and concerns about class and distribution that had been at the heart of Progressive political economy were shunted out of the political mainstream. The phrase "full employment" lived on in postwar America, but with a different meaning. Many mainstream New Dealers, along with Pauli Murray, had conceived of full employment as a political economy that offered decent jobs for all. But the postwar economists instead defined full employment in terms of unemployment figures. It became a macroeconomic variable to trade off against inflation. During the anticommunist purges of the Cold War, those who stuck to the older vision of jobs for all were hounded out of government and universities, which helped cement the new technocratic consensus. The decline of Progressive political economy, and its replacement by modern economics, had profound consequences for progressive thought during the Cold War and beyond.

On the other side, in conservative constitutional politics, political economy never disappeared, and it never lost its constitutional dimension. Instead, under the aegis of Chicago School economics and a new constitutional brand of Lochnerism, it gained a powerful new set of conservative architects and patrons and a new conceptual vocabulary that more effectively justified aggressive right-wing interventions in American political economy. The nation continues to wrestle with the consequences of these shifts.

There is an underlying argument that runs beneath the stories in this chapter: The three threads of the democracy-of-opportunity tradition cannot succeed when separate and isolated. Racial inclusion tends to become thinned out in the absence of a broad, secure, and wide-open middle class. As the middle class becomes hollowed out, efforts at racial inclusion tend to run into a buzzsaw of racial resentment, which thwarts efforts to address either racial exclusion *or* class inequality. Meanwhile, protecting a broad and open middle class is difficult if not impossible under conditions of oligarchy. It is politically and economically impossible to carve out space for a broad and open middle class when a smaller, wealthier elite has too much economic and political power. In the twentieth century, these three strands of the democracy-of-opportunity tradition were separated in a way that led to the country's turn to "pluto-cratic populism." In Chapter 9, we return to these themes and imagine a constitutional politics capable of knitting them back together.

The Preeminence of the Court—for Liberals

The Supreme Court of *Brown* and civil rights—the modern Court that would so thoroughly capture the hearts and the constitutional imagi-nation of liberals in the second half of the twentieth century—is closely and indelibly identified with its great leader, Chief Justice Earl Warren. But much of the groundwork for this new Court was laid long before Warren entered the scene. In the late nineteenth century, Reconstruc-tion Republicans had built up and empowered the federal courts for their own purposes, which included providing a short-lived federal forum for the claims of Southern Blacks and securing a long-lasting and powerful guardian of the interests of national corporations.[5]

By the 1920s, Chief Justice William Howard Taft began to envision a true constitutional court—a court that would stand, as one Taft biogra-pher put it, "freed from its obligatory jurisdiction over 'minor' litigation" and therefore "in a stronger position to perform its 'higher function'—constitutional interpretation in general, the defense of property in par-ticular."[6] At Taft's urging, Congress dramatically reduced the Court's mandatory jurisdiction so that it could control its docket and focus on important national questions, particularly constitutional ones.[7] But Taft's timing was terrible. The Supreme Court became the constitutional court he envisioned; but just as it did, the bruising confrontation with FDR led the Court to abandon its project of policing economic matters. Then, gradually, the Justices embraced a new constitutional agenda centered on civil liberties and civil rights.[8]

The switch was presaged by the now-famous footnote four in *Carolene Products*, which promised "rational basis" review of ordinary economic questions but suggested a need for "more exacting judicial scrutiny" of violations of the Bill of Rights, political process failures, and the pro-tection of "discrete and insular minorities."[9] The Court soon began to incorporate the Bill of Rights against the states, using its discretion over its docket to hear increasing numbers of individual-rights challenges to state laws.[10]

New Dealers saw a role for the courts in protecting such individual rights, even as they argued that Congress rather than the courts ought to control questions of political economy; and with the Court increasingly stacked with New Dealers, that is just the division of labor that emerged. As political scientist Richard Pacelle notes in an exhaustive empirical study of the shift in the composition of the Court's docket, "individual rights and liberties would become the reason for the existence of the modern Supreme Court."[11] Yet one important note of caution is in order. Opponents of New Deal economic policy never gave up on the courts. As Pacelle notes, certain claims that might have been framed in terms of economic liberty before 1937 began to be repackaged as other sorts of claims, including ones about procedural due process or First Amendment free expression.[12] In other words, the "weaponizing" of the First Amendment, as Justice Elena Kagan described it in her recent dissent in *Janus*,[13] is not a new story. But it is a story that will have to wait for Chapter 9. For now, the question is what this transformation of the Court's agenda meant for the trajectory of the democracy-of-opportunity tradition.

ENTER WARREN, HERO—TO SOME

The legal scholar Larry Kramer suggests in his book *The People Themselves* that *Brown v. Board of Education* and especially *Cooper v. Aaron*, the dramatic 1958 confrontation between the Court and a recalcitrant white South over desegregation in Little Rock, set in motion a powerful turn toward acceptance of judicial supremacy in the American popular imagination. From the 1960s onward, Kramer notes, the idea that the Court was just one interpreter of the Constitution, and that much of the most meaningful constitutional work occurs outside the courts, was decidedly on the wane.[14]

Kramer is partly right. The importance of *Brown* and *Cooper* to the trajectory of judicial supremacy in America is hard to overstate. But the turn was not uniform across the American political spectrum. The real story of judicial supremacy in the 1950s and into the 1960s is one in which love for the Court's newly confident assertions of judicial supremacy was concentrated among American liberals.[15] For them, *Brown* galvanized support for the Court—and ever more so over time, because of the character of the backlash *Brown* provoked. *Brown* was hailed in Northern and even border-state newspapers as "a great and just act of judicial statesmanship" by a Court that had acted "as the conscience of the nation."[16] Public opinion in most of the nation outside the South favored desegregating the South, but action in Congress was impossible because of the hammerlock that powerful Dixiecrats continued to enjoy.[17] Section 5 of the Fourteenth Amendment authorized Congress to enforce equal protection. Congress had the power to uproot segregation, but not the will.

Just as it did in the reapportionment cases, the Court broke through the logjam, reaching a widely popular result that seemed otherwise out of reach. *Brown v. Board of Education* led liberals and Northerners to believe that the Court was the institution uniquely able to give force to important constitutional guarantees of individual rights and equality. In that way, for liberals and Northerners, *Brown* helped to link faith in the Court with faith in the Constitution itself. The decision was viewed immediately (and correctly) as a salvo in the Cold War, with the Court cast as the great redeemer of the core underlying principles of American democracy.[18] Outside the South, newspapers cheered *Brown* as a welcome blow against the lamentable advantage Jim Crow was providing the Soviet Union in the battle for the hearts and minds of people of color in the newly independent nations of Africa and Asia.[19]

Into that patriotic picture stepped the segregationists, with a series of forceful attacks on the constitutional authority of the Court. By 1956, most of the senators and representatives of the former Confederacy lined up together behind the Southern Manifesto, a direct challenge to the Court and its authority over constitutional interpretation, delivered as a formal joint statement on the Senate floor. The manifesto cast *Brown* as a decision "contrary to the Constitution" and "a clear abuse of judicial power [that] climaxes a trend in the federal judiciary of trying to legislate."[20] This language echoed themes in the democracy-of-opportunity tradition going back to the Jacksonians—themes that had often enjoyed broad national appeal.

By 1956, the Southern position was more isolated. The manifesto was signed by nineteen senators and eighty-two representatives, every one of them from the former Confederacy.[21] The rhetoric of the reserved rights of the states and the people was no longer being mustered in defense of any political economy claims with cross-sectional appeal, but solely as a naked defense of the brutal Southern system of Jim Crow whose violence was dramatized on the evening news by a steady stream of images of white sheriffs and white mobs attacking Black schoolchildren and college students.

So, as the legal scholar Justin Driver writes, "an aversion to white supremacy and an adherence to judicial supremacy" became "inextricably connected in the American legal imagination."[22] Republican president Dwight Eisenhower wrote: "There must be respect for the Constitution—*which means the Supreme Court's interpretation of the Constitution*—or we shall have chaos."[23] Two months later he sent in federal troops to enforce court-ordered desegregation in Little Rock. A prominent group of lawyers and legal scholars responded to the manifesto with a collective public statement, drafted by Harvard law professor Paul Freund, arguing that "[t]he Constitution is our supreme law" and "in cases of disagreement *we have established the judiciary to interpret the Constitution for us.*"[24] In September 1958, in *Cooper v. Aaron,* the Supreme Court itself offered an uncompromising statement of its interpretive preeminence, demanding that the Southerners respect "the interpretation of the Fourteenth Amendment enunciated by this court" as "the supreme law of the land."[25]

Liberals in Congress demanded white Southern obedience to the Court.[26] This was no time for arguing about the wisdom of the Court's rulings or the merits of racial integration. The institutional stakes were more fundamental. Southerners engaging in constitutionalism outside the courts weren't just wrong on the merits—they were illegitimately undermining the rule of law. This position would have been anathema to prior generations of Jeffersonian Democrats, Lincolnian Republicans, Gilded Age Populists, and twentieth-century Progressives and New Dealers. They had all understood their work, in significant part, in terms of a struggle *against* judicial supremacy.[27] But judicial supremacy was now the mainstream liberal view.

In the light of this new conflict over desegregation decrees, FDR's epic battle with a hostile court over core New Deal political-economic reforms took on a sinister cast. The court-packers of 1937 were like the manifesto signers of 1956.[28] Franklin Roosevelt's urgent effort to "save the Constitution from the Court and the Court from itself," as he put it in a fireside chat announcing the court-packing plan,[29] was unpopular enough at the time, even though it led the Court to back down and accept the New Deal. In light of the liberal vision of judicial supremacy that emerged in response to the claims of the segregationists, the old court-packing plan appeared positively lawless. It began to function as a negative precedent for proponents of the authority of the Court, even for former New Dealers.

Two Views of the Court

Thus, the end result of the dramatic confrontations set off by *Brown* was to cement the faith of Northerners and liberals in the constitutional preeminence of the Supreme Court. This went hand in glove with the new sense of the Court's purpose and agenda after World War II, as a protector of civil liberties and civil rights. When the Court made an unpopular decision to strike down school prayer in New York State in 1962, President Kennedy urged the public to support the Court's decisions, even though they might disagree with them. He urged his fellow citizens to "support the Constitution and the responsibility of the Supreme Court in interpreting it."[30] Meanwhile, a local conservative leader on Long Island who vowed to keep school prayer concluded that Robert Welch, the head of the John Birch Society, "had the right idea in asking for the impeachment of the Supreme Court."[31] Some called the school prayer decision communist; opposition to it helped draw together disparate currents of conservative opposition to the Court.[32]

This last point is critical. While liberals, Northerners, and much of the American political center and center-left came to love the supremacy of the Court in the 1950s and 1960s, others took away a very different lesson. For the white Southerners who had formed the backbone of the Democratic Party—and who soon switched parties, and would become the backbone of the Republican Party by the twenty-first century—the lesson was *not* that the Court's constitutionalism was beyond question. Instead, the lesson was that to change the Court, they had to develop a better set of arguments for why the Warren Court was wrong, and then find ways to transmit those arguments into the politics of presidential elections and judicial appointments to break the Warren Court's liberal majority. The consolidation of a full-spectrum conservative coalition aligned against the Court and aimed at changing it would have to wait until the 1970s, but its core began to take shape even before most of the South complied with *Brown.*

Between the New Deal and the 1960s, liberals switched sides regarding the Court. Anti-Court views became concentrated heavily among Southern segregationists and their sympathizers. Respect for judicial supremacy became an article of liberal faith with remarkable staying power. The "nine old men" had become the nation's first mover on civil rights and its guardian of (certain) civil liberties. Even more significant was the shift this signaled about what a constitutional claim is. The emerging new paradigm was a claim about civil liberties or a claim about civil rights like *Brown.* This shift bypassed Progressives' older economic rights claims, such as workers' rights to organize and bargain collectively. But it left plenty of room to litigate the new kinds of rights claims in court.

Liberals learned this lesson well. By the 1970s, they had developed a broad agenda of legal claims, constitutional and otherwise, aimed straight at courts, in the service of racial justice, gender equality, consumer safety, environmental protection, and a wide array of other liberal causes. They embraced judicial governance and judicial supervision of administrative governance in ways their Progressive forebears had shunned. At the same time, they largely abandoned the old Progressive constitutional agenda centered on structural economic reforms and collective freedoms, believing wrongly that the work was done.

Meanwhile, the Court's opponents drew on elements of the democracy-of-opportunity tradition as they searched for a language to describe how and why the Court was wrong. The Dixiecrats jettisoned the old Populist focus on monopoly and wealth, but in other respects sounded much like old Southern anti-oligarchy Populists. In opposition to the Warren Court reapportionment cases such as *Reynolds v. Sims,*[33] which promised to break the rural Dixiecrat lock on political power across the South, Dixiecrat William Tuck of Virginia introduced a bill to strip the Court's jurisdiction over certain claims. He defended it as a necessary check on the "judicial oligarchy," and an effort "to liberate the people of the United States from the clutches of the Federal-judicial octopus."[34] Dixiecrat Elijah Forrester of Georgia, like the Southern Populists before him, implored his colleagues to think about interpretive authority in a less Court-centered way. No branch of government, not even the Court, "has complete, undiluted power," he argued. "Let me say this to you: You have some responsibilities of your own."[35] Forrester proceeded to weave together familiar small-r republican tropes, likening the Supreme Court to the English king during the American Revolution.

This now sounded like what it was: the special pleading of segregationists. The "oligarchy," the antirepublican king, and the "octopus" were no longer great monopolies that threatened the economic prospects of ordinary Americans. Now they were the Justices of the Supreme Court, and the threat they posed was enforcing *Brown*. So *Brown*'s defenders doubled down on judicial supremacy. Liberal congressman Emanuel Celler, a New York Democrat, declared that jurisdiction-stripping bills and other attacks on the Court "stand forth naked and undisguised as an attack upon our theory of government under the written Constitution."[36] The young Celler had been a firebrand congressman championing the New Deal, expounding its legislative constitutional political economy and assailing the Court. Now, however, he set out a full-throated attack on FDR's plan of 1937, treating it as a *negative* precedent of insufficient respect for the Court and the Constitution. Or consider Stephen Young. As a young Democratic congressman from Ohio in 1935, Young lacerated the Supreme Court for its assault on the New Deal, comparing the Court's work to *Dred Scott* and questioning whether the Court should have the constitutional authority to strike down statutes of Congress.[37] By 1963, as an Ohio senator, Young denounced attacks on the Court as "an organized effort . . . [to] undermine the Constitution of the United States."[38] On the now-ascendant liberal view, to attack the authority of the Court was to attack the Constitution itself.

This view of courts and constitutionalism, combined with the Court's shift from a docket of disputes over constitutional political economy to one of civil liberties and civil rights, posed serious problems for the democracy-of-opportunity tradition. The three strands of that tradition as we have defined them—wide-open access to the middle class, anti-oligarchy, and racial inclusion—were being pulled apart. The movement for racial inclusion was gaining political strength. But in the configuration of American constitutional politics *Brown* inaugurated, constitutional questions of racial inclusion had become questions of judge-made law, and liberals and progressives now held that the Court's constitutional interpretations were not open to question.

Meanwhile, the other two strands of the democracy-of-opportunity tradition—a broad and open middle class, and opposition to concentrated economic power—no longer seemed like constitutional issues at all. Most of the key arguments in these two strands of the tradition had been directed in the first instance at legislatures rather than courts. It can hardly be otherwise. Economic reform is rarely a project courts can initiate.[39] The Sherman Act and the Wagner Act were constitutional projects, by a Congress with its own views of constitutional political economy, independent of those of the Court. In the post-*Brown* world, the ideas of *legislative* and *popular constitutionalism* began to evoke not the Sherman Act or the Wagner Act but the Southern Manifesto.

On the right, the challenge was different, and more surmountable. Conservatives, especially in the South, were comfortable with a political discourse of resistance to liberal courts, and they developed a sustained set of tropes and arguments that helped frame a politics of constitutional opposition. This was a form of coalition politics: Not everyone had the same grievances with the Court. But over time, opposition to liberal federal courts became central to the Republican Party's overall electoral coalition and strategy.[40]

There is a broad consistency in the politics of conservative opposition to liberal federal courts from the 1950s to the present, despite many changes in the subject matter of this constitutional conflict—and despite the remarkable fact that since the 1970s, it is conservatives, not liberals, who have controlled the center of the Court. That has meant a

Court that, despite conservative complaints about high-profile social issues, has been remarkably hospitable, for half a century, to the claims of the Chamber of Commerce, specifically, and business generally.[41] Chapter 9 will discuss the Court's remarkable efforts on the business elite's behalf, striving to remake American political economy by reinvigorating political-economic ideas from the *Lochner* era in new forms.

But for now, the most critical point is this: Since the 1950s, liberals and progressives have almost never responded to the Court's neo-Lochnerism with affirmative constitutional arguments contesting the Court's interpretations—arguments of the kind one would have expected from New Dealers, Progressives, and their forebears in the democracy-of-opportunity tradition. How could they? The dominant liberal approach toward the Court and the Constitution since the 1950s has been one of vigorous *defense* of the Court and its interpretive authority. (Beginning in the late 1990s, some voices within liberal legal academia began to dissent from this view, but they were exceptions—and at first, rather lonely ones.)[42] The dominant liberal view also embraces the idea of an irreversible shift of the core subject matter of constitutional dispute. The work of racial inclusion remained constitutional work—and it involved arguments that liberals and others could take to court. But the democracy-of-opportunity tradition we have described in this book—a tradition centered on claims of constitutional duty, aimed at legislatures first and courts second—disappeared from liberals' increasingly court-centered constitutional world.

Liberals often describe that constitutional world as the product of a "New Deal settlement": an idea that, since 1937, economic questions have been taken off the table in constitutional argument. There is little evidence of any two-sided "settlement,"[43] but in the minds of the New Dealers–turned-judicial-liberals who controlled the Court at mid-century, the purported "settlement" had led them to abandon and forget the old premise that opposition to oligarchy and demands for a broad and open middle class were constitutional principles. At first, the notion seemed to be that these precepts remained important but could be put into action through ordinary politics. But soon enough, liberals backed away from the ideas themselves. Political economy itself receded from the liberal agenda—with enormous consequences. The next section examines why.

The Great Society and the Eclipse of Progressive Political Economy

The shift to a more court-centered constitutionalism on the left entailed an increased respect for the special expertise of lawyers and judges. But the Constitution was not the only domain that saw a change of that kind between the early twentieth century and the postwar years. Economic matters, like constitutional ones, came increasingly to be seen as a domain best governed by those with special expertise. That expertise was not political, but instead a kind of scientific expertise based in the discipline of economics. The term "political economy" fell into disuse.[44] It was replaced by "economics."[45]

The story of how that occurred is complex. It involved the transformation and differentiation of the social sciences into distinct academic disciplines in the twentieth century and important changes within the discipline of economics itself. It is also a story of the exuberant postwar flowering of the Progressive Era ideal of competent management by professionals with apolitical expertise.[46] Finally, it is a Cold War story, about the brutal purge of communists, socialists, and other radical economic thinkers from policy debates and mainstream public conversations where they had long been important participants—indispensable ones, as far as the democracy of opportunity is concerned. Flowing from this Cold War expulsion of vital thinkers and ideas was a confining "bipartisan consensus" around economic policy, conceived as expert management of inflation and growth.

There was room for political debate about some economic policy questions, such as the proper tax rate and the design of government spending programs. But the broader debates about political economy, central to American politics in the nineteenth and early twentieth centuries, were no more. Those who continued to espouse socialist and social-democratic views were tarred as communist sympathizers and purged from mainstream politics and government jobs.

One result of this postwar boundary-setting was that a central strand of the democracy-of-opportunity tradition—the opposition to concentrations of economic power—was marginalized for the entire period from the middle of the twentieth century until very recently. Even so, the middle class has continued to have enormous salience in American politics. If anything, gestures toward sustaining it have become *more* constant in our politics as the fortunes of middle-class Americans have eroded since the 1970s.

But as a matter of actual policy, efforts to build and maintain a broad, universally accessible middle-class standard of living have been paltry. In part, that is because keeping a relatively egalitarian class structure requires the repair and maintenance of an institutional framework to support an empowered working class. That kind of policy thinking— central to New Deal constitutional political economy—was drummed out of the economics profession, the universities, and the government, and never allowed to return.

Thus, the story of how the democracy-of-opportunity tradition was forgotten by the actors in mainstream American politics who might have shared its aspirations is a story of the enervation, among mainstream liberals, of constitutionalism-outside-the-courts *and* a parallel enervation of political economy. By the 1960s, there was little room for any of the strands of the democracy-of-opportunity tradition, except the one strand the Warren Court adopted and advanced: the principle of racial inclusion. With its links to the rest of the tradition severed, this idea ran into a whirlwind of trouble.

Economics Supplants Political Economy

The term "political economy" has an antique ring. It was in wide use from the eighteenth century into the early part of the twentieth—a long period in which what we now call "economics" was not yet really distinct from other branches of social theory. The work of the great political economists such as Adam Smith and Karl Marx ranged widely across territory that today would be identifiable as sociology, political theory, psychology, and anthropology. It was not obvious in the mid-nineteenth century that John Stuart Mill, the foundational modern political theorist, would someday be viewed as a progenitor of a different discipline than Smith or Marx. "Political economy" had the breadth to capture all this work.

To be a political economist at the turn of the twentieth century was to be concerned with such topics as currencies, prices, wages, and rents; taxation; the distribution of income and wealth; production and trade; relations between social classes and between capital and labor; industrialization and technological change; the organization of enterprise; the distribution of political power; monopoly and antitrust; and the policies governments ought to adopt in relation to all these matters. If there was one question that could fairly be called "the principal problem in Political Economy" it was probably still, as the preeminent classical political economist David Ricardo argued in 1817, the fundamental distributional question of how the "produce of the earth" (and later, the wealth generated by industrial enterprise) should be divided among the "classes of the community."[47]

Because it blends the normative with the analytical and the economic with the political, political economy always has lent itself to constitutional discussion. That is why during the eighteenth, nineteenth, and early twentieth centuries, judges, lawmakers, reformers, advocates, constitution makers, and policymakers of all stripes looked at and argued about the Constitution through a political-economy lens and the political economy through a constitutional lens. Economics is far less suited to such discussion. In general, economics is more focused on topics such as production, investment, exchange, aggregate demand, and inflation; it tends to sideline questions about the distribution of social and political power that are central to constitutional debate. Even the distribution of wealth—Ricardo's question—has been a relatively neglected topic in economics until quite recently. Worse, economics aspires to be a value-free "science."[48]

By the late nineteenth century, some scholars began to leave classical political economy behind and instead trace patterns of methodology and emphasis that came closer to modern economics. Léon Walras, a pioneering mathematician and political economist, proposed in 1874 that part of economics ought to be "a science which resembles the physico-mathematical sciences in every respect."[49] He demonstrated the power of deductive reasoning by imagining a model of the production and prices of goods across an entire economy, using simultaneous equations to describe different individual actors and their utility functions, laying the groundwork for modern general equilibrium theory.[50] However, he wrote, "I do not claim that this science constitutes the whole of economics." Classical questions of distribution mattered too, but Walras argued that it was important to keep those "applied" questions separate, to distill the "pure" part of economic science.[51] By the turn of the twentieth century, a number of economists who shared the aspiration to build a mathematical science of economics were developing the main moving parts of the model an undergraduate encounters today in an introductory microeconomics course: rational individual agents, attempting to maximize their self-interest, with utility functions and indifference curves, transacting on a plane of perfect competition.[52]

But as significant as these developments turned out to be for mainstream, mid-twentieth-century economics, it is entirely anachronistic to imagine that debates about political economy in the late nineteenth or early twentieth century unfolded under the aegis of this newly developing economic science. The reality was altogether different. Political economy was a subject of both academic debate and popular mobilization. Many prominent political economists were public intellectuals. Henry George, the Gilded Age radical, was one. (We met him debating the classical "new liberal," David Dudley Field, in Chapter 4.) George's best-selling masterwork, *Progress and Poverty,* is an equation-free work of classical political economy.

There was also a robust academic and public-intellectual base underneath the politics of the so-called laissez-faire side of that era's great debates over political economy—but it, too, involved little in the way of modern mathematical economics. When Justice Oliver Wendell Holmes, dissenting in *Lochner,* argued that the Constitution did not enact a laissez-faire political economy, he said it by stating that "[t]he Fourteenth Amendment does not enact Mr. Herbert Spencer's Social Statics."[53] Spencer's views in *Social Statics,* far from being rooted in deductive economics, were grounded in the application of Darwin's evolutionary theory to human society and political economy. Spencer coined the phrase "survival of the fittest"; his core case against redistribution and "law-enforced charity" was that they would impede the evolutionary "adaptation" that society (and especially the poor) needed to undergo.[54]

Arguments like these saturated the late nineteenth- and early twentieth-century debates about constitutional political economy discussed in this book, from the income tax to the gold standard to the creation of labor law and antitrust law. They were framed in terms that many Americans could understand. Politicians understood them well. They put political-economic questions—and the class-based distributional claims that gave political economy much of its potency—at the center of American politics.

In that period, economics itself, as it began to crystallize into a distinct academic discipline, remained protean, diverse, and mixed with the other nascent social sciences. The London School of Economics was founded in 1895 not by classical liberals or deductive mathematical economists, but by social reformers. Similarly, in the United States, Richard Ely helped found the American Economic Association while working closely with social reformers on labor laws and developing a historically inflected "institutional" economics that emphasized questions of distribution and power.[55] Privately, Ely called himself a "socialist," and publicly he associated with the Knights of Labor. This nearly cost him his academic post, amid the Gilded Age's rehearsal of the twentieth century's red scares and increasingly harsh purges of radical economic thinkers from mainstream institutions.[56]

Meanwhile, there was more than enough economic crisis and upheaval throughout this period to give political leaders and ordinary people a sense that policymakers and economists had not discovered any magic solution to complex, recurrent economic crises. With the crash of 1929 and the Great Depression of the 1930s, this became painfully obvious. John Maynard Keynes became the most important economist of the twentieth century because his work offered a fuller picture of macroeconomics than what had come before. Keynes's *General Theory of Employment, Interest, and Money*, published in 1936, offered the first clear account of the hitherto unacknowledged macroeconomic possibility of what he called "involuntary unemployment," which had become, by the mid-1930s, a widespread and hard-to-ignore situation of labor sitting idle because of insufficient aggregate demand.[57] This core idea resonated deeply for New Dealers whose own understanding of the Depression, as we saw in Chapter 6, emphasized underconsumption—that is, that poor and unemployed people didn't have enough money to spend to get the economy moving.

Keynes offered a more systematic and elegant picture, departing from the formal economic models that had come before (which he dubbed "neo-classical"). But he also embraced a version of the neoclassical aspiration for what economics could be. His book was methodologically diverse. Large swaths were devoted to the deductive development of more precise definitions of economic concepts such as savings and investment, but the book also did empirical work, and engaged in a dialogue with classical political economists and their philosophical predecessors going back to John Locke.

The book's subject matter was challenging, and it portended something of how the focus of economics was diverging from that of classical political economy. In place of questions of class power and distribution, Keynesian macroeconomics turned toward questions involving abstract forces such as economic growth, aggregate demand, and inflation, and the relationship of those forces to broad levers of fiscal and monetary policy. This focus was helpful to New Dealers in important respects. For instance, it made it obvious why a national economic problem like the Depression demanded a federal solution like the New Deal: only the national government could plausibly reach and manipulate those big macroeconomic levers. Keynes also introduced the critically important concept of "full employment"—a level of employment at which, he argued, his predecessors' economic models of supply and demand would work, a level that the Depression-era United States conspicuously lacked.[58]

The concept of full employment had distributional implications, and it became a political rallying cry. Chapter 7 described the "social Keynesians" who led the National Resources Planning Board, helped Roosevelt draft his Second Bill of Rights, and put Keynes's ideas to work. They did so in service of a conception of full employment that envisioned ongoing government assessments of regional shortfalls in private employment, to be remedied by public investment that boosted economic growth and provided middle-class livelihoods for the nation's people.

But this school of Keynesian thinking, inflected with a great deal of what was really political economy, lost influence after the counterrevolution, in politics and within the economics profession.

The enormous debt-fueled boom in government spending on the war effort in the 1940s cured the Great Depression in the United States in a way that seemed like a sweeping vindication of Keynes's model. By the 1950s, economists developed and extended the model (in a way that Keynes himself seems to have found overly deductive and axiom-driven) to fashion a new, mathematically sophisticated Keynesian macroeconomics that had a growing sense of itself as a science, separate from any normative claims about fairness or distribution that smacked of politics.[59] In the mid-1970s, new economic circumstances, specifically stagflation (simultaneous slow growth and high inflation), created problems for the Keynesian model and openings for other theories. But during those critical twenty-five years from the end of the war through the early 1970s—the heyday of postwar liberalism, the Warren Court, and the Great Society—a broad pro-business Keynesian consensus dominated discourse about the economy, and that discourse was dominated by professional economists. This consensus consolidated the shift from what had once been political economy to what was now economics.

"Few things are more evident in modern social history," the economist John Kenneth Galbraith wrote in 1958, "than the decline of interest in inequality as an economic issue."[60] The debt-fueled production boom of World War II had turned out to be such an overwhelmingly effective antidote to stubborn Depression that, as Galbraith put it, "production did more than impress the liberal. It became his program, and it established something akin to a monopoly over his mind."[61] He added: "Keynes concentrated the eyes of liberals on production, and their political success gave them a vested interest in it. Keynesian attitudes became, as ever, the new conventional wisdom."[62]

THE GREAT COMPRESSION

The "new conventional wisdom" emphasizing growth over distribution was well suited to the economic moment of the 1950s, in which economic inequality seemed to be slowly melting. The critical quarter century from the end of the war through the early 1970s was a period of enormous economic growth combined with historically low levels of inequality, a highly unusual period in American economic history that the economists Claudia Goldin and Robert Margo have called the "Great Compression."[63]

The social democracy–inflected command economy of FDR's war effort helped usher in an era with a rising minimum wage and rising wages for unskilled workers. There was also, as Goldin and Margo emphasized, a boom in the number of highly educated and skilled workers, outpacing employers' demand for them, which had the effect of keeping highly educated workers' wages lower, and therefore closer to those of unskilled workers, which kept wage inequality low. Private wealth collapsed during the war, and wartime taxes on the wealthy were exceptionally high by today's standards, with top marginal rates on the highest incomes above 90 percent.[64] Union pressure helped extend these high rates through 1964 and keep the top rate above 70 percent thereafter; estate taxes on the largest estates similarly ran above 70 percent.

Unions exerted both upward pressure on wages and, more interestingly, downward pressure on executive pay.[65] An executive pay manual from 1951 explained that boards of directors setting pay for CEOs should "consider the effect upon the company's next collective bargaining negotiation": Excessively high CEO pay could be "provocative of labor problems."[66] All told, as the economist Thomas Piketty has shown, the proportion of all income (not just wages) going to the top 1 percent plummeted during the war and remained in an unprecedented trough for a quarter century thereafter.[67] It appeared, for a time, that the tide of growth was lifting all boats.[68] In real terms, Galbraith observed, between 1941 and 1950, the average after-tax family income of the bottom fifth of all households increased 42 percent in real dollars, while the income of the top 5 percent slightly *declined*.[69]

It was not just the pay structure. With potential labor negotiations always present in the background, and the recent war mobilization fresh in mind, a whole range of surprisingly egalitarian social norms complemented (and helped explain) the surprisingly egalitarian wage and income structure. "Management does not go out ruthlessly to reward itself," Galbraith would explain in 1967; "a sound management is expected to exercise restraint."[70] *Fortune* magazine published an article in 1955 called "How Top Executives Live," which described CEOs living basically middle-class lives of "unpretentious and relatively small" houses and dinner parties—a world away from the mansions, lavish parties, yachts, and servants of the pre-Depression years, then still in living memory.[71] The article noted that there was hardly a market anymore for the "outsized mansions" of Newport, Rhode Island, built by the financiers and industrialists of the first Gilded Age. In the end, the ratio of pretax CEO pay to average employee pay in the 1950s was about 20:1, compared to today's ratios in the hundreds or even thousands.

Why did the Great Compression occur? Was it a product of political choices, or simply the working out of economic forces? At the time, the rise of economics and the eclipse of political economy made the latter answer feel far more plausible than it should have. Surveying the income data the world was presenting to him in 1955, the economist Simon Kuznets observed that inequality in developed countries had exploded in the late nineteenth century with industrialization, peaked in the Gilded Age, and declined by the mid-twentieth century to an all-time low.[72] Kuznets famously conjectured that industrial development first greatly increases, then decreases, economic inequality. The question was the causal mechanism. Kuznets had some ideas, but he closed his article with a plea to his colleagues in economics to move beyond their discipline's usual boundaries. Noting that even his brief analysis required "references to political aspects of social life," Kuznets argued that "[e]ffective work in this field necessarily calls for a shift from market economics to political and social economy."[73]

Kuznets's crucial methodological plea for revisiting political economy went unheeded. Instead, just as Keynes's work would undergird a more deductive and axiomatic Keynesian economic model, so the "Kuznets curve"—the empirical claim that industrialization and development first increases, then decreases, inequality—emerged as a free-floating conjecture that tended to bolster the dominant postwar view that economic growth and development, rather than inequality, was what mattered most. Half a century later, the economists Daron Acemoglu and James Robinson took up a version of Kuznets's invitation and reached a very different conclusion: "In our view, the decline in inequality was not an unavoidable consequence of economic development, but an outcome of political changes forced on the system by the mobilization of the masses."[74]

They were right, and the surprise is that Kuznets did not see it. Most of the core economic diagnoses and prescriptions at the center of New Deal politics—still in living memory at mid-century—hinged on class inequality and the maldistribution of wealth. In 1955, the tangible results of New Deal politics were everywhere: the economic clout of labor, the war-mobilization-like rates of income tax, and the growing mass middle class itself, whose grand, publicly subsidized, private welfare state had recently come to include pensions, health insurance, job security, federally guaranteed housing loans, and many other benefits secured through various combinations of bargaining and politics.

The redistributive politics that did so much to build this mid-century middle class was so successful—for white men and their "dependents," that is—that it was possible to forget that this success was the product of a profound struggle over rival visions of constitutional political economy. As Galbraith told the story, as the memories of those battles faded, along with memories of the Depression itself, political slogans "have come to stress the expanding economy. . . . The question of the distribution of the product so produced—who gets it—is decidedly secondary. To be concerned with it is to seem a trifle old-fashioned."[75]

It was worse than that. What Galbraith did not say is that by the 1950s, distributional class talk was becoming not just old-fashioned, but radical—not necessarily Communist perhaps, but at least a little red. To be concerned with the political and economic importance of maintaining an empowered working class was simply out of bounds.

Overall economic growth became a kind of widely shared, apolitical goal for expert economic management that could displace the distributional fights of the past.[76] This sort of economic thinking, in other words, was well-suited for what the historian Arthur Schlesinger Jr. approvingly called the "vital center": an emerging, pragmatic postwar democratic politics, equally at war with fascism on the right and communism on the left.[77] It was the latter that seemed the more urgent domestic threat.

The Silencing of the Left

Not everybody on the left forgot about the old political-economy questions of class and distribution. But in many cases, the drumbeat of loyalty investigations and anticommunist purges prompted them to speak and act as though they had forgotten. In the great political-economic ferment of early twentieth-century America, there had always been important socialist voices and currents. More than one in twenty Americans who cast a vote for president in 1912 chose Eugene Debs.[78] Communists and socialists were vital to the industrial union movement. But in the 1950s, anticommunist conservatives and liberals (including many erstwhile New Deal liberals) banished talk of political economy with any Marxist or socialist undertones from the universities, government, the mainstream of American politics, and even the mainstream of organized labor. America had seen red scares before—the purge of socialists from universities in the 1890s, the first great red scare of 1919, following the Russian Revolution—but this time was different. The global geopolitical struggle of the Cold War gave the anticommunist purges of the 1950s more sweeping repressive power.

The historian Landon Storrs traced the trajectories of a variety of important figures in the administration of the New Deal who, in the face of "a relentless stream of disloyalty allegations . . . were forced to modify their political rhetoric and moderate their policy proposals."[79] Leon Keyserling and Mary Dublin Keyserling were prominent economists in Washington. Leon was a staffer for Senator Robert Wagner and played a central role in drafting the Wagner Act; he went on to become the chairman of the Council of Economic Advisers under President Harry Truman. Mary was an assistant to Eleanor Roosevelt during the war who later served in the Commerce Department and ran the Women's Bureau of the Department of Labor from 1964 to 1969.

In the 1930s, both were socialists. By the 1940s, both dramatically revised their political-economic views in public and private in the face of repeated, extensive, and humiliating loyalty investigations by Senator Joseph McCarthy and the Washington loyalty apparatus. This meant purging "the language of class conflict" that had been central to their thinking.[80] Ultimately, in his role as the second chairman of the Council of Economic Advisers, a new body designed to inject more expertise in economics into presidential policymaking, Leon Keyserling became a central and prominent advocate of the view that "liberals should concentrate not on reslicing the economic pie but rather on enlarging it."[81] It was a startling departure for this drafter of the Wagner Act, whom we saw in Chapter 6 boasting of the act's broad and deep redistributive ambitions.[82]

The Keyserlings were not an isolated case. The loyalty program that culminated in the famous McCarthy hearings ran from 1947 to 1956 and investigated more than five million federal workers; about 25,000 got stigmatizing "full field investigations," 2,700 were dismissed, and 12,000 resigned.[83] But as Storrs noted, the numerous and often low-level federal employees who were purged during this period do not tell the whole story. Many of those accused of disloyalty "reinvented themselves as Cold War liberals who celebrated American capitalism and advocated an aggressively anticommunist foreign policy."[84] In this way, McCarthyism helped construct Cold War liberalism—coercively defining Schlesinger's "vital center"—by policing the boundaries of mainstream political debate in the 1950s in a way that consummated the counterrevolution, banishing the social-democratic thrust of New Deal political economy. In its place were forms of economic argument that suppressed distributional thinking and assumed that economic growth would continue to lift all boats.

THE SLOW TRIUMPH OF THE TECHNOCRATS

Despite all this, it would be an exaggeration to say that the old themes of oligarchy and a broad middle class, mainstays of the democracy-of-opportunity tradition, vanished by mid-century. The process was slow and uneven. But over time, various policy domains once viewed as focal points of political and constitutional conflict over oligarchy, class domination, and class distribution came to be seen as domains for expert economic management.

This transformation seemed nearly complete in the early twentieth century in the domain of currency regulation with the creation and early development of the Federal Reserve. A central site of anti-oligarchy political argument and conflict became instead a domain for expert economic management.[85] But the real story is less tidy, the trajectory less linear. During FDR's presidency, through depression and war, the transformation reversed course, with the political branches asserting greater control over monetary policy, not less.[86] In the recession of 1953–1954, President Eisenhower's treasury secretary "put the utmost pressure" on the Fed to loosen credit to get the country out of the recession.[87] That seemed to work, and when the next recession hit, as President Kennedy came into office in 1960, he similarly applied political pressure on the Fed to use monetary policy to lower long-term interest rates to speed the recovery.[88]

But let us be clear: William Jennings Bryan this was not. For Bryan and the Populists at the turn of the twentieth century, monetary policy had been distributional at its core, a politics of opposition to the "plutocracy ruling in the name of the dollar."[89] For the Kennedy administration, monetary policy was a tool of macroeconomic management. The administration was populated by prominent Keynesian economists who had been brought in-house.[90] The political pressure the White House put on the Fed in the Kennedy years was not driven by any particular view of the distributional implications of monetary policy. Instead, it was about pressing long-serving postwar Fed chair William McChesney Martin, who was not especially interested in economic theory, to operate in a more aggressively Keynesian way.[91] Martin gave in to many of the administration's political demands, but also stood up just enough for the Fed's self-conception as a technocratic expert body independent from politics that his tenure paved the way for the Fed to become what it has been ever since: "a fourth and autonomous branch of government" run primarily by economists.[92] After the disastrous stagflation of the late 1970s, the view that the Fed needed to be independent would gain additional strength as economics focused increasingly on the importance of inflation expectations. In order to credibly threaten to take tough measures to fight inflation, the Fed needed to be perceived as independent and technocratic, uncorrupted by politics.[93]

Between 1979 and 1982, Fed chair Paul Volcker provided the decisive lesson in this new way of thinking—and showed how a massive intervention in American political economy could be framed, and widely accepted, as technocratic economic policymaking. A Carter appointee, reappointed by Reagan, Volcker faced a complex and difficult problem of persistently high inflation. His monetarist solution was straightforward and seemingly aridly technocratic: The Fed had to ignore unemployment, focus on inflation, and simply tighten monetary policy very aggressively, for years on end, even through recessions, until Americans learned to expect that high inflation was gone and low inflation was the new normal.[94]

Unlike some of his predecessors, Volcker did not blame workers and their wage demands for causing the problem of high inflation.[95] But his policy solution worked by crushing those wage demands, as Volcker freely acknowledged.[96] Indeed, Volcker would later cite Ronald Reagan's dramatic busting of the air traffic controllers' union as an "important but little-recognized contribution to the fight against inflation" because it helped blunt union demands for higher wages.[97] The "Volcker shock" caused a double-dip recession and double-digit unemployment—levels not seen since the Depression. It had a catastrophic effect on workers' bargaining power and led to widespread union concessions. It was a classic, and highly consequential, intervention in American poltical economy. It helped usher in a perspective that many policymakers remain locked into even today, which holds that any increase in wages is a potential inflation emergency.[98] The "Volcker shock" drew protests from farmers, builders, car dealers, and others affected by high interest rates, but Volker earned bipartisan praise as a policy technocrat, just following the science.[99]

Antitrust was similarly transformed from a political and constitutional domain to a technocratic one—but here, too, the constitutional political economy arguments at the heart of antitrust persisted for a considerable period of time before policymakers finally abandoned them. It is striking today to read the debate in Congress in 1950 about the Anti-Merger Act (the Celler–Kefauver Act), aimed at strengthening antitrust law. The substance of the act had to do with broadening the definition of what could count as a monopoly for antitrust purposes, to include more kinds of mergers—vertical and conglomerate mergers as well as horizontal ones, mergers regardless of the method by which the companies merge—that "tend to create a monopoly" in "any line of commerce in any section of the country."[100] Technical enough, perhaps, but from the point of view of its advocates, the act's purpose was squarely in the democracy-of-opportunity tradition.

The war effort had brought significant corporate consolidation; advocates of the act worried that the more concentrated corporate landscape of the 1950s would lead large conglomerates to gain greater influence on politics as well as markets. Senator George Aiken, Republican of Vermont, argued that the Anti-Merger Act was needed "to maintain political and economic opportunity for our people."[101] A few years after the Anti-Merger Act's passage, the old New Dealer from New York, Emanuel Celler, by then chair of the Antitrust Subcommittee in the House, pressed for even more legislation to strengthen antitrust on the grounds that a "floodtide" of mergers was "contributing in large measure to the concentration of economic power" that threatened to create an "oligopolistic national economy." Invoking Justice William O. Douglas, Celler observed that "there is the effect on the community when independents are swallowed up. Entrepreneurs become employees of absent owners. Local leadership is diluted. He who was a leader in the community becomes dependent on outsiders for his action and policy."[102]

This was a classic political economy argument, reaching all the way back through New Deal antitrust and echoing the founders of the anti-monopoly movement.[103] Such worries retained real force for Celler, as he looked out at a new wave of corporate conglomeration and tried to fathom its potentially vast effects on American society and politics. The decade closed with President Eisenhower's stark and related political-economic warning that "we must guard against the acquisition of unwarranted influence, whether sought or unsought, by the military-industrial complex."[104]

Still, it seems fair to describe these broader political economy arguments as the exception in postwar debates over antitrust regulation. Most of the substance of those debates was gradually turning more specialized and technical, as lawyers confronted an increasingly complex thicket of precedents in the field. Antitrust law after the 1970s took a sharp economics-inflected turn that we discuss in Chapter 9. It became all about reducing the prices that consumers pay.[105] What is striking about the debates in the 1950s is that this turn was nowhere on the horizon. These debates scarcely mention the effect of monopolies on consumers at all. The advocates of the Anti-Merger Act were not economic technocrats, although they increasingly found themselves wrestling with technically complex judicial precedents; instead, like their forebears, they saw antitrust as part of the project of ensuring that economic, social, and political power were widely distributed.

Likewise, the idea of a broad and universally accessible middle class remained important in American politics even as it lost its constitutional dimension in the shift to the post-1937, post-*Brown* constitutional world of court-centered civil liberties and civil rights claims. In 1950, Congress did much to shore up the middle class by expanding Social Security, making it substantially more generous, especially to lower-income retirees, and extending its coverage to undo the racialized exclusions of farm workers and domestic workers that had excluded the majority of Black workers in the South from coverage.[106] It was one of the only successful legislative moves to "complete the New Deal." In the hearings over the bill, one heard echoes of arguments that linked access to middle-class economic security with equal republican citizenship. As one union representative described those excluded under the original act, "it is no exaggeration to say these workers are second-class citizens and national pariahs."[107] Meanwhile, scattered conservative opponents continued to argue for the essential unconstitutionality of the whole regime, although this now required some explaining. "The Constitution . . . is as much an economic document as a political document, [and it] set forth the doctrine of contract," one witness insisted. By growing "the cancer of welfare-statism," Social Security builds a "society of status" rather than contract and is therefore "inconsistent with the operation of a free society."[108] These constitutional arguments gained no traction. Social Security was now part of the firmament of American life, and extending it to more working-age adults improved its finances. The extensions passed almost unanimously and President Truman signed them.[109]

By the second half of the twentieth century, in an economic policy environment where arguments about class and distribution were marginalized in favor of expert macroeconomic management of growth and inflation, the idea of protecting the "middle class" became a rhetorical cipher. Sometimes it meant targeted, middle-class tax cuts; sometimes broad tax cuts; sometimes fighting inflation; sometimes general prescriptions for economic growth. Rarely if ever, though, did it mean measures that sustain the political and economic power of the working class. Until recently, when scholars such as Thomas Piketty and Emmanuel Saez revived economists' interest, mainstream economics did not much engage with questions of class and distribution, and this abetted a rising confusion about how exactly the middle class might be helped.

A problem like stagnant wages is relatively easy for ordinary people to understand and for politicians to discuss. So is the problem of inflation during periods of high inflation. But economic experts in the second half of the twentieth century offered up technocratic solutions to economic problems that had the advantage of seeming essentially apolitical, and were at best only tangentially connected to questions of distribution. By contrast, many of the older political-economy prescriptions for the same ills—for instance, strong unions as a bulwark for real wages—had been expressly distributional, more clearly political, and more comprehensible to ordinary people. But in postwar America, these ideas became specialized domains of their own, disconnected from larger questions of political economy. Fights about labor law, as we have seen, came to be viewed as specialized legal and political battles of interest mainly to the two combatants, unions and employers, as unions turned inward to protect their members and bargained for the job protections, higher wages, pensions, and health care plans that formed the private welfare state supporting the postwar middle class.[110]

When the Great Compression came to an end in the 1970s, the middle class entered a period of true stagnation and the wealthy began their climb to the heady unequal heights of the new Gilded Age. The diagnosis of middle-class anxiety became ever more politically potent. But the old adage that mounting class inequality demanded seriously rethinking American political economy—let alone the possibility that this rethinking might have a constitutional dimension, even a constitutional mandate—was forgotten.

Poverty, Race, and the Abandonment of Political Economy in the Great Society

In 1958, John Kenneth Galbraith observed that poverty, once "massive" and the object of intense interest and reform, had become an "afterthought" in the postwar boom, the poor "a small and also inarticulate minority" of scant interest to political leaders.[111] Few of his observations would prove so dated so quickly. In 1962, the socialist writer and activist Michael Harrington published *The Other America*, a searing account of the "invisible" urban and rural poverty, Black and white, of Americans who were falling "beneath the welfare state," struggling or destitute in large numbers in the richest country in the world.[112] Presciently, Harrington argued that racial emancipation and the alleviation of poverty could work only if done together. Race-based antidiscrimination alone, he suggested, would be an empty shell: "There will be speeches on equality, there will be gains as the nation moves toward a constitutional definition of itself as egalitarian. The Negro will watch all this from a world of double poverty. . . . [T]hat other America which is the ghetto will still stand."[113]

The Other America became part of a great awakening of American liberals to the urgency of poverty in the early 1960s—particularly the poverty of Black people in Northern inner cities and white people in Appalachia—an awakening that soon reached all the way to the Kennedy White House, where President Kennedy assigned his close adviser Walter Heller to develop an antipoverty program for the federal government in 1963. At the same time, Kennedy seemed wary of focusing an economic agenda *too* exclusively on poverty: It was also important to "make clear that we're doing something for the middle-income man in the suburbs."[114]

At the same moment, the civil rights movement was pressing a set of moral and constitutional claims outside the courts that extended the constitutional project of Reconstruction far beyond *Brown* and *Cooper v. Aaron*. For Martin Luther King Jr., as for the Radical Republicans a century before, it was clear that material economic opportunity was inextricable from antidiscrimination and inclusion, and that both had a constitutional dimension. In August 1963, when King addressed the March on Washington for Jobs and Freedom in his most famous speech, he reached for constitutional materials beyond the Equal Protection Clause that the Court had interpreted in *Brown*.

On the steps of the Lincoln Memorial, he began his speech with the Emancipation Proclamation, declaring that "one hundred years later . . .

the Negro is still not free." Instead, "crippled by the manacles of poverty and the chains of discrimination . . . the Negro lives on a lonely island of poverty in the midst of a vast ocean of material prosperity."[115] King then turned the dial further back, to 1776: "When the architects of our republic wrote the magnificent words of the Constitution and the Declaration of Independence, they were signing a promissory note to which every American was to fall heir." The promise was not in the Constitution but rather, as Lincoln had argued, in the Declaration: "inalienable rights of life, liberty, and the pursuit of happiness." The civil rights movement had "come to cash this check."[116]

President Kennedy saw that Jim Crow subverted constitutional ideals. But he called for civil rights legislation primarily in moral rather than constitutional terms. In 1963, in his most important speech on civil rights, he came at the Constitution from an oblique angle: "We are confronted primarily with a moral issue," he told the American people. "It is as old as the scriptures and is as clear as the American Constitution. The heart of the question is whether all Americans are to be afforded equal rights and equal opportunities, whether we are going to treat our fellow Americans as we want to be treated."[117]

After Kennedy was assassinated that November, it fell to President Lyndon Johnson to develop the federal response to both poverty and Jim Crow. His answer drew the two issues together: civil rights and the War on Poverty became the two pillars of his Great Society, the collection of ideas he persuaded Congress to "write . . . in the books of law," in landmark legislation that defined the high-water mark of postwar American liberalism.[118] For Johnson, the two pillars were deeply interconnected. "[M]any Americans live on the outskirts of hope," he told Congress, "some because of their poverty, and some because of their color, and all too many because of both. Our task is to help replace their despair with opportunity."[119] He urged Congress to move civil rights legislation and to declare "all-out war on human poverty and unemployment."[120]

However, these two issues were no longer similarly situated in their connection to the Constitution. Jim Crow remained unambiguously a constitutional problem. The task there was to craft legislation that could get through Congress—and at the same time, crucially, avoid any confrontation with the Supreme Court, whose absolute preeminence over constitutional interpretation liberals now defended. Poverty seemed an urgent moral problem, but not a constitutional one—even though lawyers won some victories for poor people protecting their rights to legal process on constitutional grounds.[121] Meanwhile, both racial equality and "poverty and unemployment" were tightly linked to larger questions about the distribution of wealth and the structure of American political economy, which the Cold War liberals trying to build the Great Society were no longer even attempting to address—to their (and the nation's) great detriment.

A War on Poverty in the Midst of Plenty

Unlike the mass unemployment of the 1930s, poverty by the 1960s seemed relatively localized, a string of lonely islands in the ocean of postwar prosperity. For such a rich and successful country, poverty seemed anomalous, a "paradox of poverty in the midst of plenty" rather than an indicator of anything deeply wrong with the nation's economic structure.[122] Thanks to the New Deal reforms and the post–World War II boom, more and more working-class, white Americans were enjoying a middle-class way of life. Many of them enjoyed a measure of dignity and voice at work, underwritten by strong unions, high wages, and a generous combination of private-employment-based benefits and public social insurance.[123]

It seemed in the early 1960s that what remained to be done was to open these bountiful opportunities to Black Americans, and to the overlapping category of the marginalized rural poor. As Congress put it, with plenty of all-American self-congratulation, in the preamble to the Economic Opportunity Act of 1964: "Although the economic well-being and prosperity of the United States have progressed to a level *surpassing any achieved in world history, and although these benefits are widely shared throughout the Nation,* poverty continues to be the lot of a substantial number of our people."[124] And so, the architects of the Great Society fatefully laid aside the old idea that equal rights demands a constitutional political economy that pays careful attention to the distribution of wealth and opportunity among economic classes.

The Great Society did not aim, as nineteenth- and early twentieth-century reformers had aimed, to redistribute wealth and power between capital and labor, the few and the many, or private business elites and government. Those demands in various forms had been at the center of the project of the democracy-of-opportunity tradition in the hands of the Jacksonians, the Populists, the Progressives, and the New Dealers who have populated this book. They were gone from the Great Society agenda. No tax hikes, large-scale redistribution, or structural changes to American political economy would be needed.[125]

Indeed, President Johnson and his allies in Congress insisted that the nation could pay for the War on Poverty out of the increased revenues that would flow from economic growth.[126] In his address to Congress in which he called for civil rights legislation and the "all-out war on human poverty," Johnson also called in the very same sentence for "the most far-reaching tax cut of our time." Johnson declared that his "war" "can be done without any increase in spending"—indeed, "it can be done with an actual reduction in Federal expenditures and Federal employment."[127] The War on Poverty would be war on the cheap.

When President Johnson urged Congress to enact the Economic Opportunity Act of 1964—which included such programs as a job corps and federal work-study in addition to community action programs—he reached tentatively back to the old democracy-of-opportunity tradition, framing the act's economic purposes in the old constitutional language of legislative constitutional obligation to promote the general welfare. However, this move was somewhat undercut by the widespread perception, which Johnson shared, that the *general* welfare was faring quite well. "Congress is charged by the Constitution to 'provide . . . for the general welfare of the United States,'" he told Congress. "Our present abundance is a measure of its success in fulfilling that duty."

He argued, however, that that was not the end of the story: "Now Congress is being asked to extend that welfare to all of our people." The president, he said, "holds a special responsibility to the distressed and disinherited, the hungry and the hopeless of this abundant nation."[128] This attempt to tie the new and relatively targeted moral commitments of the War on Poverty back to the older constitutional idea of a legislative obligation to promote the general welfare was important. But the complexity of the connection tended to highlight the discontinuity as much as the continuity. In the end, the political economy of the War on Poverty turned out to be surprisingly thin. If the overall economic structure was sound—its results abundant and widely distributed and likely to remain so—then the War on Poverty was war on an anomaly.

For all that, the Great Society retained deep connections to the thread of the democracy-of-opportunity tradition focused on the need for a broad and open middle class—connections pushed underground by the increasingly court-centered locus of post-1937 constitutional law. Consider Medicare and Medicaid. These programs substantially altered the nation's political economy. They provided millions of Americans with a more secure foothold in the middle class by socializing the provision of health insurance to two large groups (the elderly and the poor) who are among those who need it most.

Medicare in particular stands out as a broad intervention in American political economy: Like Social Security, it is not a targeted, means-tested program for the poor (as Medicaid is), but rather a universal program of socialized medicine to which almost everyone aged sixty-five and above is entitled by law.[129] Despite this, Johnson framed even Medicare primarily as an antipoverty program—not reshaping American political economy, but rather devoting some of American prosperity to the cause of caring for a particularly vulnerable population. Johnson understood (correctly) that to be elderly and sick without insurance is to be in both economic and medical peril. When he signed the Social Security amendments creating Medicare, he invoked a biblical tradition that "commands us never to turn away from helplessness" and "directs us never to ignore or to spurn those who suffer untended in a land that is bursting with abundance."[130]

Still, the bitter fight over the creation of Medicare and Medicaid was in part a constitutional fight. Some of the old patterns of constitutional argument and counterargument recurred on new terrain. The idea that the federal government might socialize health insurance had long been a constitutional nightmare for conservatives. Their arguments against the programs' constitutionality provoked defenders to make constitutional claims of their own; retracing old debates, those arguments often reached, at least obliquely, for constitutional obligation as well as for constitutional power.

But this was not a fight about the Court's Constitution. Even in the 1930s, as we have seen, the Court never struck down a single federal statute for exceeding congressional power to spend for the general welfare. In the 1960s, conservatives had not yet developed any new court-focused arguments against social insurance programs; that came later.[131] So the fight had to take place on terrain distant from the Court's Constitution. In 1961, Ronald Reagan offered an extended argument against "socialized medicine" in a speech widely distributed as a vinyl LP record.[132] (The record was paid for by the American Medical Association, which viewed supporters of what became Medicare as "followers of the Moscow party line.")[133] Reagan, an excellent rhetorician, never precisely calls socialized medicine "unconstitutional." Instead, he invokes James Madison and refers to the "Founding Fathers" as a way of staking a broader claim on the meaning of the American Revolution—"the greatest revolution that has ever taken place in world's history"—which "established the idea that you and I had within ourselves the God-given right and ability to determine our own destiny."[134] This broad conception of American freedom was unenforceable in court, and fundamentally pre-constitutional on its own terms, but deeply felt. Unless Americans stopped Medicare, he argued, "other federal programs . . . will invade every area of freedom as we have known it in this country," until "you and I are going to spend our sunset years telling our children, and our children's children, what it once was like in America when men were free."[135]

In response to claims that Medicare and Medicaid limited American freedom, with all their Cold War antisocialist overtones, defenders of these statutes reached backward for the language of legislative constitutional obligation. But this language, too, was becoming gauzier and more attenuated as the democracy-of-opportunity tradition receded into history. President Kennedy concluded a long and detailed address on the need for Medicare with a peroration invoking the Declaration: "Good health is a prerequisite to the enjoyment of 'pursuit of happiness.'"[136] Kennedy's secretary of health, education, and welfare, Abraham Ribicoff, one of the central advocates and architects of Medicare, responded to opponents' constitutional objections to the federal nature of the program by pointing out that both sides' views had deep roots in our tradition: "This argument is as old as the Constitution, when Alexander Hamilton and Thomas Jefferson crossed horns on this," he said. But, he added rather loosely: "[I]t was Alexander Hamilton who wrote the general welfare clause of the Constitution."[137]

Ribicoff could have drawn a far stronger connection. Like the Progressives before us, he might have said, we aim for Jeffersonian ends—specifically, outfitting Americans for equal citizenship—through Hamiltonian means.[138] However, in the post-1937 constitutional world of the middle of the twentieth century, the federal government's Hamiltonian powers were so sweeping, and the court-centered Constitution seemingly so distant, that there would have been no obvious need for such arguments. Today, that is no longer true.

Fair Employment without Full Employment

Before the ink was dry on the Civil Rights Act of 1964, figures like Martin Luther King Jr., Bayard Rustin, and A. Philip Randolph warned Congress that achieving "our full citizenship" demanded large-scale economic reforms as well as civil rights.[139] Decently paid industrial jobs, they pointed out, were already declining, most notably in the "relatively high-wage heavy industries into which Negroes ha[d] been moving since World War I."[140] Nothing was taking their place. "[G]reat city minorities [were feeling] the pressures of increasing unemployment and poverty."[141] Forcing white workers to make room for Blacks in every tier of industrial employment was essential, but leaders like King and Rustin predicted that this inclusionary effort would fail on its own terms if not combined with a different thread of the democracy-of-opportunity tradition: reforms to preserve a broad and open middle class. They argued that "it would be dangerous and misleading to call for [enforcement of antidiscrimination norms] without at the same time callling [sic] attention to the declining number of employment opportunities in many fields."[142] But even as they made pointed calls for economic policies to address particular economic sectors and geographic regions, civil rights leaders also adopted some of the language of the now-dominant

Keynesian paradigm, warning, "We cannot have fair employment until we have full employment."[143]

The term can be misleading. By "full employment," King did not mean what most economists had come to mean by that phrase: a specific numerical rate of unemployment, typically the lowest rate consistent with a given target rate of inflation. King meant to evoke an older meaning of the idea in New Deal thought: full employment in the sense of every American's right to a decent job. Full employment, from that perspective, is a stand-in for a broader claim about how the economy needs to operate—providing good job opportunities to all—to fulfill the promise of equal rights and equal citizenship under the Constitution.[144] Evoking FDR's Second Bill of Rights, which operated at a similar remove from the courts, Dr. King told rallies, demonstrations, Congress, and the White House that "the full emancipation and equality of Negroes and the poor" demanded a "contemporary social and economic Bill of Rights."[145]

King often articulated these rights in terms of the Declaration. But over time, like W. E. B. Du Bois and other visionary Black leaders before and after him, King also reached for a language of human rights that was more cosmopolitan and universal, and more distant still from the Court's Constitution.[146] What was clear to King about both the civil rights statutes and the War on Poverty, as enacted, was that while they did important work, "[t]he limited reforms we won have been obtained at bargain rates for the power structure. There are no expenses involved, no taxes are required for Negroes to share lunch counters, libraries, parks, hotels, and other facilities."[147] The next stage would be more costly; it would require deeper interventions into American political economy.

It was time, said Bayard Rustin, for the civil rights movement to turn from its nearly victorious fight against Jim Crow to campaigning for economic justice and structural reform—time "to propose alternatives to technological unemployment, urban decay, and the rest," and to call "for public works and training, for national economic planning . . . for attractive public housing, all this on a sufficiently massive scale to make a difference."[148] Such a campaign would require alliances with trade unionists. After all, white workers were facing many of the same economic challenges, and "the labor movement, despite its obvious faults, has been the largest single organized force in this country pushing for progressive social legislation."[149] For Rustin, LBJ's 1964 landslide victory, in which most white voters chose a desegregated Great Society over reactionary racial appeals, "proved . . . that economic interests are more fundamental than prejudice." That lesson, he said, "must be kept alive, for the civil rights movement will be advanced only to the degree that social and economic welfare gets to be inextricably entangled with civil rights."[150]

So far, the War on Poverty had provided job counseling but no jobs—and worse, precisely because of its targeted and limited nature, it had fostered the "mischievous" notion that "the War on Poverty is solely to aid the colored poor."[151] Instead, the right idea was to fold Black America—so conspicuously excluded from the New Deal—into a new New Deal political economy, one that was suited for the wrenching loss of industrial jobs Rustin and King and other clear-eyed reformers saw coming. Entwining racial inclusion "inextricably" with programs and policies for the "social and economic welfare" of all, it would be Black people's "New Deal thirty years late."[152] Once again, as it had been for a century, it was the activists, thinkers, and spokespeople of Black freedom struggles who insisted most forcefully that the inclusionary and the political-economic strands of democracy of opportunity must not be pulled apart.

So, King, Rustin, and Randolph proposed a far more expansive, and expensive, War on Poverty aimed at restoring "full employment" (and at assuring adequate incomes, perhaps through a universal basic income), doing away with the slum ghettos, "and provid[ing] a decent home for every American family."[153] To that end, the Poor People's Campaign, led by Rev. Ralph Abernathy after King's death, converged on the Washington Mall in the summer of 1968 with detailed demands for different agencies of the federal government, many of them seeking to wring broader political-economic leverage from the War on Poverty's limited programs.

The campaign demanded that the Department of Housing and Urban Development, or HUD, restrict all of its grant programs "to communities which have a 'fair share' of a metropolitan area's supply of low and moderate income housing."[154] It demanded that the Labor Department move beyond jobs programs that were "little more than public relations gimmicks" by making government "the employer of *first* resort": "The Automation Commission estimated that there are 5.3 million jobs in public service that would meet pressing social needs of the country and would, at the same time, provide permanent employment at decent wages for those who are now idle."[155] Such a program of job creation via public investment to meet social needs was central to Black people's "New Deal thirty years late."[156]

This kind of broad reimagining of the nation's economic life would involve enormous and controversial economic redistribution. Before King's death, he and Randolph had proposed a "Freedom Budget," a "multi-billion dollar social investment to destroy the racial ghettoes of America, decently house both the Black and white poor, and to create full and fair employment in the process."[157] They found support within the Johnson administration in the Department of Labor, where Secretary Willard Wirtz launched his own sustained campaign against the "partial and piecemeal" approach of the War on Poverty, particularly its emphasis on social services and work counseling without doing anything about the actual mix of jobs the economy offered.[158] Wirtz built carefully documented accounts of the "human slag heap" of widespread unemployment in industrial regions and central cities, where, in contrast to national unemployment numbers, Black unemployment had begun to "explode."[159]

In concert with King, the organizers of the March on Washington for Jobs and Freedom, and Walter Reuther of the UAW, Wirtz urged an expanded War on Poverty that would include substantial sectoral and regional public investment and incentives for job creation, along with coordinated employment services and training.[160] Meanwhile, King, Randolph, and leaders of the AFL–CIO turned to their top ally among economists in the government—Leon Keyserling, the brilliant young New Dealer, now transformed, perhaps, by the purges of the 1950s into a Cold War liberal—to develop a joint "Freedom Budget" proposal.

Keyserling viewed the redistributive parts of the plan as political nonstarters, but also unnecessary. What mattered most, he thought, was achieving full employment, which he understood in numerical macroeconomic terms, and which he thought could be accomplished through government spending of any kind. Keyserling came back with a shocking "Freedom Budget" that would achieve full employment through massive spending on military hardware—militarized Keynesianism.[161] The proposal faced opposition from nearly every point on the political spectrum. Most economists, along with conservatives, opposed it for focusing too much on expenditures and failing to recognize the threat of inflation, while anti–Vietnam War liberals opposed it for seeming to validate Johnson's war.[162] It went nowhere. Soon, the window of liberal political dominance would close, and reforms on such a scale became unthinkable.

The Great Society thus left the nation with a set of core civil rights statutes that demand fair employment but not full employment. Yet these landmark statutes nonetheless implemented a number of profoundly important political-economic insights, in a distinctly legal-liberal way. First, collectively, these statutes embody the idea that, as FDR had put it, "freedom is no half-and-half affair": "[E]qual opportunity in the polling place" and "equal opportunity in the market place" work only if you have both together.[163] Second, prodded and inspired by civil rights activism, President Johnson articulated a surprisingly thick and substantive conception of equal opportunity. He insisted that equality before the law for the Black citizen must translate into "equality as a fact and equality as a result."[164] To that end, the civil rights statutes he signed gave the administration and the judiciary broad powers to achieve (among other things) substantive school integration, which they used, in concert, to develop requirements for integration that went beyond *Brown*.[165] Third, the statutes created a whole new framework for civil rights class action litigation in employment and other spheres.

They created, through direct funding and indirect fee-shifting, an entire ecosystem of public-interest firms that, in concert with the NAACP, the Justice Department, and the Equal Employment Opportunity Commission, brought hundreds of class actions that changed the racial composition of large numbers of workplaces.[166] In that way, like the Wagner Act, these statutes built institutions that could have their own long-run impact on the trajectory of future political and economic decision-making. Title VII of the Civil Rights Act had a sweeping institutional reach across American economic life. It applied, by its terms, to employers, but also to unions, apprenticeship programs, joint labor-management committees, and employment agencies.[167]

The problem was that the entire industrial order in which blue-collar workplaces were expanding and offering good jobs at good wages—the great mid-century "affluent society" economy into which the Civil Rights Act aimed to integrate minorities and women—was about to collapse. Civil rights leaders like King and Abernathy, social-democratic policymakers like Wirtz, and labor economists in the union movement lobbied for public investments and trade and industrial policies to anticipate and avert the harshness of this outcome on the nation's jobs landscape and opportunity structures. They were ignored.[168]

By the late 1970s, it was painfully clear that employment was not expanding but contracting in most of the private sector industries, including iconic ones like automobiles and steel, with the high-paid blue-collar jobs over which Title VII aimed to end the white male monopoly.[169] Great Society liberals had conceived of their work in terms of targeted interventions to make an increasingly prosperous working class more inclusive. By the late 1970s, what had emerged instead was a world where race-conscious measures like hiring quotas and affirmative action in employment appeared to be at the center of a bitter game of redistributing a shrinking pie between white and Black workers.[170]

This was an exquisite vulnerability that politicians easily exploited. Beginning with George Wallace, a long line of white politicians channeled white resentment into populist opposition to elite national actors—liberal federal judges, lawmakers, and attorneys—and the "arrogant" interventions of these "despots" in local white middle-class and working-class spheres of governance.[171] Such foes of civil rights enforcement drew on elements of the democracy-of-opportunity tradition to depict school integration and affirmative action as threats to white children's basic initial endowments of opportunity and to their parents' economic livelihoods.[172] They found a broad white audience for populist claims that the new oligarchy, arrogating power to itself, was liberal judges and lawmakers and their allies in the civil rights movement. President Nixon found a way to make the same arguments without sounding like a racist like Wallace. Nixon appealed to many of the same working-class white constituents in his successful bid for the White House in 1968, which led to four crucial Supreme Court appointments.[173]

A century earlier, in the late nineteenth century, the old idea of Jacksonian equal protection, with its political economy of opposing "class legislation" that favored the wealthy few, was flipped by conservative elites into a ban on "class legislation" aiding industrial workers.[174] The core ideas of equal protection embodied in the civil rights statutes of the 1960s were now similarly flipped and reinterpreted. Conservative lawyers and politicians held that instead of promoting "equality as a fact and equality as a result," instead of aiming to end racial subordination, these statutes and *Brown* itself should be viewed as embodying a ban on racial classification, which condemned many measures that Great Society liberals had thought essential to equality.[175] As economic opportunity became more precarious in the 1970s and 1980s, the core programs of the War on Poverty became powerful targets for an ideology of populist white racial resentment.

And then the window of liberal political dominance closed. American political economy began to tilt decisively toward business and its owners and enrich the oligarchs of a new Gilded Age. During and after the Reagan years, mainstream politicians of both parties came to channel a more conservative vision of political economy, declaring that the era of big government was over—and promising to end welfare as we know it, with its handouts to the racialized poor. The War on Poverty gave way to a war on crime and a war on drugs. Tough-on-crime statutes, along with militarized policing and prison-building initiatives, enjoyed considerable bipartisan support in statehouses and in Congress during the last two decades of the twentieth century, devastating poor communities—Black and brown and white.[176] Instead of building on the Great Society to make the nation's public / private welfare state more accessible to more Americans, the nation's political and economic elites mounted a long crusade against corporate and governmental responsibility for individual welfare. That crusade swept like a grim reaper through pension plans, health insurance, and labor standards, cutting the bonds of social solidarity and shifting the burdens of economic risk from employers and governments to individuals and families.[177]

The Great Unraveling

Four snapshots will help to trace the shape and magnitude of the collapse of progressive constitutional political economy in the late twentieth century. This section tells four brief stories from the 1960s and 1970s. They are meant to be a suggestive, not comprehensive survey. We could have told other stories. But together, these four snapshots suggest what happened as the democracy-of-opportunity tradition went decisively into eclipse. Legal liberals won some major victories in this period, but they tended to be victories of legal liberalism at its thinnest, without much to connect them to the thicker claims about political economy once at the heart of progressive American constitutional argument.

WELFARE RIGHTS AND THE CONSTITUTION

First, consider the trajectory of the constitutional claims of the welfare rights movement. Why did a right to welfare for the very poor become the model of an affirmative, social right among progressive constitutional thinkers in the 1960s and 1970s? And what became of it? We saw how Dr. King and other civil rights leaders with the Poor People's Campaign lobbied and marched on Washington for a broader agenda of public investment, job creation, and social rights in the democracy-of-opportunity tradition—a New Deal for Black America "thirty years late." This would have altered the trajectory of the nation's political economy. But the mass constituencies to win such big demands were not there. In the highest liberal policy-making circles, this agenda was spurned; the War on Poverty did not make these public investments. It did, however, create community action centers and supply thousands of federally funded attorneys, social workers, and community-resident organizers, often veterans of civil rights activism. They set about working to get poor people the benefits to which they were entitled, under the broadest imaginable reading of Aid to Families with Dependent Children (AFDC), which from its inception as part of the Social Security Act of 1935 had functioned as a separate, decentralized, and deeply gendered and racialized benefits program, stamped with many of the centuries-old degradations of poor relief. The welfare rights movement organized around the improbable goal of transforming AFDC into a dignifying right to a guaranteed income.[178]

Never before in American history had a national social movement for economic justice been centered on and led by Black women. Its leaders and activists departed from the long history of economic citizenship conceived of and built in a gendered fashion around the presumptively male (and white) wage earner and his dependents. Poor Black women had always toiled outside their homes, but they had never been welcomed into the producers' republic of earlier reformers.[179] By the 1960s, poor Black women had gained enough experience in urban labor markets to know that decent jobs were hard to find, and had enough experience with workfare programs to think them coercive and demeaning. Instead, the National Welfare Rights Organization (NWRO), consisting primarily of Black mothers, contended that a "guaranteed adequate income" was an unconditional right of citizenship, necessary for equal respect, and an appropriate touchstone of equality in an affluent nation.[180]

Thwarted in the quest for new legislation, the NWRO went to court, where the links and continuities with the civil rights struggle were not lost on federal judges as they decided hundreds of cases undoing the exclusion of Black women from welfare rolls. Here was an opportunity to intervene in the political economy of social provision in a fashion suited to *judicial* endeavor and the new postwar liberal legal outlook. The plaintiffs were quintessential members of a "discrete and insular minority" for whom a measure of judicial activism was warranted, in the view of mainstream legal liberals. Indeed, there were early signs from the Warren Court in the 1960s that even if most questions of political economy were no longer constitutional questions, the specific problem of poverty might warrant heightened judicial scrutiny. In *Harper v. Virginia Board of Elections,* in 1966, when it struck down Virginia's poll tax, the Court wrote: "Lines drawn on the basis of wealth or property, like those of race, are traditionally disfavored."[181]

In this context, the NWRO took aim at injustices perpetrated under the AFDC statute. Originally titled Aid to Dependent Children (ADC), it was renamed AFDC in the 1950s.[182] It descended from the state-based

Mothers' Pensions programs of the early twentieth century, themselves a modern variant of the age-old practice of giving poor relief to "deserving widows."[183] Like the other branches of the Social Security Act of 1935, the original ADC was drafted to appease the white South. States could determine benefit levels, and local administrators enjoyed vast discretion in eligibility decisions. Local white officials deemed poor Black women "employable mothers"; Southern states kept payments far below official poverty levels.[184] Everywhere, including Northern cities, welfare officials enforced "man-in-the-house rules," which broadly denied benefits to children when there was an able-bodied man in the household who could ostensibly provide child support. The rules were intended to prevent public money from going to "immoral women" and "unsuitable mothers," but also to keep poor men from using AFDC to escape the low-wage labor market. Even for its target universe of impoverished single-parent families, AFDC reached a tiny fraction of the whole. Most did not even apply.[185]

Into this bleak landscape stepped the NWRO, its federally funded legal services attorneys, and their allies on the federal bench. It won some major legal victories, including *King v. Smith*,[186] which struck down an Alabama man-in-the-house eligibility rule. Under this rule, Alabama had dropped sixteen thousand children—90 percent of them Black—from its welfare rolls. The three-judge court below invalidated the rule as unconstitutional race discrimination.[187] But the plaintiff's legal services attorney sought a broader ruling, not based on race, so as to "stop similar practices in other states," where man-in-the-house rules might not have an identifiable racially discriminatory purpose or effect. Instead, counsel asked the Court for "a decision interpreting the Social Security Act as having rejected the concept of a worthy and an unworthy poor."[188]

For a unanimous Court, Chief Justice Warren did just that. The record made plain that Jim Crow had played a big role in the decentralized administrative design of the federal welfare program; it also dramatized the continuing entanglement between racial subordination and the deprivations and indignities inflicted on the "unworthy poor" of all races. And so, as the Warren Court was doing in spheres such as criminal procedure and the right to counsel, the Court acted to expand rights at the intersection of poverty, racial subordination, and the exercise of fundamental rights.[189] In the face of legislative history running in the opposite direction, *King v. Smith* read the preamble of the 1935 Social Security Act to mean that Congress intended AFDC to reach every destitute child, and thus required the invalidation of Alabama's man-in-the-house rule.[190] It was a victory for the welfare rights movement's vision of women's autonomy, and also a victory for the possibility that the War on Poverty could be waged through the courts. After *King,* the Supreme Court invalidated a series of other restrictions excluding would-be AFDC recipients, and the lower courts struck down hundreds of them.[191]

In 1970, in *Goldberg v. Kelly,* the Court articulated an explicitly constitutional rule protecting the welfare benefits of the poor—but the case was about procedural due process, not welfare's substantive scope. The Court held that the Due Process Clause required pretermination hearings, before government could cut off an individual's welfare benefits.[192] The Court reached back to the constitutional discourse of FDR and the New Deal, arguing that "[f]rom its founding the Nation's basic commitment has been to foster the dignity and well-being of all persons within its borders. We have come to recognize that forces not within the control of the poor contribute to their poverty."[193] And like FDR, the Court rang out the changes on the Preamble to the Constitution—only now on behalf of the children and grandchildren of Americans who had been conspicuously left out of the New Deal: "Welfare . . . can help bring within the reach of the poor the same opportunities that are available to others to participate meaningfully in the life of the community." Public assistance was a means to "promote the general Welfare, and secure the Blessings of Liberty to ourselves and our Posterity."[194] The case seemed to hold out the possibility of judicially enforced constitutional protections for the welfare rights of the poor.

Constitutional scholars like Frank Michelman drew on the work of the preeminent liberal moral philosopher John Rawls, building a moral and constitutional case for the idea of a needs-based right that extended beyond procedural due process to distributive justice.[195] They consulted historical works excavating the republican tradition in eighteenth-century constitutional thought, whose emphasis on a broad distribution of property and opportunities for material independence we explored in Chapter 1.[196] Michelman and the others worked mightily to forge the normative underpinnings for a substantive right to welfare. But it was not to be.

The Warren Court was teaching liberals to frame their claims in terms of rights to be litigated in court. It was teaching conservatives that advancing their constitutional politics would require changing the Court's personnel. After Richard Nixon's razor-thin victory in the 1968 presidential election, in which Nixon had campaigned in part on ending federal-judge-imposed school busing, he reshaped the Court. By 1972, he had appointed four new Justices, including Chief Justice Warren Burger, who replaced Earl Warren. Some of this was luck, but some of it was not. Recognizing the power of changing the Court's personnel, Nixon took unprecedented steps to hound liberal Justices into leaving the Court, and in the case of Justice Abe Fortas he succeeded, opening up what turned out to be the crucial fourth seat.[197] The transformed Court left many important Warren Court decisions standing, but it bent the arc of doctrinal development in a new, conservative direction.[198] Heightened scrutiny of welfare measures came to a screeching halt.

Before the Burger Court stepped in, *Goldberg v. Kelly* and other Warren Court decisions inspired lower courts to start down the heightened scrutiny path.[199] Maryland, for example, was one of several states that put a cap on how much welfare money poor families could receive, no matter the size of the family. Plaintiffs challenged this in district court, arguing it was arbitrary discrimination against poor children of big families in respect of a constitutionally vital interest; and the court agreed, striking down the state limit. The case was *Dandridge v. Williams,*[200] and it supplied the occasion for the Burger Court to announce that, past intimations notwithstanding, the Court's Constitution has nothing substantive to say about the terms of social provision for the poor. Hadn't the *Lochner* era and its dramatic reversal taught us that "state regulation in the social and economic field" was no place for heightened scrutiny?[201] "To approve the [lower court's] invalidation of state economic or social regulation" in this case, the Court wrote, "would be far too reminiscent of an era when the Court thought the Fourteenth Amendment gave it power to strike down state laws 'because they may be unwise [or] improvident.'"[202]

The *Dandridge* Court acknowledged that the precedents it quoted for this lesson in judicial restraint involved "state regulation of business or industry," while this one concerned "the most basic economic needs of impoverished human beings."[203] But that "real factual difference" provided "no basis for applying a different constitutional standard."[204] The New Deal precedents thus supplied the ground on which the Court declared it stood, as it shut down the liberal legal War on Poverty.

The orientation and approach of the movement lawyers who had brought constitutional welfare rights arguments into court would have been almost unrecognizable to New Deal lawyers and lawmakers. The New Dealers made their affirmative constitutional arguments in the polity and styled them as structural claims about constitutional political economy; the rights to social provision they championed were for Congress to redeem. The courts' job was to acknowledge Congress's authority and then get out of the way.

But the movement lawyers in the 1960s had a new model and a different set of precedents. They self-consciously modeled their campaigns on those of the ACLU and the NAACP Legal Defense Fund.[205] They styled their arguments not as structural claims about constitutional political economy but instead as claims of individual right. Proceeding that way, they won some real victories. Ultimately, the NWRO and its lawyers played the hand that was dealt them. Broadening access to AFDC through the courts gave the movement something concrete to gain for its politically marginalized rank and file.

But in virtue of the constitutional world the 1960s made, the Court's Constitution has become *the Constitution*. And the Court's Constitution came to recognize welfare rights, and indeed many rights claims of the poor, *only* when those claims were at their most procedural and legalistic. Because we live in such a Court-centered constitutional world, word from the Court tends to feed back into popular constitutional understandings. Thus, from the 1960s onward, Americans have come to understand that there is a constitutional issue when a poor person seeks a hearing, a trial transcript, or relief from a court-imposed fee—but not when that same poor person seeks a place to live, health care, a decent income, or a job.[206]

The Women's Movement and the Right to Childcare

The women's movement gained strength late in the long 1960s. Its demands, like those of the civil rights movement, drew on strands of the democracy-of-opportunity tradition. The women's movement transformed American society, but the very different trajectories of some of its major demands illustrate the challenges of implementing a constitutional principle of inclusion when broader questions of political economy have moved outside the political frame.

The women's movement was internally complex, and rich with competing moral and constitutional claims. For our limited purposes here, we focus on the "Strike for Equality," which represented one coalition's set of demands at one unique moment in time. The strike was a series of marches and demonstrations organized by Betty Friedan and others in August 1970.[207] These strikers made three main demands: "(1) free abortion on demand, (2) free 24-hour childcare centers, and (3) equal opportunity in jobs and education."[208]

These three demands were conceptually linked. Access to abortion and childcare were necessary if women were going to be able to make use of the equal opportunities in jobs and education. The three demands had a common purpose: Reconstructing the internal economic and political dynamics of the family on a new basis that would make equal citizenship possible. As Friedan put it, "[W]omen would not secure equal citizenship with men until family life was organized on terms that presupposed the equal participation of both its adult members in public life."[209]

The strike took place on the fiftieth anniversary of the ratification of the Nineteenth Amendment, in which women had won the right to vote. The new effort was thus, at its core, a constitutional claim that the Nineteenth Amendment's promise of equal citizenship for women was not yet fulfilled.[210] This constitutional claim was not aimed squarely at the Court. But the women's movement would ultimately have an enormous impact on the Court's Constitution. In a series of cases brought by Ruth Bader Ginsburg of the ACLU Women's Rights Project, the Court held that the Fourteenth Amendment's guarantee of equal protection meant that the state could not enforce sex classifications in the law based on stereotyped conceptions of women's and men's roles.[211] However, those successful constitutional arguments in court did not translate into the broad changes to American political economy that many in the women's movement, including the strikers of 1970, had sought.

Consider the radically different trajectories of the demand for equal opportunity in jobs and education and the demand for free, public twenty-four-hour childcare centers. Equal opportunity in jobs and education is the kind of rights-enforcing change that courts can, in principle, enforce. In practice, the entry of women into formerly all-male work and educational settings, and the eventual entry of men into some all-female work settings, required legislation. Congress acted first with Title VII of the Civil Rights Act of 1964, which prohibited sex discrimination in private (and later also public) employment, and then with Title IX of the Education Amendments Act of 1972, which prohibited sex discrimination by educational entities receiving federal funds. Initially, the effect of these statutory protections was minimal; it took years of sustained campaigns by ordinary women and national advocacy organizations to get them to be enforced and effective. But eventually these provisions spurred broad changes to the structure of work by integrating women into many formerly all-male jobs, and by encouraging structural changes in the governance of the workplace ranging from sexual harassment law to family-leave policy. If the strikers of 1970 could have seen the United States today, they would see a nation that went a long way toward granting one of their three demands.

The contrast with the demand for free, public twenty-four-hour childcare centers is revealing. That demand was the most expensive. It would have required substantial intervention into American political economy, moving large swaths of the enormous and hidden private economy of care work into the sphere of state-provided public goods, with day care centers "established by law on the same basis as parks, libraries, and public schools."[212] Many feminists framed childcare as a "right," but that right would require vast infrastructure and substantial government expenditures, some large portion of which would be redistributive in character. Even among feminists, there were disagreements over how universal versus how targeted (means-tested) to make a national childcare program. The economic scale of the more universal approach made it politically daunting.[213]

From a feminist perspective, the more universal approach was the most rights-like, and it had the greatest potential to transform economic and political relations within the family. As it turned out, this approach allowed for a pro-childcare coalition with liberals who were more concerned with child development than with feminism.[214] Marian Wright Edelman of the Children's Defense Fund built a coalition of labor, civil rights, and child development–related organizations in support of the Comprehensive Child Development Act (CCDA). The bill passed both houses of Congress in 1971. Universal in scope (with families above the poverty line paying on a sliding scale), the CCDA would have used day care centers to provide medical and nutritional as well as educational services.[215]

President Nixon was initially supportive of the bill. He viewed preschool and related services for poor children as a promising anticrime measure. But he balked at the CCDA's scale and cost; several of his key advisers, concerned about a conservative primary challenge in 1972, saw a political opportunity.[216] With the help of speechwriter Pat Buchanan, Nixon vetoed the legislation with a veto message that cast it as a socialist assault on the family, a law that would create "a new army of bureaucrats" and commit America "to the side of communal approaches to child-rearing over against the family-centered approach."[217]

After that consequential veto, childcare policy in the United States proceeded along the two tracks common to many present interventions in political economy: means-tested, limited, and stigmatized programs for the poor, and an entirely separate regime of private subsidies (including in the tax code) enabling more affluent Americans to buy their own childcare in the market. (Medicare and Medicaid functioned then and now in the same way. Medicare operates as a more generous universal entitlement for the elderly, while Medicaid offers a narrower, targeted, means-tested, and less generous program for the poor, subject to limitations and administration by the states, reproducing racialized divisions in social provision that began in the New Deal.)[218] No serious attempt has been made since Nixon's veto to restructure the political economy of childcare in the United States.[219]

The trajectory of the strikers' first demand—"free abortion on de-mand"—is the most revealing of all. This demand was both a claim of right, to bodily autonomy and equality, and a demand that society build out an infrastructure of provision to give women practical and "free" access to this medical procedure.[220] States in the 1960s were liberalizing their abortion laws, in a bipartisan way and for reasons that mostly had little to do with feminism and more to do with the public health crisis of self-abortion.[221] These changes stirred opposition, mostly among re-ligious Catholics.[222] But they did not make abortion an important issue in national politics.

In 1973, the Supreme Court held in a 7–2 decision (with five of the seven Justices in the majority appointed by Republican presidents) that abortion "is inherently, and primarily, a medical decision, and basic re-sponsibility for it must rest with the physician," and therefore states were generally unable to restrict women's access to the procedure prior to fetal viability.[223] *Roe* had limited political impact at the time; rising support for abortion in public opinion polls either continued to rise or remained high after the decision.[224] However, in the late 1970s, political entrepreneurs who became architects of the New Right—figures like Richard Vigurie, the direct mail pioneer, and Paul Weyrich of the Heri-tage Foundation—recognized that *Roe* could be a goldmine in consti-tutional politics.[225]

The post-Watergate Republican Party needed to find its way beyond its "country club–big business image," as future president Ronald Reagan put it in 1977. He argued for bringing "social" conservatives focused on "law and order, abortion, busing, [and] quota systems" together with "economic" conservatives focused on "inflation, deficit spending and big government" and "the mind-numbing economic idiocy of the liberals in Washington."[226] Reagan saw that there was a political opportunity to build what became the New Right by peeling off the "blue-collar, ethnic and religious groups themselves traditionally associated with the Demo-cratic Party" who were conservative on the "social" issues he named.[227]

With the exception of abortion, all these issues were about race. All of them could be framed in the same institutional terms. These were issues that pitted liberal courts—above all, the Supreme Court—against the political opinions of socially conservative voters. Anti-Court constitutional politics became a powerful glue, unifying the Southern racial conservatives opposed to busing, who became the core of the New Right, with a much broader set of constituencies: working-class Catholics, gender traditionalists attracted to Phyllis Schlafly's campaign against the Equal Rights Amendment (ERA), whites anxious about crime, and the catchall category of those who found the protests of the late 1960s and 1970s an affront to authority and to "law and order."[228] Opposition to the Court helped align all these constituencies. Southern racial conservatives took up the pro-life cause, linking it with an anti-Court message while also borrowing the political maneuvers of the anti-busing fight, such as jurisdiction-stripping bills, and applying them in the abortion context.[229] For these groups, the Court functioned as a stand-in for a broader and vaguer idea of the liberal "elite"[230]—the Court has always been the most elite branch of the government in many senses of the word.

Roe thus provided a fulcrum for advancing the epic political realignment of the second half of the twentieth century.[231] That realignment built a Republican Party whose contours were not entirely clear until President Trump's decisive primary victory exposed them in 2016: a party whose elites and officials are committed to protecting businesses and wealthy people from regulations and taxes, but most of whose voters focus on "social" conservatism, and within that, racial conservatism. As George Wallace put it in 1964, for once ahead of his time: "Being a southerner is no longer geographic. It's a philosophy and an attitude."[232] But the elites and the voters of the modern Republican Party share enough to make it work, including an attitude of unstinting disdain for the liberal "elite."

This great realignment also cemented a broader asymmetry in liberal and conservative understandings of constitutional politics that has lasted half a century. For liberals, *Roe* redoubled the effect of *Brown:* Liberal constitutional politics became, and remains, heavily about defending the Court and its precedents *from* politics. For conservatives, *Roe* became the white whale of constitutional politics, driving generations of activists' views of the relationship between politics and the Constitution. To them, the lesson of *Roe* was the need to recruit different and more conservative judges who would cease imposing liberal values, and instead impose conservative values ostensibly found in the Constitution. The

Republican Party has seen its share of internal tensions, but President Trump's judicial appointments were the most party-unifying act of his improbable presidency—perhaps the one thing that all parts of his party coalition convinced themselves they could believe in.

Left out of this story of realignment and constitutional conflict around *Roe* is that the most successful litigants before the Court since the mid-1970s have not been abortion-rights activists or racial minorities, but representatives of the Chamber of Commerce.[233] Business interests have been unafraid to advance legal and constitutional arguments for a more laissez-faire constitutional political economy. Ironically, that line of constitutional thought is the one that has had the greatest limiting effect on *Roe* itself, as the Court held in the late 1970s that *Roe* does not require the government to actually *pay* for anyone's abortion: Abortion is a personal liberty, not a claim on the state's resources.[234] This broader constitutional political economy has implications far beyond abortion. With conservatives' slowly increasing dominance of the judiciary since the mid-1970s, its full implications have not yet been felt.

HUMPHREY–HAWKINS AND THE RIGHT TO A JOB

Even as the ground was beginning to shift underneath the two party coalitions in the late 1970s, liberals made one last major legislative attempt to realign the nation's political economy with the interests of working people. Since 1964, Martin Luther King Jr. and many others had viewed the work of the March on Washington for Jobs and Freedom as incomplete. It had yielded landmark legislation for freedom, but no jobs.[235] By the late 1970s, inflation and unemployment were rising and economic pain was increasing. Old New Dealer Augustus Hawkins, an ally of A. Philip Randolph and now a congressman from California, made a plan with Senator Hubert Humphrey for a new full employment bill, to complete the work of the eviscerated 1946 Employment Act.[236]

Hawkins argued that his bill would "commit the entire society to rethinking the operations and purposes of our economic system." It would aim for full employment not in the sense of a numerical goal "tied to some limited, managed and manipulated notion of the labor supply as reflected in . . . unemployment data," but instead as "the right of each and every person to a full- or part-time job, if he or she so chooses."[237] Despite Hawkins's protestations, the bill quickly came to include a precise labor-supply definition of full employment. Full employment meant 3 percent unemployment, and the bill aimed (wildly ambitiously) to achieve that within eighteen months.[238] In early drafts, local planning councils would initiate public and private projects that met local needs and created work for a massively expanded federal job corps, while the president and the Joint Economic Committee in Congress would hammer out national plans to achieve full employment through fiscal and monetary policy.[239] Those national policies might include controls on wages and prices (which seemed a good deal more realistic then than now, as President Nixon had recently imposed a sweeping series of temporary price controls).[240] As a legal backstop, the bill would create a court-enforced statutory guarantee of employment, a right to a job.[241] However, as the historian Jefferson Cowie recounted, by the time the congressional battle over Humphrey–Hawkins reached its brutal conclusion two years later, every one of the elements just mentioned was stricken from the bill, with the exception of the statutory definition of full employment as an unemployment level of 3 percent.[242]

Coretta Scott King was the most important advocate for Humphrey–Hawkins outside Congress. After her husband's death, she cofounded a new national organization called the Full Employment Action Council (FEAC).[243] Testifying in front of Senator Humphrey at a hearing in Atlanta, she argued once more that those two strands of the democracy-of-opportunity tradition, inclusion and broad access to the middle class, can work only in tandem. "[W]hat good is the promise of fair employment when there is no employment?" she asked.[244] As she told the story, "Black people were drawn to central cities of our country by the promise of jobs. But, even as they were arriving, the jobs were passing them in the other direction."[245] The Humphrey–Hawkins Bill was needed to "fulfill the promise of full employment that [the Government] made 30 years ago, in the 1946 Employment Act." The promise, she argued, was "the clear, uncompromised right of every American to a job."[246]

King saw, and grappled mightily with, the increasingly dominant view that the way to full employment was through expert macroeconomic management. "The unemployed," King insisted, "are not pawns to be sacrificed in some economic chess game, but American citizens whom our leaders are elected to serve." She held fast to the idea that "[t]he problem of unemployment is at base a political problem," rather than some natural fact of economic life. Still, she understood that experts were going to translate Humphrey–Hawkins into policy by framing it as a commitment to "fiscal, monetary, and other measures" aimed at raising employment. And she knew the bill was being widely attacked as "unworkable and unrealistic." Her reply was that "France, Sweden, and many other European countries have done the job." Surely America could as well, rather than leaving "[t]he poor, minorities, and [the] average workingman" to "bear the brunt of our economic policy."[247]

Economists pilloried the bill. President Gerald Ford's chairman of the Council of Economic Advisers, Alan Greenspan, called it "foolish," while Treasury Secretary William Simon blasted Democrats for peddling political snake oil and relying on "the economic illiteracy of the American people." Milton Friedman called it "close to a fraud."[248] But it was not Simon or Greenspan but the *liberal* economists who really destroyed it, leaving Hubert Humphrey to fume privately that supporters of full employment had been "stabbed in the back." The bill took fire from what *Business Week* called "a *Who's Who* of liberal economists." Charles Schultze, who had been budget director under Lyndon Johnson, declared that spending your way to full employment was likely to provoke an inflationary spiral, while offering public-sector jobs at better pay than the lowest-paying private sector jobs would make that spiral worse. Privately, he called the bill "economically illiterate." Even Galbraith was skeptical.[249]

Humphrey was up against the economics profession, which had collectively decided in the 1970s that substantial unemployment was *necessary* to fight inflation. They were operating with a first-generation understanding of an unemployment-inflation trade-off known as the Phillips curve, although the stagflation all around them had begun to suggest that the relationship might be more complex. Humphrey, for his part, saw it as an "immoral trade-off": It could not possibly be worth it to let millions of Americans languish to achieve price stability.

But inflation was a politically potent force in the late 1970s, and although the unemployed numbered in the millions, the vast majority of voters had jobs. The Democratic Party sided with its economists. President Jimmy Carter declared: "[T]he achievement of full employment and price stability must be sought through the use of monetary and fiscal policies, together with structural measures designed to improve the functioning of the Nation's labor and capital markets—not through government planning or control of private production, wages, and prices."[250] He would probably have preferred to kill off the Humphrey–Hawkins Bill entirely, but many Democratic constituencies were demanding it, so instead, the administration negotiated away most of the bill's substance. The final act simply declared a national policy goal of full employment, ordered the Fed and the executive branch to pursue that goal (along with others such as stable prices), and created some new economic coordination and reporting mechanisms. The challenges of achieving both full employment and low inflation would be left to the experts.[251]

This strategy marked the end of a political era. In purely economic terms, manipulating the dials of monetary and fiscal policy, as if from some elite control room, can do some real work; economists have gotten better at this since the 1970s. In the 1990s, in particular, Alan Greenspan, of all people, took note of the Fed's dual mandate and gave priority to growth and employment over fear of inflation, yielding actual wage gains for ordinary people.[252] But such macroeconomic management is no solution to the problem of providing decent jobs and livelihoods for all. As a political program, moreover, this technocratic approach is too remote, incomprehensible, and ultimately irrelevant to too many Americans.

If the goal of preserving a broad middle class has a future in American politics, it will require bridging the gulf between the ever-increasing sophistication of economic science and the politically salient questions of how economic policy affects and is understood by ordinary people. It will require a relentless focus on the distributional questions that were always at the heart of political economy.

Coretta Scott King was right that an economic problem like unemployment is "at base a political problem." Political economists, for most of American history, agreed. Since then, advances in economic thinking have given us better tools to understand our political choices. But they remain fundamentally political choices. And they shape the economic base on which the constitutional order rests.

The Collapse of Labor and the Rise of a New Oligarchy

The *other* great political-economic reform bill of the late 1970s, besides Humphrey–Hawkins, was a labor bill titled the Labor Reform Act of 1977.[253] Its demise illustrates the deep trouble that resulted when liberals lost the anti-oligarchy thread of the democracy-of-opportunity tradition in the middle of the twentieth century.

In the late 1970s, organized labor was still aiming to repeal key elements of the Taft–Hartley regime, especially the provision authorizing states to enact "right to work" laws, which had generally resulted in a nonunion South that organized labor viewed as its greatest threat. The AFL–CIO also wanted card-check elections as an alternative to secret-ballot elections, and a provision to protect contracts from corporate consolidation (a rule that would require new owners to honor existing union contracts when they acquired a firm). But in the end, they were willing to drop all three of these big-ticket items, preferring a very modest bill mainly providing for speedier elections and NLRB decisions and giving unions an opportunity to speak to employees about unionization if management was doing so. The idea was to make sure the more modest bill could pass.[254]

The failure of even that modest bill was a critical inflection point in the history of labor and capital in America. It marked the end of the mid-century era of testy collaboration and the beginning of a new offensive by organized capital to destroy organized labor's economic and political clout.[255] The bill fell victim to a concerted campaign by the Chamber of Commerce, the Business Roundtable, and the National Association of Manufacturers (NAM), along with more specialized groups like the National Right to Work Committee, flexing their political and economic muscles in a Washington that was fast leaving the Great Society behind. As recently as 1971, corporate lawyer and future Supreme Court Justice Lewis Powell had authored a memo for the Chamber of Commerce lamenting that "few elements of American society today have as little influence in government as the American businessman, the corporation, or even the millions of corporate stockholders." Powell's famous memo called for "a full-court press by business in politics, universities, the media, and the courts 'for the preservation [of free enterprise] itself.'"[256] It presaged an explosion in corporate money and lobbying in Washington.[257]

The idea behind business's campaign against the Labor Reform Bill was to hand labor a massive defeat by destroying a seemingly harmless bill. The Chamber of Commerce, NAM, and the rest of the business and anti-union outfits spent heavily to do it. A diffident Carter administration viewed the bill as a relatively targeted service for just one Democratic constituency. The business lobby saw the political-economic stakes more clearly. They mobilized a vast publicity campaign focused on "union bosses," "labor racketeering," "destroying small business," and other slogans that were basically unrelated to the specifics of the bill. Senators on the margin felt the heat.[258] And the bill died, narrowly failing to overcome a Senate filibuster, in a "stinging humiliation" for labor. Since its defeat, there has been no federal pro-labor legislation in the United States. A renewed effort to pass card-check elections and related elements failed again in 2009.[259] Instead, new state laws and increasingly shameless union-busting hastened labor's decline—a decline that has had a profound impact on American political economy.[260]

In the summer of 1981, the politics of labor hit one more crucial inflection point when President Ronald Reagan, in his first year in office, fought the air traffic controllers' union. When the dust settled, the president had decertified the union for striking—and permanently replaced the striking workers.[261] It was an outcome that seemed straight out of the Gilded Age, but in fact it was ahead of its time, as the administration's hardball tactics provided the green light and the model for a new era of corporate aggression against labor. In this new era, employers routinely fired and replaced employees who exercised their right to strike; they found new ways to subcontract work to avoid collective bargaining; and they closed union plants to open nonunion plants in new locations. In short, the president's crackdown helped launch what one historian of the era describes as an all-out corporate "assault" on unions and other working-class institutions.[262] Meanwhile, from the 1980s through the early 2000s, a listless Democratic Party attempted with varying degrees of success to build a political coalition that bypassed questions of political economy—and viewed labor as just one Democratic constituency, and a dwindling one.[263]

As it turned out, the political rise of the business lobby was just a prelude. On the horizon, an even more formidable political and intellectual force was moving into view: a roaring resurgence of constitutional political economy on the economic-libertarian right. First, it emerged as an intellectual framework; then, a great wave of institution-building made it a mobilized force in American politics and in constitutional law. What has come to be called "neoliberalism" (originally by some of its advocates, now almost exclusively by its critics)[264] is a reconstruction, on different and more sophisticated intellectual foundations, of the classical liberal side of the great conflicts over political economy of the late nineteenth and early twentieth centuries. For our purposes, the single most important thing about this set of ideas is that it is, quite self-consciously, a revival, from the right, of constitutional political economy.

Toward a Neoliberal Constitutional Political Economy

In the postwar years, liberals had good reason to assume that many foundational debates about political economy were basically over. The United States had adopted an economic model that combined market capitalism with significant government regulation, high taxes, trade unions, and a substantial welfare state. In those respects it was not so different from the "mixed economies" of Western Europe, which had even more substantial welfare states, more economic planning, and peak-level bargaining between capital and labor. Alongside all these arrangements, an increasingly sophisticated science of macroeconomic management was building an edifice of technocratic expertise on Keynesian foundations.

However, to one set of thinkers, this dominant way of thinking about political economy was anathema. It meant altogether too much state control of the economy—and such control was dangerous because government control itself was dangerous. Austrian-born political economist Friedrich Hayek, the foremost intellectual leader of this group, saw in postwar Western democracies a dangerous tendency toward retaining in peacetime "the organization of the nation we have achieved for purposes of defense." This was happening, he wrote, "because nearly everybody wants it." But nearly everybody was wrong.[265] Defining freedom to include "freedom from necessity" or "compulsion" or "want"—the conceptual move we saw FDR making in Chapter 6, and which Hayek rightly saw everywhere in mainstream postwar Western European thought—was an epochal mistake. Real freedom, Hayek argued, was "political freedom," which Hayek understood as "freedom from the arbitrary power of other men." And that was just what the postwar government interventions in economic affairs—including the welfare state—threatened, putting government on the road to totalitarianism, and individuals on the road to serfdom.[266]

Hayek reached backward to draw on the political economy of classical "nineteenth-century liberalism."[267] His generative work would, in turn, be drawn on by advocates like Lewis Powell, the future Supreme Court Justice whose 1971 memorandum argued that "[t]he threat to the enterprise system . . . also is a threat to individual freedom." Powell would perfectly track Hayek when he argued that "the only alternatives to free enterprise are varying degrees of bureaucratic regulation of individual freedom—ranging from . . . moderate socialism to the iron heel of the leftist or rightist dictatorship."[268]

In 1947, Hayek's position was more isolated. That year, he convened a group of thirty-nine European and American intellectuals in Switzerland. They were mostly economists, but also historians, philosophers, journalists, and some free-market-minded activists.[269] They formed the Mont Pelerin Society, which aimed to provide an intellectual home for those who thought that "a decline of belief in private property and the competitive market" and the "extensions of arbitrary power" by governments were threatening "human dignity and freedom."[270] They gathered at a moment when nineteenth-century classical liberal political economy was at its nadir. Even many conservative economists suspected that the expansions of government wrought by the war would never fully be reversed.[271]

Some of the American participants in Mont Pelerin, such as the future Nobel Prize–winning public choice economist James McGill Buchanan, went on to build institutions, in Buchanan's case at the University of Virginia and later at George Mason University, designed to incubate a new generation of scholars and advocates for a neoliberal "Virginia school of political economy."[272] Buchanan was inspired in the 1950s by massive resistance to *Brown* in Virginia, which he saw as an opportunity to resist federal power, but also as something more than that: a chance to disband the public school system. Buchanan developed a talent for leveraging grants from right-wing foundations to create neoliberal institutions aimed at countering the mainstream academic "establishment."[273]

Unusually among the early neoliberals, Buchanan understood his project in explicitly constitutional terms. He often couched his writing in abstractions about the rules of hypothetical poker games and other parables of free exchange, but he was entirely clear about the constitutional stakes. In a world where the grasping many can outvote the propertied few, he argued, "effective constitutional limits must . . . effectively constrain overt political intrusions into rights of property. . . . If individual liberty is to be protected, such constitutional limits must be in place prior to and separate from any exercise of democratic governance."[274]

The University of Chicago, several of whose economists went to Mont Pelerin, had long been the main home in the United States of opposition to Keynesian economics. In the postwar years, Chicago became a center of economics conceived as a value-free science, while at the same time, it served as the incubator for normative public-intellectual political economists such as Milton Friedman, who made a forceful case outside the academy for "markets as an *unremitting good*."[275]

In the 1970s, stagflation posed problems for the mainstream Keynesian economic consensus. Friedman had a theory that seemed, for a time, well suited to explaining those problems. (His theory of monetarism held that fiscal policy was largely useless, and that governments should instead focus on managing the money supply, which was the real driver of inflation, through monetary policy.) Even if he never wholly adopted Friedman's view of fiscal policy, Fed chair Paul Volcker did more than anyone else to put Friedman's monetarism into practice. Volcker reports that as he fought inflation by sharply tightening the money supply, he "came to appreciate Friedman's basic contention" as sound "common sense."[276]

Like Keynes, Friedman became his generation's foremost public-intellectual economist. As a public expositor of ideas, Friedman was far more effective than Keynes, with a broader range and an uncompromising Hayekian focus: the pathologies of government intervention in economic life. Friedman argued, for instance, against federal disaster aid, contending that "the bureaucratizing of charity" tends to "destroy a sense of human community, of individual responsibility for assisting the less fortunate."[277] He argued for replacing the income tax with a flat tax, eliminating the estate tax, and even repealing most of antitrust law. (In earlier years, he had identified antitrust enforcement as an important role for a properly limited state, but by the 1970s, he adopted a downright preindustrial view of monopoly: "[T]here has hardly ever been a private monopoly that has been able to maintain its monopoly position without assistance from the government."[278]) Friedman's advocacy of these ideas gained enormous clout from his 1976 Nobel Prize, awarded for his pioneering work on monetary theory and consumer behavior. Friedman's success proved that the expert authority of scientific economics could be converted into persuasive authority in political-economic debate.

Friedman and other, lesser royalty of the economics profession of a similar mind became intellectual sages for an era that saw an epochal shift in American political economy. The last quarter of the twentieth century became an age of deregulation and tax-cutting, leveraged buyouts by empire-building financiers, skyrocketing "superstar" executive salaries, and a steep decline in union density, all of which helped usher in a new and considerably more unequal political economy.[279] Here an important feedback loop began to operate. The winners, in this new political economy, would have the means to exert substantial influence on politics if their money could be converted into political power. Some of them were determined to make this happen.

Beginning in the 1970s, wealthy conservative donors embarked on an ambitious institution-building crusade of the kind Powell had outlined in his memorandum to the Chamber of Commerce.[280] Facing what they, with Powell, saw as opposition from major players in American public

life, such as the media, academia, and the Washington policy establishment, they created a new, parallel set of countervailing institutions, which were more explicitly ideological than the institutions they
were created to oppose.[281] These included important think tanks such
as the Heritage Foundation (founded in 1973), whose focus was broad
enough to mirror the assorted ideologies of the then-emerging conservative coalition, and the Cato Institute (founded in 1977), which was
self-consciously libertarian.[282]

Almost all of these institutions faced internal tensions about the relative balance between research objectivity and political engagement.
Over time, the balance shifted to the latter.[283] By the mid-1990s, the
Mont Pelerin Society itself chose as its president Edwin Feulner, the
longtime president of the Heritage Foundation. Charles and David Koch,
the sons of John Birch Society cofounder Fred Koch, built one of the
largest fortunes in the United States through their oil and chemical conglomerate; they moved from being the central funders of institutions
like the Cato Institute and the Liberty Fund to presiding over their own
sprawling political operation. That remarkable operation, in turn, has
taken over many of the traditional functions of the Republican Party,
operating as a kind of shadow party, a machine for converting economic
resources into political power.[284]

In retrospect, it seems almost inevitable that these ideological revolutionaries would pursue a strategy of making claims on the Constitution in court. The idea that courts and the Constitution can help protect private property from the predations of the voting public was hardly
invented by James M. Buchanan. These ideas were among the conflicting
lines of argument present at the birth of the republic. Daniel Webster
and John Marshall did their part to burnish them; they had their heyday
in the constitutional political economy of the *Lochner* era.[285] It is true
that liberals reoriented themselves mid-century to defend the federal
courts, while conservatives made a corresponding move to oppose the
perceived excesses of liberal justices. Yet, we know that over the long arc
of American history, the more common institutional configuration has
been the opposite. In conflicts between the many and the propertied few,
it is completely unsurprising that most of the time, the democratic representatives of the many have squared off against the legal arguments

of the few. It is the courts, after all, who have the power to build a po-litical economy less democratic than the one the people's representa-tives choose. (Think here of *Citizens United*.) Courts can also shape the ground rules underneath the allocation of power in representative politics.

Thus, in the 1970s and 1980s, the same conservative billionaires who embarked on the institution-building spree of those decades also grasped the importance of constitutional political economy. They looked for ways to build a lattice of lawyers, law professors, and ultimately judges, who could rebuild on new foundations the old claims of Lochnerian consti-tutional political economy. The new neoliberal constitutional political economy arguments of the late twentieth century did not rely, as their predecessors had a century before, on substantive due process or natural rights. Instead, as the political scientist Steven Teles explains in his his-tory of the conservative legal movement of the late twentieth century, the key wedge for prying open the postwar liberal legal and constitu-tional order was by way of introducing the power and prestige of "eco-nomics" into the legal academy.[286]

Elite law schools welcomed money from large conservative founda-tions such as the Scaife and Olin Foundations to establish programs in law and economics, in part because law and economics is not inherently conservative. It offered some genuinely useful new tools for legal analysis that could be deployed in the service of a variety of values and goals.[287] But the donors understood what they were getting for their money. They were terraforming the legal academy and elite legal thought—where neo-liberal political-economic ideas had hitherto been thoroughly alien—into vastly more hospitable terrains for these ideas.

Aaron Director, a pioneer in law and economics at the University of Chicago Law School, was one of the original participants in Hayek's Mont Pelerin Society (and intervened with the University of Chicago Press to publish Hayek's *The Road to Serfdom*, a wildly successful inter-vention to save a book that would go on to sell hundreds of thousands of copies). Director's ideas, developed by younger colleagues like Robert Bork and Richard Posner, helped achieve the first great victory of the law and economics movement: completing the transformation of anti-trust law from a constitutional restraint on oligarchy to a legal framework that, as Bork put it in a seminal article, "can be legitimately interpreted only according to the canons of consumer welfare."[288]

Antitrust provided the perfect starting point. Because it involves the analysis of complex economic phenomena, courts and enforcement agencies have a felt need for economic expertise, making law and economics a natural tool kit. In the post-*Brown* world, there was little resistance to the idea that antitrust was fundamentally economic, aimed at safeguarding the prices consumers pay, rather than an intervention in our constitutional political economy, aimed at thwarting oligarchy.[289] Over time, the legal academy assimilated law and economics. Its methodological tools proved useful to liberals as well as neoliberals. But in the long run, to advance a neoliberal vision of constitutional political economy, advocates needed something more powerful than academic credentials and expertise. They needed a movement linked to a political party.

That is why the single most important investment in constitutional political economy that these same ideologically motivated foundations made was undoubtedly their investment in underwriting the recently formed Federalist Society. The group began as a home for disaffected, conservative students at elite law schools, but quickly expanded, with foundation help, into a wide network of thousands (now tens of thousands) of lawyers and judges.[290] Almost as soon as it began, the Federalist Society helped hone the accuracy of the Reagan administration's efforts to select an army of conservative lawyers to staff the executive branch and the federal judiciary.[291] The group also turbocharged a new generation of libertarian-conservative public-interest litigation firms—the Center for Individual Rights and the Institute for Justice—by giving these public-interest organizations a way to locate like-minded private lawyers at corporate firms to assist them pro bono.[292]

By the mid-1980s, Reagan's attorney general, Ed Meese, was beginning to turn the Justice Department's attention to long-term questions of strategy and tactics for "nudging our institutions of government toward greater constitutional fidelity" to the principle of preserving "economic liberty and private property."[293] As Solicitor General Charles Fried recalled, "Meese and his young advisers—many drawn from the ranks of the then-fledgling Federalist Societies and often devotees of the extreme libertarian views of Chicago law professor Richard Epstein—had a specific, aggressive, and, it seemed to me, quite radical project in mind: to use the Takings Clause of the Fifth Amendment as a severe brake upon federal and state regulation of business and property."[294]

The project extended well beyond the Takings Clause. Recognizing that "substantive due process on behalf of economic liberty has to some extent fallen out of favor" and wary of accusations of "Lochnerizing,"[295] lawyers within the Office of Legal Policy produced a lengthy roadmap for how constitutional doctrine might be remade. The aim was to "shield[] individual economic liberties from government assault."[296] The report imagined a jurisprudence reinvigorating the Contracts Clause as a sword against state laws such as the debtor protections the Court upheld in 1934 in *Blaisdell*.[297] The report singled out that case as "one of the most explicitly unprincipled Constitutional decisions ever rendered by the Court."[298]

As history has unfolded since the 1980s, the direct constitutional attack that Ed Meese and his young Federalist Society–affiliated advisers imagined has not yet become constitutional law, although recent Takings Clause jurisprudence is veering in that direction.[299] But so far, neoliberal constitutional political economy has made its most important inroads in other areas of constitutional doctrine. For instance, as Chapter 9 will discuss, the First Amendment has been hammered into an effective sword for slashing legislative efforts, old and new, to shape economic and political life in more democratic and less oligarchic ways. On the near horizon are plans to use judge-made separation-of-powers doctrine to destroy major parts of the administrative state that Progressives and New Dealers built.

The advocates of these major changes to the country's political economy have already achieved a great deal, and may soon achieve more, for one main reason: the relatively tight connection between the elite legal understandings forged within their movement and the broader political coalition of the contemporary Republican Party. To a great extent, the Federalist Society stands for full-spectrum conservative constitutional politics, which offers something to each major constituency of the current Republican Party coalition.

Abortion, gay rights, and Christian religious liberty claims may appeal to some, while cutting back on affirmative action programs and voting rights enforcement may appeal to others. However, for many of the wealthiest and most important supporters of the coalition, including Charles Koch and his late brother David Koch, the central constitutional and legal questions are questions of constitutional political economy—or as they would frame them, questions of economic liberty—in the many contexts where the logic of the market conflicts with the logic of democracy.

As we write these words, we have just witnessed four years of the presidency of Donald Trump, a man who identified himself as a populist and who featured a large portrait of Andrew Jackson in the Oval Office.[300] His presidency was the apotheosis of a long and successful effort by the Republican Party to convince large numbers of Americans that the real oligarchy to be concerned about is not the latter-day robber barons who are transforming American economic and political life, but rather, some combination of groups such as celebrities, journalists, academics, Black athletes, and so on, who espouse liberal views on questions of race, religion, and gender.[301]

This radical refashioning of the anti-oligarchy concept has enabled a self-proclaimed populist to help build a Supreme Court that, on questions of political economy, continues to inch closer to the Courts built from the elite corporate bar of the first Gilded Age.[302] President Trump's Supreme Court appointees—three Justices vetted by the Federalist Society's Leonard Leo, two of them scions of elite Washington, D.C., Republican families—will do nothing to reverse this trend and may do much to advance it. Reinvigorating the democracy-of-opportunity tradition will require not just new and better arguments in the courts, but a different form of constitutional politics.

9

BUILDING A DEMOCRACY OF OPPORTUNITY TODAY

Reinventing the Anti-Oligarchy Tradition

American liberals and progressives are now living in an antiquated, inherited constitutional world. According to the axioms of this inherited world, the Constitution is separate from politics, constraining politics, setting the boundaries of politics. It is the object of interpretation by courts, with a decidedly limited role for other interpreters. Legislatures retain the power to help fill in certain blanks the Court leaves open—say, the precise reach of Section 5 of the Fourteenth Amendment—although lately, even these openings have narrowed. When popular movements such as the LGBTQ rights movement make constitutional claims, according to these axioms, they do so for the purpose of influencing courts.

Past generations of progressive reformers operated under a different set of constitutional axioms. In their view, constitutional obligations impelled the legislature to act. The elected branches could and often did challenge the Court's interpretation of the Constitution through politics, especially in cases of profound disagreement about the trajectory of the nation's political economy. By the mid-twentieth century, as Chapter 8 showed, those older ideas were beginning to seem archaic, even paradoxical. That is how they have felt for over half a century. During that time, liberals have come to assume that the Constitution has little to say about economic matters—and that this has been so since an imagined settlement of 1937.

These inherited axioms and assumptions fit snugly together with a different idea inherited from the liberals of the second half of the twentieth century: the supposedly sharp boundary between politics and economics. According to this idea, the most important economic questions are best left to experts, such as the professional economists who run the Federal Reserve. Such expert choices about how to manipulate the great levers of macroeconomic policy should be informed by economic science and insulated from politics. On this inherited view, the job of government in economic life is important but limited: regulate externalities, address market failures, and impose carefully calibrated taxes and forms of redistribution where they least damage the economy. On this view, it is not the job of government to shape the nation's political economy in any fundamental way.

In other words, among liberals in the second half of the twentieth century, economics supplanted political economy. Liberals unlearned the political economy arguments of their progressive forebears and learned to frame that subject matter in terms of questions of economic policy, to be debated on the technocratic merits. The job of the sober, moderate liberal became to bend political leaders toward enacting and implementing the policies preferred by liberal technocrats. Liberals lost, among many other things, their forebears' understanding that economic policies function as *inputs* to politics, distributing social and political power and helping to define the political-economic landscape that drives future politics and moves the boundaries of what is possible in politics.[1]

These inherited ideas can be summed up in two phrases: the autonomy of economics from politics, and the autonomy of constitutional law from politics. For liberals in the second half of the twentieth century, these ideas fit together well. Both took matters that had once been at the center of progressive politics and moved those matters outside the political frame, into specialized expert spheres ruled by judges or by economists, with a much more passive and limited role for the people and those they elect. Today, both these inherited ideas feel exceedingly familiar, even anodyne. But each has become the object of renewed challenge from the left—and for good reason.

Consider the fight over Obamacare in the decade since the law's enactment. This is fundamentally a fight about constitutional political economy. Obamacare (the Affordable Care Act) was the most important legislative effort of the early twenty-first century to shore up the shaky foundations of the American middle class. But according to the inherited axioms that frame the mainstream liberal view, that point is hardly even relevant to the constitutional debate. Bolstering the middle class is one of many legitimate legislative ends Congress might pursue. The constitutional debate about Obamacare runs along various tracks, all of them disconnected from the political-economic purposes of the statute and instead consumed with court-centered questions about whether Congress, in pursuit of whatever legitimate ends, has transgressed some court-made limit on its powers. Indeed, even to most of its defenders, in constitutional terms, the statute was simply a permissible means to a legitimate goal. Obamacare might be morally important, on this view, even morally necessary, but enacting it was no more *constitutionally* compelled than launching a mission to Mars.

It would be one thing if conservatives shared these inherited axioms and assumptions. But they do not. Conservatives never accepted either the autonomy of constitutional law from politics *or* the autonomy of economics from politics. Instead, like the Jacksonian Democrats or the Reconstruction Republicans before them, the modern legal and ideological core of the Republican Party aims self-consciously to alter the nation's political economy through constitutional advocacy. Conservatives have appreciated the constitutional political economy of many ostensibly economic fights—especially those concerning organized labor—where liberals, in general, have not. Conservatives have also understood far better than liberals that the membrane between movement politics and constitutional argument in court is thin and permeable.[2] They have methodically placed movement judges on the courts and watched them embrace the novel political-economy arguments conservatives advanced outside the courts.

The constitutional fight over Obamacare brought this dynamic into sharp relief. According to the core beliefs of the modern conservative legal movement, the underlying problem with Obamacare is simple: it is a large and novel form of social insurance. Like Medicare before it, Obamacare threatens certain foundational commitments—in favor of economic individualism, against social insurance and solidaristic thinking—that lie very close to the heart of a neo-Lochnerian vision of political economy. This view of the underlying constitutional political economy of Obamacare impelled a variety of novel legal moves in seemingly distant doctrinal domains—commerce, federalism, statutory interpretation, and the law of severability[3]—to find some legal means to thwart the threat.

Because of their inherited late twentieth-century axioms and assumptions, liberals have tended to believe that this is not how constitutional politics is supposed to work—and certainly not how social and economic policy is supposed to be made. Liberals' sense of unfairness here is genuine and understandable, given the axioms they have inherited. But the consternation is somewhat misplaced. This is how constitutional politics always works.[4] And this is part of how our political economy has always been made and remade, and how it can be remade again.

As America plunges deeper into a second Gilded Age, liberals' inherited assumptions and axioms about economics, politics, and constitutional law are beginning to dissolve. It is no longer tenable for liberals to presume, as they did in the late twentieth century, that the economy will largely police itself, with government fixing certain problems at the margins. Just as in the last Gilded Age, elites who command immense concentrations of economic power have gained obvious forms of political power at the expense of ordinary Americans. Meanwhile, it has become obvious that the United States does not have a Court that sits separate from politics, constraining politics, setting the boundaries of politics. Instead, we have a Court that is openly engaged in a branch-transcending struggle in partisan constitutional politics. The vision of political economy at the core of that struggle is now squarely in view, just as it was a century ago.

These changes are so wrenching that they have led some liberals and progressives to yearn for a mythic liberal constitutional golden age. Confronting the collapse of the old liberal axioms, some present-day progressives advocate thoughtful and well-meaning reforms aimed at restoring some of those axioms. In particular, some hope to restore an imagined past in which the Supreme Court was a nonpartisan body, sitting outside of politics and setting the boundaries of politics.[5]

Court reform legislation in the name of nonpartisanship seems a tidy solution to the looming constitutional confrontations over rival substantive visions of our social and economic future. But it is the wrong answer to the present challenge. The goal of nonpartisanship bypasses the most important part: persuading the American people of the substantive case against the constitutional politics and vision that animate the Court's present majority, along with its patrons and allies outside the courts. Making the substantive case for a rival constitutional political economy is what reform-minded lawmakers, activists, and intellectuals did in the past—Republicans during Reconstruction, Democrats during the New Deal—before taking up the idea of curbing a reactionary Court. This remains the only sound course today. Prescriptions for reform should flow from, and should be shaped by, a substantive view of what is wrong with the present Court's constitutional politics.

The Court is always engaged in constitutional politics. That is part of its role. The question is whether the Court's constitutional politics have strayed too far from the constitutional politics of the elected branches and the American people—and if so, what can be done to push the Court back into line.

CONSTITUTIONAL POLITICS, THE AMERICAN WAY

The project of this book is to help readers imagine a different constitutional political economy and a different way of fighting about constitutional political economy. Both, we think, are likely to emerge from the wreckage of the postwar twentieth-century liberal constitutional and political-economic order. The history of constitutional conflict that you read about in the first two-thirds of this book shows that the assumptions and axioms inherited by modern liberals are not permanent or necessary features of the American constitutional order. They are not even especially enduring.

Instead, they are products of the constitutional politics of a specific time and place: American liberalism in the second half of the twentieth century. From their inception, they had some evident flaws—not least the fact that, despite a sort of simulacrum of a "settlement" imagined by many liberals, these axioms were never actually accepted by postwar liberalism's conservative opponents. Today the flaws are more glaring. These familiar axioms and assumptions seem nothing like a plausible description of either America's political economy or our constitutional order. What can take their place?

The point of this chapter is to imagine answers to this question. We make no attempt to outline a comprehensive agenda of answers, but offer a few illustrative ones. The first section discusses how progressives can contest the "weaponized" First Amendment in both campaign finance law and labor law and put constitutional political economy to work as they set about reinventing those fields. The second section explores what would happen if we situated racial inclusion, once again, in the democracy-of-opportunity tradition. When racial inclusion is brought back together with political economy, the constitutional lens widens to include not only fields such as antidiscrimination law and voting rights, but also mass incarceration; health care; public investment in social insurance and job creation; and wealth inequality and the possibility of a wealth tax. These are statutory domains, and we argue that constitutional political economy plays an essential role both in framing statutes and in statutory interpretation. The third section explores the implications of reviving the democracy-of-opportunity tradition for what is now viewed largely as economic policy: antitrust, corporate law, banking and monetary policy, and proposals for a universal basic income. Our coda returns to the question of party constitutionalism. We ask what it would mean to make the democracy-of-opportunity tradition (once again) a partisan cause.

Our answers in all these areas look to the future, in significant part, by drawing on America's past. We think that approach is inevitable when making constitutional claims and arguments. It is central to the American constitutional tradition to bring the past constantly to bear on the present, as we try to build a future constitutional order that Americans can recognize as authentically ours.

We also think there is another, deeper reason why the future of progressive constitutional political economy will draw on its past. Advocates of the democracy-of-opportunity tradition we have described in this book have advanced arguments that are many and various. We hardly endorse all of them, but in their main outlines, they are powerfully persuasive. The problem of oligarchy is not new, nor is the danger of losing the American middle class and becoming a nation of haves and have-nots. Nor, finally, is the problem of racial exclusion and other group-based exclusion a new one in American history. Quite the contrary! The intertwined and mutually reinforcing nature of these problems is also not new. The core arguments of the democracy-of-opportunity tradition speak to this combination of problems in ways that are indigenous to American constitutionalism. However, these arguments cannot get off the ground within the postwar liberal axioms and assumptions with which this chapter began.

Americans need to expand their present cramped view of what kind of constitutional politics is possible in this country. Americans need to recover an older set of understandings of how constitutional politics works. For the first two-thirds of American history—and the first two-thirds of this book, from the founding through the New Deal—all sides in our main constitutional conflicts saw the Constitution as not merely a force outside politics, constraining politics. It was also the engine of a democratic constitutional politics.

Political economy was a large part of the subject matter of this constitutional politics. Generations of reformers held that the Constitution *required* legislatures to act to restrain oligarchies that undermined American democracy, and to preserve a robust middle class broad enough for all. They thought the Constitution demanded, not just permitted, laws attacking racial exclusion—and that the fate of those laws was inextricably linked with the trajectory of the nation's political-economic development. The advocates of these arguments often made them in the teeth of hostile courts determined to impose on Americans a very different and far less democratic political economy, one in which Court-made constitutional doctrine protects the economic power of elites against democratic encroachment.

Advocates of the democracy of opportunity won some stunning victories. By the middle of the twentieth century, a number of those victories helped build the mid-twentieth-century white middle class. Ironically, the very success of the legislatively driven constitutional political economy of the New Deal helped make it possible for liberals in affluent, mid-century America to forget the constitutional fights of the first Gilded

Age. It led liberals to invent the axioms of constitutional politics whose inadequacies have now become so clear. On the other hand, conservatives never forgot. They did not mourn; they organized. More and more, we now live in the constitutional political economy that they have built.

In the first decades of the twenty-first century, these long-standing conservative efforts at constitutional change and retrenchment have become open and explicit and are achieving highly visible successes. This has an unintended, welcome consequence: to awaken the rest of America to the possibility of new forms of constitutional politics (which really are not new, but feel new to modern liberals). If Americans can once more see and understand the vision of constitutional political economy that is being imposed by undemocratic courts, it will become possible to run campaigns on, and elect leaders who strongly advocate, a rival, egalitarian constitutional political economy that aims to restore a democracy of opportunity.

Such future leaders will need to challenge not only their opponents holding political office but also, when necessary, their opponents on the bench. We are beginning to see Democratic lawmakers and progressive activists do this, as they demand structural reforms of the courts and link these demands with accounts of the constitutional politics driving right-wing judicial activism.[6] It is almost inconceivable that we will not see future rounds of constitutional conflict that reprise core elements of the battles between FDR and his opponents, including those who sat on the Supreme Court.

Modern-day progressives can win those battles. Winning them begins with understanding that the Justices are not umpires. They are, as often as not, specialized players on the opposing team. They are constrained in various respects by important norms of the judicial role and of the legal profession. They are not *simply* politicians in robes. Sometimes those legal and judicial norms can be usefully leveraged to drive critical wedges between the Justices and their political allies outside the Court, or between different Justices inside the court. But this does not make the judges umpires. In American constitutional politics, the only real umpires are the American people. In the end, it is up to them to judge whether and when the Court is out of bounds.

CONSTITUTIONAL ARGUMENTS IN THE FACE
OF HOSTILE COURTS

Some liberals sympathetic to the broad project of this book may none-theless worry that it is a mistake to "constitutionalize" political ques-tions, especially questions of political economy, either in general or es-pecially at this moment, in the face of hostile, conservative, activist courts. As we discussed at the start of this book, that worry is misplaced. Political economy has always been central to constitutional politics. Today that is especially so. The conservative opponents of the New Deal never agreed to any "settlement," and their descendants are busily ad-vancing constitutional and statutory-but-really-constitutional objections to many of the central pillars of progressive and liberal governance, from social insurance and labor rights to racial and gender inclusion and even the administrative state itself. To respond to these arguments, liberals and progressives need to make better arguments. The alternative liberal strategy of deemphasizing the Constitution—hoping that the courts will just leave their legislative program alone and that any constitutional ob-jections made in court will stay in court, rather than shaping the terms of political debate—is profoundly wrongheaded.

However, progressives should not aim to reproduce, in mirror image, the conservative approach to constitutional political economy. Progres-sives are differently situated, with different aims that call for different means.

There are three distinct ways that arguments about constitutional po-litical economy can operate in relation to a piece of legislation: as a sword, as a shield, and as a guide.[7] Today's conservatives, like their fore-bears in the *Lochner* era, wield their vision of constitutional political economy primarily as a *sword:* it drives and motivates their constitu-tional arguments for striking down legislation. To return to our first example, neo-Lochnerian constitutional political economy demands that some way be found to strike down Obamacare, simply because of the kind of program that Obamacare is and the direction in which it moves the nation's political economy. Outside the courts, this view found its strongest expression in the broccoli argument: that it is as wrong for the government to require individuals to purchase health insurance as it would be for the government to force individuals to buy (or perhaps even eat) broccoli. In court, of course, opponents of Obamacare claimed the statute violated the Constitution because it violated a variety of judge-made constitutional doctrines about the Commerce Clause and federalism. You go to court with the tools of constitutional doctrine and legal argument, not evocative libertarian imagery about a particular vision of political economy. But the broccoli argument was never as far in the background as a doctrinal sort of lawyer might expect. One of the Justices raised it at oral argument, and in the end, it appeared in three of the four opinions in the case.[8]

For progressives, now and in the future, the primary role of constitutional political economy arguments is *not* to invalidate legislation but instead to motivate and defend it—that is, to use constitutional political economy as a *shield*. This shield can defend legislation that does essential constitutional work from various forms of constitutional attack, both in politics and in court. This means doing more than just arguing, for instance, that campaign finance regulations are permissible under existing First Amendment doctrine. Conservatives will simply change that doctrine to eviscerate campaign finance regulations that violate their vision of constitutional political economy. Instead, progressives must argue that these laws do essential constitutional work. They help preserve the democracy contemplated by the Constitution and prevent it from sliding into oligarchy.

Finally, constitutional political economy arguments can function as an interpretive *guide:* not as an argument for preserving legislation or striking it down, but as an argument for how to interpret legislation. Where legislation does constitutionally necessary work, judges ought to put great weight on interpreting that legislation in ways that allow that work to be accomplished.[9]

Today, as at the dawn of the New Deal, progressives face a hostile Supreme Court majority that is very unlikely to accept arguments in the democracy-of-opportunity tradition. In court, such arguments are likely to be far more relevant to dissenters. That could be true for some time. Such arguments serve a useful function in dissent. As we have seen many times in this book, the membrane between constitutional adjudication and constitutional politics is highly porous. As swiftly as the broccoli trope found its way into judicial discourse, an effective dissent can send arguments the opposite way, providing energy and legitimacy to a constitutional politics bluntly opposed to that of the majority. We saw the early twentieth-century labor movement draw on Holmes's and Brandeis's dissents to build their arguments, when the movement defied antistrike decrees and lobbied for legislative repeal of the judge-made law of labor injunctions. We heard FDR invoke judicial dissents as he called on the American people to decide for themselves the great constitutional political-economic questions of the day. In the end, it is outside the courts that we expect our arguments will make the most difference.

Making arguments in the democracy-of-opportunity tradition does not require inventing novel constitutional doctrines or using any particular magic words. It requires acknowledging the continuity between the Constitution and the political economy on which it rests. That continuity has been there for all of American history; many of our progressive forebears built their arguments on it. Right now, the same continuity is turbocharging a host of conservative claims.

In moments of conflict like the ones on the near horizon, it is helpful and clarifying to reestablish the following proposition: Both the elected branches and the courts can legitimately engage in constitutional politics. In most of the past eras of constitutional conflict we have described in this book, that proposition was obvious. For the reasons we discussed in Chapters 7 and 8, it is now less so.[10] As a practical matter, when courts use constitutional law to advance a vision of constitutional political economy that a great majority of the people and their representatives do not share, the elected branches have a variety of potential responses.

The Federalists and the Reconstruction Republicans employed what is perhaps the simplest tactic: changing the size of the Court in order to shape the Court's composition—in particular, to prevent the wrong president from appointing Justices, when those Justices would thwart these parties' core constitutional projects. The Reconstruction Republicans succeeded. They knew President Andrew Johnson would appoint Justices who were hostile to the constitutional project of remaking the South's political economy through Reconstruction. By shrinking the Court from ten Justices to six, they blocked Johnson from making any appointments. Once President Ulysses S. Grant, our most pro-Reconstruction president, was safely inaugurated, they raised the number of Justices to nine, and Grant ultimately appointed four.

That was the main precedent for Franklin Roosevelt when he framed the message of his 1936 campaign as a challenge to both the "economic royalists" and the constitutional ideas animating the Supreme Court. FDR argued that the Court's conservative vision of constitutional political economy, which threatened to strangle the New Deal, was a "new despotism wrapped . . . in the robes of legal sanction."[11] His most famous tactical move, in the wake of his sweeping electoral triumph—his threat to pack the Court with new Justices—is remembered today as a failure. Court-packing split Roosevelt's party, never had the votes to pass the Senate, and hurt the president politically. But in strategic terms, Roosevelt's overall political campaign against the Court, from the arguments in the 1936 campaign through the court-packing plan, was a success in the way that matters most: The Supreme Court did not strike down a single New Deal statute after 1937. Instead, the Court acquiesced to a new constitutional vision of national power, vested in Congress, to regulate the national economy.

Should a future White House and Congress with a strong reform mandate find themselves locked in conflict with a hostile Court, and inclined to alter the size of the Court, the Reconstruction and New Deal precedents will be surpassingly important. It is essential to understand the constitutional political economy claims at their core. As we write these words, some Democrats outraged by Republicans' recent ruptures of institutional norms in the judicial nomination process have proposed "court-packing" essentially as a tit-for-tat response, restoring a balance that Republican constitutional hardball upended. That idea is fair enough as far as it goes. But to convince a broad, reform-minded American public of the need for such dramatic measures, political leaders must offer arguments about constitutional substance, not just righting partisan wrongs.

This is why it is important to understand the substance of past fights about court-packing. On the last two occasions when Congress took up the idea of changing the Court's size, once under Republican leadership and once under Democratic leadership, it came forward with the same argument: A reactionary Court has allied itself with a powerful (but distinctly minoritarian) social and political bloc on the side of oligarchy and racial and class domination. What the Joint Committee on Reconstruction dubbed the "spirit of oligarchy" was what animated the old Southern Slave Power hell-bent on restoring its dominance, and the Court was its chief ally in the federal government. Likewise, the central political argument for expanding the Court during the New Deal was that the Court had firmly allied itself with what Louis Brandeis called "our financial oligarchy" and FDR our "industrial despots."

It is time to revive these arguments. The place to challenge the Court is not on the procedural unfairness in how the current Court was constituted, but on the substance of the vision of constitutional political economy the Court is working to impose on the United States. It is true that liberals and progressives remain attached to a politics of defending, deferring to, and trusting the Court.[12] But it has become increasingly obvious that this Court does not deserve that trust. Liberal and progressive voters, not to mention the elected officials who listen to them, now need to reorient their thinking toward a politics of challenging a hostile Court.

Threats to change the size of the Court will continue to be part of Congress's playbook for confronting the Court. But there is much more Congress can do. The Constitution grants the Justices life tenure, but Congress might be able to accomplish certain large-scale structural reforms by statute—for instance, causing individual Justices to rotate into a secondary role after a set term of years so that new Justices may be appointed.[13] Of course, the Court may or may not agree with Congress about the constitutionality of such statutory structural reforms. Such statutes—or the threat of them—are best understood not as good-government reforms, but as moves in an interbranch struggle over constitutional meaning. Fights about restructuring the Court are part of that struggle. It is a struggle that Congress and the president can win.

Congress has other possible tactical moves that are more focused on specific substantive areas of disagreement. Congress can strip the federal courts of jurisdiction to hear particular types of challenges to its legislation.[14] It can develop subtler tools for effectively delaying rather than eliminating federal court adjudication of such challenges.[15] Congress can threaten to do any of these things, up to and including expanding the Court.

Threats, however, must be credible. So, Congress needs an array of tactical options that vary in their political explosiveness, and in their potential to damage the respect Americans have for courts in their other role, as nonpartisan adjudicators of questions of justice. That respect—and that other role—remain important, perhaps especially important to liberals, who still need the Court to stand up for the unpopular minorities and rights claims central to liberalism. Yet it is possible for partisans on the Court to hide behind the public's respect for courts as they implement their movement's vision of constitutional political economy. Having a range of realistic tactics rather than just the single, controversial tactic of "court-packing" helps make it possible to calibrate political challenges to courts more carefully.

Consider this one: Congress could make considerably more use of clauses specifying what happens in the event that a court strikes down a particular statutory provision.[16] It would be interesting to know, for instance, whether the Justices who struck down the Affordable Care Act's expansion of Medicaid benefits as too coercive of the states would have stood their ground if the statute had been written to say that if that particular provision fell in court, in its place would appear a nationalized Medicaid, paid for wholly with federal dollars and not involving the states.

The purpose of this kind of trigger provision is to confront the objecting Justices with a choice that could leave them politically exposed. They might, of course, invent novel doctrines to strike down the backup national program as well. But because especially strong precedents support the constitutionality of such a national program, such novel inventions on the Justices' part would further strain norms of legal reasoning and judicial craft, thereby exposing the Justices' actions as nakedly political. Some Justices might well get off the train before that point, splitting with their political allies on and off the Court.

Or perhaps the majority would hold. That would hardly be the end of the matter. Strategies of political confrontation with the courts are only partly about changing outcomes in court. They are part of a complex and iterative contest over constitutional meaning that today takes place largely between the two major political parties—in the elected branches and in the courts. That is why we see arguments regularly jump across the ostensible gap separating politics from judging, in both directions. The American people are both the audience for this larger contest and its only referee.

Repairing the First Amendment to Rebuild Countervailing Power

As was the case a century ago, those who wish to impose a neo-Lochnerian political economy on the United States have found the federal courts to be a more congenial venue than any elected branch of government. A century ago, defending so-called economic liberties in court primarily involved constitutional claims about the Fourteenth Amendment. Today the battle revolves around the First Amendment. This is not your grandfather's First Amendment, which justly earned a special place at the center of the twentieth-century liberal constitutional pantheon by underwriting new constitutional protections for actual political speech—often deeply unpopular speech, often in wartime.[17] Instead, it is the weaponized First Amendment, to use Justice Kagan's memorable term: As she saw it, her conservative colleagues were "weaponizing the First Amendment, in a way that unleashes judges, now and in the future, to intervene in economic and regulatory policy."[18]

The real problem is not judges intervening in economic and regulatory policy. These new First Amendment interventions have a more specific character, highly reminiscent of the political economy of the Gilded Age. They all implement a neo-Lochnerian vision of political economy. It is too simple to refer to this vision as "libertarian." That word tends to paper over the gaps between the First Amendment claims advanced by civil libertarians in the twentieth century and the newer, antidemocratic, anti-egalitarian vision of political economy that animates the weaponized First Amendment today.

The two areas where the weaponized First Amendment has so far wreaked the most havoc have been campaign finance and labor law. In both, the key jurisprudential move is the same: to confer special constitutional status on certain carefully chosen types of claims of individual right—claims that explode progressive regulatory regimes whose purpose and effect was to make economic and political power less concentrated and less unequal. In campaign finance law, the key claimants have been wealthy political spenders and donors who wish to use the First Amendment to unravel campaign finance laws. In labor law, the claimants have (at least nominally) been workers who want the First Amendment to excuse them from paying dues or fees to the unions who represent them, torpedoing those unions' financial base.[19]

The core idea of the twentieth-century First Amendment was protecting dissenting speakers' unpopular speech. This helped secure one of the foundations of liberal democracy. For a time, prevailing ideas of the First Amendment also protected workers' freedoms of communicative and collective action, promoting efforts to diminish the inequalities of power between labor and capital. The thrust of the new weaponized First Amendment is instead to attack egalitarian forms of democratic self-government—the labor unions workers elect, the campaign finance regimes elected representatives enact—and in that way, to weaken or destroy sources of countervailing power against oligarchy.[20]

For conservatives on the federal bench with neo-Lochnerian sympathies, there is plenty of continuity between the old First Amendment and the new, weaponized one. For them, legal frameworks that establish egalitarian baselines in labor law or campaign finance are not safeguards of democracy, but instead are most likely vehicles for, as one critical commentary puts it, "the self-perpetuating rule of a bureaucratic state acting on behalf of well-organized or ideologically sympathetic interest groups."[21] This is Hayek reborn as First Amendment doctrine. In this view, oligarchy and democracy do not matter. It is irrelevant whether there are *private* accumulations of oligarchic power. It is irrelevant whether there are sources of countervailing power that enable ordinary citizens to fight back against oligarchy. All that matters is the reach of the bureaucratic state.

In this respect, the claims of the weaponized First Amendment are recognizably "libertarian": Their starting premise is that the only relevant constitutional actors are one individual standing against a hostile government. Court-made First Amendment doctrine tends to facilitate this narrow focus by keeping our attention on the "speech" claims of one individual, pitted against the regulatory goals of the state.

The key to understanding what is wrong with the weaponized First Amendment, in constitutional terms, is to bring democracy back into the picture. That means bringing other people into the frame, beyond the lone plaintiff and the state. Specifically, it means seeing "the many": the numerous not-rich people whose power, in politics and in economic life, depends on building egalitarian forms of collective self-government as a bulwark against oligarchy. Building and preserving those forms of self-government is at the heart of the constitutional project of the democracy-of-opportunity tradition.

CAMPAIGN FINANCE AND REPUBLICAN GOVERNMENT

When in 1912 the Populists and Progressives of Montana enacted their Corrupt Practices Act—a campaign finance law that, among other things, prohibited corporate expenditures in elections—they understood their project as a "fight to preserve to the people of Montana the right of self-government."[22] A single company had so "clearly dominated the Montana economy and political order" that it had "convert[ed] the state government into a political instrument" serving the interests of absentee stockholders rather than the people of Montana.[23] These lawmakers correctly understood their project as not merely constitutionally permitted, but constitutionally required. A republican government, they saw, was one controlled by the people, rather than by monied interests through corrupt campaign contributions, expenditures, and outright bribes. The key constitutional actor in this story was the Montana legislature, acting on behalf of the people to defend a republican political-economic order.

A century later and a world away, when the Supreme Court shredded that 1912 Montana statute in its First Amendment buzzsaw, there was no mention of this constitutional actor or its central argument that legislation like the Corrupt Practices Act was constitutionally compelled.[24] Instead, there was the new logic of the weaponized First Amendment, as articulated by the twenty-first-century Court in a series of linked cases striking down campaign finance laws. These cases are not comprehensible in terms of the core logic of the old First Amendment, which aimed, in its most famous distillation, for "uninhibited, robust, and wide open" public debate.[25] Instead, in a run of cases beginning in 2008, a 5–4 conservative majority targeted a series of campaign finance laws because those laws aimed, in the five Justices' view, to "level the playing field" or "equalize" the power of different actors in the political sphere.[26]

That leveling or equalizing is now what the weaponized First Amendment forbids, rather than anything to do with prohibiting or limiting speech. What gets a law struck down, in this upside-down doctrinal universe, is when that law intervenes in our political economy in a way that inhibits the conversion of economic power into political power. In two important cases, the 5–4 conservative majority struck down a "millionaire's amendment" that allowed federal congressional candidates to raise extra money when faced with a rich self-funded opponent, and then a similar Arizona law that gave extra public matching funds to candidates who faced especially well-financed opposition.[27] What is so stark about these cases is that, as Justice Kagan noted in dissent, these laws "do[] not restrict any person's ability to speak," but instead, by their express terms, "create[] more speech."[28] Still, even without blocking any speech, such laws do indirectly create a disincentive for wealthy candidates and independent groups to spend their money in political ways, thereby making it somewhat trickier and less efficient for them to convert their economic might into political power. That is the point of the laws; it is how they inhibit oligarchy; and it is why the Court struck them down.[29]

In 2010, in the most famous of this line of cases, *Citizens United v. FEC*, the same 5–4 majority held that Congress could not bar corporations from spending their treasuries on political advertising.[30] American law had long drawn a line between corporations themselves, whose political activities were restricted, and political action committees (PACs), which are often affiliated with a corporation but are legally separate, and funded by the corporation's individual executives and other human supporters. The point of that distinction, as the Court articulated it in 1990, was to "ensure[] that expenditures reflect actual public support for the political ideas" rather than only "the unique state-conferred corporate structure that facilitates the amassing of large treasuries."[31] Wealthy corporate executives are human members of the polity, choosing to spend their own money. To that extent, their actions fall somewhere within the ambit of government by the people—republican government—in a way that direct corporate political spending does not. In *Citizens United*, the majority swept that distinction away. If corporations want to spend money to speak about politics, Justice Anthony Kennedy held, "the Government" (capitalization in original) must not "impose restrictions on certain disfavored speakers."[32] Through the lens of the weaponized First Amendment, protecting the power of human citizens to control their politics was a dangerously egalitarian effort to suppress the political speech rights of some of our largest agglomerations of economic power.

After *Citizens United*, the Montana Supreme Court nonetheless found a way to uphold the Montana Corrupt Practices Act.[33] The Supreme Court summarily and unanimously reversed: the statute was basically the same as the one *Citizens United* struck down. The Montana Supreme Court had seen it differently because, that court held, Montana's history showed unmistakably that the state had a compelling justification for protecting its "republican form of government" through the act. When the act passed, the state's republican government was teetering on the brink of collapse: A wealthy out-of-state corporation controlled most of the state's political system.[34] The Montana Supreme Court asked, "[W]hen in the last 99 years did Montana lose the power or interest sufficient to support the statute"?[35] The answer to this question is simple: it happened in the early twenty-first century, when five Justices weaponized the First Amendment as a means of advancing a vision of constitutional political economy.

In this vision of constitutional political economy, economic power is freely convertible into political power, and attempts to block this conversion are a new form of forbidden class legislation. Much of what an ordinary person might call "corruption" is reconceived as normal politics and subject to constitutional protection. "Corruption" is redefined so narrowly that it is almost limited to explicit quid pro quo bribery.[36] The five-Justice majority in all of these cases is entirely dismissive of alternative, more democratic visions of political economy that would distinguish the actual citizens a politician represents from that politician's financial backers—so dismissive that they occasionally fail to register the distinction in their own writing, and refer to a campaign contributor as a "constituent."[37]

In their dissents in these cases, the four liberal Justices were aware that something deeper was afoot than merely a strained extension of First Amendment doctrine. But what? From the perspective of the axioms with which this chapter began, the problem with these rulings was that the majority was using the Constitution to engage in economic policymaking. The dissents made that familiar point more than once. But something about the sweeping nature of these rulings also led the dissenters to begin to reach back to the democracy-of-opportunity tradition.

Justice Kagan argued in her dissent in the Arizona case that the law the Court struck down actually "promotes the values underlying both the First Amendment and our entire Constitution by enhancing the 'opportunity for free political discussion to the end that government may be responsive to the will of the people.'"[38] The internal quote there comes from a preeminent old First Amendment precedent.[39] But in the phrase "our entire Constitution" one detects an echo of the older, deeper republican stakes as the Montana legislature might have articulated them in 1912. In a single line in his *Citizens United* dissent, Justice John Paul Stevens came even closer to the heart of the issue. He wrote: "Our lawmakers have a compelling constitutional basis, *if not also a democratic duty,* to take measures designed to guard against the potentially deleterious effects of corporate spending."[40] That reference to "democratic duty" is highly unusual today. It evokes a lost world of democratic lawmaking in which lawmakers acknowledged and acted on their duty to build up the countervailing political power of the many—of the democratic majority of the people—as against the wealthy few and their potentially oligarchic agglomerations of economic power.[41]

The Constitutional Duty to Spend

The project of rebuilding a constitutional political economy in which there are robust sources of countervailing power against oligarchy, and in which economic power is not so easily and endlessly converted into political power, falls first to legislatures, not courts. And there is a great deal that both Congress and state legislatures can do. As the New Dealers well understood, the Spending Power is just as important—perhaps more important—than any form of direct regulation. Campaign finance is once again an instructive domain to illustrate the point.

After *Citizens United,* much attention has focused on what avenues of regulation are left open (direct-contribution limits and disclosure requirements, for now). But the most promising approaches to preserving government by the people now lie in direct government expenditure. Give candidates campaign money, and lots of it, without conditions. Then they will have considerably less of a need to kiss the rings of oligarchs.

Both state legislatures and Congress should proceed one of two ways. First, they can give large unconditional sums of campaign money—money that does not require agreeing to any spending limit or other restriction—to any serious candidate for office. Second, arguably even better, they should create public small-donor matching funds, as in New York City, where the city matches small (under about $250) contributions from residents of the city at an 8:1 ratio.[42] Donors are free to give more, but only the first $X is matched. The higher the ratio—and, up to a point, the lower the X—the closer the system comes to democratizing campaign finance, by giving ordinary voters the clout to shape who runs for office and who wins.[43] H.R. 1, the democracy reform bill that the Democratic House of Representatives passed in 2021, would create a nationwide small-donor match system for congressional elections.[44]

Democratizing does not mean equalizing. Proposals like this do not give all candidates the same funds or all voters the same influence. What they do is untilt the political economy of running for office, so that appealing to "the many" becomes a more viable pathway to political opportunity, perhaps one nearly as viable as appealing to the rich and powerful. This will shape who even considers running for office as well as who wins.[45]

Finally, lawmakers can alter the political economy of running for office—and improve the prospects of candidates and movements with poor and working-class constituencies and few wealthy friends—by making it less expensive to run a campaign. Existing Federal Communications

Commission rules require broadcasters to offer certain modestly favorable terms for candidates' political advertising.[46] Congress could go much further, adapting this rule to apply to internet platform advertising, and requiring broadcasters and internet platforms to provide a floor of very inexpensive or even free advertising to political candidates. Meanwhile, lawmakers must pursue reforms that facilitate organizing and make voting easier: for instance, universal, automatic voter registration, so that campaigns would need only organize voters to vote, rather than first needing to organize them to register. Congress has the power to require universal automatic voter registration in federal elections through the Elections Clause, and could strongly encourage states to follow suit through spending.[47] It could also preempt state laws that criminalize and otherwise make difficult a range of forms of political organizing.[48]

All of these ideas are realistic, immediate-term legislative actions that are consistent with even the current Court's judge-made doctrinal Constitution. But we do not propose them here in the spirit of finding paths forward that treat the Court's Constitution as a constraint. Just the opposite: we expect that there will likely be constitutional challenges to most of these proposals, even though they fit squarely within existing doctrine. Such right-wing challenges will begin with ideas that seem "off the wall," but will soon be treated as serious grounds for invalidating reforms.[49]

Without predicting the precise doctrinal form such challenges will take, we can reasonably predict that they will recall the judicial jihad more than a century ago against what were then (derisively) called "labor laws." Courts invalidated those laws on a wide array of doctrinal grounds.[50] The real constitutional issue was that the laws were aimed at shifting the balance of power away from employers and toward workers. Similarly, in campaign finance law, we are already seeing the emergence of doctrine under the weaponized First Amendment in which any effort to make speakers' or candidates' or voters' influence less unequal—whether or not this involves a limit on speech—is presumptively suspect. To meet those arguments, what progressives now and in the future need is not court-centered claims, incomprehensible to the public, about doctrinal tests and stare decisis. Those arguments have their place in court, where norms of judicial craft can provide some leverage. Sometimes they can change the outcome of a case. But to engage in the struggle over constitutional meaning in which conservatives are already deeply engaged, progressives need to press the broader constitutional arguments on the other side.

The best version of those arguments draws deeply on the democracy-of-opportunity tradition. The case is straightforward and begins with constitutional essentials. The American Constitution is the constitution of a republic, not an oligarchy. It can continue to function as such only if Americans prevent would-be oligarchs from accumulating excessive political and economic power. Americans also need to maintain a broad, open, and racially inclusive middle class. To do that, it is necessary to restore the political power of ordinary workers, as represented by labor, as a counterweight to wealth and capital. It is also necessary to build and maintain pathways to political office for those who can win popular support but not the support of wealthy would-be oligarchs. These are not merely constitutionally permissible goals. They are constitutional necessities. Legislators and citizens who hope to halt the slide from a republican form of government into oligarchy need to take these arguments down from the shelf, revise them, and deploy them to help rebuild the democratic foundations of our republic.

Labor as Countervailing Power

In the twentieth century, New Dealers used legislation to build the political-economic clout of labor as a countervailing power. They did this for reasons of constitutional political economy. President Franklin Roosevelt and his congressional allies argued that constitutional democracy and political self-rule could not exist alongside industrial "despotism."[51] Working Americans had become "industrial slaves."[52] They could regain their economic independence—and the social and political power it imparted—not through individual property-holding, but instead collectively, through the security, voice, and authority that came with unions. Recalling the Jacksonians' core anti-oligarchy insight, that the laboring "many" needed mass organizations with the clout to counter the wealthy "few," New Dealers declared that their labor law reforms would come to the republic's rescue by finally "incorporat[ing] the industrial workers in the polity of the United States" as a "check upon the power of 'Big Business.'"[53] Jacksonians had once defended the invention of the mass party as a structural constitutional necessity; New Dealers similarly defended the invention of the industrial union.

Today most legal scholars, when they think of this New Deal moment of constitutional lawmaking, understand it in terms of the expansion of national power through the Commerce Clause. That was part of the story. It was the ground on which a conservative Supreme Court chose to surrender. But at the time, the era's leading scholar of the Supreme Court, Edward Corwin, who coined the phrase "constitutional revolution," saw the substance of what was happening quite differently. What made the "constitutional revolution" revolutionary was not a reinterpretation of commerce. It was a vision of constitutional political economy in which some important fundamental rights were by their nature collective, redistributive, enforceable against private actors (industrial employers), and protected through the administrative state. Safeguarding workers' collective freedoms against private employers' coercion, Corwin wrote at the time, and guaranteeing "the economic security of the common man" through social insurance, were now "affirmative" governmental obligations. Those were the core of the "revolution." In the late 1930s and early 1940s, even the Supreme Court took this core meaning on board and began fashioning new constitutional doctrine and new constructions of the antitrust laws to protect what it agreed were "fundamental rights" of a collective and redistributive character.[54]

Unsurprisingly, for decades, the remnants of this vision have been squarely in the crosshairs of conservative politicians and judges. Starting with the counterrevolution of the late 1940s and continuing through today, the "right-to-work" movement has waged an ongoing campaign of legislation and litigation, funded and supported by corporate executives and employers' associations as well as wealthy anti-union ideological activists, to destroy the New Deal vision and the politically powerful unions it yielded. This movement has scored many big victories, and the Supreme Court has never been more actively allied with the antilabor movement than it is today.

A consistent aim of this long campaign has been to neuter unions' political role. Instead of a source of countervailing social and political power against oligarchy, on this view, unions should be entirely private collective bargainers, acting exclusively on behalf of current members in their negotiations with a single employer. This campaign's first great success, the Taft–Hartley Act of 1947, prohibited so-called secondary boycotts, in which workers act in solidarity to aid fellow workers in a dispute with a different employer.[55] Taft–Hartley also prohibited "closed shops" (where an employer agrees to make union membership a condition of employment). This meant that, from then on, there would be nonunion workers in unionized workplaces, who would not pay the usual union dues. But would the nonunion workers have an unfettered right to free ride on everything that the union had bargained for? Taft–Hartley allowed states to say yes, through "right-to-work" laws, which some (mostly Southern) states promptly enacted. Elsewhere, unions often negotiated for "agency fees," in which those who didn't join the union would nonetheless pay a fee, reducing the free-riding problem. This raised a new issue: workers who disagreed with a union's politics, and refused to join for that reason, might now be supporting some of its political speech.

In *Abood v. Detroit Board of Education,* in 1977, the Court saw a First Amendment problem with this arrangement and drew a careful line. A union could charge agency fees for the costs of collective bargaining, contract administration, and grievances (all of which it was required by law to undertake on behalf of all the workers at the workplace, whether union members or not).[56] But it could not use agency fees for political speech. This line, which attempted to separate the private-bargaining function of a union from its political function, would have been entirely unsatisfactory to the architects of the New Deal constitutional revolution. They understood the entire project of unions to be inextricably political—and they initially won the Supreme Court's agreement on that point. Wages, labor standards, and union efforts to boost them were "not matters of mere local or private concern," the Court noted in *Thornhill v. Alabama* in 1940, but part and parcel of how workers were using "the processes of popular government . . . to shape the destiny of modern industrial society."[57] Later, however, the Court retreated from this position and came to view collective bargaining and union activity as essentially private and economic, not public and political. That was how the Court justified upholding Taft–Hartley's various limitations on union activity such as boycotts and picketing against First Amendment challenge.[58]

In 2018, in *Janus v. AFSCME,* the Court brought the hammer down, overturning *Abood* and holding that at least in the case of public employers (the private-employer case is still to come), the First Amendment requires that every state be a "right-to-work" state.[59] Unions must fully allow nonmembers to free ride, charging them no fees for the services the unions must provide them. The political-economy implications of this ruling were lost on no one. They were why the case was brought.[60] The American Federation of State, County, and Municipal Employees (AFSCME) is such a prominent political actor and supporter of the Democratic Party that President Donald Trump summarized the decision in one sentence: "Big loss for the coffers of the Democrats!"[61] In that way, the case was part of a much broader conservative political economy project: using constitutional law to weaken groups—especially unions, but also plaintiffs' lawyers and others—that contribute to the Democratic Party.[62]

It is striking how frankly Justice Samuel Alito, writing for the five-Justice conservative majority in *Janus,* assessed the political economy of public-sector unions as part of the basis of his First Amendment decision, as though acknowledging Justice Kagan's point in dissent that this "weaponized First Amendment" was "unleash[ing] judges . . . to intervene in economic and regulatory policy." "Th[e] ascendance of public-sector unions," Alito wrote, "has been marked by a parallel increase in public spending." He cited statistics about the growth of state and local government spending over the decades, pension systems underfunded "as a result of generous public-employee retirement packages," and in general, "the mounting costs of public-employee wages, benefits, and pensions." On all these points, Alito echoed the public statements of Bruce Rauner, the anti-union Republican governor of Illinois who originally filed the case.[63] Alito concluded: "These developments, and the political debate over public spending and debt they have spurred, have given collective-bargaining issues a political valence that *Abood* did not fully appreciate."[64]

This was a conclusion rich with historical irony. Yes, public-sector bargaining, like all collective bargaining, has a political valence as well as an economic one. That truth was central to the purpose of the Wagner Act; it was how the New Deal worked its "constitutional revolution." Unions are engaged in fights about political economy that are never private in nature. Having successfully convinced themselves that unions' sole legitimate function is to bargain for the private benefits of their members, union opponents such as Alito have now come full circle: They have discovered that even so-called private benefits have a public, political-economy dimension, and decided that they can pull on that thread to unravel unions' membership and financial base.

Felix Frankfurter, an architect of the National Labor Relations Act (NLRA), became the Justice with by far the greatest familiarity with American labor laws. He had sought to stop the Court from ever proceeding down the road it chose in cases like *Abood,* of trying to distinguish unions' "economic" and "political" functions. Frankfurter pointed out that both the champions and the foes of the Wagner Act had been crystal clear that under the statute, unions would go on doing what they had always strived to do: engage in the industrial arena by bargaining collectively, waging strikes, and representing workers in arbitration; and engage in the political arena in support of candidates and policies that favored unions and workers' interests. That was the point! The law rested on a core insight of progressive constitutional political economy: In a modern capitalist economy, power relations between labor and capital are such that citizen-workers simply cannot enjoy a constitutionally fair measure of either bargaining power or political clout without protections of the kind Congress attempted to build in the NLRA. As a matter of First Amendment law, Frankfurter argued, the claim of compelled speech flowing from mandatory dues spent on union politicking was far too "fine-spun."[65] Neither members nor dues-paying nonmembers were in any "way subjected to . . . suppression of their true beliefs or sponsorship of views they do not hold. . . . No one's desire or power to speak his mind is checked or curbed. The individual member may express his views in any public or private forum as freely as he could before the union collected his dues."[66]

Like Alito and the present Court, Frankfurter rejected the notion that union political advocacy coerced and injured the political liberty of dissenting employees in a way that union bargaining or grievance processing did not. Indeed, Frankfurter observed, "[t]he notion that economic and political concerns are separable is pre-Victorian. . . . It is not true in life that political protection is irrelevant to, and insulated from, economic interests. It is not true for industry or finance. Neither is it true for labor."[67] But for Frankfurter, as for us, this point cuts just the opposite way that it cuts for Alito. Unions throughout American history have served their members at the bargaining table *and* by advocating in the legislature for improved working conditions and countless "other social reforms."[68] By constructing dubious First Amendment exemptions from union dues, Frankfurter persuasively argued, the Court was throwing out of whack a carefully constructed congressional project of constitutional political economy. Congress had crafted a system of workplace democracy to bring constitutional precepts to bear on the relations between capital and labor, compelling employers to deal with a union where a majority of workers voted for one, while compelling unions to represent and honor the interests and freedom of expression of all workers, including those who shunned union membership.[69]

As today's liberal Justices stare down a far bolder and more sweeping antilabor intervention than *Abood,* Frankfurter's insights are nowhere to be found. Kagan's dissent in *Janus* focused primarily on the majority's abuses of First Amendment doctrine and stare decisis. She raised alarms about the majority's decision to "pick the winning side in what should be—and until now, has been—an energetic policy debate" about right-to-work laws by "turning the First Amendment into a sword, and using it against workaday economic and regulatory policy."[70] But on the substantive questions of political economy at the heart of that energetic debate, which was now taking place inside the Court, Kagan offered only that an agency fee clause might "facilitate peaceful and stable labor relations."[71]

What was missing in *Janus*, even more starkly than in the campaign finance dissents, was any account of the constitutional stakes on the other side. For the Wagner Act's chief architects, the goal of promoting industrial peace and stability was just one goal among many. The primary objective was to secure the collective freedoms the act enshrined. *That* would have been the apt constitutional counterweight for Justice Kagan to put on the scale against Alito's new-model First Amendment. The architects of the Wagner Act saw a constitutional mandate to protect the right to organize, and to build and protect the power of organized labor, as a countervailing institution against economic and political oligarchy.[72] As the Populists, Progressives, and the New Dealers each understood, America needs such countervailing institutions. They include but are certainly not limited to unions. Through them, "the many" can organize and gain the social and political power to block rule by the oligarchic few and in that way preserve the democratic foundations of our constitutional order.

For lawyers focused on the action inside the Court, it might not be obvious what the point would be in making such arguments. Such arguments would not have convinced any of the five Justices in the majority in *Janus*. However, the arguments would have had a function in our public debate about constitutional political economy that includes, yet transcends, the Court. Such arguments would have put the majority's arguments into sharper relief. They would have sent a clearer signal to the political branches and the American people about what cases like *Janus* and *Arizona Free Enterprise* are really about—not speech, but constitutional political economy.

A Duty to Rebuild Labor and Employment Law

Today, organized labor is near its nadir. Unions represent less than 10 percent of American workers. Meanwhile, 40 percent of Americans live without any savings, and if they need a job, as most do, they must accept an unequal bargain to stay alive.[73] The great majority of unorganized workers say they would like to have a union, if they were not worried about fierce reprisals without redress.[74] The NLRA framework, however, has been so hollowed out that it overwhelmingly fails to protect workers' organizing efforts or any other form of collective action.[75] Union attempts to repair the statute have failed in Congress even during moments of Democratic control.[76]

As we write these words, there are strong indications that this is changing. Democrats truly committed to labor law reform have gained power within the party.[77] A new Democratic president has put labor law reform high on his agenda. Not since Harry Truman vetoed Taft–Hartley in 1947 (and was then overridden by the conservative Dixiecrat / Republican coalition in Congress) has the White House spoken about workers' right to organize the way Joe Biden now does.[78] Indeed, the House has just passed a sweeping labor law reform bill, Protecting the Right to Organize Act (the PRO Act), which aims to repeal crucial elements of Taft–Hartley and boost efforts to organize unions.[79] Meanwhile, far from Washington, despite the bleak legal landscape that currently prohibits many forms of labor action, we have begun to see workers pursue actions like the flatly illegal—but also surprisingly popular—statewide teachers' strikes.[80]

Enacting transformative labor law reform will involve fierce and protracted battles, not only in the Senate, but in the courts—where challenges are inevitable—and in workplaces and in the public sphere. Getting there will require *both* Democratic majorities committed to such change *and* considerable labor organizing and action on the ground. As in the 1930s, workers will need to exercise their rights to organize, strike, and act in solidarity in contexts where this is now illegal, in order to back up (and drive home what is at stake in) their demands for recognition of those rights in today's political economy.[81] When they do, unions will face large fines, and workers will face jail time, for defying judicial injunctions against their illegal strikes. They will encounter a barrage of political, legal, and constitutional challenges and objections aimed at lawmakers, courts, and public opinion, as they contend for recognition of their still unsanctioned freedoms.

It is not hard to imagine the constitutional core of the conservative opposition to any such recognition. In Congress and public debate, as well as in court, conservatives will resurrect versions of the old Lochnerian claims that any measures broadly protecting workers' collective action are violations of the constitutional property rights of employers to be free from class-based coercion. In 2021, the Supreme Court advanced this project in *Cedar Point Nursery v. Hassid,* in which the Court improbably recast the protection of agricultural workers' right to organize as a "taking" of their employers' property.[82] The Court held that California's labor regulation allowing union organizers to go onto farmers' property to meet with workers at certain times was a taking under the Takings Clause—and not just a regulatory taking but apparently a *"per se* physical taking"—so that California must pay compensation to the growers. The Court acknowledged the obvious point that many government regulatory actions involve intruding on someone's property—a search by police, for instance, or the investigation of a nuisance—but found that these "will not amount to takings because they are consistent with longstanding background restrictions on property rights."[83]

This "longstanding background restrictions" maneuver is an innovative way of smuggling in and constitutionalizing an imagined Lochnerian common-law baseline that conveniently predates, and thereby somehow excludes, government efforts to protect "the self-organization rights of employees."[84] As the dissent in *Cedar Point Nursery* pointedly asks: "Do only those exceptions that existed in, say, 1789 count? Should courts apply those privileges as they existed at that time, when there were no union organizers?"[85] Apparently so. But against the majority's effort to enshrine that ancien regime of property rights as a constitutional baseline against labor organizing, the dissent asserts only that state legislators aimed to secure "labor peace" and "may well have believed" that union organizing yields additional public benefits as well.[86]

This sort of limited, diffident defense, focused mainly on broad legislative power, is not adequate to the challenge at hand. It will not be enough outside the courts, or inside them, to overcome the fusillade of constitutional claims that conservative advocates and judges will launch against any legislative expansion of the right to organize. Building on *Janus,* they will argue that any effort to repeal Taft–Hartley's exemption for state right-to-work laws violates the First Amendment rights of dissenting workers.[87] They will make creative First Amendment arguments against efforts to restrain employers' anti-union activity. They will make federalism arguments that Congress lacks the power to upend states' traditional common law and police-power authority to limit the allowable forms of labor solidarity. Liberals will need more than the old response: that the New Deal settled it, Congress has broad power under the Commerce Power to regulate the national economy, and Congress has exercised that power to promote labor peace.[88] This traditional response has been threadbare for some time. As the Court continues to back off from its New Deal precedents, allowing ever-more-explicitly Lochnerian challenges to federal economic policies promoting workers' economic power, the inadequacies of this response are ever more apparent—both in court and outside the courts.

In the coming constitutional debates, which will take place primarily outside the courts, labor and its allies hold a far stronger hand than this. They can begin by reaching back to the core constitutional political economy arguments that New Dealers made for enacting measures like the NLRA in the first place. Prodded and supported by workers on the streets and in the hearing rooms of Congress, the New Dealers argued that labor law reform was necessary and central to building a modern democracy of opportunity.[89] Today, a new version of that case can expose the constitutional stakes of labor law reform for our crumbling democracy, and put that case before legislators, lawyers, and the court of public opinion.[90]

Even if the NLRA had retained more of its original shape and meaning, the statutory scheme was not going to work indefinitely, without substantial reforms, as our political economy changed. The NLRA was designed for a specific set of political-economic conditions. The statute emerged out of the struggles of factory workers.[91] It strongly encourages bargaining at the firm or even the worksite level. This made some sense when so many workers were in plants with tens of thousands of coworkers, but today's postindustrial workplaces are much more fragmented, even when owned or controlled by large corporations. Fast-food workers are split among thousands of locations. Janitors labor in small groups, at night. Home health care workers, Uber drivers, and Amazon delivery drivers work alone. Many of these low-wage workers do not even fit our aging statutory definitions of who is an "employee" of whom. McDonald's cooks and cashiers are employed by franchisees, even as McDonald's itself helps screen applicants and sets workplace standards and even wages. Janitors and home health care workers, delivery drivers and warehouse workers are often employed by subcontractors and temp agencies that have little real power over those workers' livelihoods. Uber and Lyft drivers are misclassified as independent contractors, not "employees" at all. As a result, none of these workers have bargaining rights against the real parties in interest. Unions face sharp restrictions on their abilities to strike or picket against such "third party" companies, and as we discuss below, organizing "independent" workers can even run afoul of antitrust law.

Breaking out of this outdated scheme requires bold but simple statutory reforms. Congress should ensure that organized workers can bargain with the companies who actually benefit from their work by expanding the legal definition of employment. (The House's "PRO Act" does just that.)[92] Congress should also make it easier to raise wages across the board, by promoting or requiring multi-employer bargaining or so-called sectoral bargaining, which covers all companies in an industry.[93] If all bargain together, no firm is placed at a large competitive disadvantage as a result of unionization. By promoting firm-by-firm or "enterprise-level" bargaining, the NLRA only stiffens an employer's resistance to unionization, and "bakes an anti-union animus into American labor relations."[94]

Perhaps most important, Congress should reform American labor law's restrictions on strikes. Scholars tend to assume that "every liberal democracy recognizes that workers have a right to strike."[95] But the United States does not, as historian and activist James Gray Pope reminds us.[96] Our labor laws not only fail to protect but actually block workers from exercising the right to strike or organize.[97] The ban on secondary actions, Pope points out, bars workers who have some economic power, such as organized grocery workers, from aiding workers who do not, like unorganized packinghouse workers. If the grocery workers support striking packers by refusing to handle food packed by strikebreakers, they are deemed to be engaging in an illegal secondary strike. Even employees in different branches of the same firm—say, the tech workers at Uber, should they walk out in support of a drivers' strike—have no right to act in solidarity with fellow workers under current law.[98]

This problem can be fixed by statute. But it has constitutional stakes. As the House Education and Labor Committee puts it, the PRO Act would enable "unions to exercise these basic First Amendment rights."[99] Labor marched and fought for this view—that current prohibitions on secondary boycotts violate basic First Amendment rights—during its losing battle against Taft–Hartley. Workers also brought their claim to court, shortly after Taft–Hartley was enacted; the Court rejected it, and the current Court is very unlikely to think differently.[100] But exactly for that reason, it is significant that Congress is explicitly framing the project of legislative reform in these constitutional terms. Enacting this law would be the beginning, not the end, of a struggle between Congress, the courts, employers, state lawmakers, and unions over how far the new protections go, and how much they preempt state law, in the name of vindicating "these basic First Amendment rights."

We have been here before. Confronted by denials of rights by state and federal courts and legislatures, organized labor responded by acting as a "rights movement."[101] Not only labor radicals but also stodgy craft unionists proclaimed workers' constitutional rights to organize and strike. As we have seen in the pages of this book, they did so in support of open lawbreaking and mass civil disobedience, and they pushed unionism across much of the economic landscape.[102] Like abolitionists, women's suffragists, and civil rights activists, the early twentieth-century labor movement claimed its key rights by putting them at the center of organizing, protest, civil disobedience, and legislative and administrative advocacy.[103] They found support in the early twentieth-century Congress and the New Deal White House in the face of an unremittingly hostile judiciary.

These reformers well understood that big, protracted strikes are costly to all concerned. But creating a new baseline of workers' freedom was unlikely to yield a future full of mass strikes. It is worth considering why such prominent figures as Frances Perkins and Robert Wagner would proclaim that workers had a largely unfettered constitutional right to strike and boycott. Even establishment politicians like Justice Frank Murphy, when governor of Michigan in the 1930s, defended autoworkers' massive sit-down strikes.[104] Jurists like Brandeis and Oliver Wendell Holmes dissented from decisions that held any secondary action (any action against a "third party") to be illegal. They thought that to restrain exactly the broad strikes and boycotts that industry-wide organizing required was a restraint on workers' liberty akin to "involuntary servitude."[105] None of these lawmakers and jurists wanted or expected to see the nation engulfed in endless mass strikes. Instead, they believed that protecting workers' broad collective liberties would produce a new equilibrium, after a period of contestation, in which workers' greater power would yield a more stable and democratic constitutional political economy. They were right.

Race, Class, and the Reach of Public Law

Americans have been fighting about race and what the Constitution says about it for as long as there has been a Constitution. Most of the sharpest constitutional conflicts in American history have had a central racial dimension. But in recent decades, in the wake of the Great Forgetting, the scope of what Americans understand to be a debate about race and the Constitution has narrowed.[106] Americans today could reasonably be forgiven for thinking that the entire conflict over race and the Constitution consists of the constitutional law of policing and the constitutional conflict over race-conscious or race-specific efforts by government such as affirmative action. Conservatives and liberals have bound themselves tightly and publicly, in constitutional politics, to starkly opposed visions in these areas. In the case of affirmative action, liberals argue that the Equal Protection Clause and the leading case interpreting it, *Brown v. Board of Education,* are centrally about lifting up and including groups that have suffered subordination and exclusion. Conservatives argue that the same clause and *Brown* are about blocking the government from taking actions based on race—especially when this means treating one person differently from another on the basis of their individual race ("classification").[107]

Affirmative action is the crucible of this conflict in constitutional politics and its most obvious application. As movement conservatives have gained political power and appointed more judges, some have begun to articulate broader and bolder visions that go beyond anticlassification, perhaps challenging government policies that are facially neutral but aimed at assisting subordinated racial groups.[108] Even hints of that bolder conservative vision have alarmed liberals, who argue correctly that it would seem to block any effort at racial inclusion, including arguably the choice Americans made to ratify and enforce the Fourteenth Amendment itself.

However, this analysis misses most of the real action. The political and economic order of this country has been shaped by centuries of racial subordination and inequality. Interventions by government to unravel any of that subordination and inequality are possible only where and to the extent that government has the constitutional authority to displace so-called private orderings—regimes of property and contract—with public policy.[109] Think of antidiscrimination laws, labor laws, employment laws, fair housing laws, and the much larger set of laws aimed at producing a wider distribution of wealth and opportunities, rather than their concentration in the hands of those born to the right family. All these laws do the work of unraveling generations-long patterns of racial exclusion, hierarchy, and oligarchy. When judges find ways to constrain and block these laws—typically either by inventing new constraints on federal power or by aggrandizing and elevating private law norms such as property and contract over norms of public law and public policy— they hobble this work. A government so hobbled cannot do much to help subordinated racial groups or the poor; it cannot preserve a middle class; and it cannot arrest the slide of our political economy toward oligarchy.

The Radical Republicans understood this. They pushed their fellow lawmakers during Reconstruction to bring together all three strands of the democracy-of-opportunity tradition—and confront both their interdependence and the scale of the transformation of American constitutional political economy that they demanded. To the Radical Republicans, it was a nonstarter to consider solving the nation's racial problems through civil rights laws alone. Court-enforced rights against discrimination—guarantees that Black citizens would enjoy the same rights to make and enforce contracts, to sue, and so on, "as is enjoyed by white citizens"[110]—were incalculably important and central to the constitutional project of Reconstruction. But those laws needed to be embedded in a much broader project of constitutional political economy.

"How," we heard Thaddeus Stevens ask, "can republican institutions . . . exist in a mingled community of nabobs and serfs?"[111]

To eliminate the white planter oligarchy and elevate Black Americans to full citizenship, the entire hierarchical political and economic structure of Southern life needed to be upended and reconstructed on a new basis. This meant federal enforcement of Black voting rights *and* government provision of education *and* the redistribution of land from the deposed oligarchs to the freedmen who worked the land.[112] Without such interventions in political economy and social provision, the Radicals saw, generations of servitude and oligarchy would be followed by generations of other forms of hierarchy and dependence rather than full citizenship and democracy. That is basically what happened. Perhaps for that reason, those Radical Republican arguments have echoed down the subsequent decades, in a Black tradition often in dissent from the main line of white liberalism, extending from the W. E. B. Du Bois of *Black Reconstruction*, to Pauli Murray and Bayard Rustin, to Martin Luther King Jr. and Coretta Scott King, to the Movement for Black Lives and Reverend William Barber's Poor People's Campaign.[113]

What the Radical Republicans briefly saw, and this Black tradition held fast to, was this: It is not possible to unravel the layers of racial hierarchy and oppression at the heart of American political and economic life without substantially renovating American political economy. The three strands of the democracy-of-opportunity tradition are mutually reinforcing. They cannot be pulled apart without significant damage.

Opponents of racial inclusion have always understood this. They have consistently chosen lines of constitutional attack that are broader than questions about the legal meaning of discrimination or equal protection. They have endeavored to reduce the power of public law to intervene in our political economy in any manner that could promote a broader distribution of economic or political power. They have also pressed the interventions of public law downward, away from the federal government and toward the states, to give the white political elite of the South more power to block positive interventions from reaching most Black people. They have worked to carve out constitutional domains where private-law norms of contract and property trump public policy interventions such as antidiscrimination law. And they have attempted to hobble the most significant, specific government efforts to alter America's political economy through innovations in constitutional doctrine custom built for the job at hand.

RACE AND THE CONSTITUTIONAL POLITICAL ECONOMY OF HEALTH CARE—AND VOTING

To take just one tragic example of these dynamics, consider the political economy of American health care, built on top of the legal architecture of the New Deal. Back in the 1930s, FDR's Dixiecrat allies demanded that any democracy of opportunity built during the New Deal be a democracy of opportunity for whites only. In some New Deal programs, this meant de jure segregation and racial exclusion.[114] In others, it meant the careful rewriting of statutes such as the landmark Wagner and Social Security Acts to exclude most categories of Black Southern labor.[115] But there was also another crucial accommodation of Southern oligarchy. Most of the authority to administer a wide range of New Deal programs, especially those affecting the poor, was pushed downward to the state level, where Southern states in particular could and did use that authority to exclude Black people—and to make the Southern versions of these programs stingier and more punitive to people of all races.[116] White Southern politicians had all manner of constitutional arguments for why the programs had to be structured in this way. But in the end, it was their raw political power that mattered. Federalism became a way to accommodate the powerful antipathy toward programs that help the poor— especially the Black poor—on the part of a Southern white political oligarchy.[117]

This structure, designed to accommodate the demands of that Southern white oligarchy, became the Achilles' heel of American health care. It persisted and even expanded a generation later, at the high point of federal efforts to bring the poor into the fold of middle-class security. Lyndon Johnson's Great Society built Medicare, its greatest new middle-class entitlement, as essentially a purely federal program. In contrast, Medicaid, for the poor, was to be administered through the states, like Aid to Families with Dependent Children (AFDC) and other federally subsidized welfare programs. This structure enabled Southern white politicians, who ruled over the jurisdictions where the majority of all Black Americans lived, to ensure that their states' programs for the poor were limited and ungenerous.[118] In the 1980s and 1990s, efforts to cut back on federal antipoverty programs often retraced the same pattern, implementing reductions by giving states more power to make cuts, which Southern states did with particular vigor.[119] For decades, American political economy seemed hardwired to produce this sort of targeted fragmentation, with federalism calibrated to leave Black people in the South with the stingiest and most punitive safety net. This was particularly disastrous in the area of health care. That is part of what the Affordable Care Act aimed to correct.

As enacted by Congress, Obamacare aimed to alter the entire political economy of health care by giving all Americans access to affordable health insurance. To disturb as little as possible of the existing insurance regime, rather than move all Americans to a single, universal program, it built a patchwork of different coverage programs. The single most important piece was a large expansion of Medicaid. "Under the Affordable Care Act, Medicaid is transformed into a program to meet the health care needs of the entire nonelderly population with income below 133 percent of the poverty level," Chief Justice John Roberts wrote in 2012, in his majority opinion in *NFIB v. Sebelius,* kneecapping this part of the act. "It is no longer a program to care for the neediest among us, but rather an element of a comprehensive national plan to provide universal health insurance coverage."[120]

In political-economy terms the shift was as dramatic as Roberts described. That was pivotal to his opinion striking down the law. The old Medicaid had focused on certain sympathetic subgroups of the poor such as parents. It had not aimed for the political-economic transformation that universal social insurance would constitute. Because the ACA was "a shift in kind, not merely degree," Roberts held for the Court that states had to be given the opportunity to opt out of the Medicaid expansion—to keep the old, much stingier program in place, even though such opting out would create a large class of working poor people suddenly ineligible for *any* form of subsidized health insurance, a wild outcome never imagined by Congress, and one that millions of working-class Americans have suffered from since 2012.

For Southern conservative political elites, this outcome was a great political-economic gift. It amounted to the power to opt out of the commitment to universality at the heart of the ACA. It gave them the power to keep millions of their states' poorest workers from obtaining health insurance—and with it, their foothold in the economic security and independence of the middle class. To reach this surprising result, Roberts had to build new constitutional doctrine. To force states to accept a broad and universal program for the poor and the working class, or else lose the narrower and stingier program they had had before, was "coercion," Roberts held. It was a "gun to the head"[121]—and therefore unconstitutional—by dint of an account of the relationship between the federal government and the states that elevates the constitutional entitlements of states over those of citizens.[122]

The concrete result was predictable, even though the scope of the tragedy was hard to fathom in real time.[123] By limiting the federal Spending Power with this new states'-rights codicil, Roberts's opinion resulted in well over two million Americans becoming uninsured.[124] This was no random set of Americans. Today, outside the boundaries of the former Confederacy, over 95 percent of the population lives under a regime of expanded Medicaid. But within the boundaries of the former Confederacy, only 15 percent of the population does.[125] About nine out of ten of the people whom Roberts's novel doctrine deprived of health insurance live within the boundaries of the former Confederacy. A vastly disproportionate number of them are Black.[126] This result was inconsistent with the Affordable Care Act's statutory scheme, but it was entirely in line with a vision of constitutional political economy that has always had its strongest foothold in the South.

This fight might seem very distant from the hot-button political-constitutional conflicts over race. And yet it is all about race—because core questions of constitutional political economy and social provision are "inextricably entangled" with problems of racial exclusion, as Bayard Rustin put it back in the mid-1960s.[127]

In a society with vast intergenerational chasms in family wealth by race, built on centuries of laws and policies of racial exclusion, the political economy of social insurance has a profound racial dimension. Chief Justice Roberts's creative doctrinal move in *NFIB v. Sebelius* closely parallels what he did the following year in *Shelby County v. Holder*. In that case, Roberts destroyed the centerpiece of the Voting Rights Act—Section 5, which had subjected places with a long history of excluding racial minorities from voting to heightened federal oversight.[128] *Shelby County* predictably unleashed a new politics of voter disenfranchisement across the South in the formerly covered jurisdictions. But Chief Justice Roberts held that Section 5's differentiation among states was unconstitutional: it violated a kind of quasi-equal protection principle that applied to states, not people. This "equal sovereignty" principle, as Roberts called it, is not part of the Constitution's text. Nor is the anticoercion principle that limits federal spending powers in *NFIB v. Sebelius*. They are structural principles. They both sound as if they rest on general ideas about the nature of our federalism. But in fact, they are principles custom-built for targeted interventions in constitutional political economy.

To see the targeted nature of the interventions, consider that federal spending accounts for perhaps a third of state revenue. All federal grants come with strings attached. Many large federal spending programs could conceivably run afoul of a sufficiently robust anticoercion principle. Similarly, in a large and complex country in which states are differently situated from one another in almost every possible respect, many well-designed federal laws apply to one state and not another.[129] Both of these principles could potentially have quite broad applications. But in both cases, the majority carefully invented limiting principles, so that the opinions' doctrinal innovations would apply primarily, and perhaps only, to the questions presented in the two cases themselves.[130] Why?

In both cases, what stands out is the exceptionally high political-economic stakes. The prospect of altering the American social compact by creating "a comprehensive national plan to provide universal health insurance coverage" is a lot to stomach, for a Supreme Court Justice committed to an anti-redistributive, Lochnerian vision of constitutional political economy. The idea that past racial wrongs are relevant to present constitutional conflicts—as Section 5 of the Voting Rights Act forcefully asserted, correctly and with great effect, before Chief Justice Roberts destroyed it—is equally offensive to an anti-redistributive, "colorblind" vision of constitutional political economy. In the face of these challenges,

Roberts found it necessary to construct novel structural principles of constitutional constraint. The best explanation for these principles' creation does not lie in abstract principles of federalism. Yet it is also wholly unsurprising that the principles were couched in terms of conceptions of federalism and state autonomy that track antebellum understandings.

In the democracy-of-opportunity tradition, it is the principles on the *opposite* side of these fights that have special constitutional weight. The Voting Rights Act is so significant because it functions as a framework for politics, making possible a racially inclusive politics that changes what can be achieved in politics. Section 5 in particular is essential for exactly the reason Roberts rejects it: it takes account of the ongoing effects in the present of the layered racial political and economic inequalities of the past. Congress intended the statute to directly and self-consciously attack election practices that disproportionately disenfranchise minority voters because of those layered inequalities—election practices that often also affect poor voters of all races.[131]

Until recently, many courts were willing to follow the logic of the Voting Rights Act where it leads, striking down barriers to voting that affect poor voters, when minority voters are disproportionately among the poor.[132] The Roberts Court has relentlessly targeted this link, and now has largely broken it through judge-made law. In *Brnovich v. Democratic National Committee*, the Court's latest assault on the Voting Rights Act, Justice Alito opined for a majority of the Court that a Section 2 claim under the Voting Rights Act should generally not succeed when the disparate racial impact of the challenged voting restriction is traceable to "predictable disparities" caused by "the extent [to which] minority and non-minority groups differ with respect to employment, wealth, and education."[133] In other words, the Court's present majority aims to carefully isolate race from class (as well as from political party), leaving racial protections separate and weakened, because they operate only against practices that target race *alone*.[134]

The lesson of the democracy-of-opportunity tradition is the opposite: that race and class are constitutionally inseparable, and that statutes like the Voting Rights Act do constitutionally essential work, for reasons that include the fact that they address this link. In response to the Court's cynical enabling of a state-level politics of disenfranchisement, Congress must enact new, clear, and universal statutory schemes protecting voting rights—and must then be prepared for a protracted fight with this Court.[135]

The democracy-of-opportunity tradition reveals, somewhat more surprisingly, that the Medicaid expansion is also a statutory provision with constitutional weight—not merely in the sense that it is a legitimate exercise of congressional power, but because without universal social insurance that covers health care, it will not be possible to preserve a democracy of opportunity in a world of burgeoning health care expenses and thin household savings. Congress passed the ACA to fix this problem, fully conscious of its intensely disproportionate and egalitarian racial impact. That is why the Court's intervention to hobble the ACA itself had such an intensely disproportionate and reactionary racial impact. Congress still can, and should, undo the Court's constitutional intervention by enacting statutory reforms that take the question of basic health insurance coverage for working-class people of all races out of the hands of state governments that are too wrapped up in the racial politics of anti-redistribution to protect the core economic interests of their own constituents.

CLASH OF THE SUPERSTATUTES

For all of our (justified) attention to instances like these where the Court intervenes in constitutional political economy through constitutional law, it would be a mistake to assume that those are the only important interventions. You can also build out a constitutional vision through statutory interpretation. In particular, Congress and the courts often do this work when they decide which statutes are so central to the constitutional order that they deserve to be treated as framework statutes—"superstatutes"—that trump other statutes.[136]

Within the democracy-of-opportunity tradition, some of the federal laws that are obvious candidates for this status are labor and employment laws and antidiscrimination laws. By encoding in statutory language the core understandings of New Deal constitutional political economy and the Reconstruction Amendments, these bodies of law codify fundamental constitutional commitments to racial and gender inclusion and to building and preserving a broad and open middle class.[137] But within a rival vision of political economy with Lochnerian roots, these same statutes are constitutionally suspect, because they so powerfully impose public policy goals on domains otherwise characterized by private contract. And so, conservative judges in recent decades have embarked on a project, styled as statutory interpretation, but transparently aiming to implement a vision of constitutional political economy under which individuals can avoid public regimes of rights and regulation, such as antidiscrimination and labor laws, by contracting around them. This project has had the intent and effect of blasting holes in the public law aims of antidiscrimination law and labor law. To accomplish this, conservative judges had to pick different statutes to elevate to "super" status.

They found a useful if imperfect vehicle in the Federal Arbitration Act (FAA) of 1925. The FAA aimed originally to promote the arbitration of commercial disputes by protecting agreements to arbitrate from certain kinds of attack by state law and state courts. The FAA contains text that appears on its face to explicitly *exclude* employment and labor agreements from the act's scope, and there are good reasons to believe Congress meant that exclusion.[138] Undeterred, a stable 5–4 conservative majority on the Court embarked on a three-decade-long quest to expand the FAA beginning in the 1990s. Overturning old opinions to the contrary (including a unanimous one by the conservative Justice Lewis Powell),[139] this slim majority greatly expanded the reach of the act. First, it held that the FAA applies to employment and labor agreements.[140] Second, it held that the act authorizes the federal courts to insist that agreements to arbitrate in this context are binding even when, for instance, they require each employee to arbitrate her dispute alone rather than band together to engage in the "concerted activity" protected under the NLRA.[141] When confronted by dissenting colleagues with the question of why this contestable interpretation of the FAA should trump subsequently enacted labor and civil rights legislation, the majority could only offer arguments that elevate ideas of freedom of contract over public law values. "[T]he task for courts and arbitrators at bottom remains the same," the majority wrote: "'to give effect to the intent of the parties.'"[142]

But whose intent, exactly? Perhaps the most striking thing about the Court's FAA jurisprudence is the way it neatly retraces the *Lochner*-era view that there is no such (relevant) thing as unequal bargaining power in employment contracts. The Court flatly asserts in these cases that "Parties may generally shape [arbitration] agreements to their liking by specifying with whom they will arbitrate, the issues subject to arbitration, the rules by which they will arbitrate, and the arbitrators who will resolve their disputes."[143] To anyone who has been handed an arbitration clause by an employer, this is plainly ridiculous. Only one party drafts these clauses and it is essentially impossible to find an instance of an individual employee bargaining over them. But the legal fiction of bargaining and consent serves a political-economic function. As in the *Lochner* era, the aggrandizement of the FAA through these fictions of consent helps elevate the logic of private contract over the logic of public law—even public law statutes that do constitutionally essential work, such as the NLRA and the Civil Rights Act.

These same conservative Justices are also carving out a growing statutory and constitutional exception to civil rights laws from a different direction. They are rapidly building a jurisprudence that reads the Religious Freedom Restoration Act (RFRA) and the First Amendment together to give religious individuals, groups, organizations, and even corporations the power to opt out of a widening range of generally applicable public laws including antidiscrimination laws. In a striking moment in Justice Neil Gorsuch's recent landmark opinion upholding the application of Title VII's sex discrimination provision to LGBT plaintiffs, Gorsuch paused to describe RFRA explicitly as "a kind of super statute" that "might supersede Title VII's commands in appropriate cases."[144] The Court has already used this logic to undermine the universality of insurance coverage for contraceptives; the Court recently upheld a Trump administration regulation that offered any employer with "sincerely held moral objections" to contraception the opportunity to opt out of Obamacare's requirement that they provide it to their employees.[145] Expanding the exception all the way to "moral objections" seems to amount to a rule that employers need not follow the requirements of the contraceptive mandate if they strongly disagree with it.[146] This is a different but also powerful way to displace public law in favor of the prerogatives of employers and other actors with sufficient economic power to shape the rights of workers, contractors, customers, patients, and so on.[147]

To the extent that these interventions by conservative judges are statutory, Congress should reverse them. Congress should, for instance, enact a statute specifically holding that the intent of Congress is for antidiscrimination law to trump the FAA and RFRA. To the extent that the interventions are constitutional in nature, but in principle curable through statute, Congress should act to cure them. Congress must enact statutory protections for voting rights that cover all states, not merely the ones covered by the old Section 5 coverage formula—protections that go beyond antidiscrimination and toward the establishment of a fundamental right to vote, along with funding to alter the political economy of voting and make it easier, smoother, and more universal. Advocates inside and outside the halls of Congress should state with confidence that these enactments are not optional. They are matters of legislative constitutional duty. The democracy-of-opportunity tradition teaches us at least that much.

But the same tradition also teaches us that there is much more to do than restore civil rights protections. In a society marked by vast racial inequalities in wealth, educational opportunities, job opportunities, and access to capital, it is not enough to protect against discrimination and protect fundamental rights like the right to vote. It is not close to enough. As the Radical Republicans understood, there is no way to secure those rights without also enacting structural reforms to the nation's political economy. For example, we need to legislate new forms of social insurance that are equal to the task of overcoming the precariousness with which many Americans—especially (disproportionately) Black and Hispanic Americans—now cling to the edge of the middle class, or have been pushed back into poverty, or imprisoned there for generations.

Looking back to the Homestead Acts and short-lived land allotments of the Reconstruction era, the thwarted efforts to bring Black America into the fold of New Deal social provision, and Dr. King's Freedom Budget, we need to build universal basic endowments that enable people of all races and class backgrounds to participate fully in our economic life, which today would include the opportunity to pursue higher education without onerous debt. We need to end systems such as cash bail, and mass incarceration itself, which have been fueled by, and which also enable, a politics of racial exclusion and disenfranchisement. We need to alter the tax system to train its sights on taxing concentrations of accumulated wealth and the hereditary aristocracy such concentrations create. We need to reinvent our banking and credit systems in the spirit of Gilded Age and Progressive Era visions of public banking and a "citizens' currency." All this would help thwart oligarchy; it would also have a disproportionate racial effect, moving capital away from those whose ancestors owned lots of it and toward those whose ancestors suffered centuries of forced labor, expropriation, and exclusion that often involved destroying or confiscating wealth.[148]

In other words, here all three threads of the democracy-of-opportunity tradition come together. The Americans with the most wealth have increased their share of the wealth so rapidly in recent decades that today the concentration of wealth in few hands matches or perhaps exceeds the level of wealth concentration of the Gilded Age.[149] Meanwhile, the middle class is being hollowed out.[150] And after centuries of racial expropriation and exclusion, inequalities of wealth, more than almost any other form of American inequality, now fall starkly along racial lines. This is why the Movement for Black Lives, along with Reverend Barber's Poor People's Campaign for a Third Reconstruction, have proposed programs of public investment, job creation, and community economic development that resemble a twenty-first-century Freedom Budget; why the movement for reparations for Black Americans has gathered steam; and why policies for addressing wealth inequality, like baby bonds, wealth taxes, and homeownership-related asset-building are now being framed by prominent lawmakers in expressly racial terms.[151] Such advocates are engaged in arguments about constitutional political economy. The further along their proposals proceed toward possible enactment, the more certain they are to face opponents who frame their opposition in constitutional terms, inside and outside the courts.

WEALTH, RACE, AND THE DEMOCRACY OF OPPORTUNITY

To make this point concrete, consider the most straightforward and obvious way to tax accumulated wealth: a wealth tax. Proposals for wealth taxes animated two major presidential campaigns in 2020 and are unlikely to go away. But these proposals face inevitable constitutional challenge, in politics and in the courts. Here as ever, it is a mistake to assume that all the real action takes place in the courts. Opponents' constitutional arguments are likely to move freely across the courthouse threshold, in both directions, which is why it is essential for proponents to articulate the constitutional dimensions of their own arguments.

The most likely constitutional flash point is this: The Constitution provides that "direct" taxes must be apportioned among the states, meaning that each state must pay its population-weighted share. As we saw in Chapter 1, this provision originally linked Southern states' taxation to their political power: if they were going to get "extra" representation, for three-fifths of all their slaves, the argument went, then they should at least have to pay that much more if and when the federal government imposed direct taxes.[152] For a century after 1789, the Court read this rule very narrowly; basically, no federal taxes were deemed "direct." In the middle of that period, Americans fought a bloody and protracted Civil War and eliminated slavery—and with it, the point of the original apportionment compromise. It would have been fair to assume the "direct" tax limitation was dead. But it was not, and we have seen why.[153] In *Pollock*, in 1895, as Chapter 5 recounted, a slim majority of the Court mounted a rearguard action in service of its anti-redistributive vision of constitutional political economy by reviving the category of "direct" taxes to hobble progressive taxation and Progressive state-building.

They failed. Through the Sixteenth Amendment, the people reversed the Court. After a few brief feints the other way in the 1920s,[154] the Supreme Court has appeared to accept that the "direct" tax rule no longer poses a serious threat to innovations in federal taxation. However, a wealth tax might unsettle that. For the same basic reasons some judges were resistant to the innovation of the peacetime income tax in *Pollock*, some judges today will see a wealth tax as a fundamental assault on an anti-redistributive vision of constitutional political economy, according to which an individual's accumulation of wealth—his property—ought basically to lie beyond the government's reach.

If Congress decides to enact a wealth tax, it ought to prepare for a confrontation with a hostile Supreme Court by simultaneously enacting alternatives: equally powerful revenue-raising taxes aimed at taxing accumulated wealth through better-established constitutional channels, which by statutory design would kick in immediately if a wealth tax were struck down in court for any reason. There are a variety of good options. (Indeed, some may be better than a wealth tax, for independent reasons; we express no view of that here.) An inheritance tax, targeting large inheritances, with very limited exemptions and loopholes, could do the job by replacing our current enfeebled estate tax. Taxing wealth once a generation, at a high enough rate, is enough. By focusing on the person *receiving* the inheritance rather than on the estate itself, inheritance taxes get the focus right in terms of the democracy-of-opportunity tradition: What is important, as Jefferson argued, is that wealth be dispersed anew each generation, rather than concentrated in the hands of a few.[155] For heirs, inheritance is a form of income—one that Congress has simply not yet exercised its Sixteenth Amendment power to tax. To find a constitutional excuse to strike down an inheritance tax would require truly breathtaking violations of the norms of judicial craft.

There are other strategies worthy of consideration, such as ending the indefensible step-up in basis at death rule, or reshaping corporate taxes to more effectively tax wealth or rents.[156] What matters most for our purposes here is not the precise contours of the new policy, but rather the constitutional point: If Congress chooses a wealth tax, and even if it chooses a more circuitous route to the same goal, it must formulate alongside its policy a strategy for confronting hostile judges on the field of constitutional political economy.

The project of taxing concentrations of wealth—and using the money to rebuild the foundations of a democracy of opportunity for all the people—brings together all three threads of the tradition that is the focus of this book. But tax is far from the only area of public law where this is possible. Taxation is a powerful tool, but there is no reason in the twenty-first century to hew to the late twentieth-century neoliberal axiom that taxes and transfers are the best (or only) way that public choices should shape our mutual economic life. Building a democracy of opportunity has always required more than this. The recent and highly public collapse of a number of central neoliberal economic axioms provides an opportunity, not yet realized, to rethink the political and economic rules at the heart of our constitutional order.

The Power to Shape Our Political Economy:
Antitrust, Ownership, and Democracy

The assumptions and axioms with which this chapter began—the independence of economics from politics, the independence of constitutional law from politics—have become impossible to sustain. But what will take their place? The idea of a Court-led constitutionalism separate from politics, setting neutral boundaries for politics, is impossible to square with the reality of a Supreme Court lurching to the right, with many decisions breaking precisely along party lines, with judicial appointments at the very center of national Republican Party politics. Meanwhile, when society confronts a true economic crisis—such as the Great Recession of 2008–2010 or the coronavirus pandemic of 2020–2021—a variety of what were ostensibly apolitical, scientific economic rules and constraints turn out to have been political choices.

For instance, it turns out that trillions of dollars of federal deficit spending, which each of these emergencies prompted, does not always lead to runaway inflation. It turns out that it was economically possible, at least during a moment of crisis, for the country to conduct a first experiment in providing all Americans a flat general payment akin to a basic income from the federal government.[157] And most importantly, it turns out that the question of which firms and which individuals will have to weather crises on their own, and which ones will be buoyed by a substantial cushion of government support that amounts to social insurance, is a political question. Like the shape of antitrust law, the rules of corporate governance, and the contours of monetary policy—all of which this section will briefly discuss—the question of which risks must be socialized and which must be borne by individuals and firms is a political choice. In each of these areas, the best choices cannot be deduced through value-free applications of economic science. They are choices we make through constitutional politics.

RACE, RISK, AND SOCIAL INSURANCE: THE STORY OF THE PPP

The reach of social insurance—the fundamental question of which risks which parties must bear on their own, and which we bear together as a society—is a core question of constitutional political economy. In the 2020–2021 coronavirus pandemic, Congress decided that the federal government ought to bear a large share of the pandemic's enormous economic cost, and therefore enacted a blast of one-time payments, increased unemployment benefits, and child credits that together made a large difference in the lives of ordinary Americans. Widely mislabeled as macroeconomic "stimulus," this national disaster relief program was not about the management of supply and demand (and indeed was larger and less targeted than some prominent centrist macroeconomists preferred).[158] It was a political response to widespread economic dislocation, and its simple, near-universal approach (generally excluding only the highest earners) greatly reduced poverty, in all racial groups, without being specifically targeted at the poor.[159]

When it came to the protection of firms rather than individuals, Congress approached the problem differently, delegating many of the most critical decisions to the least democratic, most expert-driven of economic policy-making institutions: the Federal Reserve. The result was a macroeconomic success. The Fed bought mountains of corporate debt to protect companies' ability to borrow, keeping many solvent.[160] The Paycheck Protection Program (PPP), enacted by Congress as part of the CARES Act, offered large grants in the form of forgivable loans to businesses so that they could pay their employees and other expenses during the pandemic—a lifeline for many businesses and millions of workers.[161]

From a different perspective, this particular program was a disaster—and an illustrative one. Capped at $350 billion, the PPP aimed to push funds out the door to businesses with five hundred or fewer employees that needed funds to stay solvent. But in fact, while some not-so-small businesses obtained funds quickly and easily, smaller businesses and in particular minority-owned businesses got very little money, and an enormous number had to cease operations. From February to March 2020, the number of white-owned businesses declined by 17 percent nationwide, but the number of Hispanic-owned businesses fell by 32 percent and the number of Black-owned businesses fell by 41 percent.[162]

Observers of this collapse, and of how the PPP may have exacerbated its startling racial skew, cite a variety of factors, all of them race-neutral in the cramped constitutional vocabulary of modern equal protection law. Minority-owned businesses are on average smaller than white-owned businesses, and the program's fee structure presented a bigger barrier to the smallest businesses. A higher percentage of minority-owned businesses have no employees, and although Congress explicitly made such businesses eligible for PPP funds, the Fed set up one application process for firms with employees and a second one, which opened a week later, for firms with no employees; by the time the Fed opened the doors for the latter group, the PPP funds were almost entirely exhausted. Minority-owned businesses are considerably less likely than white-owned businesses to bank with large national banks; they are more likely, instead, either to bank with smaller community financial institutions or to have no traditional banking relationships. The Fed rolled out the PPP through federally regulated banks, and many of the banks imposed "gating" requirements that prioritized businesses with whom they had existing banking relationships. Given the cap on total PPP funds, firms with stronger existing banking relationships with larger financial institutions got the lion's share of the funds before anyone else's claims were processed. About a quarter of all the funds ended up going to the top 1 percent of borrowers.[163] (Finally, the PPP expressly excluded borrowers with past felony convictions—and, for good measure, people who have been charged with a crime but not yet tried or convicted. The racial impact of that sort of exclusion is obvious in the United States.)[164] The federal courts, for their part, intervened little in the PPP rollout. But litigation in federal court did block the distribution of some of the funds in a tiny program in Oregon earmarked for Black-owned small businesses, because *that,* according to the Court's Constitution, likely posed an equal protection problem.[165]

The striking thing about the example of the PPP is that this program was aimed at helping small businesses. It was not a program designed to increase inequality and hollow out entrepreneurial opportunity by giving more money to larger and better-financed firms, nor was it designed to worsen long-term problems of racial exclusion by excluding the vast majority of minority-owned businesses from obtaining funds. But it did all those things, and it did them for predictable structural reasons. In this way, the PPP is emblematic of a lot of choices elites have made over the past half century about how to structure our economic life.

THE CONSTITUTIONAL POLITICAL ECONOMY OF ANTITRUST

Americans seem to retain a deep attachment to the idea of the entrepreneurial small business, the family business, the family farm, and generally the idea of an open marketplace with numerous competitors and low barriers to entry. This attachment makes sense in terms of the democracy-of-opportunity tradition: this sort of marketplace is one ingredient in a political economy with widespread economic opportunity and mobility—and one in which political and economic power are widely dispersed, rather than concentrated in a few hands.

However, since the 1970s, Americans have built something quite different: a monopolistic, winner-take-all economy in which most sectors are dominated by a small number of firms, and entrepreneurial activity is at an all-time low.[166] We have done this through antitrust policy, corporate law, tax and monetary policy, the deregulation of lobbying and campaign finance, and many other areas of public law. Usually, our first step toward making our disastrously bad choices has been to forget or cast aside the constitutional principles that once undergirded these areas of regulation, back when we understood each of them to be a domain of constitutional political economy. Instead, we reconceptualized these domains as technocratic spheres of economic policy best insulated from democratic meddling. We entrusted them to the ostensibly apolitical and value-neutral expertise of economic technocrats.

Liberals since the 1970s have been particularly eager to reallocate power in this way. We saw one key chapter in that story in Chapter 8, when President Carter rejected Coretta Scott King's movement for full employment and instead sided with his administration's economists. Business interests and conservatives have never followed liberals quite so far down the road toward deference to the economics profession. Instead, they have, through a range of channels, found ways to buy influence over the technocracy: creating and funding think tanks; engaging in direct lobbying; and creating a revolving door of lucrative private firm work for former government regulators of policy areas such as antitrust—for regulators, that is, who can find their way to allowing the largest and most powerful firms to merge repeatedly with their competitors, and turn a blind eye toward other forms of predatory behavior.[167]

Antitrust law provides a particularly sharp distillation of what happened when we abandoned the democracy-of-opportunity tradition, and what might be gained by reviving it. This area of law began, as we have seen, as a quintessential domain of constitutional political economy.[168] For the antimonopoly movement in the Gilded Age, as for Republicans like Senator John Sherman (of the foundational Sherman Act), and for Louis Brandeis in the Progressive Era, the purpose of antitrust was to preserve a democratic republican constitutional order, one in which no single economic actor would be sufficiently powerful to crush competition or direct the power of the state to its own ends. Economic decentralization, competition, and businesses operating at a more human scale were essential to economic liberty and to democratic citizenship; they were an essential part of a broader project of preventing private domination and oligarchy. Brandeis urged Americans to see the "contradiction" between "our grand political liberty" and "industrial slavery": "Either political liberty will be extinguished or industrial liberty must be restored."[169]

With New Dealers like Thurman Arnold, we saw antitrust make its peace with "bigness," take a more modern, administrative turn, and begin to speak and reason in a more technical institutionalist-economics key. But New Deal antitrust policy under Arnold still took its bearings from the old precepts, monitoring the entire corporate landscape, bringing hundreds of indictments, and restructuring scores of industries, in an effort to thwart oligarchy and maintain a democracy of opportunity. We heard Justice William O. Douglas condemn the "growth of monopoly power" in steel, declaring that "[p]ower that controls the economy should be in the hands of elected representatives of the people, not . . . an industrial oligarchy."[170] When a majority of the Court demurred from this outlook, we saw that Congress responded as it had in the past—by amending the antitrust law with the Anti-Merger Act of 1950 (the Celler–Kefauver Act) to push back against monopoly capital and restore something more of the constitutional political economy of the framers of antitrust.[171] The problem with such concentrations of power as U.S. Steel was a classic problem of political economy: it was as much a problem for democracy as a problem for entrepreneurial competition.

But somehow, in the 1980s, with the help of the Reagan Justice Department, Robert Bork and his allies in what came to be called the Chicago School managed to convince judges and regulators to discard this entire tradition of antitrust thought. Instead, Bork argued (without much evidence) that the purpose of the Sherman Act was to promote "consumer welfare"—and that therefore, the only time antitrust law should enjoin mergers is when those mergers would cause higher consumer prices.[172] This view read backward into the Sherman Act an entire vision of economic well-being that was very 1980s rather than 1890s: a vision in which the real interests of Americans are our interests as consumers, not as producers, and certainly not as citizens. Bork's triumph helped spur rising economic concentration in many different sectors of the U.S. economy in the decades since. It led regulators to excuse monopolies' predatory behavior toward competitors as long as they kept consumer prices low. As in the first Gilded Age, the rise of monopoly has made some people very rich. It also seems to have been a significant factor contributing to the sharp decrease in the share of our economic output that is actually paid out to workers—and to the meteoric rise in inequality overall.[173]

From the start, there were important dissenting voices challenging this reimagining of antitrust as myopically focused on "consumer welfare."[174] But today, with monopoly itself and the concentrations of wealth and plutocratic power that it fuels reaching Gilded Age levels, a full-fledged movement is emerging to reconsider how we do antitrust and to advocate a return to a more Brandeisian conception of what antitrust law is about.[175] This means recovering the idea of antitrust as an intervention in political economy. Antitrust is a mechanism—not the only one, but a very important one—of blocking the concentration of too much economic and political power in too few hands. A decentralized economy full of smaller, independent enterprises rather than one dominated by large monopolies is valuable for reasons wholly distinct from consumer welfare: it helps prevent anyone or any one company from accumulating the sort of privileged position that gives it excessive and undemocratic power over others, either economically or politically or both. This way of thinking draws on the rich antimonopoly tradition in American constitutional thought from a century ago, and back through that tradition all the way to Jefferson.[176]

The point is not competition for its own sake. As Zephyr Teachout and Lina Khan argue, "Excessive corporate size tends to hurt democratic self-government because it enables a handful of actors to purchase disproportionate political power and to subject citizens to systems of private governance that become less accountable the bigger and fewer the corporations."[177] The neo-Brandeisians are beginning to mark out the path to a crucial old Brandeisian idea: that antitrust law is "constitutional" in nature.[178] If we want to maintain a constitutional democracy, we have to limit the convertibility of economic power into political power and vice versa, and we have to limit concentrations of both. We also have to limit the reach of private forms of regulation and private "government" over the lives of Americans—a core Brandeisian insight, which one need not be a neo-Brandeisian to appreciate.[179]

As we write these words, President Biden is installing key architects of the neo-Brandeisian turn, including Lina Khan and Tim Wu, in key administrative roles in antitrust and competition policy, and he is beginning to empower them through executive orders.[180] In the coming years it seems certain that some of the new enforcement efforts will be challenged in court, and these fights over antitrust and competition policy will likely draw in all three branches. This makes it all the more important to understand the stakes of reconceptualizing antitrust in anti-oligarchy terms. It is not simply a question of how much or how little enforcement; it is a question of what this body of law and regulation is there to do. An antitrust law focused on oligarchy would be far less tolerant of mergers, and far more likely to break up monopolies and oligopolies, than the antitrust law of recent decades. It would be a body of law considerably less confident in government's long-run ability to impose behavioral conditions on companies (a common substitute today for blocking mergers or breaking up monopolies), in part on the grounds that regulators do not sit outside of the economy, regulating it, but are instead necessarily part of our constitutional political economy, and are inevitably affected by the kinds of enterprises we decide to foster. An anti-oligarchy antitrust law would be much less inclined to grant a blanket exemption from antitrust to all political activity (the Noerr-Pennington doctrine).[181] Much political activity by corporations in concert with one another may be acceptable to antitrust law, but anti-trust law should step in when the collective political activity is an attempt to capture the power of the state for private ends—exactly the kind of conversion of economic into political power at the constitutional core of what antitrust condemns.

Of course, antitrust, by itself, cannot cultivate a landscape of firms well suited to a democratic political economy for the twenty-first century. Nor did Brandeis or other sophisticated Progressives believe it could at the dawn of the last century. A leading firm in a given industry might have the attributes of what the Progressive economist H. C. Adams, whom we met in Chapter 4, dubbed a "natural monopoly" that supplies some important public good or infrastructure (Adams was thinking of railroads, but think today of Google, or broadband internet).[182] Progressive state-builders argued that such a firm ought not be broken up in the name of competition, but could and should be owned directly by government, or regulated and run as a public utility.[183] Public utilities can also usefully compete alongside private firms, preventing the development of monopolies by providing a baseline of service to all.[184] But even leaving public utilities aside, there is more to competition policy than antitrust. Rebuilding a political economy in which economic and political power are widely dispersed instead of concentrated means curbing a wide array of oligopolistic practices in different industries where a few firms have outsized power. It means curbing employment practices such as the noncompete agreements many employers demand from workers by contract. It means curbing the power of agribusiness giants to govern and control the actions of the small producers who have become far too subordinate to and dependent on the giants.[185]

There are also areas where antitrust law in the anti-oligarchy tradition would be *much less* activist than current law—especially labor. Since the 1970s, antitrust law has once again proved unremittingly hostile to various forms of labor organizing.[186] For example, under current law, workers who are not deemed to be employees but instead are treated as "independent contractors" face potential antitrust liability if they attempt to organize and exert some collective control over the terms and conditions under which they work. (*Employees* are exempt from such liability because of the "labor exemption" in antitrust law, which labor won in the Norris–La Guardia Act in 1932.)[187] To understand this, imagine that each Uber driver were an independent firm, and they banded together to press Uber for higher wages. This would look to current antitrust law like a kind of price-fixing agreement among firms. Amazingly, it is not Uber but instead Uber drivers—along with home health aides and gig workers of all kinds—who currently face potential antitrust scrutiny.[188] As antitrust expert Sandeep Vaheesan summarizes, "Even as antitrust law permits monopolies and oligopolies to dominate the economy, it is used to thwart the efforts of many American workers to build countervailing power."[189] If anything should be drawing antitrust scrutiny here, it is not the efforts at coordination among gig workers, but the efforts of large firms to control the details of the work of these so-called independent contractors.[190]

As labor and antitrust scholar Sanjukta Paul argues, antitrust law should be asking the question of which actors ought to have "coordination rights" in terms of market power: if you have lots of market power, your cooperation and coordination with others deserves careful scrutiny as cartel-like, anticompetitive behavior. But if you have very little market power and are at the mercy of some other economic actor, similar cooperation with others looks much more like traditional labor or agrarian organizing.[191] This idea is at the center of the project of bringing antitrust back to its roots in constitutional political economy. Many of the lawmakers who created antitrust law in the first place worried about (and hoped to avoid) its misapplication to farmers and workers who ought to have the right to coordinate.[192] Farmers today who are stuck with one monopolist to sell them their seeds or buy their chickens are exactly the kind of dispersed, largely powerless economic actors that antitrust law, if returned to its anti-oligarchy roots, would aim to aid rather than attack.[193]

Progressive proponents of these new ways of thinking about antitrust (most of which are not really new) are fooling themselves if they believe business interests will accept new regulatory and congressional action in this area without a constitutional fight. Although it will require them to make some novel arguments, the stakes are too high for business interests—especially those sitting comfortably on cushy monopoly rents—not to try making them. Businesses will find ways to argue, for instance, that limiting Noerr-Pennington violates corporations' First Amendment rights, or even that treating home health aides' organizing differently from oligopolists' price-fixing somehow violates the equal protection of the laws. They will find ways to claim that antitrust regulators are taking their property, improperly invalidating bargained-for contracts with suppliers or employees, or in some way exceeding constitutional limits on federal power. Some of these arguments will sound thoroughly Lochnerian, while others will repackage the old arguments in new ways. Whatever the precise shape of the arguments, if monopolists lose in Congress and in the Department of Justice, we should expect to see constitutional fights in court.

The constitutional arguments will, as ever, take place inside and outside the courts at the same time, and will cross the membrane separating the two. That is a central reason why we need to reinvent progressive constitutional political economy. We need to rekindle the once-familiar principle that constitutional democracy requires an underlying political economy that is democratic rather than oligarchic. That insight is at the heart of why we have antitrust law. It ought to shape antitrust law. The same is true of corporate law and how we regulate the ownership and control of firms.

THE CONSTITUTIONAL POLITICAL ECONOMY OF CORPORATE LAW

The path of American corporate law has been broadly similar to the trajectory of antitrust: over time, and especially since the 1980s, a relatively pluralistic and contested conception of whose interests corporations must serve has given way to a more streamlined and economics-inflected view that corporations exist exclusively to maximize the returns to their shareholders or owners.[194] From this perspective, if a corporation can return even slightly more value to shareholders through a stock buyback than through a strategy involving more investment and wages, its obligation is to pursue the stock buyback. This narrowing of the set of stakeholders to whom corporations are responsible was a slow process, intertwined with the declining power of labor to exert its own claims on corporations.

The shareholder-value endpoint we have now reached might have surprised the architects of early American corporate law. In the early republic, as we have seen, the prevailing view, reflected in statutes and common law, was that corporations were "artificial persons," chartered to serve public purposes and in need of being supervised and held to account by legislatures and courts. The Jacksonians' democratization of access to the corporate form via general incorporation statutes loosened these public-purpose constraints, even while Jacksonian constitutional political economy and common law remained focused on the perils of concentrated economic power. Thus, the classical outlook that big corporations were artificial agglomerations of power, "adverse to the spirit of republicanism,"[195] remained active in state common law and constitutional doctrine well into the Gilded Age. Then, as we saw in Chapter 5, the doctrinal carriers of these ideas were derailed by a corporate bar and bench with new ideas about corporate personhood and the "inevitability of bigness."[196] The New Deal ushered in an era of institutional economics and corporate-law thinking that emphasized the plurality of stakeholders to whom corporations ought to be accountable, until this was derailed, in turn, by the rise of a Chicago School brand of law and economics riveted on shareholder value, much as Chicago School antitrust was riveted on consumer welfare. So, today, the idea that corporations have obligations to do anything other than maximize shareholder value has largely been lost, outside of a relatively small number of corporations that are either owned by their employees or specially chartered as benefit corporations under state law.[197]

There is nothing inevitable about this. One potential answer to the challenge lies in corporate governance. In Germany, employees elect up to half the directors of corporations, an arrangement known as co-determination that arose out of battles waged by social-democratic unions and was first lodged in collective bargaining agreements but is now codified in federal law and required of all corporations with large numbers of employees.[198] Senator Elizabeth Warren has proposed legislation to institute a similar requirement in the United States.[199] This proposal would revive an old idea we saw Theodore Roosevelt champion: requiring the largest corporations to obtain federal rather than state charters. The terms of the charters would specify that, like benefit corporations, these large corporations must "consider the interests of all corporate stakeholders—including employees, customers, shareholders, and the communities in which the company operates."[200] Employees would elect 40 percent of the seats on boards of directors.[201]

Regardless of what precise form it takes, any effort to modify U.S. corporate law in this direction will face inevitable constitutional challenge. Some conservative commentators already argue that mandating codetermination would violate the Takings Clause of the Fifth Amendment.[202] Others will argue that the federal preemption of so much state corporate law violates structural principles of federalism.[203] Or perhaps that the law violates the First Amendment rights of corporations by giving employees an effective veto over corporate speech. At the bottom of these arguments will be an objection to the sea change in constitutional political economy that would be wrought if codetermination gave workers a significant role in shaping the goals and policies of the companies they work for.[204]

The most powerful answer to such constitutional political economy arguments is not to claim the Constitution is indifferent, and gives Congress broad powers in this sphere, but rather to reply with stronger constitutional political economy arguments. In court, to be sure, the simpler line may be to use doctrine and precedent to push back against conservative objections. But constitutional law is not made only in court. Both inside and outside the courts,[205] the core argument for codetermination is straightforward. It is that we are choosing to build a regime of corporate governance that is compatible over the long run with democratic government. That was the constitutional argument Progressives like Brandeis and Herbert Croly put forward. There could be no more "political democracy" in contemporary America, we heard Brandeis argue, without workers' "participating in the decisions" of their firms as to "how the business shall be run."[206] Wagner and the other architects of New Deal political economy made the same point. Much has changed since then. But that much remains true.

ECONOMIC EXPERTISE AND CONSTITUTIONAL
POLITICAL ECONOMY

Remaking American political economy will require revising the division of labor between democratic government and economic expertise,
especially when it comes to fundamental questions of economic regulation such as the policies of the Federal Reserve. At the moment we have
veered quite far in the direction of leaving many of the big choices to
experts, with Congress abdicating much of its role. We saw this in the
PPP episode at the start of this section; it is true of a good deal of the
Fed's work. We have reached a level of democratic dysfunction in which
members of Congress are reduced to writing op-eds urging the Fed to
devote more attention to the impact of its policy choices on Black
people—for instance, to consider the rate of Black unemployment, or to
give state and local governments (which employ a disproportionate share
of Black workers) the same access to emergency credit facilities during
crises as private firms.[207] It is Congress's job to direct the Fed to pursue
such goals, and Congress should do it through legislation and oversight.

To be clear, we agree with the mainstream view that economic expertise has a central role to play in formulating policies like those of the
Fed. Economics has advanced a great deal since the last Gilded Age. But
setting policy goals is no more value-neutral now than it was then. It
remains inevitably and fundamentally political. And here, the elected
branches have largely abdicated their role. When the anti–New Deal
Dixiecrats and conservative Republicans joined hands to gut the administration's Full Employment Bill and replace it with the Employment
Act of 1946, they allowed one nontrivial trace of the original measure to
remain, charging the Fed to attend to labor markets and unemployment
levels as well as the rate of inflation.[208] The struggling middle class in
general, and Black and Hispanic workers in particular, benefit when the
Fed chooses to prioritize full employment over worries about inflation.
It is only when we approach full employment that the most marginal
workers, who are often the victims of discrimination, are likely to find
decent jobs.

That is a public choice. It is not a technical optimization problem that
can be solved using scientific tools alone. And in truth, the same can be

said of much of monetary policy. The tools are complex and technical. But the *aims*, the major policy choices, are choices about constitutional political economy. This is a truth Americans once understood in our bones. Americans knew that choices about currency, credit, and central banking were, at bottom, choices about the distribution of wealth, power, and opportunity and the kind of nation the Constitution requires that our government promote and redeem. So, we built American monetary policy through bare-knuckled constitutional politics, from the Jacksonians' vehement opposition to the constitutionality of paper money to the Populist conviction that the Constitution prohibited crucifying the nation on a cross of gold.[209] These political movements may have been quite wrong about the effects of the monetary policies they sought. (They can hardly have both been entirely right!) And yet, they both were right about something fundamental: that the choices we make in this sphere are choices about constitutional political economy.

As legal historian Christine Desan has demonstrated, money is not something that exists prior to the state.[210] Some of the most important choices we make about the trajectory of our political economy are choices about which economic entities we will license (and in what way we will license them) to create money on top of the constitutional foundation on which all our money rests: the full faith and credit of the United States.[211]

This way of framing the choices may seem unfamiliar. Today, we are accustomed to thinking of monetary policy as simply a matter of experts at the Fed dialing their target interest rates up and down to respond to economic phenomena like the business cycle. It takes a crisis like the Great Recession or the coronavirus pandemic to expose the full richness of the policy choices we did not realize we were making. It takes disasters like the PPP to begin to see how much we are choosing to make that ultimate constitutional monetary backstop—the full faith and credit of the United States—available to some and not others, mostly in ways that promote concentrations of wealth or exacerbate patterns of race-based exclusion rather than building a democracy of opportunity.

This is a truth that the Populists understood well, as they watched the credit of the United States gush through the financial institutions of New York to the manufacturers of the Northeast, even as it trickled or ran dry before it reached farmers in the hinterland.[212] Today, the wealth-concentrating results of PPP and the early pandemic response have helped build new public pressure for public banks. Such banks would compete with private banks and provide credit (and other banking functions) to local governments, businesses, and individuals in a way that self-consciously aims to promote a more broadly democratic political economy.[213] This sort of "public option" for banking exists today in extremely limited form.[214] But it could greatly expand if Congress chose to give new public banks access to funding through the Federal Reserve.[215] The promise of public banking is that the people, through their representatives, can direct these banks to promote racial inclusion, preserve access to the middle class, build up ill-served, hard-hit regions, and avoid capture by economic oligarchy.[216] Such ideas are by now familiar to any reader of this book. Each of the three strands of the democracy-of-opportunity tradition puts demands on how we direct the financial institutions and intermediaries that we license to spin money out of the full faith and credit of the United States.[217]

WORK IN A DEMOCRACY OF OPPORTUNITY

There are always problems of translation in adapting an American constitutional tradition like the democracy-of-opportunity tradition to the new circumstances of one's time. When a nation of small producers became a nation of employees, old ideas of how to build a mass middle class and secure its political and economic power gave way to new ideas, including the constitutional projects of building social insurance and labor law. Today, good jobs and even the employment relationship itself are becoming less widespread and more tenuous. Technological fears—fears that there might not be good jobs to replace those lost to automation—are prompting calls from some quarters for a universal basic income (UBI), which is getting more public attention now than in its last moment in the sun in the late 1960s.[218]

The tradition we have described in this book offers good reasons for skepticism about the UBI as a plausible *substitute* for decent remunerative work, which continues to play a central role in most Americans' conception of what it is to live a useful, meaningful life. When we frame the problem in political economy terms, the number and type of jobs that exist is not an exogenous, technologically determined fact. It is a function of political choices. There are enormous human needs, especially in areas such as childcare and early education, elder care, and health care, that would provide enormous numbers of good jobs if we chose to allocate public resources and enact laws for meeting those needs in ways that match the work's social value—and if we make it possible for workers to gain robust bargaining power in what are now highly exploitive sectors of the low-wage labor market. The same is true of investments in infrastructure, where our nation lags its peers. The jobs created in these areas would be "good jobs" to the extent that the bargaining power of the workers involved, including their political power, was sufficient to make the pay and working conditions commensurate with a middle-class life.

And yet a UBI may be a good idea anyway. It can be viewed as a strategy for increasing workers' bargaining power. It alters the political economy of low-wage work by making workers less dependent. Greatly expanded income supports for the poor would do similar work, as would universal benefits for health care and higher education—still better if all of it is funded with taxes that fall most heavily on concentrations of wealth. In addition, as labor law scholar Cindy Estlund argues, if we want more Americans to have access to decent remunerative work, a decent income or livelihood, *and* more time for pursuits other than work, we should combine these two kinds of intervention with a third: policies aimed at spreading out work among more people—including policies to improve retirement security, paid leave, and vacations.[219] There is much that the federal government could do, through spending and regulation, to move the economy in this direction. Indeed, it may be the only level of government with the resources to invest on the scale required. These are among the most important and potentially the most transformative policy planks a future progressive majority might enact.

Perhaps we can argue that these are good policy and leave it at that, leaving on the table the deep connections between these policies and the democracy-of-opportunity tradition. Perhaps liberal majorities in the elected branches will enact all of these policies, transforming American political economy, and there will be no constitutional fight about them whatsoever. Not a peep about the unconstitutionality of any of it in the halls of Congress. No trial balloons of novel constitutional arguments floated in Republican political circles, aimed at finding their way into court. No fringe, "off-the-wall" legal theories attacking these new statutes' constitutionality, which slowly gain acceptance among conservative politicians and then judges.[220] Perhaps any challenges to these laws that reach the Supreme Court will be swatted back unanimously, as the justices uphold them as applications of Congress's four great powers: to tax, to spend, to regulate commerce, and to enforce the Reconstruction Amendments.[221] That is to say, perhaps conservative political and legal actors will decide to obey the "New Deal settlement" that liberals so frequently mention, and imagine settled so much. It could happen.

But let's be serious. It won't. If we have learned anything from the past several decades of conservative constitutional activism, it is this: Constitutional political economy is alive and well on the right. When you enact major changes to our political economy that would greatly augment workers' power, or greatly increase the reach of taxes and social insurance, or greatly diminish the convertibility of wealth into political power that is so central to the machinery of the modern Republican Party, there is absolutely no way to keep the Constitution out of the story. The only question is whether the Constitution will come in on one side only, in the service of a deregulatory, anti-redistributive vision of constitutional political economy, or whether the democracy-of-opportunity tradition, too, will be heard.

Coda: The Democracy of Opportunity as a Partisan Cause

If there was one movement in the story we have told in this book that brought together the three strands of the democracy-of-opportunity tradition to strike at the foundations of our political-economic order, it was the Radical Republicans, the so-called Black Republicans, during Reconstruction. Their approach to constitutional political economy was unabashedly partisan. Like some of their Democratic forebears, they saw their Republican Party as the party of the Constitution, and they deliberately altered the American political system to build bulwarks of Republican Party power in order to ensure that the constitutional change they sought would actually take place.[222] Some of these bulwarks are still with us today. (For instance, consider the otherwise inexplicable fact that we have two Dakotas. The point was to ensure two additional Republican senators. Although sadly, by the time this was accomplished, the Republicans had morphed from the party of Reconstruction to the party of big business and its skewed version of economic nationalism.)

After Reconstruction's collapse, and through the entire twentieth century, there was no major party that brought together all three strands of the democracy-of-opportunity tradition. For much of the first half of the twentieth century, the Democrats brought together the anti-oligarchy idea and the need to build a broad and open middle class. But their coalition also included the champions of Jim Crow.

That story actually offers a modest reason for hope. As we write this book, the discourse of constitutional political economy remains largely dormant. But we are beginning to hear renewed talk of the problem of oligarchy, as well as the problem of racial exclusion. What makes our time different—what begins to offer the reason for hope—is that for the first time since Reconstruction, there is actually a political party that might bring all three strands together at the center of its political program. It is the Democratic Party, no longer anchored in the reactionary precincts of the white South. Whether or not the Democratic Party will advance a vision of constitutional politics in the democracy-of-opportunity tradition is history not yet written. There are other versions of the future in which it is a new party, or even a completely transfigured Republican Party, that adapts the core commitments of the anti-oligarchy Constitution for our time. But those latter scenarios require radical transformations of the current configuration of the parties—scenarios that presently seem extremely remote. So, for the moment, let us assume it is the Democrats.

If the Democratic Party succeeds in enacting substantial legislation aimed at building a new, multiracial democracy of opportunity, of the kind this chapter has discussed, it may well face a judiciary as hostile to such legislation as any the nation has seen since 1933. This tough fact will prompt some liberals and progressives to disdain the Constitution, to view all talk of the Constitution as essentially deradicalizing, demobilizing talk that cedes power to jurispathic courts.[223]

But just the opposite is true. It is the failure to speak about the Constitution in politics, an insistence on treating it as a thing outside of politics, setting the boundaries of politics, that cedes power to the courts. And more often than not, over the long arc of American history, courts have used their power to protect economic and political oligarchy.

What progressives must do instead is expose the fact that there is such a thing as constitutional politics. We are all engaged in it: progressives and conservatives, judges and legislators, commentators and protesters, those deeply knowledgeable about legal doctrine and those completely unschooled in it. When we make arguments about the Constitution, we do not cede all authority to courts. Instead, by making claims on the Constitution, we show that there is no judicial monopoly on the authority to engage in this fundamental democratic activity.

Today, in our polarized times, judicial confirmation battles are beginning to make the stakes of constitutional politics obvious, even to the liberals most attached to the old axioms. There is a clash of constitutional visions occurring among those senators, even as the nominees themselves pursue their script of silent refusal to engage. The next step is understanding that it is not just about judicial confirmation battles, and not just about courts: There is a tight continuity between those familiar fights and the broader ones in our polity over the future of American constitutional political economy. These fights are often partisan, even bitterly so, but they are constitutional fights.

In order to win them, the Democrats will also need to pursue structural reforms of our political system—particularly its most antidemocratic features, such as the U.S. Senate and the Electoral College. Here Democrats will take up the project of constitutional renewal that Republicans undertook during Reconstruction and Progressives embarked on at the beginning of the twentieth century. And for the same reason: the structural tilt of institutions like these are indefensible barriers to building the kind of twenty-first-century democracy of opportunity our Constitution requires. Thus, for example, like Republicans prodigiously adding states over a century ago, Democrats will likely need to use any partisan leverage they can find to deliver the admission of new states including Washington, D.C.

Critics will attack such moves as distortions of the constitutional system for partisan ends. They are the opposite. They are structural reforms that Democrats must undertake in order to build a democracy of opportunity in our time. To reform our constitutional order to vindicate its underlying principles is no contradiction. The underlying principles remain what the Bible-quoting Abraham Lincoln called them: the "apple of gold," whereas the Constitution is a *"picture of silver,* subsequently framed around it."[224] For Lincoln, the underlying principles, which he located in the Declaration of Independence, are the real lodestar. The Constitution is "made *for*" those ideals, not the other way around.[225] We have inherited a constitutional order with many pathologies, but with some core principles and ideals that are well worth defending and promoting—even when that requires significant structural change to the constitutional order itself.

These struggles are as old as the nation. Arguing about constitutional political economy is something Americans have always done. If and when progressives recover this idea, we will be able to make much more effective use of the rich tradition this book has traced, which has aimed over time, through many setbacks and challenges, to dismantle oligarchy and construct a democracy of opportunity in the United States.

NOTES

Introduction

1. The most prominent such voice, but certainly not the only one, has been Senator Bernie Sanders, whose two presidential runs have brought considerable attention to this word and idea.

2. Jack Balkin argues that this sort of judicial entrenchment is common at the tail end of a political-constitutional regime—in this case, the long regime that began with Ronald Reagan's presidency. *See* Jack M. Balkin, The Cycles of Constitutional Time 81–96 (2020).

3. We discuss this sea change in Chapter 8. *See* "Economics Supplants Political Economy," Chapter 8.

4. We discuss this asymmetry in Chapter 7; in "The Collapse of Labor and the Rise of a New Oligarchy," Chapter 8; and at the start of Chapter 9.

5. In spring 2021, the White House convened a commission to study the prospects of "reforming" the Supreme Court. This political gesture had an ambiguous relationship to the more controversial calls among progressives to expand (or "pack") the Court to change its balance of power. We will discuss the question of lawmakers' options in confronting hostile courts, which are not limited to expanding the Court, in Chapter 9. *See* "Constitutional Arguments in the Face of Hostile Courts," Chapter 9.

6. Franklin D. Roosevelt, Acceptance of the Renomination for the Presidency, 5 Pub. Papers 230, 232–34 (June 27, 1936). You can read more about this speech and about FDR's role in the democracy-of-opportunity tradition in Chapter 6.

7. The relationship between this third principle of inclusion to the rest of the tradition is more complex, as we discuss below.

8. Constitutional politics in this sense plays an especially important role in our political life because it helps to legitimate, as well as shape, the constitutional order. *See* Jack M. Balkin, Living Originalism 69–73 (2011); Robert C. Post & Reva B. Siegel, *Democratic Constitutionalism, in* The Constitution in 2020, at 25–28 (Jack M. Balkin & Reva B. Siegel eds., 2009).

9. *See* John Fabian Witt, Patriots and Cosmopolitans: Hidden Histories of American Law 1–12 (2007).

10. *See id.; see also* Paul W. Kahn, *The Constitution and United States' Culture, in* Oxford Handbook of the U.S. Constitution (Mark Tushnet, Mark A. Graber, & Sanford Levinson, eds., 2015); William E. Forbath, *Constitutionalism, Human Rights and the Genealogy of Jewish American Liberalism, in* The Law of Strangers: Jewish Lawyering and International Legal Thought in Historical Perspective (James Loeffler & Moria Paz eds. 2019).

11. This was the narrative around which the new immigrants of the 1890s–1910s from the peripheries of Europe hammered out their claims to Americanness: the true American is not the

"old stock" American by descent but the newcomer, the American by active consent, replenishing the nation's liberal ideals and contributing to the ever-new "race" of an immigrant nation. *See* Forbath, *Constitutionalism, Human Rights and the Genealogy of Jewish American Liberalism.*

12. *See, e.g.,* ROGERS M. SMITH, CIVIC IDEALS (1997).

13. The apotheosis of this vision can be found in Dred Scott v. Sandford, 60 U.S. 393, 407 (1857) (stating that neither "slaves, nor their descendants, whether they had become free or not" were acknowledged by the Constitution "as a part of the people"—and holding as a constitutional matter that Blacks had "no rights which the white man was bound to respect").

14. *See* Rick Perlstein, *I Thought I Understood the American Right. Trump Proved Me Wrong,* N.Y. TIMES MAG., Apr. 11, 2017.

15. *See* CASS R. SUNSTEIN, THE SECOND BILL OF RIGHTS: FDR'S UNFINISHED REVOLUTION AND WHY WE NEED IT MORE THAN EVER 62 (2004).

16. *See* BALKIN, CYCLES OF CONSTITUTIONAL TIME, at 50–53, for a discussion of this premise and its republican roots. It is the economic counterpart of the modern premise that the Constitution is inevitably entwined with—and not neutral with respect to—the nation's *social* order. *See* Jack M. Balkin, *The Constitution of Status,* 106 YALE L.J. 2313, 2313–14 (1997).

17. For this formulation we are indebted to Jeremy Kessler. *See* Jeremy Kessler, *The Political Economy of "Constitutional Political Economy,"* 94 TEXAS L. REV. 1527, 1529 (2016) ("Fishkin and Forbath's new constitutional history promises to recast the New Deal as a contingent and incomplete resolution of a centuries-long struggle to achieve the political-economic conditions that the Constitution requires . . . in the double sense of 'demands' and 'depends upon.'").

18. There is a certain circularity here: a robust and open middle class both depends on a fair and open opportunity structure and also helps produce and maintain such an opportunity structure. Think of it as a positive feedback loop. The inverse is also true: a collapsing middle class may both result from and fuel a decaying opportunity structure in which ordinary people face severely limited opportunities.

19. Americans' actual opportunities to live middle-class lives matter here because they shape who will have the economic security and independence that, in this tradition, is associated with republican citizenship. Americans' subjective assessments of their own opportunities matter as well, because they shape whether Americans will understand themselves as having that kind of security and independence. For more on why the objective and subjective dimensions of economic opportunity are so deeply intertwined, see JOSEPH FISHKIN, BOTTLENECKS: A NEW THEORY OF EQUAL OPPORTUNITY 200–205 (2014). For our purposes in this book, we are describing a tradition, not a single writer's philosophical argument. More objective and more subjective accounts of what it is to have the opportunity to live a middle-class life can both fit comfortably within that tradition.

20. Lyndon B. Johnson, Commencement Address at Howard University: "To Fulfill These Rights," 2 PUB. PAPERS 636 (June 4, 1965).

21. *See generally* SERENA MAYERI, REASONING FROM RACE: FEMINISM, LAW, AND THE CIVIL RIGHTS REVOLUTION (2011).

22. These words come from a retelling of the story by Martin Van Buren, whose remarkable and influential book we discuss in Chapter 1. *See* MARTIN VAN BUREN, AN INQUIRY INTO THE ORIGIN AND COURSE OF POLITICAL PARTIES IN THE UNITED STATES 214–15 (1867). *See* "The Political Economy of the Birth of Partisanship," Chapter 1.

23. Statement of John Bell (June 8, 1832), 22d Cong., 1st Sess., *in* 8 REGISTER OF DEBATES IN CONGRESS, pt. 3, 3357, 3359. *See* "Jacksonian Equal Protection," Chapter 2.

24. John Quincy Adams, *Report of the Committee on Manufactures* (May 23, 1832), *quoted in* Speech of Hon. Robert M. La Follette, of Wisconsin, in the House of Representatives (June 2, 1886), *in Appendix to the Congressional Record,* 49th Cong., 1st Session, 223, 224. *See* "The 'American System' and the Whig Constitution of Opportunity," Chapter 2.

25. Republican Party Platform of 1856, *available at* https://www.presidency.ucsb.edu/documents /republican-party-platform-1856 [https://perma.cc/SGX5-4XHK]; FORREST A. NABORS, FROM OLIGARCHY TO REPUBLICANISM 62–67 (2017) (quoting Representative George W. Julian, The Homestead Bill (Jan. 29, 1851), *in* GEORGE W. JULIAN, SPEECHES ON POLITICAL QUESTIONS 51–52 (1872)); CONG. GLOBE, 32d Cong., 1st Sess. App., 427 (1852) (Man's Right to the Soil, a speech of Rep. Grow).

26. LEON F. LITWACK, BEEN IN THE STORM SO LONG: THE AFTERMATH OF SLAVERY 149 (1979); *Report of the Joint Committee on Reconstruction,* 39th Cong., 1st Sess., Apr. 30, 1866, viii–ix; LEONARD L. RICHARDS, THE SLAVE POWER: THE FREE NORTH AND SOUTHERN DOMINATION, 1780–1860 (2000); NABORS, FROM OLIGARCHY TO REPUBLICANISM. *See* Chapter 3.

27. CONG. GLOBE, 39th Cong., 1st Sess. 682 (1866). Interestingly, Sumner believed no Fourteenth Amendment was required: the clause guaranteeing a Republican form of government in the states was sufficient, in his view, to give Congress the power to enact this proposed language.

28. 2 HISTORY OF WOMAN SUFFRAGE 635 (Elizabeth Cady Stanton, Susan B. Anthony, & Matilda Joslyn Gage eds., 1882). The quote is from a speech by Susan B. Anthony, who argued that this "hateful oligarchy" offended not only the Reconstruction Amendments but also the textual guarantee of a republican form of government. *See* "The Women's Rights Movement in the Age of Emancipation and Reconstruction," Chapter 3.

29. *Reconstruction; Hon. Thaddeus Stevens on the Great Topic of the Hour: An Address Delivered to the Citizens of Lancaster, Sept. 6, 1865,* N.Y. TIMES, Sept. 10, 1865, at 2 (emphasis added). *See* ERIC FONER, RECONSTRUCTION: AMERICA'S UNFINISHED REVOLUTION 236 (2002).

30. Franklin D. Roosevelt, Acceptance Speech of the Renomination for the Presidency, 5 PUB. PAPERS 230, 234 (June 27, 1936).

31. 21 Cong. Rec. 2461 (1890) (statement of Sen. John Sherman); LOUIS D. BRANDEIS, BUSINESS— A PROFESSION 17 (1914).

32. Racially inclusive movements for a democracy of opportunity reemerged again and again, as we shall see, making claims for racial *and* economic justice on behalf of poor, working-class, and middle-class people of color and whites alike. But it falls to us in the twenty-first century to make this the outlook of a durable majority of Americans, which it has never been. In Chapter 9, we set out why we think the time may be ripe, and what such a constitutional political-economic outlook might look like in the polity and in the courts.

33. *See* "Labor, Populism and the Updating of the Democracy of Opportunity," Chapter 4.

34. *See* "Updating the Democracy of Opportunity—Populist Constitutional Political Economy," Chapter 4.

35. *See* "The Money of the Constitution," Chapter 4.

36. Roosevelt, Acceptance of the Renomination for the Presidency.

37. Franklin D. Roosevelt, Campaign Address on Progressive Government at the Commonwealth Club, 1 PUB. PAPERS 742, 752 (Sept. 23, 1932).

38. Franklin D. Roosevelt, A "Fireside Chat" Discussing the Plan for Reorganization of the Judiciary, 1937 PUB. PAPERS 122, 127 (Mar. 9, 1937).

39. The idea that Americans have reasoned in the past about our Constitution in ways that speak to problems of economic inequality and power—and that we might do so again—is the starting point for a nascent wave of scholarship. One of us has been working on this enterprise for some time. *See, e.g.,* William E. Forbath, *Caste, Class, and Equal Citizenship,* 98 MICH. L. REV. 1 (1999); William E. Forbath, *Social and Economic Rights in the American Grain: Reclaiming Constitutional Political Economy,* in THE CONSTITUTION IN 2020, at 55 (Jack M. Balkin & Reva B. Siegel eds., 2009); William E. Forbath, *The Distributive Constitution and Workers' Rights,* 72 OHIO STATE L.J. 1115 (2011). For the recent wave of scholarship, *see, e.g.,* K. SABEEL RAHMAN, DEMOCRACY AGAINST DOMINATION (2017); AZIZ RANA, THE RISE OF THE CONSTITUTION (forthcoming); GANESH SITARAMAN, THE CRISIS OF THE MIDDLE-CLASS CONSTITUTION (2017); Benjamin Sachs &

Kate Andrias, *Constructing Countervailing Power: Law and Organizing in an Era of Political Inequality,* 130 YALE L.J. 546 (2021). Many of the participants in this conversation participated in a symposium organized by the *Texas Law Review,* part of which focused on an early draft of the manuscript of this book, in January 2016. *See* Symposium on the Constitution and Economic Inequality, 94 Tex. L. Rev. 1287 (2016), *available at* https://texaslawreview.org/wp-content/uploads/2016/09/Symposium-Introduction.pdf [https://perma.cc/QD72-KAHX]. Our initial joint exploration of these themes can be found at Joseph Fishkin & William E. Forbath, *The Anti-Oligarchy Constitution,* 94 B. U. L. REV. 669 (2014).

40. *See* Chapter 9 n.8 (tracing the trajectory of the broccoli argument).

41. *Cf.* Robert C. Post, *Foreword: Fashioning the Legal Constitution: Culture, Courts, and Law,* 117 HARV. L. REV. 4, 9–10 (2003) (discussing "the membrane separating constitutional law from constitutional culture").

42. *See* "Constitutional Arguments in the Face of Hostile Courts," Chapter 9.

43. *See* "After Slavery, What Did Freedom Mean?," Chapter 2.

44. For more about both of the examples sketched here, see "Constitutional Politics, the American Way," Chapter 9.

45. We discuss both of these tectonic shifts in liberal worldviews in Chapter 8. For more on the distinction between political economy and economics, see "The Great Society and the Eclipse of Progressive Political Economy," Chapter 8.

46. We discuss this point in the most depth at the start of Chapter 7; *see also* Chapters 6 and 8.

47. U.S. v. Carolene Products Co., 304 U.S. 144, 152 n.4 (1938).

48. BRUCE ACKERMAN, WE THE PEOPLE, VOLUME 3: THE CIVIL RIGHTS REVOLUTION 105–6 (2014).

49. *See* Chapter 6.

50. The project of inclusion extended beyond race from the beginning. It included an imperative to generate opportunities for the marginalized poor—whites as well as Blacks, poverty-stricken whites being seen as predominantly rural and, like African Americans, excluded from the prosperous industrial economy and the welfare state that had been built around it. And indeed, they *were* often excluded because their geographic and economic circumstances were similar to those of African Americans, in ways that caused them to fall outside the New Deal system by dint of the racialized lines its architects had drawn. *See* Chapter 6.

51. ALAN BRINKLEY, THE END OF REFORM: NEW DEAL LIBERALISM IN RECESSION AND WAR 7 (1995). For further discussion, see "The Slow Triumph of the Technocrats," Chapter 8.

52. *See* "The Taming of the Labor Movement and the Eclipse of Progressive Constitutional Political Economy," Chapter 7; "Poverty, Race, and the Abandonment of Political Economy in the Great Society," Chapter 8.

53. *See* WILLIAM P. JONES, THE MARCH ON WASHINGTON: JOBS, FREEDOM, AND THE FORGOTTEN HISTORY OF CIVIL RIGHTS (2013); William E. Forbath, *Constitutional Welfare Rights: A History, Critique and Reconstruction,* 69 FORDHAM L. REV. 1821, 1842–45 (2001).

54. Barack Obama, *A More Perfect Union* (Mar. 18, 2008), *in* THE AMERICAN SPIRIT: UNITED STATES HISTORY AS SEEN BY CONTEMPORARIES 663 (David M. Kennedy & Thomas A. Bailey eds., 2010).

55. *See* "Coda: The Democracy of Opportunity as a Partisan Cause," Chapter 9.

56. *See* JOSEPH E. STIGLITZ, THE PRICE OF INEQUALITY: HOW TODAY'S DIVIDED SOCIETY ENDANGERS OUR FUTURE (2012); Miles Corak, *Income Inequality, Equality of Opportunity, and Intergenerational Mobility,* 27 J. ECON. PERSPECTIVES 79 (2013); THOMAS PIKETTY, CAPITAL IN THE TWENTY-FIRST CENTURY (Arthur Goldhammer trans. 2014); Raj Chetty, Nathan Hendren, Patrick Kline, & Emmanuel Saez, *Where Is the Land of Opportunity? The Geography of Intergenerational Mobility in the United States,* 129 Q. J. ECON. 1553 (2014); Raj Chetty, John N. Friedman, Emmanuel Saez, Nicholas Turner, & Danny Yagan, *Income Segregation and Intergenerational*

Mobility Across Colleges in the United States, 135 Q. J. ECON. 1567 (2020). For a discussion of the mechanisms by which inequality exacerbates unequal opportunity, see JOSEPH FISHKIN, BOT-TLENECKS: A NEW THEORY OF EQUAL OPPORTUNITY 199–219 (2014).

57. For example, see JACOB S. HACKER & PAUL PIERSON, LET THEM EAT TWEETS (2020); MARTIN GILENS, AFFLUENCE AND INFLUENCE: ECONOMIC INEQUALITY AND POLITICAL POWER IN AMERICA (2012). This renewed attention is one piece of a revival of progressive political economy underway in multiple disciplines.

One influential recent effort at reinventing progressive political economy, building on the legacies of institutionalist economics and Marxist thought, is the work of Wolfgang Streeck. *E.g.,* Wolfgang Streeck, *Taking Capitalism Seriously: Toward an Institutionalist Approach to Contemporary Political Economy*, 9 SOCIO-ECONOMIC REV. 137 (2011); WOLFGANG STREECK, CRITICAL ENCOUNTERS: CAPITALISM, DEMOCRACY, IDEAS (2020). Working within mainstream welfare economics is, among others, the prominent iconoclast Angus Deaton, who has kept classical political economy's concern with distributional questions and political power alive in works such as ANGUS DEATON, THE GREAT ESCAPE: HEALTH, WEALTH, AND THE ORIGINS OF INEQUALITY (2010). Economists Samuel Bowles and Herbert Gintis have threaded modern behavioral economics and the study of social and cultural evolution with the legacy of the critical theory tradition. *See, e.g.,* SAMUEL BOWLES & HERBERT GINTIS, DEMOCRACY AND CAPITALISM: PROPERTY, COMMUNITY, AND THE CONTRADICTIONS OF MODERN SOCIAL THOUGHT (1987); Samuel Bowles & Herbert Gintis, *Power and Wealth in a Competitive Capitalist Economy,* 21 PHIL. & PUB. AFF. 324, 324 (1992); SAMUEL BOWLES & HERBERT GINTIS, A COOPERATIVE SPECIES: HUMAN SOCIALITY AND ITS EVOLUTION (2011); SAMUEL BOWLES, THE NEW ECONOMICS OF INEQUALITY AND REDISTRIBUTION (2012); SAMUEL BOWLES, THE MORAL ECONOMY: WHY GOOD INCENTIVES ARE NO SUBSTITUTE FOR GOOD CITIZENS (2016).

In political science, a renewal of progressive political economy is also underway, led by figures such as Jacob S. Hacker and Paul Pierson. *See, e.g.,* JACOB S. HACKER, THE DIVIDED WELFARE STATE: THE BATTLE OVER PUBLIC AND PRIVATE SOCIAL BENEFITS IN THE UNITED STATES (2002); JACOB S. HACKER & PAUL PIERSON, WINNER-TAKE-ALL POLITICS: HOW WASHINGTON MADE THE RICH RICHER—AND TURNED ITS BACK ON THE MIDDLE CLASS (2010).

58. Among legal academics and law students, these insights are at the core of a new movement that goes by the name law and political economy. The Law and Political Economy Project has become an organizing point for this movement. Four of its founders have authored an important scholarly manifesto, Jedediah Britton-Purdy, David Singh Grewal, Amy Kapczynski, & K. Sabeel Rahman, *Building a Law-and-Political-Economy Framework: Beyond the Twentieth-Century Synthesis*, 129 YALE L.J. 1784 (2020), which offers a critical account of late twentieth-century developments in legal and economic thought that chimes with our own.

As we set out to reclaim and reinvent constitutional political economy as a resource for constitutional politics and law, *Building*'s authors aim to renew political economy as a framework for progressive legal scholarship. Like us, they embrace the "foundational . . . nineteenth-century" understanding of political economy in which "the economy is always already political in both its origins and consequences." *Id.* at 1792. They begin *Building* with a critique of mainstream law and economics, unpacking how the latter operates within legal thought as "the 'normal science' familiar to legal academics today"—and how it works to uphold the profoundly mistaken and ideologically loaded "misconception" of the "autonomy of the economy." *Id.* at 1795, 1800.

Like their critical forebear Duncan Kennedy, *Building*'s authors aim to make their critical essay a "'How to Use This Argument' manual" for progressive law students, constructing their wide-ranging synthetic account around the law school curriculum. Under the influence of law and economics and the broader neoliberal turn, they argue, law school subjects have been divided into fields "considered to be 'about the market': contracts, property, antitrust, intellectual property, corporate law and so on"; and fields thought to be about politics, the "so-called political and public legal fields, centrally constitutional law." In the first set of subjects—the ones "about 'the economy'"—"efficiency analysis anchors both the descriptive framing and the normative assessment of law," providing "no framework for thinking systematically about the interrelationships between political and economic power" nor any means "to analyze . . . contemporary concentrations of wealth and power, except insofar as they interfere with overall efficiency." In the second, so-called "political and public" law fields, "economic power and other structural forms of inequality" are cordoned off from scrutiny, which "tends to be restricted to narrowly defined differential treatment of individuals . . . by the state." Constitutional law, they point out, "advances visions of equality and liberty that leave many forms of unequal power . . . unchallenged or even enshrined as constitutionally fundamental." *Id.* at 1790–91. *Cf.* DUNCAN KENNEDY, LEGAL EDUCATION AND THE REPRODUCTION OF HIERARCHY: A POLEMIC AGAINST THE SYSTEM 14–32 (1983).

The upshot is a legal education and a model of legal thought and scholarship that sends students "into powerful legal and political positions" well equipped to reproduce the status quo and ill equipped to confront the nation's "urgent problems of distribution, democracy, and ecology." *Id.* at 1789–90. What is to be done? *Building*'s authors urge a "renewed commitment to questions of political economy" with its focus on the construction and distribution of economic and political power and a "reorientation" of fields like constitutional law from the "antipolitics" of the present Court-centered constitutional universe to "a candid and risky embrace of democracy." *Id.* at 1822.

59. *E.g.,* California v. Trump, 267 F. Supp. 3d 1119, 1139 (N.D. Cal. 2017) (Chhabria, J.) (explaining that "[c]ourts (and in fact, all branches of government) should be reluctant to balance harms or apply laws in ways that exacerbate" America's "immense inequality of wealth and opportunity").

60. The conceptual distinction here—the democracy-of-opportunity tradition as sword, shield, and guide, to which we will return in Chapter 9—emerged from our useful colloquy with Frank Michelman in a symposium in the *Texas Law Review,* part of which focused on an early version of this project. *See* Frank I. Michelman, *The Unbearable Lightness of Tea Leaves: Constitutional Political Economy in Court,* 94 TEX. L. REV. 1403 (2016); Joseph Fishkin & William Forbath, *The Democracy of Opportunity and Constitutional Politics: A Response,* 94 TEX. L. REV. 1469, 1480–85 (2016). *See* "Constitutional Arguments in the Face of Hostile Courts," Chapter 9.

Michelman has long been an inspiration and interlocutor in just these precincts. In a 2001 colloquy, he anticipated more or less the argument of this book. In Frank I. Michelman, *Democracy-Based Resistance to a Constitutional Right of Social Citizenship: A Commentary on Forbath,* 69 FORDHAM L. REV. 1893 (2001), he playfully envisions battles over what today seem simply "sundry" policy battles—about education, health care, "macro-economic policy and controls . . . industrial organization including antitrust . . . [and] anti-plutocratic political institutions and practices including campaign regulation"—transmuted into "occasions for constitutional judgment or constitutional interpretation" on the part of citizens and lawmakers. Michelman painted all this as a laudable counterfactual, regulative ideal Forbath was conjuring up. *Id.* at 1897–98. In this book, we aim to show it is more than that. It is a regulative ideal that presided over much of our constitutional history.

61. Robin West has argued in a related vein that only a "legislated" Constitution, rather than a judicially enforced one, will do much for the substantive equality claims of the poor. Robin West, *The Missing Jurisprudence of the Legislated Constitution, in* THE CONSTITUTION IN 2020, at 79 (Jack M. Balkin & Reva B. Siegel eds., 2009). Larry Sager has argued forcefully that Americans need to see the daylight between the *court-enforced* Constitution and the Constitution itself. He argues that the rights of the poor (for instance, to adequate medical care) are among the clearest examples of constitutional rights that are "underenforced" by courts, but no less constitutional in nature for that. *See* LAWRENCE G. SAGER, JUSTICE IN PLAINCLOTHES 85–91 (2004).

62. For a fuller discussion of this theme, see "Constitutional Arguments in the Face of Hostile Courts," Chapter 9.

1. Constitution Making and the Political Economy of Self-Rule in the Early Republic

1. The canonical account is PHILIP PETTIT, REPUBLICANISM: A THEORY OF FREEDOM AND GOVERNMENT (1997). *See also* PHILIP PETTIT, ON THE PEOPLE'S TERMS: A REPUBLICAN THEORY AND MODEL OF DEMOCRACY (2012). For one of the first efforts by a coauthor of this book to trace this republican conception of liberty in American constitutional history, see William Forbath, *The Ambiguities of Free Labor: Labor and the Law in the Gilded Age,* 1985 WISCONSIN L. REV. 767 (1985).

2. Noah Webster, *Miscellaneous Remarks on Divizions of Property . . . in the United States* (1790), *in* 1 THE FOUNDER'S CONSTITUTION 552, 553 (Philip B. Kurland & Ralph Lerner eds., 1987).

3. Noah Webster, *An Examination into the Leading Principles of the Federal Constitution* (Oct. 10, 1787), *in* PAMPHLETS ON THE CONSTITUTION OF THE UNITED STATES PUBLISHED DURING ITS DISCUSSION BY THE PEOPLE, 1787–1788, at 59 (Paul L. Ford ed., 1888), *quoted in* CLEMENT FATOVIC, AMERICA'S FOUNDING AND THE STRUGGLE OVER ECONOMIC INEQUALITY 10 (2015).

4. JAMES HARRINGTON, THE COMMONWEALTH OF OCEANIA AND A SYSTEM OF POLITICS 20 (J. G. A. Pocock ed., 1992), *quoted in* FATOVIC, AMERICA'S FOUNDING, at 9. For a thoughtful discussion of Harrington's ideas about inequality and their influence on a number of thinkers in the founding generation, see GANESH SITARAMAN, THE CRISIS OF THE MIDDLE-CLASS CONSTITUTION 53–58, 67–74 (2017).

5. Noah Webster, *Miscellaneous Remarks on Divizions of Property . . . in the United States* (1790), *in* THE FOUNDERS' CONSTITUTION (Philip B. Kurland & Ralph Lerner eds., 1987), http://press-pubs.uchicago.edu/founders/documents/v1ch15s44.html [https://perma.cc/G7V9-L5NK], *quoted in* FATOVIC, AMERICA'S FOUNDING, at 9.

6. Letter from John Adams to James Sullivan (May 26, 1776), *in* 9 WORKS OF JOHN ADAMS 376–77 (Harry Alonzo Cushing ed., 1906), *quoted in* FATOVIC, AMERICA'S FOUNDING, at 13.

7. *Id.*

8. *See* CHRISTOPHER TOMLINS, FREEDOM BOUND: LAW, LABOR AND CIVIC IDENTITY IN COLONIZING ENGLISH AMERICA, 1580–1865, at 93–192 (2010); K-Sue Park, *Money, Mortgages, and the Conquest of America,* 41 LAW & SOC. INQUIRY 1006 (2016).

9. *See generally* CLAUDIO SAUNT, UNWORTHY REPUBLIC: THE DISPOSSESSION OF NATIVE AMERICANS AND THE ROAD TO INDIAN TERRITORY (2020).

10. *See* Joshua Rosenbloom, *Indentured Servitude in the Colonial U.S., in* EH.NET ENCYCLOPEDIA OF ECONOMIC AND BUSINESS HISTORY (Robert Whaples ed., 2008), http://eh.net/encyclopedia/indentured-servitude-in-the-colonial-u-s/; Robert C. Allen et al., *The Colonial Origins of the Divergence in the Americas: A Labor Market Approach,* 72 J. OF ECON. HIST. 863 (2012); JAMES T. LEMON, THE BEST POOR MAN'S COUNTRY: A GEOGRAPHICAL STUDY OF EARLY SOUTHEASTERN PENNSYLVANIA (1972); Stanley L. Engerman and Kenneth L. Sokoloff, *The Evolution of Suffrage Institutions in the New World,* 65 J. ECON. HIST. 891 (2005); ALEXANDER KEYSSAR, THE RIGHT TO VOTE: THE CONTESTED HISTORY OF DEMOCRACY IN AMERICA 6–7 (2000).

11. *See* AZIZ RANA, TWO FACES OF AMERICAN FREEDOM 7 (2011) (arguing that throughout American history, "democratic ideals themselves gained strength and meaning through frameworks of exclusion"); *see also id.* at 97–98 (describing tensions between republicanism and a growing "settler empire").

12. *See* EDMUND S. MORGAN, AMERICAN SLAVERY, AMERICAN FREEDOM: THE ORDEAL OF COLONIAL VIRGINIA x (2d ed. 2003) ("How republican freedom came to be supported, in large part, by its opposite, slavery, is the subject of this book.").

13. FATOVIC, AMERICA'S FOUNDING, at 5 (citing GORDON WOOD, THE RADICALISM OF THE AMERICAN REVOLUTION (1991) ("Equality was in fact the most radical and most powerful ideological force let loose in the Revolution.").

14. James Otis, *The Rights of the British Colonies Asserted and Proved* (1764), in 1 PAMPHLETS OF THE AMERICAN REVOLUTION 1750–1776, at 408, 439 (Bernard Bailyn ed., 1965).

15. Emancipation came swiftly in some Northern states, but painfully slowly in others. *See* HENDRIK HARTOG, THE TROUBLE WITH MINNA: A CASE OF SLAVERY AND EMANCIPATION IN THE ANTEBELLUM NORTH (2018) (exploring life under New Jersey's "regime of gradual emancipation").

16. JILL LEPORE, THESE TRUTHS: A HISTORY OF THE UNITED STATES 111 (2018).

17. Letter from Thomas Jefferson to Thomas Nelson (May 16, 1776), *in* 1 THE PAPERS OF THOMAS JEFFERSON 292–93 (Julian P. Boyd ed., 1950), *quoted in* LEPORE, THESE TRUTHS, at 111.

18. Christopher L. Tomlins, *Law, Police, and the Pursuit of Happiness in the New American Republic*, 4 STUDIES AM. POL. DEVELOPMENT 3, 18–19 (2008).

19. *See generally* LARRY D. KRAMER, THE PEOPLE THEMSELVES: POPULAR CONSTITUTIONALISM AND JUDICIAL REVIEW (2005).

20. *Constitution of Virginia—1776, in* 7 THE FEDERAL AND STATE CONSTITUTIONS, COLONIAL CHARTERS, AND OTHER ORGANIC LAWS OF THE STATES, TERRITORIES, AND COLONIES NOW OR HERETOFORE FORMING THE UNITED STATES OF AMERICA 3812, 3813 (Francis Newton Thorpe ed., 1909).

21. ROBERT J. DINKIN, VOTING IN REVOLUTIONARY AMERICA 27 (1982).

22. *Id.* at 31–40. The upshot: in Pennsylvania, New Hampshire, Georgia, North Carolina, and New Jersey, about 90 percent of adult white men could vote. (In New Jersey all inhabitants with 50 pounds to their names, including women, had the ballot.) In Massachusetts, 60–70 percent of adult white men in the seacoast towns could vote, while 80–90 percent did in the countryside. *Id.* However, this revolutionary liberalization was uneven; Massachusetts, then locked in a contentious period of class conflict, actually tightened its eligibility rules. *See* ALEXANDER KEYSSAR, THE RIGHT TO VOTE 16–21 (2000).

23. *Constitution of Pennsylvania—1776*, Sec. XVI, *in* 5 FEDERAL AND STATE CONSTITUTIONS 3081, 3084.

24. *See* U.S. CONST. art. I, § 9, cl. 8 ("No Title of Nobility shall be granted by the United States . . .").

25. NEW HAMPSHIRE CONST. art. IX (1784).

26. VIRGINIA CONST. art. 1, § 4, *quoted in* GORDON S. WOOD, THE RADICALISM OF THE AMERICAN REVOLUTION 181 (1991).

27. Noah Webster, *An Examination into the Leading Principles of the Federal Constitution* (Oct. 10, 1787), *in* PAMPHLETS ON THE CONSTITUTION OF THE UNITED STATES PUBLISHED DURING ITS DISCUSSION BY THE PEOPLE, 1787–1788, at 59 (Paul L. Ford ed., 1888), *available at* https://perma .cc/GB46-L5L3, *quoted in* CLEMENT FATOVIC, AMERICA'S FOUNDING AND THE STRUGGLE OVER ECONOMIC INEQUALITY 10 (2015).

28. Claire Priest, *Creating an American Property Law: Alienability and Its Limits in American History,* 120 HARVARD L. REV. 385, 394, 441 n.249 (2006).

29. Holly Brewer, *Entailing Aristocracy in Colonial Virginia: "Ancient Feudal Restraints" and Revolutionary Reform,* 52 WM. & MARY Q. 307, 311 (1997); LEE SOLTOW, DISTRIBUTION OF WEALTH AND INCOME IN THE UNITED STATES IN 1789, at 144–47 (1989) (looking at New Jersey in particular).

30. WILLI PAUL ADAMS, THE FIRST AMERICAN CONSTITUTIONS: REPUBLICAN IDEOLOGY AND THE MAKING OF THE STATE CONSTITUTIONS IN THE REVOLUTIONARY ERA 188 (1980).

31. CHRISTOPHER L. TOMLINS, LAW, LABOR, AND IDEOLOGY IN THE EARLY AMERICAN REPUBLIC 81 (1993).

32. Letter from Thomas Jefferson to James Madison (Oct. 28, 1785), *in* 8 THE PAPERS OF THOMAS JEFFERSON 682 (Julian P. Boyd ed., 1953).

33. *Id.* (Jefferson writes one means to "silently lessen[] the inequality of property is to exempt all from taxation below a certain point, and to tax the higher portions of property in geometrical progression as they rise"); Tomlins, Law, Labor, and Ideology, at 81–82; Richard K. Matthews, The Radical Politics of Thomas Jefferson: A Revisionist View 19–29, 40–42, 50 (1984). On such subjects as high taxes on large holdings and total exemptions for the smallholder, Madison consistently seconded Jefferson's views. In implementing the new constitutions, Madison held that state legislatures ought to craft laws and policies whose "silent operation" would "reduce extreme wealth towards a state of mediocrity, and raise extreme indigence towards a state of comfort." *See also* James Madison, For the *National Gazette,* [ca. Jan. 23] 1792, *in* 14 The Papers of James Madison 197 (Robert A. Rutland & Thomas A. Mason eds., 1983).

34. Thomas Jefferson, *Virginia Constitution, Third Draft [before 13 June 1776],* in 1 Papers of Thomas Jefferson, at 356, 362 (editorial annotations omitted).

35. Letter from Thomas Jefferson to James Madison (Dec. 20, 1787), *in* 12 Papers of Thomas Jefferson, at 438, 442.

36. Joyce Appleby, *What Is Still American in the Political Philosophy of Thomas Jefferson?,* 39 Wm. & Mary Q. 287, 295 (1982); Joyce Appleby, *The Radical Double-Entendre in the Right to Self-Government,* in The Origins of Anglo-American Radicalism 275, 281 (Margaret Jacob & James Jacob eds., 1984).

37. Thomas Jefferson, *Autobiography* (1821), *in* 1 The Works of Thomas Jefferson 3, 75, 77 (Paul Leicester Ford ed., 1904).

38. Thomas Jefferson, *Notes on Virginia, in* 4 Works of Thomas Jefferson, at 3, 64.

39. Paul Tractenberg, *Education, in* 3 State Constitutions for the Twenty-First Century 241–306 (G. Alan Tarr & Robert F. Williams eds., 2006); Emily Zackin, Looking for Rights in All the Wrong Places: Why State Constitutions Contain America's Positive Rights 67–84 (2013).

40. Jefferson, *Notes on Virginia,* at 62–65.

41. *Id.* at 60–62, 64.

42. *Id.* at 64.

43. Jefferson and many of his fellow republican gentlemen favored this idea when pondering the white "poor," but found it impossible or agonizing to ponder extending it to African Americans. *See* Paul Finkelman, *Jefferson and Slavery: "Treason Against the Hopes of the World," in* Jeffersonian Legacies 181, 184–86 (Peter S. Onuf ed., 1993). In *Notes on the State of Virginia,* Jefferson dwelled on his "suspicion" that "blacks, whether originally a distinct race, or made distinct by time and circumstances, are inferior to the whites in the endowments of both body and mind." Jefferson, *Notes on Virginia,* at 58.

44. David Ramsay, *An Oration on the Advantages of American Independence* (July 4, 1778), *quoted in* Gordon S. Wood, The Radicalism of the American Revolution 180 (1991).

45. *The Constitution of Virginia—1776* (June 1776), *in* 7 The Federal and State Constitutions, Colonial Charters, and Other Organic Laws of the States, Territories, and Colonies Now or Heretofore Forming the United States of America 3812, 3813 (Francis Newton Thorpe ed., 1909).

46. Joyce Appleby, *What Is Still American in the Political Philosophy of Thomas Jefferson?* 39 Wm. & Mary Q. 287, 297 (1982).

47. *Constitution of Pennsylvania—1776* (Sept. 1776), *in* 5 Federal and State Constitutions, 3081, 3082. Nearly identical language exists in the constitutions of Delaware (Sept. 1776), Maryland (Nov. 1776), North Carolina (Dec. 1776), and Georgia (Feb. 1777). *See* Willi Paul Adams, The First American Constitutions: Republican Ideology and the Making of the State Constitutions in the Revolutionary Era 288 (1980); Christopher L. Tomlins, Law, Labor, and Ideology in the Early American Republic 57 (1993).

48. TOMLINS, LAW, LABOR, AND IDEOLOGY, at 57.

49. Nicolai Rubinstein, *The History of the Word* Politicus *in Early-Modern Europe,* in THE LANGUAGES OF POLITICAL THEORY IN EARLY MODERN EUROPE 42–43 (Anthony Pagden ed., 1987); TOMLINS, LAW, LABOR, AND IDEOLOGY, at 44, 55–59, 81–88.

50. THE KEY OF LIBERTY: THE LIFE AND DEMOCRATIC WRITINGS OF WILLIAM MANNING, "A LABORER," 1747–1814, xi–xii, 131 (Michael Merrill & Sean Wilentz eds., 1993).

51. "The earth," Jefferson famously wrote, "is given as a common stock for man to labour and live on." All persons had a natural right to enough land to produce their subsistence, as well as a right to the property produced by mixing their labor with the land. This theory sanctified private property for most free inhabitants of the early republic and its cheap, fertile land. Jefferson recognized that the country was not ready "yet" to let the landless appropriate enough uncultivated land to meet their needs. But "it is not too soon," he insisted, "to provide by every possible means that as few as possible shall be without a little portion of land." Letter from Jefferson to Madison (Oct. 28, 1785), *in* 8 THE PAPERS OF THOMAS JEFFERSON 681, 682 (Julian P. Boyd ed., 1950); *see also* CHARLES SELLERS, THE MARKET REVOLUTION: JACKSONIAN AMERICA, 1815–1846, at 36 (1991); *see also* RICHARD K. MATTHEWS, THE RADICAL POLITICS OF THOMAS JEFFERSON: A REVISIONIST VIEW 28 (1984).

52. *See* TOMLINS, LAW, LABOR, AND IDEOLOGY, at 57. The people's "sole exclusive and inherent Right of governing and regulating" is from the Pennsylvania constitution (1776), with similar language in the constitutions of Delaware, Maryland, and North Carolina. *See* ADAMS, FIRST AMERICAN CONSTITUTIONS, at 288.

53. TOMLINS, LAW, LABOR, AND IDEOLOGY, at 84 (quoting Jeffrey Barnouw, *The Pursuit of Happiness in Jefferson and Its Background in Bacon and Hobbes,* 11 INTERPRETATION: J. POL. PHIL. 225, 229 (1983)).

54. *Id.*

55. Rather, by Jeffersonian lights, higher law constrained the accumulation of property to the extent it clashed with the natural right of the poor to a sufficient share of land and resources to make a livelihood. Christopher Tomlins, *Law, Police and the Pursuit of Happiness in the New American Republic,* 4 STUD. AM. POL. DEV. 28–31 (1990); David M. Post, *Jeffersonian Revisions of Locke: Education, Property-Rights, and Liberty,* 47 J. HIST. IDEAS 147, 152–153 (1986); MATTHEWS, RADICAL POLITICS OF JEFFERSON, at 40–42, 50, 122.

56. *See* William Treanor, *The Origins and Original Significance of the Just Compensation Clause of the Fifth Amendment,* 94 YALE L.J. 694 (1985).

57. *Id.*

58. Joyce Appleby, *What Is Still American in the Political Philosophy of Thomas Jefferson?* 39 WM. & MARY Q. 287, 297 (1982).

59. JILL LEPORE, THESE TRUTHS: A HISTORY OF THE UNITED STATES 114 (2018).

60. MICHAEL J. KLARMAN, THE FRAMERS' COUP: THE MAKING OF THE UNITED STATES CONSTITUTION 21 (2016).

61. *Id.* at 26.

62. WOODY HOLTON, UNRULY AMERICANS AND THE ORIGINS OF THE CONSTITUTION (2007); KLARMAN, FRAMERS' COUP, at 74–81.

63. Letter from Alexander Hamilton to Robert Morris (Aug. 13, 1782), *in* 3 PAPERS OF ALEXANDER HAMILTON 132, 135 (Harold Syrett ed., 2011), *quoted in* KLARMAN, FRAMERS' COUP, at 86.

64. James Madison, *Notes on the Debates* (June 26, 1786), *in* THE DEBATES ON THE ADOPTION OF THE FEDERAL CONSTITUTION IN THE CONVENTION HELD AT PHILADELPHIA IN 1787, at 109, 243 (Jonathan Elliott ed., 1886) ("leveling spirit"); Edmund Randolph, May 14, 1786, *quoted in* James McHenry, *Papers of Dr. James McHenry on the Federal Convention of 1787* ("democratic parts of our constitutions"), *available at* https://avalon.law.yale.edu/18th_century/mchenry.asp [https://perma.cc/NS79-NFBC].

65. KLARMAN, FRAMERS' COUP, at 86–87.

66. *Id.* at 90–95.

67. Economic historians reckon that per capita gross national product plummeted nearly 50 percent in the fifteen years between 1776 and 1791. KLARMAN, at 75 (citing Peter Lindert & Jeffrey Williamson, *American Incomes Before and After the Revolution*, 73 J. ECON. HIST. 725, 752–54 (2013) (attributing the loss to "the war itself," "the loss of overseas trade," and "an urban crisis" in cities near the coast and major rivers)); THOMAS MCCRAW, THE FOUNDERS AND FINANCE: HOW HAMILTON, GALLATIN, AND OTHER IMMIGRANTS FORGED A NEW ECONOMY 47–48 (2012).

68. HOLTON, UNRULY AMERICANS, at 110; KLARMAN, FRAMERS' COUP, at 74–81.

69. HOLTON, UNRULY AMERICANS, at 169–70 (describing practical difficulties for Western legislators).

70. KLARMAN, FRAMERS' COUP, at 89–99.

71. HOLTON, UNRULY AMERICANS, at 33–36, 85–86; KLARMAN, FRAMERS' COUP, at 90–99.

72. When peaceful forms of constitutional protest like petitioning failed, the seventeenth-century English tradition had supplied the eighteenth-century American revolutionaries with precedent and support for the startling proposition that extra-legal, forcible resistance—"mobbing," as it was called—was a legitimate form of constitutional action, and "mobbing" often spilled over into tarring and feathering, and destruction of Crown property. *See* LARRY D. KRAMER, THE PEOPLE THEMSELVES: POPULAR CONSTITUTIONALISM AND JUDICIAL REVIEW 27 (2004).

73. HOLTON, UNRULY AMERICANS, at 76 (referring to "wealthy citizens who lent the government the money it needed to suppress Shays's Rebellion"); KLARMAN, FRAMERS' COUP, at 92.

74. KLARMAN, FRAMERS' COUP, at 92n.

75. Letter from Thomas Jefferson to Abigail Adams (Feb. 22, 1787), *in* 11 THE PAPERS OF THOMAS JEFFERSON 174 (Julian P. Boyd ed., 1955), *quoted in* KLARMAN, FRAMERS' COUP, at 92.

76. JILL LEPORE, THESE TRUTHS: A HISTORY OF THE UNITED STATES 116 (2018) (citing NOAH FELDMAN, THREE LIVES OF JAMES MADISON: GENIUS, PARTISAN, PRESIDENT 82–83, 94 (2017)).

77. LEPORE, THESE TRUTHS, at 118.

78. *See, e.g.,* KLARMAN, FRAMERS' COUP; *see also* AZIZ RANA, THE RISE OF THE CONSTITUTION (forthcoming).

79. Edmund Randolph, May 14, 1786, *quoted in* James McHenry, *Papers of Dr. James McHenry on the Federal Convention of 1787* ("democratic parts of our constitutions"), *available at* https://avalon.law.yale.edu/18th_century/mchenry.asp [https://perma.cc/NS79-NFBC].

80. *Articles of Confederation, in* 1 THE FEDERAL AND STATE CONSTITUTIONS, COLONIAL CHARTERS, AND OTHER ORGANIC LAWS OF THE STATES, TERRITORIES, AND COLONIES NOW OR HERETOFORE FORMING THE UNITED STATES OF AMERICA 9, 10 (Francis Newton Thorpe ed., 1909).

81. Edmund Randolph, *Resolutions Proposed by Mr. Randolph in Convention, May 29, 1787* ("Virginia Plan," Resolution 6), *in* MAX FARRAND, 1 RECORDS OF THE FEDERAL CONVENTION OF 1787, at 20, 21 (1907), *quoted in* KLARMAN, FRAMERS' COUP, at 139. What was more, Congress also would have the power "to call forth the force of the Union [against] any member of the Union failing to fulfill its duty under the articles thereof." *Id.*

82. Virginia Plan, Res. 6, *quoted in* KLARMAN, FRAMERS' COUP, at 140.

83. Edmund Randolph, May 29, 1787, *in* FARRAND, 1 RECORDS OF THE FEDERAL CONVENTION at 27, *quoted in* CLEMENT FATOVIC, AMERICA'S FOUNDING AND THE STRUGGLE OVER ECONOMIC INEQUALITY 60 (2015).

84. James Madison, June 6, 1787, *in* FARRAND, 1 RECORDS OF THE FEDERAL CONVENTION, at 134, *quoted in* FATOVIC, AMERICA'S FOUNDING, at 60.

85. James Madison, *Vices of the Present System* (April 1787), *in* 9 THE PAPERS OF JAMES MADISON 350 (Robert A. Rutland & Thomas A. Mason eds., 1983).

86. NOAH FELDMAN, THREE LIVES OF JAMES MADISON: GENIUS, PARTISAN, PRESIDENT 123–25 (2017); *see also* KLARMAN, FRAMERS' COUP, at 157–58.

87. James Madison, *Notes on the Debates* (June 26, 1786), *in* The Debates on the Adoption of the Federal Constitution in the Convention Held at Philadelphia in 1787, at 109, 171 (Jonathan Elliott ed., 1886), *quoted in* Feldman, Three Lives of Madison, at 123–25.

88. *See* Feldman, Three Lives of Madison, at 151–54, 175; *see also* Klarman, Framers' Coup, at 158.

89. *See* Feldman, Three Lives of Madison, at 172–75.

90. U.S. Const. art. 1, § 10; Woody Holton, Unruly Americans and the Origins of the Constitution 183–84 (2007); Klarman, Framers' Coup, at 161–62.

91. U.S. Const. art. 6, § 2.

92. On the continuing enactment and implementation of debtor relief legislation by the states, see Emily Zackin's pathbreaking empirical work. Emily Zackin, *Rethinking Blaisdell: State Debt Relief and the Limits of Constitutional Doctrine,* 45 Law & Soc. Inquiry 658–77 (2020); on state banks creating paper currency, see Bray Hammond's classic account. Bray Hammond, Banks and Politics in America (1991); and for a general account of continuing contestation over state versus national authority over political economy, see Tony Freyer, Producers Versus Capitalists: Constitutional Conflicts in Antebellum America (1994).

93. Holton, Unruly Americans, at 213–16.

94. James Madison, *in* Farrand, 1 Records of the Federal Convention, at 486, *quoted in* Jill Lepore, These Truths: A History of the United States 123 (2018).

95. Klarman, Framers' Coup, at 60–61 (describing divergence of attitudes toward Jay's treaty with Spain), 265 (summarizing different economic interests).

96. *See id.* at 266.

97. *Id.* at 268.

98. *Id.* at 270.

99. *Id.* at 274.

100. Lepore, These Truths, at 156; *see also* Klarman, Framers' Coup, at 228.

101. Klarman, Framers' Coup, at 230–34.

102. Lepore, These Truths, at 164; *see also* Klarman, Framers' Coup, at 276–77.

103. Klarman, Framers' Coup, at 264–65.

104. U.S. Const. art. 1, § 9, cl. 1 (disallowing Congress's regulation of slave trade prior to 1808); art. 1, § 2, cl. 3 (congressional apportionment of representation); art. 4, § 2, cl. 3 (requiring that states assist with returning fugitive slaves).

105. *See* Sean Wilentz, No Property in Man: Slavery and Antislavery at the Nation's Founding (2018).

106. Lepore, These Truths, at 128.

107. James Madison, *Federalist No. 40,* in The Federalist Papers 198, 202, 204 (Ian Shapiro ed., 2009), *quoted in* Lepore, These Truths, at 128.

108. *See* Woody Holton, Unruly Americans and the Origins of the Constitution (2007); Saul Cornell & Gerald Leonard, The Partisan Republic: Democracy, Exclusion and the Fall of the Founders' Constitution, 1780s–1830s (2019); Saul Cornell, The Other Founders: Anti-Federalism and the Dissenting Tradition in America, 1788–1828 (1999).

109. Holton, Unruly Americans, at 247 (quoting Hugh Williamson, Speech (Nov. 8, 1787), *in* 2 Debate on the Constitution 233 (Bernard Bailyn ed., 1993)).

110. *Id.* at 241, 136 (discussing potential establishment of tariff during the Confederation).

111. Had delegates been allocated more fairly, several ratifying conventions, including Pennsylvania's and South Carolina's, could well have produced a different outcome, and defeated the new Constitution. *See id.* at 249.

112. *See* Klarman, Framers' Coup, at 398 (summarizing ratification contest). Klarman also argues that had districting been fairer to poorer, rural voters, the Constitution might well have

been defeated. The Federalist victory, he writes, "was so narrow—one North Carolina Antifed-eralist rightly noted the 'very trifling margins of victory' in 'several great adopting states'—that a small shift in any of a large number of circumstances and choices might have altered the out-come." *Id.* at 540.

113. Alexander Hamilton, *Conjectures about the New Constitution* (January 1787–May 1788), *in* 4 The Papers of Alexander Hamilton 275–77 (Harold C. Syrett ed., 1962).

114. Holton, Unruly Americans, at 236–38 (describing "the widespread expectation that the men elected . . . would far surpass their constituents in wealth").

115. Christopher L. Tomlins, *Law, Police, and the Pursuit of Happiness in the New American Re-public,* 4 Studies Am. Pol. Development 3, 18–19. Similar language can be found in the consti-tutions of Delaware, Maryland, Georgia, and North Carolina. *Id.* at 19. *See also* Willi Paul Adams, The First American Constitutions: Republican Ideology and the Making of the State Constitutions in the Revolutionary Era 287 (1980).

116. Patrick Henry, Speech at the Virginia Ratifying Convention (June 5, 1788), *in* The Anti-Federalist 297, 305 (Murray Dry ed., 1981), *quoted in* Clement Fatovic, America's Founding and the Struggle over Economic Inequality 71 (2015).

117. Melancton Smith, Speech (June 21, 1788), *in* Anti-Federalist, at 338, 341, *quoted in* Fa-tovic, America's Founding, at 74.

118. *The Address and Reasons of the Dissent of the Minority of the Convention of Pennsylvania to Their Constituents, in* Anti-Federalist, at 201, 219, *quoted in* Fatovic, America's Founding, at 73.

119. Letter from John Quincy Adams to William Cranch (Dec. 8, 1787), *quoted in* Holton, Unruly Americans, at 236.

120. George Mason, *Objections to This Constitution of Government* (Sept. 15, 1787), *quoted in* Fatovic, America's Founding, at 72.

121. Thomas Paine, *quoted in* Holton, Unruly Americans, at 242–43 (*citing* Alfred E. Young, *The Framers of the Constitution and the "Genius of the People,"* 42 Radical Hist. Rev. 8 (1988)).

122. James Madison, *Federalist No. 10, in* The Federalist Papers 47 (Ian Shapiro ed., 2009).

123. Madison, *Federalist No. 57, in* Federalist Papers 290, 290–91, *quoted in* Jill Lepore, These Truths: A History of the United States 162 (2018).

124. Madison, *Federalist No. 10, in* Federalist Papers, at 47–53. Madison said privately that the divide and conquer strategy was necessary when dealing with political opponents. Holton, Unruly Americans, at 10, 207 (citing Madison, Letter to Thomas Jefferson (Oct. 24, 1787) *in* 10 The Papers of James Madison 214 (Robert A. Rutland & Thomas A. Mason eds., 1983)).

125. James Madison, *Vices of the Political System of the United States (April 1787) in* 9 Papers of Madison 345, 357, *quoted in* Michael Klarman, The Framers' Coup: The Making of the United States Constitution 132 (2016).

126. Madison, *Federalist No. 10, in* Shapiro, Federalist Papers 47, 52 (asserting that such men will "possess the most attractive merit and the most diffusive and established characters"). *See* Klarman, Framers' Coup, at 132.

127. Melancton Smith, June 21, 1788, *in* 2 The Debates in the Several State Conventions on the Adoption of the Federal Constitution 246 (Jonathan Elliott ed., 1836), *quoted in* Holton, Unruly Americans, at 237. Smith was bitingly plainspoken about the class prejudices and dangerous moral blindness he saw in the "natural aristocracy" Federalists aimed to put in office. Such "aristocrats" "do not feel for the poor and middling class," he said. "[T]he reasons are obvious—they are not obliged to use their pains and labor to procure property . . . [and] feel not the inconveniences arising from the payment of small sums. They consider themselves above the common people [and] do not associate with them." Smith, June 21, 1788, *quoted in* Holton, Unruly Americans, at 237.

128. HOLTON, UNRULY AMERICANS, at 235–238 (citing Letter from "Brutus," *New York Journal,* Jan. 18, 1787, *in* DOCUMENTARY HISTORY OF THE RATIFICATION OF THE CONSTITUTION (Merrill Jensen ed., 1976)).

129. *Address of the Albany Antifederal Committee, April 26, 1788, in* 6 THE COMPLETE ANTI-FEDERALIST 122–27 (Herbert Storing ed., 1981).

130. Letter from Agrippa No. 12, Part 2 (Jan. 14, 1788), *in* 4 COMPLETE ANTI-FEDERALIST, at 94, 96–97.

131. Montezuma, Essay (Oct. 17, 1787), *in* 3 COMPLETE ANTI-FEDERALIST, at 53, 55.

132. James Madison, *Federalist No. 45, in* SHAPIRO, FEDERALIST PAPERS, at 234, 237–38.

133. Alexander Hamilton, *Federalist No. 33, id.* at 158, 159 (accusing opponents of painting the Necessary and Proper Clause "in all the exaggerated colors of misrepresentation") and *Federalist No. 67, id.* at 340 ("[W]riters against the Constitution seem to have taken pains to signalize their talent of misrepresentation").

134. James Madison, *Federalist No. 46, id.* at 239.

135. Madison, *Federalist No. 45, id.* at 234; *see* Madison, *Federalist No. 46, id.* at 239.

136. Alexander Hamilton, *Federalist No. 34, id.* at 162 (revenue power "leaves open to the States far the greatest part of the resources of the community" and with "means as abundant as could be desired for the supply of their own wants, independent of all external control").

137. Letter from Thomas Jefferson to James Madison, 1787, *in* 12 THE PAPERS OF THOMAS JEFFERSON 438, 440 (Julian P. Boyd ed., 1955).

138. *See* WOODY HOLTON, UNRULY AMERICANS AND THE ORIGINS OF THE CONSTITUTION 253 (2007); KLARMAN, FRAMERS' COUP, at 547–54; *but see* PAULINE MAIER, RATIFICATION: THE PEOPLE DEBATE THE CONSTITUTION, 1787–1788, at 444 (2011) (noting lack of unanimity among Constitution's critics about a bill of rights).

139. HOLTON, UNRULY AMERICANS, at 252–53; JENNIFER NEDELSKY, PRIVATE PROPERTY AND THE LIMITS OF AMERICAN CONSTITUTIONALISM: THE MADISONIAN FRAMEWORK AND ITS LEGACY 144–48 (1990); ROBERT RUTLAND, THE BIRTH OF THE BILL OF RIGHTS, 1776–1791, at 206 (1969) (quoting Madison's statement that a bill of rights would make "the constitution better in the opinion of those who are opposed to it, without weakening its frame or abridging its usefulness").

140. Saul Cornell & Gerald Leonard, *The Consolidation of the Early Federal System, 1791–1812, in* 1 CAMBRIDGE HISTORY OF LAW IN AMERICA 524 (Michael Grossberg & Christopher Tomlins eds., 2008).

141. *See* SEAN WILENTZ, THE RISE OF AMERICAN DEMOCRACY: JEFFERSON TO LINCOLN 43–49 (2005).

142. Alexander Hamilton, *Report Relative to a Provision for the Support of Public Credit (1790), reprinted in* 6 THE PAPERS OF ALEXANDER HAMILTON 61 (Harold C. Syrett & Jacob E. Cooke eds., 1962); Alexander Hamilton, *Report on the Subject of Manufactures (Dec. 5, 1791), in* 10 THE PAPERS OF ALEXANDER HAMILTON 230 (Harold C. Syrett & Jacob E. Cooke eds., 1962).

143. *See* HA-JOON CHANG, BAD SAMARITANS: THE MYTH OF FREE TRADE AND THE SECRET HISTORY OF CAPITALISM 40–55 (2010).

144. Cornell & Leonard, *Consolidation,* at 525.

145. *Id.* at 525–26.

146. Gerald Leonard, *Jefferson's Constitutions, in* CONSTITUTIONS AND THE CLASSICS: PATTERNS OF CONSTITUTIONAL THOUGHT FROM FORTESCUE TO BENTHAM 369, 382 (D. J. Galligan ed., 2015); WILENTZ, AMERICAN DEMOCRACY, at 41; SAUL CORNELL, THE OTHER FOUNDERS: ANTI-FEDERALISM AND THE DISSENTING TRADITION IN AMERICA, 1788–1828, at 177–79 (1999); Cornell & Leonard, *Consolidation,* at 524–27.

147. Leonard, *Jefferson's Constitutions,* at 383–84; RALPH KETCHAM, PRESIDENTS ABOVE PARTY: THE FIRST AMERICAN PRESIDENCY 1789–1829, at 103–7 (1984); RICHARD HOFSTADTER, THE IDEA

OF A PARTY SYSTEM: THE RISE OF LEGITIMATE OPPOSITION IN THE UNITED STATES, 1780–1840, at 122–28 (1969).

148. Leonard, *Jefferson's Constitutions,* at 25–26.

149. GERALD LEONARD, THE INVENTION OF PARTY POLITICS: FEDERALISM, POPULAR SOVEREIGNTY, AND CONSTITUTIONAL DEVELOPMENT IN JACKSONIAN ILLINOIS 161–62 (2002) (focusing on Illinois politics); *id.* at 181 (describing Van Buren's belief that corporations "opposed the will of the people" as a "law of their nature").

150. MARTIN VAN BUREN, AN INQUIRY INTO THE ORIGIN AND COURSE OF POLITICAL PARTIES IN THE UNITED STATES 166 (1867).

151. *Id.* at 214–15.

152. *See* CHARLES SELLERS, THE MARKET REVOLUTION: JACKSONIAN AMERICA, 1815–1846, at 37–46, 71, 79, 100–101 (1991); *see also* WILENTZ, AMERICAN DEMOCRACY, at 203–5.

153. Letter from James Madison to William Eustis (May 22, 1823), *in* 3 PAPERS OF JAMES MADISON, RETIREMENT SERIES 57, 58 (David B. Mattern et al. eds., 2013), *quoted in* SELLERS, MARKET REVOLUTION, at 101.

154. *See* SELLERS, MARKET REVOLUTION, at 89–90.

155. *Id.* at 132–33.

156. *Id.* at 134 (citing THOMAS P. GOVAN, NICHOLAS BIDDLE, NATIONALIST AND PUBLIC BANKER, 1786–1844 (1959)); *id.* at 135.

157. Letter from Jefferson to Colonel Yancey (Jan. 6, 1816), *in* 9 THE PAPERS OF THOMAS JEFFERSON 328–31 (Julian P. Boyd ed., 1950), *quoted in* SELLERS, MARKET REVOLUTION, at 133.

158. Letter from Jefferson to Nathaniel Macon (Jan. 12, 1819), *in* 10 PAPERS OF THOMAS JEFFERSON, at 71–72, *quoted in* SELLERS, MARKET REVOLUTION, at 133.

159. SELLERS, MARKET REVOLUTION, at 137.

160. *Id.*

161. WILENTZ, AMERICAN DEMOCRACY, at 210–16.

162. Andrew Jackson, Farewell Address (Mar. 4, 1837), *in* 3 A COMPILATION OF THE MESSAGES AND PAPERS OF THE PRESIDENTS 1789–1897, at 303, 305 (James D. Richardson ed., 1896).

2. CLASHING CONSTITUTIONAL POLITICAL ECONOMIES IN ANTEBELLUM AMERICA

1. For this formulation we are indebted to Gerald Leonard, *Party as a "Political Safeguard of Federalism": Martin Van Buren and the Constitutional Theory of Party Politics,* 54 RUTGERS L. REV. 221, 224–25, 277 (2001).

2. CHARLES SELLERS, THE MARKET REVOLUTION: JACKSONIAN AMERICA, 1815–1846, at 180 (1991).

3. *Id.* at 180, 301–31; Andrew Jackson, Veto Message (July 10, 1832), *reprinted in* 2 COMPILATION OF THE MESSAGES AND PAPERS OF THE PRESIDENTS, 1879–1897, at 576–91 (James Daniel Richardson ed., 1897).

4. *See* United States v. Carolene Prods. Co., 304 U.S. 144, 152 n.4 (1938).

5. Jackson, Veto Message (July 10, 1832), at 576, 591; Michael Les Benedict, *Laissez-Faire and Liberty: A Re-Evaluation of the Meaning and Origins of Laissez-Faire Constitutionalism,* 3 LAW & HIST. REV. 293, 317–18 (1985) (discussing equal rights, equal protection, and class legislation); THOMAS M. COOLEY, A TREATISE ON THE CONSTITUTIONAL LIMITATIONS WHICH REST UPON THE LEGISLATIVE POWER OF THE STATES OF THE AMERICAN UNION 393, 573 (1868) (on equal rights).

6. *See generally* SELLERS, MARKET REVOLUTION; GERALD LEONARD, THE INVENTION OF PARTY POLITICS: FEDERALISM, POPULAR SOVEREIGNTY, AND CONSTITUTIONAL DEVELOPMENT IN JACKSONIAN ILLINOIS (2002). Quotes are from Andrew Jackson, Farewell Address (Mar. 4,

1837), *reprinted in* 3 COMPILATION OF THE MESSAGES AND PAPERS OF THE PRESIDENTS, 1789–1907, at 292–308 (James Daniel Richardson ed., 1908).

7. Jackson, Farewell Address, at 302.

8. For a brief and readable summary, see George Rogers Taylor, *A Brief History of the Second Bank of the United States, in* JACKSON VS. BIDDLE'S BANK 1–10 (George Rogers Taylor ed., 2d ed. 1972).

9. William Leggett, *The Monopoly Banking System,* EVENING POST, Dec. 1834, *reprinted in* 1 A COLLECTION OF THE POLITICAL WRITINGS OF WILLIAM LEGGETT 96, 103 (Theodore Sedgwick Jr. ed., 1840).

10. Andrew Jackson, Maysville Road Veto (May 27, 1830), *reprinted in* MESSAGES OF GEN. ANDREW JACKSON 69 (John F. Brown & William White eds., 1837). In the Maysville Road Veto, Jackson stated: "That a constitutional adjustment of this power [of the federal government to appropriate] is, in the highest degree, desirable, can scarcely be doubted; nor can it fail to be promoted by every sincere friend to the success of our political institutions. . . . It would seem to me that an honest application of the conceded powers of the General Government to the advancement of the common weal, presents a sufficient scope to satisfy a reasonable ambition." *Id.* at 82; Andrew Jackson, Veto Message (July 10, 1832), *reprinted in* 2 COMPILATION OF THE MESSAGES AND PAPERS, at 576; MARTIN VAN BUREN, INQUIRY INTO THE ORIGIN AND COURSE OF POLITICAL PARTIES IN THE UNITED STATES 311–52 (1867).

11. Leggett, *Monopoly Banking System,* at 97.

12. William Leggett, *The Reserved Rights of the People,* EVENING POST, Dec. 13, 1834, *reprinted in* DEMOCRATICK EDITORIALS: ESSAYS IN JACKSONIAN POLITICAL ECONOMY 7, 8 (Lawrence H. White ed., 1984); William Leggett, *Despotism of Andrew Jackson,* EVENING POST, May 23, 1834, *reprinted in* 1 A COLLECTION OF THE POLITICAL WRITINGS 285, 290; William Leggett, *The Division of Parties,* EVENING POST, Nov. 4, 1834, *reprinted in id.* at 64, 66.

13. Jackson, Veto Message, at 590 (emphasis added).

14. Statement of John Bell (June 8, 1832), 22d Cong., 1st Sess., *in* 8 REGISTER OF DEBATES IN CONGRESS pt. 3 at 3357, 3359 (1833).

15. *Id.* at 3359. *See also* VAN BUREN, POLITICAL PARTIES, at 47–49 & 419 (on distribution).

16. Statement of John Bell, at 3357–59.

17. Andrew Jackson, Seventh Annual Message (Dec. 7, 1835), *reprinted in* 3 COMPILATION OF THE MESSAGES AND PAPERS 164, 165, 167; Jackson, Farewell Address, *id.* at 305 ("moneyed interest").

18. Jackson, Veto Message, at 582–585, 590.

19. For this critical perspective on Jacksonian democracy, see generally DANIEL WALKER HOWE, WHAT HATH GOD WROUGHT: THE TRANSFORMATION OF AMERICA, 1815–1848, at 347–49, 352–65 (2007); ALEXANDER SAXTON, THE RISE AND FALL OF THE WHITE REPUBLIC: CLASS POLITICS AND MASS CULTURE IN NINETEENTH-CENTURY AMERICA 148–54, 247 (1990); STEPHANIE MCCURRY, MASTERS OF SMALL WORLDS: YEOMAN HOUSEHOLDS, GENDER RELATIONS, AND THE POLITICAL CULTURE OF THE ANTEBELLUM SOUTH CAROLINA LOW COUNTRY (1995).

20. One such Whig foe was the young Illinois politician Abraham Lincoln, who probed those contradictions as an antislavery friend of corporations and spokesman for the Whig vision of capitalist development, which, as we will see, he outfitted in a vocabulary of equal opportunity largely borrowed from his Democratic adversaries.

21. CLAUDIO SAUNT, UNWORTHY REPUBLIC: THE DISPOSSESSION OF NATIVE AMERICANS AND THE ROAD TO INDIAN TERRITORY 75–79 (2020); *id.* at 81–82.

22. *Id.* at 165.

23. PIERRE L. VAN DEN BERGHE, RACE AND RACISM: A COMPARATIVE PERSPECTIVE 18 (1967).

24. "States' rights" and "strict construction" likewise were bound up in antebellum constitutional discourse with democracy of opportunity for the "humbler [white male] members of so-

ciety." As Tony Freyer has shown, the constant antebellum battles between state and federal courts, and between federal courts and state lawmakers, frequently pitted small and middling producers against larger, regional and national players: the mercantile, corporate, and financial elites and their allies on the federal bench. State judges and attorneys championed a broad state police power and broad readings of state versus federal jurisdiction; they linked "strict construction" and "states' rights" to ideals of safeguarding broad structures of opportunity and a fair chance for "humbler members of society" and of averting oligarchy. *See* TONY FREYER, PRO-DUCERS VERSUS CAPITALISTS: CONSTITUTIONAL CONFLICT IN ANTEBELLUM AMERICA (1994).

25. GERALD LEONARD, THE INVENTION OF PARTY POLITICS: FEDERALISM, POPULAR SOVER-EIGNTY, AND CONSTITUTIONAL DEVELOPMENT IN JACKSONIAN ILLINOIS 43, 162, 173 (2002) (quoting delegates at an 1837 Illinois Democratic congressional convention).

26. *See generally* MARTIN J. SKLAR, THE UNITED STATES AS A DEVELOPING COUNTRY: STUDIES IN U.S. HISTORY IN THE PROGRESSIVE ERA AND THE 1920S (1992); HA-JOON CHANG, KICKING AWAY THE LADDER: DEVELOPMENT STRATEGY IN HISTORICAL PERSPECTIVE (2003); John R. Van Atta, *"A Lawless Rabble": Henry Clay and the Cultural Politics of Squatters' Rights*, 28 J. EARLY AM. REPUBLIC 337 (2008).

27. ROBERT V. REMINI, DANIEL WEBSTER: THE MAN AND HIS TIME 162, 208 (1999); EVERETT PEPPERRELL WHEELER, DANIEL WEBSTER: THE EXPOUNDER OF THE CONSTITUTION (1905) (collecting oral arguments).

28. *See generally* DANIEL WALKER HOWE, THE POLITICAL CULTURE OF THE AMERICAN WHIGS (1979); SEAN WILENTZ, THE RISE OF THE AMERICAN DEMOCRACY: JEFFERSON TO LINCOLN (2005).

29. Abraham Lincoln, *reprinted in* 1 THE COLLECTED WORKS OF ABRAHAM LINCOLN 172, 395–405 (Roy Basler ed., 1953), *quoted in* GABOR S. BORITT, LINCOLN AND THE ECONOMICS OF THE AMERICAN DREAM 128 (1978).

30. BORITT, LINCOLN, at 128.

31. Richard B. Latner, *Preserving "the Natural Equality of Rank and Influence": Liberalism, Republicanism, and Equality of Condition in Jacksonian Politics, in* THE CULTURE OF THE MARKET: HISTORICAL ESSAYS 189, 219–20 (Thomas L. Haskell & Richard F. Teichgraeber III eds., 1996); Statement of John Bell (June 8, 1832), 22d Cong., 1st Sess., *in* 8 REGISTER OF DEBATES IN CONGRESS pt. 3 at 3357–84 (1833).

32. Lincoln, *reprinted in* 1 COLLECTED WORKS, at 395–405.

33. Compare the Jacksonian John Bell's view that an American political economy built on true constitutional principles would never aim for the "European" goal of maximizing national wealth "without regard to the manner of its distribution," Statement of John Bell (June 8, 1832), at 3359, with Clay's oft-expressed view (in speeches on the bank, currency, and the tariff): "The great desideratum in political economy is the same as in private pursuits; that is, what is the best application of the aggregate industry of a nation, that can be made honestly to produce the largest sum of national wealth?" Henry Clay, Speech of Henry Clay on American Industry, in the House of Representatives (Mar. 30, 31, 1824) *reprinted in* STATE PAPERS AND SPEECHES ON THE TARIFF 252, 269 (F. W. Taussig ed., 1893). For a discussion of the uses of this metaphor of a rising tide lifting all boats, see Chapter 8 n.68.

34. Statement of Henry Clay (Feb. 2, 1832), 22d Cong., 1st Sess., *in* 8 REGISTER OF DEBATES IN CONGRESS 277 (1833).

35. SEAN WILENTZ, CHANTS DEMOCRATIC: NEW YORK CITY AND THE RISE OF THE AMERICAN WORKING CLASS, 1788–1850, at 115 (2d ed. 2004). Nationwide in 1890, on average only 13.3 employees worked in each manufacturing workplace. Richard Stott, *Artisans and Capitalist Development*, 16 J. EARLY REPUBLIC 257, 266 n.28 (1996).

36. *See* BORITT, LINCOLN.

37. HOWE, POLITICAL CULTURE OF THE AMERICAN WHIGS, at 16, 32–34; WILENTZ, RISE OF AMERICAN DEMOCRACY, at 482–546; JOHN LAURITZ LARSON, INTERNAL IMPROVEMENT:

National Public Works and the Promise of Popular Government in the Early United States 218–20 (2001).

38. The parties also shared the view that free education and cheap or free land were essential initial endowments. They differed on how to implement them. Howe, Political Culture of the American Whigs, at 22, 196.

39. Henry Clay, *Speech of Henry Clay, In Defence of the American System, Against the British Colonial System, Delivered in the Senate of the United States (Feb. 2d, 3d, & 6th, 1832)*, 33 (1832), Internet Archive (Aug. 15, 2008), https://archive.org/details/speechhenryclayooclay/page/n2.

40. Henry Clay, Speech of Henry Clay (Jan. 20, 1840), *reprinted in* 9 The Papers of Henry Clay: The Whig Leader, January 1, 1837–December 31, 1843, at 378, 378–79 (Robert Seager II ed., 1988) (speech on the sub-treasury bill before the U.S. Senate).

41. John Quincy Adams, Report of the Committee on Manufactures (May 23, 1832), *quoted in* Speech of Hon. Robert M. La Follette, of Wisconsin, in the House of Representatives (June 2, 1886), *in Appendix to the Congressional Record* 223–29.

42. *Id.*

43. Clay, *In Defence of the American System,* at 32.

44. John Calhoun argued that with protective tariffs, Congress had abused its constitutional power, which was restricted to using the tariff to raise revenue and not to prevent the import of foreign goods that compete with Northern manufacturers' goods. However, he continued, the courts could not look behind a facially allowable exercise of power to uncover and condemn the illegitimate use of it; this was a matter for Congress alone. Calhoun set out a congressionally constructed constitutional norm that required supermajorities to secure the constitutional principle of states as equals by preventing a majority of states whose economic interests align from oppressing a minority. Keith Whittington, Constitutional Construction: Divided Powers and Constitutional Meaning 72–112 (1999); John C. Calhoun, *South Carolina Exposition* (1828), *in* 1 Documents of American Constitutional and Legal History: From the Founding Through the Age of Industrialization 238, 238–41 (Melvin I. Urofsky & Paul Finkelman eds., 2002); Larson, Internal Improvement, at 176–181.

45. Alexander Hamilton, *Alexander Hamilton's Final Version of the Report on the Subject of Manufactures [Dec. 5, 1791],* Founders Online, https://founders.archives.gov/documents /Hamilton/01-10-02-0001-0007 [https://perma.cc/CXF5-X275] (emphasis in original).

46. Theodore Sky, To Provide for the General Welfare: A History of the Federal Spending Power 19, 79, 93–105 (2005).

47. Andrew Jackson, Maysville Road Veto (May 27, 1830), *reprinted in* Messages of Gen. Andrew Jackson 69 (John F. Brown & William White eds., 1837); James Monroe, Veto Message of "An act for the preservation and repair of the Cumberland road" (May 4, 1822), https://www .presidency.ucsb.edu/documents/veto-message [https://perma.cc/27S8-4ZD4].

48. Michele Landis Dauber, The Sympathetic State: Disaster Relief and the Origins of the American Welfare State 20 (2013).

49. *Id.*

50. *Id.*

51. Joseph Story, Commentaries on the Constitution of the United States §462 (Melville M. Bigelow ed., 5th ed. 1891).

52. *Id.*

53. James Buchanan, *Veto Message Regarding Land-Grant Colleges* (Feb. 24, 1859), University of Virginia Miller Center, https://millercenter.org/the-presidency/presidential-speeches /february-24-1859-veto-message-regarding-land-grant-colleges [https://perma.cc/E2K8-TCVL].

54. In 1862, with the Southern Democrats gone and President Lincoln in the White House, Congress again passed, and Lincoln signed, the legislation inaugurating the land-grant college system, as a general welfare measure. So, too, in January 1866, with the war over and the war

power unavailing, the first Reconstruction Congress relied on the Spending Power and General Welfare Clause for authority to extend the life and replenish the resources of the Freedmen's Bureau, over the objections of Northern Democrats.

55. DAUBER, SYMPATHETIC STATE, at 20–34.

56. ERIC FONER, THE SECOND FOUNDING: HOW THE CIVIL WAR AND RECONSTRUCTION REMADE THE CONSTITUTION (2019); Garrett Epps, *Second Founding: The Story of the Fourteenth Amendment,* 85 OR. L. REV. 895 (2006).

57. The phrase belongs to Hendrik Hartog. See his canonical *The Constitution of Aspiration and "The Rights That Belong to Us All,"* 74 J. AM. HIST. 1013 (1987).

58. *See generally* ORLANDO PATTERSON, FREEDOM: VOLUME I: FREEDOM IN THE MAKING OF WESTERN CULTURE (1991); DAVID BRION DAVIS, THE PROBLEM OF SLAVERY IN WESTERN CULTURE (1966); DAVID BRION DAVIS, THE PROBLEM OF SLAVERY IN THE AGE OF REVOLUTION, 1770–1823 (1975); DAVID BRION DAVIS, THE PROBLEM OF SLAVERY IN THE AGE OF EMANCIPATION (2014). On the distinction between "slave societies" and "societies with slaves," see DIXA RAMÍREZ, COLONIAL PHANTOMS: BELONGING AND REFUSAL IN THE DOMINICAN AMERICAS, FROM THE 19TH CENTURY TO THE PRESENT 4 (2018); IRA BERLIN, MANY THOUSANDS GONE: THE FIRST TWO CENTURIES OF SLAVERY IN NORTH AMERICA 7–14 (1998).

59. DAVIS, AGE OF REVOLUTION, at 299–306; GERALD LEONARD & SAUL CORNELL, THE PARTISAN REPUBLIC: DEMOCRACY, EXCLUSION, AND THE FALL OF THE FOUNDERS' CONSTITUTION, 1780S–1830S, at 19–21, 146–177 (2019); MICHAEL J. KLARMAN, THE FRAMERS' COUP: THE MAKING OF THE UNITED STATES CONSTITUTION 257–304 (2016). *See generally* EVA SHEPPARD WOLF, RACE AND LIBERTY IN THE NEW NATION: EMANCIPATION IN VIRGINIA FROM THE REVOLUTION TO NAT TURNER'S REBELLION (2006). *See also* ERIC FONER, THE STORY OF AMERICAN FREEDOM (1998). The volume of abolitionist voices rose in the 1780s, as Black and white abolitionists seized on the "contagion of liberty" set loose by the Revolution; during the 1780s, "every state from New Hampshire to Pennsylvania took steps toward emancipation." *Id.* at 35. This sentiment rose again, as we shall see, in the 1830s–1850s, as abolitionists found cautious welcome and mainstream allies in the party of antislavery.

60. FONER, STORY OF AMERICAN FREEDOM, at 5–8, 29–46; LINDA K. KERBER, FEDERALISTS IN DISSENT: IMAGERY AND IDEOLOGY IN JEFFERSONIAN AMERICA 23–66 (1970). On Jefferson and race, *see* ANNETTE GORDON-REED, THOMAS JEFFERSON AND SALLY HEMINGS: AN AMERICAN CONTROVERSY 133–35 (1997); JILL LEPORE, THESE TRUTHS: A HISTORY OF THE UNITED STATES 175 (2018).

61. WILLIAM W. FREEHLING, 2 THE ROAD TO DISUNION: SECESSIONISTS TRIUMPHANT, 1854–1861, at 27–47 (2007). Prevailing liberal and republican discourse also cast gender as a "natural" boundary of freedom and full membership in the self-governing republic. KERBER, FEDERALISTS IN DISSENT, at 23–66. On race, gender, and innate inferiority, see STEPHANIE MCCURRY, MASTERS OF SMALL WORLDS: YEOMAN HOUSEHOLDS, GENDER RELATIONS, AND THE POLITICAL CULTURE OF THE ANTEBELLUM SOUTH CAROLINA LOW COUNTRY 208–38 (1995); STEPHANIE MCCURRY, CONFEDERATE RECKONING: POWER AND POLITICS IN THE CIVIL WAR SOUTH 12, 32, 225 (2010).

62. On proslavery critiques of "wage slavery" in the North, see NANCY COHEN, THE RECONSTRUCTION OF AMERICAN LIBERALISM: 1865–1914, at 33–34 (2002); LEPORE, THESE TRUTHS, at 254–57.

63. SVEN BECKERT, EMPIRE OF COTTON: A GLOBAL HISTORY 98–135 (2014); Sven Beckert, *Cotton and the US South: A Short History, in* PLANTATION KINGDOM: THE AMERICAN SOUTH AND ITS GLOBAL COMMODITIES 39–60 (Richard Follett, Sven Beckert, Peter Coclanis, & Barbara Hahn eds., 2016). *See generally* KERI LEIGH MERRITT, MASTERLESS MEN: POOR WHITES AND SLAVERY IN THE ANTEBELLUM SOUTH (2017); WALTER JOHNSON, SOUL BY SOUL: LIFE INSIDE THE ANTEBELLUM SLAVE MARKET (1999); WALTER JOHNSON, RIVER OF DARK DREAMS: SLAVERY AND EMPIRE IN THE COTTON KINGDOM (2013); MCCURRY, MASTERS OF SMALL WORLDS; EDMUND MORGAN, AMERICAN SLAVERY, AMERICAN FREEDOM (1975). Plantation slavery had seemed on

shaky economic ground in the 1780s, when tobacco was still the planters' principal crop. Tobacco ravaged the soil, and this helps explain why at the time of the founding, many Southern statesmen expected plantation slavery might gradually decline and wither away. But the invention of a new cotton gin in 1793 and the shift to cotton as the South's—and the nation's—main export commodity changed that. BECKERT, EMPIRE OF COTTON, at 102–3. By 1860, 0.11 percent of Southern whites held over one hundred slaves. MERRITT, MASTERLESS MEN, at 8. One in three people in the Southern states was a slave; and their net worth in the region's slave markets was roughly half a billion in today's U.S. dollars. Henry Louis Gates Jr., *Slavery, by the Numbers,* THE ROOT (Feb. 10, 2014), https://www.theroot.com/slavery-by-the-numbers-1790874492 [https://perma.cc/6V5L-NN9L]; JOHNSON, SOUL BY SOUL, at 6. Plantation slavery became the basis of the South's social and economic orders, and the planter elite dominated its politics and culture.

64. Leon Fink, *From Autonomy to Abundance: Changing Beliefs About the Free Labour System in Nineteenth-Century America, in* TERMS OF LABOR: SLAVERY, SERFDOM, AND FREE LABOR 121–23 (Stanley L. Engerman ed., 1999); RICHARD WHITE, THE REPUBLIC FOR WHICH IT STANDS: THE UNITED STATES DURING RECONSTRUCTION AND THE GILDED AGE, 1865–1896, at 213–52 (2017); ERIC FONER, FREE SOIL, FREE LABOR, FREE MEN: THE IDEOLOGY OF THE REPUBLICAN PARTY BEFORE THE CIVIL WAR ix–xlii, 11–39 (2d ed. 1995); GABOR S. BORITT, LINCOLN AND THE ECONOMICS OF THE AMERICAN DREAM 175–94 (1978); JAMES OAKES, SLAVERY AND FREEDOM: AN INTERPRETATION OF THE OLD SOUTH 134–36 (1990). The phrase "the right to rise" is historian Gabor Boritt's. BORITT, LINCOLN.

65. *See* COHEN, RECONSTRUCTION OF AMERICAN LIBERALISM, at 143–76; ERIC FONER, THE FIERY TRIAL: ABRAHAM LINCOLN AND AMERICAN SLAVERY 92–131 (2010). *See generally* PAUL K. CONKIN, PROPHETS OF PROSPERITY: AMERICA'S FIRST POLITICAL ECONOMISTS (1980); WILLIAM E. GIENAPP, THE ORIGINS OF THE REPUBLICAN PARTY, 1852–1856 (1987); JOSEPH RAYBACK, FREE SOIL: THE ELECTION OF 1848 (1970).

66. Abraham Lincoln, Agriculture: Annual Address Before the Wisconsin State Agricultural Society, Milwaukee, Wisconsin (September 30, 1859), *in* LINCOLN ON AGRICULTURE (1943).

67. *Id.*

68. On proslavery critiques of "wage slavery" in the North, see COHEN, RECONSTRUCTION OF AMERICAN LIBERALISM, at 33–34; LEPORE, THESE TRUTHS, at 254–57.

69. James Henry Hammond, Speech on the Admission of Kansas, Under the Lecompton Constitution, Delivered in the Senate of the United States (Mar. 4, 1858), *reprinted in* SELECTIONS FROM THE LETTERS AND SPEECHES OF THE HON. JAMES H. HAMMOND 302–22 (1866).

70. *Id.*

71. GEORGE FITZHUGH, CANNIBALS ALL! OR, SLAVES WITHOUT MASTERS (1857). On Fitzhugh, see WHITE, REPUBLIC, at 78–81. On Southern intellectuals addressing the poverty of Northern white mill workers and making the case that slavery is more humane, see SEAN WILENTZ, CHANTS DEMOCRATIC: NEW YORK CITY AND THE RISE OF THE AMERICAN WORKING CLASS, 1788–1850, at 299–390 (Twentieth-Anniversary ed. 2004).

On the conditions of the working class in the North, see generally SETH ROCKMAN, SCRAPING BY: WAGE LABOR, SLAVERY, AND SURVIVAL IN EARLY BALTIMORE (2009); CHARLES SELLERS, THE MARKET REVOLUTION: JACKSONIAN AMERICA, 1815–1846, at 6, 103–36, 396 (1991) (on wage labor); SCOTT SANDAGE, BORN LOSERS: A HISTORY OF FAILURE IN AMERICA 1–21 (2005). On New York and industrializing cities, see ANTHONY F. C. WALLACE, ROCKDALE: THE GROWTH OF AN AMERICAN VILLAGE IN THE EARLY INDUSTRIAL REVOLUTION 33–70 (1972) (on hierarchy of factory managers with respect to workers); CHRISTINE STANSELL, CITY OF WOMEN: SEX AND CLASS IN NEW YORK, 1789–1860 (1987) (on young women, mills, and women's labor).

72. *See* FITZHUGH, CANNIBALS ALL!, at 24 ("Nothing written on the subject of slavery . . . is worth reading, until the days of the modern Socialists. Nobody . . . thought it worth while to en-

quire from history and statistics, whether the physical and moral condition of... slaves had been improved or rendered worse by emancipation. None would condescend to compare the evils of domestic slavery with the evils of liberty without property. The relations of capital and labor ... were things about which no one had thought or written" until the socialists began "analysing, detecting and exposing the existing relations of labor, skill and capital."). *See also* ERIC FONER, POLITICS AND IDEOLOGY IN THE AGE OF THE CIVIL WAR 57–77 (1980); FONER, FIERY TRIAL, at 97 (on Lincoln and Fitzhugh); ALEX GOUREVITCH, FROM SLAVERY TO THE COOPERATIVE COMMONWEALTH: LABOR AND REPUBLICAN LIBERTY IN THE NINETEENTH CENTURY 38–40, 47–96 (2015) (on wage slavery); WILENTZ, CHANTS DEMOCRATIC, at 326–90 (on wage slavery); JONATHAN GLICKSTEIN, CONCEPTS OF FREE LABOR IN ANTEBELLUM AMERICA 144–45 (1991) (on socialism and proslavery critiques of wage slavery); ALLAN KULIKOFF, ABRAHAM LINCOLN AND KARL MARX IN DIALOGUE 1–45 (2018) (on relations between Lincoln, socialism, and wage slavery critiques). *See generally* ROBIN BLACKBURN, AN UNFINISHED REVOLUTION: KARL MARX AND ABRAHAM LINCOLN (2011); Matt Karp, *The World the Slaveholders Craved: Proslavery Internationalism in the 1850s, in* THE WORLD OF THE REVOLUTIONARY AMERICAN REPUBLIC 414 (Andrew Shankman ed., 2014).

73. FONER, POLITICS AND IDEOLOGY, at 73.

74. *Id.*

75. Abraham Lincoln, Agriculture, at 11.

76. *Id.* at 10.

77. *Id.* at 10–11.

78. *Id.* at 11.

79. ERIC FONER, THE STORY OF AMERICAN FREEDOM 47–68 (1998); WHITE, REPUBLIC, at 136–367; GLICKSTEIN, CONCEPTS, at 91–92 (on countermodels of truly free labor in the antislavery movement). On mortgages, see Jonathan Levy, *The Mortgage Worked the Hardest: The Fate of Landed Independence in Nineteenth-Century America, in* CAPITALISM TAKES COMMAND: THE SOCIAL TRANSFORMATION OF NINETEENTH-CENTURY AMERICA 39 (Gary J. Kornblith & Michael Zakim eds., 2012); JONATHAN LEVY, FREAKS OF FORTUNE: THE EMERGING WORLD OF CAPITALISM AND RISK IN AMERICA 60–103 (2012).

80. Lincoln, Agriculture, at 11.

81. Letter from Abraham Lincoln to Albert G. Hodges (Apr. 4, 1864) ("If Slavery Is Not Wrong, Nothing Is Wrong"), *reprinted in* LINCOLN ON DEMOCRACY 316 (Mario M. Cuomo & Harold Holzer eds., 2004).

82. As they legislated and decided in favor of emancipation, Northern courts and lawmakers had invoked the Declaration-repeating "free and equal" and "inalienable rights" clauses in their state constitutions. And now in this 1830s–1850s "heyday of natural rights talk" among Northern jurists, even the steely positivist Lemuel Shaw, chief justice of the Massachusetts Supreme Judicial Court and the most widely respected of antebellum state high court judges, remarked that the Declaration itself—or if not, then the Declaration-embracing language in the 1780 state constitution—probably abolished slavery in Massachusetts. *See* William E. Forbath, *Lincoln, the Declaration, and the "Grisly, Undying Corpse of States' Rights": History, Memory, and Imagination in the Constitution of a Southern Liberal,* 92 GEO. L.J. 709, 721–22 (2004).

83. WHITE, REPUBLIC, at 62, 87 (on Southern elites); JAMES OAKES, FREEDOM NATIONAL: THE DESTRUCTION OF SLAVERY IN THE UNITED STATES, 1861–1865, at 32–34, 42–48 (2014) (on critique of slaveholders wielding power in the federal government); WILENTZ, CHANTS DEMOCRATIC, at 299–390.

84. Abolitionists were such an unpopular and despised minority because they pressed forward the cause of Black bondsmen in the South and insisted on dramatizing—via fugitive slave cases and via abolitionist press—the complicity of Northern states and the federal government in supporting slavery.

85. *See generally* ERIC FONER, FREE SOIL, FREE LABOR, FREE MEN: THE IDEOLOGY OF THE REPUBLICAN PARTY BEFORE THE CIVIL WAR (2d ed. 1995); MICHAEL LES BENEDICT, PRESERVING THE CONSTITUTION: ESSAYS ON POLITICS AND THE CONSTITUTION IN THE RECONSTRUCTION ERA (2006); WILLIAM W. FREEHLING, 2 THE ROAD TO DISUNION: SECESSIONISTS TRIUMPHANT, 1854–1861, at 27–47 (2007); MARK GRABER, DRED SCOTT AND THE PROBLEM OF CONSTITUTIONAL EVIL (2008); ELIZABETH R. VARON, DISUNION! THE COMING OF THE AMERICAN CIVIL WAR, 1789–1859 (2008).

86. *See generally* FONER, FREE SOIL, at 40–72; DAVID M. POTTER, THE IMPENDING CRISIS: AMERICA BEFORE THE CIVIL WAR, 1848–1861 (1976); RICHARD H. SEWELL, BALLOTS FOR FREEDOM: ANTISLAVERY POLITICS IN THE UNITED STATES, 1837–1860 (1980).

87. CHRISTOPHER L. TOMLINS, LAW, LABOR, AND IDEOLOGY IN THE EARLY AMERICAN REPUBLIC 12–13, 164, 385–88 (1993); WILENTZ, CHANTS DEMOCRATIC, at 332–33.

88. *An Address of the Workingmen of Charleston, Mass., to Their Brethren Throughout the Commonwealth and the Union*, 4 BOSTON QUARTERLY REVIEW 112, 113–114 (1841) *quoted in* TOMLINS, LAW, LABOR, AND IDEOLOGY, at 12 n.36.

89. Orestes Brownson, *The Laboring Classes, An Article from the Boston Quarterly Review* (1840), *quoted in* TOMLINS, LAW, LABOR, AND IDEOLOGY, at 385.

90. *Id.* at 387, quoting Brownson.

91. *Id.*

92. *See* Chapters 4–6.

93. BARRINGTON MOORE JR., SOCIAL ORIGINS OF DICTATORSHIP AND DEMOCRACY 112 (1967).

94. FONER, FREE SOIL, at 18–23, 26, 66.

95. *Id.* at 26–29.

96. *Id.* at 92–93; MICHAEL HOLT, THE POLITICAL CRISIS OF THE 1850S (1983). For years, the Democratic Party had advocated a policy of easy access to government land, "to afford every American citizen of enterprise," as Jackson had put it, "the opportunity of securing an independent freehold." WILLIAM B. SCOTT, IN PURSUIT OF HAPPINESS: AMERICAN CONCEPTIONS OF PROPERTY FROM THE SEVENTEENTH TO THE TWENTIETH CENTURY 59–66 (1977). But Jackson had never proposed barring slavery from all new territories. Leader of a party with robust Northern and Southern bases, he was content with the Missouri Compromise's pragmatic "36 / 30" line on the map. Now, however, the annexation of Texas and vast new territories ceded by Mexico in the Southwest arrived just as the nation's most severe depression (1837–1842) had stirred up a politics of class feelings: a felt crisis of free labor and brittle opportunity structures in the North. The pragmatic line on the map promised the spread of slavery throughout the new territories, which would turn soon enough into a fleet of new slave states. In this context, many Northern Whigs and Jacksonians alike were drawn to a more militant line—not 36 / 30, but instead "free soil" throughout the new territory. Stemming the power of slaveholders in the national government— stemming what Republicans were coming to call "the Slave Power"—was equally central to the enterprise. LEONARD L. RICHARDS, THE SLAVE POWER: THE FREE NORTH AND SOUTHERN DOMINATION, 1780–1860 (2000).

97. FONER, FREE SOIL, at 92–96.

98. *Republican Party Platform of 1856* (June 18, 1856), THE AMERICAN PRESIDENCY PROJECT (Gerhard Peters & John T. Woolley eds.), https://www.presidency.ucsb.edu/node/273293 [https:// perma.cc/SGX5-4XHK].

99. *Id.*

100. *Report of the Joint Committee on Reconstruction*, 39th Cong., 1st Sess., viii–ix (Apr. 30, 1866). On the Republican Party leadership's understanding of the party's constitutional purpose as one of thwarting the return of the Slave Power and its oligarchic designs, see "Black Suffrage and Electoral Arithmetic: A Biracial Republic or a White Oligarchy," Chapter 3; see also RICHARDS, SLAVE POWER; FORREST NABORS, FROM OLIGARCHY TO REPUBLICANISM: THE GREAT TASK OF RECONSTRUCTION (2017).

101. FONER, FREE SOIL, at 73–102; Matthew Adams Axtell, American Steamboat Gothic: Disruptive Commerce and Slavery's Liquidation, 1832–1865 (2016) (unpublished Ph.D. dissertation, Princeton University); Randy E. Barnett, *From Antislavery Lawyer to Chief Justice: The Remarkable but Forgotten Career of Salmon P. Chase,* 63 CASE W. RES. L. REV. 653 (2013); NABORS, FROM OLIGARCHY, at 105–86.

102. FONER, FREE SOIL, FREE LABOR, at ix, 80, 87.

103. *Id.;* SEAN WILENTZ, NO PROPERTY IN MAN: SLAVERY AND ANTISLAVERY AT THE NATION'S FOUNDING 266–68 (2018); MARK GRABER, DRED SCOTT AND THE PROBLEM OF CONSTITUTIONAL EVIL 91–172 (2008); NABORS, FROM OLIGARCHY, at 31–222.

104. FONER, FREE SOIL, at 87.

105. NABORS, FROM OLIGARCHY, at 31–222; Axtell, American Steamboat Gothic.

106. Matthew A. Axtell, *What Is Still "Radical" in the Antislavery Legal Practice of Salmon P. Chase?* 11 HASTINGS RACE & POVERTY L.J. 269, 271–72 (2014).

107. Axtell, American Steamboat Gothic; NABORS, FROM OLIGARCHY, at 31–222.

108. FONER, FREE SOIL, at 73–102; GABOR S. BORITT, LINCOLN AND THE ECONOMICS OF THE AMERICAN DREAM 195–222 (1978); WILENTZ, NO PROPERTY, at 206–62.

109. WILENTZ, NO PROPERTY, at 225–42; RICHARD S. NEWMAN, THE TRANSFORMATION OF AMERICAN ABOLITIONISM: FIGHTING SLAVERY IN THE EARLY REPUBLIC 100–30 (2002); RICHARDS, SLAVE POWER, at 2, 77; JOHN STAUFFER, THE BLACK HEARTS OF MEN: RADICAL ABOLITIONISTS AND THE TRANSFORMATION OF RACE 22–33, 153 (2001).

110. Abraham Lincoln, Springfield Speech (June 26, 1857), *in* 2 COLLECTED WORKS OF ABRAHAM LINCOLN, at 398, 405–6 (Roy P. Basler ed., 1953), *quoted in* GEORGE ANASTAPLO, ABRAHAM LINCOLN: A CONSTITUTIONAL BIOGRAPHY 18 (1999).

111. ANASTAPLO, LINCOLN, at 18, 165. Quoting Scripture, Lincoln would write that the principles of the Declaration were the "apple of gold" and the Constitution and the Union were a "*picture of silver,* subsequently framed around it. The picture was made, not to *conceal,* or *destroy* the apple; but to *adorn,* and *preserve* it. The *picture* was made *for* the apple—*not* the apple for the picture." Lincoln, Fragment on the Constitution and the Union, *in* 4 THE COLLECTED WORKS, 168–69.

112. Lincoln, Springfield Speech, at 398, 405; *see* CREATED EQUAL? THE COMPLETE LINCOLN-DOUGLAS DEBATES OF 1858, at 111–12 (Paul M. Angle ed., 1958).

113. Lincoln, Fragment on the Constitution and the Union, *in* 4 COLLECTED WORKS, at 169.

114. The platform reads:

> Resolved: That the maintenance of the principles promulgated in the Declaration of Independence, and embodied in the Federal Constitution are essential to the preservation of our Republican institutions. . . .
>
> Resolved: That, with our Republican fathers, we hold it to be a self-evident truth, that all men are endowed with the inalienable right to life, liberty, and the pursuit of happiness, and that the primary object and ulterior design of our Federal Government were to secure these rights to all persons under its exclusive jurisdiction; that, as our Republican fathers, when they had abolished Slavery in all our National Territory, ordained that no person shall be deprived of life, liberty, or property, without due process of law, it becomes our duty to maintain this provision of the Constitution against all attempts to violate it for the purpose of establishing Slavery in the Territories of the United States by positive legislation, prohibiting its existence or extension therein. That we deny the authority of Congress, of a Territorial Legislation, of any individual, or association of individuals, to give legal existence to Slavery in any Territory of the United States, while the present Constitution shall be maintained.

Republican Party Platform of 1856.

115. "[W]e hold that the Federal Government has no right . . . whatever to distinguish between the domestic institutions of one State or section and another, in order to favor one and discourage the other. As the Federal representative of each and all the States, it is bound to deal out, within the sphere of its powers, equal and exact justice and favour to all." *The Address of the Southern Delegates in Congress to Their Constituents*, 3 Am. Q. Reg. & Mag., Sept. 1849, at 276, 282.

116. *Cf.* Shelby County v. Holder, 570 U.S. 529 (2013) (espousing a modern analogue of this principle).

117. John C. Calhoun, Mr. Calhoun's Address to the People of the Southern States (1849).

118. Elizabeth Varon, Disunion!: The Coming of the America Civil War, 1789–1859, at 235–336 (2008).

119. Dred Scott v. Sandford, 60 U.S. (19 How.) 393, 543 (1857) (McLean, J., dissenting).

120. *Id.* at 529, 527 (Catron, J., concurring).

121. *Id.* at 527.

122. David M. Potter, The Impending Crisis: America Before the Civil War, 1848–1861, at 61–62 (1976).

123. The Labor Movement: The Problem of To-day 67–123 (George E. McNeill ed., 1886).

124. *See* Eric Foner, Politics and Ideology in the Age of the Civil War 73 (1980).

125. Wendell Phillips, *The Question of Labor*, Liberator, July 9, 1847, *quoted in* Jonathan Glickstein, *"Poverty Is Not Slavery": American Abolitionists and the Competitive Labor Market, in* Antislavery Reconsidered: New Perspectives on the Abolitionists 195, 210–11 (Lewis Perry & Michael Fellman eds., 1979). Evangelical abolitionists often contrasted the "degrading" coercion of the lash with the "kindly" stimulus of poverty. *Id.* at 200.

126. *See* Foner, Politics and Ideology, at 63–71.

127. *Id.* at 64.

128. *Id.*

129. *See* Chapter 3.

3. The Second Founding

1. Eric Foner, The Second Founding: How the Civil War and Reconstruction Remade the Constitution (2019); Garrett Epps, *Second Founding: The Story of the Fourteenth Amendment*, 85 Oregon L. Rev. 895, 905–7 (2006).

2. *See* James Oakes, Freedom National: The Destruction of Slavery in the United States, 1861–1865 (2012). *See also* Harold M. Hyman & William M. Wiecek, Equal Justice Under Law 170 (1982).

3. Civil Rights Act of 1866, ch. 31, 14 Stat. 27.

4. Forrest A. Nabors, From Oligarchy to Republicanism 307 (2017); Eric Foner, Reconstruction: America's Unfinished Revolution, 1863–1877, at 301 (1988).

5. Report of the Joint Committee on Reconstruction, 39th Cong., 1st Sess., Apr. 30, 1866, at xiii.

6. *Reconstruction.; Hon. Thaddeus Stevens on the Great Topic of the Hour. An Address Delivered to the Citizens of Lancaster, Sept. 6, 1865,* N.Y. Times, Sept. 10, 1865, at 2.

7. Abraham Lincoln, Address Delivered at the Dedication of the Cemetery at Gettysburg (Nov. 19, 1863), *in* 7 Collected Works of Abraham Lincoln 22, 23 (Roy P. Basler et al. eds., 1953).

8. Foner, Reconstruction, at 240. Privately, Johnson supposedly declared, "[T]his is a country for white men, and, by God, as long as I am President, it shall be a government for white men." Richard White, The Republic for Which It Stands 62 (2017).

9. Foner, Reconstruction, at 240.

10. *See* White, Republic, at 54 (citing Gregory P. Downs, After Appomattox: Military Occupation and the Ends of War, 84–87 (2015); Joseph A. Ramney, In the Wake of

SLAVERY: CIVIL WAR, CIVIL RIGHTS, AND THE RECONSTRUCTION OF SOUTHERN LAW 45–46 (2006)). In Alabama, for example, "any runaway, stubborn servant or child," any worker "who loiters away his time," or failed to comply with a labor contract was deemed a vagrant. The laws thus produced vagrants en masse, who could be punished by forced labor, usually leased to planters by local courts and sheriffs—putting the Thirteenth Amendment's "except as punishment for a crime" to work for a new system of bound Black labor. S. REP. No. 53–113, pt. 2, at 6 (1894); *see also* WHITE, REPUBLIC, at 54.

11. CONG. GLOBE, 39th Cong., 1st Sess. App. 140 (1866) (Representation of Rebel States, a speech by Sen. Wilson).

12. FONER, RECONSTRUCTION, at 252. *See* CONG. GLOBE, 39th Cong., 1st Sess. 683 (1866) (speech of Sen. Sumner noting increased representation in the South based on unfranchised population). *See also Report of the Joint Committee on Reconstruction,* H.R. Rep. No. 39-30, at xiii (1866).

13. CONG. GLOBE, 39th Cong., 1st Sess. 6 (1865).

14. Slavery also had been a system of sexual exploitation and gender domination. For accounts and analysis of how the constitutional politics of Reconstruction addressed (and how it ignored) these dimensions of sex and gender in the aftermath of slavery, see Amy Dru Stanley, *Instead of Waiting for the Thirteenth Amendment: The War Power, Slave Marriage, and Inviolate Human Rights,* 115 AMERICAN HISTORICAL REV. 732 (2010); Amy Dru Stanley, *Slave Emancipation and the Revolutionizing of Human Rights, in* THE WORLD THE CIVIL WAR MADE (Greg Downs and Kate Masur eds., 2015); TERA W. HUNTER, BOUND IN WEDLOCK: SLAVE AND FREE BLACK MARRIAGE IN THE NINETEENTH CENTURY 121–95 (2017).

15. In today's dollars.

16. Abraham Lincoln, Annual Message to Congress (Dec. 3, 1861), *in* 5 COLLECTED WORKS OF ABRAHAM LINCOLN 35, 49 (Roy P. Basler et al. eds., 1953).

17. *See* OLAV THULESIUS, HARRIET BEECHER STOWE IN FLORIDA: 1867–1884 (2001).

18. ERIC FONER, A SHORT HISTORY OF RECONSTRUCTION 104 (1990).

19. *Id.*

20. *Id.* at 104–5.

21. JAMES BREWER STEWART, WENDELL PHILLIPS: LIBERTY'S HERO 289 (1998).

22. FORREST A. NABORS, FROM OLIGARCHY TO REPUBLICANISM 68 (2017) (quoting CONG. GLOBE, 38th Cong., 1st Sess. 506 (1864) (statement of H. Wilson)).

23. ERIC FONER, RECONSTRUCTION 234 (1988) (quoting Horace Greeley to Thomas Dixon (June 2, 1865) (on file with N. Y. Pub. Libr.)).

24. NABORS, FROM OLIGARCHY TO REPUBLICANISM, at 70 (quoting Representative George W. Julian, Homesteads for Soldiers on the Lands of Rebels (Mar. 18, 1864), *in* GEORGE W. JULIAN, SPEECHES ON POLITICAL QUESTIONS 212, 224–25 (1872)).

25. Charles Sumner, Part Execution of the Guaranty of a Republican Form of Government, Bill in the Senate (Dec. 4, 1865) *in* 13 CHARLES SUMNER; HIS COMPLETE WORKS 14, 14 (George Frisbie Hoar ed., Project Gutenberg 2015) (ebook).

26. Charles Sumner, The Equal Rights of All, *in* 13 CHARLES SUMNER; HIS COMPLETE WORKS, at 115; CONG. GLOBE, 39th Cong., 1st Sess. 673–87 (1866) (statement of Sen. Sumner). We are indebted to Richard White for leading us to this speech. See RICHARD WHITE, THE REPUBLIC FOR WHICH IT STANDS 65 (2017).

27. NABORS, FROM OLIGARCHY TO REPUBLICANISM, at 39–40 (quoting CONG. GLOBE, 39th Cong., 1st Sess. 1280 (1866)).

28. Sumner, Guaranty of a Republican Form of Government, *in* 13 CHARLES SUMNER; HIS COMPLETE WORKS, at 14.

29. CONG. GLOBE, 39th Cong., 1st Sess. 675 (1866) (statement of Sen. Sumner).

30. U.S. CONST. art. IV, § 4.

31. CONG. GLOBE, 40th Cong., 1st Sess. 614 (1867); Sumner, Equal Rights of All, *in* 13 CHARLES SUMNER; HIS COMPLETE WORKS, at 136..

32. Cong. Globe, 39th Cong., 1st Sess. 684 (1866) (statement of Sen. Sumner) (quoting Luther v. Borden, 48 U.S. 1, 42 (1849)).

33. Sumner, Equal Rights of All, *in* 13 Charles Sumner; His Complete Works, at 143.

34. Cong. Globe, 39th Cong., 1st Sess. 676 (1866) (statement of Sen. Sumner).

35. Sumner, Equal Rights of All, *in* 13 Charles Sumner; His Complete Works, at 136, 148.

36. *Id.* at 125, 163.

37. Cong. Globe, 39th Cong., 1st Sess. 684 (1866) (statement of Sen. Sumner).

38. *Id.*

39. *Id.* at 681.

40. Sumner, Equal Rights of All, *in* 13 Charles Sumner; His Complete Works, at 120. For a contemporary historian's effort to clinch the case that this reading of the founders' design is, in fact, historically accurate, see Sean Wilentz, No Property in Man: Slavery and Antislavery at the Nation's Founding (2018).

41. Sumner, Equal Rights of All, *in* 13 Charles Sumner; His Complete Works, at 143.

42. *Id.*

43. *See* Forrest A. Nabors, From Oligarchy to Republicanism 69 (2017). Sumner's bill was only "in part execution of the guaranty [clause]." He presented five others, one of which conferred possessory rights on freed people settled by army officials on abandoned plantations. S. 5, 39th Cong. (1865); Sumner, Part Execution of the Guaranty of a Republican Form of Government, Bill in the Senate (December 4, 1865) *in* 13 Charles Sumner; His Complete Works at 14.

44. Mark Graber, *The Second Freedmen's Bureau Bill's Constitution*, 94 Tex. L. Rev. 1361, 1384 (2016) (quoting Cong. Globe, 39th Cong., 1st Sess. 942 (1866) (statement of Sen. Trumbull)).

45. Abraham Lincoln, Speech at Springfield, Ill. (June 26, 1857), *in* 2 Collected Works of Abraham Lincoln 398, 406 (Roy P. Basler et al. eds., 1953).

46. Civil Rights Act of 1866, ch. 31, 14 Stat. 27.

47. Graber, *Second Freedmen's Bureau*, at 1361, 1366–70; Eric Foner, The Second Founding 63–65 (2019).

48. Civil Rights Act of 1866, ch. 31, 14 Stat. 27.

49. Graber, *Second Freedmen's Bureau*, at 1375 (quoting Cong. Globe, 39th Cong., 1st Sess. 654 (statement of Rep. McKee)); *see also id.* at 1376 (quoting Cong. Globe, 39th Cong., 1st Sess. 340 (1865) (statement of Rep. Wilson)).

50. *Id.* at 1384 (quoting Cong. Globe, 39th Cong., 1st Sess. 942 (1866) (statement of Sen. Trumbull)).

51. Emily Zackin, Looking for Rights in All the Wrong Places 39–40 (2013). *See, e.g.,* DeShaney v. Winnebago County Dep't of Soc. Servs., 489 U.S. 189, 195–96 (1989) ("[The Fourteenth Amendment's] language cannot be fairly extended to impose an affirmative obligation on the State. . . . [It confers] no affirmative right to government aid, even where such aid may be necessary to secure life, liberty, or property"); Collins v. City of Harker Heights, Tex., 503 U.S. 115, 126–27 (1992). *See also, e.g.,* Harris v. McRae, 448 U.S. 297, 318 (1980).

52. Graber, *Second Freedmen's Bureau*, at 1384 (quoting Cong. Globe, 39th Cong., 1st Sess. 656 (1866) (statement of Rep. Eliot)).

53. *Id.* at 1367–68 (citing The American Nation: Primary Sources 92–94 (Bruce P. Frohnen ed., 2008)).

54. *Id.* at 1368 (quoting The American Nation: Primary Sources 92, 93). For the least familiar of these clauses, see U.S. Const. art. IV, § 3 ("The Congress shall have Power to dispose of and make all needful Rules and Regulations respecting the Territory or other Property belonging to the United States").

55. *See* Forrest A. Nabors, From Oligarchy to Republicanism 46–49 (2017).

56. *See generally* Nabors, From Oligarchy to Republicanism.

57. *Id.* at 50 (quoting Cong. Globe, 37th Cong., 2d Sess. 1077, 1075 (1862) (statement of Sen. Morrill)).

58. *Id.* (quoting CONG. GLOBE, 38th Cong., 1st Sess. 507 (1864) (statement of Rep. Wilson)).

59. *Id.* at 51 (quoting James Abram Garfield, Speech Delivered in the House of Representatives: The National Bureau of Education (June 8, 1866), *in* 1 THE WORKS OF JAMES ABRAM GARFIELD 126, 142 (Burke A. Hinsdale ed., 1882)).

60. Graber, *Second Freedmen's Bureau,* at 1361, 1387 (quoting CONG. GLOBE, 39th Cong., 1st Sess. 588 (1865) (statement of Rep. Donnelly)).

61. NABORS, FROM OLIGARCHY TO REPUBLICANISM, at 51 (quoting CONG. GLOBE, 38th Cong., 1st Sess. 2115 (1864) (statement of Rep. Allison)).

62. *See generally* RONALD E. BUTCHART, SCHOOLING THE FREED PEOPLE: TEACHING, LEARNING, AND THE STRUGGLE FOR BLACK FREEDOM, 1861–1876 (2010); WILLIAM P. VAUGHN, SCHOOLS FOR ALL: THE BLACKS AND PUBLIC EDUCATION IN THE SOUTH, 1865–1877 (1974); ADAM FAIRCLOUGH, A CLASS OF THEIR OWN: BLACK TEACHERS IN THE SEGREGATED SOUTH (2007).

63. BUTCHART, SCHOOLING THE FREED PEOPLE, at 79–80.

64. FAIRCLOUGH, CLASS OF THEIR OWN, at 27.

65. *Id.* at 27–28.

66. *Id.*

67. *Id.* at 48.

68. *Id.* at 48–49.

69. *Id.* at 57.

70. *See generally* FAIRCLOUGH, CLASS OF THEIR OWN; VAUGHN, SCHOOLS FOR ALL.

71. NABORS, FROM OLIGARCHY TO REPUBLICANISM, at 46–63 (quoting Representative George W. Julian, The Homestead Bill (Jan. 29, 1851), *in* GEORGE W. JULIAN, SPEECHES ON POLITICAL QUESTIONS 51 (1872)).

72. CONG. GLOBE, 32d Cong., 1st Sess. App., 426–29 (1852) (Man's Right to the Soil, a speech of Rep. Grow). The authors are indebted to Yochai Benkler for bringing this speech as well as the general constitutional political-economic outlook of Galusha Grow to their attention.

73. *Id.* at 427.

74. NABORS, FROM OLIGARCHY TO REPUBLICANISM, at 62–67 (quoting Julian, Homestead Bill, *in* JULIAN, SPEECHES ON POLITICAL QUESTIONS, at 51–52); CONG. GLOBE, 32d Cong., 1st Sess. App., 427 (1852) (Man's Right to the Soil, a speech of Rep. Grow).

75. CONG. GLOBE, 32d Cong., 1st Sess. App., 427 (1852) (Man's Right to the Soil, a speech of Rep. Grow).

76. Republican Party Platform of 1860, *reprinted in* NATIONAL PARTY PLATFORMS 32 (Kirk H. Porter & Donald Bruce Johnson eds., 2d ed. 1961).

77. Homestead Act of 1862, Pub. L. No. 37–64, 12 Stat. 392 (1862).

78. CONG. GLOBE, 39th Cong., 1st Sess. 91 (1865) (statement of Sen. Sumner).

79. Mark Graber, *The Second Freedmen's Bureau Bill's Constitution,* 94 TEX. L. REV. 1361, 1386 (2016) (quoting CONG. GLOBE, 39th Cong., 1st Sess. 299 (1866) (statement of Sen. Trumbull)).

80. *Id.* at 1384 (quoting CONG. GLOBE, 39th Cong., 1st Sess. 942 (1866) (statement of Sen. Trumbull)). Others had much the same response: "The second section of that amendment confers the power and so creates the duty for just such legislation as this bill contains, to give [the freed people] shelter, and food, to lift them from slavery." *Id.* (quoting CONG. GLOBE, 39th Cong., 1st Sess. 656 (1866) (statement of Rep. Eliot)).

81. Graber, *Second Freedmen's Bureau,* at 1386 (quoting CONG. GLOBE, 39th Cong., 1st Sess. 299 (1866) (statement of Sen. Trumbull)).

82. NABORS, FROM OLIGARCHY TO REPUBLICANISM , at 69 (quoting CONG. GLOBE, 38th Cong., 1st Sess. 2115 (1852) (statement of Rep. Allison)).

83. CONG. GLOBE, 38th Cong., 1st Sess. 506 (1864) (statement of Sen. Wilson). *See also* CONG. GLOBE, 38th Cong., 1st Sess. 2115 (1852) (statement of Rep. Allison).

84. CONG. GLOBE, 38th Cong., 1st Sess. 507 (1864) (statement of Sen. Wilson).

85. *Id.* (quoting CONG. GLOBE, 38th Cong., 1st Sess. 506 (1864) (statement of Sen. Wilson)). *See also* CONG. GLOBE, 38th Cong., 1st Sess. 2115 (1852) (statement of Rep. Allison) ("We must restore the great body of that people . . . by a division of the large estates, now abandoned, into small farms, which shall be tilled by their owners. This division is also necessary to eradicate slavery.").

86. *Reconstruction.; Hon. Thaddeus Stevens on the Great Topic of the Hour. An Address Delivered to the Citizens of Lancaster, Sept. 6, 1865,* N.Y. TIMES, Sept. 10, 1865, at 2.

87. NABORS, FROM OLIGARCHY TO REPUBLICANISM, at 70 (quoting Rep. George W. Julian, Homesteads for Soldiers on the Lands of Rebels (Mar. 18, 1864), *in* GEORGE W. JULIAN, SPEECHES ON POLITICAL QUESTIONS 224 (1872)).

88. CONG. GLOBE, 38th Cong. 1st Sess. 1186 (1864) (statement of Rep. Julian); *see* LaWanda Cox, *The Promise of Land for the Freedmen,* 45 MISSISSIPPI VALLEY HIST. REV. 413, 431–40 (1958).

89. Letter from Merrimon Howard to Adelbert Ames (Nov. 28, 1973) (on file with Ames Family papers, Sophia Smith Collection, Smith College, Northampton, Mass.), *quoted in* Eric Foner, *The Meaning of Freedom in the Age of Emancipation,* 81 J. AM. HIST. 435, 458 (1994).

90. Garrison Frazier, *Colloquy with Colored Ministers,* 16 J. NEGRO HIST. 88, 90–91 (1931), *quoted in* Foner, *Meaning of Freedom,* at 457.

91. BARRINGTON MOORE JR., SOCIAL ORIGINS OF DEMOCRACY AND DICTATORSHIP 153 (1967).

92. MAREK D. STEEDMAN, JIM CROW CITIZENSHIP: LIBERALISM AND THE SOUTHERN DEFENSE OF RACIAL HIERARCHY 101 (2012).

93. *See id. See also* NEIL R. MCMILLEN, DARK JOURNEY: BLACK MISSISSIPPIANS IN THE AGE OF JIM CROW 120 (1990); RICHARD WHITE, THE REPUBLIC FOR WHICH IT STANDS 149 (2017).

94. CONG. GLOBE, 40th Cong., 3d Sess. 912 (1869) (statement of Sen. Willey).

95. CONG. GLOBE, 39th Cong., 1st Sess. 72 (1865) (Reconstruction, a speech by Rep. Stevens).

96. *See generally* Mark Graber, *Constructing Constitutional Politics: Thaddeus Stevens, John Bingham, and the Forgotten Fourteenth Amendment* 65 (University of Maryland Legal Studies Research Paper No. 2014–37), https://ssrn.com/abstract=2483355.

97. U.S. CONST. amend. XIV, § 5.

98. Mark Graber, *The Second Freedmen's Bureau Bill's Constitution,* 94 TEX. L. REV. 1361, 1381 (2016) (quoting CONG. GLOBE, 39th Cong., 1st Sess. app. 110 (1866) (statement of Sen. Stewart)).

99. U.S. CONST. amend. XIV, § 2.

100. *Id.* § 3.

101. *See generally* Graber, *Constructing Constitutional Politics,* at 73–74.

102. ERIC FONER, A SHORT HISTORY OF RECONSTRUCTION 148–61 (2014).

103. *Id.*

104. JILL LEPORE, THESE TRUTHS: A HISTORY OF THE UNITED STATES 323 (2018).

105. *Id.*

106. For more detailed accounts of the implementation of Reconstruction Amendments and legislation under the Black Republicans, see ERIC FONER, RECONSTRUCTION 281–411 (1988); THOMAS HOLT, BLACK OVER WHITE: NEGRO POLITICAL LEADERSHIP IN SOUTH CAROLINA DURING RECONSTRUCTION (1977); EDWARD MAGDOL, A RIGHT TO THE LAND: ESSAYS ON THE FREEDMEN'S COMMUNITY (1977); DONALD G. NIEMAN, TO SET THE LAW IN MOTION: THE FREEDMEN'S BUREAU AND THE LEGAL RIGHTS OF BLACKS, 1865–1868 (1979); Donald G. Nieman, *African Americans and the Meaning of Freedom: Washington County, Texas as a Case Study, 1865–1886—Freedom: Politics,* 70 CHICAGO-KENT L. REV. 541 (1994); Donald G. Nieman, *Black Political Power and Criminal Justice: Washington County, Texas, 1868–1884,* 55 J. S. HIST. 391 (1989).

107. *See generally* FONER, RECONSTRUCTION, at 281–411; HOLT, BLACK OVER WHITE; Nieman, *African Americans and the Meaning of Freedom;* Nieman, *Black Political Power and Criminal Justice.*

108. *See generally* GREGORY P. DOWNS, AFTER APPOMATTOX: MILITARY OCCUPATION AND THE ENDS OF WAR (2015).

109. LePore, These Truths, at 329.

110. Reva Siegel, *She the People: The Nineteenth Amendment, Sex Equality, Federalism, and the Family,* 115 Harvard L. Rev. 948, 969 n.58 (quoting 2 History of Woman Suffrage 91 (Elizabeth Cady Stanton, Susan B. Anthony, and Matinda Joslyn Gage eds., 1882)).

111. *See, e.g.,* Judith Shklar, American Citizenship: The Quest for Inclusion 57 (1991) (describing how the suffragists' "bitter resentment" over this exclusion illustrates what Shklar calls "the darker side of citizenship as standing": to be consigned to a lower status than enfranchised Black men brought out a "deep racism" among some suffragists).

112. Susan B. Anthony delivered this speech to multiple audiences in Monroe and Ontario Counties in advance of her trial on June 17, 1873. 2 History of Woman Suffrage, at 630, 635.

113. *See* Serena Mayeri, Reasoning from Race (2014).

114. *See* Kenneth Karst, *The Coming Crisis of Work in Constitutional Perspective,* 82 Cornell L. Rev. 523, 531 (1997).

115. *See* Proceedings of the Woman's Rights Convention, Held at Worcester, October 23d & 24th, 1850, at 4–5 (Prentiss & Sawyer 1851), *quoted in* Reva B. Siegel, *Home as Work: The First Woman's Rights Claims Concerning Wives' Household Labor, 1850–1880,* 103 Yale L.J. 1073, 1100 (1994); *see also* Norma Basch, In the Eyes of the Law: Women, Marriage, and Property in Nineteenth-Century New York 162–99 (1982) (discussing the links between women's battles for equality in the domestic sphere, contract and property rights, and suffrage).

116. *See* Amy Dru Stanley, *Conjugal Bonds and Wage Labor: Rights of Contract in the Age of Emancipation,* 75 J. Am. Hist. 471, 479–81 (1988); Amy Dru Stanley, From Bondage to Contract: Wage Labor, Marriage, and the Market in the Age of Slave Emancipation (1998).

117. *See* Siegel, *Home as Work,* at 1100.

118. Proceedings of the Woman's Rights Convention, Held at Worcester, October 15th & 16th, 1851, at 18 (1852), *quoted in* Reva B. Siegel, *Home as* Work, at 1115. In this way, nineteenth-century feminists did not challenge the gender division of labor so much as the gendered definition of labor, in the useful phrase offered by Jeanne Boydston, Home and Work: Housework, Wages, and the Ideology of Labor in the Early Republic xi–xv (1990).

119. *See* Siegel, *Home as Work,* at 1112–18.

120. National Woman Suffrage Association, Declaration of Rights for Women, July 4, 1876, *in* 3 History of Woman Suffrage 31–34 (Elizabeth Cady Stanton et al. eds., 1886).

121. *Id.*

122. *Id.* at 33.

123. 2 History of Woman Suffrage 635 (Elizabeth Cady Stanton et al. eds., 1882).

124. *Id.* at 631–32 (emphasis added).

4. Constitutional Class Struggle in the Gilded Age

1. George E. McNeill, *The Problem of To-Day, in* The Labor Movement: The Problem of Today 459 (George E. McNeill ed. 1887).

2. Citizens United v. FEC, 558 U.S. 310 (2010); Janus v. AFSCME, 138 S. Ct. 2448 (2018); National Fed'n of Indep. Bus. v. Sebelius, 567 U.S. 519 (2012). For a discussion, see "Repairing the First Amendment to Rebuild Countervailing Power," Chapter 9; "Race and the Constitutional Political Economy of Health Care—and Voting," Chapter 9.

3. *See, e.g.,* Philip Pettit, Republicanism: A Theory of Freedom and Government 21–27 (1997) (defining the republican ideal of nondomination, as distinct from positive and negative liberty); *id.* at 163–65 (discussing republican economic thought, and contrasting the republican and classical liberal conceptions of economic freedom); Michael J. Sandel, Democracy's Discontent: America in Search of a Public Philosophy 185–89 (1996) (describing the political

theory of labor republicanism); ALEX GOUREVITCH, FROM SLAVERY TO THE COOPERATIVE COMMONWEALTH: LABOR AND REPUBLICAN LIBERTY IN THE NINETEENTH CENTURY 7–17 (2015) (discussing the salience of labor republicanism for contemporary republican theory); K. SABEEL RAHMAN, DEMOCRACY AGAINST DOMINATION (2017) (exploring the connection between political and economic power in republican thought).

4. *See* ERIC FONER, RECONSTRUCTION: AMERICA'S UNFINISHED REVOLUTION, 1863–1877, at 524–34 (1988); J. MORGAN KOUSSER, THE SHAPING OF SOUTHERN POLITICS: SUFFRAGE RESTRICTION AND THE ESTABLISHMENT OF THE ONE-PARTY SOUTH, 1880–1910, at 11–44 (1974); LAURA F. EDWARDS, A LEGAL HISTORY OF THE CIVIL WAR AND RECONSTRUCTION: A NATION OF RIGHTS 149–53 (2015).

5. *See* FONER, RECONSTRUCTION, at 517–22; HEATHER COX RICHARDSON, TO MAKE MEN FREE: A HISTORY OF THE REPUBLICAN PARTY 109–38 (2014).

6. DAVID MONTGOMERY, BEYOND EQUALITY: LABOR AND THE RADICAL REPUBLICANS 1862–1872, at 340 (1967).

7. E. L. Godkin, *The Labor Crisis,* 105 N. AM. REV. 177, 188 (1867).

8. *Id.* at 188–89.

9. *Id.* at 186, 207–8.

10. *Id.* at 197, 208, 213.

11. *See, e.g.,* International Labor Union of Am., Declaration of Principles, Measures, and Methods (1873), *quoted in* LABOR MOVEMENT, at 161 (denouncing the reign of "property-right rulers"); *Home News,* N.Y. TRIBUNE, Oct. 17, 1870, at 8 (describing a meeting of the International Association of Workingmen of New York at which members called for unity against "wages-slavery and military despotism"); Samuel Johnson, *Labor Parties and Labor Reform,* RADICAL, Nov. 1871, at 14–16 (criticizing the "managers of the Eight-Hour Movement" for trying to "set aside the working of demand and supply"), *reprinted in* SAMUEL JOHNSON, LECTURES, ESSAYS, AND SERMONS 299 (1883).

12. E. L. Godkin, *Labor and Politics,* NATION, June 13, 1872, *reprinted in* 14 NATION 386, 386–87 (1872).

13. E. L. Godkin, *Some Questions for the Labor Commission,* NATION, Jan. 4, 1872, *reprinted in* 14 NATION 5, 6 (1872).

14. Godkin, *Labor and Politics,* at 386.

15. *See* JOHN G. SPROAT, "THE BEST MEN": LIBERAL REFORMERS IN THE GILDED AGE 223–25 (1968); HAROLD M. HYMAN, A MORE PERFECT UNION: THE IMPACT OF THE CIVIL WAR AND RECONSTRUCTION ON THE CONSTITUTION 347–66 (1973).

16. *See* E. L. Godkin, *Classes in Politics,* NATION, June 27, 1867, *reprinted in* 4 NATION 519, 520 (1867); ERIC FONER, POLITICS AND IDEOLOGY IN THE AGE OF THE CIVIL WAR 97–127 (1980); HYMAN, MORE PERFECT UNION, at 359–61.

17. William E. Forbath, *The Ambiguities of Free Labor: Labor and the Law in the Gilded Age,* 1985 WIS. L. REV. 767, 789–91; *see* MONTGOMERY, BEYOND EQUALITY, at 368–86; SPROAT, BEST MEN.

18. Forbath, *Ambiguities of Free Labor,* at 790.

19. *Id.; see* HOWARD GILLMAN, THE CONSTITUTION BESIEGED: THE RISE AND DEMISE OF LOCHNER ERA POLICE POWERS JURISPRUDENCE 6–7, 10 (1993).

20. Forbath, *Ambiguities of Free Labor,* at 790–91; Michael Les Benedict, *Laissez-Faire and Liberty: A Re-Evaluation of the Meaning and Origins of Laissez-Faire Constitutionalism,* 3 L. & HIST. REV. 293, 312–14 (1985). On common-law restraints on corporate expansion, see the section titled "Updating the Democracy of Opportunity—Populist Constitutional Political Economy" in this chapter; *see also* William E. Forbath, *Politics, State-Building, and the Courts, 1870–1920, in* 2 THE CAMBRIDGE HISTORY OF LAW IN AMERICA 643, 658–62 (Michael Grossberg & Christopher Tomlins eds., 2008).

21. *See* Forbath, *Ambiguities of Free Labor,* at 791. The classic treatment of this ambivalence is Robert W. Gordon's essay, *"The Ideal and the Actual in the Law": Fantasies and Practices of New York City Lawyers, 1870–1910, in* THE NEW HIGH PRIESTS: LAWYERS IN POST–CIVIL WAR AMERICA 51 (Gerard W. Gawalt ed., 1984).

22. David Dudley Field, *Industrial Co-Operation,* 140 N. AM. REV. 411, 412 (1885).

23. *Id.* at 418.

24. *Id.* at 416.

25. David Dudley Field & Henry George, *Land and Taxation: A Conversation,* 141 N. AM. REV. 1, 9 (1885).

26. *Id.* at 10.

27. *See* Forbath, *Politics, State-Building, and the Courts,* at 647–48; Robert W. Gordon, *Legal Thought and Legal Practice in the Age of American Enterprise, 1870–1920, in* PROFESSIONS AND PROFESSIONAL IDEOLOGIES IN AMERICA 70 (Gerald L. Geison ed., 1983); Gordon, *Ideal and Actual;* WILLIAM M. WIECEK, THE LOST WORLD OF CLASSICAL LEGAL THOUGHT: LAW AND IDEOLOGY IN AMERICA, 1886–1937, at 64–122 (1998).

28. DUNCAN KENNEDY, THE RISE AND FALL OF CLASSICAL LEGAL THOUGHT (2d ed. 2006).

29. *See generally id.*

30. *See generally id.*

31. *See* United States v. Joint Traffic Ass'n, 171 U.S. 505, 569 (1898); OWEN M. FISS, TROUBLED BEGINNINGS OF THE MODERN STATE, 1888–1910, at 123 (1993); see discussion infra.

32. Howard Gillman, *How Political Parties Can Use the Courts to Advance Their Agendas: Federal Courts in the United States, 1875–1891,* 96 AM. POL. SCI. REV. 511, 518 (2002). Peckham himself was an appointee of the only Democratic president of the era, Grover Cleveland. He nonetheless exemplifies this new pattern of judicial appointments, which was a substantial departure from the prior makeup of the federal bench.

33. *Government by Injunction Established,* AM. NONCONFORMIST, May 30, 1895, at 4.

34. THOMAS M. COOLEY, A TREATISE ON THE CONSTITUTIONAL LIMITATIONS WHICH REST UPON THE LEGISLATIVE POWER OF THE STATES OF THE AMERICAN UNION (1868). Cooley's *Treatise* was reissued seven times following its publication in 1868. The eighth and most recent edition was published in 1927.

35. On Cooley, see William E. Forbath, *The Ambiguities of Free Labor: Labor and the Law in the Gilded Age,* 1985 WIS. L. REV. 767, 792–94; Alan Jones, *Law and Economics v. A Democratic Society: The Case of Thomas M. Cooley, Charles H. Cooley, and Henry C. Adams,* 36 AM. J. LEGAL HIST. 119, 123–28 (1992); Paul D. Carrington, *Law as "The Common Thoughts of Men": The Law-Teaching and Judging of Thomas McIntyre Cooley,* 49 STAN. L. REV. 495 (1997). For a compelling account of Cooley's emergence as a proto-Progressive during his impressive stint as first chief of the Interstate Commerce Commission, when he memorably reproached the Supreme Court for giving short shrift to the capacity of administrative hearings to safeguard due process principles, see GERALD BERK, ALTERNATIVE TRACKS: THE CONSTITUTION OF AMERICAN INDUSTRIAL ORDER, 1865–1917, at 100–12 (1994).

36. THOMAS M. COOLEY, A TREATISE ON THE CONSTITUTIONAL LIMITATIONS WHICH REST UPON THE LEGISLATIVE POWER OF THE STATES OF THE AMERICAN UNION (5th ed. 1883), at 356–57.

37. *See* Forbath, *Ambiguities of Free Labor,* at 792 n.87.

38. *See* WILLIAM E. FORBATH, LAW AND THE SHAPING OF THE AMERICAN LABOR MOVEMENT 37–58 (1991).

39. 6 A. 354 (Pa. 1886).

40. *Id.* at 356.

41. Slaughter-House Cases, 83 U.S. 36, 110 n.39 (1872) (Field, J., dissenting); *Godcharles,* 6 A. at 356.

42. *See* FORBATH, LAW AND SHAPING, at 49–51. For an inventory of cases, see *id.* at 177–92.

43. 198 U.S. 45 (1905). For a good, sustained study of *Lochner,* see PAUL KENS, *LOCHNER V. NEW YORK:* ECONOMIC REGULATION ON TRIAL (1998); for a spirited libertarian take, see DAVID E. BERNSTEIN, REHABILITATING *LOCHNER:* DEFENDING INDIVIDUAL RIGHTS AGAINST PROGRESSIVE REFORM (2011).

44. *Lochner,* 198 U.S. at 57.

45. *See* FORBATH, LAW AND SHAPING, at 52–60.

46. Jas. F. Hudson, *Railways: Their Uses and Abuses, and Their Effect upon Republican Institutions and Productive Industries, No. 2,* NAT'L ECONOMIST, May 18, 1889, at 137.

47. *See generally* LEON FINK, WORKINGMEN'S DEMOCRACY: THE KNIGHTS OF LABOR AND AMERICAN POLITICS (1983); MATTHEW HILD, GREENBACKERS, KNIGHTS OF LABOR, AND POPULISTS: FARMER-LABOR INSURGENCY IN THE LATE-NINETEENTH-CENTURY SOUTH (2007); CRAIG PHELAN, GRAND MASTER WORKMAN: TERENCE POWDERLY AND THE KNIGHTS OF LABOR (2000); KIM VOSS, THE MAKING OF AMERICAN EXCEPTIONALISM: THE KNIGHTS OF LABOR AND CLASS FORMATION IN THE NINETEENTH CENTURY (1993).

48. On the size and composition of the Knights, see VOSS, MAKING OF AMERICAN EXCEPTIONALISM, at 72–79. On the Knights' social vision and political-economic outlook, see *id.* at 80–89; and FINK, WORKINGMEN'S DEMOCRACY, at 3–17. On their political and economic reform initiatives and institution-building, see FINK, WORKINGMEN'S DEMOCRACY, at 18–37; and ROBERT E. WEIR, BEYOND LABOR'S VEIL 19–101 (1996). And on their strikes and boycotts, see HILD, GREENBACKERS, at 66–78; and PHELAN, GRAND MASTER WORKMAN, at 171–225. *See also* William E. Forbath, *The Ambiguities of Free Labor: Labor and the Law in the Gilded Age,* 1985 WIS. L. REV. 767, 808–9 (describing the role of the Knights in expounding the idea of a working-class republicanism).

49. *See* FORBATH, LAW AND SHAPING, at 37–58; DAVID R. ROEDIGER & PHILIP S. FONER, OUR OWN TIME: A HISTORY OF AMERICAN LABOR AND THE WORKING DAY 81–122 (1989).

50. *See* Forbath, *Ambiguities of Free Labor,* at 809–10.

51. E. L. Godwin, *The Eight-Hour Movement,* NATION, Nov. 16, 1865, *reprinted in* 1 NATION 615, 615 (1865).

52. SINCLAIR TOUSEY, A BUSINESS MAN'S VIEWS OF PUBLIC MATTERS 9–10 (1865).

53. NANCY COHEN, THE RECONSTRUCTION OF AMERICAN LIBERALISM, 1865–1914, at 38–40 (2002) (quoting Horace White, *Industrial Legislation,* CHI. TRIBUNE, May 1, 1867; Horace White, *The Eight-Hour Riots,* CHI. TRIBUNE, May 5, 1867).

54. Ira Steward, *Poverty, in* MASS. BUREAU OF STATISTICS OF LABOR, HOUSE REPORT NO. 173, FOURTH ANNUAL REPORT OF THE BUREAU OF STATISTICS OF LABOR 411, 412 (1873), https://archives.lib.state.ma.us/handle/2452/757007 [https://perma.cc/743Y-GT8T].

55. DAVID MONTGOMERY, BEYOND EQUALITY: LABOR AND THE RADICAL REPUBLICANS 1862–1872, at 239 (1967) (quoting REVOLUTION, Dec. 24, 1868, at 395, which quotes the PHILADELPHIA DAILY NEWS) (emphasis in original).

56. *Id.* at 252 (quoting GEORGE E. MCNEILL, ARGUMENT ON THE HOURS OF LABOR, DELIVERED BEFORE THE LABOR COMMITTEE OF THE MASSACHUSETTS LEGISLATURE 13 (1874)).

57. THE LABOR MOVEMENT: THE PROBLEM OF TODAY 479 (George E. McNeill ed. 1887).

58. *Id.* at 478.

59. *See* Forbath, *Ambiguities of Free Labor,* at 806; William E. Forbath, *Caste, Class, and Equal Citizenship,* 98 MICH. L. REV. 1, 28–30 (1999); *see also* ALEX GOUREVITCH, FROM SLAVERY TO THE COOPERATIVE COMMONWEALTH, at 97–173 (2015) (explaining labor republicans' argument that industrial capitalism created new forms of economic dependence).

60. LABOR MOVEMENT (McNeill ed.), at 459.

61. *See* Preamble and Declaration of Principles of the Knights of Labor of North America, art. II (1881) ("To secure to the toilers a proper share of the wealth . . . necessary to make them ca-

pable of enjoying, appreciating, defending and perpetuating the blessings of good government."),
reprinted in 5 OFFICIAL DOCUMENTS, COMPRISING THE DEPARTMENT AND OTHER REPORTS
MADE TO THE GOVERNOR, SENATE AND HOUSE OF REPRESENTATIVES OF PENNSYLVANIA, OFF.
DOC. NO. 12, at G33–G35 (1888).

62. LABOR MOVEMENT (McNeill ed.), at 456, 462.

63. *See* Forbath, *Ambiguities of Free Labor,* at 808, 813 (citing Terence Powderly, *Address of the Grand Master Workman, in* PROCEEDINGS OF THE KNIGHTS OF LABOR GENERAL ASSEMBLY (1881), for the phrase "republicanization of industry").

64. *See generally* WILLIAM E. FORBATH, LAW AND THE SHAPING OF THE AMERICAN LABOR MOVEMENT 1–58 (1991); William E. Forbath, *Courts, Constitutions, and Labor Politics in England and America: A Study of the Constitutive Power of Law,* 16 L. & SOC. INQUIRY 1 (1991).

65. FORBATH, LAW AND SHAPING, at 37–58.

66. *See* Forbath, *Courts, Constitutions, and Labor Politics,* at 6–7; *see also* JULIE GREENE, PURE AND SIMPLE POLITICS: THE AMERICAN FEDERATION OF LABOR AND POLITICAL ACTIVISM, 1881–1917, at 17–70 (1998).

67. A VERBATUM [*sic*] REPORT OF THE DISCUSSION ON THE POLITICAL PROGRAMME AT THE DENVER CONVENTION OF THE AMERICAN FEDERATION OF LABOR, DECEMBER 14, 15, 1894, at 19–20 (1895), *quoted in* FORBATH, LAW AND SHAPING, at 54.

68. *Id.* at 19, 21.

69. FORBATH, LAW AND SHAPING, at 55–56. Also, Gompers and Strasser sprang from the émigré Marxist syndicalism of New York City's English- and German-born labor leadership, an outlook that championed workers' self-organization, and opposed the Knights' old-fashioned "middle class" faith in the efficacy of political reform.

70. *Id.* at 63; *see also* DAVID MONTGOMERY, WORKERS' CONTROL IN AMERICA: STUDIES IN THE HISTORY OF WORK, TECHNOLOGY, AND LABOR STRUGGLES 1–31 (1979); FRED S. HALL, SYMPATHETIC STRIKES AND SYMPATHETIC LOCKOUTS (1898); David Montgomery, *Strikes in Nineteenth-Century America,* 4 SOC. SCI. HIST. 81, 89–93 (1980).

71. *See* GREENE, PURE AND SIMPLE POLITICS, at 58–64.

72. *See* "The Labor Question," Chapter 5.

73. GERALD G. EGGERT, RAILROAD LABOR DISPUTES: THE BEGINNINGS OF FEDERAL STRIKE POLICY 37 (1967) (quoting Telegram (July 24, 1877) and Letter (July 25, 1877) from Judge Thomas S. Drummond to Attorney General Charles Devens, *in* Source Chronological, N. Ill., Gen. Records of the Justice Dep't, Record Group 60, Nat'l Archives).

74. FORBATH, LAW AND SHAPING, at 66–79.

75. *Id.* at 80; *see, e.g.,* Carleton v. Rugg, 22 N.E. 55, 57 (Mass. 1889) ("It would be an anomalous proceeding for a court to issue an injunction against a defendant's committing . . . ordinary crimes. . . ."); *see also* Haggai Hurvitz, *American Labor Law and the Doctrine of Entrepreneurial Property Rights: Boycotts, Courts, and the Judicial Reorientation of 1886–1895,* 8 INDUS. REL. L.J. 307, 313–18 (1986) (describing how late nineteenth-century precedent prevented courts from enjoining boycotts).

76. State v. Patterson, 37 S.W. 478, 480 (Tex. Civ. App. 1896).

77. *Against Injunction,* 2 AM. FEDERATIONIST 163, 163 (1895) (quoting U.S. Circuit Court Judge Hallet of Colorado denying mining company's application for injunction against union miners' interference with strikebreakers).

78. *In re* Debs, 158 U.S. 564 (1895).

79. 157 U.S. 429 (1895).

80. The confrontation between the Populists and the judiciary pushed both sides to sharpen their rival constitutional political economies. We cannot understand the fierce and innovative anti-oligarchic constitutional outlook the Populists were fashioning apart from the Court's stunning efforts to save the bourgeois order from the rise of the People's Party and their radical

program on the politics front, and the burgeoning railway strikes on the field of labor. On this theme, see Gerard N. Magliocca, The Tragedy of William Jennings Bryan: Constitutional Law and the Politics of Backlash 48–52 (2011).

81. Hon. David J. Brewer, *The Nation's Safeguard, in* Proceedings of the New York State Bar Association Sixteenth Annual Meeting Held at the City of Albany 37 (1893).

82. *Id.* at 39.

83. *Id.* at 39, 47.

84. *Id.* at 47.

85. William E. Forbath, Law and the Shaping of the American Labor Movement 74 (1991); *see also* Nick Salvatore, Eugene V. Debs: Citizen and Socialist 114–46 (1982); Ray Ginger, The Bending Cross: A Biography of Eugene Victor Debs 108–51 (1949); Almont Lindsey, The Pullman Strike: The Story of a Unique Experiment and of a Great Labor Upheaval (1942).

86. Eugene Victor Debs, *Labor Strikes and Their Lessons, in* Striking for Life, Labor's Side of the Labor Question: The Right of the Workingman to a Fair Living 319, 330 (John Swinton ed., 1894).

87. Charles Claflin Allen, *Injunction and Organized Labor*, 28 Am. L. Rev. 828, 847 (1894).

88. *See* David Ray Papke, *The* Debs *Case: Labor, Capital, and the Federal Courts of the 1890s,* at 4 (Federal Judicial Center 2008), https://www.fjc.gov/sites/default/files/trials/debs.pdf [https://perma.cc/9R54-FXK6] ("The Attorney General appointed Edwin Walker as a special deputy U.S. attorney in the Northern District of Illinois. Walker was a long-time attorney for a railroad company . . .").

89. *Id.* at 23.

90. Judith Icke Anderson, William Howard Taft: An Intimate History 63 (1981) (quoting 1894 letter from William H. Taft to Helen H. Taft (1894)).

91. Magliocca, Tragedy of William Jennings Bryan, at 59 (quoting Letter from John P. Altgeld to Grover Cleveland, *reprinted in* W. F. Burns, The Pullman Boycott: A Complete History of the Great R. R. Strike 63–64 (1894)).

92. U.S. Const. art. IV, § 4 ("The United States shall guarantee to every State in this Union a Republican Form of Government, and shall protect each of them against Invasion; and on Application of the Legislature, or of the Executive (when the Legislature cannot be convened) against domestic Violence.").

93. Magliocca, Tragedy of William Jennings Bryan, at 59 (quoting Letter from Grover Cleveland to John P. Altgeld, *reprinted in* W. F. Burns, The Pullman Boycott 64–65 (1894)).

94. *See* Papke, Debs *Case,* at 4; Forbath, Law and Shaping, at 76.

95. Biennial Message of John P. Altgeld, Governor of Illinois, to the 39th General Assembly 57, 53 (1895).

96. Pub. L. No. 49–104, 24 Stat. 379 (1887); Pub. L. No. 51–647, 26 Stat. 209 (1890); *see* Papke, Debs *Case,* at 47–48.

97. *THE GOVERNMENT'S RIGHT—Argument by the Attorney General in the Debs Case—*the united states was a trustee*—Not only the Privilege but the Duty of the Government to Prevent Restrictions of Inter-State Commerce,* N.Y. Times, Mar. 27, 1895, at 16.

98. *See* Papke, Debs *Case,* at 8 ("Attorney General Richard Olney told his secretary that the Supreme Court 'took my argument and turned it into an opinion' . . .").

99. *Id.* at 7–8, 19–20; *see also ARGUING THE DEBS CASE—Habeas-Corpus Hearing in the Supreme Court—*constitutional questions raised*—Ex-Senator Lyman Trumbull of Illinois Appears for the President of the American Railway Union,* N.Y. Times, Mar. 26, 1895, at 9.

100. *In re* Debs, 158 U.S. 564 (1895).

101. *Id.* at 600.

102. *Id.* at 582–84.

103. *Id.*

104. *Id.* at 582–83.

105. Justice Jackson's great opinion in Youngstown Sheet & Tube Co. v. Sawyer, 343 U.S. 579, 634 (1952) (Jackson, J., concurring), is commonly viewed as the canonical text on the executive's power in national emergency. A classic discussion is Samuel Issacharoff & Richard H. Pildes, *Between Civil Libertarianism and Executive Unilateralism: An Institutional Process Approach to Rights During Wartime,* 5 THEORETICAL INQUIRIES L. 1 (2004). *In re Debs* tells a darker story—it may be part of the anticanon, presaging the outlook of President Trump and his Department of Justice.

106. *In re Debs,* 158 U.S. at 583.

107. *Id.* at 581–82.

108. *Id.* at 582.

109. President Andrew Jackson, Proclamation Regarding Nullification, December 10, 1832, THE AVALON PROJECT, https://avalon.law.yale.edu/19th_century/jack01.asp [https://perma.cc/YD7W -X3DL].

110. *In re Debs,* 158 U.S. at 582, 595.

111. *See, e.g., id.* at 597 (analogizing strikers to "Lee's army during the late Civil War"); *id.* at 596–98 (discussing the *"inter arma leges silent"* doctrine and threats of "rebellion or revolution" as opposed to instances of mere "mob violence").

112. WILLIAM E. FORBATH, LAW AND THE SHAPING OF THE AMERICAN LABOR MOVEMENT 74 (1991).

113. *See In re Debs,* 158 U.S. at 600 ("[W]e prefer to rest our judgment on the broader ground which has been discussed in this opinion, believing it of importance that the principles underlying it should be fully stated and affirmed.").

114. *Id.* at 598–99.

115. *Id.* at 599.

116. *Id.*

117. William E. Forbath, *Politics, State-Building, and the Courts, 1870–1920, in* 2 THE CAMBRIDGE HISTORY OF LAW IN AMERICA 643, 659–62 (Michael Grossberg & Christopher Tomlins eds., 2008).

118. United States v. E. C. Knight Co., 156 U.S. 1 (1895). For discussion, see Forbath, *Politics, State-Building, and the Courts.*

119. *Populist Party Platform* (1896), DIGITAL HISTORY, http://www.digitalhistory.uh.edu/disp _textbook.cfm?smtID=3&psid=4067 [https://perma.cc/7AVM-28WY] ("The arbitrary course of the courts in assuming to imprison citizens for indirect contempt and ruling by injunctions should be prevented by proper legislation.").

120. KIM VOSS, THE MAKING OF AMERICAN EXCEPTIONALISM: THE KNIGHTS OF LABOUR AND CLASS FORMATION IN THE NINETEENTH CENTURY (1993).

121. *See* LAWRENCE GOODWYN, DEMOCRATIC PROMISE: THE POPULIST MOMENT IN AMERICA (1976); LAURA GRATTAN, POPULISM'S POWER: RADICAL GRASSROOTS DEMOCRACY IN AMERICA 69–86 (2016); MATTHEW HILD, GREENBACKERS, KNIGHTS OF LABOR, AND POPULISTS: FARMER-LABOR INSURGENCY IN THE LATE-NINETEENTH-CENTURY SOUTH 122–49 (2007); MICHAEL KAZIN, THE POPULIST PERSUASION: AN AMERICAN HISTORY 27–46 (1995); CHARLES POSTEL, THE POPULIST VISION 137–72 (2007).

122. *See* GOODWYN, DEMOCRATIC PROMISE, at 110–53; POSTEL, POPULIST VISION, at 137–71; KAZIN, POPULIST PERSUASION, at 37–42; MICHAEL KAZIN, AMERICAN DREAMERS: HOW THE LEFT CHANGED A NATION 102–8 (2011).

123. William E. Forbath, *Caste, Class, and Equal Citizenship,* 98 MICH. L. REV. 1, 43 (1999); *see also* GOODWYN, DEMOCRATIC PROMISE, at 351–86 (describing the Populist press's role in both reflecting and shaping the content of the Populist message).

124. Jas. F. Hudson, *Railways: Their Uses and Abuses, and Their Effect Upon Republican Institutions and Protective Industries,* NAT'L ECONOMIST, May 11, 1889, at 113, 114.

125. *Id.* at 137; *see also* Harry Tracey, *Some Questions About "Vested Rights" Answered*, Nat'l Economist, June 22, 1889, at 214–15 (arguing that corporate monopolies on "any field of labor" abridged the equal rights of citizens and were "consequently unconstitutional"); G. Campbell, *The Early History of the Farmers' Alliance*, 2 Advocate 1, 2 (Topeka, Kansas) Apr. 8, 1891 (claiming that private railroad and banking corporations usurp functions assigned by Constitution to government).

126. Forbath, *Caste, Class, and Equal Citizenship*, at 45. *See* Morton J. Horwitz, The Transformation of American Law, 1870–1960: The Crisis of Legal Orthodoxy 9–33, 65–109 (1992) (tracing the development of the legal concept of the corporation from artificial entity to natural entity).

127. Henry D. Lloyd, Notebook *quoted in* Chester McArthur Destler, Henry Demarest Lloyd and the Empire of Reform 129 (1963).

128. Forbath, *Caste, Class, and Equal Citizenship*, at 45–46.

129. *Id.*

130. Hudson, *Railways*, at 137.

131. Sylvester Pennoyer, Speech at Pendleton, Oregon (May 9, 1888) (on file with Sylvester Pennoyer Scrapbook, University of Oregon, Eugene, Oregon), *quoted in* Margaret K. Holden, Legal Theory, Political Culture and Public Policy: The Rise and Fall of Oregon Populism, 1865–1896, at 459 (1993) (unpublished Ph.D. dissertation, University of Virginia) (on file with the Lillian Goldman Law Library, Yale Law School).

132. Jacksonian fare, which, as we have seen, the great new liberal treatise writer Thomas Cooley carried over into his discussion of corporate charters and the Contracts Clause.

133. For more on this see the discussion of Cyclone Davis below.

134. 16 Cong. Rec. 1208 (1885) (statement of Sen. McKenna).

135. *See* James B. Weaver, A Call to Action 5, 264–65, 436 (1892).

136. *Id.* at 436.

137. *Populist Party Platform* (1896), Digital History, http://www.digitalhistory.uh.edu/disp_textbook.cfm?smtID=3&psid=4067 [https://perma.cc/7AVM-28WY]. The platform imagined the government owning the railroads directly and operating them "in the interest of the people and on a non-partisan basis," with equal treatment for all. *Id.* at 30.

138. James H. Davis, A Political Revelation 97 (1894).

139. *Id.* at 75.

140. *Id.*

141. *Id.* at 72–73.

142. *Id.* at 70–71, 82.

143. *Id.* at 15.

144. *The National People's Party Platform of 1892*, *in* A Populist Reader, Selections from the Works of American Populist Leaders 90–96 (George Brown Tindall ed., 1966), *available at* Digital History, http://historymatters.gmu.edu/d/5361/ [https://perma.cc/D5YA-SADW].

145. For extended Populist discussions of the right and duty of coordinate branches to make and enforce their own interpretations of the Constitution, see James H. Davis, A Political Revelation 23–67 (1894); S. M. Jelley, The Voice of Labor 26–63 (1893); Weaver, A Call to Action, at 73–77, 134–35. For this theme among Progressives, see David E. Kyvig, Explicit and Authentic Acts: Amending the U.S. Constitution, 1776–2015, at 188–215 (2016); William Forbath, *Politics, State-Building, and the Courts, 1870–1920*, *in* 2 The Cambridge History of Law in America 643, 650–54 (Michael Grossberg & Christopher Tomlins eds., 2008); Aziz Rana, *Progressivism and the Disenchanted Constitution*, *in* The Progressives' Century: Political Reform, Constitutional Government, and the Modern American State 41 (Stephen Skowronek et al. eds., 2016).

146. Howard Gillman, *How Political Parties Can Use the Courts to Advance Their Agendas: Federal Courts in the United States, 1875–1891*, 96 AMER. POL. SCI. REV. 511, 518 (2002).

147. DEBORAH J. BARROW ET AL., THE FEDERAL JUDICIARY AND INSTITUTIONAL CHANGE 30 (1996).

148. Kermit L. Hall, *The Children of the Cabins: The Lower Federal Judiciary, Modernization, and the Political Culture, 1789–1899*, 75 NORTHWESTERN UNIV. L. REV. 423, 437 (1980).

149. *Id.* at 436.

150. The federal bench had never been the friend of small business or the workingman against bigger players, but it had never exerted so much power over economic developments, nor been populated by such a narrow band of elite attorneys with such a small band of giant clients as the new corporate bar. *See* Robert W. Gordon, *"The Ideal and the Actual in the Law": Fantasies and Practices of New York City Lawyers, 1870–1910, in* THE NEW HIGH PRIESTS: LAWYERS IN POST-CIVIL WAR AMERICA 51 (Gerard W. Gawalt ed., 1984); MORTON J. HORWITZ, THE TRANSFORMATION OF AMERICAN LAW, 1870–1960: THE CRISIS OF LEGAL ORTHODOXY 16–31 (1992); WILLIAM G. ROY, SOCIALIZING CAPITAL 144–75 (1999).

151. Sylvester Pennoyer, Speech at Pendleton, Oregon (May 9, 1888) (on file with Sylvester Pennoyer Scrapbook, University of Oregon, Eugene, Oregon), *quoted in* Holden, Legal Theory, Political Culture and Public Policy.

152. *See id.* For extended discussions of the right and duty of coordinate branches to make and enforce their own interpretations of the Constitution, see JAMES H. DAVIS, A POLITICAL REVELATION 9–67 (1894); JAMES B. WEAVER, A CALL TO ACTION 73–77, 134–35 (1892).

153. *See* WILLIAM G. ROSS, A MUTED FURY: POPULISTS, PROGRESSIVES, AND LABOR UNIONS CONFRONT THE COURTS, 1890–1937 (1994). For a discussion of these innovations in the Progressive Era, see "The Structure of Politics Itself," Chapter 5.

154. *See* Thomas E. Watson, *The People's Party Paper* (1892), *in* THE POPULIST MIND 374–75 (Norman Pollack ed., 1967).

155. *See The National People's Party Platform of 1892, in* A POPULIST READER, SELECTIONS FROM THE WORKS OF AMERICAN POPULIST LEADERS 90–96 (George Brown Tindall ed., 1966), *available at* DIGITAL HISTORY, http://historymatters.gmu.edu/d/5361/ [https://perma.cc/D5YA-SADW] ("TRANSPORTATION—Transportation being a means of exchange and a public necessity, the government should own and operate the railroads in the interest of the people."). For discussion, see CHARLES POSTEL, THE POPULIST VISION 146–50 (2007).

156. *See* NORMAN POLLACK, THE JUST POLITY: POPULISM, LAW, AND HUMAN WELFARE 14 (1987) (finding in Populist accounts of political economy and fundamental rights: "an inclusive entitlement to labor (and . . . a political economy organized to provide work for all who are willing)"). An example of Populist advocacy for public works and counter-cyclical spending to address unemployment may be found in "Unemployment: A 'Natural' Calamity," Chapter 6, describing Kansas Populist senator Pfeffer's efforts during the 1890s depression.

157. Under the much-criticized National Banking System that governed U.S. monetary policy from the Civil War through 1913, banks were arranged in a pyramid, with local county banks at the bottom and the national banks in New York City at the top. All were required to hold funds in reserve, and banks deposited their reserves with other banks higher in the pyramid, which is one straightforward piece of the story of why so much of the nation's money was in the national banks in New York. *See* GRETCHEN RITTER, GOLDBUGS AND GREENBACKS: THE ANTIMONOPOLY TRADITION AND THE POLITICS OF FINANCE IN AMERICA 67–70 (1997).

158. *Id.*

159. *Id.* at 78.

160. *See* LAWRENCE GOODWYN, DEMOCRATIC PROMISE: THE POPULIST MOMENT IN AMERICA (1976).

161. WEAVER, CALL TO ACTION, at 297.

162. *Id.* at 23.

163. *Id.* at 299.

164. It is not clear how much bimetallism in particular actually would have accomplished for poor farmers struggling with tight money and onerous debt. But that is not our focus here. As a political and constitutional argument in the democracy-of-opportunity tradition, the call for bimetallism proved a potent force in American constitutional politics.

165. On Bryan and the 1896 election, see generally MICHAEL KAZIN, A GODLY HERO: THE LIFE OF WILLIAM JENNINGS BRYAN 45–79 (2006).

166. William Jennings Bryan, Speech Concluding Debate on the Chicago Platform (July 9, 1896) [The "Cross of Gold" speech], *in* WILLIAM JENNINGS BRYAN, THE FIRST BATTLE: A STORY OF THE CAMPAIGN OF 1896, at 199–206 (1896).

167. *Id.*

168. U.S. CONST. art. I, § 8, cl. 5.

169. U.S. CONST. art. I, § 10, cl. 1.

170. 31 CONG. REC. 1098 (1898) (statement of Rep. Jeremiah Vardaman Cockrell of Texas, a Democrat who had just narrowly defeated his Populist (People's) Party opponent).

171. William Jennings Bryan, Madison Square Garden Speech (Aug. 10, 1896), *in* BRYAN, FIRST BATTLE, at 315, 316.

172. *Id.* at 316, 323. Not unrelatedly, Populists also argued that the gold standard was essentially sectional legislation, favoring the people of the Northeast over those of the South and West, and that it violated equal protection for that reason. These lines of argument tracked the constitutional arguments of Senator John C. Calhoun and others in the 1820s and 1930s for why the tariff amounted to unconstitutional discrimination against the South (an agricultural, exporting region disproportionately burdened by tariffs). *See* "Proslavery Constitutional Political Economy as 'Minority Rights,'" Chapter 2. For an extended discussion of that debate and the uneasy compromise these constitutional arguments yielded, see KEITH E. WHITTINGTON, CONSTITUTIONAL CONSTRUCTION: DIVIDED POWERS AND CONSTITUTIONAL MEANING 93–106 (1999).

173. WEAVER, CALL TO ACTION, at 221.

174. Here, the Populists echoed the Gilded Age labor movement's critique of "wage slavery," which, as we have shown, attacked the characteristic forms of economic dependency and domination attending the "wage labor system" and common-law rules of labor-capital relations as depriving industrial workers of both economic and political independence.

Ironically, the Populists' arguments also echoed the *pro*-slavery constitutional discourse that had attacked federal laws that benefited the North over the South—including, to choose a pointed example, banning slavery in the territories. Those arguments, from Calhoun and others, would have been familiar to the Populists, and their echoes are unmistakable.

175. WEAVER, CALL TO ACTION, at 314.

176. William Jennings Bryan, Address before the Federation of Labor in Chicago (Sept. 7, 1908), *in* 2 WILLIAM JENNINGS BRYAN, SPEECHES OF WILLIAM JENNINGS BRYAN 164, 167–68 (1909).

177. For example, Foote repeatedly quotes Alexander Hamilton for this point, that "creditors, both of the public and of individuals, would lose a part of their property." *See, e.g.,* ALLEN RIPLEY FOOTE, THE MONEY OF THE CONSTITUTION 96 (1896) (quoting Alexander Hamilton, *Report on the Subject of a Mint,* 2 ANNALS OF CONG. 2073 (1791)).

178. *Id.*

179. *Id.* at 85, 90, 116.

180. GRETCHEN RITTER, GOLDBUGS AND GREENBACKS: THE ANTIMONOPOLY TRADITION AND THE POLITICS OF FINANCE IN AMERICA 244 (1997) (quoting members of Massachusetts's Sound Money League).

181. The Federal Reserve Act represented a painful compromise for Bryan himself, who as President Wilson's secretary of state fought for a Federal Reserve that would keep control of the currency

in the hands of the government, not the banks; instead, a complex hybrid system was enacted. *See* Michael Kazin, A Godly Hero: The Life of William Jennings Bryan 225–26 (2007).

182. U.S. Const. art. I, § 2, cl. 3 ("Representatives and direct Taxes shall be apportioned among the several States which may be included within this Union, according to their respective Numbers, which shall be determined by adding to the whole Number of free Persons . . . three fifths of all other Persons."); U.S. Const. art. I, § 9, cl. 4 ("No Capitation, or other direct, Tax shall be laid, unless in Proportion to the Census or enumeration herein before directed to be taken."); U.S. Const. art. I, § 8, cl. 1 ("all Duties, Imposts and Excises shall be uniform throughout the United States"). As the tail end of the first clause suggests, the direct tax apportionment language was part of the original constitutional compromise over slavery. *See* Bruce Ackerman, *Taxation and the Constitution*, 99 Colum. L. Rev. 1, 6–13 (1999).

183. *See, e.g.,* Hylton v. United States, 3 U.S. (3 Dall.) 171 (1796) (holding that a tax on carriages "of course is not a direct tax"); Springer v. United States, 102 U.S. 586 (1880) (holding that an income tax is not a direct tax). On the view that became the main thread running through this line of cases, the only "direct" taxes were "capitation taxes" and "taxes on real estate." See *Springer*, 102 U.S. at 602 (discussing *Hylton*).

184. Thomas M. Cooley, A Treatise on the Law of Taxation 35–36 (1st ed. 1881).

185. Cooley recognized that policing the boundaries of "public purpose" would necessarily involve judges evaluating legislators' choices, but he argued that here and in other cases of constitutional limitations on the power to tax, courts should apply a strong presumption in favor of the legislature's judgments. *Id.* at 67–83.

186. Ajay K. Mehrotra, Making the Modern American Fiscal State: Law, Politics, and the Rise of Progressive Taxation, 1887–1929, at 65 (2013).

187. *See The National People's Party Platform of 1892, in* A Populist Reader, Selections from the Works of American Populist Leaders 90–96 (George Brown Tindall ed., 1966), *available at* Digital History, http://historymatters.gmu.edu/d/5361/ [https://perma.cc/D5YA-SADW]; *Populist Party Platform* (1896), Digital History, http://www.digitalhistory.uh.edu/disp_textbook.cfm?smtID=3&psid=4067 [https://perma.cc/7AVM-28WY].

188. Mehrotra, Making the Modern American Fiscal State, at 86–140.

189. *Id.* at 132; Gerard N. Magliocca, The Tragedy of William Jennings Bryan: Constitutional Law and the Politics of Backlash 77–85 (2011).

190. In this sense it is certainly fair to accuse the majority, which focused on arcane distinctions surrounding the meaning of direct taxation, of an "unwillingness to address the real issue." Owen M. Fiss, Troubled Beginnings of the Modern State, 1888–1910, at 100 (1993).

191. Pollock v. Farmers' Loan & Trust Co. (*Pollock II*), 158 U.S. 601, 621 (1895).

192. Given states' huge differences in per-capita income, forcing each state to pay its per-person share of the tax would mean taxing income in poor states at wildly higher rates than in rich states.

193. *Pollock II,* 158 U.S. at 671 (Harlan, J., dissenting).

194. Slaughter-House Cases, 83 U.S. 36, 110 (1872) (Field, J., dissenting).

195. Pollock v. Farmers' Loan & Trust Co. (*Pollock I*), 157 U.S. 429, 596 (1895) (Field, J., concurring).

196. *Id.* Field also invoked the bar on class legislation to condemn an exemption in the statute for certain types of financial corporations—mutual savings banks, mutual insurance corporations, and buildings and loans—that Congress had decided to shield from the tax. These relatively smaller-scale financial institutions favored by the law are "in no sense benevolent or charitable," Justice Field writes. Why should they be "singled out for the special favor of congress" and exempted from the taxes their larger competitors must pay? *Id.* at 598. An antimonopolist, aiming to build a democracy of opportunity, might well have smiled on a tax favoring small farmers, small producers, and the relatively small-scale financial institutions that tended to serve their

needs. But this outlook was eclipsed in the new liberal refashioning of the old Jacksonian bar on "class legislation" into a defense of the "equal rights" of powerful economic actors.

197. *Id.* at 607.

198. *Id.*

199. Decisions of the United States Supreme Court in Corporation Tax Cases and Income Tax Cases with Dissenting Opinions, H.R. Doc. No. 62–601, at 108, 121 (1912) (*Pollock* oral argument transcript).

200. *Pollock II,* 158 U.S. at 685–86 (Harlan, J., dissenting).

201. *Id.* at 672–74.

202. *Id.* at 672, 685.

203. *Id.* at 672.

204. William Jennings Bryan, Speech Concluding Debate on the Chicago Platform (July 9, 1896) [The "Cross of Gold" speech], *in* William Jennings Bryan, The First Battle: A Story of the Campaign of 1896, at 203 (1896).

205. It was in exactly these years that Finley Peter Dunne's fictional political observer Tom Dooley memorably opined that the Supreme Court follows "th' iliction returns." Finley Peter Dunne, Mr. Dooley's Opinions 26 (1901). This is no coincidence. It was a period of high-stakes battles in constitutional politics, which brought politics and constitutional law into especially obvious contact.

206. Dep't of the Treasury, Legislative History of Death Taxes 11 (1963) (quoting Sen. Oscar Underwood of Alabama) (on file with authors).

207. Knowlton v. Moore, 178 U.S. 41 (1900).

208. Theodore Roosevelt, *American Problems, in* 18 The Works of Theodore Roosevelt 578 (Memorial ed. 1925); Theodore Roosevelt, *State Papers as Governor and President, in* 17 The Works of Theodore Roosevelt 433–34 (Memorial ed. 1925).

209. Roosevelt, *State Papers as Governor and President,* at 504–5. The actual estate tax would have to wait until the revenue demands of World War I made it a fiscal necessity.

210. The concentration of wealth in this period was more extreme than at any other point in American history. By 1910, at the peak, the top 10 percent of American households held over 80 percent of the nation's wealth. Today that figure is rising again and is around 75 percent. *See* Thomas Piketty, Capital in the Twenty-First Century 441 fig.10.6 (Arthur Goldhammer trans., 2014).

211. *See* Alexander Keyssar, The Right to Vote 105–16 (2000). There were several waves of attacks on Black voting rights after Reconstruction, some legislative and some through Klan violence. The Lodge Force Bill, which died in the Senate in 1891 amid Republican infighting, would have enforced Black voting rights in the South. The exact date of the dramatic drop in Black participation varied by state, as Southern states enacted the poll taxes, literacy tests, and other devices that locked in the Jim Crow voting regime. *Id.*

212. Peter J. Rachleff, Black Labor in the South: Richmond, Virginia, 1865–1890, at 145 (1984).

213. *See id.;* Eric Foner, Reconstruction: America's Unfinished Revolution, 1863–1877 (1988); The Black Worker: A Documentary History from Colonial Times to the Present (Phillip S. Foner & Ronald L. Lewis eds., 1978); Steven Hahn, A Nation Under Our Feet: Black Political Struggles in the Rural South from Slavery to the Great Migration 317–411 (2003); William E. Forbath, *Caste, Class, and Equal Citizenship,* 98 Mich. L. Rev. 1, 49–51 (1999).

214. C. Vann Woodward, Tom Watson: Agrarian Rebel 216 (1963).

215. *Id.* at 220.

216. *Id.* at 221.

217. The political dynamics were shifting and unstable until, arguably, the failure in Congress of the Lodge Force Bill, which gave the Southern states a final clear green light to violate the Fifteenth Amendment with wholesale disenfranchisement. *See* KEYSSAR, RIGHT TO VOTE, at 107–8.

218. CELESTE M. CONDIT & JOHN L. LUCAITES, CRAFTING EQUALITY: AMERICA'S ANGLO-AFRICAN WORD (1993); KEVIN K. GAINES, UPLIFTING THE RACE: BLACK LEADERSHIP, POLITICS, AND CULTURE IN THE TWENTIETH CENTURY (1996); Barnor Hesse, *Escaping Liberty: Western Hegemony, Black Fugitivity*, 42 POL. THEORY 288 (2014); Stephen R. Robinson, *Rethinking Black Urban Politics in the 1880s: The Case of William Gaston in Post-Reconstruction Alabama*, 66 ALA. REV. 3 (2013).

219. Woodward's classic book is largely the tale of this sad and important transformation of Watson's views of race, which was emblematic of the trajectory of Populism itself. See also ROBERT C. MCMATH JR., AMERICAN POPULISM: A SOCIAL HISTORY, 1877–1898 (1992); MICHAEL KAZIN, A GODLY HERO: THE LIFE OF WILLIAM JENNINGS BRYAN 142–68 (2007); MICHAEL KAZIN, POPULIST PERSUASION: AN AMERICAN HISTORY 1–48 (1995); Forbath, *Caste, Class, and Equal Citizenship*, at 50.

220. ARTHUR F. RAPER, PREFACE TO PEASANTRY: A TALE OF TWO BLACK BELT COUNTIES 4 (Arno Press ed. 1971) (1936); *see also* DEWEY W. GRANTHAM, THE LIFE AND DEATH OF THE SOLID SOUTH: A POLITICAL HISTORY (1988); V. O. KEY JR. WITH ALEXANDER HEARD, SOUTHERN POLITICS IN STATE AND NATION (1949); J. MORGAN KOUSSER, THE SHAPING OF SOUTHERN POLITICS: SUFFRAGE RESTRICTION AND THE ESTABLISHMENT OF THE ONE-PARTY SOUTH, 1880–1910 (1974); ARTHUR F. RAPER & IRA D. READ, SHARECROPPERS ALL (1941); C. VANN WOODWARD, ORIGINS OF THE NEW SOUTH, 1877–1913 (2d ed. 1971) (1951); Lee J. Alston & Joseph P. Ferrie, *Paternalism in Agricultural Labor Contracts in the U.S. South: Implications for the Growth of the Welfare State*, 83 AM. ECON. REV. 852 (1993).

221. *See, e.g.,* United States v. Cruikshank, 92 U.S. 542 (1875); United States v. Harris, 106 U.S. 629 (1883); The Civil Rights Cases, 109 U.S. 3 (1883); Plessy v. Ferguson, 163 U.S. 537 (1896); Williams v. Mississippi, 170 U.S. 213 (1898); Giles v. Harris, 189 U.S. 475 (1903). *See also* PAMELA BRANDWEIN, RETHINKING THE JUDICIAL SETTLEMENT OF RECONSTRUCTION (2011); C. VANN WOODWARD, THE STRANGE CAREER OF JIM CROW 69–72 (2d ed. 1966); Richard H. Pildes, *Democracy, Anti-Democracy, and the Canon*, 17 CONST. COMMENT. 295 (2000).

5. PROGRESSIVE CONSTITUTIONAL FERMENT IN THE NEW CENTURY

1. *See* William E. Forbath, *The Long Life of Liberal America: Law and State-Building in the U.S. and England*, 24 LAW & HIST. REV. 179 (2006); William E. Forbath, *Courting the State: An Essay for Morton Horwitz, in* 2 TRANSFORMATIONS IN AMERICAN LEGAL HISTORY 70–80 (Daniel W. Hamilton & Alfred L. Brophy eds., 2010); William E. Forbath, *Politics, State-Building, and the Courts: 1870–1920, in* 2 THE CAMBRIDGE HISTORY OF LAW IN AMERICA 643, 653–58 (Michael Grossberg & Christopher Tomlins eds., 2008).

2. Aziz Rana, *Progressivism and the Disenchanted Constitution, in* THE PROGRESSIVES' CENTURY: POLITICAL REFORM, CONSTITUTIONAL GOVERNMENT, AND THE MODERN AMERICAN STATE 45–49 (Stephen Skowronek, Stephen M. Engel & Bruce Ackerman, eds., 2016).

3. *See* JACK KIRBY, DARKNESS AT THE DAWNING: RACE AND REFORM IN THE PROGRESSIVE SOUTH 4 (1972); C. VANN WOODWARD, TOM WATSON: AGRARIAN REBEL 370–95 (1938). A standard bearer of "advanced" Progressive thinking in the nation's capital, the *New Republic* bluntly declared that constitutional challenges to "grandfather clauses" and other disenfranchising measures in the South were folly. "Whatever happens, the whites in the South will not allow the negroes to vote." What possible good could come from court judgments whose only possibility of enforcement would require "the actual presence at the polls throughout the South of national

policemen"? *See* Editorial, THE NEW REPUBLIC, June 26, 1915, at 186; *see also* DAVID W. BLIGHT, RACE AND REUNION: THE CIVIL WAR IN AMERICAN MEMORY 338–66 (2001).

4. KIRBY, DARKNESS AT THE DAWNING, at 63, 66–67. *See also* BLIGHT, RACE AND REUNION; KIMBERLEY JOHNSON, REFORMING JIM CROW: SOUTHERN POLITICS AND STATE IN THE AGE BE-FORE BROWN (2010); MICHAEL PERMAN, STRUGGLE FOR MASTERY: DISENFRANCHISEMENT IN THE SOUTH, 1888–1908 (2001); RICHARD M. VALELLY, THE TWO RECONSTRUCTIONS: THE STRUGGLE FOR BLACK ENFRANCHISEMENT (2004).

5. KIRBY, DARKNESS AT THE DAWNING, at 67.

6. *See* CHARLES A. BEARD & MARY R. BEARD, 2 THE RISE OF AMERICAN CIVILIZATION 166–253 (1933); RICHARD HOFSTADER, THE PROGRESSIVE HISTORIANS: TURNER, BEARD, PARRINGTON 207–45 (1968); KIRBY, DARKNESS AT THE DAWNING, at 89–107.

7. *See* WOODROW WILSON, DIVISION AND REUNION, 1829–1889, at 286–87, 290 (1902); NICH-OLAS PATLER, JIM CROW AND THE WILSON ADMINISTRATION: PROTESTING FEDERAL SEGREGA-TION IN THE EARLY 20TH CENTURY 9–89 (2004).

8. William English Walling, *The Race War in the North,* INDEPENDENT, Sept. 3, 1908, at 1, *re-printed in* A SOCIAL HISTORY OF RACIAL VIOLENCE 46, 51 (Allen D. Grimshaw ed., 2009); Plat-form Adopted by the National Negro Committee, 1909 [renamed the NAACP in 1910], https://www .loc.gov/exhibits/naacp/founding-and-early-years.html#obj10 [https://perma.cc/9CLW-AU4Q].

9. *See, e.g.,* AZIZ RANA, THE TWO FACES OF AMERICAN FREEDOM 176–325 (2010) (contrasting them with older Gilded Age radicals); NANCY COHEN, RECONSTRUCTION OF AMERICAN LIBER-ALISM, 1865–1914, at 110–256 (2002); ALAN DAWLEY, STRUGGLES FOR JUSTICE: SOCIAL RESPONSI-BILITY AND THE LIBERAL STATE (1991); LAWRENCE GOODWYN, DEMOCRATIC PROMISE: THE POP-ULIST MOMENT IN AMERICA (1976); CHRISTOPHER LASCH, THE NEW RADICALISM IN AMERICA, 1889–1963: THE INTELLECTUAL AS SOCIAL TYPE (1965); CHRISTOPHER LASCH, THE TRUE AND ONLY HEAVEN: PROGRESS AND ITS CRITICS (1991). For a recent treatment of Gilded Age and Pro-gressive Era reformers in tune with our own, see K. SABEEL RAHMAN, DEMOCRACY AGAINST DOMINATION (2017).

10. Quoted in BLAKE EMERSON, THE PUBLIC'S LAW: ORIGINS AND ARCHITECTURE OF PROGRES-SIVE DEMOCRACY 124 (2019).

11. HERBERT CROLY, PROGRESSIVE DEMOCRACY 215, 380, 384 (1914).

12. *Id.* at 125.

13. *See id.* at 58, 125, 215, 381.

14. *See id.* at 208–9.

15. *Id.* at 116, 119.

16. *See id.* at 143–44, 152.

17. *Id.* at 144.

18. *See id.* at 144,150, 215.

19. *Id.* at 145–46.

20. *See id.* at 144, 210–11.

21. *See id.* at 150.

22. *Id.* at 240.

23. *Id.* at 209.

24. *Id.* at 217, 229–30.

25. *Id.* at 230–37.

26. *See* SIDNEY M. MILKIS, THEODORE ROOSEVELT, THE PROGRESSIVE PARTY, AND THE TRANS-FORMATION OF AMERICAN DEMOCRACY (2009); Sidney M. Milkis & Daniel J. Tichenor, *"Direct Democracy" and Social Justice: The Progressive Party Campaign of 1912,* 8 STUD. AM. POL. DEV. 282 (1994).

27. *Progressive Party Platform of 1912 (Aug. 7, 1912),* TEACHING AMERICAN HISTORY, http:// teachingamericanhistory.org/library/document/progressive-platform-of-1912/ [https://perma

.cc/7X3Z-X6F5]. *See also* Theodore Roosevelt, *A Charter of Democracy—Address Before the Ohio Constitutional Convention,* OUTLOOK, Feb. 24, 1912, at 390.

28. *Id.;* STEFAN LORANT, THE LIFE AND TIMES OF THEODORE ROOSEVELT 374 (1959).

29. Theodore Roosevelt, *A Charter of Democracy,* at 398.

30. *See id.* at 395, 400.

31. Theodore Roosevelt, *The Right of the People to Rule* (Mar. 20, 1912), *in* S. DOC. NO. 62–473, at 4, https://teachingamericanhistory.org/library/document/the-right-of-the-people-to-rule/ [https://perma.cc/8L6V-3CWM].

32. *Id.* at 5.

33. Roosevelt, *Charter of Democracy,* at 400.

34. *Id.* at 399.

35. *Id.*

36. *Id.* at 399–400.

37. *Id.* at 400.

38. *Id.* at 391.

39. *See id.* at 398.

40. For superb recent treatments of Progressives and civil liberties, see LAURA WEINRIB, THE TAMING OF FREE SPEECH: AMERICA'S CIVIL LIBERTIES COMPROMISE (2016); Jeremy K. Kessler, *The Administrative Origins of Modern Civil Liberties Law,* 114 COLUM. L. REV. 1083 (2014); Jeremy K. Kessler & David E. Pozen, *The Search for an Egalitarian First Amendment,* 118 COLUM. L. REV. 1953 (2018).

41. Louis D. Brandeis, *True Americanism: Fourth of July Oration, 1915, in* BUSINESS—A PROFESSION 364, 366 (1933); *see also* Louis Brandeis, *How Far Have We Come on the Road to Industrial Democracy?—An Interview,* LA FOLLETTE'S WKLY. MAG., May 24, 1913, *reprinted in* LOUIS D. BRANDEIS, THE CURSE OF BIGNESS: MISCELLANEOUS PAPERS OF LOUIS D. BRANDEIS 43–47 (Osmond K. Fraenkel ed., 1934).

42. Brandeis, *True Americanism,* at 367–68, 370.

43. LOUIS BRANDEIS, ON INDUSTRIAL RELATIONS, UNITED STATES COMM. ON INDUSTRIAL RELATIONS, S. DOC. NO. 26–6936, at 7657–81 (1915), *reprinted in* BRANDEIS, CURSE OF BIGNESS, at 73–74.

44. For more on Brandeis and this experiment in industrial democracy, see William E. Forbath, *Class Struggle, Group Rights and Socialist Pluralism on the Lower East Side—Radical Lawyering and Constitutional Imagination in the Early Twentieth Century* (Univ. of Texas Law, Public Law Research Paper no. 712), https://papers.ssrn.com/sol3/papers.cfm?abstract_id=3485241.

45. *See "In re Debs: 'A Lesson Which Cannot Be Learned Too Soon,'"* Chapter 4.

46. A. L. A. Schechter Poultry Corp. v. United States, 295 U.S. 495 (1935); Morehead v. New York *ex rel.* Tipaldo, 298 U.S. 587 (1936); West Coast Hotel Co. v. Parrish, 300 U.S. 379 (1937); NLRB v. Jones & Laughlin Steel Corp., 301 U.S. 1 (1937).

47. *See* WILLIAM E. FORBATH, LAW AND THE SHAPING OF THE AMERICAN LABOR MOVEMENT 98–127 (1991).

48. *See id.* at 58–97.

49. *Id.* at 82–83.

50. Barr v. Essex Trades Council, 30 A. 881, 886, 883 (N.J. Ch. 1894).

51. *See* William E. Forbath, *Ambiguities of Free Labor: Labor and the Law in the Gilded Age,* 1985 WIS. L. REV. 767, 787–90 (1985). FORBATH, LAW AND SHAPING, at 84.

52. *See* David Scobey, *Boycotting the Politics Factory: Labor Radicalism and the New York City Mayoral Election of 1884,* 28–30 RADICAL HIST. REV. 280 (1984).

53. People v. Wilzig, 4 N.Y. Crim. Rptr. 403, 425 (1886).

54. Crump v. Commonwealth, 84 Va. 927, 946 (1888).

55. FORBATH, LAW AND SHAPING, at 84.

56. *Id.* at 90.

57. *See, e.g., To the Order Wherever Found, Greetings,* J. Knights of Lab., Sept. 10, 1891, at 3, col. 2 (presenting a circular directing Knights to "leave the boots and shoes made by Messrs. Thomas and Co. severely alone" and reproducing the brand marks used by the firms); *St. Louis Cigars,* J. Knights of Lab., Dec. 9, 1897, at 3, col. 4; *St. Louis Theatre Boycotted,* J. Knights of Lab., Jan. 28, 1897, at 3, col. 2; *Boycott Worthley's Shoes,* J. Knights of Lab., Feb. 9, 1893, at 4, col. 1.

58. Forbath, Law and Shaping, at 91.

59. Leo Wolman, The Boycott in American Trade Unions 101–28 (1916) (describing labor's ability to foment far-flung boycotts and their use in obtaining employer concessions).

60. *See generally* Cause Lawyers and Social Movements (Austin Sarat & Stuart A. Scheingold eds., 2006).

61. Sherman Antitrust Act, ch. 647, § 1, 26 Stat. 209 (1890), the current version of which is codified as amended at 15 U.S.C. § 1–38.

62. Forbath, Law and Shaping, at 90–93.

63. *Sending Labor Leaders to Jail,* Literary Digest, Jan. 2, 1909, at 1–2.

64. *Id.; Justice Wright's Decision,* 16 Am. Federationist 101, 122 (1909).

65. *Id.,* quoting the N.Y. World.

66. *Id.* at 1.

67. Gompers v. Buck's Stove and Range Co., 221 U.S. 418 (1911).

68. *See* Harry W. Laidler, Boycotts and the Labor Struggle: Economic and Legal Aspects 63–64, 118–19 (1913); Wolman, Boycott in American Trade Unions, at 134–35.

69. Forbath, Law and Shaping, at 59–97.

70. On the "state of courts and parties," see Stephen Skowronek, Building a New American State: The Expansion of National Administrative Capacities, 1877–1920 (1982).

71. Samuel Gompers, Labor and Common Welfare 45 (1919) (excerpt from Annual Report of AFL Convention, Detroit, Mich., Dec. 11, 1899).

72. *The Predicament of Organized Labor,* New Republic, Dec. 2, 1916, at 114.

73. *Id.*

74. *Id.*

75. Christopher L. Tomlins, The State and the Unions: Labor Relations, Law, and the Organized Labor Movement in America, 1880–1960, at 60–69 (1985).

76. Forbath, Law and Shaping, at 96–97.

77. Samuel Gompers, Seventy Years of Life and Labour 385 (1925).

78. *See* William E. Forbath, *Caste, Class, and Equal Citizenship,* 98 Mich. L. Rev. 1, 58–61 (1999).

79. Forbath, Law and Shaping, at 128–66; *see also* James Pope, *Labor's Constitution of Freedom,* 106 Yale L.J. 941 (1997).

80. Forbath, Law and Shaping, at 128–66.

81. *See* "A Court Transformed," Chapter 6.

82. James Schouler, A Treatise on the Law of the Domestic Relations 599 (1870), *quoted in* Christopher L. Tomlins, Law, Labor, and Ideology in the Early American Republic 292 (1993).

83. *See* Karen Orren, Belated Feudalism: Labor, the Law, and Liberal Development in the United States (1991); Robert Steinfeld, The Invention of Free Labor: The Employment Relation in English and American Law and Culture, 1350–1870 (1991); Tomlins, Law, Labor, and Ideology; Christopher Tomlins, Freedom Bound: Law, Labor, and Civic Identity in Colonizing English America, 1580–1865, at 231–400 (2010).

84. Carter v. Carter Coal Co., 298 U.S. 238, 308 (1936).

85. Hitchman Coal & Coke Co. v. Mitchell, 245 U.S. 229, 259 (1917).

86. Forbath, Law and Shaping, at 79–97. For the canonical legal realist critique of *Hitchman* and this conception of "property right," see Walter Wheeler Cook, *Privileges of Labor Unions in the Struggle for Life,* 27 Yale L.J. 779 (1918).

87. FORBATH, LAW AND SHAPING, 98–127.

88. *See* Victor A. Olander, *The Constitution, the Free Man, and the Slave* (radio talk), *reprinted in* ILL. STATE FED'N LAB. NEWSL., May 30, 1925, at 5, col. 1–3; *see also* Andrew Furuseth, *No Property Rights in Man: The Essential Principle of Protest Against Injunctions in Labor Disputes*, 13 AM. FEDERATIONIST 310, 313 (1906) ("[The typical injunction violates the] fundamental principle of American law . . . that there shall be no property rights in man.").

89. Bedford Cut Stone Co. v. Journeymen Stone Cutters' Ass'n, 274 U.S. 37, 56 (1927) (Brandeis, J., dissenting).

90. *See* Samuel Gompers, *Government by Injunction*, 4 AM. FEDERATIONIST 82 (1897); Samuel Gompers, *Taft, the Injunction Standard Bearer*, 14 AM. FEDERATIONIST 785, 788 (1907) ("It is an indirect assertion of a property right in men . . ."); *To a Federal Judge*, 13 UNITED MINE WORKERS' J. 3, col. 3 (1902) (poem deriding judges' use of antistrike decrees to "drive [workers] back to slav'ry days again").

91. John Frey, *Yellow Dog Contracts and Contempt Charges*, ILL. STATE FED'N LAB. WKLY. NEWSL., Aug. 14, 1926, at 1, col. 2.

92. 40 IRON MOLDERS' J. 750, 750 (1904), *quoted in* Howell John Harris, *Industrial Democracy and Liberal Capitalism, 1890–1925, in* INDUSTRIAL DEMOCRACY IN AMERICA: THE AMBIGUOUS PROMISE 46–47 (Nelson Lichenstein & Howell John Harris eds., 1993).

93. In industrializing nineteenth-century America, we saw, this inherited republican outlook gave rise to the working-class expression "wage slave," whose everyday experience of power and authority was one of subjection, of being governed without a voice or a vote—a live countermodel to democratic or republican self-rule in a sphere of life central to one's social identity and social power or powerlessness.

94. These phrases would find a home in the preamble to the National Labor Relations (Wagner) Act, ch. 372, 49 Stat. 449 (1935) (codified as amended at 29 U.S.C. §§ 151–69 (2006)).

95. JAMES B. WEAVER, A CALL TO ACTION: AN INTERPRETATION OF THE GREAT UPRISING, ITS SOURCE AND CAUSES 103 (1892).

96. CHRISTOPHER G. TIEDEMAN, A TREATISE ON STATE AND FEDERAL CONTROL OF PERSONS AND PROPERTY IN THE UNITED STATES 611 (1900), *quoted in* Louis A. Halper, *Christopher G. Tiedeman, Laissez-Faire Constitutionalism, and the Dilemmas of Small-Scale Property in the Gilded Age*, 51 OHIO ST. L.J. 1349, 1356 (1990); *see also* William E. Forbath, *Caste, Class, and Equal Citizenship*, 98 MICH. L. REV. 1, 37–46 (1999).

97. *See* William E. Forbath, *Politics, State-Building, and the Courts: 1870–1920, in* 2 THE CAMBRIDGE HISTORY OF LAW IN AMERICA 643, 658–665 (Michael Grossberg & Christopher Tomlins eds., 2008); GERALD BERK, ALTERNATIVE TRACKS: THE CONSTITUTION OF AMERICAN INDUSTRIAL ORDER 153–78 (1994); MARTIN SKLAR, THE CORPORATE RECONSTRUCTION OF AMERICAN CAPITALISM, 1890–1916: THE MARKET, THE LAW, AND POLITICS (1988).

98. Theodore Roosevelt, Speech at Providence, R.I. (Aug. 23, 1902), *in* ADDRESSES AND PRESIDENTIAL MESSAGES OF THEODORE ROOSEVELT, 1902–1904, at 11, 15 (1907).

99. *See* SKLAR, CORPORATE RECONSTRUCTION, at 179–332; WILLIAM G. ROY, SOCIALIZING CAPITAL: THE RISE OF THE LARGE INDUSTRIAL CORPORATION IN AMERICA 41–114 (1997).

100. 21 CONG. REC. 2457 (1890) (statement of Sen. John Sherman).

101. 21 CONG. REC. 2461, 2457; *see also* 21 CONG. REC. 1765–71, 2460–65.

102. *See* MORTON J. HORWITZ, THE TRANSFORMATION OF AMERICAN LAW, 1780–1860, at 79–90 (1992).

103. OWEN M. FISS, TROUBLED BEGINNINGS OF THE MODERN STATE, 1888–1910, at 111 (1993) ("The populists had little interest in the Sherman Act. They railed against monopolies, but for the most part they did not seek to perfect the market and restore the competitive ethic. Nor did they have the least confidence in the enforcement mechanism of the Sherman Act, relying as it did on the federal courts and suits by the attorney general. Populists feared that the statute would be used, if at all, against their interests, probably to impede the growth of agrarian cooperative enterprises.").

104. *Id.* at 107.

105. *Id.* at 108.

106. United States v. Trans-Missouri Freight Ass'n, 166 U.S. 290, 323 (1897).

107. TIM WU, THE CURSE OF BIGNESS: ANTITRUST IN THE NEW GILDED AGE 54 (2018).

108. *Id.* at 54.

109. *Id.* at 54 (quoting United States v. Columbia Steel Co., 334 U.S. 495 (1948) (Douglas, J., dissenting)).

110. For a discussion of some of the scholars and arguments that constitute this movement, see "The Constitutional Political Economy of Antitrust," Chapter 9.

111. H. D. Lloyd, *The Story of a Great Monopoly,* ATLANTIC MONTHLY, Mar. 1881, at 317.

112. HORWITZ, TRANSFORMATION OF AMERICAN LAW, at 211–52; Morton J. Horwitz, *Santa Clara Revisited: The Development of Corporate Theory,* 88 W. VA. L. REV. 173 (1985).

113. *Id.; see also* Western Union Tel. Co. v. Kansas, 216 U.S. 1 (1910); Pullman Co. v. Kansas, 216 U.S. 56 (1910); Ludwig v. Western Union Tel. Co., 216 U.S. 146 (1910); Southern Ry. Co. v. Greene, 216 U.S. 400 (1910).

114. *See* 1890 ILL. ATT'Y GEN. BIENNIAL REP. 40.

115. Statement of Facts, Brief, and Argument of State of Missouri in Reply to the Briefs and Arguments of Respondents at 126–29, State *ex rel.* Hadley v. Standard Oil Co., 116 S.W. 902 (Mo. 1909), *quoted in* James May, *Antitrust in the Formative Era: Political and Economic Theory in Constitutional and Antitrust Analysis 1880–1918,* 50 OHIO ST. L.J. 257, 340 (1989).

116. People v. North River Sugar Ref. Co., 24 N.E. 834, 840 (N.Y. 1890).

117. HENRY C. ADAMS, RELATION OF THE STATE TO INDUSTRIAL ACTION 64 (1887), *quoted in* HORWITZ, TRANSFORMATION OF AMERICAN LAW, at 82.

118. *See* William J. Novak, *The Public Utility Idea and the Origins of Modern Business Regulation, in* CORPORATIONS AND AMERICAN DEMOCRACY 139–76 (Naomi R. Lamoreaux & William J. Novak eds., 2017). Public utilities doctrine would come to cover the railways, other forms of transportation and communication, power and water, and other industries "affected with a public interest," and allowed for lumbering and court-like (and court-supervised and -confined) commission hearings on rates, along with some shining experiments in more robust, participatory forms of regulation and municipal and state ownership. *See* William E. Forbath, *Politics, State-Building, and the Courts: 1870–1920, in* 2 THE CAMBRIDGE HISTORY OF LAW IN AMERICA 643 (Michael Grossberg & Christopher Tomlins eds., 2008); BLAKE EMERSON, THE PUBLIC'S LAW: ORIGINS AND ARCHITECTURE OF PROGRESSIVE DEMOCRACY 61–130 (2019).

119. Lincoln Steffens, *New Jersey: A Traitor State,* MCCLURE'S MAG., Apr. 1905, at 41.

120. Sherman Antitrust Act, c. 647, § 1, 26 Stat. 209 (1890), the current version of which is codified at 15 U.S.C. § 1–38; *see* HANS B. THORELLI, THE FEDERAL ANTITRUST POLICY: ORIGINATION OF AN AMERICAN TRADITION 169–70 (1955).

121. United States v. Trans-Missouri Freight Ass'n, 166 U.S. 290, 337 (1897).

122. *Id.* at 323–24.

123. *Id.*

124. OWEN M. FISS, TROUBLED BEGINNINGS OF THE MODERN STATE, 1888–1910, at 121 (1993).

125. *Trans-Missouri Freight Ass'n,* 166 U.S. at 323.

126. *Id.* at 337. *Trans-Missouri*'s total ban on price-fixing contracts prompted a vigorous dissent from Justice Edward White. White and the other dissenters contended that the Sherman Act codified the common law of restraint of trade as a matter of substantive doctrine and changed the law only as it authorized new remedies and new suits by the federal government. This meant that the substantive standard prohibited only "unreasonable" restraints of trade; and as far as *Trans-Missouri* was concerned, it was quite possible that a price-fixing contract eliminating "ruinous competition" passed muster.

127. EDMUND MORRIS, THEODORE REX (2001), *quoted in* TIM WU, THE CURSE OF BIGNESS: ANTITRUST IN THE NEW GILDED AGE 45 (2018).

128. *Id.* at 46.
129. Wu, Curse of Bigness, at 45–77.
130. *Id* at 50.
131. Northern Securities Co. v. United States, 193 U.S. 197 (1904).
132. *Id.* at 411 (Holmes, J., dissenting).
133. Standard Oil Co. of N.J. v. New Jersey, 221 U.S. 1 (1911).
134. *Id.* at 83–84 (1911) (Harlan, J., dissenting).
135. *Id.* at 84.
136. 51 Cong. Rec. 12,742 (1914) (Sen. Cummins speaking in hearing over FTCA).
137. People v. North River Sugar Ref. Co., 24 N.E. 834, 840 (N.Y. 1890).
138. Martin Van Buren, Inquiry into the Origin and Course of Political Parties in the United States 166 (1867).
139. George Henry Haynes, The Election of Senators 165 (1906).
140. *See* "Updating the Democracy of Opportunity—Populist Constitutional Political Economy," Chapter 4.
141. *See* Thomas Piketty, Capital in the Twenty-First Century (Arthur Goldhammer trans., 2014).
142. Bryan himself was a latecomer to Prohibitionism but became an important advocate; by his late career he was a champion of all four of the Article V amendments of this period.
143. Lisa McGirr, The War on Alcohol: Prohibition and the Rise of the American State (2015).
144. *Id.*
145. For detailed tables, see Alexander Keyssar, The Right to Vote, 399–401 (2000). Broadly, states in the West enfranchised women most often, and states in the South by far the least. In a state like Colorado, where suffragists had allied themselves successfully with the People's Party, they won full suffrage as early as 1893. *Id.* at 195. The Nineteenth Amendment thus had its greatest impact in the South.
146. *See* Reva B. Siegel, *She the People: The Nineteenth Amendment, Sex Equality, Federalism, and the Family,* 115 Harv. L. Rev. 947, 1045 (2002); *see id.* ("The generations of Americans who debated 'the woman question' understood woman suffrage as a question concerning the family."). Unsurprisingly, the ruling class of the white South bitterly opposed this federal intervention in domestic relations. *See* Keyssar, Right to Vote, at 217–18.
147. *See* Kristi Andersen, After Suffrage: Women in Partisan and Electoral Politics Before the New Deal (1996); Celeste K. Carruters & Marianne K. Wanamaker, *Municipal Housekeeping: The Impact of Women's Suffrage on Public Education,* 50 J. Hum. Resources 837 (2015) (finding significant increases in education spending following suffrage—but greater increases in white schools than Black schools). Theda Skocpol notes, however, that during the 1920s most women did not "retain[]" the "self-consciousness and organization" that had marked the fight for suffrage, while red-baiting seriously scaled back the agenda of maternalist policies the suffragists had advocated, diminishing the expected impact that suffrage would have on the shape of American economic and social policy. Theda Skocpol, Protecting Soldiers and Mothers: The Political Origins of Social Policy in the United States 52–53 (1992).
148. Andersen, After Suffrage, at 9. One small example of a piece of legislation exercising federal regulatory power in a novel way, in the years immediately following women's suffrage, whose passage may be attributable to women's suffrage, was the ban on shipping "filled milk" that the Court upheld in *Carolene Products. Id.* at 154–55.
149. Adkins v. Children's Hospital, 261 U.S. 525 (1923).
150. Muller v. Oregon, 208 U.S. 412 (1908).
151. *Adkins,* 261 U.S. at 553.
152. *See* Siegel, *She the People,* at 1012–19.

153. *See, e.g.,* Reva B. Siegel, *Home as Work: The First Woman's Rights Claims Concerning Wives' Household Labor, 1850–1880,* 103 YALE L.J. 1073 (1994). For a brief discussion of some of the ways the early suffrage movement made use of central threads of the democracy-of-opportunity tradition, see "The Women's Rights Movement in the Age of Emancipation and Reconstruction," Chapter 3.

154. STEVEN L. PIOTT, GIVING VOTERS A VOICE: THE ORIGINS OF THE INITIATIVE AND REFERENDUM IN AMERICA 33 (2003); *see also* David Schuman, *The Origin of State Constitutional Direct Democracy: William Simon U'Ren and "The Oregon System,"* 67 TEMP. L. REV. 947, 949–51 (1994). The classical general treatment of transatlantic commerce in Progressive Era reform ideas is DANIEL T. RODGERS, ATLANTIC CROSSINGS (2000), which treats direct democracy and other reforms in what we now call the law of democracy.

155. Samuel Gompers was a fan. THOMAS GOEBEL, A GOVERNMENT BY THE PEOPLE: DIRECT DEMOCRACY IN AMERICA, 1890–1940, at 33–38 (2002). These ideas may have found particularly fertile soil in western Oregon, in an area populated by many Swiss immigrants. *See* Schuman, *State Constitutional Direct Democracy,* at 950 n.28.

156. On Americans' use of such European models in the Progressive Era, see RODGERS, ATLANTIC CROSSINGS, at 52–75. The European imports of the Progressive Era included the term "Progressive" itself, which made its way from London to the United States in the 1910s. *Id.* at 52.

157. ROBERT GRUNDSTAD, THE HISTORY AND DEVELOPMENT OF THE INITIATIVE AND REFERENDUM IN OREGON AND OTHER STATES 4 (1978) (Legislative Administration Committee Report); *see* Schuman, *State Constitutional Direct Democracy,* at 948–49.

158. LINCOLN STEFFENS, UPBUILDERS 324 (1909).

159. GRUNDSTAD, HISTORY AND DEVELOPMENT, at 4.

160. These quotes are from a remarkable essay by Edgar Lee Masters, *The Federal Courts,* WATSON'S MAG., Sept. 1906, at 372, 380–81. *See* GANESH SITARAMAN, THE CRISIS OF THE MIDDLE-CLASS CONSTITUTION 168 (2017).

161. STEFFENS, UPBUILDERS, at 285–326, 287–88.

162. *Id.*

163. GOEBEL, GOVERNMENT BY THE PEOPLE, at 26–28.

164. *Initiative and Referendum States,* NATIONAL COUNCIL OF STATE LEGISLATURES, http://www.ncsl.org/research/elections-and-campaigns/chart-of-the-initiative-states.aspx [https://perma.cc/8XJD-LA3E]; *The Canvass: States and Election Reform,* NATIONAL COUNCIL OF STATE LEGISLATURES, http://www.ncsl.org/research/elections-and-campaigns/cnv-the-canvass-vol-xx-may-2011.aspx#Primer [https://perma.cc/8XK5-5Z5V]. That is, in half the states, the legislature is not the exclusive gatekeeper of what questions go on the ballot; the voters have some means of bypassing their legislators.

165. OREGON CONST. art. 4, § 1 (amended 1902).

166. The dramatic story is told in STEFFENS, UPBUILDERS, at 307–18.

167. PAUL THOMAS CULBERTSON, A HISTORY OF THE INITIATIVE AND REFERENDUM IN OREGON 69 (1941). The vote was 62,024 to 5,668. *Id.*

168. *See* ALLEN H. EATON, THE OREGON SYSTEM: THE STORY OF DIRECT LEGISLATION IN OREGON 92–98 (1912). This had a powerful and immediate effect. Some Republicans who refused to sign "Statement No. 1" pledging to support the people's choice for U.S. Senate were defeated, and from then on "Statement No. 1 men" dominated the legislature and Oregon's U.S. Senate seats. Oregon's Senate delegation, long the product of corrupt bargains and boodle, became, in effect, popularly elected. *See* George A. Thatcher, *The Initiative, Referendum, and Popular Election of Senators in Oregon,* 2 AM. POL. SCI. REV. 601 (1908). This creative workaround did nothing to free state legislative elections from being dominated by U.S. Senate elections: voters were still choosing state legislators in significant part on the basis of their role in selecting U.S. senators. *Cf.* David Schleicher, *The Seventeenth Amendment and Federalism in an Age of National Political Parties,*

65 HASTINGS L.J. 1043 (2014). Changing that required the amendment itself. But this did not provide a way to choose U.S. senators by popular vote, and in that way helped pave the way for the amendment.

169. ROBERT D. JOHNSTON, THE RADICAL MIDDLE CLASS: POPULIST DEMOCRACY AND THE QUESTION OF CAPITALISM IN PROGRESSIVE ERA PORTLAND, OREGON 137 (2006). The *Oregonian* newspaper, a voice of the conservative establishment, groused that "In Oregon the state government is divided into four departments—the executive, judicial, legislative, and Mr. U'Ren. . . . To date, the indications are that Mr. U'Ren outweighs any one." David Schuman, *The Origin of State Constitutional Direct Democracy: William Simon U'ren and "The Oregon System,"* 67 TEMP. L. REV. 947, 963 (1994) (quoting PORTLAND OREGONIAN, July 17, 1906, at 8).

170. William H. Brown, secretary of the Chicago Civic Federation, in 1905, *quoted in* GOEBEL, GOVERNMENT BY THE PEOPLE, at 51.

171. Pacific States Telephone & Telegraph Co. v. State of Oregon, 223 U.S. 118, 138 (1912).

172. *Id.* at 151.

173. J. Allen Smith, *Recent Institutional Legislation,* 4 PROC. AM. POL. SCI. ASS'N: FOURTH ANN. MEETING 141, 141 (1907); *see* GOEBEL, GOVERNMENT BY THE PEOPLE, at 54.

174. *See* GOEBEL, GOVERNMENT BY THE PEOPLE, at 56.

175. *See* Jonathan Bourne Jr., *Functions of the Initiative, Referendum and Recall,* 43 ANNALS AM. ACAD. POL. & SOC. SCI. 3, 3 (1912).

176. 26 CONG. REC. 7766–70 (1894) (statement of Rep. McEttrick).

177. JOHNSTON, RADICAL MIDDLE CLASS, at 122 (quoting Harvey Scott).

178. For a discussion, see *id.* at 140–41.

179. *Id.* at 133.

180. *Id.*

181. JOHNSTON, RADICAL MIDDLE CLASS, at 144–45. The state did pass an initiative giving the legislature the power to enact a ranked-choice version of proportional representation, prompting one optimistic commentator in 1908 to opine that "the gerrymander cannot be considered as permanently established in a democracy." Thatcher, *Initiative, Referendum, and Popular Election,* at 603. The gerrymander has proved altogether more durable.

182. *See* Coleman v. Miller, 307 U.S. 433, 436 n.1 (1939) (quoting the amendment's text). This amendment gave Congress (a limited version of) a constitutional power it successfully claimed through the Fair Labor Standards Act in 1938. *See* "The Fair Labor Standards Act," Chapter 6.

183. *Progressive Party Platform of 1912 (Aug. 7, 1912),* TEACHING AMERICAN HISTORY, http://teachingamericanhistory.org/library/document/progressive-platform-of-1912/ [https://perma.cc/7X3Z-X6F5].

184. *Id.*

185. In more thoroughgoing fashion than the Populists or most Progressives, Debs's Socialist Party assailed the many antidemocratic and oligarchy-prone features of the Constitution, which stood in the way of transforming the political economy into their version of a Co-operative Commonwealth. *See* Aziz Rana, The Rise of the Constitution, ch. 1, "Settler Crisis and Constitutional Disillusionment" (unpublished manuscript).

186. 44 CONG. REC. 533–34 (1909).

187. *Id.* at 536.

188. *Id.* at 534–35.

189. *Id.*

190. *See* 44 CONG. REC. 3344 (1909) (reprinting the message).

191. *Id.*

192. *See, e.g.,* DAVID E. KYVIG, EXPLICIT AND AUTHENTIC ACTS: AMENDING THE U.S. CONSTITUTION, 1776–2015, at 202–3 (2d ed. 2016).

193. 23 CONG. REC. 6072–75 (1892) (statement of Rep. Kem of Nebraska).

194. *Id.* ("[I]f all classes of our people in the years gone by could have been represented in the halls of Congress fairly and alike, no class receiving any advantage over another, millions of people would have good, comfortable, happy homes to-day who are eking out a miserable existence and paying tribute to some landlord or corporation for the privilege of doing it.").

195. *Id.*

196. JOSEPH L. BRISTOW, RESOLUTION FOR THE DIRECT ELECTION OF SENATORS, S. Doc. No. 62–666, at 5 (2d Sess. 1912).

197. *Id.*

198. H.R. REP. No. 62-2 (1911) (Rep. William Waller Rucker, Democrat of Missouri).

199. 31 CONG. REC. 4809–12 (1898) (statement by Rep. Corliss). In forthcoming work, Aziz Rana explores the way that Eugene Debs and other leaders, lawyers, public intellectuals, and activists attached to the Socialist Party made use of the same tropes of constitutional fidelity—calling for radical revision of inherited constitutional structures and institutions, while proclaiming constancy to the principles of the Declaration of Independence. And like Beard, Croly, and others, the Socialists called for an end to Constitution worship and a pragmatic assessment of the features of the original structure that stood in the way of political economic transformation. *See* Aziz Rana, The Rise of the Constitution, ch. 2, "Constitutional Disillusionment" (unpublished manuscript).

200. 35 CONG. REC. 2617–18 (1902) (statement by Sen. Stewart).

201. *Id.*

202. *See* GEORGE HENRY HAYNES, THE ELECTION OF SENATORS 53, 69–70, 164–66 (1912).

203. *Id.* at 165.

204. DAVID GRAHAM PHILLIPS, THE TREASON OF THE SENATE 59–60 (George E. Mowry & Judson A. Grenier eds., 1964); *id.* at 97–98. *See* Donald R. Matthews, *Review: The Treason of the Senate (1906),* 30 PUB. OPINION Q. 326, 326 (1966).

205. *See* Sara Brandes Crook & John R. Hibbing, *A Not-So-Distant Mirror: The 17th Amendment and Congressional Change,* 91 AM. POL. SCI. REV. 845 (1997).

206. On the varied meanings of "corruption," and ways Americans have used this term of disapprobation to attack methods of transmuting economic into political power and vice versa, see ZEPHYR TEACHOUT, CORRUPTION IN AMERICA: FROM BENJAMIN FRANKLIN'S SNUFF BOX TO CITIZENS UNITED (2014).

207. MICHAEL P. MALONE, THE BATTLE FOR BUTTE: MINING AND POLITICS ON THE NORTHERN FRONTIER, 1864–1906, at 173–74 (1981).

208. MICHAEL P. MALONE & RICHARD B. ROEDER, MONTANA: A HISTORY OF TWO CENTURIES 158–59 (1976); C. B. GLASSCOCK, THE WAR OF THE COPPER KINGS: BUILDERS OF BUTTE AND WOLVES OF WALL STREET 290 (1935).

209. No one's hands are clean in this story; the rival, Frederick Heinze, was playing an aggressive economic game of his own, digging from his own claims to ore underneath land owned by Amalgamated, raising complex problems that had to be fought out in court. MALONE, BATTLE FOR BUTTE, at 137–48.

210. K. ROSS TOOLE, MONTANA: AN UNCOMMON LAND 208–9 (1959).

211. MALONE & ROEDER, MONTANA, at 175.

212. STEVEN L. PIOTT, GIVING VOTERS A VOICE: THE ORIGINS OF THE INITIATIVE AND REFERENDUM IN AMERICA 57–59 (2003).

213. 1913 Mont. Laws 593. *See* Jeff Wiltse, *The Origins of Montana's Corrupt Practices Act: A More Complete History,* 73 MONT. LAW REV. 299, 322–26, 333 (2013).

214. *Tom Walsh Sounds Keynote of the Democratic Campaign for Montana at Coliseum Meeting,* BILLINGS GAZETTE, Sept. 24, 1912, at 6, *quoted in* Wiltse, *Montana's Corrupt Practices Act,* at 331.

215. Western Tradition P'ship v. Attorney General of Montana, 271 P.3d 1, 8, 9 (Mont. 2011) (internal quotation marks omitted) (first quoting MALONE & ROEDER, MONTANA, at 176; then

quoting HELEN FISK SANDERS, 1 HISTORY OF MONTANA 429 (1913)), *rev'd sub nom.* American Tradition P'ship v. Bullock, 567 U.S. 516 (2012) (per curiam).

216. *American Tradition P'ship,* 567 U.S. at 516.

217. Citizens United v. FEC, 558 U.S. 310 (2010).

218. *American Tradition P'ship,* 567 U.S. at 516.

6. THE NEW DEAL "DEMOCRACY OF OPPORTUNITY"

1. ARTHUR M. SCHLESINGER JR., THE AGE OF ROOSEVELT: THE CRISIS OF THE OLD ORDER, 1919–1933 (1957).

2. Herbert Hoover, Campaign Speech at Madison Square Garden, New York City (Oct. 31, 1932), *in* 2 THE STATE PAPERS AND OTHER PUBLIC WRITINGS OF HERBERT HOOVER 408, 408–9 (William Starr Myers ed., 1934).

3. Franklin D. Roosevelt, Acceptance of the Renomination for the Presidency, 5 PUB. PAPERS 230, 231–33 (June 27, 1936).

4. *Id.* at 233.

5. Franklin D. Roosevelt, Address at the Texas Centennial Exposition, 5 PUB. PAPERS 209, 212 (June 12, 1936).

6. Franklin D. Roosevelt, Message to the Congress Reviewing the Broad Objectives and Accomplishments of the Administration, 3 PUB. PAPERS 287, 288, 292 (June 8, 1934).

7. Franklin D. Roosevelt, Campaign Address on Progressive Government at the Commonwealth Club, 1 PUB. PAPERS 742, 752 (Sept. 23, 1932); Franklin D. Roosevelt, Address on Constitution Day, 1937 PUB. PAPERS 359, 366 (Sept. 17, 1937); Roosevelt, Acceptance of the Renomination, at 234.

8. Roosevelt, Progressive Government, at 754.

9. Daniel Vickers, *Competency and Competition: Economic Culture in Early America,* 47 WM & MARY Q. 3 (1990).

10. *See* Roosevelt, Acceptance of the Renomination, at 231–34; Roosevelt, Broad Objectives and Accomplishments, at 292; Franklin D. Roosevelt, Address at Jefferson Day Dinner, 1 PUB. PAPERS 627, 638 (Apr. 18, 1932). The *locus classicus* from the Progressive Era was HERBERT CROLY, THE PROMISE OF AMERICAN LIFE (1909).

11. For this eye-opening passage from Corwin and many other insights, we are indebted to Laura Weinrib's account of early twentieth-century contests and compromises over the meaning of labor's freedom—and scores of other crucial civil liberties ideas and battles—as they unfolded in the work and world of the American Civil Liberties Union. *see* LAURA WEINRIB, THE TAMING OF FREE SPEECH: AMERICA'S CIVIL LIBERTIES COMPROMISE 224 (2016) (quoting Edward S. Corwin, *The Passing of Dual Federalism,* 36 VA. L. REV. 1, 1 (1950)); *see also* Corwin, *The Passing,* at 23 ("[B]y the constitutional revolution which once went by the name of the 'New Deal' . . . [government] has been converted into an instrument for the achievement of . . . economic security for 'the common man'. . . .").

12. *See* WEINRIB, TAMING OF FREE SPEECH, at 224 (quoting Corwin's article in *The New Republic*).

13. Roosevelt, Progressive Government, at 752.

14. *See* W. Coast Hotel Co. v. Parrish, 300 U.S. 379 (1937) (upholding Washington state's minimum wage for women); NLRB v. Jones & Laughlin Steel Corp., 301 U.S. 1 (1937) (upholding the Wagner Act as a legitimate exercise of Congress's power to regulate interstate commerce). See below "The Wagner Act and New Deal Constitutional Political Economy."

15. For a detailed discussion of this history, see FEDERAL RESERVE BOARD, TWENTIETH ANNUAL REPORT OF THE FEDERAL RESERVE BOARD (1933), https://fraser.stlouisfed.org/title/annual -report-board-governors-federal-reserve-system-117/1933-2491 [https://perma.cc/ZV4C-TRXR]. There have been three excellent accounts of this story by legal scholars. Kenneth W. Dam, *From*

the Gold Clause Cases to the Gold Commission: A Half Century of American Monetary Law, 50 U. CHI. L. REV. 504 (1983); Anna Gelpern, *Financial Crisis Containment,* 41 CONN. L. REV. 1051, 1088–96 (2009); Gerard N. Magliocca, *The Gold Clause Cases and Constitutional Necessity,* 64 FLA. L. REV. 1243 (2012).

16. Exec. Order No. 6102, https://www.presidency.ucsb.edu/documents/executive-order-6102 -requiring-gold-coin-gold-bullion-and-gold-certificates-be-delivered [https://perma.cc/L9NJ -JWC2]; *see* Dam, *From the Gold Clause Cases,* at 509–10; Gelpern, *Financial Crisis Containment,* at 1088–89.

17. Gold Reserve Act of 1934, ch. 6, § 5, 48 Stat. 337, 340.

18. *See* Dam, *From the Gold Clause Cases,* at 516.

19. Joint Resolution of June 5, 1933, ch. 48, § 1, 48 Stat. 112, 113 (rendering gold clauses in public and private contracts void as against public policy); *see* Dam, *From the Gold Clause Cases,* at 512.

20. *See* "The Money of the Constitution," Chapter 4.

21. *See* "The Constitutional Convention," Chapter 1; "Labor, Constitutional Laissez-Faire, and *Lochner v. New York,*" Chapter 4.

22. Norman v. Baltimore & Ohio R.R. Co., 294 U.S. 240 (1935) (consolidated for review with *United States v. Bankers Trust Co.*); Nortz v. United States, 294 U.S. 317 (1935); Perry v. United States, 294 U.S. 330 (1935).

23. Brief for Respondents, United States v. Bankers Trust Co., 294 U.S. 240 (1935), (Nos. 270, 471, 472), 1935 WL 32780, at *59 (consolidated for review with Norman v. Baltimore & Ohio RR. Co.).

24. Phanor J. Eder, *The Gold Clause Cases in the Light of History: Part One,* 23 GEO. L.J. 359, 360 (1935).

25. *Perry,* 294 U.S. at 369.

26. *Id.* at 375 (citing 17 U.S. 316, 421 (1819)).

27. *Id.*

28. *Id.* at 367.

29. *Justice McReynolds' Remarks on the Gold Case Decision,* WALL ST. JOURNAL, Feb. 23, 1935, at 1. This is the most extensive news account of his oral dissent.

30. "Revision of Report Concerning Justice McReynolds' Remarks on Gold Clause Decision, Published by the *Wall Street Journal* February 23, 1935" (Papers of Justice James Clark McReynolds, MSS 85-1, Box 1, Special Collections, University of Virginia School of Law Library).

31. ROBERT H. JACKSON, THE STRUGGLE FOR JUDICIAL SUPREMACY 101–2 (1941).

32. *Wall Street Glad Suspense Is Ended,* N.Y. TIMES, Feb. 19, 1935, at 16 (describing a financial community that reacted with "unmixed relief" and "welcomed" the fact that "the decisions had supported the government's monetary policy").

33. Osborn v. Nicholson, 80 U.S. 654, 662 (1871); *see Perry,* 294 U.S. at 376 (Reynolds, J., dissenting).

34. *Nicholson,* 80 U.S. at 662–63 (1871).

35. *Id.*

36. Perhaps reflecting the extraordinary level of interest in these cases, some of the oral arguments were transcribed and reprinted in the United States Reports. *See* Norman v. Baltimore & Ohio R.R. Co., 294 U.S. 240, 251–72 (1934); Perry v. United States, 294 U.S. 330, 342–46 (1934).

37. *See* "The Money of the Constitution," Chapter 4.

38. *Norman,* 294 U.S. at 257.

39. Brief for the United States and Reconstruction Finance Corporation, United States v. Bankers Trust Co., 294 U.S. 240 (1935), (Nos. 471, 472), 1934 WL 32075, at *84–85.

40. *Norman,* 294 U.S. at 268–70.

41. *Id.* at 254–56. He consigned to a sentence the plaintiffs' claims that the law's real purpose was redistribution. "In view of the foregoing, it is not necessary to discuss the irrelevant and unsubstantial allegation that the purpose of the legislation was to transfer wealth from one class of our citizens to another." *Id.* at 259.

42. *Id.* at 268.

43. Home Building & Loan Assn. v. Blaisdell, 290 U.S. 398, 439–440 (1934).

44. *Norman v. B. & O,* 294 U.S. at 303. As Anna Gelpern observes, this sweeping holding authorized Congress to "strike contracts that interfered with its macroeconomic powers, broadly defined," rather than being limited to the questions of money and coinage. Anna Gelpern, *Financial Crisis Containment,* 41 CONN. L. REV. 1051, 1092 (2009).

45. Because all this happened *before* 1937, the Gold Clause Cases are at the center of arguments that complicate the timeline and narrative of the court's "switch in time." *See, e.g.,* Richard D. Friedman, *Switching Time and Other Thought Experiments: The Hughes Court and Constitutional Transformation,* 142 U. PA. L. REV. 1891, 1927 (1994).

46. *Perry,* 294 U.S. at 352.

47. *See* 294 U.S. 330, 357–58. *See* Gerard N. Magliocca, *The Gold Clause Cases and Constitutional Necessity,* 64 FLA. L. REV. 1243, 1265–73 (2012). The Chief Justice similarly disposed of the parallel claim in the last of the four cases, which concerned gold clauses in government-issued gold certificates. *Nortz,* 294 U.S. 317.

48. A young Henry Hart wrote in the *Harvard Law Review* that "[f]ew more baffling pronouncements . . . have ever issued from the United States Supreme Court." Henry M. Hart Jr., *The Gold Clause in United States Bonds,* 48 HARV. L. REV. 1057, 1057 (1935).

49. *See* Magliocca, *Gold Clause Cases,* at 1262–65. Magliocca's excellent article about this confrontation also includes as an appendix a draft of the prepared speech. *See id.* at 1275. 1275, 1276.

50. *Id.* at 1277.

51. *Id.; see* Abraham Lincoln, First Inaugural Address (Mar. 4, 1861), *in* 4 COLLECTED WORKS OF ABRAHAM LINCOLN 262, 268 (Roy P. Basler et al. eds., 1953), https://quod.lib.umich.edu/l /lincoln/lincoln4/1:389?rgn=div1;view=fulltext [https://perma.cc/6JSZ-RCVW].

52. National Industrial Recovery Act, Pub. L. No. 73-67, 48 Stat. 195 (1933) [hereinafter NIRA].

53. A. L. A. Schechter Poultry Corp. v. United States, 295 U.S. 495 (1935).

54. *See, e.g.,* NELSON LICHTENSTEIN, A CONTEST OF IDEAS: CAPITAL, POLITICS, AND LABOR 81 (2013) ("Corporatism . . . called for government agencies composed of capital, labor, and 'public' representatives to substitute rational, democratic planning for the chaos and inequities of the market.").

55. NIRA § 7(a), 48 Stat. at 198–99.

56. Michael L. Wachter, *Labor Unions: A Corporatist Institution in a Competitive World,* 155 U. PA. L. REV. 581, 605 (2007).

57. Exec. Order No. 6173 (1933), *terminated by* Exec. Order No. 7252 (1935).

58. For good accounts of the administration's campaign to launch the NRA, see generally ROBERT F. HIMMELBERG, THE ORIGINS OF THE NATIONAL RECOVERY ADMINISTRATION 181–218 (1993); IRA KATZNELSON, FEAR ITSELF: THE NEW DEAL AND THE ORIGINS OF OUR TIME 227–52 (2013).

59. As for labor's long-sought and long-denied collective rights, § 7(a) of the NIRA seemed to demand exactly what the Court's Constitution forbade. True, in 1917, the Court had upheld a wartime eight-hours law for interstate railway workers. Wilson v. New, 243 U.S. 332, 359 (1917). That same year, however, in *Hitchman Coal,* the Court reaffirmed the proposition that employers had a constitutional right to refuse to employ unionized workers, and it relied on this to uphold a savage antistrike injunction against mine workers organizing. Hitchman Coal & Coke Co. v. Mitchell, 245 U.S. 229, 251 (1917). The 1920s saw the Court reaffirm that any federal effort to regulate manufacturing labor was beyond Congress's authority. *See, e.g.,* Oliver Iron Mining Co. v. Lord, 262 U.S. 172, 178 (1923) (maintaining that manufacturing and mining were "not interstate commerce" but "local business," subjects left by the Constitution "to local regulation"). And *Tipaldo* seemed to confirm that any governmental effort, state or federal, to set minimum rates of pay remained beyond the constitutional pale. Morehead v. New York *ex rel.* Tipaldo, 298 U.S. 587, 610–11 (1936).

60. NIRA § 1, 48 Stat. at 195.

61. Franklin D. Roosevelt, First Inaugural Address (Mar. 4, 1933), https://avalon.law.yale.edu /20th_century/froos1.asp [https://perma.cc/TZ2G-8U6N]. As though to underscore the rupture with constitutional laissez-faire, one of Roosevelt's principal brain trusters, the economist Rexford Tugwell, explained that the Recovery Act authorized "the national Government to assume the leadership of private enterprise." REXFORD G. TUGWELL, THE BATTLE FOR DEMOCRACY 5 (1935). The very idea of an independent and free market was no longer compelling. "The jig is up," said Tugwell. "There is no invisible hand. There never was. If the depression has not taught us that, we are incapable of education." *Id.* at 14. With the NRA, he announced, Washington was "recapturing the vision of a government equipped to fight and overcome the forces of economic disintegration. A strong government with an executive amply empowered by legislative delegation is the one way out of our dilemma, and on to the realization of our vast social and economic possibilities." *Id.* at 14–15.

62. Herbert Hoover, *The Challenge to Liberty,* SATURDAY EVENING POST, Sept. 8, 1934, at 6, 69, *quoted in* KATZNELSON, FEAR ITSELF, at 235.

63. KATZNELSON, FEAR ITSELF, at 162–63 (observing that the NIRA's architects and champions embraced "features of planning that had been identified mainly with the radical program of the Bolsheviks" and "features of corporatism that principally had been associated with Fascist Italy," along with "delegation of great power to administrative agencies that regulated the private economy in a manner that had a family resemblance" to the policies of Nazi Germany).

64. Here, we are indebted to Ira Katznelson's pioneering work for his insights into the New Dealers' views of the constitutional stakes. *See generally* KATZNELSON, FEAR ITSELF.

65. *Id.*

66. *Richberg's Warning to Industry on Recovery,* N.Y. TIMES, July 7, 1933, at 4, *quoted in* KATZNELSON, FEAR ITSELF, at 233.

67. 78 CONG. REC. 3443 (1934).

68. J. R. PERITZ, COMPETITION POLICY IN AMERICA: HISTORY, RHETORIC, LAW 126 (1996). Johnson opposed "general rules of what should and what should not be in codes" or rules "requiring the Administrator to include or not to include this or that thing." *Id.* at 125 (quoting Johnson).

69. *Id.* at 126. Most cases that reached the courts dealt with businesses like "gas stations, auto dealerships, laundries and drycleaners, and lumber yards." Responding to widespread grievances, Roosevelt created a board to investigate the codes' effects on small businesses; it reported that they were "cruelly oppressed" under the NRA codes. *Id.*

70. Franklin D. Roosevelt, Statement on the Appointment of the First National Labor Board (Aug. 5, 1933), https://www.presidency.ucsb.edu/documents/statement-the-appointment-the-first -national-labor-board [https://perma.cc/9EDM-MF3U].

71. Exec. Order No. 6511, § 1 (1933); *see* Beulah Amidon, *Section 7-A: The Clash Over the Most Disputed Clause in the Recovery Act,* 23 SURVEY GRAPHIC 213, 214 (1934).

72. During its first six months, the board and its regional offices "handled 1818 cases, involving some 914,000 workers." "'The record has a disquieting aspect. Its percentages of settlements are too low, and some settlements have been unsatisfactory.'" Amidon, *Most Disputed Clause,* at 215, quoting Labor Board's Report to President.

73. *See* IRVING BERNSTEIN, THE TURBULENT YEARS: A HISTORY OF THE AMERICAN WORKER, 1933–1940, at 92–171 (2d ed. 2010) (discussing employer intransigence, role of courts, and resulting unrest at length). Professor Bernstein summarizes the situation: "Man-days lost due to strikes, which had not exceeded 603,000 in any month in the first half of 1933, spurted to 1,375,000 in July and to 2,378,000 in August.... The overriding issue in these disputes was the fundamental right to bargain collectively. Workers formed unions and demanded recognition ... employers, especially in the heavy industries, refused to negotiate with the new organizations." *Id.* at 172–

73; *see also* JAMES A. GROSS, THE MAKING OF THE NATIONAL LABOR RELATIONS BOARD: A STUDY IN ECONOMICS, POLITICS, AND THE LAW, 1933–1937 (1974).

74. BERNSTEIN, TURBULENT YEARS, at 41.

75. *Id.*

76. Amidon, *Most Disputed Clause,* at 225.

77. 295 U.S. 495 (1935).

78. Frederick H. Wood, a litigation partner at Cravath, would argue multiple high-profile Supreme Court cases during the New Deal, including *Carter Coal,* discussed below, where he was counsel for the plaintiffs successfully challenging the statute. (He also argued one of the Gold Clause cases—*Norman v. Baltimore & Ohio Railroad*—but in that case, being a frequent lawyer for major railroads, he had represented B & O, which was on the same side as the Roosevelt administration.)

79. Brief for Petitioners at 157, *reprinted in* 28 LANDMARK BRIEFS AND ARGUMENTS OF THE SUPREME COURT OF THE UNITED STATES: CONSTITUTIONAL LAW 550 (Philip B. Kurland & Gerhard Casper eds., 1975).

80. Transcript of Oral Argument at 54, A. L. A. Schechter Poultry Corp. v. United States, 295 U.S. 495 (1935) (Nos. 854, 864), *reprinted in* 28 LANDMARK BRIEFS AND ARGUMENTS, at 855.

81. *See, e.g.,* Oral Argument at 18, *reprinted in* 28 LANDMARK BRIEFS AND ARGUMENTS, at 819.

82. *Id.* at 2, 7, 17. Furthermore, the power to regulate interstate commerce was not "merely the power to prohibit wrongdoing." It was a power to "promote and foster commerce," to "encourage and to organize cooperation." *Id.* at 3.

83. *Id.* at 2.

84. *Id.* at 18 (internal quotation marks removed).

85. Black Monday saw three more unanimous decisions that clashed with the New Deal's aims. In *Radford,* the Court struck down the Frazier-Lemke Farm Bankruptcy Act—a federal statute limiting repossession of farms and allowing bankrupt farmers to stay on their land. The Court held that the act exceeded Congress's "bankruptcy power," which "like the other great substantive powers of Congress, is subject to the Fifth Amendment." Writing for the Court, Justice Brandeis said that *Blaisdell* lent "no support" to the farmer's position. Echoing the *Lochner* era, he continued, "[H]owever great the nation's need . . . resort must be had to proceedings by eminent domain; so that, through taxation, the burden of the relief afforded in the public interest may be borne by the public [rather than private parties]." Louisville Joint Stock Land Bank v. Radford, 295 U.S. 555, 589, 597, 602 (1935). Next, in *Humphrey's Executor,* the Court denied FDR the power to remove anti–New Deal officials from "quasi-legislative" and "quasi-judicial" agencies, such as the Federal Trade Commission, the Interstate Commerce Commission, and the U.S. Tariff Commission. Humphrey's Ex'r v. United States, 295 U.S. 602 (1935). Finally, in *Mobley,* the Court affirmed a directed verdict for the New York Life Insurance Company in a dispute with a disabled policyholder. Mobley v. N.Y. Life Ins. Co., 295 U.S. 632 (1935).

86. A. L. A. Schechter Poultry Corp. v. United States, 295 U.S. 495, 553 (1935) (Cardozo, J., concurring).

87. *See, e.g.,* Cass R. Sunstein, *Constitutionalism After the New Deal,* 101 HARV. L. REV. 421, 447–48 (1987) (arguing that the nondelegation doctrine's demise following *Schechter* "altered the constitutional system in ways so fundamental as to suggest that something akin to a constitutional amendment had taken place"); *see also* PAUL BREST ET AL., PROCESSES OF CONSTITUTIONAL DECISIONMAKING: CASES AND MATERIALS 598 (7th ed. 2018) ("The non-delegation doctrine . . . was largely abandoned within a decade, as the country came to terms with the administrative state.").

88. This paragraph and the next rely heavily on Keith Whittington and Jason Iuliano's effective debunking of the "myth of the nondelegation doctrine." Keith E. Whittington & Jason Iuliano, *The Myth of the Nondelegation Doctrine,* 165 U. PA. L. REV. 379 (2017).

89. Recent scholarship has shown rather conclusively that, contrary to the wishful thinking of present-day advocates of a robust nondelegation doctrine, there was no such doctrine in the early years of the Republic either. *See* Julian Davis Mortenson & Nicholas Bagley, *Delegation at the Founding,* 121 COLUM. L. REV. 277 (2021); Nicholas R. Parrillo, *A Critical Assessment of the Originalist Case Against Administrative Regulatory Power: New Evidence from the Federal Tax on Private Real Estate in the 1790s,* 130 YALE L. J. 1288 (2021).

90. Whittingon & Iuliano, *Myth of the Nondelegation Doctrine.*

91. *Id.* at 405 ("With a modicum of specificity, Congress could provide the 'adequate' policy guidance that the Court had long required for a statute to pass constitutional muster.").

92. Contrary to the Justices' fantasies, nondelegation simply never was the constitutional ground on which even the most conservative jurists fought their battles to constrain and shape the administrative state that was under construction in the late nineteenth and early twentieth centuries. That ground was judicial review of administrative process and an insistence that due process meant judicial process, whenever "private rights" were at stake. Thus, as we saw in Chapter 4, Gilded Age controversies over the railroads brought forth the Interstate Commerce Commission, the first significant federal regulatory agency to reach beyond the traditional agency business of veterans' pensions and federal land and postal services. The judiciary greeted the new federal agency with fierce hostility: limiting its jurisdiction, gutting its remedial powers, and reviewing its rate-making with a fine-tooth comb—until finally, over two decades or so, the judiciary's familiarity with the ICC's lumbering court-like procedures, court-crafted formulae, and sound, lawyerly expertise bred a deferential posture. This deference did not extend to state rate-makers or other, newer federal agencies. The Supreme Court continued to demand that lower courts redo agency fact-finding, pick through the details of agency decision-making, and second-guess agencies on hosts of other issues within their expertise—all in the name of due process.

As for Chief Justice Hughes, however, he was the very model of a moderate, mildly Progressive member of the elite bar and bench who saw full well the necessity of the new administrative state and set out to make it safe for the courts, the Constitution, and the elite bar, by molding the new state institutions in their own image, laden with more or less court-like processes, and subject to some significant measure of judicial review. Thus, here, in *Schechter,* Hughes approvingly observed that the FTC's decision-making process made it "a quasi[-]judicial body," and grimly noted that in creating the NRA, Congress has "dispense[d] with this administrative procedure and with any administrative procedure." *Schechter,* 295 U.S. at 533. We will return soon to Hughes's role as a cautious Progressive tacking back and forth between the old liberalism and the new. Congress got the chief's message, and New Deal state-building met no more rebuffs on nondelegation grounds.

We'll also return to the broader battles over the shape of administrative process and the extent of judicial review, and we'll find it is constitutional ground that foes of New Deal state-building would reclaim in the mid-1940s. Still hoping to tie the New Deal agencies in knots, the ABA would take due process claims for extensive judicial review of agency action to Congress, seeking relief through legislation—and gaining what would become, in a more moderate iteration, with greater emphasis on court-like administrative process and less on judicial review, the 1946 Administrative Procedure Act.

93. *Id.* at 547–49.

94. *See* Oral Argument at 2, *reprinted in* 28 LANDMARK BRIEFS AND ARGUMENTS, at 803 ("[T]he problem presented to Congress was not an isolated need for the regulation of the live-poultry industry. The problem was to check the progressive destruction of an economic system upon which depended the welfare of the people and the maintenance of the Government itself. . . . When this nationwide system of production, exchange, and employment was breaking down, only the National Government could bring about an orderly improvement through concerted action."); *see also id.* at 13 (arguing that if even 10 percent of employers failed

to pay their workers adequate wages, they would "destroy [Congress's] health-giving, life-giving effort to improve economic conditions . . . [and] force down the 90 percent to a continuation of sweatshop operation and the worst evils in trade and industry.").

95. *Schechter,* 295 U.S. at 547–48.

96. *Id.* at 554 (Cardozo, J., concurring).

97. United States v. A. L. A. Schechter Poultry Corp., 76 F.2d 617, 624 (2d Cir. 1935) (Hand, J., concurring) ("It may indeed follow that the nation cannot as a unit meet any of the great crises of its existence except war, and that it must obtain the concurrence of the separate states; but that to some extent at any rate is implicit in any federation, and the resulting weaknesses have not hitherto been thought to outweigh the dangers of a completely centralized government. If the American people have come to believe otherwise, Congress is not the accredited organ to express their will to change.").

98. Franklin D. Roosevelt, The Two Hundred and Ninth Press Conference, 4 PUB. PAPERS 200, 201, 205 (May 31, 1935).

99. BRUCE ACKERMAN, 2 WE THE PEOPLE: TRANSFORMATIONS 297 (2000).

100. *Id.* at 298.

101. Roosevelt, Two Hundred and Ninth Press Conference, at 201, 208.

102. *Id.* at 207, 210–12.

103. *Id.* at 204, 208–10, 216; United States v. E. C. Knight Co., 156 U.S. 1 (1895).

104. Roosevelt, Two Hundred and Ninth Press Conference, at 210.

105. *Id.* at 208, 210, 214, 221.

106. *Id.* at 219.

107. *Id.* at 215.

108. Beulah Amidon, *Section 7-A: The Clash Over the Most Disputed Clause in the Recovery Act,* 23 SURVEY GRAPHIC 213, 225 (May, 1934).

109. *See, e.g.,* Truax v. Raich, 239 U.S. 33, 38 (1915) (insisting on "the freedom of the employer to exercise his judgment without illegal interference or compulsion"); Coppage v. Kansas, 236 U.S. 1, 19 (1915) ("Conceding the full right of the individual to join the union, he has no inherent right to do this and still remain in the employ of one who is unwilling to employ a union man. . . ."); Adair v. United States, 208 U.S. 161, 174 (1908) ("[T]here [i]s no disagreement as to the general proposition that there is a liberty of contract which cannot be unreasonably interfered with by legislation."); *see also* REBECCA E. ZIETLOW, ENFORCING EQUALITY: CONGRESS, THE CONSTITUTION, AND THE PROTECTION OF INDIVIDUAL RIGHTS 75 (2006) (recounting the argument of business interests that the Wagner bill was unconstitutional); KIM PHILLIPS-FEIN, INVISIBLE HANDS: THE MAKING OF THE CONSERVATIVE MOVEMENT FROM THE NEW DEAL TO REAGAN 14–15 (2009) (same).

110. ZIETLOW, ENFORCING EQUALITY, at 75 (quoting Emery's testimony before the Senate).

111. 78 CONG. REC. 3679 (1934), *quoted in* James Gray Pope, *The Thirteenth Amendment Versus the Commerce Clause: Labor and the Shaping of American Constitutional Law, 1921–1957,* 102 COLUM. L. REV. 1, 48 (2002).

112. *Id.* at 47–48.

113. *Id.* at 48.

114. 78 CONG. REC. 3679 (1934), *quoted in* ZIETLOW, ENFORCING EQUALITY, at 75.

115. Joyce Appleby, *What Is Still American in the Political Philosophy of Thomas Jefferson?,* 39 WM. & MARY Q. 287, 295 (1982); Joyce Appleby, *The Radical Double-Entendre in the Right to Self-Government, in* THE ORIGINS OF ANGLO-AMERICAN RADICALISM 275, 281 (Margaret Jacob & James Jacob eds., 1984).

116. Robert Wagner, *"Industrial Democracy" and Cooperations,* Radio Address at the National Democratic Club 4–5 (May 8, 1937), *quoted in* Mark Barenberg, *The Political Economy of the Wagner Act: Power, Symbol, and Workplace Cooperation,* 106 HARV. L. REV. 1379, 1424 n.208 (1993).

117. ZIETLOW, ENFORCING EQUALITY, at 78 (quoting an interview of Wagner).

118. Pope, *Thirteenth Amendment,* at 47 (quoting a letter from Furuseth to Wagner).

119. *Id.;* William E. Forbath, *The New Deal Constitution in Exile,* 51 DUKE L.J. 165, 196 (2001).

120. JAMES A. GROSS, THE MAKING OF THE NATIONAL LABOR RELATIONS BOARD: A STUDY IN ECONOMICS, POLITICS, AND THE LAW, 1933–1937, at 144 (1974).

121. A. L. A. Schechter Poultry Corp. v. United States, 295 U.S. 495, 554 (1935) (Cardozo, J., concurring).

122. United States v. A. L. A. Schechter Poultry Corp., 76 F.2d 617, 625 (2d Cir. 1935) (Hand, J., concurring).

123. National Labor Relations Act, Pub. L. No. 74–198, § 1, 49 Stat. 449, 449 (1935) [hereinafter NLRA].

124. Pope, *Thirteenth Amendment,* at 53.

125. *Id.* at 53 n.249.

126. NLRA § 1, 49 Stat. at 449 ("The inequality of bargaining power between employees who do not possess full freedom of association or actual liberty of contract, and employers . . . tends to aggravate recurrent business depressions, by depressing wage rates and the purchasing power of wage earners. . . . Experience has proved that protection by law of the right of employees to organize and bargain collectively . . . promotes the flow of commerce by removing certain recognized sources of industrial strife and unrest, by encouraging practices fundamental to the friendly adjustment of industrial disputes . . . and by restoring equality of bargaining power. . . .").

127. *Id.* at 449–50; *see* Pope, *Thirteenth Amendment,* at 53 ("[Wagner] insisted that the [NLRA's] statement of policy retain its references to inequality of bargaining power and inadequate consumer purchasing power. Unlike the precedent-bound Labor Department lawyers, [Wagner was] engaged in a forthrightly transformative project.").

128. NLRA § 1, 49 Stat. at 449–50.

129. *Id.* at 449.

130. *Id.* §§ 3–6, 49 Stat. at 451–52. Courts' role in the process was reduced to as modest a measure of review as its drafters thought could pass judicial muster. Trial courts had no role at all. Here was the nation's first "wrongful discharge" and employment antidiscrimination law, forbidding discrimination against workers who chose union, but unlike the civil rights employment statutes of the 1960s and 1970s, the law abjured any private right of action in federal court. Federal trial courts had been the engineers and enforcers of the labor injunction, and labor and labor's friends in Congress sought to exclude them from the Wagner Act process. *See id.* § 10(f), 49 Stat. at 455 (providing for review of NLRB orders in the federal courts of appeals, thus bypassing the district courts).

131. William E. Forbath, *Caste, Class, and Equal Citizenship,* 98 MICH. L. REV. 1, 60–61 (1999); *see also* Pope, *Thirteenth Amendment,* at 46–54 (discussing the debate on the NLRA, which was seen by its proponents as a way to end wage slavery and to secure equality in fact between employees and their employers); William E. Forbath, *New Deal Constitution in Exile,* 51 DUKE L.J. 165, 195 (2001) ("Historians have amply shown the centrality of citizenship rights in the outlook and arguments of the Wagner Act's proponents."); *see generally* DAVID PLOTKE, BUILDING A DEMOCRATIC POLITICAL ORDER: RESHAPING AMERICAN LIBERALISM IN THE 1930S AND 1940S (1996); Mark Barenberg, *The Political Economy of the Wagner Act: Power, Symbol, and Workplace Cooperation,* 106 HARV. L. REV. 1379 (1993); Craig Becker, *Democracy in the Workplace: Union Representation Elections and Federal Labor Law,* 77 MINN. L. REV. 495 (1993).

132. Pope, *Thirteenth Amendment,* at 47–48.

133. *Id.* at 79.

134. *Id.* at 47 (quoting a letter from Furuseth to Wagner).

135. Robert F. Wagner, Address Before the National Democratic Forum (May 8, 1937), *quoted in* Leon H. Keyserling, *Why the Wagner Act?, in* THE WAGNER ACT: AFTER TEN YEARS 13 (Louis G. Silverberg ed., 1945).

136. *To Create a National Labor Board, 1934: Hearings on S. 2926 Before the Senate Comm. on Educ. and Labor,* 73d Cong. 109, at 51 (1934) (statement of Robert L. Hale).

137. S. Rep. No. 1184, at 4 (1934).

138. *To Create a National Labor Board,* at 302 (statement of Richard W. Hogue).

139. Pope, *Thirteenth Amendment,* at 60.

140. *Id.*

141. 298 U.S. 238 (1936).

142. Pub. L. No. 74–402, 49 Stat. 991 (1935) (also called the Guffey-Snyder Act and the Bituminous Coal Conservation Act).

143. *Carter Coal,* 298 U.S. at 308–9.

144. *See* Pope, *Thirteenth Amendment,* at 71 n.353 (collecting cases).

145. Franklin D. Roosevelt, Acceptance of the Renomination for the Presidency, 5 Pub. Papers 230, 232–33 (June 27, 1936).

146. Republican Party Platform of 1936 (June 9, 1936), The American Presidency Project, https://www.presidency.ucsb.edu/documents/republican-party-platform-1936 [https://perma.cc /BX77-FBG2]; *see also* Pope, *Thirteenth Amendment,* at 72–73 (recounting attacks by Landon and supporters on the New Deal administration).

147. Roosevelt, Acceptance of the Renomination.

148. *Id.* at 231.

149. *Id.* at 232.

150. *Id.* at 233.

151. *Id.* at 233–34.

152. *Id.* at 234.

153. Alan Brinkley, The End of Reform: New Deal Liberalism in Recession and War 10 (1995).

154. Roosevelt, Acceptance of the Renomination, at 234.

155. *See* Bruce Ackerman, Revolutionary Constitutions: Charismatic Leadership and the Rule of Law 390–91 (2019).

156. 81 Cong. Rec. 1291 (1937) (remarks of Sen. McKellar).

157. 81 Cong. Rec. App. 307 (1937) (reprinting radio address by Hon. Hugo L. Black).

158. *Id.*

159. 81 Cong. Rec. 1291 (1937) (remarks of Sen. McKellar). Parallel to this action in Congress, President Roosevelt was urging states to ratify a child labor amendment to the U.S. Constitution. He would use that amendment's failure to justify non–Article V approaches to responding to a reactionary Court. *See* Gerard Magliocca, *Court-Packing and the Child Labor Amendment,* 27 Const. Comment. 455 (2011).

160. James T. Patterson, Congressional Conservatism and the New Deal: The Growth of the Conservative Coalition in Congress 1933–1939, at 86 (1967).

161. *Id.* at 88–89.

162. Franklin D. Roosevelt, A "Fireside Chat" Discussing the Plan for Reorganization of the Judiciary (Mar. 9, 1937), 1937 Pub. Papers 122, 122, 124 (1941).

163. Franklin D. Roosevelt, "The Constitution of the United States Was a Layman's Document, Not a Lawyer's Contract," Address on Constitution Day (Sep. 17, 1937), *in* 1937 Pub. Papers 359, 361, 362, 364, 365 (1941).

164. Roosevelt, A "Fireside Chat" Discussing the Plan for Reorganization of the Judiciary, at 126.

165. *Id.* at 131.

166. *Id.* at 124.

167. *See generally* Sidney Fine, Sit-Down: The General Motors Strike of 1936–1937 (1969) (detailing the emergence and spread of sit-down strikes in 1936 and 1937); Robert Zieger, The CIO, 1935–1955, at 50 (1995) (noting that sit-down strikes offered advantages over outside strikes

because they shut down production at once, minimized violence, and masked "union's numerical weaknesses").

168. *See* Drew D. Hansen, *The Sit-Down Strikes and the Switch in Time*, 46 WAYNE L. REV. 49, 51–53 (2000) (arguing that the sit-down strikes had a profound influence on the "switch in time of 1937").

169. ZIEGER, CIO, at 50–53 (recounting strikes at General Motors and Chrysler).

170. Hansen, *Sit-Down Strikes*, at 73–107 (explaining the pervasiveness of the strikes and their effects on the Court).

171. *Id.* at 51–53; James Gray Pope, *Thirteenth Amendment Versus the Commerce Clause: Labor and the Shaping of American Constitutional Law, 1921–1957*, 102 COLUM. L. REV. 1, 78–80 (2002).

172. We are indebted to Jeremy Kessler and David Pozen for this elegant encapsulation of the changed character of these new basic rights. *See* Jeremy K. Kessler & David E. Pozen, *The Search for an Egalitarian First Amendment*, 118 COLUM. L. REV. 1953 (2018).

173. 301 U.S. 1 (1937).

174. *See* West Coast Hotel Co. v. Parrish, 300 U.S. 379 (1937) (upholding a state minimum wage statute, in what is conventionally viewed as the first case marking this "switch in time"). *But see* note 45 above. For a discussion of the case, see the section titled "The Fair Labor Standards Act," below.

175. NLRB v. Jones & Laughlin Steel Co., 301 U.S. 1, 29 (1937).

176. *Id.* at 29–30.

177. *Id.* at 30–32.

178. *Id.* at 34–41.

179. NLRB v. Fruehauf Trailer Co., 301 U.S. 49 (1937); NLRB v. Friedman-Harry Marks Clothing Co., 301 U.S. 58 (1937).

180. *Friedman-Harry Marks Clothing*, 301 U.S. at 75.

181. *Jones & Laughlin Steel Co.*, 301 U.S. at 33.

182. *Id.* at 33–34 (quoting Texas & New Orleans R.R. Co. v. Brotherhood Ry. & S.S. Clerks, 281 U.S. 548, 570 (1930)).

183. LAURA WEINRIB, THE TAMING OF FREE SPEECH: AMERICA'S CIVIL LIBERTIES COMPROMISE 224 (2016) (quoting Corwin's article in *The New Republic*).

184. *Id.*

185. *Id.*

186. *Storm-Clouds in Legislative Sky: "Judicial Reform," "Collective Bargaining" Twin Headaches*, LITERARY DIG., Apr. 24, 1937, at 3.

187. *Judgment Day: Supreme Court Gives Its Blessing to Labor Relations Act and Hands Roosevelt a Victorious Defeat*, NEWSWEEK, Apr. 17, 1937, at 7.

188. *Id.*

189. *See* Jeremy K. Kessler & David E. Pozen, *The Search for an Egalitarian First Amendment*, 118 COLUM. L. REV. 1953 (2018).

190. 301 U.S. 468, 473–75 (1937).

191. *Id.* at 478, 482.

192. Charles O. Gregory, *Peaceful Picketing and Freedom of Speech*, 26 A.B.A. J. 709, 710 (1940).

193. *Id.* at 710, 714.

194. For primary strikes, see Thornhill v. Alabama, 310 U.S. 88 (1940). For secondary actions, see AFL v. Swing, 312 U.S. 321, 326 (1941) ("A state cannot exclude workingmen from peacefully exercising the right of free communication by drawing the circle of economic competition between employers and workers so small. . . . The interdependence of economic interest of all engaged in the same industry has become a commonplace. . . . The right of free communication cannot therefore be mutilated by denying it to workers, in a dispute with an employer, even though they are not in his employ.").

195. Edward S. Corwin, *The Passing of Dual Federalism,* 36 Va. L. Rev. 1, 1 (1950).

196. *Id.*

197. *See* "From Gilded Age Radicalism to 'Progressive Democracy,'" Chapter 5.

198. Michele Landis Dauber, The Sympathetic State: Disaster Relief and the Origins of the American Welfare State 148 (2013); Alan Brinkley, Voices of Protest: Huey Long, Father Coughlin, and the Great Depression 222–26 (1982); Luke Norris, *The Workers' Constitution,* 87 Fordham L. Rev. 1459, 1484–85 (2019); *see generally* Abraham Holtzman, The Townsend Movement: A Political Study (1963).

199. Senator Huey P. Long, "Every Man a King": Share Our Wealth Radio Speech (Feb. 23, 1934), https://www.hueylong.com/programs/share-our-wealth-speech.php [https://perma.cc/G5PE -XJ7M]. On Long and "Share Our Wealth," see Brinkley, Voices of Protest, at 79–81, 166–75, 179–86.

200. Robert Zieger, The cio, 1935–1955, at 39–40 (1995).

201. *See* Lizabeth Cohen, Making a New Deal: Industrial Workers in Chicago, 1919–1939 (2d ed. 2008); *see also* Irving Bernstein, The Turbulent Years: A History of the American Worker, 1933–1940 (2d ed. 2010).

202. *See* Cohen, Making a New Deal.

203. *See id.* at 252–83.

204. Franklin D. Roosevelt, Message to the Congress Reviewing the Broad Objectives and Accomplishments of the Administration, 3 Pub. Papers 287, 291–92 (June 8, 1934).

205. *Id.* at 292.

206. *See* "Congressional Constructions of Spending for the General Welfare," Chapter 2.

207. Dauber, Sympathetic State, at 20–34.

208. *See* "Congressional Constructions of Spending for the General Welfare," Chapter 2 (discussing President Buchanan's veto of the land-grant college bill, which Congress enacted a few years later as a general welfare measure under President Lincoln).

209. Dauber, Sympathetic State, at 20–34.

210. *Id.* at 48 (quoting 2 Cong. Rec. 3151 (1874) (remark of Rep. Cox, a New York Democrat)). Dauber's book brings the whole arc of this story to light and we rely on it in these paragraphs.

211. William E. Forbath, *Caste, Class, and Equal Citizenship,* 98 Mich. L. Rev. 1, 22 (1999).

212. Alexander Keyssar, Out of Work: The First Century of Unemployment in Massachusetts 251 (1986), *quoted in* Dauber, Sympathetic State, at 48–49.

213. Dauber, Sympathetic State, at 49.

214. *Id.* at 51 (quoting 26 Cong. Rec. 386 (1893)).

215. *Id.* at 48 (quoting 26 Cong. Rec. 388 (1893)).

216. *Id.*

217. United States v. Realty Co., 163 U.S. 427 (1896). The tariffs and subsidies benefited the Sugar Refining Trust, along with domestic raw sugar producers. Congress had repealed the subsidy, and the sugar producers were claiming reliance on the unpaid federal bounty.

218. Dauber, Sympathetic State, at 59 (quoting Brief for the United States at 187–88, United States v. Realty Co., 163 U.S. 427 (1896) (No. 870)).

219. *Realty Co.,* 163 U.S. at 441, 444; Dauber, Sympathetic State, at 61.

220. William N. Eskridge Jr. & John Ferejohn, A Republic of Statutes: The New American Constitution 182, 184 (2010) (quoting *Ex-President Hoover's Call to Republicans,* N.Y. Times, Mar. 24, 1935, at 32 (quoting Hoover)).

221. *Schechter* was the first big NIRA case, and the Supreme Court immediately took it up, granting certiorari fourteen days after the Second Circuit's decision. A. L. A. Schechter Poultry Corp. v. United States, 295 U.S. 495, 520 (1935); United States v. A. L. A. Schechter Poultry Corp., 76 F.2d 617, 625 (2d Cir. 1935). Other circuit courts had barely weighed in. *See, e.g.,* Locke v. United States, 75 F.2d 157, 159 (5th Cir. 1935) ("An act of Congress which assumes to regulate interstate

commerce even by indirection is presumptively constitutional."); Ryan v. Amazon Petroleum Corp., 71 F.2d 1 (5th Cir. 1934) (upholding NIRA provisions pertaining to petroleum), *rev'd sub nom.* Panama Ref. Co. v. Ryan, 293 U.S. 388 (1935). The district courts, on the other hand, had a lot to say and were quite active in dismantling the NIRA. *See, e.g.,* United States v. National Garment Co., 10 F. Supp. 104, 110 (E.D. Mo. 1935) (holding that the federal government had "no valid power" to regulate hours and wages in the underwear manufacturing industry); Hart Coal Corp. v. Sparks, 7 F. Supp. 16, 25 (W.D. Ky. 1934) ("[T]he lack of power in the national government, under the commerce clause, to regulate manufacture and production . . . is as axiomatic as is the proposition that no state is entitled to more than two Senators under the Constitution."). *But see* Annotation, *National Industrial Recovery Act and Similar State Statutes,* 95 A.L.R. 1391 (1935) (collecting cases upholding the NIRA).

The D.C. Supreme Court had also struck down the Railroad Retirement Act of 1934, Congress's first modest foray into national old-age insurance, also under the Commerce Power. *See* Railroad Ret. Bd. v. Alton R.R. Co., 295 U.S. 330, 346 (1935); Brief for Respondents at 1–2, Railroad Ret. Bd. v. Alton R.R. Co., 295 U.S. 330 (1935) (No. 566), 1935 WL 32944, at *1–2; Brief for Petitioners at 1–2, Railroad Ret. Bd. v. Alton R.R. Co., 295 U.S. 330 (1935) (No. 566), 1934 WL 32082, at *1–2.

222. DAUBER, SYMPATHETIC STATE, at 132.

223. David J. Danelski, *The Propriety of Brandeis's Extrajudicial Conduct, in* BRANDEIS AND AMERICA 11, 26 (Nelson L. Dawson ed., 1989) (quoting Brandeis) (citing Florida v. Mellon, 273 U.S. 12 (1927)).

224. DAUBER, SYMPATHETIC STATE, at 138 (using the professors' words).

225. *Id.* (quoting EDWARD S. CORWIN, THE TWILIGHT OF THE SUPREME COURT: A HISTORY OF OUR CONSTITUTIONAL THEORY 178–79 (1934)).

226. *Id.* at 134–39.

227. Child Labor Tax Case, 259 U.S. 20 (1922) (official case name). In the unofficial *Supreme Court Reporter,* this case is called: Bailey v. Drexel Furniture Co., 42 S. Ct. 449 (1922).

228. Again, Dauber's *Sympathetic State* is the key work demonstrating how the CES lawyers and economists favored a straight national plan. *See* DAUBER, SYMPATHETIC STATE, at 134–39.

229. ESKRIDGE & FEREJOHN, REPUBLIC OF STATUTES, at 181 (quoting Roosevelt).

230. HARVARD SITKOFF, A NEW DEAL FOR BLACKS: THE EMERGENCE OF CIVIL RIGHTS AS A NATIONAL ISSUE 104 (1978) (quoting Sen. Carter Glass of Virginia).

231. 79 CONG. REC. 5555 (1935) (statement of Rep. Burdick).

232. DAUBER, SYMPATHETIC STATE, at 148–50; *see generally* ARTHUR J. ALTMEYER, THE FORMATIVE YEARS OF SOCIAL SECURITY 34 (1966); FRANCES PERKINS, THE ROOSEVELT I KNEW 296–301 (1946); EDWIN E. WITTE, THE DEVELOPMENT OF THE SOCIAL SECURITY ACT 143–45 (1962); Kenneth Finegold, *Agriculture and the Politics of U.S. Social Provision, in* THE POLITICS OF SOCIAL POLICY IN THE UNITED STATES 199–234 (Margaret Weir et al. eds., 1988).

233. *Old-Age Pensions: Hearings Before the H. Comm. on Labor,* 71st Cong. 246 (1930) (supplemental statement by Abraham Epstein, founder of the American Association for Social Security), *quoted in* ESKRIDGE & FEREJOHN, REPUBLIC OF STATUTES, at 52, 184.

234. 79 CONG. REC. 5811 (1935) (statement of Rep. Dirksen).

235. 79 CONG. REC. 8224 (statement of Sen. Bachman).

236. *Id.*

237. 79 CONG. REC. 5476–77 (statement of Rep. Doughton).

238. 79. CONG. REC. 9283 (statement of Sen. Wagner).

239. 295 U.S. 330 (1935).

240. *Id.* at 350.

241. *Id.* at 368.

242. *Id.* at 351.

Notes to Pages 304–308 **551**

243. *Id.*

244. *Id.* Put simply, as the dissenters pointed out, the Court had put any "pension act for railroad employees . . . no matter . . . how sound" beyond Congress's power to regulate interstate commerce. *Id.* at 374–5.

245. Helvering v. Davis, 301 U.S. 619, 641, 645 (1937).

246. *Id.* at 641.

247. Decided the same day, *Steward Machine Co. v. Davis*, 301 U.S. 548 (1937) upheld the unemployment insurance provisions of the SSA, and *Helvering v. Davis*, 301 U.S. 619 (1937) its old-age pension program. Much as the constitutional law professoriate and the CES legal staff predicted, the straight national program, old-age pensions, had an easier time in the Court. The federal-state unemployment insurance scheme, the "Brandeis idea," drew four dissents. But two of them, Justices Sutherland and Van Devanter, were at pains to say that they would have approved the scheme if it had been crafted like the old-age insurance program, along national lines. *Steward Machine*, 301 U.S. at 609–16 (Sutherland, J., concurring in part and dissenting in part). Even more strikingly: Sutherland, Van Devanter, and Butler—all the horsemen but McReynolds—ended up endorsing the federal–state unemployment insurance scheme as Wisconsin had carried it out, in a later 1937 case. Carmichael v. Southern Coal & Coke Co., 301 U.S. 495, 530–31 (1937) (Sutherland, J., dissenting).

248. *Steward Machine*, 301 U.S. at 600 (1937) (McReynolds, J., dissenting).

249. *Id.* at 602–3.

250. *Id.* at 616–17 (Butler, J., dissenting).

251. *Id.* at 617–18.

252. The joint dissent forthrightly embraces the argument that making states an offer too big to refuse is a form of coercion. National Fed'n of Indep. Bus. v. Sebelius, 567 U.S. 519, 646 (Scalia, Kennedy, Thomas, & Alito, J. J., dissenting). And indeed, the majority, by a 7–2 vote, *see id.* at 579–85 (Roberts, C. J.), also concludes that the Medicaid expansion was too coercive, but emphasizes the way the statute leveraged an existing program, Medicaid, to press states to accept the large new program, expanded Medicaid. The coercive nature of this "leveraging" led the Court to create an option for states to refuse the new money and keep their old Medicaid program in place. *See* Samuel R. Bagenstos, *The Anti-Leveraging Principle and the Spending Clause After NFIB*, 101 Georgetown L.J. 861 (2013); "Race and the Constitutional Political Economy of Health Care—and Voting," Chapter 9.

253. *Steward Machine*, 301 U.S. at 589–90.

254. *Id.* at 589.

255. Pub. L. No. 75–718, 52 Stat. 1060 (1938) [hereinafter FLSA].

256. Luke Norris, *The Workers' Constitution*, 87 Fordham L. Rev., 1459, 1499 (2019) (quoting 83 Cong. Rec. 7310 (1938) (statement of Rep. Fitzgerald)); *id.* (quoting 83 Cong. Rec. 7283 (1938) (statement of Rep. Curley)); *id.* at 1500 (quoting 83 Cong. Rec. 7311 (1938) (statement of Rep. Sirovich)). We are much indebted to Luke Norris's explorations of the legislative constitutional history of both the Social Security and the Fair Labor Standards Acts. See the section titled "The Fair Labor Standards Act" later in this chapter.

257. Morehead v. New York ex rel. Tipaldo, 298 U.S. 587 (1936).

258. Arthur M. Schlesinger Jr., The Politics of Upheaval 1935–1936, at 489 (1960).

259. 261 U.S. 525 (1923); *see* "The Structure of Politics Itself," Chapter 5.

260. *Id.* at 558.

261. 300 U.S. 379 (1937).

262. *Id.* at 391.

263. *Id.* at 399.

264. Indeed, the suffrage movement itself had been somewhat divided over the question of sex-specific protective labor legislation. *See* "The Structure of Politics Itself," Chapter 5.

265. Muller v. Oregon, 208 U.S. 412, 421 (1908).

266. Deborah M. Figart et al., Living Wages, Equal Wages: Gender and Labour Market Policies in the United States 100 (2002).

267. *Id.*

268. FLSA §§ 5–8, 52 Stat. at 1062–65.

269. We are indebted to Kate Andrias for her brilliant reconstruction of these forgotten dimensions of the FLSA. *See* Kate Andrias, *An American Approach to Social Democracy: The Forgotten Promise of the Fair Labor Standard Act*, 128 Yale L.J. 616 (2019).

270. *Id.*

271. Gerald Mayer, Cong. Research Serv., Union Membership Trends in the United States 23 (2004).

272. *See* Andrias, *American Approach to Social Democracy,* at 661–63 (summarizing the legislative debate); *see also id.* at 680–83 (explaining how the AFL and the CIO capitalized on the FLSA to organize workers).

273. *Id.* at 662 (quoting 81 Cong. Rec. 7652 (1937) (statement of Sen. Walsh)); *see also* 81 Cong. Rec. 7800 (1937) (statement of Sen. Walsh).

274. 81 Cong. Rec. 7800 (1937) (statement of Sen. Walsh).

275. United States v. Darby, 312 U.S. 100 (1941).

276. *Id.* at 115.

277. *Id.* at 114.

278. Luke Norris, *The Workers' Constitution,* 87 Fordham L. Rev., 1459, 1499 (2019) (quoting 83 Cong. Rec. 7311 (1938) (statement of Rep. Sirovich)).

279. 83 Cong. Rec. 7312 (1938) (statement of Rep. Sirovich).

280. Andrias, *American Approach to Social Democracy,* at 678–83.

281. *Id.* at 682 (quoting Sean Farhang & Ira Katznelson, *The Southern Imposition: Congress and Labor in the New Deal and Fair Deal,* 19 Stud. Am. Pol. Dev. 1, 2 (2005)).

282. *See* "The Slow Triumph of the Technocrats," Chapter 8.

283. For an important account of antitrust's constitutional dimensions along these lines, see Tim Wu, The Curse of Bigness: Antitrust in the New Gilded Age (2019). See especially Wu's persuasive interpretation of Theodore Roosevelt's trust-busting as constitutional enforcement. *Id.* at 45–77.

284. *See* Matt Stoller, Goliath: The 100-Year War Between Monopoly Power and Democracy 25–51 (2019). Commissioned by Mellon's son, the most comprehensive account of Mellon's life, at 779 pages, is David Cannadine, Mellon: An American Life (2006).

285. Stoller, Goliath, at 144–46.

286. That Mellon also had created cartels with European counterparts, committing them not to export aluminum to the United States, only made ALCOA's notoriety greater. *Id.* at 148.

287. Stoller, Goliath, at 129.

288. *Id.* at 126.

289. Alan Brinkley, The End of Reform: New Deal Liberalism in Recession and War 106 (1995).

290. Means was coauthor, with the Columbia corporate law professor and New Deal brain truster Adolph Berle, of the New Deal classic *The Modern Corporation and Private Property* (1932). The book is known today for its pioneering insights about the "separation of ownership and control," and its evidence and argument that shareholders no longer exercised any effective authority over the big companies they owned, and corporate management ruled the roost. The book also deconstructed the efficiency claims neoclassical economists made on behalf of the giant corporation, and offered an up-to-date institutional-economics and legal realist rendering of the old Populist political-economic case that unregulated corporate capitalism had devolved into oligarchy—an oligarchy composed of the executives who ran the nation's biggest corporations and exerted unprecedented sway over economic and political life. The solution, argued Berle

and Means, was not what corporate governance scholars take from their work today: re-upping shareholder sovereignty. Rather, the book called for a more radical reconstruction of corporate governance to make the "law of corporations" a "constitutional law for the new economic state," making the corporate elite accountable not only to shareholders but also to workers, consumers, and other stakeholders. ADOLF A. BERLE & GARDINER C. MEANS, THE MODERN CORPORATION AND PRIVATE PROPERTY 357 (1932).

291. WILLIAM N. ESKRIDGE JR. & JOHN FEREJOHN, A REPUBLIC OF STATUTES: THE NEW AMERICAN CONSTITUTION 136–37 (2010); GARDINER C. MEANS, U.S. DEP'T OF AGRIC., INDUSTRIAL PRICES AND THEIR RELATIVE INFLEXIBILITY (Jan. 17, 1935), reprinted in S. Doc. 13, 74th Cong., 1st Sess. (1935).

292. ESKRIDGE & FEREJOHN, REPUBLIC OF STATUTES, at 136–37.

293. THURMAN W. ARNOLD, THE BOTTLENECKS OF BUSINESS 122, 202, 211–12 (1940).

294. Spencer Weber Waller, *The Antitrust Legacy of Thurman Arnold*, 78 ST. JOHN'S L. REV. 569, 582 (2004).

295. ESKRIDGE & FEREJOHN, REPUBLIC OF STATUTES, at 138 (quoting Arnold).

296. *Id.* (quoting Arnold).

297. *Id.* at 138–39.

298. *Id.* at 140.

299. *Id.* at 143 (quoting Berge).

300. United States v. Aluminum Co. of Am., 148 F.2d 416 (2d Cir. 1945).

301. United States v. Aluminum Co. of Am., 44 F. Supp. 97, 116, 153–61 (S.D.N.Y. 1941), *aff'd in part, rev'd in part*, 148 F.2d 416 (2d Cir. 1945).

302. *Aluminum Co.*, 148 F.2d at 421.

303. *Id.* at 427–28, 430.

304. *Id.* at 427–28, 428 n.1, 431 (quoting 21 CONG. REC. 2460 (1890) (statement of Sen. Sherman)).

305. *Id.* at 428 n.1 (quoting 21 CONG. REC. 2457 (statement of Sen. Sherman)).

306. United States v. Columbia Steel Co., 334 U.S. 495, 535 (1948) (Douglas, J., dissenting).

307. *Id.* at 534.

308. *Id.* at 534–35.

309. *Id.* at 535.

310. *Id.* at 536.

311. WILLIAM N. ESKRIDGE JR. & JOHN FEREJOHN, A REPUBLIC OF STATUTES: THE NEW AMERICAN CONSTITUTION 143 (2010).

312. For a superb account of Glass-Steagall from this perspective, see K. Sabeel Rahman, *Democracy and Productivity: The Glass-Steagall Act and the Shifting Discourse of Financial Regulation*, 24 J. POL'Y HIST. 612 (2012).

7. CONSTITUTIONAL COUNTERREVOLUTION AND THE LEGACIES OF A TRUNCATED NEW DEAL

1. It is widely held that the New Deal "settlement" consisted of two parts: (1) judicial deference to Congress in matters of economic and social legislation enshrined in two cases, United States v. Darby, 312 U.S. 100 (1941) (upholding the FLSA), and Wickard v. Filburn, 317 U.S. 111 (1942) (upholding the Agricultural Adjustment Act), and (2) some measure of judicial enforcement of civil and political rights and liberties. *See, e.g.*, Laura M. Weinrib, *Civil Liberties Outside the Courts*, 2014 SUP. CT. REV. 297, 322–23; Jamal Greene, *What the New Deal Settled*, 15 U. PA. J. CONST. L. 265, 280 (2012); Larry D. Kramer, *The Supreme Court, 2000 Term—Foreword: We the Court*, 115 HARV. L. REV. 5, 122 (2001).

2. Preliminary Report of the Staff of the Committee on Economic Security 415 (Sept. 1934), *reprinted in* STATUTORY HISTORY OF THE UNITED STATES: INCOME SECURITY 72, 73 (Robert B. Stevens ed., 1970).

3. 79 Cong. Rec. 9283–84 (1935) (remarks of Sen. Wagner).

4. *See* Alvin H. Hansen, After the War—Full Employment (1942); James Tobin, *Hansen and Public Policy*, 90 Q. J. Econ. 32 (1976). Margaret Weir and Theda Skocpol coined the phrase "social Keynesianism." *See* Margaret Weir, *The Federal Government and Unemployment: The Frustration of Policy Innovation from the New Deal to the Great Society, in* The Politics of Social Policy in the United States 149, 298–99 (Margaret Weir et al. eds., 1988); Margaret Weir, *Innovation and Boundaries in American Employment Policy*, 107 Pol. Sci. Q. 249 (1992).

5. *Full Employment Act of 1945: Hearings Before a Subcomm. of the Senate Comm. on Banking and Currency on S. 380*, 79th Cong. 1248–59 (1945) (statement of John R. Ellingston, member of the drafting committee of the Statement of Essential Human Rights) [hereinafter *Full Employment Act Hearings*].

6. *Id.*

7. *Id.* at 1248–51.

8. *Id.* at 1254.

9. *Id.; see* Stephen Holmes & Cass R. Sunstein, The Cost of Rights: Why Liberty Depends on Taxes 39–43 (1999) (discussing the negative / positive rights dichotomy and its origin in the New Deal era).

10. *Full Employment Act Hearings*, at 1252–53, 1255, 1258.

11. Charles A. Beard, An Economic Interpretation of the Constitution of the United States (1913).

12. Clyde W. Barrow, *Building a Workers' Republic: Charles A. Beard's Critique of Liberalism in the 1930s*, 30 Polity 29, 40 (1997).

13. *Id.* (quoting Charles A. Beard, The Open Door at Home: A Trial Philosophy of National Interest 227 (1934)).

14. *Id.* at 31 (quoting Charles A. Beard, *The World as I Want It*, 91 Forum & Century 332, 333 (1934)).

15. The tools were at hand in the law of eminent domain and of public utilities, which, like many New Dealers, he favored extending to a host of "highly concentrated industries." *Id.* at 38 (quoting Charles A. Beard, The Open Door at Home 210 (1934)).

16. *Id.* at 36.

17. *Id.* at 52, 54 (quoting Charles A. Beard, Foreword to René Brunet, The New German Constitution v, vii (Joseph Gollomb trans., 1922) (1921)).

18. Charles A. Beard, *The Living Constitution*, 185 Annals Am. Acad. Pol. & Soc. Sci. 29 (1936).

19. *Id.* at 31.

20. *Id.* at 34.

21. *Id.* at 31.

22. Aziz Rana's forthcoming Rise of the Constitution offers a thoughtful discussion of Beard's "Living Constitution" essay, situating it in the context of other constitutional thinkers on the left in the New Deal era. Rana identifies two important currents of 1930s radical thought about constitutional change—"formalist" and "anti-formalist." The first current carried forward the early twentieth-century Socialist Party focus—in common with other "advanced" Progressive thinking—on formal structural amendments like abolishing the Senate and Electoral College and enlarging national over state regulatory power, in order to create "the type of governing order [that would be] responsive to mass democratic pressure." The anti-formalist current—and Beard and Thurman Arnold are Rana's chief exemplars—instead emphasized "the text's open-endedness" and aimed to educate Americans to see the Constitution as a "pliable instrument of social improvement," as long as Americans understood that the Constitution was a "living thing" and the "product of what workable popular majorities could achieve through political action." In this way, the Living Constitution / anti-formalist outlook, Rana points out, was well suited to a moment when formal constitutional change of the kind that the left hoped for would have rough sledding in view of the reactionary elements in any supermajority the New Deal could muster behind formal amendments. *See* Aziz Rana, Rise of the Constitution, ch. 6 (forthcoming).

23. Franklin D. Roosevelt, The Nine Hundred and Twenty-Ninth Press Conference (Excerpts), 1943 Pub. Papers 569, 571 (Dec. 28, 1943).

24. *See* Meg Jacobs, *"How About Some Meat?": The Office of Price Administration, Consumption Politics, and State Building from the Bottom Up, 1941–1946*, 84 J. Am. Hist. 910 (1997); Nelson Lichtenstein, *From Corporatism to Collective Bargaining: Organized Labor and the Eclipse of Social Democracy in the Postwar Era, in* The Rise and Fall of the New Deal Order, 1930–1980, at 122 (Steve Fraser & Gary Gerstle eds., 1989).

25. Alan Brinkley, The End of Reform: New Deal Liberalism in Recession and War (Vintage Books 1996) (1995).

26. *See* Theodore J. Lowi, *The Roosevelt Revolution and the New American State, in* Comparative Theory and Political Experience 188 (Peter J. Katzenstein et al. eds., 1990); David M. Kennedy, Freedom from Fear: The American People in Depression and War, 1929–1945, at 322 (1999); James T. Sparrow, Warfare State: World War II Americans and the Age of Big Government 3–4, 197, 247–52 (2011); Andrew A. Workman, *Creating the National War Labor Board: Franklin Roosevelt and the Politics of State Building in the Early 1940s*, 12 J. Pol'y Hist. 233 (2000); Ira Katznelson & Bruce Pietrykowski, *Rebuilding the American State: Evidence from the 1940s*, 5 Studies in Am. Pol. Dev. 301 (1991); Philip W. Warken, A History of the National Resources Planning Board, 1933–1943 (1979); James B. Atleson, Labor and the Wartime State: Labor Relations and Law During World War II, at 1–2 (1998); Nelson Lichtenstein, Labor's War at Home: The CIO in World War II (reprt. 2003) (1982).

27. *See* Nat'l Res. Planning Bd., National Resources Development Report for 1942, at 3–4 (1942), *reprinted in part in* 1942 Pub. Papers 52, 53–54 (Jan. 14, 1942) (affirming nine sets of rights, including rights to (1) work; (2) fair pay; (3) "adequate food, clothing, shelter, and medical care"; (4) social security; (5) "a system of free enterprise, free from compulsory labor, irresponsible private power, arbitrary public authority, and unregulated monopolies"; (6) movement, speech, and privacy; (7) "equality before the law, with equal access to justice in fact"; (8) education; and (9) "rest, recreation, and adventure").

28. *Id.* at 3.

29. Samuel I. Rosenman, ed., Explanatory Note, 1942 Pub. Papers 52, 53 (1950).

30. Franklin D. Roosevelt, State of the Union Message to Congress (Jan. 11, 1944), https://www.presidency.ucsb.edu/documents/state-the-union-message-congress [https://perma.cc/M3AV-83ZR].

31. *Id.*

32. *Id.*

33. *Id.*

34. *Id.*

35. V. O. Key Jr., Southern Politics in State and Nation 9, 345–46, 351 (1949).

36. *See* Ira Katznelson, Kim Geiger, & Daniel Kryder, *Limiting Liberalism: The Southern Veto in Congress, 1933–1950*, 108 Pol. Sci. Q. 283 (1993); *see also* Ira Katznelson, Fear Itself: The New Deal and the Origins of Our Time 156–94 (2014) (describing the "Jim Crow Congress").

37. *Id.*

38. Harvard Sitkoff, A New Deal for Blacks: The Emergence of Civil Rights as a National Issue 104 (1978) (quoting Sen. Carter Glass of Virginia); *see also* The New Deal and the South (James C. Cobb & Michael V. Namorato eds., 1984); Gavin Wright, Old South, New South: Revolutions in the Southern Economy Since the Civil War (1986).

39. Wright, Old South, New South, at 219.

40. Sitkoff, New Deal for Blacks, at 103.

41. *Id.* at 106.

42. *Id.* at 109–10; *see also* Nancy Joan Weiss, Farewell to the Party of Lincoln: Black Politics in the Age of F.D.R. 186 (2020).

43. *See generally* SIDNEY BALDWIN, POVERTY AND POLITICS: THE RISE AND DECLINE OF THE FARM SECURITY ADMINISTRATION (1968); DAVID EUGENE CONRAD, THE FORGOTTEN FARMERS: THE STORY OF SHARECROPPERS IN THE NEW DEAL (1965); DONALD H. GRUBBS, CRY FROM THE COTTON: THE SOUTHERN TENANT FARMERS' UNION AND THE NEW DEAL (1971); EDWIN G. NOURSE ET AL., THREE YEARS OF THE AGRICULTURAL ADJUSTMENT ADMINISTRATION (1937); Lee J. Alston & Joseph P. Ferrie, *Resisting the Welfare State: Southern Opposition to the Farm Security Administration, in* EMERGENCE OF THE MODERN POLITICAL ECONOMY 83 (Robert Higgs ed., 1985).

44. 300 U.S. 379 (1937); NLRB v. Jones & Laughlin Steel Corp., 301 U.S. 1 (1937).

45. JAMES T. PATTERSON, CONGRESSIONAL CONSERVATISM AND THE NEW DEAL: THE GROWTH OF THE CONSERVATIVE COALITION IN CONGRESS, 1933–1939, at 198–210 (1967).

46. 82 CONG. REC. 1936 (1937) (statement of Sen. Bailey).

47. *Id.* at 1936–38.

48. 83 CONG. REC. 1379 (1938) (statement of Sen. Bridges) (opposing Roosevelt's executive reorganization plan).

49. William E. Forbath, *The New Deal Constitution in Exile*, 51 DUKE L.J. 165, 206–7 (2001).

50. *See, e.g.*, IRA KATZNELSON, FEAR ITSELF: THE NEW DEAL AND THE ORIGINS OF OUR TIME 383–88 (2014) (discussing failed attempts to reform labor policy and Social Security).

51. *See To Establish a National Health Program: Hearings Before a Subcomm. of the Comm. on Educ. & Labor U.S. Senate*, 76th Cong. (1939) (considering S. 1620, the Wagner National Health Act of 1939); INTERDEPARTMENTAL COMM. TO COORDINATE HEALTH AND WELFARE ACTIVITIES, THE NEED FOR A NATIONAL HEALTH PROGRAM (1938), https://www.ssa.gov/history/reports /Interdepartmental.html [https://perma.cc/2CBY-FRYC].

52. Full Employment Act of 1945, H.R. 2202 & S. 380, 79th Cong. (1945), *reprinted in Full Employment Act of 1945: Hearings Before a Subcomm. of the Comm. on Banking & Currency U.S. Senate*, 79th Cong. 6–9 (1945).

53. *See* MARION CLAWSON, NEW DEAL PLANNING: THE NATIONAL RESOURCES PLANNING BOARD 225–36 (1981) (describing Congress's destruction of the NRPB following the conservative swing in the 1942 midterms). Stephen Bailey provides the most detailed legislative history of the administration's Full Employment Bill. Bailey chronicles the efforts of President Truman and his cabinet to pressure Congress into passing the administration's 1945 bill. He makes clear that the key players in gutting the bill were all Southern Democrats—Congressmen Carter Monasco of Alabama and Will Whittington of Mississippi in particular. Their key positions on the Expenditures Committee, on the subcommittee that drafted the House substitute bill, as well as on the Conference Committee enabled them to engineer a bill that would "exclude the last remnants of what [they] considered to be dangerous federal commitments and assurances, including the words of the title," as well as the original bill's provisions for new planning and budget offices and capacities. STEPHEN KEMP BAILEY, CONGRESS MAKES A LAW: THE STORY BEHIND THE EMPLOYMENT ACT OF 1946, at 165 (1950). "The emasculation, or as some wit put it, the 'Manasco-lation' of the policy commitments and the economic program of the original bill needs no further elucidation here." *Id.* at 167. *See also* Ira Katznelson et al., *Limiting Liberalism: The Southern Veto in Congress, 1933–1950*, 108 POL. SCI. Q. 283, 285–86, 294–99 (1993) (observing the existence of a conservative, anti-labor coalition, joining Southern Democrats and Republicans).

54. *See* Forbath, *New Deal Constitution;* KATZNELSON, FEAR ITSELF, at 398–402; Katznelson et al., *Limiting Liberalism*, at 301–2.

55. *See* RISA GOLUBOFF, THE LOST PROMISE OF CIVIL RIGHTS (2007).

56. *Id.*

57. *See* HORACE R. CAYTON & GEORGE S. MITCHELL, BLACK WORKERS AND THE NEW UNIONS (1939); NELSON LICHTENSTEIN, THE MOST DANGEROUS MAN IN DETROIT: WALTER REUTHER AND THE FATE OF AMERICAN LABOR (1995); HERBERT R. NORTHRUP, ORGANIZED LABOR AND THE NEGRO (2d ed. 1944); ROBERT H. ZIEGER, THE CIO, 1935–1955 (1995).

58. *See generally* IRA KATZNELSON, BLACK MEN, WHITE CITIES: RACE, POLITICS, AND MIGRATION IN THE UNITED STATES, 1900–30 AND BRITAIN, 1948–68 (1973); NICHOLAS LEMANN, THE PROMISED LAND: THE GREAT BLACK MIGRATION AND HOW IT CHANGED AMERICA (1991); HARVARD SITKOFF, A NEW DEAL FOR BLACKS: THE EMERGENCE OF CIVIL RIGHTS AS A NATIONAL ISSUE 89–92 (1978).

59. *See generally* CAYTON & MITCHELL, BLACK WORKERS AND THE NEW UNIONS; LICHTENSTEIN, MOST DANGEROUS MAN IN DETROIT; NORTHRUP, ORGANIZED LABOR AND THE NEGRO; ZIEGER, CIO.

60. Harold Preece, *The South Stirs: Brothers in the Union,* CRISIS, Oct. 1941, at 317, 318.

61. ROBIN D. G. KELLEY, HAMMER AND HOE: ALABAMA COMMUNISTS DURING THE GREAT DEPRESSION 99 (2019).

62. *Id.; see generally* KELLEY, HAMMER AND HOE; GLENDA E. GILMORE, DEFYING DIXIE: THE RADICAL ROOTS OF CIVIL RIGHTS, 1919–1950, at 67–105 (2008).

63. KELLEY, HAMMER AND HOE, at xxviii.

64. *Id.* at 99.

65. SITKOFF, NEW DEAL FOR BLACKS, at 52; KATZNELSON, FEAR ITSELF, at 268–70.

66. Robert Korstad & Nelson Lichtenstein, *Opportunities Found and Lost: Labor, Radicals, and the Early Civil Rights Movement,* 75 J. AM. HIST. 786, 787 (1988).

67. *Id.*

68. *See* PAULA F. PFEFFER, A. PHILIP RANDOLPH, PIONEER OF THE CIVIL RIGHTS MOVEMENT 45–118 (1990).

69. A. Philip Randolph, *Call to Negro America* (on file with C. R. Dellums Papers, Bancroft Library, U.C. Berkeley, Carton 23, Folder: *March on Washington; Statement of Facts*), *quoted in* Eileen Boris, *"The Right to Work is the Right to Live!": Fair Employment and the Quest for Social Citizenship, in* TWO CULTURES OF RIGHTS: THE QUEST FOR INCLUSION AND PARTICIPATION IN MODERN AMERICA AND GERMANY 121, 125 (Manfred Berg & Martin H Geyer eds., 2002).

70. *See generally* MERL E. REED, SEEDTIME FOR THE MODERN CIVIL RIGHTS MOVEMENT: THE PRESIDENT'S COMMITTEE ON FAIR EMPLOYMENT PRACTICE, 1941–1946 (1991) (recounting the history of the Fair Employment Practices Committee).

71. *See generally id.*

72. Daniel Bell, *A. Philip Randolph Leads Drive for Permanent FEPC,* NEW LEADER, Sept. 18, 1943, at 1.

73. *See* REED, MODERN CIVIL RIGHTS MOVEMENT, at 321–43 (discussing the plans for reconversion of the Fair Employment Practices Committee).

74. 90 CONG. REC. A3031–32 (1944) (extension of remarks of Rep. La Follette); 91 CONG. REC. A2882 (1945) (extension of remarks of Rep. Patterson).

75. *See* SERENA MAYERI, REASONING FROM RACE: FEMINISM, LAW AND THE CIVIL RIGHTS REVOLUTION 69 (2011).

76. *See* TROY R. SAXBY, PAULI MURRAY: A PERSONAL AND POLITICAL LIFE 133–35 (2020).

77. Pauli Murray, *The Right to Equal Opportunity in Employment,* 33 CAL. L. REV. 388 (1945)

78. *Id.* at 432.

79. *Id.* at 431.

80. 94 CONG. REC. A4280, A4281 (extension of remarks of Rep. Williams quoting Sen. Hawkes).

81. 83 U.S. (16 Wall.) 36, 82 (1873) (holding that the states should have the power to regulate "civil rights—the rights of person and of property").

82. 109 U.S. 3, 24–25 (1883).

83. 91 CONG. REC. 3680 (1945) (statement of Rep. Hays).

84. 94 CONG. REC. A4282 (1948) (extension of remarks of Rep. Williams).

85. William E. Forbath, *The New Deal Constitution in Exile,* 51 DUKE L. J. 165, 213–15 (2001).

86. 91 CONG. REC. 3673 (1945) (citing Steele v. Louisville & Nashville R.R. Co., 323 U.S. 192, 203 (1944)) (extension of remarks of Rep. La Follette).

87. *Id.* at 3673–74.

88. 90 CONG. REC. A3032 (1944) (extension of remarks of Rep. La Follette).

89. *Id.* at A3031–32.

90. 91 CONG. REC. 3673 (1945) (remarks of Rep. La Follette).

91. *See* EDWARD S. CORWIN, CONSTITUTIONAL REVOLUTION, LTD. 67 (1941) (italics removed).

92. Civil Rights Cases, 109 U.S. 3, 42–43 (1883) (Harlan, J., dissenting).

93. *Id.* at 58–59.

94. Thus, the Wagner Act:

> § 151. Findings and declaration of policy . . .
> The inequality of bargaining power between employees who do not possess full freedom of association or actual liberty of contract, and employers who are organized in the corporate or other forms of ownership association substantially burdens and affects the flow of commerce, and tends to aggravate recurrent business depressions, by depressing wage rates and the purchasing power of wage earners in industry and by preventing the stabilization of competitive wage rates and working conditions within and between industries. (29 U.S.C. § 151 (2018)).

95. *See* Osmond K. Fraenkel, *The Federal Civil Rights Laws*, 31 MINN. L. REV. 301, 323 (1947) (expressing hope that Justice Harlan's dissent would be "particularly persuasive" given "recent judicial authority" barring unions' discriminatory use of government-granted bargaining authority).

96. S. 101, 79th Cong. § 2 (1946), *reprinted in* 92 CONG. REC. 82 (1946).

97. *See* MERL E. REED, SEEDTIME FOR THE MODERN CIVIL RIGHTS MOVEMENT: THE PRESIDENT'S COMMITTEE ON FAIR EMPLOYMENT PRACTICE, 1941–1946 (1991).

98. STEPHEN KEMP BAILEY, CONGRESS MAKES A LAW: THE STORY BEHIND THE EMPLOYMENT ACT OF 1946, at 165–67 (1950).

99. *See* PATRICIA SULLIVAN, DAYS OF HOPE: RACE AND DEMOCRACY IN THE NEW DEAL ERA 66 (1996) (noting that, because "the poll tax and other restrictions kept most blacks and a majority of low-income whites from voting," the people in the South most likely to support the New Deal were also those unable to participate in elections).

100. *Id.* at 65; THOMAS A. KRUEGER, AND PROMISES TO KEEP: THE SOUTHERN CONFERENCE FOR HUMAN WELFARE, 1938–1948, at 11–12 (1967).

101. *E.g.,* Franklin D. Roosevelt, Fireside Chat on Party Primaries (June 24, 1938), 1938 PUB. PAPERS 391, 399 (1941).

102. GLENDA E. GILMORE, DEFYING DIXIE: THE RADICAL ROOTS OF CIVIL RIGHTS, 1919–1950, at 232–33 (2008).

103. *Quoted in* SULLIVAN, DAYS OF HOPE, at 66.

104. RALPH J. BUNCHE, THE POLITICAL STATUS OF THE NEGRO IN THE AGE OF FDR 384–437 (1973).

105. *See* KRUEGER, AND PROMISES TO KEEP, at 18–20 (suggesting that both President Roosevelt and the Southern Conference for Human Welfare's founders sought "an informal alliance between the progressive South and the National Administration").

106. Clark H. Foreman & James Dombrowski, Memo for the CIO Exec. Bd. (Nov. 13, 1944) (on file with Records of the Southern Conference for Human Welfare, Box 43, Tuskegee Institute Archives), *quoted in* NUMAN V. BARTLEY, THE NEW SOUTH, 1945–1980, at 24 (1995).

107. *Id.*

108. *Id.*

109. Osceola McKaine, *For Victory at the Ballot Box,* S. Negro Youth Cong., at 3 (on file with John McCray Papers, Box 2), *quoted in* SULLIVAN, DAYS OF HOPE, at 191.

110. RANDOLPH BOURNE, THE RADICAL WILL: SELECTED WRITINGS, 1911–1918, at 375 (Olaf Hansen ed., 1977).

111. *See* ELIZABETH A. FONES-WOLF, SELLING FREE ENTERPRISE: THE BUSINESS ASSAULT ON LABOR AND LIBERALISM, 1945–1960 (1994).

112. *See id.; see also* HOWELL JOHN HARRIS, THE RIGHT TO MANAGE: INDUSTRIAL RELATIONS POLICIES OF AMERICAN BUSINESS IN THE 1940S (1982); JOEL SEIDMAN, AMERICAN LABOR FROM DEFENSE TO RECONVERSION (1953).

113. *See generally* HARRIS, RIGHT TO MANAGE; FONES-WOLF, SELLING FREE ENTERPRISE.

114. *Id.*

115. *See generally* HARRIS, RIGHT TO MANAGE; 2 JAMES GROSS, RESHAPING OF THE NATIONAL LABOR RELATIONS BOARD: A STUDY IN ECONOMICS, POLITICS, AND THE LAW (1981); FONES-WOLF, SELLING FREE ENTERPRISE.

116. *Quoted in* NELSON LICHTENSTEIN, STATE OF THE UNION: A CENTURY OF AMERICAN LABOR 109–10 (rev. ed. 2013). *See also* LICHTENSTEIN, THE MOST DANGEROUS MAN IN DETROIT: WALTER REUTHER AND THE FATE OF AMERICAN LABOR 230 (1995).

117. *See* HARRIS, RIGHT TO MANAGE.

118. *Quoted in* Nelson Lichtenstein, *Politicized Unions and the New Deal Model: Labor, Business and Taft-Hartley, in* THE NEW DEAL AND THE TRIUMPH OF LIBERALISM 135, 144 (Sidney M. Milkis & Jerome M. Mileur eds., 2002). Our account of Taft–Hartley and its significance for postwar labor politics and the postwar fortunes of New Deal liberalism is deeply indebted to Lichtenstein's work. *See also* Nelson Lichtenstein, *From Corporatism to Collective Bargaining: Organized Labor and the Eclipse of Social Democracy in the Postwar Era, in* THE RISE AND FALL OF THE NEW DEAL ORDER, 1930–1980, at 122 (Steve Fraser & Gary Gerstle eds., 1989); Nelson Lichtenstein, *Taft-Hartley: A Slave Labor Law?*, 47 CATH. U. L. REV. 763, 766–67 (1998).

119. Labor Management Relations Act, Pub. L. No. 80–101, 61 Stat. 136 (1947).

120. 93 CONG. REC. 3515 (1947) (remarks of Rep. Smith).

121. Employment Act of 1946, Pub. L. 79–304, 60 Stat. 23 (1946).

122. *See* SOPHIA Z. LEE, THE WORKPLACE CONSTITUTION: FROM THE NEW DEAL TO THE NEW RIGHT 56–78 (2014).

123. *See* "Labor as Countervailing Power," Chapter 9.

124. 93 CONG. REC. 3444 (1947) (remarks of Rep. Gwinn).

125. *Id.* at 3616 (extension of remarks of Rep. Hoffman).

126. *Id.* at 3617.

127. For the analogy to mini-constitutional conventions, we are indebted to Jedediah Purdy, *Beyond the Bosses' Constitution: The First Amendment and Class Entrenchment,* 118 COLUM. L. REV. 2161 (2018).

128. The old, Lochnerian "right to work" constitutional outlook proved longer-lived in our constitutional politics than the New Deal conception of labor's collective constitutional liberties. The latter vanished into what labor law scholars call a constitutional "black hole," as antistrike, antiboycott, and antipicketing decrees were subsumed into what the courts chose to call a statutory scheme of social and economic regulation in the service of "private ordering" and insulated from meaningful constitutional scrutiny. *See* James G. Pope, *The Three-Systems Ladder of First Amendment Values: Two Rungs and a Black Hole,* 11 HASTINGS CON. L. Q. 189 (1984).

129. 93 CONG. REC. 5000 (1947) (remarks of Sen. Wiley).

130. *Id.* at 5004 (remarks of Sen. Hatch).

131. Nelson Lichtenstein, *Taft-Hartley: A Slave Labor Law?*, 47 CATH. U. L. REV. 763, 766–67 (1998).

132. George Meany, *The Taft-Hartley Law: A Slave Labor Measure,* 14 VITAL SPEECHES OF THE DAY 119, 120–21 (1947).

133. *Id.* at 120.

134. *Id.*

135. *Id.*

136. *Id.*

137. *Id.* (quoting Bedford Cut Stone Co. v. Journeymen Stone Cutters' Ass'n, 274 U.S. 37, 65 (1927) (Brandeis, J., dissenting)).

138. *Id.* at 121.

139. *Id.* Meany is quoting from AFL v. Swing, 312 U.S. 321, 326 (1941). The Court continues: "The right of free communication cannot therefore be mutilated by denying it to workers, in a dispute with an employer, even though they are not in his employ. Communication by such employees of the facts of a dispute, deemed by them to be relevant to their interests, can no more be barred because of concern for the economic interests against which they are seeking to enlist public opinion. . . ." *Id.*

140. Harry S. Truman, Radio Address to the American People on the Veto of the Taft–Hartley Bill, PUB. PAPERS 298 (June 20, 1947).

141. *See* JACK BALKIN, LIVING ORIGINALISM 3–34 (2011).

142. Wages, labor standards, and union efforts to boost them were "not matters of mere local or private concern," the Court noted in *Thornhill v. Alabama,* but part and parcel of how workers were using "the processes of popular government to shape the destiny of modern industrial society." Peaceful picketing of a nonunion shop, therefore, warranted First Amendment protection. 310 U.S. 88, 103 (1940). And that protection was not restricted by old common-law conceptions of "direct" disputes between individual employers and their employees. The "interdependence" of workers in the same industry or region was now a "commonplace." AFL v. Swing, 312 U.S. 321, 326 (1941).

143. *See* Katherine Van Wezel Stone, *The Post-War Paradigm in American Labor Law,* 90 YALE L.J. 1509 (1981); STUART CHINN, RECALIBRATING REFORM: THE LIMITS OF POLITICAL CHANGE 237–69 (2014).

144. Stone, *Post-War Paradigm,* at 1513, 1525 n.80, 1526.

145. James Gray Pope, *Labor and the Constitution: From Abolition to Deindustrialization,* 65 TEX. L. REV. 1071, 1074–76 (1987); James G. Pope, *The Three-Systems Ladder of First Amendment Values: Two Rungs and a Black Hole,* 11 HASTINGS CONST. L.Q. 189 (1984).

146. *See generally* Nelson Lichtenstein, *From Corporatism to Collective Bargaining: Organized Labor and the Eclipse of Social Democracy in the Postwar Era, in* THE RISE AND FALL OF THE NEW DEAL ORDER, 1930–1980, at 122 (Steve Fraser & Gary Gerstle eds., 1989).

147. Federally guaranteed housing loans had their genesis in the New Deal's Federal Housing Administration (FHA). Created by Congress in 1934, the FHA transformed the home mortgage market and the financing of large-scale, single-family housing developments, making homeownership affordable for blue- and white-collar workers for the first time. By guaranteeing private home mortgages and construction loans, the FHA and, later, the Veterans Administration (VA) (which got into the home loan business with the G.I. Bill of Rights, in 1944) ushered in the distinctly mid-twentieth-century American phenomenon of mass homeownership and the suburbanization of the entire nation during the postwar boom. It also was "the greatest mass-based opportunity for wealth accumulation" in the nation's history. MELVIN L. OLIVER & THOMAS M. SHAPIRO, BLACK WEALTH / WHITE WEALTH: A NEW PERSPECTIVE ON RACIAL INEQUALITY 18 (2d ed. 2006).

It was a whites-only suburbanization and a whites-only opportunity for wealth accumulation. The FHA did not simply tolerate private actors' policies of restricting insurance and lending to whites-only neighborhoods and developments. Instead, the FHA took up the so-called ethics codes of realtors' associations and the practices of private banks and made them mandatory; it "exhorted segregation and enshrined it as public policy." KENNETH T. JACKSON, CRABGRASS FRONTIER: THE SUBURBANIZATION OF THE UNITED STATES 213 (1985). The G.I. Bill of Rights included measures to give veterans assured access to low-interest home loans; but the VA followed the FHA's lead in enshrining and enforcing the racist policies of private lenders.

While their white working-class comrades-in-arms moved to the burgeoning postwar suburbs, Black veterans "simply . . . could not use this particular title" of the legislation. KATHLEEN J. FRYDL, THE GI BILL 237 (2009).

By 1960, more than 60 percent of Americans were homeowners. "'Homeownership became an emblem of American citizenship.'" But as Ta-Nehisi Coates writes, "'That emblem was not to be awarded to Blacks." Ta-Nehisi Coates, *The Case for Reparations,* THE ATLANTIC (June 2014), https://www.theatlantic.com/magazine/archive/2014/06/the-case-for-reparations/361631/ (quoting THOMAS J. SUGRUE, SWEET LAND OF LIBERTY: THE FORGOTTEN STRUGGLE FOR CIVIL RIGHTS IN THE NORTH 204 (2008)). The New Deal's housing policies ensured that these key features of mid-twentieth-century America's mass middle class—homeownership and the family wealth-building it afforded—would be for whites only. Coates and others put this racialized piece of wealth distribution, class formation, and social engineering at the heart of their case for reparations for Black America. We discuss the racial dimensions of wealth-building and contemporary progressive constitutional political economy in Chapter 9.

8. THE GREAT SOCIETY AND THE GREAT FORGETTING

1. We noted in Chapter 6 how the New Dealers managed to grab hold of the label "liberal" and the brand "liberalism" from conservative classical liberals. "New Deal liberalism" came to mean an American variant of what in most Western countries would be called social democracy. Later, however, as the subject matter of both constitutional politics and "liberalism's" reform energies shifted dramatically—a story we tell in this chapter—the "liberal" label came to be attached chiefly to advocates of civil liberties and civil rights, rather than to the social-democratic and labor-based commitments of New Deal liberalism. (Nor did "liberal" refer anymore to defenders of the old-school economic liberties, who eventually came to be called "classical liberals.") Many former "progressives" became "liberals," but the words did not mean the same thing because the subject of constitutional conflict itself had changed.

2. *See, e.g.,* Brown v. Board of Education, 347 U.S. 483, 495 (1954); Heart of Atlanta Motel, Inc. v. United States, 379 U.S. 241, 250 (1964) (upholding the Civil Rights Act's prohibition on discrimination in places of public accommodation); Loving v. Virginia, 388 U.S. 1, 12 (1967) (striking down miscegenation law as unconstitutional under the Fourteenth Amendment).

3. Congress deferred to the Court in its framing of these landmark statutes in a variety of respects. Perhaps the most obvious was Congress's refusal to use its enforcement powers to challenge the Court's precedents holding that the Fourteenth Amendment did not reach private conduct. *See* The Civil Rights Cases, 109 U.S. 3 (1883). Instead, Congress used its Commerce Power—building on key precedents in which the Court had accepted the New Deal vision of the scope of the Commerce Power—to enact civil rights laws that reached private conduct. *See* BRUCE ACKERMAN, WE THE PEOPLE, VOLUME 3: THE CIVIL RIGHTS REVOLUTION 109 (2014) (calling this "the New Deal-Civil Rights synthesis"). An even more striking example was Congress's effort in the Voting Rights Act to outlaw poll taxes. Here, Congress's ultimate aim was to reverse the Court's unanimous 1937 decision upholding poll taxes. Rather than challenge the Court directly on this point, Congress reached a complex compromise: issuing findings explaining why the tax ought to be viewed as unconstitutional, then directing the attorney general to bring lawsuits in an attempt to get the Court to strike it down. *See id.* at 92–113 (describing the roots and trajectory of this compromise).

4. The significant popular backlash against the *Citizens United* decision in 2010 may in retrospect prove a turning point. It may be a sign that these long-standing dynamics are beginning to change.

5. *See* Howard Gillman, *How Political Parties Can Use the Courts to Advance Their Agendas: Federal Courts in the United States, 1875–1891*, 96 Am. Pol. Sci. Rev. 511 (2002).

6. Alpheus Thomas Mason, William Howard Taft: Chief Justice 64 (1964). The National Association of Manufacturers would appreciatively deem the Taft Court the "'safest repository of power' and the protector of property from the 'babel voices of the mob.'" *See* Melvin Urofsky & Paul Finkelman, 1 A March of Liberty: A Constitutional History of the United States: From the Founding to 1900, at 715 (3d ed. 2011).

7. *See* William Howard Taft, *The Jurisdiction of the Supreme Court Under the Act of February 13, 1925*, 35 Yale L.J. 1, 2–3 (1925) (arguing that after his 1925 Judges Bill, "[t]he function of the Supreme Court is conceived to be, not the remedying of a particular litigant's wrong," but broad questions of principle: "issues of Federal constitutional validity of statutes, Federal and State, genuine issues of constitutional right of individuals, the interpretation of Federal statutes when it will affect large classes of people," etc.). Taft also persuaded Congress to move the Court from a cramped room in the Capitol to the permanent and august building where it remains today, to give the Court more staff, and to consolidate authority over the rest of the federal judiciary in the Chief Justice. *See* Urofsky & Finkelman, March of Liberty, at 700; David M. O'Brien, Storm Center: The Supreme Court in American Politics 105–21 (10th ed. 2014); Richard Davis, Decisions and Images: The Supreme Court and the Press 29–36 (1994).

8. *See* Jeremy K. Kessler & David E. Pozen, *The Search for an Egalitarian First Amendment*, 118 Colum. L. Rev. 1953, 1964–70 (2018) (collecting recent scholarship on this shift); Richard Primus, The American Language of Rights 180–234 (1999) (emphasizing the antitotalitarian roots of this conceptual shift). For an account of the ACLU's transformation from an organization centered on class conflict and labor action to one focused on neutral principles of free speech and other civil liberties, enforced through litigation, see Laura Weinrib, The Taming of Free Speech: America's Civil Liberties Compromise (2016).

9. United States v. Carolene Products Co., 304 U.S. 144, 153 n.4 (1938). On the same day it decided *Carolene Products*, the Court held that it would get out of the business of making federal common-law rules in its large docket of commercial diversity cases, which meant immediately scaling back a large part of its docket. Erie Railroad Co. v. Tompkins, 304 U.S. 64, 78–80 (1938). For an empirical discussion of the shift in the Court's docket following *Erie*, see Richard Pacelle, The Transformation of the Supreme Court's Agenda: From the New Deal to the Reagan Administration 62–71 (1991).

10. Gitlow v. People of State of New York, 268 U.S. 652, 666 (1925) (holding that states were bound by the First Amendment). As Edward Hartnett argues, it is impossible to imagine that the Court would have incorporated the Bill of Rights against the states had it been obligated to hear every appeal, however nonmeritorious, from each prisoner and other litigant across the nation who would have a federal constitutional claim as a result of incorporation. Edward A. Hartnett, *Questioning Certiorari: Some Reflections Seventy-Five Years After the Judges' Bill*, 100 Colum. L. Rev. 1643, 1644–48 (2000).

11. Pacelle, Transformation, at 90.

12. *See id.* at 93 ("[A] number of similar fact situations that were formerly found under the rubric of Economic issues were converted to Civil Liberties issues that might raise civil due process concerns, freedom of expression questions, or equal protection.").

13. Janus v. Am. Fed'n of State, County, & Municipal Employees (AFSCME), 138 S. Ct. 2448, 2501 (2018) (Kagan, J., dissenting).

14. Larry D. Kramer, The People Themselves: Popular Constitutionalism and Judicial Review 220–21 (2004).

15. *See* Lucas A. Powe, Jr., The Warren Court and American Politics (2000). This story fits into a larger pattern, as articulated by Jack Balkin: over the life cycle of a regime in American constitutional politics, a dominant poltical party—such as the Democrats of the "New Deal / Civil

Rights" regime that stretched from 1932 to 1980—tends to gradually switch from arguing for judicial restraint to arguing for judicial engagement. JACK BALKIN, THE CYCLES OF CONSTITUTIONAL TIME 85–96 (2020).

16. POWE, WARREN COURT, at 36–37 (quoting articles from the *St. Louis Post-Dispatch* and the *Cincinnati Enquirer*).

17. *See id.* at 37 (citing polls). The question of desegregation in the North would not squarely reach the national agenda for years.

18. *See generally* MARY DUDZIAK, COLD WAR CIVIL RIGHTS 79–114 (2000).

19. *Id.* at 107–11.

20. 102 CONG. REC. 4515–16 (1956) (Southern Manifesto text).

21. POWE, WARREN COURT, at 61.

22. Justin Driver, *Supremacies and the Southern Manifesto*, 92 TEX. L. REV. 1053, 1058–59 (2014).

23. Letter from President Dwight Eisenhower to Captain Hazlett (July 22, 1957), *in* DWIGHT D. EISENHOWER, THE WHITE HOUSE YEARS: WAGING PEACE, 1956–1961, at 157 (1965) (emphasis added); *see* Driver, *Supremacies and the Southern Manifesto*, at 1117.

24. George Wharton Pepper et al., *Recent Attacks upon the Supreme Court: A Statement by Members of the Bar*, 42 A.B.A. J. 1128, 1128 (1956) (emphasis added). *See* Driver, *Supremacies and the Southern Manifesto*, at 1118.

25. Cooper v. Aaron, 358 U.S. 1, 18 (1958).

26. For instance, Republican senator Jacob Javits of New York posited that *Cooper* "should be universally approved," and "called on 'reasonable people' in areas opposing integration to recognize that 'enforcement of law is superior in their own and the national interests to even deeply held social views.'" *Court Decision Gets Criticism, Praise*, DALLAS MORNING NEWS, Sept. 30, 1958, at 2.

27. See discussions in Chapters 4 and 5. For a clear distillation of the view, see (future justice) ROBERT H. JACKSON, THE STRUGGLE FOR JUDICIAL SUPREMACY (1941).

28. Paul Freund's statement for those distinguished lawyers and legal scholars made the point explicit. "[T]he American Bar" had stood firmly against both the court-packers of 1937 *and* the signers of the Southern Manifesto, he wrote, in an effort to "defend the judiciary against assaults which would undermine the Rule of Law." *Recent Attacks upon the Supreme Court*, at 1128.

29. Franklin Delano Roosevelt, Fireside Chat on the Reorganization of the Judiciary (Mar. 9, 1937), https://www.docsteach.org/documents/document/fireside-chat-on-reorganization-of-the-judiciary [https://perma.cc/7TSQ-B2G9].

30. *President Urges Court Be Backed on Prayer Issue*, N. Y. TIMES, June 28, 1962, at 1. *See* Engel v. Vitale, 370 U.S. 421 (1962).

31. Alexander Burnham, *Court's Decision Stirs Conflicts*, N.Y. TIMES, June 27, 1962, at 1, 20.

32. *See* POWE, WARREN COURT, at 85 (describing how, similarly, the Court's forays into protecting the civil liberties of those accused of communist ties "were a godsend to southerners [because] [t]he decisions gave them allies against the Court—national security conservatives" who had not necessarily opposed *Brown*. "With a little care," he writes, "anti-Court criticism . . . could be made on the newer and higher ground of anticommunism without mentioning race.").

33. Reynolds v. Sims, 377 U.S. 533 (1964).

34. 110 CONG. REC. 20223 (1964) (statement of Rep. Tuck).

35. 110 CONG. REC. 20225 (1964) (statement of Rep. Forrester).

36. 110 CONG. REC. 20227 (1964) (statement of Rep. Celler). Celler pointedly noted, for whatever it was worth, that the above quoted language was a quote from none other than John W. Davis, the Southern lawyer on the losing side of *Brown*. Celler argued that the Supremacy Clause would be "dead as a dodo" if such assaults on the Court's authority were to succeed. *Id.*

37. *See* 79 CONG. REC. 8862–63 (1935).

38. *See* 109 CONG. REC. 10036 (1963).

39. There are exceptions. Certain narrow types of economic reforms center on creating new forms of liability. That is something common-law courts can and do initiate. However, most economic reforms do not work that way.

40. *See* Linda Greenhouse & Reva B. Siegel, *Before (and After) Roe v. Wade: New Questions About Backlash*, 120 YALE L.J. 2028 (2011) (describing the consolidation of the conservative coalition around these ideas by the late 1970s, when abortion became central to this kind of politics). See discussion toward the end of this chapter.

41. For the leading empirical paper on the overall shift in business' favor—significant at the end of the Warren Court, but even more dramatic after Justice Samuel Alito replaced Justice Sandra Day O'Connor in 2006—see Lee Epstein, William M. Landes, & Richard Posner, *How Business Fares in the Supreme Court*, 97 MINN. L. REV. 1431, 1472 (2013). *See also* ADAM WINKLER, WE THE CORPORATIONS: HOW AMERICAN BUSINESSES WON THEIR CIVIL RIGHTS 311, 322 (2018) ("Today, the [National Chamber Litigation Center] wins nearly 70 percent of its Supreme Court Cases."); Jeffrey Rosen, *Supreme Court, Inc.*, N.Y. TIMES MAG., Mar. 16, 2008; J. Mitchell Pickerill, *Is the Roberts Court Business Friendly? Is the Pope Catholic?, in* BUSINESS AND THE ROBERTS COURT 35 (Jonathan H. Adler ed., 2016). For periodically updated tables on the litigation record of the Chamber of Commerce, see *Corporations and the Supreme Court*, CONSTITUTIONAL ACCOUNTABILITY CENTER, https://www.theusconstitution.org/series/chamber-study/ [https:// perma.cc/RXJ5-2F94] (showing that the Roberts Court has ruled "for the Chamber's position 70% of the time").

42. *See* MARK TUSHNET, TAKING THE CONSTITUTION AWAY FROM THE COURTS (1999); JEREMY WALDRON, LAW AND DISAGREEMENT (1999); LARRY D. KRAMER, THE PEOPLE THEMSELVES: POPULAR CONSTITUTIONALISM AND JUDICIAL REVIEW (2004). *See also* William E. Forbath, *Caste, Class, and Equal Citizenship*, 98 MICH. L. REV. 1 (1999); William E. Forbath, *The New Deal Constitution in Exile*, 51 DUKE L.J. 165 (2001); Robert C. Post & Reva B. Siegel, *Legislative Constitutionalism and Section Five Power: Policentric Interpretation of the Family and Medical Leave Act*, 112 YALE L.J. 1943 (2003) (offering a "policentric" constitutionalism in which nonjudicial actors have some space to interpret the Constitution for themselves). To the extent that this work truly dissented from judicial supremacy, it was controversial among liberals. *See, e.g.,* Laurence H. Tribe, *"The People Themselves": Judicial Populism*, N.Y. TIMES BOOK REV., Oct. 24, 2004, at 32 (reviewing Kramer).

43. *See* "The Taming of the Labor Movement and the Eclipse of Progressive Constitutional Political Economy," Chapter 7; "Constitutional Politics, the American Way," Chapter 9; "Constitutional Arguments in the Face of Hostile Courts," Chapter 9.

44. Confusingly, "political economy" was half-revived in the late twentieth century, as a field centered on public choice economics. The most important advocate of this half-revival was James M. Buchanan. His colleagues in the field argue that "Buchanan literally founded the field of constitutional political economy." Robert D. Tollison, Foreword, *in* 16 GEOFFREY BRENNAN & JAMES BUCHANAN, COLLECTED WORKS OF JAMES M. BUCHANAN: CHOICE, CONTRACT, AND CONSTITUTIONS xi (2001). Buchanan saw continuities between his project and some of the traditions we discuss in this book. Like us, Buchanan urged his fellow "modern economists" to return to "the early tradition in 'political economy.'" 10 BRENNAN & BUCHANAN, COLLECTED WORKS: THE REASON OF RULES: CONSTITUTIONAL POLITICAL ECONOMY xvi–xviii (1985). However, the word "constitutional" in Buchanan's title and throughout his work has an unusual and not especially legal meaning—one that sometimes overlaps with our usage in this book but is not the same. Buchanan's conception of a constitution is any set of rules that constrain majority rule in some way; he calls all such rules "constitutional rules." *See id.* at xvii–xix; *see also* 9 BRENNAN & BUCHANAN, COLLECTED WORKS: THE POWER TO TAX: ANALYTICAL FOUNDATIONS OF A FISCAL CONSTITUTION §1.3 (2000) (discussing the potential usefulness of "nonelectoral constitutional rules" limiting the government's power to tax). Thus he could simultaneously argue for a balanced budget

amendment and for the proposition that an idea of keeping the government's books in balance had long been part of the "fiscal constitution." Still, within his rather capacious conception of what counts as constitutional for purposes of the term "constitutional political economy," there is much that we recognize. *See, e.g.,* 16 BRENNAN & BUCHANAN, COLLECTED WORKS: CHOICE CONTRACT AND CONSTITUTIONS 339 ("In effect, the New Deal rewrote the political economic constitution."). *See* "Toward a Neoliberal Constitutional Political Economy," this chapter.

45. We are hopeful about a nascent revival of political economy, which is afoot today. For example, consider the law and political economy movement in the legal academy, *see* Introduction n.58, and parallel revivals in political science and economics, *see* Introduction n.56-57.

46. *See, e.g.,* K. SABEEL RAHMAN, DEMOCRACY AGAINST DOMINATION 7 (2016) (exploring the roots of liberals' turn to "a 'managerial' approach to economic governance" in the Progressive and New Deal eras).

47. DAVID RICARDO, THE PRINCIPLES OF POLITICAL ECONOMY AND TAXATION iii-iv (1817).

48. At the same time, economics tends to privilege efficiency, variously defined—sometimes, simply as wealth maximization—as its quasi-normative touchstone. *See* Jedediah Britton-Purdy, David Singh Grewal, Amy Kapczynski, & K. Sabeel Rahman, *Building a Law-and-Political-Economy Framework: Beyond the Twentieth-Century Synthesis,* 129 YALE L.J. 1784 (2020). *See* Introduction n.58.

49. LÉON WALRAS, ELEMENTS OF PURE ECONOMICS, OR THE THEORY OF SOCIAL WEALTH 71 (William Jaffe trans., 2013) (1874).

50. *Id.*

51. *Id.*

52. *See, e.g.,* F. Y. EDGEWORTH, MATHEMATICAL PSYCHICS: AN ESSAY ON THE APPLICATION OF MATHEMATICS TO THE MORAL SCIENCES 16 (1881) (on self-interested actors); VILFREDO PARETO, MANUAL OF POLITICAL ECONOMY 77 (Aldo Montesano et al. eds., 2014) (1906) (on utility functions).

53. Lochner v. New York, 198 U.S. 45, 75 (1908) (Holmes, J., dissenting).

54. HERBERT SPENCER, SOCIAL STATICS 355-56 (1880) (1851).

55. *See* BENJAMIN G. RADER, THE ACADEMIC MIND AND REFORM: THE INFLUENCE OF RICHARD T. ELY IN AMERICAN LIFE 53 (1966). For a summary of the state of the field, see BO SANDELIN ET AL., A SHORT HISTORY OF ECONOMIC THOUGHT, ch. 5 (2014).

56. DOROTHY ROSS, THE ORIGINS OF AMERICAN SOCIAL SCIENCE 117 (rev'd ed. 2008). Chastened after a public trial by the university regents at Wisconsin, he left radicalism behind. *Id.* at 117-38.

57. *See* JOHN MAYNARD KEYNES, THE GENERAL THEORY OF EMPLOYMENT, INTEREST, AND MONEY 15-17 (1936).

58. *Id.* at 16.

59. This work arguably began with J .R. Hicks, *Mr. Keynes and the "Classics": A Suggested Interpretation,* 5 ECONOMETRICA 147 (1937). *See* ALVIN H. HANSEN, A GUIDE TO KEYNES (1953); PAUL A. SAMUELSON, ECONOMICS: AN INTRODUCTORY ANALYSIS (3d ed. 1955). Keynes himself was frustrated with the methodological approaches of some of his colleagues and successors, who seemed to be building "a contraption proceeding from premises which are not stated with precision to conclusions which have no clear application." John Maynard Keynes, *quoted in* FRANCISCO LOUÇÃ, THE YEARS OF HIGH ECONOMETRICS 63 (2007). But the field was fast becoming a mathematically driven science. By the mid-1960s, the National Science Foundation would become the largest funder of social science research in the United States, and the largest share of the social science funding went to economics; NSF funding would eventually become "a cornerstone of a successful career in economics." *See* Tiago Mata & Tom Scheiding, *National Science Foundation Patronage of Social Science, 1970s and 1980s: Congressional Scrutiny, Advocacy Network, and the Prestige of Economics,* 50 MINERVA 423, 447 (2012).

60. JOHN KENNETH GALBRAITH, THE AFFLUENT SOCIETY 82 (1958).

61. *Id.* at 189.

62. *Id.* at 192.

63. Claudia Goldin & Robert A. Margo, *The Great Compression: The U.S. Wage Structure at Mid-Century,* 107 Q J. ECON. 1 (1992).

64. To be sure, during this period few households earned enough to owe the very highest marginal rate. Still, the decision to impose progressivity even at the top, as between the wealthy and very wealthy, is notable. On the wartime collapse in private wealth, which actually was not as severe in the United States as in Europe, but was nonetheless quite large, see THOMAS PIKETTY, CAPITAL IN THE TWENTY-FIRST CENTURY 152–56 (Arthur Goldhammer trans., 2014).

65. *See* Steven A. Bank et al., *Executive Pay: What Worked?,* 42 J. CORP. L. 59, 93–96 (2016) (on executive pay); William J. Collins & Gregory T. Niemesh, *Unions and the Great Compression of Wage Inequality in the US at Mid-Century: Evidence From Local Labour Markets,* 72 ECON. HIST. REV. 691 (2019) (on wages).

66. GEORGE THOMAS WASHINGTON & V. HENRY ROTHSCHILD, COMPENSATING THE CORPORATE EXECUTIVE 9, 16 (2d ed. 1951); *see* Bank et al., *Executive Pay,* at 94.

67. PIKETTY, CAPITAL IN THE TWENTY-FIRST CENTURY, at 291–94.

68. This expression gained national fame after President Kennedy used it on the campaign trail in September 1960, in a speech in Ohio where he discussed the St. Lawrence Seaway: "I was proud, though I came from Massachusetts, to vote for it, because it is a national asset and a rising tide lifts all boats." Senator John F. Kennedy, Remarks at Municipal Auditorium, Canton, Ohio (Sept. 27, 1960), https://www.jfklibrary.org/archives/other-resources/john-f-kennedy-speeches/canton-oh-19600927 [https://perma.cc/2USK-9LAB]. The context illustrates that the economic policy measure to which Kennedy originally attached the phrase was not specifically Keynesian: building a canal to spur economic development would have been entirely familiar and congenial to Alexander Hamilton. However, the phrase gained a Keynesian connotation from Kennedy's broader economic policy agenda.

69. GALBRAITH, AFFLUENT SOCIETY, at 86.

70. JOHN KENNETH GALBRAITH, THE NEW INDUSTRIAL STATE 146 (rev'd ed. 2007) (1967). *See* Paul Krugman, *For Richer,* N.Y. TIMES MAG., Oct. 20, 2002, at 62.

71. Duncan Norton-Taylor, *How Top Executives Live,* FORTUNE, July 1955.

72. Simon Kuznets, *Economic Growth and Income Inequality,* 45 AM. ECON. REV. 1, 22 (1955).

73. *Id.* at 28.

74. Daron Acemoglu & James A. Robinson, *The Political Economy of the Kuznets Curve,* 6 REV. DEV. ECON. 183, 184 (2002). There is much debate about the Kuznets curve's validity and its causes, which are undoubtedly complex. We cite Acemoglu and Robinson here primarily for the proposition that improving our answers to these questions requires taking seriously the political side of political economy.

75. GALBRAITH, AFFLUENT SOCIETY, at 190.

76. *Cf.* Senator John F. Kennedy, Speech to the Associated Business Publications Conference, Biltmore Hotel, New York, N.Y. (Oct. 12, 1960), https://www.presidency.ucsb.edu/documents/speech-senator-john-f-kennedy-the-associated-business-publications-conference-biltmore [https://perma.cc/RU8J-QD8A] (making his case in a campaign speech that "[n]o President—Democratic or Republican—will be satisfied with growing unemployment, lagging economic growth or excessive price inflation," and that the two candidates are "equally opposed to excessive, unjustified or unnecessary government intervention in the economy").

77. *See* ARTHUR M. SCHLESINGER JR., THE VITAL CENTER: THE POLITICS OF FREEDOM (1949).

78. *1912 Electoral Vote Tally,* NATIONAL ARCHIVES: CENTER FOR LEGISLATIVE ARCHIVES, https://www.archives.gov/legislative/features/1912-election [https://perma.cc/Q8UD-9P99].

79. LANDON R. Y. STORRS, THE SECOND RED SCARE AND THE UNMAKING OF THE NEW DEAL LEFT 147 (2013).

80. *See id.* at 155–64.

81. Alonzo Hamby, *The Vital Center, the Fair Deal, and the Quest for a Liberal Political Economy,* 77 AM. HIST. REV. 653, 663–64 (1972). As Hamby recounts, Keyserling successfully persuaded the Truman administration to adopt this perspective during debates over how to respond to the economic dislocations of the Korean War. *Id.* at 675–78.

82. *See* "The Wagner Act and New Deal Constitutional Political Economy," Chapter 6.

83. STORRS, SECOND RED SCARE at 2.

84. *Id.* at 3.

85. *See* "'The Money of the Constitution,'" Chapter 4.

86. *See* 1 ALLAN H. MELTZER, A HISTORY OF THE FEDERAL RESERVE: 1913–1951, at 415–724 (2003).

87. 2 ALLAN H. MELTZER, A HISTORY OF THE FEDERAL RESERVE, bk. 1: 1951–1969, at 87–88 (2010).

88. *Id.* at 318–24.

89. William Jennings Bryan, Address Before the Federation of Labor in Chicago (Sept. 7, 1908), *in* 2 WILLIAM JENNINGS BRYAN, SPEECHES OF WILLIAM JENNINGS BRYAN 167–68 (1909).

90. *See* ALLEN J. MATUSOW, THE UNRAVELING OF AMERICA: A HISTORY OF LIBERALISM IN THE 1960S, at 45 (1984).

91. 2 MELTZER, FEDERAL RESERVE, bk. 1, at 6.

92. Bart Barnes, *Longtime Fed Chairman William Martin Jr. Dies,* WASH. POST, July 29, 1998.

93. *See* 2 MELTZER, FEDERAL RESERVE, bk. 2, at 1216–42.

94. *See id.* at 1014–63.

95. *Id.* at 1097 n. 112 ("Unlike Burns, Volcker did not blame labor unions for inflation. . . . 'Labor and management were in large part reflecting inflationary forces originating elsewhere'" (quoting Volcker's papers).

96. *See, e.g.,* Statement by Paul A. Volcker before the Joint Economic Committee of the U.S. Congress, January 26, 1982, 68 FED. RESERVE BULLETIN 88, 89 (1982) ("Our current inflation did not originate as a 'wage-push' phenomenon. But in an economy like ours, with wages and salaries accounting for two-thirds of all costs," reducing inflation requires slowing "the growth of *nominal* wages" and unfortunately, so far "general indexes of worker compensation still show relatively little improvement."). "Improvement" here means relatively lower wages.

97. PAUL A. VOLCKER, KEEPING AT IT: THE QUEST FOR SOUND MONEY AND GOOD GOVERNMENT 113 (2018).

98. *See* 2 MELTZER, FEDERAL RESERVE, bk. 2, at 1033–36 (describing the paradigm shift toward the single-minded focus on inflation); Daniel J. B. Mitchell, *Inflation, Unemployment and the Wagner Act: A Critical Reappraisal,* 38 Stan. L. Rev. 1065, 1079 (1986) (observing, just a few years after the Volcker shock, that the entire paradigm of unions bargaining for higher wages now appeared to be "on a collision course with monetary policy").

99. *See Renomination of Paul A. Volcker to be Chairman, Board of Governors, Federal Reserve System, Hearing Before the Committee on Banking, Housing, and Urban Affairs,* S. Hearing 98–238 (July 14, 1983), at 3 (Statement of Democratic Senator William Proxmire) (citing "the support you have won with the American public" and "the warm approval of almost everyone"); *id.* at 5 (Statement of Republican Senator John Heinz) (Volcker has "attained a level of sophistication in monetary policy and its implementation" that has earned "the respect of the financial community," even as "the economy itself is defying traditional theories of economic beahavior"); 2 MELTZER, FEDERAL RESERVE, bk. 2, at 1074 (lauding Volcker for restoring the "independence" of the Fed from politics that had been lost in prior years).

100. Celler-Kefauver Anti-Merger Act, Pub. L. 81–899, 62 Stat. 1125, 1126 (1950), codified as rev. at 15 U.S.C. § 18.

101. 96 CONG. REC. 16,504 (1950) (statement of Sen. Aiken).

102. *Amending the Clayton Act by Requiring Prior Notification of Certain Corporate Mergers and for Other Purposes: Hearing on H.R. 6748, H.R. 7229, and H.R. 8332 Before the Antitrust Subcomm. of the H. Comm. on the Judiciary,* 84th Cong. 6 (1956) (statement of Rep. Emanuel Celler, Chairman of the Antitrust Subcommittee). Celler was drawing here on Justice Douglas's dissent in Standard Oil Co. of California v. U.S., 337 U.S. 293, 320–21 (1949) (Douglas, J., dissenting) (arguing that when large oil companies "supplant" independent stations with their own stations, "there will be a tragic loss to the nation. The small, independent business man will be supplanted by clerks"; by approving this, he argues, the Court "helps remake America in the image of the cartels.").

103. *See* "The New Dealers Take Up the Mantle of Antitrust," Chapter 6; "Updating the Democracy of Opportunity—Populist Constitutional Political Economy," Chapter 4.

104. President Dwight D. Eisenhower, Farewell Radio and Television Address to the American People, PUB. PAPERS 1035, 1038 (Jan. 17, 1961).

105. *See* "The Constitutional Political Economy of Antitrust," Chapter 9.

106. *See* Wilbur J. Cohen & Robert J. Myers, *Social Security Act Amendments of 1950: A Summary and Legislative History,* 13 SOCIAL SECURITY BULLETIN 3 (Oct. 1950); *Social Security Act Amendments of 1949: Hearings on H.R. 2893 Before the H. Comm. on Ways and Means: Part 2: Old Age, Survivors, and Disability Insurance,* 81st Cong. 1878 (1949) (statement of Edgar G. Brown, Director, National Negro Council) ("Unfortunately, 80 percent of the Negroes are outside of the benefits of the act; so that we have had serious discrimination from the point of view of not being covered.").

107. *Social Security Act Amendments of 1949: Hearings on H.R. 2893 Before the H. Comm. on Ways and Means: Part 2: Old Age, Survivors, and Disability Insurance,* 81st Cong. 2344 (1949) (statement of Elizabeth Sasuly, Washington Representative, Food, Tobacco, Agricultural, and Allied Workers Union of America).

108. *Id.* at 1823–24 (statement of Dr. H. M. Griffith, Staff Director of Public Relations, National Economic Council [a private organization in New York, not the later-created executive branch agency]).

109. Cohen & Myers, Social Security Act Amendments of 1950, at 6 (votes of 333–14 and 81–2). On how the extension improved its finances, *see id.* at 7 tbl. 5.

110. *See* "The Taming of the Labor Movement and the Eclipse of Progressive Constitutional Political Economy," Chapter 7.

111. JOHN KENNETH GALBRAITH, THE AFFLUENT SOCIETY 323, 328 (1958).

112. MICHAEL HARRINGTON, THE OTHER AMERICA: POVERTY IN THE UNITED STATES 80 (1962).

113. *Id.* at 81.

114. Lyndon Baines Johnson Library, *Walter Heller: An Oral History, quoted in* ROBERT CARO, THE PASSAGE OF POWER 538–39 (2012).

115. Martin Luther King Jr., Remarks at March on Washington for Jobs and Freedom: I Have a Dream (Aug. 28, 1963).

116. *Id.*

117. President John F. Kennedy, Radio and Television Report to the American People on Civil Rights, PUB. PAPERS 468, 469 (June 11, 1963) (video https://www.jfklibrary.org/learn/about-jfk /historic-speeches/televised-address-to-the-nation-on-civil-rights).

118. President Lyndon B. Johnson, Address Before a Joint Session of the Congress, 1 PUB. PAPERS 8, 9 (Nov. 27, 1963) ("We have talked long enough in this country about equal rights. It is time now to write the next chapter—and to write it in the books of law.").

119. President Lyndon B. Johnson, Annual Message to the Congress on the State of the Union, 1 PUB. PAPERS 112, 113–14 (Jan. 8, 1964).

120. *Id.* at 112.

121. *Compare* President Lyndon B. Johnson, Remarks at the University of Michigan, 1 PUB. PAPERS 704, 706 (May 22, 1964) (describing "the battle to give every citizen an escape from the crushing weight of poverty," without reference to law or the Constitution) with *id.* (describing

"the battle to give every citizen the full equality which God enjoins and the law requires" on the basis of race in more explicitly legal and constitutional terms). On the important procedural due process victories for the poor, and the thwarted possibility of a more substantive set of constitutional rights for the poor, see "Welfare Rights and the Constitution," this chapter. *See also* SUSAN E. LAWRENCE, THE POOR IN COURT: THE LEGAL SERVICES PROGRAM AND SUPREME COURT DECISION MAKING (1990); William E. Forbath, *Constitutional Welfare Rights: A History, Critique and Reconstruction,* 69 FORDHAM L. REV. 1821 (2001).

122. Preamble to the Economic Opportunity Act of 1964, Pub. Law No. 88–452, § 2, 78 Stat. 508, 508 (1964).

123. *See* THOMAS PIKETTY, CAPITAL IN THE TWENTY-FIRST CENTURY 309, 324 (2014) (showing the peak of the purchasing power of the minimum wage in 1970, and the low level of inequality from 1950 to 1970 in terms of the share of all income going to the top decile); Rosemary A. Stevens, *Health Care in the Early 1960s,* HEALTH CARE FINANCING REV., Winter 1996, at 11, 11 http://www.ssa.gov/history/pdf/HealthCareEarly1960s.pdf [https://perma.cc/5KWS-GJGT] (showing that in "a country blessed by plenty," a solid majority of Americans had various forms of health insurance by 1965); George Friedman, *The Crisis of the Middle Class and American Power,* STRATFOR WORLDVIEW: GEOPOLITICAL WEEKLY (Dec. 31, 2013), http://www.stratfor.com /weekly/crisis-middle-class-and-american-power#axzz3775wPoM1 [https://perma.cc/9MVP -FMJU] (suggesting that a median income in the 1950s and 1960s would provide a modest and proper standard of living).

124. Economic Opportunity Act of 1964, Pub. Law No. 88–452, § 2, 78 Stat. 508 (1964) (emphasis added).

125. *See* IRVING BERNSTEIN, GUNS OR BUTTER: THE PRESIDENCY OF LYNDON JOHNSON 38–39 (1996).

126. *See* ALLEN J. MATUSOW, THE UNRAVELLING OF AMERICA: A HISTORY OF LIBERALISM IN THE 1960S, at 56, 59 (1984); *see generally* BERNSTEIN, GUNS OR BUTTER, at 38–42.

127. President Lyndon B. Johnson, Annual Message to the Congress on the State of the Union, 1 PUB. PAPERS 112, 112 (Jan. 8, 1964). The tax cut was yet another proposal that had stalled in Congress under President Kennedy.

128. President Lyndon B. Johnson, Special Message to the Congress Proposing a Nationwide War on the Sources of Poverty, 1 PUB. PAPERS 375, 380 (Mar. 16, 1964).

129. Like Social Security, Medicare requires you or your spouse to have worked and paid taxes for at least ten years during your life, but unlike Social Security, the benefits do not vary based on how much you worked or earned. In that way, Medicare is more redistributive, and more purely a form of *social* insurance, than is Social Security itself.

130. President Lyndon B. Johnson, Remarks with President Truman at the Signing in Independence of the Medicare Bill, 2 PUB. PAPERS 811, 814 (July 30, 1965).

131. We discuss the Affordable Care Act (Obamacare) in Chapter 9.

132. RONALD REAGAN, RONALD REAGAN SPEAKS OUT AGAINST SOCIALIZED MEDICINE (Am. Med. Ass'n 1961) audio, https://www.americanrhetoric.com/speeches/ronaldreagansocialized medicine.htm [https://perma.cc/HLS6-45VT]. *See* Max J. Skidmore, *Ronald Reagan and "Operation Coffeecup": A Hidden Episode in American Political History,* J. AM. CULTURE, Fall 1989, at 89.

133. Julian E. Zelizer, *How Medicare Was Made,* NEW YORKER, Feb. 15, 2015.

134. REAGAN, RONALD REAGAN SPEAKS OUT.

135. *Id.*

136. President John F. Kennedy, Special Message to the Congress on National Health Needs, PUB. PAPERS 165, 173 (Feb. 27, 1962).

137. *Health Services for the Aged Under the Social Security Insurance System: Hearing on H.R. 4222 Before the H. Committee on Ways and Means,* Vol. 1, 87th Cong. 2408 (1961) (statement of Abraham Ribicoff, Secretary of Health, Education, and Welfare).

138. *See* "Social-Democratic State-Building and the Second Bill of Rights," Chapter 7.

139. Dr. Martin Luther King Jr., Statement before the Platform Committee of the Democratic National Convention, Atlantic City, N.J. (Aug. 1964), *in* Bayard Rustin Papers, Reel 3, at 27 (Univ. Pub. of Am. 1988).

140. *Bills Relating to Equal Employment Opportunities: Hearing on S.B. 773, S.B. 1210, S.B. 1211, and S.B. 1937 Before the Subcomm. on Employment and Manpower of the S. Comm. on Labor and Public Welfare,* 88th Cong. 1st Sess. 172 (1964) (statement of A. Philip Randolph, President, Negro American Labor Council, Brotherhood of Sleeping Car Porters, and Vice President, AFL–CIO); *see* Bayard Rustin, Draft Testimony Before the FEPC, *in* Rustin Papers, Reel 4, at 4; *see* William E. Forbath, *Caste, Class, and Equal Citizenship,* 98 MICH. L. REV. 1, 86 (1999).

141. Rustin, Draft Testimony, at 5.

142. *Id.* at 7.

143. *Id.* This formulation had considerable power, and would be adopted by others including liberals in Congress. *See Bills Relating to Equal Employment Opportunities: Hearing on S.B. 773, S.B. 1210, S.B. 1211, and S.B. 1937 Before the Subcomm. on Employment and Manpower of the S. Comm. on Labor and Public Welfare,* 88th Cong. 1st Sess. 172 (1964) (remarks of Sen. Joseph Clark) ("[W]e will not have fair employment until we have full employment").

144. For a thoughtful discussion of this phrase before it became so fully identified with modern Keynesian macroeconomics, *see* Michael Dennis, *The Idea of Full Employment: A Challenge to Capitalism in the New Deal Era,* 14 LABOR: STUDIES IN WORKING-CLASS HISTORY OF THE AMERICAS 69 (May 2017).

145. *See* MARTIN LUTHER KING JR., WHERE DO WE GO FROM HERE: CHAOS OR COMMUNITY? 193, 199–200 (1967).

146. *See, e.g.,* Martin Luther King Jr., Address to Local 1199 (Mar. 10, 1968), *in* ALL LABOR HAS DIGNITY 155, 162 (Michael Honey ed., 2012) (highlighting the Declaration's idea that there are "certain basic rights that are neither derived from nor conferred by the state"); Martin Luther King Jr., Address to AFSCME (Mar. 18, 1968), *in* ALL LABOR HAS DIGNITY 170–74 (describing the trajectory of the movement as "going beyond purely civil rights to questions of human rights"). On the continuities between King's growing emphasis on economic justice and a "refashioning of capitalism" and the thinking of earlier generations of left-leaning Black leaders like Du Bois, *see* Reuel Schiller, *Mourning King: The Civil Rights Movement and the Fight for Economic Justice,* 27 NEW LAB. F. 1, 2 (2018), https://newlaborforum.cuny.edu/2018/05/10/mourning-king/.

147. Martin Luther King Jr., Address to Shop Stewards of Local 815 (May 2, 1967), *in* ALL LABOR HAS DIGNITY, 125–29.

148. Bayard Rustin, *From Protest to Politics: The Future of the Civil Rights Movement,* COMMENTARY, Feb. 1965, https://www.commentarymagazine.com/articles/bayard-rustin-2/from-protest-to-politics-the-future-of-the-civil-rights-movement/ [https://perma.cc/D28A-NTJZ]. For leading us to this striking essay by Rustin, and many other insights, we are indebted to Cindy Estlund's AUTOMATING THE FUTURE: WHY AND HOW TO SAVE AND SPREAD WORK IN AN ERA OF LESS OF IT 149 (2021).

149. Rustin, *From Protest to Politics.*

150. *Id.*

151. Bayard Rustin, Address to Democratic National Convention, Atlantic City, N.J. (Aug. 1964), *in* Rustin Papers, Reel 3, at 27 (Univ. Pub. of America. Inc. 1988).

152. Bayard Rustin, Untitled Article on the Freedom Budget, *in* Rustin Papers, Reel 13, at 1.

153. On King and the UBI, *see* King, Address to Shop Stewards, *in* ALL LABOR HAS DIGNITY, at 131, 133. Rustin, Untitled Article on the Freedom Budget, *in* Rustin Papers, Reel 13, at 3–4.

154. Poor People's Campaign, Statements of Demands for Rights of the Poor Presented to Agencies of the U.S. Government by the Southern Christian Leadership Conference and Its Com-

mittee of 100 (SCLS-PPC Information Office 1968), at 31 (statement of Rev. Bernard Lafayette, Apr. 30, 1968).

155. *Id.* at 11–12 (statement of Rev. Ralph Abernathy, Apr. 29, 1968) (emphasis in original).

156. Rustin, Untitled Article on the Freedom Budget, *in* Rustin Papers, Reel 13, at 1.

157. *Id.*

158. *See* Memorandum from Secretary of Labor, Willard Wirtz, to the Chairman of the Council of Economic Advisers (Nov. 19, 1963), *in* The Administrative History of the Department of Labor, Vol. 3, Documentary Supplement, Section III-B, Box 12 at the LBJ Library. *See* William E. Forbath, *Caste, Class, and Equal Citizenship,* 98 MICH. L. REV. 1, 87–89 (1999).

159. Memorandum from Willard Wirtz.

160. *Id.*

161. *See* Edmund F. Wehrle, *Guns, Butter, Leon Keyserling, the AFL–CIO, and the Fate of Full-Employment Economics,* 66 THE HISTORIAN 730, 746 (2004).

162. *See id.* at 745–48. The criticism that Keyserling failed to see the inflation threat seems entirely fair.

163. President Franklin Delano Roosevelt, Acceptance of the Renomination for the Presidency, Philadelphia, Pa., 5 PUB. PAPERS 230, 234 (June 27, 1936).

164. President Lyndon B. Johnson, Commencement Address at Howard University: "To Fulfill These Rights," 2 PUB. PAPERS 635, 636 (June 4, 1965).

165. *See* Mark G. Yudof, *Equal Educational Opportunity & the Courts,* 51 TEX. L. REV. 411, 465 (1973).

166. *See, e.g.,* SEAN FARHANG, THE LITIGATION STATE: PUBLIC REGULATION AND PRIVATE LAWSUITS IN THE U.S. 94–213 (2010); NANCY MACLEAN, FREEDOM IS NOT ENOUGH: THE OPENING OF THE AMERICAN WORKPLACE 76–113 (2006); Neal Devins, *I Love You, Big Brother,* 87 CALIF. L. REV. 1283, 1293 (1999).

167. Civil Rights Act of 1964 § 703, 42 U.S.C. § 2000e-2.

168. *See generally* JUDITH STEIN, RUNNING STEEL, RUNNING AMERICA: RACE, ECONOMIC POLICY, AND THE DECLINE OF LIBERALISM (2000).

169. *See generally* JEFFERSON COWIE, STAYIN' ALIVE: THE 1970S AND THE LAST DAYS OF THE WORKING CLASS (2010).

170. *See, e.g.,* MACLEAN, FREEDOM IS NOT ENOUGH, at 233–36.

171. *See* Governor George C. Wallace, The Civil Rights Movement: Fraud, Sham, and Hoax (July 4, 1964), BLACKPAST.ORG, http://www.blackpast.org/1964-george-c-wallace-civil-rights-movement-fraud-sham-and-hoax [https://perma.cc/7PUA-25UF].

172. *Id.*

173. On Nixon's racial appeals, see IAN HANEY LÓPEZ, DOG WHISTLE POLITICS 17–54 (2014); on his construction of himself as a tribune of working-class whites against liberals, see COWIE, STAYIN' ALIVE, at 118–45.

174. *See* "Liberalism and the Aggrandizement of Capital," Chapter 4.

175. Reva Siegel, *Foreword: Equality Divided,* 127 HARV. L. REV. 1 (2013); Jack M. Balkin & Reva B. Siegel, *The American Civil Rights Tradition: Anticlassification or Antisubordination?,* 58 U. MIAMI L. REV. 9, 9–10, 30–31 (2003).

176. *See generally* JONATHAN SIMON, GOVERNING THROUGH CRIME: HOW THE WAR ON CRIME TRANSFORMED AMERICAN DEMOCRACY AND CREATED A CULTURE OF FEAR (2007); RUTH GILMORE, GOLDEN GULAG: PRISONS, SURPLUS, CRISIS AND OPPOSITION IN GLOBALIZING CALIFORNIA (2007); LOÏC WAQUANT, PUNISHING THE POOR: THE NEOLIBERAL GOVERNMENT OF INSECURITY (2009); JAMES FOREMAN, LOCKING UP OUR OWN: CRIME AND PUNISHMENT IN BLACK AMERICA (2017).

177. *See generally* JACOB S. HACKER, THE GREAT RISK SHIFT: THE NEW ECONOMIC INSECURITY AND THE DECLINE OF THE AMERICAN DREAM (2019); GABRIEL WINANT, THE NEXT SHIFT: THE FALL OF INDUSTRY AND THE RISE OF HEALTH CARE IN RUST BELT AMERICA (2020).

178. *See* William E. Forbath, *Constitutional Welfare Rights: A History, Critique and Reconstruction*, 69 FORDHAM L. REV. 1821, 1845–67 (2001); FELICIA ANN KORNBLUH, THE BATTLE FOR WELFARE RIGHTS: POLITICS AND POVERTY IN MODERN AMERICA (2007).

179. *See generally* JACQUELINE JONES, LABOR OF LOVE, LABOR OF SORROW: BLACK WOMEN, WORK, AND THE FAMILY FROM SLAVERY TO THE PRESENT (1985).

180. *Id.* at 249–52.

181. Harper v. Virginia Bd. of Elections, 383 U.S. 663, 668 (1966).

182. Its direct successor today is the Temporary Assistance for Needy Families (TANF) program.

183. WINIFRED BELL, AID TO DEPENDENT CHILDREN 9 (1965) (internal quotation omitted); *see* MOLLY LADD-TAYLOR, MOTHER-WORK: WOMEN, CHILD WELFARE, AND THE STATE, 1890–1930 136–66 (1994); SONYA MICHEL, CHILDREN'S INTERESTS / MOTHERS' RIGHTS: THE SHAPING OF AMERICA'S CHILD CARE POLICY 73–78 (1999); THEDA SKOCPOL, PROTECTING SOLDIERS AND MOTHERS: THE POLITICAL ORIGINS OF SOCIAL POLICY IN THE UNITED STATES 424–79 (1992).

184. BELL, AID TO DEPENDENT CHILDREN, at 33–34, 63–65, 76–82, 108–9.

185. *See id.* at 4–6, 76–92, 213 n.7; R. SHEP MELNICK, BETWEEN THE LINES: INTERPRETING WELFARE RIGHTS 57, 85–90, 98, 121–22, 130 (1994).

186. 392 U.S. 309 (1968).

187. Smith v. King, 277 F. Supp. 31, 41 (M.D. Ala. 1967).

188. MARTIN GARBUS, READY FOR THE DEFENSE 194–95 (1971).

189. *See* LUCAS A. POWE JR., THE WARREN COURT AND AMERICAN POLITICS 239–41, 386 (2000); MORTON J. HORWITZ, THE WARREN COURT AND THE PURSUIT OF JUSTICE (1998); Cary Franklin, *The New Class Blindness*, 128 YALE L.J. 2, 8–13 (2018).

190. MELNICK, BETWEEN THE LINES, at 85–92.

191. *See id.;* SUSAN E. LAWRENCE, THE POOR IN COURT: THE LEGAL SERVICES PROGRAM AND SUPREME COURT DECISION MAKING 123–48 (1990).

192. Goldberg v. Kelly, 397 U.S. 254 (1970).

193. *Id.* at 264–65.

194. *Id.*

195. *See generally* Frank Michelman, *Foreword: On Protecting the Poor Through the Fourteenth Amendment*, 83 HARVARD L. REV. 7 (1969); Frank I. Michelman, *In Pursuit of Constitutional Welfare Rights: One View of Rawls' Theory of Justice*, 121 U. PA. L. REV. 962 (1973). For an extended discussion of Michelman's reading of Rawls and its relationship to the War on Poverty and the welfare rights movement, see William E. Forbath, *Not So Simple Justice: Frank Michelman on Social Rights, 1969–Present*, 39 TULSA L. REV. 597 (2004). For discussion of other constitutional scholars' work along similar lines, see generally William E. Forbath, *Constitutional Welfare Rights: A History, Critique and Reconstruction*, 69 FORDHAM L. REV. 1821 (2001).

196. *See, e.g.,* Frank I. Michelman, *Possession vs. Distribution in the Constitutional Idea of Property*, 72 IOWA L. REV. 1319 (1987); Frank Michelman, *Law's Republic*, 97 YALE L.J. 1493 (1988).

197. *See* ADAM COHEN, SUPREME INEQUALITY 24–30 (2020) (telling this story and situating it in terms of its impact on the trajectory of the Court). Nixon initiated a Justice Department investigation of Fortas's financial dealings and used strategic leaks from that investigation to convince Fortas to resign.

198. LINDA GREENHOUSE & MICHAEL J. GRAETZ, THE BURGER COURT AND THE RISE OF THE JUDICIAL RIGHT (2016).

199. *See* LAWRENCE, POOR IN COURT, at 60 n.51, 123–47 (analyzing the Legal Services Program's role in shaping legal doctrines of fundamental rights as applied to poverty).

200. 397 U.S. 471 (1970).

201. *Id.* at 484.

202. *Id.* (citing Wiliamson v. Lee Optical Co., 348 U.S. 483, 488 (1955)).

203. *Id.* at 485.

204. *Id.* To punctuate the point, the 1980s Court would proclaim that the Constitution confers "no affirmative right to government aid, even where such aid may be necessary to secure life, liberty, or property. . . ." DeShaney v. Winnebago Cty. Soc. Servs. Dept., 489 U.S. 189, 196 (1989).

205. *See* Forbath, *Constitutional Welfare Rights,* at 1856.

206. Three years later, in San Antonio Independent School District v. Rodriguez, 411 U.S. 1 (1973), the Burger Court shut down the other notable 1960s effort to use constitutional litigation to enlist the federal courts in creating constitutional rights to social provision for the racialized poor. Texas's school district lines, and its property-tax-based school finance regime, left schools separate and deeply unequal in financial terms by class and race. Overturning lower court decisions that would have required the state to make financing less unequal, the Court extended *Dandridge.* Education was a social good of "undisputed importance"—but that would not "cause this Court to depart from the usual standard for reviewing a State's social and economic legislation." *Id.* at 35.

Writing for the new conservative majority was Nixon appointee Justice Lewis F. Powell, who had been chair of Richmond, Virginia's Board of Education throughout the 1950s. Just two years earlier, in 1971, Powell wrote his memorandum urging corporate America to launch a legal and political counterattack against the redistributive laws and policies of New Deal and Great Society liberalism. Memorandum from Lewis F. Powell Jr. to Eugene B. Sydnor Jr., Attack on American Free Enterprise System (Aug. 23, 1971), https://scholarlycommons.law.wlu.edu/powellmemo /1/ [https://perma.cc/6ST6-ZNJN].

207. For a discussion of the strike, see Robert C. Post & Reva B. Siegel, *Legislative Constitutionalism and Section Five Power: Policentric Interpretation of the Family and Medical Leave Act,* 112 Yale L.J. 1943, 1988–89 (2003).

208. *See id.* at 1989; Judy Klemesrud, *A Herstory-Making Event,* N.Y. TIMES MAG., Aug. 23, 1970, at 6, 14.

209. Post & Siegel, *Legislative Constitutionalism and Section Five Power,* at 1991 (quoting Betty Friedan).

210. *Id.* at 1989–96.

211. *See* Cary Franklin, *The Anti-Stereotyping Principle in Constitutional Sex Discrimination Law,* 85 N.Y.U. L. REV. 83 (2010) (describing these cases and Ginsburg's legal campaign).

212. National Organization for Women (N.O.W.), Bill of Rights for 1969, *reprinted in* Terrie Epstein & Heidi Hursh, *Teaching About the 60's,* OAH MAG. HIST., Apr. 1985, at 27. *See* Deborah Dinner, *The Universal Childcare Debate: Rights Mobilization, Social Policy, and the Dynamics of Feminist Activism, 1966–1974,* 28 LAW & HIST. REV. 577, 628 (2010).

213. *See* Dinner, *Universal Childcare Debate,* at 601–14.

214. Dinner argues that rights talk was important both for the mobilization and "political imagination." *Id.* at 579.

215. *See* MARY FRANCES BERRY, POLITICS OF PARENTHOOD: CHILD CARE, WOMEN'S RIGHTS, AND THE MYTH OF THE GOOD MOTHER 137–40 (1993). The legislation was bundled into the Economic Opportunity Amendments of 1971.

216. *Id.*

217. President Richard Nixon, Veto of the Economic Opportunity Amendments of 1971, PUB. PAPERS 1174, 1178 (Dec. 10, 1971).

218. Tomiko Brown, *Two Americas in Healthcare: Federalism and Wars over Poverty from the New Deal–Great Society to Obamacare,* 62 DRAKE L. REV. 981 (2014).

219. Recent proposals by some progressive politicians suggest that there is renewed interest in such a potential restructuring today. *See, e.g.,* Universal Child Care and Early Learning Act, S. 1398, 117th Cong. (2021) (Senator Elizabeth Warren's bill).

220. *See* Cary Franklin, *The New Class Blindness,* 128 YALE L.J. 2, 47 (2018).

221. Linda Greenhouse & Reva B. Siegel, *Before (and After) Roe v. Wade: New Questions About Backlash,* 120 YALE L.J. 2028, 2036 (2011).

222. *Id.* at 2046.

223. Roe v. Wade, 410 U.S. 113, 166 (1973).

224. Greenhouse & Siegel, *Before (and After) Roe v. Wade,* at 2058–59, 2081 n.183.

225. *Id.* at 2082–85.

226. Ronald Reagan, Speech before the Conservative Political Action Coalition (Feb. 6, 1977).

227. *Id.*

228. Presidents Nixon and Reagan both emphasized explicitly that their judicial selections were aimed at advancing "law and order." *See, e.g.,* President Richard Nixon, Remarks on Accepting the Presidential Nomination of the Republican National Convention (Aug. 23, 1972), PUB. PA-PERS 787, 791 (1973) ("the first civil right of every American is to be free from domestic violence. . . . I shall continue to appoint judges who share my philosophy that we must strengthen the peace forces as against the criminal forces in the United States."); President Ronald Reagan, 1988 Leg-islative and Administrative Message: A Union of Individuals (Jan. 25, 1988), 1 PUB. PAPERS 91, 95 (1990) ("Federal court records indicate that between 1981, when I first took office, and 1984, the average sentence handed down by a Federal court per conviction increased dramatically—by over 100 percent for rape, over 100 percent for burglary, and over 60 percent for murder. I will con-tinue to nominate judges who are tough on crime.").

229. *See, e.g.,* S. 158, 97th Cong. (1981); *see also* 127 CONG. REC. S8420 (daily ed. July 24, 1981) (state-ment of Sen. Helms and text of proposed jurisdiction-stripping bill on abortion). *See* Cary Franklin, *Roe As We Know It,* 114 MICH. L. REV. 867, 879–81 (2016); Lawrence Gene Sager, *The Supreme Court, 1980 Term—Foreword: Constitutional Limitations on Congress's Authority to Reg-ulate the Jurisdiction of the Federal Courts,* 95 HARV. L. REV. 17, 17–18 & nn.3–5 (1981) (detailing the flurry of such bills on abortion, school prayer, and busing).

230. This concept of an elite was usefully plastic, and in a pinch could encompass much of the federal government, such as the IRS, whose threat to withdraw tax-exempt status from racially segregated private Christian schools operated as a foundational motivator for the involvement of evangelicals in politics and in the New Right coalition in the late 1970s. *See* Greenhouse & Siegel, *Before (and After) Roe v. Wade,* at 2067 n.141 and accompanying text (discussing Weyrich's account of the centrality of this tax exemption issue, more than abortion, to the formation of the Moral Majority).

231. *Id.* at 2079–86.

232. Governor George C. Wallace, The Civil Rights Movement: Fraud, Sham, and Hoax (July 4, 1964), BLACKPAST.ORG, http://www.blackpast.org/1964-george-c-wallace-civil-rights-movement -fraud-sham-and-hoax [https://perma.cc/7PUA-25UF].

233. We use "Chamber of Commerce" here mostly figuratively, to refer to the success of busi-ness interests more generally, but the success of the actual Chamber itself as a litigant is also quite striking. *See* note 41 above.

234. *See* Cary Franklin, *The New Class Blindness,* 128 YALE L.J. 2, 47 (2018), on what these cases did and did not hold.

235. *See* JEFFERSON COWIE, STAYIN' ALIVE: THE 1970S AND THE LAST DAYS OF THE WORKING CLASS 269–71 (2010).

236. The bill was the Full Employment and Balanced Growth Act of 1978. For a discussion of the 1946 act, see Chapter 7.

237. Augustus F. Hawkins, *Planning for Personal Choice: The Equal Opportunity and Full Employ-ment Act,* 418 ANNALS AM. ACAD. POL. & SOC. SCI. 13, 14 (1975); *see* DEAN BAKER ET AL., CTR. FOR ECON. & POLICY RESEARCH, THE FULL EMPLOYMENT MANDATE OF THE FEDERAL RESERVE (2017).

238. Full Employment and Balanced Growth Act of 1978, 15 U.S.C. § 1022(a)–(b)(1) (1978); *see* COWIE, STAYIN' ALIVE, at 270.

239. COWIE, STAYIN' ALIVE, at 270–71.

240. *See* Executive Order 11615—Providing for Stabilization of Prices, Rents, Wages, and Salaries, 36 Fed. Reg. 15727 (Aug. 15, 1971).

241. COWIE, STAYIN' ALIVE, at 269.

242. *See id.* at 283–86.

243. BAKER ET AL., FULL EMPLOYMENT MANDATE, at 10.

244. *Jobs and Prices in Atlanta: Hearing Before the Joint Econ. Comm.*, 94th Cong. 28 (1975) (statement of Coretta Scott King, Co-Chair, Full Employment Action Council).

245. *Id.*

246. *Id.* at 29.

247. *Id.*

248. Edward Cowan, *Greenspan Scores Employment Bill*, N.Y. TIMES, June 21, 1976, at 23; *Full Employment Bill Stirs Partisan Battle*, 34 CONG. Q. 1171, 1171–75 (1976); Milton Friedman, *Humphrey-Hawkins*, NEWSWEEK, Aug. 2, 1976, at 55; *see* COWIE, STAYIN' ALIVE, at 274–75.

249. *What Humphrey-Hawkins Would Mean*, BUSINESS WEEK, May 31, 1976, at 66; *Full Employment and Balanced Growth Act: Hearings on S. 50 and S. 472 Before the Sen. Comm. on Labor and Public Welfare, Subcomm. on Unemployment, Poverty, and Migratory Labor*, 94th Cong. 142–44 (1976) (statement of Charles Schultze, Brookings Institution); *see* COWIE, STAYIN' ALIVE, at 274–80.

250. President Jimmy Carter, Statement on the Full Employment and Balanced Growth Bill, 2 PUB. PAPERS 2023, 2023 (Nov. 14, 1977); *see* COWIE, STAYIN' ALIVE, at 283–86.

251. *See id.* The watered-down act also set the somewhat implausible goal of achieving zero inflation within a decade. The new reporting requirements were repealed in 2000. *See* Pub. L. 106–569, Title X, Sec. 1003(a).

252. BAKER ET AL., FULL EMPLOYMENT MANDATE, at 19.

253. *See* H.R. 8410, Labor Reform Act, 95th Cong. (1977–1978).

254. Memorandum from Stu Eizenstat on Labor Law Reform to President Jimmy Carter (June 29, 1977), https://www.jimmycarterlibrary.gov/digital_library/cos/142099/35/cos_142099_35_16 -Labor_Law_Reform_Bill.pdf [https://perma.cc/PLJ2-Z5HX] (explaining how labor had dropped the major provisions in part to get the Carter administration's support for a more modest bill); *see* COWIE, STAYIN' ALIVE, at 291–92.

255. *See* COWIE, STAYIN' ALIVE, at 292 ("The compromise bill was lean, moderate, and basically unchallenging to the corporate order, which is why the opposition it raised was so historically significant.").

256. Memorandum from Lewis F. Powell Jr. to Eugene B. Sydnor Jr., Attack on American Free Enterprise System (Aug. 23, 1971), https://scholarlycommons.law.wlu.edu/powellmemo/1/ [https:// perma.cc/6ST6-ZNJN]; *see also* Jedediah Purdy, *Beyond the Bosses' Constitution: The First Amendment and Class Entrenchment*, 118 COLUM. L. REV. 2161, 2166 (2018).

257. *See* LEE DRUTMAN, THE BUSINESS OF AMERICA IS LOBBYING: HOW CORPORATIONS BECAME POLITICIZED AND POLITICS BECAME MORE CORPORATE 58 (2015) ("Between 1971 and 1982, the number of firms with registered lobbyists in Washington grew from 175 to 2,445. Between 1976 and 1980, the number of corporations with political action committees more than quadrupled, from 294 to 1,204.").

258. COWIE, STAYIN' ALIVE, at 293–95.

259. For the Employee Free Choice Act, *see, e.g.*, Employee Free Choice Act of 2009, H.R. 1409, 111th Cong. (2009).

260. *See, e.g.*, Bruce Western & Jake Rosenfeld, *Unions, Norms, and the Rise in U.S. Wage Inequality*, 76 AM. SOC. REV. 513 (2011) (finding that, especially for men, union decline has contributed substantially to overall wage inequality, in part because of the loss of unions' effect on social "norms of equity" in pay); LARRY BARTELS, UNEQUAL DEMOCRACY: THE POLITICAL ECONOMY

OF THE NEW GILDED AGE 217–28 (2017) (describing the practical effect of unions' decline on the politics of the minimum wage).

261. JOSEPH A. MCCARTIN, COLLISION COURSE: RONALD REAGAN, THE AIR TRAFFIC CONTROLLERS, AND THE STRIKE THAT CHANGED AMERICA (2011) (analyzing President Reagan's firing of air traffic controllers and its impact on the labor movement).

262. *See id. See also* COWIE, STAYIN' ALIVE, at 362–64 (describing an "assault" against unions and other working-class institutions after President Reagan's crackdown on air traffic controllers).

263. *See, e.g.,* Daniel Schlozman & Sam Rosenfeld, The Hollow Parties, ch. 9 (unpublished manuscript, on file with the authors).

264. For an early use of the term by its most prominent twentieth-century spokesperson, see Milton Friedman, *Neo-Liberalism and Its Prospects,* FARMAND, Feb. 17, 1951, at 89, *in* COLLECTED WORKS OF MILTON FRIEDMAN PROJECT (Robert Leeson & Charles G. Palm eds., Hoover Institution), and https://perma.cc/EQ9G-L6VF. For the story of the evolution of the term, from a moderate, pragmatic revival of classical liberalism to a term more often used as a critique of excessive market fundamentalism, see Taylor C. Boas & Jordan Gans-Morse, *Neoliberalism: From New Liberal Philosophy to Anti-liberal Slogan,* 44 STUD. COMP. INT'L DEV. 137 (2009).

265. F. A. HAYEK, THE ROAD TO SERFDOM 2–3 (1945).

266. *Id.* at 18–20.

267. *Id.* at 2. Indeed, he lamented that "[n]ot merely nineteenth- and eighteenth-century liberalism, but the basic individualism inherited by us from Erasmus and Montaigne, from Cicero and Tacitus, Pericles and Thucydides, is progressively relinquished." *Id.* at 10.

268. Memorandum from Lewis F. Powell Jr. to Eugene B. Sydnor Jr., Attack on American Free Enterprise System (Aug. 23, 1971), at 32, https://scholarlycommons.law.wlu.edu/powellmemo/1/ [https://perma.cc/6ST6-ZNJN].

269. For more on the Mont Pelerin Society, its generative role, and its internal disagreements, see ANGUS BURGIN, THE GREAT PERSUASION: REINVENTING FREE MARKETS SINCE THE DEPRESSION (2015). The gathering was funded by the Volker Fund, a Kansas City charity controlled by an advocate of laissez-faire economics, which became one of the first of several large American ideological funders of this work. At that initial gathering of the Mont Pelerin Society, this foundation intervened to remove some of the more heterodox names from Hayek's draft list of invitees. *Id.* at 100–102.

270. *Statement of Aims,* THE MONT PELERIN SOCIETY (Apr. 8, 1947), https://www.montpelerin .org/statement-of-aims/ [https://perma.cc/9Q2B-R2ZH].

271. *See* BURGIN, GREAT PERSUASION, at 13–16.

272. For an in-depth account of Buchanan and his circle, see NANCY MACLEAN, DEMOCRACY IN CHAINS (2017).

273. On massive resistance, see *id.* at 68–71. On institution-building, see *id.* at 88–126, 171–87.

274. James Buchanan, *Property as a Guarantor of Liberty, in* 18 FEDERALISM, LIBERTY, AND THE LAW: THE COLLECTED WORKS OF JAMES BUCHANAN 259 (2001). On Buchanan's use of the word "constitutional," see the discussion in note 44 above.

275. This language is Burgin's. BURGIN, GREAT PERSUASION, at 185 (emphasis added); *see id.* at 152–85. Indeed, Friedman himself exemplifies the tension. His influential early work advocated a methodologically positivist approach to economic theory, which differs from axiomatic deduction but shares its distinctly normativity-free aspirations. Over time, he became more politically active and a far more doctrinaire advocate of free markets against government intervention. *See id.* at 170–80. Friedman and Chicago colleagues, such as Aaron Director, in that way left behind their teachers, who had been skeptics of the New Deal but also skeptics of dogmatic laissez-faire. *Id.* at 33–45.

276. Paul A. Volcker, Keeping At It: The Quest for Sound Money and Good Government 103, 33 (2018). *See* "The Slow Triumph of the Technocrats," earlier in this chapter.

277. Milton Friedman, *Federal Flood Relief,* Newsweek, Sept. 4, 1972, *in* Collected Works of Milton Friedman (Robert Leeson & Charles G. Palm eds., Hoover Institution) [https://perma.cc/PJ6N-ZKN5].

278. *See* Burgin, Great Persuasion, at 180 (quoting Friedman).

279. We are telling this part of the story far too tersely. There is only so much one book can do. For a nuanced discussion of these dynamics and the changing social norms they produced, see Yochai Benkler, A Political Economy of Oligarchy: Winner-Take-All Ideology, Superstar Norms, and the Rise of the 1% (Sept. 2017) (unpublished manuscript, on file with the authors).

280. Memorandum from Lewis F. Powell Jr. to Eugene B. Sydnor Jr., Attack on American Free Enterprise System (Aug. 23, 1971), at 30, https://scholarlycommons.law.wlu.edu/powellmemo/1/ [https://perma.cc/6ST6-ZNJN]; *see* Adam Winkler, We the Corporations: How American Businesses Won Their Civil Rights 281 (2018). Although this memorandum has become especially infamous among its progressive opponents, and it presaged a massive rise in legal and ideological activism of exactly the sort it urged, its causal influence is a matter of some dispute. As Ann Southworth notes, the Chamber itself did not take on the central role Powell envisioned. *See* Ann Southworth, Lawyers of the Right: Professionalizing the Conservative Coalition 15 (2008).

281. For a discussion of this institutional dynamic, see Joseph Fishkin & David Pozen, *Asymmetric Constitutional Hardball,* 118 Colum. L. Rev. 915, 952–56 (2018). We refer to the Cato Institute as libertarian because its interests have extended beyond economic neoliberalism to encompass certain additional causes such as drug legalization, although no one would mistake its docket for that of the ACLU. For a discussion of the role of the Scaife Foundations in providing much of the crucial early funding for the Heritage Foundation, see Robert G. Kaiser & Ira Chinoy, *Scaife: Funding Father of the Right,* Wash. Post, May 2, 1999, at A1.

282. *See* Fishkin & Pozen, *Asymmetric Constitutional Hardball,* at 952–56.

283. Jonathan Mahler, *How One Conservative Think Tank Is Stocking Trump's Government,* N.Y. Times Mag., June 20, 2018, https://www.nytimes.com/2018/06/20/magazine/trump-government -heritage-foundation-think-tank.html. For a further discussion of the Mont Pelerin Society, see Burgin, Great Persuasion, at 141.

284. *See* Jane Mayer, Dark Money: The Hidden History of the Billionaires Behind the Rise of the Radical Right 6 (2016); Nancy MacLean, Democracy in Chains 128–43 (2017). As operators of a shadow party, the Koch brothers are not unique; their version is simply (by far) the best funded of the shadow party groups that have gradually given political donors more control of parties in our relatively deregulated environment of political law. *See* Joseph Fishkin & Heather K. Gerken, *The Party's Over: McCutcheon, Shadow Parties, and the Future of the Party System,* 2014 Sup. Ct. Rev. 175 (2015). For a thorough analysis of the role of the Koch-funded political network in Republican politics, see Theda Skocpol & Alexander Hertel-Fernandez, *The Koch Network and Republican Party Extremism,* 14 Persp. on Pol. 681 (2016). Skocpol and Hertel-Fernandez argue that the role of the Koch network in relation to the Republican Party is now similar to the role of the labor movement, at its height, in the politics of the Democratic Party. *Id.* at 690.

285. For discussions of this theme in different parts of this book, see "Proslavery Constitutional Political Economy as 'Minority Rights,'" Chapter 2; "Labor, Constitutional Laissez-Faire, and Lochner v. New York," Chapter 4.

286. Steven M. Teles, The Rise of the Conservative Legal Movement: The Battle for Control of the Law 90–134 (2008).

287. *See id.* at 99 (discussing how debates between two early law-and-economics powerhouses, the conservative Richard Posner and the liberal Guido Calabresi, were central to building the

credibility and reach of the field); *id.* at 201 (graph showing dominance of Scaife and Olin Foundation money in early law and economics programs).

288. Robert Bork, *The Goals of Antitrust Policy,* 57 Am. Econ. Rev. 242 (1967). *See* "The Constitutional Political Economy of Antitrust," Chapter 9. Because Director's publications were few, it can be difficult to assess his influence, but those close to the field find it "profound." Sam Peltzman, *Aaron Director's Influence on Antitrust Policy,* 48 J. L. & Econ. 313 (2005). For an interesting personal reflection on the normative core of the early law and economics movement, see George L. Priest, The Limits of Antitrust *and the Chicago School Tradition,* 6 J. Competition Law & Econ. 1 (2010). Priest explains that Director's *Journal of Law and Economics* was at its inception more of a pro-market journal of political economy. "[T]he underlying aim of the antitrust program was only partially scientific advance; more centrally, it was to ridicule the grounds upon which courts interfered with the marketplace." *Id.* at 4.

289. The Court adopted Bork's standard. *See, e.g.,* Reiter v. Sonotone Corp., 442 U.S. 330, 343 (1979) ("Congress designed the Sherman Act as a 'consumer welfare prescription.' R. Bork, The Antitrust Paradox 66 (1978).").

290. For a discussion of the crucial contributions of the leaders of the Olin, Bradley, and Scaife Foundations to the Federalist Society in its early years, where personal "bonds of trust" between leaders of these foundations and leaders of the Federalist Society enabled "a more aggressive and long-term style of grant-making," see Teles, Rise of the Conservative Legal Movement, at 151. (Later, the Federalist Society developed its own base of wealthy lawyer donors.)

291. *See id.* at 158–59.

292. *See id.* at 249. On the effectiveness of the new foundation-funded conservative and libertarian public-interest firms, as against their less effective predecessors who were funded mainly by business interests, see *id.* at ch. 7.

293. Attorney General Edward Meese, Speech before the Department of Justice Conference on the Constitution, Economic Liberties, and the Extended Commercial Republic (June 14, 1986) (on file with the Hoover Institution, Stanford, Calif.).

294. Charles Fried, Order and Law: Arguing the Reagan Revolution—A Firsthand Account 183 (1991).

295. Meese, Speech before the Department of Justice Conference, at 12–14. This conference is remembered today exclusively because of a speech Justice Scalia gave about constitutional interpretation. But Meese's agenda for the conference was broader and focused specifically on reinvigorating the Takings and Contract Clauses, bringing them out of the shadow of *Lochner. See id.* at 13–16; *see* Attorney General's Conference on Economic Liberties (June 14, 1986) (on file with Hoover Institution, Stanford, Calif.).

296. Office of Legal Policy, U.S. Dep't of Justice, Report to the Attorney General on Economic Liberties Protected by the Constitution (1988). The quoted phrase is from the unpaginated Executive Summary. This report preceded, and is cited in, the broader memoranda about constitutional change that the Meese Justice Department's Office of Legal Policy produced later that year. Office of Legal Policy, U.S. Dep't of Justice, Report to the Attorney General: The Constitution in the Year 2000: Choices Ahead in Constitutional Interpretation (1988); Office of Legal Policy, U.S. Dep't of Justice, Guidelines on Constitutional Litigation (1988). *See* Dawn E. Johnsen, *Ronald Reagan and the Rehnquist Court on Congressional Power: Presidential Influences on Constitutional Change,* 78 Ind. L.J. 363 (2003).

297. Home Building & Loan Assn. v. Blaisdell, 290 U.S. 398 (1934).

298. Office of Legal Policy, Economic Liberties, at 74.

299. *See, e.g.,* Koontz v. St. Johns River Water Management Dist., 570 U.S. 595 (2013) (requiring heightened scrutiny of land-use agency's imposition of a requirement to pay money into conservation fund as a condition of receiving development permit, making monetary exaction an unconstitutional taking); Cedar Point Nursery v. Hassid, 141 S.Ct. 2063 (2021) (holding that it was

a "per se physical taking" of private land for California to enact regulations allowing labor organizers to meet with farmworkers on privately owned farms).

300. *See* Zach Schonfeld, *Understanding Donald Trump's Weird Obsession with Andrew Jackson,* NEWSWEEK, May 1, 2017, https://www.newsweek.com/understanding-donald-trumps-obsession-andrew-jackson-592635 [https://perma.cc/68XD-JY9S].

301. *See* JACOB S. HACKER & PAUL PIERSON, LET THEM EAT TWEETS: HOW THE RIGHT RULES IN AN AGE OF EXTREME INEQUALITY (2020) (explaining the political strategy they call "plutocratic populism").

302. *See generally* J. Mitchell Pickerill, *Is the Roberts Court Business Friendly? Is the Pope Catholic?, in* BUSINESS AND THE ROBERTS COURT (Jonathan Adler ed. 2016) (describing the Roberts Court's exceptional degree of solicitude for business interests as less a departure than the continuation of a trend that has been underway since the mid-1970s).

9. Building a Democracy of Opportunity Today

1. Sabeel Rahman offers perhaps the most sustained and powerful contemporary effort to revive this older understanding. *See* K. SABEEL RAHMAN, DEMOCRACY AGAINST DOMINATION (2016) and K. SABEEL RAHMAN & HOLLIE RUSSON GILMAN, CIVIC POWER (2019).

2. *See* Robert C. Post, *Foreword: Fashioning the Legal Constitution: Culture, Courts, and Law,* 117 HARV. L. REV. 4, 9 (2003) (using this metaphor to depict the "free and continuous exchange between constitutional law and constitutional culture"). Post especially emphasizes how courts can move to allow more or less of this exchange to occur. Political actors outside the courts likewise make moves that shape what and how much is crossing this membrane each way.

3. A Republican Congress in 2017 failed to repeal the ACA, but eliminated one provision, the individual tax penalty for not having insurance. Some conservative states saw an opening for the most implausible challenge yet to the ACA. They claimed that because various parts of the act were "inseverable" from the individual mandate to purchase insurance, but that mandate was unconstitutional without the tax penalty, the whole act was now unconstitutional and unenforceable. This wild argument—which required contorting both the law of severability and the law of standing—won two votes at the Supreme Court. California v. Texas, No. 19-1019, 2021 WL 2459255, at *26 (U.S. June 17, 2021) (Alito, J., joined by Gorsuch, J., dissenting). The whole sorry episode suggests that a nontrivial number of conservative elected officials, judges, and justices are willing to champion nearly any conceivable argument for the unconstitutionality of the ACA, whatever its doctrinal form.

4. For a long period in American constitutional politics, roughly the first two-thirds of the twentieth century, these normal aspects of conflict in American constitutional politics were relatively muted because of the nonpolarized, ideologically mixed nature of the two political parties and elements of a constitutional consensus among the (white) American elite. On the relationship between this depolarized period and the dynamics of constitutional politics inside and outside the courts, see JACK BALKIN, THE CYCLES OF CONSTITUTIONAL TIME 112–55 (2020).

5. *See, e.g.,* Daniel Epps & Ganesh Sitaraman, *How to Save the Supreme Court,* 129 YALE L.J. 148, 170 (2019) (proposing two structural reforms "designed to preserve the Court as an institution that is not partisan": either populating the Court with a bipartisan balance of fifteen justices, five from each party and five chosen by the others, or else filling the Court with circuit judges chosen by lottery for short stints).

In spring 2021, the White House convened a commission to study the prospects of "reforming" the Supreme Court—an effort that sits in a complex relationship to the various calls among Democrats for more aggressive reforms, including enlarging the Court by adding new progressive Justices. The convening of this commission reflects the fact that the attention of Democratic voters and elected officials has begun to turn to the Court, but these are early days. It remains to be seen whether today's wave of would-be court reformers embrace a model of restoring a nonpartisan court, or challenging a partisan court through politics.

6. *See, e.g.,* Amicus Curiae Brief of Senator Sheldon Whitehouse et al., New York State Rifle & Pistol Ass'n, Inc. v. New York, No. 18–280 (explaining efforts of the Federalist Society and related gun rights advocacy groups to shape the Supreme Court's composition and enlist it in the "project" of expanding gun rights. The brief concludes: "Perhaps the Court can heal itself before the public demands it be 'restructured in order to reduce the influence of politics'"). We discuss structural reform proposals below.

7. We developed this conceptual typology in an early dialogue with Frank Michelman, to whom we are extremely grateful for pressing us on these points. *See* Frank I. Michelman, *The Unbearable Lightness of Tea Leaves: Constitutional Political Economy in Court,* 94 TEX. L. REV. 1403 (2016); Joseph Fishkin & William Forbath, *The Democracy of Opportunity and Constitutional Politics: A Response,* 94 TEX. L. REV. 1469 (2016).

8. *See* James B. Stewart, *How Broccoli Landed on Supreme Court Menu,* N.Y. TIMES, June 13, 2012 (tracing the argument's trajectory). All of the opinions in the case other than Justice Thomas's discuss the libertarian dystopian hypothetical of a government that requires individuals to purchase broccoli. National Federation of Independent Businesses v. Sebelius, 132 S. Ct. 2566, 2591 (2012) ("But cars and broccoli are no more purchased for their 'own sake' than health insurance."); *id.* at 2619–20 (Ginsburg, J., concurring in part, concurring in the judgment in part, and dissenting in part) (arguing that, although individuals may elect not to purchase broccoli during their lifetimes, they are certain to use health care services); *id.* at 2650 (joint dissent) (positing that, even if individuals elect not to purchase broccoli, such an election is not an activity that the government can regulate). For accounts of how such partisan arguments found their way into court in the ACA litigation, see Brian Highsmith, *Partisan Constitutionalism: Reconsidering the Role of Political Parties in Popular Constitutional Change,* 4 WISC. L. REV. 911 (2019); Mark D. Rosen & Christopher W. Schmidt, *Why Broccoli? Limiting Principles and Popular Constitutionalism in the Health Care Case,* 61 UCLA L. REV. 66 (2013).

9. This would have been the strongest argument for defending the constitutionality of the ACA in the second of its trips to the Supreme Court, King v. Burwell, 576 U.S. 473 (2015). But that was not the way the case was framed by either side.

10. For a helpful account of how judicial appointments became disconnected from constitutional politics in the twentieth century, under conditions of depolarized parties, *see* Mark Graber, *Judicial Supremacy and the Structure of Partisan Conflict,* 50 INDIANA L. REV. 141 (2016).

11. *See* "The Constitution: A 'Layman's Document,'" Chapter 6.

12. *See* "The Preeminence of the Court—For Liberals," Chapter 8.

13. *See, e.g.,* BALKIN, CYCLES OF CONSTITUTIONAL TIME, at 152–54.

14. The authority here begins with the Constitution's text, which refers to Congress creating "Exceptions" to the Court's jurisdiction. *See* U.S. CONST. art. III, § 2 ("the supreme Court shall have appellate Jurisdiction . . . with such Exceptions, and under such Regulations as the Congress shall make."). There is a large body of legal scholarship debating the potential scope of the jurisdiction-stripping power, which we will not attempt to summarize. The limits of this power are largely unknown; they will be defined and revised through future struggles between Congress and the Court. The Court, for instance, has staked out an important but narrow limitation on the jurisdiction-stripping power to the effect that Congress cannot strip courts of the jurisdiction to hear writs of habeas corpus by people in government custody. *See* Boumediene v. Bush, 553 U.S. 723, 771 (2008). However, the existence of some congressional power to remove jurisdiction is, as Charles Black once put it, "the rock on which rests the legitimacy of the judicial work in a democracy." Charles L. Black Jr., *The Presidency and Congress,* 32 WASH. & LEE L. REV. 841, 846 (1975). *See* Christopher Jon Sprigman, *Congress's Article III Power and the Process of Constitutional Change,* 95 N.Y.U. L. REV. 1778 (2020) (developing much more fully this argument that

congressional power to strip jurisdiction helps build the democratic legitimacy of the judgments of the courts).

15. This is not as unprecedented as it might sound. For example, Congress has exercised this power in statutes such as the Prison Litigation Reform Act (PLRA), 42 U.S.C. § 1997e (enacted 1996), to constrain and slow but not eliminate the federal courts' ability to hear constitutional claims by prisoners.

16. Michael Dorf has dubbed such provisions "fallback laws." *See* Michael C. Dorf, *Fallback Law*, 107 COLUMBIA L. REV. 303 (2007). Dorf argues that such fallbacks can be constitutionally questionable in certain circumstances—specifically, where the legislature is using them to coerce the Court for purposes that are arguably themselves constitutionally impermissible. In the cases we have in mind here, the purpose is more than merely permissible: it is arguably a matter of legislative constitutional obligation to enact such laws.

17. *See, e.g.,* Schenk v. United States, 249 U.S. 47 (1919) (socialist advocating draft resistance); Terminiello v. Chicago, 337 U.S. 1 (1949) (a Father Coughlin–like figure whose political diatribes provoked protesters into a near riot).

18. Janus v. AFSCME, 585 U.S. ___ (2018), 138 S. Ct. 2448, 2501 (2018).

19. The interests initiating and funding these claims have not necessarily been the objecting workers themselves. *See* "Labor as Countervailing Power," this chapter.

20. *See* David Singh Grewal & Jedediah Purdy, *Law and Neoliberalism,* 77 LAW & CONTEMP. PROBLEMS 1 (2015); K. SABEEL RAHMAN, DEMOCRACY AGAINST DOMINATION 109 (2016); Benjamin Sachs & Kate Andrias, *Constructing Countervailing Power: Law and Organizing in an Era of Political Inequality,* 130 YALE L.J. 546 (2021); Daryl J. Levinson, *The Supreme Court, 2015 Term—Foreword: Looking for Power in Public Law,* 130 HARVARD L. REV. 31, 101 (2016); Kate Andrias, *An American Approach to Social Democracy: The Forgotten Practice of the Fair Labor Standards Act,* 128 YALE L.J. 616, 641 (2019).

21. Jedediah Purdy, *Beyond the Bosses' Constitution: The First Amendment and Class Entrenchment,* 118 COLUMBIA L. REV. 2159, 2168 (2018).

22. *See* "The Copper Kings," Chapter 5.

23. Western Tradition Partnership v. Attorney General of Montana, 271 P.3d 1, 8, 9 (Mont. 2011) (internal quotation marks omitted) (first quoting MICHAEL P. MALONE & RICHARD B. ROEDER, MONTANA: A HISTORY OF TWO CENTURIES 176 (1976); then quoting HELEN FISK SANDERS, 1 HISTORY OF MONTANA 429 (1913)), *rev'd sub nom.* American Tradition Partnership v. Bullock, 132 S. Ct. 2490 (2012) (per curiam).

24. *See* American Tradition Partnership v. Bullock, 132 S. Ct. 2490 (2012) (per curiam).

25. New York Times Co. v. Sullivan, 376 U.S. 254, 270 (1964).

26. Arizona Free Enterprise Club's Freedom Club PAC v. Bennett, 564 U.S. 721, 749–50 (2011).

27. Davis v. Federal Election Commission, 554 U.S. 724 (2008) (federal millionaire's amendment); Arizona Free Enterprise Club's Freedom Club PAC v. Bennett, 564 U.S. 721 (2011) (invalidating Arizona's law granting extra public funds to candidates participating in public financing who faced either candidates or independent groups spending above certain threshold amounts to defeat them).

28. *Bennett,* 564 U.S. at 756 (Kagan, J., dissenting).

29. *See Bennett,* 564 U.S. at 746 (citing this disincentive).

30. Citizens United v. Federal Election Commission, 558 U.S. 310 (2010).

31. Austin v. Michigan Chamber of Commerce, 494 U.S. 652, 660 (1990).

32. *Citizens United,* 558 U.S. at 341.

33. Western Tradition Partnership, Inc. v. Attorney General, 271 P.3d 1 (Mont. 2011), *rev'd sub nom.* American Tradition Partnership, Inc. v. Bullock, 567 U.S. 516 (2012).

34. *See* "The Copper Kings," Chapter 5.

35. *Western Tradition Partnership,* 271 P.3d at 11.

36. *See* United States v. Sun Diamond Growers of California, 526 U.S. 398 (1999) (deciding that lavishing gifts does not necessarily constitute bribery); Skilling v. United States, 561 U.S. 358 (2010) (holding that mail-services fraud covers only bribery and kickback schemes); McDonnell v. United States, 579 U.S. ___, 136 S. Ct. 2355 (2016) (narrowly defining an "official act" for the purpose of federal bribery statutes); Kelly v. United States, 590 U.S. ___, 140 S. Ct. 1565 (2020) (holding that there can be no criminal fraud violation without intent to obtain money or property).

37. *See* Joseph Fishkin, *Who Is a Constituent?*, Balkinization (Apr. 3, 2014), https://balkin.blogspot.com/2014/04/who-is-constituent.html [https://perma.cc/FF9M-SA2G].

38. Arizona Free Enterprise Club's Freedom Club PAC v. Bennett, 564 U.S. 721, 757 (2011) (Kagan, J., dissenting) (citing New York Times Co. v. Sullivan, 376 U.S. 254, 269 (1964)). After all, the law simply gives some candidates additional money to pay for additional speech; it does not limit or block any speech.

39. *Sullivan,* 376 U.S. 254 (1964).

40. Citizens United v. Federal Election Commission, 558 U.S. 310, 394 (2010) (Stevens, J., concurring in part, dissenting in part) (emphasis added). Stevens, who retired later that year, was the only sitting Justice who would have been old enough to have any memory of FDR and the New Deal.

41. This sort of argument made the very occasional appearance in the congressional debate about the Bipartisan Campaign Reform Act (BCRA) itself. *See, e.g.,* Remarks of Senator Carl Levin (Congress has "the right to protect our democratic institutions from being undermined . . ."), 147 Cong. Rec. S3249 (daily ed. Apr. 2, 2001).

42. *Matching Funds Program: How It Works,* New York City Campaign Finance Board, https://www.nyccfb.info/program/how-it-works [https://perma.cc/P5VV-G39P]; *Matching Funds Program: What's New,* New York City Campaign Finance Board, https://www.nyccfb.info/program/what-s-new-in-the-campaign-finance-program-2/ [https://perma.cc/GW37-PN6F].

43. A related proposal would simply give "democracy vouchers" to all citizens of a jurisdiction, which citizens can give to campaigns, and campaigns can give to the state for cash. *Democracy Voucher Program: About the Program,* Seattle.gov, https://www.seattle.gov/democracyvoucher/about-the-program [https://perma.cc/R2C5-74V4].

44. *See* H.R. 1, For the People Act of 2021, § 5111 (offering a 6:1 match). Critics of this model of campaign finance argue that it can increase polarization in legislatures by pushing candidates to reflect the highly polarized views of the more politically engaged part of the public. *See* Richard H. Pildes, *Small-Donor-Based Campaign-Finance Reform and Political Polarization,* 129 Yale L. J. Forum 149 (2019). That is a perfectly good reason to support direct public financing regimes (which we support); perhaps such regimes are in some respects ideal. However, especially in a highly polarized and fractured polity, it is difficult to determine in a fair way which candidates deserve public financing—and most mechanisms for answering that question are subject to some degree of capture by those with significant political and economic power. Small donor match is a way of deciding who should get the public campaign money that is less subject to capture by oligarchy.

45. *See* Brian J. McCabe & Jennifer A. Herwig, *Diversifying the Donor Pool: How Did Seattle's Democracy Voucher Program Reshape Participation in Municipal Campaign Finance?*, 18 Election L.J. 323, 336–37 (2019); Elisabeth Genn, Sundeep Iyer, Michael J. Malbin, & Brendan Galvin, *Donor Diversity Through Public Matching Funds,* Brennan Center For Justice (May 12, 2012), https://www.brennancenter.org/sites/default/files/2019-08/Report_DonorDiversity-public-matching-funds.PDF [https://perma.cc/24DE-EWPS].

46. The FCC's "lowest unit charge" rule, *see* 47 C.F.R. §73.1942 (1992), means that when a campaign buys even a single advertisement, it gets the same discounts as the largest advertiser buying many; the rule insulates campaigns from the bidding wars that sometimes occur as deep-pocketed interests buy up advertising in close races.

47. Indeed, this is part of congressional Democrats' current election reform package. *See* For the People Act of 2021, H.R. 1, 117th Cong. (2021), Title I. On the potential reach of the Elections Clause, see generally FRANITA TOLSON, IN CONGRESS WE TRUST? THE EVOLUTION OF FEDERAL VOTING RIGHTS ENFORCEMENT FROM THE FOUNDING TO THE JIM CROW ERA (forthcoming).

48. *See, e.g.,* H.B. 1355 (Fla. 2011) (introducing restrictions on voter-registration drives and reducing early voting days and hours); Michael C. Herron & Daniel A. Smith, *The Effects of House Bill 1355 on Voter Registration in Florida,* 13 STATE POLITICS & POLICY Q. 279, 281–82 (2013); Fla. Stat. § 97.0575(3)(a) (2011) (reducing the window of time for organizations conducting voter-registration drives to submit voter-registration applications from ten days to forty-eight hours), *invalidated by* League of Women Voters of Florida v. Browning, 863 F. Supp. 2d 1155 (N.D. Fla. 2012); S.B. 9, 86th Leg. (Tex. 2019) (bill that passed the Senate but failed in the House that proposed escalating the penalty for mistakes on a voter registration form from a Class B misdemeanor to a state jail felony and adding obstacles to individuals transporting voters to the polls); Tex. Elec. Code § 13.031 (requiring re-registration for volunteer deputy registrants conducting voter-registration drives every two years); Tex. Elec. Code § 13.044 (1986) (making it a misdemeanor to register voters from another county).

49. Novel doctrinal ideas become politically and then legally plausible, at least within one side's political coalition, as they propagate back and forth across the thin membrane separating politics outside the courts from law inside. *See* Jack M. Balkin, *From Off the Wall to On the Wall: How the Mandate Challenge Went Mainstream,* THE ATLANTIC (June 4, 2012), https://www.theatlantic.com/national/archive/2012/06/from-off-the-wall-to-on-the-wall-how-the-mandate-challenge-went-mainstream/258040/ [https://perma.cc/ZJ9F-EEG7]; JACK M. BALKIN, LIVING ORIGINALISM 330–32 (2011).

50. *See* "Labor, Constitutional Laissez-Faire, and *Lochner v. New York*," Chapter 4; "The Labor Question," Chapter 5.

51. Robert Wagner, *"Industrial Democracy" and Cooperations,* Radio Address at the National Democratic Club 4–5 (May 8, 1937), *quoted in* Mark Barenberg, *The Political Economy of the Wagner Act: Power, Symbol, and Workplace Cooperation,* 106 HARVARD L. REV. 1379, 1424 n. 208 (1993).

52. 79 Cong. Rec. 9714 (1935) (statement of Rep. Truax); *see* James Gray Pope, *The Thirteenth Amendment Versus the Commerce Clause: Labor and the Shaping of American Constitutional Law, 1921–1957,* 102 COLUM. L. REV. 1, 49 (2002); "The Wagner Act and New Deal Constitutional Political Economy," Chapter 6.

53. Pope, *The Thirteenth Amendment,* at 47 (2002) (quoting letter from Andrew Furuseth to Robert Wagner). *See* "The Wagner Act and New Deal Constitutional Political Economy," Chapter 6.

54. *See* "The New Dealers Take Up the Mantle of Antitrust," Chapter 6 (discussing inter alia the U.S. Steel case).

55. *See* "The Taming of Labor and the Eclipse of Progressive Constitutional Political Economy," Chapter 7.

56. Abood v. Detroit Board of Education, 431 U.S. 209, 235–36 (1977).

57. Thornhill v. Alabama, 310 U.S. 88, 103 (1940).

58. *See, e.g.,* NLRB v. Retail Store Employees Local 1001, 447 U.S. 607 (1980). For recent cases relying on the Court's teaching that the First Amendment does not safeguard labor boycotts and picketing, because they are economic and not political activity, *see, e.g.,* NLRB v. Teamsters Union Local No. 70, 668 F. App'x 283, 284 (9th Cir. 2016) (upholding the NLRA's prohibition against peaceful secondary picketing against constitutional challenge because the Supreme Court "has recognized that picketing might have a coercive effect, not entitling it to full First Amendment protection").

59. Janus v. AFSCME, 585 U.S. ___, 138 S. Ct. 2448, 2486 (2018).

60. The case was brought by a Republican politician, Illinois governor Bruce Rauner, who attempted to eliminate agency fees by executive order, and brought this lawsuit seeking to create a legal basis for this action. (When a district judge determined that Rauner lacked standing, Mark Janus, a teacher who did not want to pay the fee, was added and became the lead plaintiff. *See* Rauner v. AFSCME, 2015 WL 2385698 (N.D. Ill. May 19, 2015)).

61. Donald J. Trump (@realDonaldTrump), TWITTER (June 27, 2018, 10:11 A.M.) https://twitter .com/realDonaldTrump/status/1011975204778729474 [https://perma.cc/U7E5-SNZJ].

62. *See* MARK TUSHNET, TAKING BACK THE CONSTITUTION 59–65 (2020) (detailing this effort to defund the contributors to the Democratic Party).

63. *See* Ill. Exec. Order No. 15-13 (Feb. 9, 2015), https://www2.illinois.gov/Documents/ExecOrders /2015/ExecutiveOrder2015-13.pdf [https://perma.cc/45GH-GP3D] (detailing similar arguments that "at least in part because of the cost of wage, benefits, and pension packages obtained by state employee unions . . . with the use of compelled 'fair share' fees, the State of Illinois currently has a staggering structural budget deficit and unfunded pension liability").

64. Janus v. AFSCME, 585 U.S. ___, 138 S. Ct. 2448 (2018).

65. *See* Int'l Ass'n. of Machinists v. Street, 367 U.S. 740, 806 (1961) (Frankfurter, J., dissenting).

66. *Id.* at 805–6. He noted that life is full of "analogies" where "a minority of a legally recognized group may at times see an organization's funds used for promotion of ideas opposed by the minority." Governments, to take the most obvious such analogy, regularly "expend[] revenue collected from individual taxpayers to propagandize ideas which many taxpayers oppose." *Id.* at 808.

67. *Id.* at 814–15.

68. *Id.* at 800.

69. For an account of this congressionally constructed system, and a careful analysis of how the Court's First Amendment attack on agency fees ignores and subverts the logic of that system, see Cynthia Estlund, *Are Unions a Constitutional Anomaly?*, 114 MICH. L. REV. 169 (2015). For a defense of the proposition that workers who vote against union representation may fairly be constrained to abide with the majority of their fellow workers' decision in favor of union representation and collective bargaining—one grounded in democratic theory and an outlook on constitutional political economy akin to our own—see Jedediah Purdy, *Beyond the Bosses' Constitution: The First Amendment and Class Entrenchment*, 118 COLUM. L. REV. 2161 (2018).

70. *Janus,* 138 S. Ct. at 2501 (Kagan, J., dissenting).

71. *Id.* at 2489.

72. *See* "The Wagner Act and New Deal Constitutional Political Economy," Chapter 6.

73. *See* Jeff Larrimore et al., *Report on the Economic Well-Being of U.S. Households in 2017,* FEDERAL RESERVE (May 2018), at 21, https://www.federalreserve.gov/publications/files/2017-report -economic-well-being-us-households-201805.pdf [https://perma.cc/G4EZ-3QD2] (noting that four in ten adults would need to sell property or borrow money, or would not be able to pay at all, if confronted with a $400 expense).

74. *See generally* RICHARD B. FREEDMAN & JOEL ROGERS, WHAT WORKERS WANT (2006); JAKE ROSENFELD, WHAT UNIONS NO LONGER DO (2014).

75. Kate Andrias, *Peril and Possibility: Strikes, Rights, and Legal Change in the Age of Trump,* 40 BERKELEY J. EMP. & LAB. L. 135, 137 n.19 (collecting sources on failure of labor law to protect concerted action); Kate Andrias, *The New Labor Law,* 126 YALE L.J. 2, 25–32 (2016) (summarizing scholarly consensus that the hollowing out of the NLRA is an important cause of labor's decline); Cynthia L. Estlund, *The Ossification of American Labor Law,* 102 COLUM. L. REV. 1527, 1529–30 (2002).

76. *See* Estlund, *Ossification of American Labor Law,* at 1535–40; Eric Levitz, *Democrats Paid a Huge Price for Letting Unions Die,* NY MAG.: DAILY INTELLIGENCER, Jan. 26, 2018, http://nymag

.com/daily/intelligencer/2018/01/democrats-paid-a-huge-price-for-letting-unions-die.html (last visited June 28, 2021) ("[U]nder Jimmy Carter, Bill Clinton, and Barack Obama[,] Democrats failed to pass labor law reforms that would [] bolster the union cause. In hindsight, it's clear that the Democratic Party didn't merely betray organized labor with these failures, but also, itself.").

77. This change was visible in the platforms of prominent presidential candidates and the Democratic Party platform itself. *See The Workplace Democracy Plan*, BERNIE, https://berniesanders.com/issues/workplace-democracy [https://perma.cc/5PCP-AQCH]; *Empowering American Workers and Raising Wages*, WARREN DEMOCRATS, https://elizabethwarren.com/plans/empowering-american-workers [https://perma.cc/N7PK-RHXJ]; DEMOCRATIC NAT'L CONVENTION, 2020 DEMOCRATIC PARTY PLATFORM 14–16 (2020), https://www.demconvention.com/wp-content/uploads/2020/08/2020-07-31-Democratic-Party-Platform-For-Distribution.pdf [https://perma.cc/PZF8-Y2A6].

78. *See* President Biden (@POTUS), TWITTER (March 1, 2021, 1:01 A.M.), https://twitter.com/potus/status/1366191901196644354 [https://perma.cc/SK8E-CZJS] (President Biden posts a tweet and video referencing an organizing drive in Alabama and championing workers' right to organize and form unions free from employer interference).

79. Protecting the Right to Organize Act of 2021, H.R. 842, 117th Cong. (2021). The bill would, among other things, repeal restrictions on secondary boycotts and preempt key features of state "right-to-work" laws.

80. On the illegalities of the teachers' strikes and how the strikers contended with them, see Andrias, *Peril and Possibility*, at 140–48; *see also* William E. Forbath, *Janus in Appalachia*, LAW & POLITICAL ECONOMY (Feb. 13, 2019), https://lpeproject.org/blog/janus-in-appalachia/.

81. *Cf.* James Gray Pope et al., *The Right to Strike*, BOSTON REV., May 22, 2017, http://bostonreview.net/forum/james-gray-pope-ed-bruno-peter-kellman-right-strike [https://perma.cc/YMA3-4DSM] ("American workers have never won a significant piece of workers' rights legislation without first engaging in exactly the kind of strikes and other forms of noncooperation that current labor laws forbid.").

82. Cedar Point Nursery v. Hassid, 141 S. Ct. 2063 (2021).

83. *Id.* at 2072, 2079.

84. *Id.* at 2069. The majority duly notes that this was the point of the regulation, but does not mention or discuss it any further, except by way of holding that such "self-organization rights of employees" fall outside the Court's newly crafted constitutionalized common-law baseline.

85. *Id.* at 2089 (Breyer, J., dissenting).

86. *Id.* The dissent mentions "higher standards of living," but does not develop the idea or suggest that it could have any constitutional relevance.

87. If the PRO Act were to become law, such a *Janus*-based challenge would certainly confront its Section 111 ("Fair Share Agreement Permitted"), which would preempt state right-to-work laws so that unions could negotiate agreements with employers that require nonunion members to pay a fee for union administration of collective contracts. *See* H.R. 842, 117th Cong. §111 (2021) (adding language to NLRA to preempt state prohibitions on voluntary fair share agreements). This is the kind of agreement that *Abood* allowed, and the *Janus* Court struck down, in the context of public employee unions. We have not yet seen the private sector version of this case. Labor law scholars and union activists have strong arguments (based mainly on the state action doctrine) for why the private sector context is different from the public sector. But there is reason to be skeptical of whether those arguments will prevail in the Roberts Court.

88. U.S. v. Lopez, 514 U.S. 549, 568–583 (1995) (Kennedy, J., concurring).

89. *See* Chapter 6.

90. A cohort of the country's leading union lawyers and labor law academics (along with labor economists, sociologists, and activists) have begun making that case. Calling themselves the "Clean Slate for Worker Power" project, they have framed their lengthy array of proposals around

the proposition that sweeping labor law reform is a constitutional essential. Their 2020 report, *Clean Slate for Worker Power: Building a Just Economy and Democracy,* begins, like this book, at the beginning: "Since the founding of the country, concentration of power in the hands of a small minority has been recognized as a threat—perhaps the primary threat to the viability of American democracy." If "we are to have a republican form of government, not an oligarchy or an aristocracy," if we are going to "preserve democracy in the face of [our time's] . . . dual crises [of mutually reinforcing economic and political] inequality," then it is indispensable to "rewrit[e] American labor law in a manner that is explicitly designed to enable workers to build collective economic and political power," write the project's directors. Sharon Block & Benjamin Sachs, *Clean Slate for Worker Power: Building a Just Economy and Democracy* 7 (2020), https://perma .cc/4JZP-4UKU.

91. This paragraph and the next draw heavily on William E. Forbath and Brishen Rogers, *New Workers, New Labor Laws,* N.Y. Times, Sept. 4, 2017, at A21.

92. *See* H.R. 842, 117th Cong. §101(b) (2021) (broadening the NLRA's definition of employee to include any "individual performing any service" no matter her immediate employer, unless that individual meets a stringent definition of freedom from control "both under the contract for performance of the service and in fact" to prevent mischaracterization of workers as independent contractors); *see also* H.R. 842, 117th Cong. §104(1) (2021) (making it an unfair labor practice under NLRA to "communicate or misrepresent" to employees that they are not defined as an employee under the amended NLRA).

93. We saw in Chapter 6 that the New Deal Congress originally built a role for industry-wide, tripartite (capital, labor, government) negotiations right into the administration of the Fair Labor Standards Act (FLSA) with respect to minimum wages and maximum hours. This corporatist idea of authorizing unions to represent all workers (and employers' associations, all employers) in industry-wide settling of minimum standards has been revived in a bill amending the FLSA that the Service Employees International Union (SEIU) has brought to Congress. *See* Kate Andrias, *The New Labor Law,* 126 Yale L.J. 2, 46–51 (2016). It has been rekindled and put into practice on the state level in New York, the site of the key subnational dress rehearsal for New Deal labor law reform. *See id.* at 64–66.

The details matter here; calling a scheme "sectoral bargaining" does not ensure that the balance of bargaining power is fair to workers. For discussion and a wise set of proposals about implementing sectoral bargaining, see Block & Sachs, *Clean Slate for Worker Power,* at 37–45.

94. *See* Block & Sachs, *Clean Slate for Worker Power,* at 13.

95. Alex Gourevitch, *The Right to Strike: A Radical View,* 112 Am. Pol. Sci. Rev. 905, 905 (2018) (describing scholarly consensus).

96. *See* Pope et al., *Right to Strike* (on which this paragraph draws heavily). *See also* James Gray Pope, *Labor's Constitution of Freedom,* 106 Yale L.J. 941 (1997); James Gray Pope, *Republican Moments: The Role of Direct Popular Power in the American Constitutional Order,* 139 U. Penn. L. Rev. 287 (1990).

97. The Committee on Freedom of Association of the International Labor Organization has held that the United States is violating international standards (to which it has signed on) by failing to protect the right to organize, by banning all secondary strikes and boycotts, and by allowing employers to permanently replace workers who strike. *See* Lance A. Compa, Unfair Advantage: Workers' Freedom of Association in The United States under International Human Rights Standards 18, 31, 171–90, 209–13 (2000).

98. *See* Pope et al., *Right to Strike.*

99. House Education & Labor Committee, Protecting the Right to Organize Act: Section by Section, https://edlabor.house.gov/imo/media/doc/Section%20by%20Section%20-%20PRO%20 Act.pdf [https://perma.cc/WV3H-QTML]. *See* PRO Act, Section 104, H.R. 842, 117th Cong. §104(2) (2021) (deleting prohibitions on secondary actions from the NLRA). For the current pro-

hibitions, *see* 29 U.S.C. §158(b)(4) (prohibitions on secondary actions). Section 104 of the act also removes paragraph (7), which outlaws any union effort "to picket or cause to be picketed, or threaten to picket or cause to be picketed, any employer where an object thereof is forcing or requiring an employer to recognize or bargain with a labor organization as the representative of his employees. . . ." 29 U.S.C. §158.

100. *See* Int'l Brotherhood of Electric Workers v. NLRB, 341 U.S. 694 (1951) (Section 8(b)(4)(A) of NLRA, barring secondary picketing and boycotts, "carries no unconstitutional abridgement of free speech.").

101. Here again, we draw the work of James Gray Pope, cited above.

102. *See "In re Debs:* 'A Lesson Which Cannot Be Learned Too Soon,'" Chapter 4; "The Labor Question," Chapter 5.

103. *See* Pope et al., *Right to Strike.*

104. *See* Sidney Fine, *The General Motors Sit-Down Strike: A Re-Examination*, 70 AM. HISTORICAL REV. 691, 698 (1965) (Governor Murphy "saw the union as using the means at its disposal to safeguard its rights and as fighting back against the employer violation of the Wagner Act and . . . told the GM negotiators that the occupation of their factories went 'deeper into social and economic questions' than did the ordinary violation of property rights.").

105. *See, e.g.,* Duplex v. Deering, 254 U.S. 443, 479–88 (1921) (Brandeis, Holmes, and Clarke, J., dissenting); Bedford Cut Stone Co. v. Journeymen Stone Cutters' Ass'n of North America, 274 U.S. 37, 65 (1927) (Brandeis, J., dissenting).

106. Among other sites of resistance, this cultural and legal forgetting has been resisted by important movements in legal thought—critical race theory, above all. From the start, critical race scholars spotlighted the ways in which racial subordination was baked into the nation's distribution of wealth and power and educational and employment opportunities in ways that even the most robust judicial accounts of race discrimination obscured—and that conservative doctrinal developments in the antidiscrimination law of the 1980s and 1990s seemed designed to perpetuate and protect, instead of helping to undo. *See, e.g.,* Derrick A. Bell Jr., Brown v. Board of Education *and the Interest-Convergence Dilemma*, 93 HARV. L. REV. 518 (1980); Kimberlé Williams Crenshaw, *Race, Reform, and Retrenchment: Transformation and Legitimation in Antidiscrimination Law*, 101 HARV. L. REV. 1331 (1988); Cheryl I. Harris, *Whiteness as Property*, 106 HARV. L. REV. 1709 (1993); DARIA ROITHMAYR, REPRODUCING RACISM: HOW EVERYDAY CHOICES LOCK IN WHITE ADVANTAGE (2014).

107. To understand the shape of this conflict in constitutional politics, inside and outside the legal system, see Reva B. Siegel, *Equality Talk: Antisubordination and Anticlassification Values in Constitutional Struggles over Brown*, 117 HARV. L. REV. 1470 (2004). For an analysis of the conflict as it emerged, see Crenshaw, *Race, Reform, and Retrenchment.*

108. *See, e.g.,* Ricci v. DeStefano, 557 U.S. 557, 594–96 (Scalia, J., concurring) (suggesting that the disparate-impact provision of Title VII violates the equal protection guarantee of the Fourteenth Amendment). *See also* Richard Primus, *The Future of Disparate Impact*, 108 MICH. L. REV. 1341, 1384–87 (2010); Michelle Adams, *Is Integration a Discriminatory Purpose?*, 96 IOWA L. REV. 837 (2011).

109. Why "so-called"? Because in reality, a private ordering is hardly an ordering at all unless it is built on the public enforcement power of government. *See generally* JOSEPH W. SINGER, NO FREEDOM WITHOUT REGULATION: THE HIDDEN LESSON OF THE SUBPRIME CRISIS (2015). We will use the term anyway, lacking a better one. For exploration focused on racial subordination, see ROITHMAYR, REPRODUCING RACISM; Harris, *Whiteness as Property.*

110. Civil Rights Act of 1866, ch. 31, 14 Stat. 27 (codified as amended at 42 U.S.C. § 1981 (1991)).

111. Thaddeus Stevens, Address to Pennsylvania Republican Convention (1865), quoted in ERIC FONER, THE RECONSTRUCTION ERA AND THE FRAGILITY OF DEMOCRACY 236 (1988).

112. *See* Chapter 3.

113. *See* "Poverty, Race, and the Abandonment of Political Economy in the Great Society," Chapter 8.

114. *See* IRA KATZNELSON, FEAR ITSELF: THE NEW DEAL AND THE ORIGINS OF OUR TIME 159–61 (2013).

115. *See* "The Conservative Counterrevolution Begins," Chapter 7. These exclusions were undone by the Social Security Act Amendments of 1950; *see* Chapter 8 n.106.

116. *See* KATZNELSON, FEAR ITSELF, at 163.

117. Similarly, as Judith Resnik has shown, we have systematically pushed authority to adjudicate claims of gender-related injustice downward from the federal level to lower levels of government—with similar effect. *See* Judith Resnik, *"Naturally" Without Gender: Women, Jurisdiction, and the Federal Courts,* 66 N.Y.U. L. REV. 1682, 1759 (1991).

118. *See* Tomiko Brown-Nagin, *Two Americas in Healthcare: Federalism and Wars over Poverty from the New Deal–Great Society to Obamacare,* 62 DRAKE L. REV. 981, 991–98 (2014).

119. *See* SHANNA ROSE, FINANCING MEDICAID: FEDERALISM AND THE GROWTH OF AMERICA'S HEALTH CARE SAFETY NET (2013); Stephen Griffin, *Race, Federalism, and Constitutional Change* (paper presented at The Present and Future of Civil Rights Movements: Race and Reform in 21st Century America, Duke Law School, Nov. 20–21, 2015).

120. National Fed'n of Indep. Bus. v. Sebelius, 567 U.S. 519, 583 (2012).

121. *Id.* at 583, 579, 581.

122. *See* Joseph Fishkin, *The Dignity of the South,* 123 YALE L.J. ONLINE 175, 180 (2013) (discussing Shelby County). *See* Griffin, *Race, Federalism, and Constitutional Change* (discussing the lack of attention to the Civil War and Reconstruction in the constitutional assumptions underlying this part of *Sebelius*).

123. As it turned out, the Medicaid holding of *Sebelius*, and the subsequent nonexpansion across the South, resulted in an estimated 15,000 otherwise preventable deaths in just the first four years, just among adults aged fifty-five to sixty-four (the most vulnerable group), according to the best estimate available. *See* Sarah Miller et al., *Medicaid and Mortality: New Evidence from Linked Survey and Administrative Data,* NBER Working Paper No. 26081 (2021), https://www.nber.org/papers/w26081 [https://perma.cc/32JJ-HN2U]. For each of those deaths, a much larger but harder-to-estimate number of Americans were consigned to various degrees of economic precarity and personal risk, and in that way lost the security of being truly in the middle class.

124. *See* Rachel Garfield et al., *The Coverage Gap: Uninsured Poor Adults in States That Do Not Expand Medicaid,* KAISER FAM. FOUND. (2021), https://www.kff.org/medicaid/issue-brief/the-coverage-gap-uninsured-poor-adults-in-states-that-do-not-expand-medicaid/ [https://perma.cc/HXX9-987R].

125. Authors' calculations, based on *Status of State Medicaid Expansion Decisions: Interactive Map,* KAISER FAM. FOUND. (2020), https://www.kff.org/medicaid/issue-brief/status-of-state-medicaid-expansion-decisions-interactive-map/ [https://perma.cc/MH2W-7H7L], and 2019 Census population estimates.

126. *See* Samantha Artiga et al., *Changes in Health Coverage by Race and Ethnicity Since Implementation of the ACA, 2013–2017,* KAISER FAM. FOUND. (2020), https://www.kff.org/disparities-policy/issue-brief/changes-in-health-coverage-by-race-and-ethnicity-since-implementation-of-the-aca-2013-2017/ [https://perma.cc/M55Y-AW52]. As this book was going to press, the Congressional Black Caucus, Congressional Hispanic Caucus, and Congressional Asian Pacific Islander Caucus wrote a joint open letter to congressional leaders urging them to close this Medicaid "coverage gap," noting that "almost 60 percent of people affected by the coverage gap are Black, Hispanic, Asian, or Pacific Islander." Robin L. Kelly et al., Tri-Caucus Letter to Close Medicaid Coverage Gap, June 16, 2021, at 1, https://perma.cc/XHY2-ZL4W.

127. Bayard Rustin, *From Protest to Politics: The Future of the Civil Rights Movement,* COMMENTARY, Feb. 1965, https://www.commentarymagazine.com/articles/bayard-rustin-2/from

-protest-to-politics-the-future-of-the-civil-rights-movement/ [https://perma.cc/D28A-NTJZ]. *See* Chapter 8.

128. Shelby County v. Holder, 570 U.S. 529, 540 (2013).

129. *See* Fishkin, *Dignity of the South,* at 193; Zachary S. Price, *NAMUDNO's Non-Existent Principle of State Equality,* 88 N.Y.U. L. REV. ONLINE 24, 27–29 (2013).

130. It is hardly worthy of mention, but the Court signaled its novel anti–Voting Rights Act equal sovereignty principle a few years earlier, in NAMUDNO v. Holder, 557 U.S. 193 (2009). More interestingly, the leading permissive spending clause case, South Dakota v. Dole, 483 U.S. 203 (1987), did contemplate the potential for an anticoercion jurisprudence, perhaps akin to what the Court built in *Sebelius.* But *Dole* never remotely contemplated a scenario in which the Constitution would require that states be given the option to revive their older, stingier federal program in place of a new, more comprehensive (and more political-economy-altering) one. To reach that outcome, as the Court did in *Sebelius,* one must take the political economy of health care very seriously—and view states as having a kind of implicit entitlement to maintain theirs.

131. *See* S. Rep. No. 97-417, 97th Cong., 2d Sess. (1982), at 28–29 (listing "the extent to which minority group members bear the effects of discrimination in areas such as education, employment, and health, which hinder their ability to participate effectively in the political process" as one of the factors relevant to whether, in the totality of the circumstances, an election practice violates Section 2).

132. *See, e.g.,* Texas v. Holder, 888 F. Supp. 2d 113 (D.D.C. 2012), vacated and remanded, 570 U.S. 928 (2013). That special three-judge trial court held: "A law that forces poorer citizens to choose between their wages and their franchise unquestionably denies or abridges their right to vote. . . . To be sure, a section 5 case cannot turn on wealth alone. In Texas, however, the poor are disproportionately racial minorities," and racial minorities also disproportionately lack access to a vehicle. *Id.* at 140. Therefore, Texas' voter ID law "will almost certainly have [a] retrogressive effect" under Section 5 of the Voting Rights Act. *Id.* at 144. This decision was vacated following *Shelby County's* evisceration of Section 5.

133. Brnovich v. Democratic Nat'l Comm., No. 19-1257, 2021 WL 2690267, at *13 (U.S. July 1, 2021).

134. Regarding the impossibility of isolating race from party, see Richard L. Hasen, *Race or Party, Race as Party, or Party All the Time: Three Uneasy Approaches to Conjoined Polarization in Redistricting and Voting Cases,* 59 WM. & MARY L. REV. 1837 (2018).

135. On the reach of congressional power in this field, see FRANITA TOLSON, IN CONGRESS WE TRUST?: THE EVOLUTION OF FEDERAL VOTING RIGHTS ENFORCEMENT FROM THE FOUNDING TO THE JIM CROW ERA (forthcoming 2021).

136. *See* WILLIAM N. ESKRIDGE JR. & JOHN FEREJOHN, A REPUBLIC OF STATUTES (2010).

137. Indeed, there are strong grounds for viewing these statutes in this way without reference to the anti-oligarchy tradition. *See id.* at 9–24 (discussing these statutes and the indicia that they are best understood as superstatutes).

138. Circuit City Stores, Inc. v. Adams, 532 U.S. 105, 124–27 (2001) (Stevens, J., dissenting); *id.* at 133–40 (Souter, J., dissenting).

139. Alexander v. Gardner-Denver Co., 415 U.S. 36 (1974) (8–0 decision). Claims by more recent and narrower majorities to have limited rather than overturned *Gardner-Denver* are unconvincing.

140. Gilmer v. Interstate/Johnson Lane Corp., 500 U.S. 20 (1991); 14 Penn Plaza LLC v. Pyett, 556 U.S. 247 (2009). *See* J. Maria Glover, *Disappearing Claims and the Erosion of Substantive Law,* 124 YALE L.J. 3052, 3059–64 (2015).

141. Epic Systems Corp. v. Lewis, 138 S. Ct. 1612 (2018).

142. Lamps Plus, Inc. v. Varela, 139 S. Ct. 1407, 1416 (2019) (quoting Stolt-Nielsen S.A. v. Animal-Feeds Int'l Corp., 599 U.S. 662, 684 (2010)).

143. *Lamps Plus,* 139 S. Ct. at 1416.

144. Bostock v. Clayton County, 140 S. Ct. 1731, 1754 (2020).

145. *See* Little Sisters of the Poor Saints Peter and Paul Home v. Pennsylvania, 140 S. Ct. 2367 (2020).

146. *Cf.* Burwell v. Hobby Lobby Stores, 573 U.S. 682 (2014) (pressing the limits in a different way, by holding that corporations, at least closely held ones, have First Amendment free exercise rights that can trump public law protections for employees).

147. *See generally* Elizabeth Sepper, *Free Exercise Lochnerism*, 115 Colum. L. Rev. 1453 (2015).

148. For more on the staggering Black–white wealth gap, *see* Kriston McIntosh et al., *Examining the Black-White Wealth Gap*, Brookings Institution (Feb. 27, 2020), https://perma.cc/P2NL-GKVA. For more about the historical roots of the gap, see Melvin L. Oliver & Thomas M. Shapiro, Black Wealth/White Wealth: A New Perspective on Racial Inequality 13–23, 39–47 (2d ed. 2006). On historical and modern examples of the expropriation of Black wealth and the rigorous de jure exclusion of Black America from the great federally sponsored opportunities for mass homeownership and wealth accumulation in the banking and housing contexts, respectively, see Mehrsa Baradaran, The Color of Money: Black Banks and the Racial Wealth Gap (2017); Richard Rothstein, The Color of Law: A Forgotten History of How Our Government Segregated America 153–75 (2017).

149. Thomas Piketty, Capital in the Twenty-First Century 348 (Arthur Goldhammer trans., 2014); Emmanuel Saez & Gabriel Zucman, *Wealth Inequality in the United States Since 1913: Evidence from Capitalized Income Tax Data*, 131 Q. J. of Econ. 519, 520 (2016); *see also* Ethan Wolff-Mann, Super Rich's Wealth Concentration Surpasses Gilded Age Levels, Yahoo Finance, July 7, 2021, https://uk.finance.yahoo.com/news/super-richs-wealth-concentration-surpasses-gilded-age-levels-210802327.html [https://perma.cc/DK6K-X7HR] (reporting unpublished calculations by Gabriel Zucman, based on new data as this book was going to press, showing that as of 2021, the richest 0.01 percent of families, about 18,000 families, hold 10 percent of the nation's wealth, surpassing the 9 percent that such families owned in 1913 at the peak of the last Gilded Age, and as compared to 2 percent that such families owned in the 1970s).

150. We discuss these points, and the literatures exploring them, in the Introduction.

151. On the economic justice platform and policy vision of Movement for Black Lives, see *Economic Justice*, Movement 4 Black Lives, https://m4bl.org/policy-platforms/economic-justice [https://perma.cc/9KB5-9UXT]. On Barber's Third Reconstruction, see William J. Barber, The Third Reconstruction: Moral Mondays, Fusion Politics, and the Rise of a New Justice Movement (2016). For leading lawmakers' proposals to address the racial wealth gap, *see, e.g., Booker, Pressley Reintroduce "Baby Bonds" Legislation to Combat Wealth Inequality*, Cory Booker (July 26, 2019), https://www.booker.senate.gov/news/press/booker-pressley-reintroduce-and-ldquobaby-bonds-and-rdquo-legislation-to-combat-wealth-inequality [https://perma.cc/AQ5C-9T9Q] (reintroducing legislation for "baby bonds" that would "giv[e] all American children an opportunity to generate wealth" and would "nearly close the racial wealth gap"); Elizabeth Warren, *Leveling the Playing Field for Entrepreneurs of Color*, Medium: Team Warren (June 14, 2019), https://medium.com/@teamwarren/leveling-the-playing-field-for-entrepreneurs-2a585aa2b6d7 [https://perma.cc/CJ9B-QMKX] (proposing a Small Business Equity Fund, funded by a wealth tax, and framing its purpose in terms of closing racial wealth gaps and boosting capital access for entrepreneurs of color); *Tom Will Fight for Economic Justice*, Tom Steyer 2020, https://perma.cc/KS52-FR6W (proposing to "close the racial wealth gap" by, inter alia, "enact[ing] a wealth tax on the richest families").

152. *See* "The Political Economy of Slavery," Chapter 1. *See also* Bruce Ackerman, *Taxation and the Constitution*, 99 Colum. L. Rev. 1, 4 (1999). As we observed in Chapter 1, the constitutional text itself clearly reflects this compromise. The same sentence in Article I, Section 2, Clause 3 apportions both "Representatives and direct Taxes"—and all according to "the whole number of

free persons . . . and three fifths of all other Persons" (slaves) in each state. *See* U.S. CONST. art. 1, § 2, cl. 3.

153. *See* "The Court and the Income Tax," Chapter 4.

154. *See* Eisner v. Macomber, 252 U.S. 189 (1920).

155. *See* "Thomas Jefferson and Initial Endowments as Constitutional Essentials," Chapter 1. This strategy would also require finding a way to tax the new forms of dynastic intergenerational trusts, such as "Dynasty Trusts," whose very existence would have utterly appalled Jefferson and for good reason. *See* Note, *Dynasty Trusts and the Rule Against Perpetuities,* 116 Harv. L. Rev. 2588, 2590–95 (2003) (describing the rise of "Dynasty Trusts" in state law).

156. Ending the step-up in basis at death rule would go a long way by itself toward taxing wealth. *See* Calvin Johnson, *Gain Realized in Life Should Not Disappear by a Step-Up in Basis,* 156 TAX NOTES 1305 (2017), available at https://ssrn.com/abstract=3068814. Others argue for a tax on capital, rather than returns to capital, by taxing securities (and separately taxing corporate assets outside of securities markets). *See* Mark Gergen, A Securities Tax and the Problems of Taxing Global Capital (June 2, 2020) (unpublished manuscript), https://ssrn.com/abstract=3619211. Still others would raise and reshape corporate taxes in an effort to capture more of what economists call "rents," the extraordinary returns that firms so often earn in our increasingly concentrated, winner-take-all economy. *See* Edward Fox & Zachary Liscow, *A Case for Higher Corporate Tax Rates,* 167 TAX NOTES FEDERAL, June 22, 2020, at 2021, https://ssrn.com/abstract=3657324. Fox and Liscow point out that corporate income taxes now may (or could be changed so that they) tax economic rents, rather than income more generally. Ultimately, the owners of corporations would bear most of the cost of taxes on their rents, and such taxes would serve an especially useful anti-oligarchy function by targeting the big firms whose position is sufficiently monopoly-like that they earn disproportionate rents.

157. Perhaps such payments are politically possible only in a time of national crisis. But there are reasons to doubt this, including the fact that similar payments have been the law in Alaska for decades. Alaska's constitution requires that 25 percent of mineral revenues be deposited into a permanent fund—which, in turn, is partially distributed as a lump sum payment to every registered Alaskan, regardless of age or income. The lump sum payment is typically between $1,000 and $2,000 per person per year. *See* ALASKA CONST. art. IX, § 15; Dylan Matthews, *The Amazing True Socialist Miracle of the Alaska Permanent Fund,* VOX (Feb. 13, 2018), https://www.vox.com/policy-and-politics/2018/2/13/16997188/alaska-basic-income-permanent-fund-oil-revenue-study.

158. *See, e.g.,* Lawrence H. Summers, *Trump's $2,000 Stimulus Checks Are a Big Mistake,* Bloomberg Opinion (December 27, 2020), https://www.bloomberg.com/opinion/articles/2020-12-27/larry-summers-trump-pelosi-2-000-stimulus-checks-are-a-mistake [https://perma.cc/7TBG-BEP9].

159. Indeed, these programs, which did not specifically target the poor, apparently managed the remarkable feat of *reducing* the overall poverty rate in the early months of the pandemic even as millions of poor and working-class Americans lost their jobs. *See, e.g.,* Jeehoon Han, Bruce D. Meyer, & James X. Sullivan, *Income and Poverty in the COVID-19 Pandemic,* NBER Working Paper 2779 (Aug. 2020), https://www.nber.org/papers/w27729.

160. This was carried out using existing Fed authority: the Fed has long had the power to assist businesses beyond banks. *See* Federal Reserve Act § 13(3), 12 U.S.C. 343 (2010). But that authority was largely dormant until the Fed confronted the coronavirus pandemic in 2020. *See* Federal Reserve, *Primary Market Corporate Credit Facility* (Apr. 9, 2020), https://www.federalreserve.gov/newsevents/pressreleases/files/monetary20200409a5.pdf [https://perma.cc/TJJ7-YV7T].

161. Coronavirus Aid, Relief, and Economic Security Act, Pub. L. No. 116–136, § 1102, 134 Stat. 281 (2020).

162. These figures are based on Census Current Population Survey data. Robert Fairlie, *The Impact of COVID-19 on Small Business Owners: Evidence of Early-Stage Losses from the April 2020 Current Population Survey* 5 (NBER Working Paper No. 20-022, 2020), https://siepr.stanford.edu /sites/default/files/publications/20-022.pdf [https://perma.cc/GJ2H-RGT8].

163. That is approximately 600 firms, which included some nationally prominent boutique law firms, among others. *See* Stacy Cowley & Ella Koeze, *1 Percent of P.P.P. Borrowers Got over One-Quarter of the Loan Money*, N.Y. Times, Dec. 2, 2020, https://www.nytimes.com/2020/12/02 /business/paycheck-protection-program-coronavirus.html.

164. *See* Elise Gould & Valerie Wilson, *Black Workers Face Two of the Most Lethal Preexisting Conditions for Coronavirus—Racism and Economic Inequality*, Econ. Policy Inst. (June 1, 2020), https://perma.cc/7PKK-QA3T; Center for Responsible Lending, *The Paycheck Protection Program Continues to Be Disadvantageous to Smaller Businesses, Especially Businesses Owned by People of Color and the Self-Employed* 2–3 (Apr. 6, 2020), https://www.responsiblelending.org/sites/default /files/nodes/files/research-publication/crl-cares-act2-smallbusiness-apr2020.pdf [https://perma .cc/LR66-5GPT]; Lauren Leatherby, *Coronavirus Is Hitting Black Business Owners Hardest*, N.Y. Times, June 18, 2020, https://www.nytimes.com/interactive/2020/06/18/us/coronavirus-black -owned-small-business.html. Despite the facially race-neutral character of these barriers, at least one lawsuit claimed a Fifth Amendment violation in the way that the federal government distributed PPP funds. *See* Complaint, Infinity Consulting Group, LLC, et al. v. United States et al., No. 8:20-cv-00981-GJH (D. Md. Apr. 17, 2020).

165. *See* Jamie Goldberg, *State's $62 Million Relief Fund for Black Oregonians Suspends Operations, Hands Over Remaining Money to Federal Court*, The Oregonian, Dec. 17, 2020, https://www .oregonlive.com/business/2020/12/states-62-million-relief-fund-for-black-oregonians -suspends-operations-hands-over-remaining-money-to-federal-court.html (discussing Great Northern Resources, Inc. v. Coba).

166. *See* Lina Khan & Sandeep Vaheesan, *Market Power and Inequality: The Antitrust Counterrevolution and Its Discontents*, 11 Harv. L. & Pol'y Rev. 235, 273–75 (2017) (discussing the rise of monopolies in light of antitrust precedent); Stacy Mitchell, *Monopoly Power and the Decline of Small Business*, Inst. for Local Self-Reliance (Aug. 2016), https://ilsr.org/wp-content/uploads /downloads/2016/08/MonopolyPower-SmallBusiness.pdf [https://perma.cc/BQP5-3XQW] (discussing trends in market concentration); Council of Economic Advisers, *Benefits of Competition and Indicators of Market Power* (Apr. 2016), https://obamawhitehouse.archives.gov/sites/default /files/page/files/20160414_cea_competition_issue_brief.pdf [https://perma.cc/U9R6-NVMM].

167. David Dayen, Monopolized: Life in the Age of Corporate Power 281–85 (2020); Zephyr Teachout, Break 'Em Up: Recovering our Freedom from Big Ag, Big Tech, & Big Money 109–125 (2020); Steven M. Teles, The Rise of the Conservative Legal Movement: The Battle for Control of the Law 90–134 (2008).

168. *See* "The Trust Question," Chapter 5.

169. Louis D. Brandeis, The Curse of Bigness 39 (1934).

170. United States v. Columbia Steel Co., 334 U.S. 495, 535–6 (1948) (Douglas, J., dissenting).

171. *See* "The Slow Triumph of the Technocrats," Chapter 8.

172. *See* Robert H. Bork, The Antitrust Paradox: A Policy at War with Itself 66 (1978) ("The legislative histories . . . of the antitrust statutes . . . do not support any claim that Congress intended the courts to sacrifice consumer welfare to any other goal. The Sherman Act was clearly presented and debated as a consumer welfare prescription."); Reiter v. Sonotone Corp., 442 U.S. 330, 343 (1979) (quoting Bork and declaring that "Congress designed the Sherman Act as a 'consumer welfare prescription'"); U.S. Dep't of Justice, 1982 Merger Guidelines 2 (1982), https://www.justice.gov/sites/default/files/atr/legacy/2007/07/11/11248.pdf [https://perma.cc/78UJ -28QS] (asserting that mergers "should not be permitted to create or enhance 'market power,'" defined as the "ability of one or more firms profitably to maintain prices above competitive levels").

173. The leading economics paper on this point is David Autor, David Dorn, Lawrence F. Katz, Christina Patterson, & John Van Reenen, *Concentrating on the Fall of the Labor Share,* 107 AM. ECON. REV. 180 (2017). For a view from the law, with a more granular account of some pathways by which concentration fuels inequality, see Khan & Vaheesan, *Market Power and Inequality,* at 236.

174. Robert Pitofsky, *The Political Content of Antitrust,* 127 U. PA. L. REV. 1051 (1979); Eleanor M. Fox, *The Battle for the Soul of Antitrust,* 75 CAL. L. REV. 917 (1987).

175. For a few important voices and arguments that help constitute this movement, see Maurice E. Stucke, *Reconsidering Antitrust's Goals,* 53 B.C. L. REV. 551 (2012); Barak Orbach, *How Antitrust Lost Its Goal,* 81 FORDHAM L. REV. 2253 (2013); Harry First & Spencer Weber Waller, *Antitrust's Democracy Deficit,* 81 FORDHAM L. REV. 2543 (2013); Zephyr Teachout & Lina Khan, *Market Structure and Political Law: A Taxonomy of Power,* 9 DUKE J. CONST. L. & PUB. POL'Y 37 (2014); K. Sabeel Rahman, *From Economic Inequality to Economic Freedom: Constitutional Political Economy in the New Gilded Age,* 35 YALE L. & POL'Y REV. 321 (2016); Khan & Vaheesan, *Market Power and Inequality;* Lina Khan, *Amazon's Antitrust Paradox,* 126 YALE L.J. 710 (2017); TIM WU, THE CURSE OF BIGNESS: ANTITRUST IN THE NEW GILDED AGE (2018); Sandeep Vaheesan, *The Twilight of the Technocrats' Monopoly on Antitrust?,* 127 YALE L.J. F. 980 (2018); Marshall Steinbaum & Maurice E. Stucke, *The Effective Competition Standard: A New Standard for Antitrust,* 87 U. CHI. L. REV. 595 (2020); Lina M. Khan, *The End of Antitrust History Revisited,* 133 HARV. L. REV. 1655 (2020); Hiba Hafiz, *Labor Antitrust's Paradox,* 86 U. CHI. L. REV. 381 (2020); Sanjukta Paul, *Antitrust as Allocator of Coordination Rights,* 67 UCLA L. REV. 378 (2020); *see also* BARRY C. LYNN, CORNERED: THE NEW MONOPOLY CAPITALISM AND THE ECONOMICS OF DESTRUCTION (2010).

176. As Kate Andrias shows, the antimonopoly tradition also had significant life within the labor movement, especially in the thinking of leaders like Eugene Debs. Kate Andrias, *Beyond the Labor Exemption: U.S. Labor's Antimonopoly Tradition and the "Desire for Greater Democracy," in* THE ANTIMONOPOLY TRADITION (Tobin Project, Daniel Crane & Bill Novak eds., forthcoming); ZEPHYR TEACHOUT, BREAK 'EM UP.

177. Teachout & Khan, *Market Structure and Political Law,* at 40. On how these systems of private governance impinge on worker freedoms, *see* ELIZABETH ANDERSON, PRIVATE GOVERNMENT: HOW EMPLOYERS RULE OUR LIVES (AND WHY WE DON'T TALK ABOUT IT) (2017).

178. *See, e.g.,* WU, CURSE OF BIGNESS, at 54.

179. *See* Thomas Nachbar, *The Antitrust Constitution,* 99 IOWA L. REV. 57 (2013) (offering an argument in this vein about the constitutional problem of "private regulation" from the point of view of economic liberty).

180. *See* Gilad Edelman, *Biden Is Assembling a Big Tech Antitrust All-Star Team,* WIRED, Mar. 9, 2021, https://www.wired.com/story/lina-khan-ftc-antitrust-biden-administration/ [https://perma .cc/2XRR-5VLY]; President Joseph R. Biden, Executive Order 14036 Promoting Competition in the American Economy, 86 FR 36987 (2021), *see* https://www.whitehouse.gov/briefing-room/statements -releases/2021/07/09/fact-sheet-executive-order-on-promoting-competition-in-the-american -economy/ [https://perma.cc/89CG-89XZ].

181. Tim Wu, *Antitrust & Corruption: Overruling* Noerr (Columbia Public Law Research Paper No. 14–66, 2020), https://ssrn.com/abstract=3630610.

182. Telecommunications giants have waged an intense battle, through lobbying and litigation, to maintain their monopoly positions and block municipalities and municipally owned utilities from creating publicly owned broadband internet. The residents of Chattanooga, Tennessee, enjoy by far the fastest and cheapest broadband internet in the nation, because it is provided by a municipally owned electric utility that is not seeking a profit. The question of the future reach of this model, which so far exists in only a few dozen mostly small jurisdictions in the United States, is a classic problem of political economy. *See, e.g.,* Emily Stewart, *Give Everybody the Internet,*

Vox (Sept. 10, 2020), https://www.vox.com/recode/2020/9/10/21426810/internet-access-covid-19
-chattanooga-municipal-broadband-fcc.

183. *See* K. Sabeel Rahman, *The New Utilities: Private Power, Social Infrastructure, and the Revival of the Public Utility Concept,* 39 CARDOZO L. REV. 1621 (2018).

184. *See* GANESH SITARAMAN AND ANNE L. ALSTOTT, THE PUBLIC OPTION: HOW TO EXPAND FREEDOM, INCREASE OPPORTUNITY, AND PROMOTE EQUALITY (2019).

185. Some of these changes, too, are now finding their way onto the new administration's agenda. *See* President Joseph R. Biden, Executive Order on Promoting Competition. For especially sharp accounts of the current problem of concentrated power in agribusiness, see DAVID DAYEN, MONOPOLIZED: LIFE IN THE AGE OF CORPORATE POWER 43–63 (2020) (mapping the historical rise of agribusiness and its monopolistic dominance in, inter alia, chicken, dairy, and seed markets); ZEPHYR TEACHOUT, BREAK 'EM UP: RECOVERING OUR FREEDOM FROM BIG AG, BIG TECH, & BIG MONEY 17–38 (2019) (focusing on the shocking state of purportedly independent small chicken producers, who are in fact entirely dependent on agribusiness giants).

186. *See* Andrias, *Beyond the Labor Exemption.*

187. *See* 29 U.S.C. § 52; *See* Chapter 6.

188. *See* Paul, *Antitrust as Allocator of Coordination Rights,* at 378.

189. Sandeep Vaheesan, *Accommodating Capital and Policing Labor: Antitrust in the Two Gilded Ages,* 78 MD. L. REV. 766, 824 (2019).

190. Marshall Steinbaum argues that if reconceived in this way, antitrust law could helpfully disincentivize the misclassification of employees as independent contractors, which would itself be beneficial in untilting the playing field of relative bargaining power between such workers and their employers-in-all-but-name. Marshall Steinbaum, *Antitrust, the Gig Economy, and Labor Market Power,* 82 L. & CONTEMP. PROBS. 45, 62 (2019).

191. Paul, *Antitrust as Allocator of Coordination Rights.*

192. *Id.* at 412–13; Vaheesan, *Accommodating Capital and Policing Labor,* at 824.

193. *See* DAYEN, MONOPOLIZED 43–63; TEACHOUT, BREAK 'EM UP 17–38.

194. *See* LYNN STOUT, THE SHAREHOLDER VALUE MYTH: HOW PUTTING SHAREHOLDERS FIRST HARMS INVESTORS, CORPORATIONS, AND THE PUBLIC 16–23 (2012) (tracing this trajectory).

195. *New-York Diary,* Feb. 1, 1793, *quoted in* Eric Hilt, *Early American Corporations and the State, in* CORPORATIONS AND AMERICAN DEMOCRACY 37, 42 (Naomi R. Lamoreaux & William J. Novak eds., 2017).

196. Legal historian William Novak has forcefully argued that as the older legal vehicles for protecting the public interest were scrapped in the late nineteenth and early twentieth centuries, they were replaced by a new one focused on the concept of "public utility": that a vast variety of business enterprises, not only railroads and telegraphs but everything from sawmills and grain elevators to hospitals and hotels, were public utilities obligated by law to serve the public interest. William J. Novak, *The Public Utility Idea and the Origins of Modern Business Regulation, in* CORPORATIONS AND AMERICAN DEMOCRACY, at 139, 142.

197. *See* DANA BRAKMAN REISER & STEVEN A. DEAN, SOCIAL ENTERPRISE LAW: TRUST, PUBLIC BENEFIT AND CAPITAL MARKETS 52–60 (2017) (explaining the benefit corporation legal form and the set of stakeholders beyond shareholders that directors are obligated to consider). *See generally* Henry Hansmann, *When Does Worker Ownership Work? ESOPs, Law Firms, Codetermination, and Economic Democracy,* 99 YALE L.J. 1749 (1990).

198. Ewan McGaughey, *The Codetermination Bargains: The History of German Corporate and Labor Law,* 23 COLUM. J. EUR. L. 135, 166–72 (2016) (detailing the history of German decisions to mandate worker representation on boards and the codification of this principle).

199. Accountable Capitalism Act, S. 3348, 115th Cong. § 6(b) (2018).

200. *See* Warren Introduces Accountable Capitalism Act, Press Release, August 15, 2018, https://www.warren.senate.gov/newsroom/press-releases/warren-introduces-accountable -capitalism-act [https://perma.cc/V3M9-K29E]; *see* Acccountable Capitalism Act at § 4, 5 (2018).

201. Any political activities by the corporation would require supermajority approval of both the board and the shareholders. (For large, publicly held corporations, this rule would surely be a significant impediment to choosing to engage in direct political activity at all.)

202. Carol D. Rasnic, *Germany's Statutory Works Councils and Employee Codetermination: A Model for the United States,* 14 LOY. L.A. INT'L & COMP. L. REV. 275, 294–95 (1992).

203. *See, e.g.,* Stephen Bainbridge, *A Critique of Senator Elizabeth Warren's "Accountable Capitalism Act": Introduction and Links to My Posts,* PROFESSORBAINBRIDGE.COM (Aug. 15, 2018), https://perma.cc/ZE2Y-Y6GB (in a series of blog posts, arguing inter alia that proponents of greater federal preemption in this area miss the connection between federalism and liberty—an argument that one can easily imagine framed in constitutional terms in court).

204. *Id.* (arguing inter alia that the Accountable Capitalism Act "is blatantly intended to defund the GOP").

205. The strategic question of which arguments to deploy in different venues, such as courts and Congress, is necessarily complex. The New Dealers used an especially two-pronged strategy, offering a conservative Supreme Court a much different and narrower set of arguments than their arguments outside the courts. This made sense at the time, although we now can see it contributed to the Great Forgetting. *See* Chapter 6.

206. Louis Brandeis, *On Industrial Relations,* UNITED STATES COMM. ON INDUSTRIAL RELATIONS, S. DOC. NO. 26–6936, at 7657–81, *reprinted in* THE CURSE OF BIGNESS: MISCELLANEOUS PAPERS OF LOUIS D. BRANDEIS 73–74 (Osmond K. Fraenkel ed., 1934).

207. Ayanna Pressley & David Stein, *Op-Ed: The Fed Has a "Responsibility" to Help Reduce High Unemployment in the Black Community,* CNBC (Jul. 21, 2020), https://www.cnbc.com/2020/07/21 /op-ed-fed-policies-have-contributed-to-black-unemployment.html (calls for considering Black unemployment levels in Fed policymaking are also coming from inside the house of the economics profession, from luminaries ranging from Jared Bernstein to Narayana Kocherlakota); Heather Long, *Calls Grow for the Federal Reserve to Target Lowering the Black Unemployment Rate,* WASH. POST, June 10, 2010, https://www.washingtonpost.com/business/2020/06/10/black -unemployment-rate-fed/. *See also Senator Warren's Questions for the Record to Federal Reserve Chairman Jerome Powell During the Semiannual Monetary Policy Report to Congress* (June 16, 2020), https://perma.cc/Y3GV-UN2W (probing Chairman Powell on how the racial wealth gap figures into Federal Reserve policy).

208. *See* Employment Act of 1946, Pub. L. 79–304, 60 Stat. 23, §§ 2–3 (1946).

209. *See* "Jacksonian Equal Protection," Chapter 2; "The Money of the Constitution," Chapter 4.

210. *See* CHRISTINE DESAN, MAKING MONEY: COIN, CURRENCY, AND THE COMING OF CAPITALISM (2014).

211. *See* Robert C. Hockett & Saule T. Omarova, *The Finance Franchise,* 102 CORNELL L. REV. 1143 (2017); Christine Desan, *The Monetary Structure of Economic Activity* (Harvard Public Law Working Paper No. 20-04, 2020), https://ssrn.com/abstract=3557233.

212. *See* "The Money of the Constitution," Chapter 4.

213. *See, e.g.,* California Public Banking Act of 2019, AB 857 (creating a framework for chartering public banks in California).

214. For an account of the century-old Bank of North Dakota, and its unique role in sustaining an ecosystem of healthy local banks in its state as well as promoting democratic access to credit, see Will Peischel, *How a Brief Socialist Takeover in North Dakota Gave Residents a Public Bank,* Vox (October 1, 2019), https://www.vox.com/the-highlight/2019/9/24/20872558/california-north -dakota-public-bank.

215. Congresswoman Rashida Tlaib has proposed a federal public banking act that would do exactly this, giving state-chartered public banks seed grants and access to funds through the Federal Reserve. *See* Public Banking Act of 2020 (proposed legislation), https://tlaib.house.gov/sites /tlaib.house.gov/files/PublicBanking.pdf [https://perma.cc/7VKH-X7XF].

216. They can also pursue other public goals. *See id.* (discussing prohibitions on public banks investing, for example, in fossil fuel companies).

217. For the idea that what banks are doing in our system is licensing or franchising the government's power to create money, see Hockett & Omarova, *Finance Franchise.*

218. *See, e.g.,* Andrew Yang, Opinion, *Yes, Robots Are Stealing Your Job,* N.Y. TIMES, Nov. 15, 2019, at A23. *See* "Fair Employment Without Full Employment," Chapter 8.

219. Cynthia Estlund, *Three Big Ideas for a Future of Less Work and a Three-Dimensional Alternative,* 82 L. & CONTEMP. PROBS. 1 (2019).

220. This conceptual framework is Jack Balkin's. *See* Jack M. Balkin, *From Off the Wall to On the Wall: How the Mandate Challenge Went Mainstream,* THE ATLANTIC (June 4, 2012), https://www.theatlantic.com/national/archive/2012/06/from-off-the-wall-to-on-the-wall-how -the-mandate-challenge-went-mainstream/258040/ [https://perma.cc/73S3-QHEK]; JACK M. BALKIN, LIVING ORIGINALISM 330–32 (2011).

221. *See* Pamela S. Karlan, *No Respite for Liberals,* Sunday Review, N.Y. TIMES, June 30, 2012 (offering this memorable formulation of the four greatest powers and showing how conservative judges are mounting novel attacks on the Spending, Commerce, and Reconstruction Powers).

222. *See* Mark Graber, *Constructing Constitutional Politics: Thaddeus Stevens, John Bingham, and the Forgotten Fourteenth Amendment,* at Part III (University of Maryland Legal Studies Research Paper No. 2014–37, 2014), https://ssrn.com/abstract=2483355. For our account, building on Graber's work, see Chapter 3.

223. For the idea of judging as jurispathic—destroying other potential meanings of law—see Robert M. Cover, *The Supreme Court, 1982 Term—Foreword:* Nomos *and Narrative,* 97 HARV. L. REV. 4, 4 (1983).

224. Abraham Lincoln, Fragment on the Constitution and Union, 4 THE COLLECTED WORKS OF ABRAHAM LINCOLN 168–69 (Roy Basler ed., 1953). *See* Proverbs 11:23 ("A word fitly spoken is like apples of gold in pictures of silver.").

225. Lincoln, Fragment, at 169.

ACKNOWLEDGMENTS

A book this long in the making incurs abundant debts. That is truer for this book than most. When we began this project we had in mind a short article. Over time it became something more. We found ourselves helping build a new movement in legal and constitutional thought and scholarship—and we gladly drew on other voices in that movement as it came into its own. Whatever virtues this book has, they are largely thanks to the amazing generosity of fellow scholars. By no means would all of them associate their own work with "constitutional political economy" or "law and political economy." Most would situate their work elsewhere in the precincts of law, history, and government, but all were willing to get on board long enough to lend a hand. All this means we have a lot of people to thank!

First, though, we should thank our editors at Harvard University Press, who have been uncommonly patient and supportive throughout this book's evolution. Before she took her many talents to other precincts of the university, Elizabeth Knoll gave our proposed book a warm welcome. James Brandt shared her vision of what the book could be. Sharmila Sen believed in the project and persuaded Ian Malcolm to pick it up as it neared the finish line. Happily for us, Ian made the book his own, shepherding the manuscript through the many stages to completion with all his considerable publishing expertise and intellectual energy and enthusiasm.

Next, we thank the institutions that have supported our work. First and foremost is the University of Texas School of Law. Dean Ward Farnsworth has led the school since the project's inception, and we are grateful for his confidence in the worth of the project throughout that time. Ward provided substantial material support for the project, not only in underwriting our research over these many years, but also in helping to foot the bill for the ambitious *Texas Law Review* Symposium on the Constitution and Economic Inequality back in 2014, when we were embarking on this project in earnest. We would also like to thank the editors at *TLR,* who helped make that symposium into a great gathering and a great volume of essays. Joey Fishkin thanks Yale Law School for supporting a small army of research assistants during a visit there in 2016–2017. Willy Forbath thanks Princeton University's Law and Public Affairs Program, its splendid director, Paul Frymer, and his associates Leslie Gerwin, Jennifer Bolton, and Judi Rivkin for an invaluable semester in spring 2018. Finally, we gratefully acknowledge a University of Texas at Austin Subvention Grant awarded by the Office of the President.

Writing this book involved a daunting amount of exploration in primary sources and numerous secondary literatures. It would not have been possible without several generations of gifted research assistants, most of them students at Texas Law, others at Yale Law, still others in the UT-Austin departments of history or government or the Princeton History Department. We are indebted to Stephanie Agu, Patrick Baker, Sebastian Brady, Ben Chang, Shane Davitt, Anne Derrig, Haris Durrani, Ricardo Gelb, Brian Highsmith, Barrett Hollingsworth, Joseph Hughes, Jerry Klaristenfeld, Austin Lee, Gabe Levine, Sam McNutt, Phill Melton, Zachary Montz, Austin Nelson, Jackie Odum, Kayla Oliver, Lulu Ortiz, Ian Petersen, Reid Pillifant, Aaron Roper, Eyad Saqr, Rohan Shetty, Anderson Tuggle, Jonah Wacholder, Claudia Wack, Henry Weaver, and Zoe Zissu. Throughout this long journey, one research librarian, Kasia Solon Cristobal of the University of Texas School of Law library, has been our constant collaborator, and she has been boundlessly helpful and resourceful.

We wrote the first version of the project that became this book as part of a symposium hosted by the *Boston University Law Review* in 2013. We thank the organizers and the student editors of that symposium and also many of the faculty there who engaged with the arguments we were beginning to articulate, including among others (and here and throughout we will undoubtedly omit names we should have included, for which we apologize!): Jack Balkin, Sot Barber, Jim Fleming, Mark Graber, Ellen Katz, Ken Kersch, Linda McClain, and Robin West.

It was that *Texas Law Review* symposium in 2014, on the Constitution and economic inequality, that first gave us a real sense that our collaboration on this book was part of a larger scholarly and intellectual movement. Although the phrase *law and political economy* was not yet in wide circulation—much less *constitutional political economy*—we were lucky enough to have the chance to engage with a remarkable group of historians, constitutional theorists, and other scholars in Austin, some of whom were, like us, beginning to think in these terms. Several wrote compelling critical and constructive commentaries on our manuscript-in-the-making and transformed it with their insights; others wrote essays of their own. All of them contributed immeasurably to the work of this book, and many of them continued doing so in the years that followed: Kate Andrias, Jack Balkin, Cindy Estlund, Cary Franklin, Bob Gordon, Mark Graber, David Grewal, Bob Hockett, Olati Johnson, Jeremy Kessler, Frank Michelman, Bill Novak, Jim Pope, Jed Purdy, Sabeel Rahman, Brishen Rogers, Reva Siegel, and Ganesh Sitaraman. The project also benefited, at this early stage and beyond, from conversations with Larry Sager, whose intellectual generosity and engagement we will always appreciate.

As the project developed, we were fortunate to be invited, sometimes jointly and sometimes separately, to present papers drawn from this book, as a work in progress, at many great venues. At every step in its evolution, the project gained from a wonderful range of incredulous, skeptical, cautiously sympathetic, and enthusiastic readers and interlocutors at these conferences, workshops, seminars, and colloquia—what mattered was the precious time and thought they gave to it and to us. Rather than attempt to highlight everyone who organized these events and engaged with our work we will just list the events themselves: the Faculty Colloquium at the University of Texas School of Law; the Faculty Workshop at Loyola School of Law; the Political Economy of Modern Capitalism Seminar at Harvard University; the Law, Economics, and Politics Colloquium at NYU School of Law; the Center for the Study of Law and Society at UC Berkeley School of Law; the Elizabeth Clark

Legal History Workshop at Boston University School of Law; the Faculty Workshop at Cornell Law School; the Faculty Workshop at Vanderbilt Law; the Faculty Workshop at the University of Minnesota School of Law; the Hewlett Foundation's Conference on New Approaches to Political Economy; the Faculty Workshop at Yale Law School; the Conference on "Understanding Constitutional Change: The State of the Field" at Tulane Law School; the Conference on "Law and Politics under Stress" at the Wayne Morse Center, University of Oregon; the Public Law Workshop at the University of Chicago Law School; the Faculty Workshop at the University of Michigan School of Law; and both the Public Law Colloquium and the Faculty Workshop at Northwestern University School of Law.

As this project grew and developed, we gained enormously from a series of fellow scholars—friends, colleagues, mentors, comrades in arms—who read the drafts of chapters we sent their way. They gave us generative insights, clarifying formulations, historical nuances, superb sources, and challenging counterevidence, as well as ruthless editorial counsel from which the work has emerged immeasurably better. We are especially thankful to Bruce Ackerman, Les Benedict, Yohai Benkler, Chris Desan, Cindy Estlund, Eric Foner, Steve Griffin, Dirk Hartog, Sam Issacharoff, Susannah Jacobs, Lina Khan, Andy Koppelman, Sandy Levinson, Gerard Magliocca, Susie Morse, Robert Post, Jed Purdy, Aziz Rana, Brishen Rogers, Larry Sager, Reva Siegel, Jonathan Simon, Jordan Steiker, Chris Tomlins, Gerald Torres, Natasha Wheatley, Adam Winkler, Laura Weinrib, Tim Wu, and Emily Zackin. Then, finally, there were some who read the entire manuscript and offered all this—insights, framings, clarifications, and skeptical counters, along with great, sometimes sentence-by-sentence, editorial counsel—across more pages than we dared ask: Kate Andrias, Lincoln Caplan, Sabeel Rahman, Daniel Rodgers, and John Witt.

Joey Fishkin thanks his parents, Shelley and Jim Fishkin, not only for reading and discussing this book but for encouraging him to dive headfirst into the project. He thanks Cary Franklin—his partner in all things and his first, last, and most incisive reader—for all that she gave to this project over a period of years, even in the thick of work on projects of her own.

Willy Forbath thanks Mitch Bernard, Jane Cohen and Larry Sager, Kari and Nate McBride, Isolde and Joel Motley, Alison Roberts and Theo Forbath, and Kem and Jon Sawyer for their steadfast friendship, long before this book got underway, and all through its long growing season. For their amazing patience and support he thanks Zoey and Aaron Forbath, and their mates, Tom Langer and Haley Perkins, along with the newest member of the family, Henry Langer. The first four have been more engaged with this project than he had any right to expect, and Henry brought a burst of joy to its completion. Most of all, he thanks Judy Coffin for her unshakable confidence and camaraderie; as the others mentioned in this paragraph well know, she is his inspiration and anchor.

INDEX

Abernathy, Ralph, 388, 391
abolition of slavery and abolitionists, 11, 36, 53, 95, 133, 496n15, 509n84
Abood v. Detroit Board of Education (1977), 443–46, 585n87
Accountable Capitalism Act (introduced by Warren, 2018), 594–95nn199–204
Acemoglu, Daron, 371–72, 566n74
Ackerman, Bruce, 24, 274, 492n48, 526–27n181, 545n99, 547n155, 561n3, 590n152
Adams, Henry Carter, 175, 219–20, 222, 475
Adams, John, 34–35, 46, 56
Adams, John Quincy, 13, 60, 78, 82
Adams, Willi Paul, 39
Addams, Jane, 185, 189
Address of Workingmen of Charlestown (October 1840), 96
Adkins v. Children's Hospital (1923), 235, 307–8
Administrative Procedure Act of 1946, 544n92
affirmative action, 252, 391, 418, 453
Affordable Care Act of 2010 (Obamacare or ACA): court challenges to, 19, 427–28, 579n3, 580nn8–9; as fight over constitutional political economy, 420–22; Medicaid expansion and, 20, 305, 432, 457–59, 461, 551n252, 588nn122–23; race and, 457–59, 461, 588n126; religious

carve-outs from contraceptive mandate of, 463
AFL. *See* American Federation of Labor
AFL–CIO, 389, 408
AFL v. Swing (1941), 345, 560n139
agrarian reformers. *See* Populists and People's Party
Agricultural Adjustment Act of 1933 (reauthorized 1938), 319, 328
Aid to Families with Dependent Children (AFDC), 393–96, 398, 456
Aiken, George, 377
Alabama: Black Codes in, 513n10; Black suffrage in, 130, 336; Communist Party's Black membership in, 330; welfare requirement of "man-in-the-house" for eligibility, 395–96
A. L. A. Schechter Poultry Corp. v. United States. See Schechter Poultry Corp. v. United States
ALCOA, 312, 314–15
Alito, Samuel, 444–47, 460, 564n41
Allison, William, 124
Altgeld, John, 158–59, 160
Amalgamated Copper Company, 248–50
Amazon, 216, 450
American Anti-Boycott Association, 199–200
American Civil Liberties Union (ACLU), 398, 539n11, 562n8; Women's Rights Project, 399

American Economic Association, 367
American Federation of Labor (AFL),
  154–57, 162, 197, 199–205, 207, 276, 279,
  295, 343
American Federation of State, County,
  and Municipal Employees (AFSCME),
  444
American Law Institute (ALI): "Statement
  of Essential Human Rights," 321–22
American Medical Association, 385
American Railway Union (ARU), 157–59,
  163, 181
American Revolution, 4, 32–33, 37, 38
American Socialist Party. *See* Socialist
  Party
"American System" of political economy
  of Whig Party, 71–72, 78–83, 99
American Tobacco Company, 226
*American Tradition Partnership v.
  Bullock* (2012), 250
American West: corporations' capture of
  state governments in, 231, 238, 249;
  Oregon System's popularity in, 241,
  248; slavery's expansion in, 95, 96–99,
  103–5, 510n96; state constitutional
  changes in, 237. *See also specific states*
Andrias, Kate, 309, 311, 491–2n39, 552n269,
  581n20, 584n75, 585n80, 593n176
antebellum America, 13, 71–108; "American System" of Whigs, 71–72, 78–83,
  99; Congress's affirmative constitutional duties, 72, 73–78, 83–84, 89,
  94–95, 99; Congress's constructions
  of spending for the general welfare,
  85–88; democracy-of-opportunity
  tradition and, 74–78; equal protection
  and, 74–78; Jacksonians and Jacksonian
  democracy, 71–83; proslavery arguments,
  103–5; slavery and free labor, 88–91;
  slavery's expansion restricted, 99–103;
  state autonomy arguments' contemporary resonance, 460
Anthony, Susan B., 134–37, 491n28

antidiscrimination law: Congress's need
  to enact statute to undo judicial constructions of FAA, RFRA, and other
  court interventions, 464; critical race
  theory and, 587n106; forgotten links
  to other elements of democracy of
  opportunity, 380, 453–55, 460; formalist versus substantive interpretations of, 390, 554n22; recent Supreme
  Court interpretations, 455, 463; as
  superstatutes, 461–62; widening constitutional lens on racial inequality
  beyond, 424. *See also* race and racism;
  sex equality; *specific civil rights legislation*
Anti-Federalists, 50, 57–64
Anti-Merger Act of 1950, 376–78, 472
anti-oligarchy: Anti-Federalist arguments
  in Ratification debates, 49–50, 57–64;
  antitrust regulation and, 215–16, 314,
  472, 474–77; constitutional amendments of Progressive Era, 233, 247;
  contemporary reforms needed to
  address, 465, 485; Jacksonians and,
  115, 128, 154, 163, 441–42; Jeffersonian
  constitutionalism and, 67, 86, 87, 98,
  99, 115, 128, 154; middle class and, 209,
  353, 441; New Deal and, 252–54; populists and, 16, 181, 211–14, 359, 521–22n80,
  552n290; principle defined, 9; state
  constitutions in early republic and,
  14, 33, 37–39; as strand of democracy-
  of-opportunity tradition, 8–9, 27, 30,
  141, 181, 229, 253, 361, 374, 494n60
antipoverty program. *See* War on Poverty
antitrust law, 9, 10, 15, 29; administrative
  state-building and litigation as regulation, 312–13; agribusiness and, 476,
  594n185; ambiguous progressive
  legacies, 229–30; Anti-Merger Act
  of 1950, 376–78; anti-oligarchy and,
  215–16, 314, 472, 474–77; bigness and,
  186, 216–20, 472, 474; Brandeis
  and, 472–75; capitalism and political

economics: autonomy of economics from politics in mid-twentieth century liberal thought, 420–21, 468; competition and antitrust in, 219–20; constitutional political economy and economic expertise, 480–82; economies of scale and the idea of natural monopolies, 226; Humphrey–Hawkins Bill (1978) vs. economics profession, 404–7; ignoring issues of class and distribution, 379; introduction into the legal academy, effect of, 412, 415; "Kuznets curve," 371, 566n74; macroeconomic management of inflation and full employment, 405–7; modern equilibrium theory, 366; replacing "political economy," 2, 26, 311, 353, 363, 364–69, 420; stagflation of late 1970s, 369, 375, 406; as technocratic domain, 146, 351, 353, 363, 374–79, 407, 420, 471, 480–82, 565n59; wealth maximization and neoclassical and welfare economics, 565n48. *See also* Chicago School; Keynesian economics; neoliberalism

economic security, legislation for: as affirmative government obligation, 286, 294, 442; Committee on Economic Security and, 295–97, 300–302; constitutional liberty as requiring, 253, 294–97, 349; democracy of opportunity and, 286; Fair Labor Standards Act and, 306, 310; Medicaid expansion of Obamacare as, 20–21, 305, 432, 456–58, 461, 588nn122–23; racial inclusion and, 27; universal basic income (UBI) proposals, 424, 482–83. *See also* full employment; social insurance

Edelman, Marian Wright, 401

education: Black schools in the South, 119, 121–22, 131, 455; as essential endowment, 40–41, 464, 506n38; school integration, 390

Education Amendments Act of 1972 (Title IX), 400

Eighteenth Amendment, 233–34, 339, 535n142

Eisenhower, Dwight, 357, 375, 377

elections: direct primaries, 193, 237, 240; proportional representation systems, 242, 537n181; of senators by popular vote, 17, 232–33. *See also* presidential elections; Seventeenth Amendment; voting rights

Elections Clause, 440, 583n47

Electoral College, 56, 129, 486

elite domination: alternative parties formed to counter, 230–31; of contemporary society and politics, 422; early American fear of, 61–62; FDR and New Deal vs., 284, 319, 328, 337–38; framers viewed as elitists, 192, 241; of National Recovery Administration, 267–68; Teddy Roosevelt's view of corporate elite, 224, 226; of Supreme Court membership in 1880s, 168; today's Supreme Court's favoring of business elite, 362, 404, 425, 564n41, 574n233. *See also* Gilded Age; oligarchy

Ely, Richard, 175, 367, 565n56

Emancipation Proclamation, 126, 380

emergency powers doctrine, 160–61

Emery, James, 277

Employment Act of 1946, 340, 404, 405, 480

employment regulation. *See* labor and employment

Engel v. Vitale, 358

enumerated powers, 13, 82–85, 87, 167, 484, 596n221

Epstein, Richard, 417

Equal Employment Opportunity Commission (EEOC), 390

equal opportunity, 12, 15, 25, 27; in conservative constitutional arguments, 477; Court as institution to enforce, limitations of, 356; in Gilded Age, 150;

and, 231; post-WWII, 337–46; Progressives and, 187, 231, 233, 351, 352, 363–79; public choice economics and, 564n44; racial equality and, 464–65; Reagan era and after, conservative vision of, 392; rebuilding democracy of opportunity and, 31, 422, 455, 464, 468–84, 565n45; replaced by economics, 2, 26, 311, 353, 363, 364–69, 420; revival of progressive political economy today, 420, 493–94nn57–58; slavery and, 53–57;. *See also* antitrust law; constitutional political economy; Lochnerism; monetary policy

political parties, formation of, 12, 65–66, 78. *See also specific parties*

Pollock v. Farmers' Loan & Trust Co. (1895), 157, 176–77, 232, 243–44, 466; Harlan's dissent, 178, 243, 260

Poor People's Campaign (1968), 388–89, 393, 455, 465

Pope, James Gray, 451, 545n109, 546, nn118, 124–27, 131, 132, 547nn139, 144, 146, 548n171, 559n128, 560n145, 572n79, 582nn52, 53, 585n81, 586nn96, 98, 587nn101, 103

popular sovereignty, 142, 148, 154, 164, 169, 191, 246, 249

populism of twenty-first century, right-wing 28; plutocratic, 354; racism and, 391–92

Populists and People's Party, 15–17, 141, 150–85; 1892 and 1896 platform of, 166, 171, 524n137; affirmative constitutional duties and, 72; Black activism and, 330; constitutional amendments, and, 236; constitutional political economy and, 133, 162–66; corporate power, attempts to restrain, 16, 164, 210; to counter traditional two-party system, 230, 236; federal income tax and, 16–17, 175, 179–80; gold standard and monetary policy and, 170–72, 258, 259, 375,

481–82, 526n172; public works advocacy by, 169, 298, 525n156; Southern Populists, 359–60

Posner, Richard, 415, 577n287

Post, Robert C., 489n8, 492n41, 564n42, 573n207, 579n2

post-WWII economic boom. *See* Great Compression

Pound, Roscoe, 187

poverty. *See* War on Poverty

Powderly, Terence, 153

Powe, Lucas A., Jr., 563n32

Powell, Lewis F., 408–9, 411, 413, 462, 573n206, 577n280

Pozen, David, 548n171

Priest, George L., 578n288

primaries. *See* elections

Prison Litigation Reform Act of 1996 (PLRA), 581n15

procedural due process, 355, 393–98, 569n121

Progressives, 15–17, 185–250; affirmative constitutional duties and, 72; as alternative to two traditional parties, 230, 236; antitrust and, 211–12, 229–30, 472, 475; constitutional amendments and, 187, 188, 236–37, 242–48; constitutional political economy and, 150, 190, 198, 220; contemporary revival of, 493–94nn57–58; democracy-of-opportunity tradition and, 6, 486; direct democracy and, 193, 232, 237–42; economic liberty and, 307; European models used by, 238, 536n156; federal income tax and, 17, 175; forgetting of constitutional politics of, 22, 25, 363–79, 392–418, 420, 487; Great Society compared to, 383, 386; industrial democracy and, 196, 202–5, 208, 279; judicial philosophies of, 202–10, 238, 359; labor reform and, 197–201; "Living Constitution" and philosophy of, 554n22; participatory